Contents

First published in 1991 by

Philip's, a division of Octopus Publishing Group Ltd,
2–4 Heron Quays, London E14 4JP

www.philips-maps.co.uk

Thirteenth edition 2004 First impression 2004

Ordnance Survey® This product includes mapping data licensed from Ordnance Survey®, with the permission of the Controller of Her Majesty's Stationery Office © Crown copyright 2004. All rights reserved. Licence number 100011710.

This product includes mapping data licensed from Ordnance Survey of Northern Ireland® reproduced by permission of the Chief Executive, acting on behalf of the Controller of Her Majesty's Stationery Office. © Crown Copyright 2004 Permit No 40351

To the best of the Publisher's knowledge, the information in this atlas was correct at the time of going to press. No responsibility can be accepted for any errors or their consequences.

The representation in this atlas of any road, drive or track is not evidence of the existence of a right of way.

The mapping on page 126 and the town plans of Edinburgh and London are based on mapping data licenced from Ordnance Survey with the permission of the Controller of Her Majesty's Stationery Office. © Crown Copyright 2004. All rights reserved. Licence number 100011710.

The maps of Ireland on pages 18 to 21 and the town plan of Dublin are based on Ordnance Survey Ireland by permission of the Government Permit Number 7735 © Ordnance Survey Ireland and Government of Ireland, and Ordnance Survey Northern Ireland on behalf of the Controller of Her Majesty's Stationery Office © Crown Copyright 2004 Permit Number 40351

Cartography by Philip's. Copyright © Philip's 2004
Printed and bound in Spain by Cayfosa-Quebecor

Cover photograph: Lake Sylvenstein (Sylvensteinsee) 62 C2
Pictor International / Alamy

Legend to route

	Motorway – tunnel, und...
	Toll motorwa...
	Main through under cons...
	Other majo...
	Other road
25 50	European road number, motorway number
55	National road number
56	Distances – in kilometres
	International boundary, national boundary
LE HAVRE	Car ferry and destination
✈ 1089	Mountain pass, international airport, height – in metres
	National park

Town – population

MOSKVA ▣	5 million +	Ikast ○	10000–20000
BERLIN ▣	2–5 million	Skjern ○	5000–10000
MINSK ▣	1–2 million	Lillesand ○	0–5000
Oslo ◉	500000–1million		
Århus ◉	200000–500000		
Turku ◎	100000–200000		
Gävle ◉	50000–100000		
Nybro ○	20000–50000		

Scale 1: 4 250000
approximately 67 miles to 1 inch

0 20 40 60 80 miles

0 40 80 120 km

Legend to road maps pages 18–114

⑦ ◇	Motorway with junctions – numbered, not numbered services tunnel, under construction
	Toll Motorway tunnel
	Principal trunk highway – single / dual carriageway tunnel, under construction
	Other main highway – single / dual carriageway tunnel, under construction
	Other important road under construction
	Other road
E25 A49	European road number, motorway number
135	National road number
Col Bayard 1248	Mountain pass
	Scenic route, gradient – arrow points uphill
143 28	Distances – in kilometres major minor
	Principal railway tunnel
Nápoli 15:30	Ferry route with journey time – hours:minutes
	Short ferry route
	International boundary
	National boundary
✈	Airport
⏟	Ancient monument
⚓	Beach
⌂	Castle or house
◠	Cave
	National park
	Natural park
✦	Other place of interest
❀	Park or garden
✝	Religious building
⛷	Ski resort
754▲	Spot height
Verona	Town of tourist interest

Scale 1: 1000000 • Pages 18–110
approximately 16 miles to 1 inch

0 5 10 15 20 miles

0 10 20 30 km

Scale 1: 2000000 • Pages 111–114
approximately 32 miles to 1 inch

0 10 20 30 40 miles

0 10 20 30 40 50 60 km

GW00420047

Driving regulations

A national vehicle identification plate is always required when taking a vehicle abroad.

It is important for your own safety and that of other drivers to fit headlamp converters or beam deflectors when taking a right-hand drive car to a country where driving is on the right (every country in Europe except the UK and Ireland). When the headlamps are dipped on a right-hand drive car, the lenses of the headlamps cause the beam to shine upwards to the left – and so, when driving on the right, into the eyes of oncoming motorists.

The symbols used are:

🏛	Motorway
⚠	Dual carriageway
▲	Single carriageway
🚗	Surfaced road
🚗	Unsurfaced / gravel road
🏙	Urban area
🕐	Speed limit in kilometres per hour (kph)
🔗	Seat belts
👶	Children
♈	Blood alcohol level
△	Warning triangle
🗀	First aid kit
💡	Spare bulb kit
🔥	Fire extinguisher
🪖	Motorcycle helmet
⊖	Minimum driving age
📰	Additional documents required
📱	Mobile phones
★	Other information

All countries require that you carry a driving licence, green card/insurance documentation, registration document or hire certificate, and passport.

The penalties for infringements of regulations vary considerably from one country to another. In many countries the police have the right to impose on-the-spot fines (you should always request a receipt for any fine paid). Penalties can be severe for serious infringements, particularly for drinking when driving which in some countries can lead to immediate imprisonment. Insurance is important, and you may be forced to take out cover at the frontier if you cannot produce acceptable proof that you are insured.

Please note that driving regulations often change.

The publishers have made every effort to ensure that the information given here was correct at the time of going to press. No responsibility can be accepted for any errors or their consequences.

Andorra (AND)

🕐	🏛	⚠	▲	🏙
	n/a	90	90	50

🔗 Compulsory in front seats

👶 Over 10 only allowed in front seats if over 150cm

♈ 0.05%

△ Compulsory

🗀 Recommended

💡 Compulsory

🔥 Recommended

🪖 Compulsory for all riders

⊖ 18 (16-18 accompanied)

📱 Use not permitted whilst driving

Austria (A)

🕐	🏛	⚠	▲	🏙
	130	100	100	50

If towing trailer under 750kg

🕐	🏛	⚠	▲	🏙
	100	100	100	50

If towing trailer over 750kg

🕐	🏛	⚠	▲	🏙
	100	100	80	50

🔗 Compulsory in front seats and rear seats

👶 Under 14 and under 150cm in front seats only in child safety seat; under 14 and over 150cm, must wear adult seat belt

♈ 0.05%

△ Compulsory

🗀 Compulsory

💡 Recommended

🔥 Recommended

🪖 Compulsory for all riders

⊖ 18 (16 for mopeds)

📰 Third party insurance

📱 Use permitted only with hands-free speaker system

★ If you intend to drive on motorways or expressways, a motorway vignette must be purchased at the border. These are available for 10 days, 2 months or 1 year.

★ Dipped headlights must be used at all times on motorbikes.

Belarus (BY)

🕐	🏛	⚠	▲	🏙
	110	90	90	60

If towing trailer under 750kg

🕐	🏛	⚠	▲
	90	70	70

Vehicle towing another vehicle 50 kph limit

🔗 Compulsory in front seats, and rear seats if fitted

👶 Under 12 in front seats only in child safety seat

♈ 0.5

△ Compulsory

🗀 Compulsory

Belgium (B)

🕐	🏛	⚠	▲	🏙
	120*	120	90	50

*Minimum speed of 70kph on motorways

If towing trailer

🕐	🏛	⚠	▲	🏙
	90	90	90	50

🔗 Compulsory in front and rear seats

👶 Under 12 in front seats only in child safety seat

♈ 0.05%

△ Compulsory

🗀 Compulsory

💡 Recommended

🔥 Compulsory

🪖 Compulsory for all riders

⊖ 18 (16 for mopeds)

📰 Third party insurance

📱 Use only allowed with hands-free kit

Bulgaria (BG)

🕐	🏛	⚠	▲	🏙
	120	80	80	50-60

If towing trailer

🕐	🏛	⚠	▲	🏙
	100	70	70	50

🔗 Compulsory in front seats; advised in rear

👶 Under 12 not allowed in front seats

♈ 0.00%

△ Compulsory

🗀 Compulsory

💡 Recommended

🔥 Compulsory

🪖 Compulsory for all riders

⊖ 18

📰 Driving licence with translation or international driving permit, third party insurance

📱 Use only allowed with hands-free kit

★ $10 fee at border plus $2 disinfection fee

Recommended / Belgium (continued column 2)

🗀 Recommended

🔥 Compulsory

🪖 Compulsory for all riders

⊖ 18 (16 for motorbikes)

📰 Third party insurance; visa (ensure it's specific to driving); vehicle technical check stamp; international driving permit

📱 Use only allowed with hands-free kit

Croatia (HR)

🕐	🏛	⚠	▲	🏙
	130	80	80	50

If towing

🕐	🏛	⚠	▲	🏙
	110	80	80	50

🔗 Compulsory if fitted

👶 Under 12 not allowed in front seats

♈ 0.05%

△ Compulsory

🗀 Compulsory

💡 Compulsory

🪖 Compulsory for all riders

⊖ 18

📱 No legislation

Czech Republic (CZ)

🕐	🏛	⚠	▲	🏙
	130	130	90	50

If towing

🕐	🏛	⚠	▲	🏙
	80	80	80	50

🔗 Compulsory in front seats and, if fitted, in rear

👶 Under 12 or under 150cm not allowed in front seats

♈ 0.00%

△ Compulsory

🗀 Compulsory

💡 Compulsory

🪖 Compulsory for all riders (unless maximum speed is 40kph or less)

⊖ 18 (17 for motorcycles over 50cc, 16 for motorcycles under 125 cc)

📰 International driving permit

📱 Use only allowed with hands-free kit

★ Permit needed for motorway driving

Denmark (DK)

🕐	🏛	⚠	▲	🏙
	110/130	80	80	50

If towing

🕐	🏛	⚠	▲	🏙
	80	70	70	50

🔗 Compulsory in front seats and, if fitted, in rear

👶 Under 3 not allowed in front seat except in a child safety seat; in rear, 3 to 7 years in a child safety seat or on a booster cushion

♈ 0.05%

△ Compulsory

🗀 Recommended

💡 Recommended

🔥 Recommended

🪖 Compulsory for all riders

⊖ 18

📰 Third party insurance

Estonia (EST)

🕐	🏛	⚠	▲	🏙
	n/a	90	70	50

🔗 Compulsory in front seats and if fitted in rear seats

👶 Under 12 not allowed in front seats; under 7 must have child safety seat in rear

♈ 0.00%

△ Compulsory

🗀 Compulsory

💡 Recommended

🔥 Compulsory

🪖 Compulsory for all riders

⊖ 18 (16 for motorcycles, 14 for mopeds)

📰 International driving permit recommended

📱 Use only allowed with hands-free kit

Finland (FIN)

🕐	🏛	⚠	▲	🏙
	120	100	80	30-60

If towing

🕐	🏛	⚠	▲	🏙
	80	80	80	30-60

If towing a vehicle by rope, cable or rod, max speed limit 60 kph.

Maximum of 80 kph for vans and lorries

Speed limits are often lowered in winter

🔗 Compulsory in front and rear

👶 Children must travel with a safety belt or in special child's seat

♈ 0.05%

△ Compulsory

🗀 Recommended

💡 Recommended

🔥 Recommended

🪖 Compulsory for all riders

⊖ 18

📰 Third party insurance

📱 Use only allowed with hands-free kit

★ Dipped headlights must be used at all times

France (F)

🕐	🏛	⚠	▲	🏙
	130	110	90	50

On wet roads

🕐	🏛	⚠	▲	🏙
	110	90	80	50

50kph on all roads if fog reduces visibility to less than 50m. Licence will be lost and

Estonia note (top of column 4)

📱 Use only allowed with hands-free kit

★ Dipped headlights must be used at all times

driver fined for exceeding speed limit by over 40kph

- Compulsory in front seats and, if fitted, in rear
- Under 10 not allowed in front seats unless in approved safety seat facing backwards; in rear, if 4 or under, must have a child safety seat (rear facing if up to 9 months); if 5 to 10 may use a booster seat with suitable seat belt
- 0.05%
- Compulsory unless hazard warning lights are fitted; compulsory for vehicles over 3,500kgs or towing a trailer
- Recommended
- Recommended
- Compulsory for all riders
- 18 (16 for light motorcycles, 14 for mopeds)
- Use not permitted whilst driving
- ★ Tolls on motorways

Germany (D)

*	*	100	50
If towing			
*	*	80	50

*no limit, 130 kph recommended

- Compulsory
- Children under 12 and under 150cm must have a child safety seat, in front and rear
- 0.05%
- Compulsory
- Compulsory
- Recommended
- Recommended
- Compulsory for all riders
- 18 (motorbikes: 16 if not more than 125cc and limited to 11 kW)
- Third party insurance
- Use permitted only with hands-free kit – also applies to drivers of motorbikes and bicycles
- ★ Motorcyclists must use dipped headlights at all times.

Greece (GR)

120	110	110	50
If towing			
90	70	70	40

- Compulsory in front seats and, if fitted, in rear
- Under 12 not allowed in front seats except with suitable safety seat; under 10 not allowed in front seats
- 0.025%
- Compulsory

- Compulsory
- Recommended
- Compulsory
- Compulsory for all riders
- 18 (16 for low cc motorcycles)
- Third party insurance
- Use only allowed with hands-free kit

Hungary (H)

130	110	90	50
If towing			
80	70	70	50

- Compulsory in front seats and if fitted in rear seats
- Under 12 or under 140cm not allowed in front seats
- 0.00%
- Compulsory
- Compulsory
- Compulsory
- Recommended
- Compulsory for all riders
- 18
- Third party insurance
- Use only allowed with hands-free kit
- ★ All motorways are toll and operate the vignette system, tickets are available for 4 days, 10 days, 1 month, 1 year
- ★ Dipped headlights are compulsory during daylight hours (cars exempted in built-up areas)

Iceland (IS)

n/a	90	80	50

- Compulsory in front and rear seats
- Under 12 or under 140cm not allowed in front seats
- 0.00%
- Compulsory
- Compulsory
- Compulsory
- Recommended
- Compulsory for all riders
- 18
- Third party insurance
- Use only allowed with hands-free kit
- ★ Headlights are compulsory at all times
- ★ Highland roads are not suitable for ordinary cars
- ★ Driving off marked roads is forbidden

Ireland (IRL)

112	96	96	48
If towing			
80	80	80	48

- Compulsory in front seats and if fitted in rear seats. Driver responsible for ensuring passengers under 17 comply.
- Under 4 not allowed in front seats unless in a child safety seat or other suitable restraint
- 0.08%
- Recommended
- Recommended
- Recommended
- Recommended
- Compulsory for all riders
- 17 (16 for motorbikes up to 125cc; 18 for over 125cc; 18 for lorries; 21 bus/minibus)
- Third party insurance; international driving permit for non-EU drivers
- No specific legislation
- ★ Driving is on the left

Italy (I)

130	110	90	50
If towing			
80	70	70	50

- Compulsory in front seats and, if fitted, in rear
- Under 12 not allowed in front seats except in child safety seat; children under 3 must have special seat in the back
- 0.08%
- Compulsory
- Recommended
- Compulsory
- Recommended
- Compulsory for all motorcylists
- 18 (14 for mopeds, 16 for up to 125cc, 20 for up to 350cc)
- International Driving Licence unless you have photocard licence
- Use only allowed with hands-free kit

Latvia (LV)

n/a	90	90	50
If towing			
n/a	80	80	50

In residential areas limit is 20kph

- Compulsory in front seats and if fitted in rear

- If under 150cm must use child restraint in front and rear seats
- 0.05%
- Compulsory
- Compulsory
- Recommended
- Compulsory
- Compulsory for all riders
- 18 (14 for mopeds, 16 for up to 125cc, 21 for up to 350cc)
- International driving permit if licence is not in accordance with Vienna Convention
- Use only allowed with hands-free kit
- ★ Dipped headlights must be used at all times all year round
- ★ Cars and minibuses under 3.5 tonnes must have winter tyres from 1Dec-1Mar

Lithuania (LT)

130	110	90	60
If towing			
70	70	70	60

- Compulsory in front seats and if fitted in rear seats
- Under 12 not allowed in front seats unless in a child safety seat
- 0.04%
- Compulsory
- Compulsory
- Recommended
- Compulsory
- Compulsory for all riders
- 18 (14 for mopeds)
- Visa
- No legislation
- ★ Dipped headlights must be used day and night from Nov to Mar (all year for motorcyclists) and from 1 to 7 Sept

Luxembourg (L)

130/110	90	90	50
If towing			
90	75	75	50

- Compulsory
- Under 12 or 150cm not allowed in front seats unless in a child safety seat; under 12 must have child safety seat or belt in rear seats
- 0.08%
- Compulsory
- Recommended
- Recommended
- Recommended

- Compulsory for all riders
- 18 (16 for mopeds)
- Third party insurance
- Use permitted only with hands-free speaker system
- ★ Motorcyclists must use dipped headlights at all times.

Macedonia (MK)

120	100	60	60
If towing			
80	70	50	50

- Compulsory in front seats; compulsory if fitted in rear seats
- Under 12 not allowed in front seats
- 0.05%
- Compulsory
- Compulsory
- Compulsory
- Recommended
- Compulsory for all riders
- 18 (mopeds 16)
- International driving permit; visa
- No legislation

Moldova (MD)

90	90	60	60

- Compulsory in front seats
- Under 12 not allowed in front seats
- 0.00%
- Compulsory
- Compulsory
- Compulsory
- Recommended
- Compulsory for all riders
- 18 (mopeds 16)
- Visa
- No legislation

Netherlands (NL)

120	80	80	50

- Compulsory in front seats and, if fitted, rear
- Under 12 not allowed in front seats except in child restraint; in rear, 0-3 child safety restraint, 4-12 child restraint or seat belt
- 0.5%
- Recommended
- Recommended
- Recommended
- Recommended
- Compulsory for all riders

🚗 18 (16 for mopeds)

Third party insurance

Use only allowed with hands-free kit

Norway (N)

90	80	80	50
If towing trailer with brakes			
80	80	80	50
If towing trailer without brakes			
60	60	60	50

- Compulsory in front seats and, if fitted, in rear
- Under 4 must have child restraint; over 4 child restraint or seat belt
- 0.02%
- Compulsory
- Recommended
- Recommended
- Recommended
- Compulsory for all riders
- 18 (16 mopeds, heavy vehicles 18/21)
- Use only allowed with hands-free kit
- Dipped headlights must be used at all times
- Tolls apply on some bridges, tunnels and access roads into major cities

Poland (PL)

130	110	90	60
If towing			
80*	80	70	60

*40kph minimum; 20kph in residential areas

- Compulsory in front seats and, if fitted, in rear
- Under 12 not allowed in front seats unless in a child safety seat or the child is 150cm tall
- 0.02%
- Compulsory
- Recommended
- Recommended
- Compulsory
- Compulsory for all riders
- 17 (mopeds – 15, motorbikes – 16)
- International permit (recommended)
- Use only allowed with hands-free kit
- Between 1 Nov and 1 Mar dipped headlights must be used day and night

Portugal (P)

120*	100	90	50
If towing			
100*	80	70	50

*40kph minumum; 90kph maximum if licence held under 1 year

- Compulsory in front seats; compulsory if fitted in rear seats
- Under 3 not allowed in front seats unless in a child seat; 3 – 12 not allowed in front seats except in approved restraint system
- 0.05%. Imprisonment for 0.12% or more
- Compulsory
- Recommended
- Recommended
- Recommended
- Compulsory for all riders
- 18 (motorcycles under 50cc 16)
- Use not permitted
- Tolls on motorways

Romania (RO)

Cars			
120	90	90	50
Vehicles seating eight persons or more			
90	80	80	50
Motorcycles			
100	80	80	50

Jeep-like vehicles: 70kph outside built-up areas but 60kph in all areas if diesel

- Compulsory in front seats and, if fitted, in rear
- Under 12 not allowed in front seats
- 0.00%
- Recommended
- Compulsory
- Recommended
- Recommended
- Compulsory for all riders
- 18 (16 for mopeds)
- Visa (only if stay over 30 days for EU citizens); third party insurance
- Use only allowed with hands-free kit
- Tolls on Bucharest to Constanta motorway and bridges over Danube

Russia (RUS)

130	120	110	60

- Compulsory in front seats
- Under 12 not allowed in front seats
- 0.00%
- Compulsory
- Compulsory
- Recommended
- Compulsory
- Compulsory
- 18
- International driving licence with translation; visa
- No legislation

Serbia and Montenegro (YU)

120	100	80	60

- Compulsory in front and rear seats
- Under 12 not allowed in front seats
- 0.05%
- Compulsory
- Compulsory
- Recommended
- Compulsory
- Compulsory
- 18 (16 for motorbikes less than 125cc; 14 for mopeds)
- International driving permit; visa
- No legislation
- Tolls on motorways and some primary roads
- All types of fuel available at petrol stations
- 80km/h speed limit if towing a caravan

Slovak Republic (SK)

130	90	90	60

- Compulsory in front seats and, if fitted, in rear
- Under 12 not allowed in front seats unless in a child safety seat
- 0.0
- Compulsory
- Compulsory
- Compulsory
- Recommended
- Compulsory for motorcyclists
- 18 (15 for mopeds)
- International driving permit

Use only allowed with hands-free kit

- Tow rope recommended

Slovenia (SLO)

130	100*	90*	50
If towing			
80	80*	80*	50

*70kph in urban areas

- Compulsory in front seats and, if fitted, in rear
- Under 12 only allowed in the front seats with special seat; babies must use child safety seat
- 0.05%
- Compulsory
- Compulsory
- Compulsory
- Recommended
- Compulsory for all riders
- 18 (motorbikes up to 125cc – 16, up to 350cc – 18)
- Use only allowed with hands-free kit
- Dipped headlights must be used at all times

Spain (E)

120	100	90	50
If towing			
80	80	70	50

- Compulsory in front seats and if fitted in rear seats
- Under 12 not allowed in front seats except in a child safety seat
- 0.05% (0.03% if vehicle over 3,500 kgs or carries more than 9 passengers, and in first two years of driving licence)
- Two compulsory (one for in front, one for behind)
- Recommended
- Compulsory in adverse weather conditions
- Recommended
- Compulsory for all riders
- 18 (18/21 heavy vehicles; 18 for motorbikes over 125cc; 16 for motorbikes up to 125cc; 14 for mopeds up to 75cc)
- Third party insurance
- Use only allowed with hands-free kit
- Tolls on motorways

Sweden (S)

110	90	70	50
If towing trailer with brakes			
80	80	70	50

- Compulsory in front and rear seats
- Under 7 must have safety seat or other suitable restraint
- 0.02%
- Compulsory
- Recommended
- Recommended
- Recommended
- Compulsory for all riders
- 18
- Third party insurance
- No legislation
- Dipped headlights must be used at all times

Switzerland (CH)

120	100	80	50/30
If towing up to 1 tonne			
80	80	80	50/30
If towing over 1 tonne			
80	80	60	50/30

- Compulsory in front and, if fitted, in rear
- Under 7 not allowed in front seats unless in child restraint; between 7 and 12 must use child restraint or seatbelt
- 0.05%
- Compulsory
- Compulsory
- Recommended
- Recommended
- Compulsory for all riders
- 18 (mopeds up to 50cc – 14)
- Third party insurance
- Use only allowed with hands-free kit
- Motorways are all toll and a vignette must be purchased at the border. Can also be purchased online at www.swisstravelsystem.com/uk/ or phone 020 7292 1550. The vignette costs £17.50 and is valid for one calendar year.

Turkey (TR)

120	90	90	50
If towing			
70	70	70	40

- Compulsory in front seats
- Under 12 not allowed in front seats
- 0.05%
- Two compulsory (one in front, one behind)
- Compulsory
- Compulsory

Left sidebar (symbols legend)

🏍Compulsory

🏍 Compulsory for all riders (except on freight motorcycles)

⊖18

📖International driving permit advised; note that Turkey is in both Europe and Asia

📱Use only allowed with hands-free kit

★ Tow rope and tool kit must be carried

Ukraine (UA)

	🏘	🛤	⚠	🏔
⊘	130	90	90	60
If towing				
⊘	80	80	80	60

Speed limit in pedestrian zone 20 kph

🔖Compulsory in front and rear seats

🧒Under 12 not allowed in front seats

🍷0.0%

△Compulsory

⛑Compulsory

💡Optional

🏍Compulsory

🏍Compulsory for all riders

⊖18 – cars; 16 motorbikes

📖International driving permit; visa

📱No legislation

★Tow rope and tool kit must be carried

United Kingdom (GB)

	🏘	🛤	⚠	🏔
⊘	112	112	96	48
If towing				
⊘	96	96	80	48

🔖Compulsory in front seats and if fitted in rear seats

🧒Under 3 not allowed in front seats except with appropriate restraint, and in rear must use child restraint if available; 3–12 and under 150cm must use appropriate restraint or seat belt in front seats, and in rear if available

🍷0.08%

△Recommended

⛑Recommended

💡Recommended

🏍Recommended

🏍Compulsory for all riders

⊖17 (16 for mopeds)

📱Use only allowed with hands-free kit

★Driving is on the left

Main text

The resorts listed are popular ski centres, therefore road access to most is normally good and supported by road clearing during snow falls. However, mountain driving is never predictable and drivers should make sure they take suitable snow chains as well as emergency provisions and clothing. Listed for each resort are: the atlas page and grid square; the altitude; the number of lifts; the season start and end dates; the nearest town (with its distance in km) and the telephone number of the local tourist information centre ('00' prefix required for calls from the UK).

Andorra

Pyrenees

Pas de la Casa / Grau Roig 91 A4 2640m 31 lifts Dec-May •Andorra La Vella (30km) ☎+376 801060 🖥www.pasgrau.com Access via Envalira Pass (2407m), highest in Pyrenees, snow chains essential.

Austria

Alps

A 24-hour driving conditions information line is provided by the Tourist Office of Austria www.austria.info +43 1 588 660

Bad Gastein 72 A3 1002m 51 lifts Dec-Apr •Bad Hofgastein (6km) ☎+43 6434 85044 🖥www.skigastein.at Snow report: +43 6432 64555.

Bad Hofgastein 72 A3 860m 51 lifts Dec-Apr •Salzburg (90km) ☎+43 6432 33930 🖥www.badhofgastein.com

Bad Kleinkirchheim 72 B3 1100m 32 lifts Dec-Apr •Villach (35km) ☎+43 4240 8212 🖥www.badkleinkirchheim.com Snowfone:+43 4240 8222. Near Ebene Reichenau.

Ehrwald 71 A5 1000m 22 lifts Dec-Apr •Imst (30km) ☎+43 5673 2395 🖥www.tiscover.at/ehrwald Weather report: +43 5673 3329

Innsbruck 71 A6 574m 75 lifts Dec-Apr •Innsbruck ☎+43 5125 9850 🖥www.innsbruck-tourismus.com Motorway normally clear. The motorway through to Italy and through the Arlberg Tunnel West to Austria are both toll roads.

Ischgl 1400m 42 lifts Dec-May •Landeck (25km) ☎+43 5444 52660 🖥www.ischgl.com Car entry to resort prohibited between 2200hrs and 0600hrs.

Kaprun 72 A2 800m, 56 lifts Jan-Dec •Zell am See (10km) ☎+43 6542 7700 🖥www.zellkaprun.at Snowfone:+43 6547 8444.

Kirchberg in Tyrol 72 A2 860m 59 lifts Dec-Apr •Kitzbühel (6km) ☎+43 5357 2309 •www.kirchberg.at Easily reached from Munich International Airport (120 km)

Kitzbühel 72 A2 800m 59 lifts Dec-Apr •Wörgl (40km) ☎+43 5356 777 🖥www.kitzbuehel.com

Lech/Oberlech 71 A5 1450m 84 lifts Dec-Apr •Bludenz (50km) ☎+43 5583 21610 🖥www.Lech.at Roads normally cleared but keep chains accessible because of altitude. Road conditions report tel +43 5583 1515.

Mayrhofen 72 A1 630m 29 lifts Dec-Apr •Jenbach (35km) ☎+43 5285 67600 🖥www.mayrhofen.com Chains rarely required.

Obertauern 72 A3 1740m 27 lifts Nov-May •Radstadt (20km) ☎+43 6456 7252 🖥www.top-obertauern.com Roads normally cleared but chains accessibility recommended. Camper vans and caravans not allowed; park these in Radstadt

Saalbach Hinterglemm 72 A2 1003m 52 lifts Dec-Apr •Zell am See (19km) ☎+43 6541 6800 68 🖥www.saalbach.com Both village centres are pedestrianised and there is a good ski bus service during the daytime

St Anton am Arlberg 71 A5 1304m 84 lifts Nov-May •Innsbruck (104km) ☎+43 5446 22690 🖥www.stantona-marlberg.com Snow report tel +43 5446 2565

Schladming 72 A4 2708m 86 lifts Nov-Apr •Schladming ☎+43 3687 22777 🖥www.schladming.com

Serfaus 71 A5 1427m 53 lifts Dec-Apr •Landeck (30km) ☎+43 5476 6239 🖥www.serfaus.com Cars banned from village, use world's only 'hover' powered underground railway.

Sölden 71 B6 1377m, 32 lifts all year •Imst (50km) ☎+43 5254 5100 🖥www.soelden.com Roads normally cleared but snow chains recommended because of altitude. The route from Italy and the south over the Timmelsjoch via Obergurgl is closed in the winter and anyone arriving from the south should use the Brenner Pass motorway. Snow information tel +43 5254 2666.

Zell am See 72 A2 758m 57 lifts Dec-Mar •Zell am See ☎+43 6542 7700 🖥www.zellkaprun.at Snowfone +43 6542 73694 Low altitude, therefore good access and no mountain passes to cross.

Zell im Zillertal (Zell am Ziller) 72 A1 580m 47 lifts Dec-Apr •Jenbach (25km) ☎+43 5282 2281 🖥www.tiscover.at/zell Snowfone +43 5282 716526.

Zürs 71 A5 1720m 84 lifts Dec-May •Bludenz (30km) ☎+43 5583 2245 🖥www.zuers.com Roads normally cleared but keep chains accessible because of altitude. Village has garage with 24-hour self-service gas/petrol, breakdown service and wheel chains supply.

France

Alps

Alpe d'Huez 79 A5 1860m 87 lifts Dec-Apr •Grenoble (63km) ☎+33 4 76 11 44 44 🖥www.alpedhuez.com Snow chains may be required on access road to resort. Road report tel +33 4 76 11 44 50.

Avoriaz 70 B1 2277m 38 lifts Dec-May •Morzine (14km) ☎+33 4 50 74 02 11 🖥www.avoriaz.com Chains may be required for access road from Morzine. Car free resort, park on edge of village. Horse-drawn sleigh service available.

Chamonix-Mont-Blanc 70 C1 1035m 49 lifts Nov-May •Martigny (38km) ☎+33 4 50 53 00 24 🖥www.chamonix.com

Chamrousse 79 A4 1700m 26 lifts Dec-Apr •Grenoble (30km) ☎+33 4 76 89 92 65 🖥www.chamrousse.com Roads normally cleared, keep chains accessible because of altitude.

Châtel 2200m 40 lifts Dec-Apr •Thonon Les Bains (35km) ☎+33 4 50 73 22 44 🖥www.chatel.com

Courchevel 70 C1 1850m 185 lifts Dec-Apr •Moûtiers (23km) ☎+33 4 79 08 00 29 🖥www.courchevel.com Roads normally cleared but keep chains accessible. Traffic 'discouraged' within the four resort bases. Traffic info: +33 4 79 37 73 37.

Flaine 70 B1 1800m 74 lifts Dec-Apr •Cluses (25km) ☎+33 4 50 90 80 01 🖥www.flaine.com Keep chains accessible for D6 from Cluses to Flaine. Car access for depositing luggage and passengers only. 1500-space car park outside resort. Near Sixt-Fer-á-Cheval.

La Clusaz 69 C6 1100m 55 lifts Dec-Apr •Annecy (32km) ☎+33 4 50 32 65 00 🖥www.laclusaz.com Roads normally clear but keep chains accessible for final road from Annecy.

La Plagne 70 C1 2100m 110 lifts Dec-Apr •Moûtiers (32km) ☎+33 4 79 09 /9 79 🖥www.la-plagne.com Ten different centres up to 2100m altitude. Road access via Bozel, Landry or Aime normally cleared.

Les Arcs 70 C1 2600m 77 lifts Dec-Apr •Bourg-St-Maurice (15km) ☎+33 4 79 07 12 57 🖥www.lesarcs.com Three base areas up to 2000 metres; keep chains accessible. Pay parking at edge of each base resort.

Les Carroz d'Araches 70 B1 1140m 74 lifts Dec-Apr •Cluses (13km) ☎+33 4 50 90 00 04 🖥www.lescarroz.com

Les Deux-Alpes 79 B5 1650m 63 lifts Dec-May •Grenoble (75km) ☎+33 4 76 79 22 00 🖥www.les2alpes.com Roads normally cleared, however snow chains recommended for D213 up from valley road (N91).

Les Gets 70 B1 1172m 53 lifts Dec-May •Cluses (18km) ☎+33 4 50 75 80 80 🖥www.lesgets.com

Les Ménuires 69 C6 1815m 197 lifts Dec-Apr •Moûtiers (27km) ☎+33 4 79 00 73 00 🖥www.lesmenuires.com Keep chains accessible for N515A from Moûtiers.

Les Sept Laux 69 C6 1350m, 29 lifts Dec-Apr •Grenoble (38km) ☎+33 4 76 08 17 86 🖥www.les7laux.com Roads normally cleared, however keep chains accessible for mountain road up from the A41 motorway. Near St Sorlin d'Arves.

Megève 1350m? 2350m 117 lifts Dec-Apr •Sallanches (12km) ☎+33 4 50 21 27 28 🖥www.megeve.com Horse-drawn sleigh rides available.

Méribel 1400m 197 lifts Dec-May •Moûtiers (18km) ☎+33 4 79 08 60 01 🖥www.meribel.com Keep chains

accessible for 18km to resort on D90 from Moûtiers.

Morzine 70 B1 1000m 217 lifts, Dec-May •Thonon-Les-Bains (30km) +33 4 50 74 72 72 www.morzine.com

Pra Loup 79 B5 1600m 53 lifts Dec-Apr •Barcelonnette (10km) +33 4 92 84 10 04 www.praloup.com Roads normally cleared but chains accessibility recommended.

Risoul 79 B5 1850m 58 lifts Dec-Apr •Briançon (40km) +33 4 92 46 02 60 www.risoul.com Keep chains accessible. Near Guillestre.

St Gervais 70 C1 850m 121 lifts Dec-Apr +33 4 50 47 76 08 www.st-gervais.com

Serre-Chevalier 79 B5 1350m 79 lifts Dec-May •Briançon (10km) +33 4 92 24 98 98 www.serre-chevalier.com Made up of 13 small villages along the valley road, which is normally cleared.

Tignes 70 C1 2100m 97 lifts Jan-Dec +33 4 79 40 04 40 www.tignes.net Keep chains accessible because of altitude. Parking information tel +33 4 79 06 39 45.

Val d'Isère 70 C1 1850m 97 lifts Nov-May •Bourg-St-Maurice (30km) +33 4 79 06 06 60 www.valdisere.com Roads normally cleared but keep chains accessible.

Val Thorens 69 C6 2300m 197 lifts Nov-May •Moûtiers (37km) +33 4 79 00 08 08 www.valthorens.com Chains essential – highest ski resort in Europe. Obligatory paid parking on edge of resort.

Valloire 69 C6 1430m 36 lifts Dec-May •Modane (20km) +33 4 79 59 03 96 www.valloire.net Road normally clear up to the Col du Galbier, to the south of the resort, which is closed from 1st November to 1st June.

Valmeinier 69 C6 2600m 32 lifts Dec-Apr •St Michel de Maurienne (47km) +33 4 79 59 53 69 www.valmeinier.com Access from north on N9 / N902. Col du Galbier, to the south of the resort closed from 1st November to 1st June. Near Valloire.

Valmorel 69 C6 1400m 55 lifts Dec-Apr •Moûtiers (15km) +33 4 79 09 85 55 www.valmorel.com Near St Jean-de-Belleville.

Vars Les Claux 79 B5 1850m 58 lifts Dec-Apr •Briançon (40km) +33 4 92 46 51 31 www.vars-ski.com Four base resorts up to 1850 metres. Keep chains accessible. Road and weather information tel +33 4 36 68 02 05 and +33 4 91 78 78 78. Snowfone +33 492 46 51 04

Villard-de-Lans 79 A4 1050m 29 lifts Dec-Apr •Grenoble (32km) +33 4 76 95 10 38 www.villard-de-lans.com

Pyrenees

Font-Romeu 91 A5 1800m 33 lifts Dec-Apr •Perpignan (87km) +33 4 68 30 68 30 www.fontromeu.com Roads normally cleared but keep chains accessible.

St Lary-Soulan 830m 32 lifts Dec-Apr •Tarbes (75km) +33 5 62 39 50 81 www.saintlary.com Access roads constantly cleared of snow.

Vosges

La Bresse-Hohneck 900m 20 lifts Dec-Mar •Cornimont (6km) +33 3 29 25 41 29 www.labresse-remy.com

Germany

Alps

Garmisch-Partenkirchen 71 A6 702m 38 lifts Dec-Apr •Munich (95km) +49 8821 180 700 www.garmisch-partenkirchen.de Roads usually clear, chains rarely needed.

Oberaudorf 62 C3 483m 21 lifts Dec-Apr •Kufstein (15km) +49 8033 301 20 www.oberaudorf.de Motorway normally kept clear. Near Bayrischzell.

Oberstdorf 71 A5 815m 31 lifts Dec-Apr •Sonthofen (15km) +49 8322 7000 www.oberstdorf.de Snow information on tel +49 8322 3035 or 1095 or 5757.

Rothaargebirge

Winterberg 51 B4 700m 55 lifts Dec-Mar •Brilon (30km) +49 2981 925 00 www.winterberg.de Roads usually cleared, chains rarely required.

Greece

Central Greece

Mountain Parnassos: Kelaria-Fterolakka 112 D4 1750-1950m 14 lifts Dec-Apr •Amfiklia +30 22340 22694

Mountain Parnassos: Gerondourachos 112 D4 1800-2390m 3 lifts Dec-Apr •Amfiklia +30 69440 470731 www.parnassos-eot.gr

Ipiros

Mountain Pindos: Karakoli 112 C3 1350-1700m 1 lift Dec-Mar •Metsovon +30 26560 41333

Mountain Pindos: Profitis Ilias 112 C3 1500-1700m 3 lifts Dec-Mar •Metsovon +30 26560 41095

Peloponnisos

Mountain Helmos: Kalavrita Ski Centre 113 D4 1650-2340m 7 lifts Dec-Mar •Kalavrita +30 26920 244514 www.kalavrita-ski.gr/en/default.asp

Mountain Menalon: Oropedio Ostrakinos 113 E4 1600m 3 lifts Dec-Mar •Tripolis +30 27960 22227

Macedonia

Mountain Falakro: Agio Pneuma 112 A6 1720m 3 lifts Dec-Mar •Drama +30 25210 62224

Mountain Vasilitsa: Vasilitsa 112 B3 1750m 2 lifts Dec-Mar •Konitsa +30 24620 84850 www.vasilitsa.com

Mountain Vermio: Seli 112 B4 1500m 4 lifts Dec-Mar •Kozani +30 23310 26237

Mountain Vermio: Tria-Pente Pigadia 112 B3 1420-2005m 4 lifts Dec-Mar •Ptolemais +30 23320 44446

Mountain Vernon: Vigla 112 B3 1650-2000m 3 lifts Dec-Mar •Florina +30 23850 22354

Mountain Vrondous: Lailias 112 A5 1847m 3 lifts Dec-Mar •Serrai +30 23210 62400

Thessalia

Mountain Pilion: Agriolefkes 112 C5 1500m 4 lifts Dec-Mar •Volos +30 24280 73719

Italy

Alps

Bardonecchia 1312m 24 lifts Dec-Apr •Bardonecchia +39 122 99137 Snowfone +39 122 907778 www.goski.com/rit/bardon.htm Resort reached through the 11km Frejus tunnel from France, roads normally cleared.

Bórmio 71 B5 1225m 16 lifts Dec-Apr •Tirano (40km) +39 342 903300 www.bormio.com Tolls payable in Ponte del Gallo Tunnel, open 0800hrs-2000hrs.

Breuil-Cervinia 2050m 73 lifts Jan-Dec •Aosta (54km) +39 166 940986 www.breuil-cervinia.it Snow chains strongly recommended. Bus from Milan airport.

Courmayeur 70 C1 1224m 27 lifts Dec-Apr •Aosta (40km) +39 165 842370 www.courmayeur.net Access through the Mont Blanc tunnel from France. Roads constantly cleared.

Limone Piemonte 80 B1 1050m 29 lifts Dec-Apr •Cuneo (27km) +39 171 929515 www.limonepiemonte.it Roads normally cleared, chains rarely required. Snow report tel +39 171 926254.

Livigno 71 B5 1816m 33 lifts Dec-May •Zernez (CH) (27km) +39 342 996379 www.aptlivigno.it Keep chains accessible. La Drosa Tunnel from Zernez, Switzerland, is open only from 0800hrs to 2000hrs.

Sestrière 79 B5 2035m 91 lifts Dec-Apr •Oulx (22km) +39 122 755444 www.sestriere.it One of Europe's highest resorts; although roads are normally cleared, chains should be accessible.

Appennines

Roccaraso – Aremogna 103 B7 1285m 31 lifts Dec-Apr •Castel di Sangro (7km) +39 864 62210 www.roccaraso.net

Dolomites

Andalo – Fai della Paganella 71 B5 1042m 22 lifts Dec-Apr •Trento (40km) www.paganella.net +39 461 585588

Arabba 72 B1 2500m 30 lifts Dec-Apr •Brunico (45km) +39 436 79130 www.arabba.it Roads normally cleared but keep chains accessible.

Cortina d'Ampezzo 1224m 48 lifts Dec-Apr •Belluno (72km) +39 436 866252 www.cortinadampezzo.it Access from north on route 51 over the Cimabanche Pass may require chains.

Corvara (Alta Badia) 1568m 54 lifts Dec-Apr •Brunico (38km) +39 471 836176 www.altabadia.it/inverno Roads normally clear but keep chains accessible.

Madonna di Campiglio 71 B5 1550m 60 lifts Dec-Apr •Trento (60km) +39 465 442000 www.campiglio.net Roads normally cleared but keep chains accessible.

Moena di Fassa (Sorte/Ronchi) 1184m 29 lifts Dec-Apr •Bolzano (40km) +39 462 602466 www.dolomitisuperski.com/valfassa

Passo del Tonale 1883m 30 lifts Dec-Aug •Breno (50km) +39 364 903838 www.adamelloski.com Located on high mountain pass; keep chains accessible.

Selva di Val Gardena/Wolkenstein Groden 1563m 82 lifts Dec-Apr •Bolzano (40km) +39 471 792277 www.valgardena.it Roads normally cleared but keep chains accessible.

Norway

Hemsedal 2 F18 650m 16 lifts Nov-May •Honefoss (150km) +47 32 055030 www.hemsedal.com Be prepared for extreme weather conditions.

Trysil (Trysilfjellet) 2 F20 465m 24 lifts Nov-May •Elverum (100km) +47 62 451000 www.trysil.com Be prepared for extreme weather conditions.

Slovakia

Chopok 65 B5 2024m 21 lifts Nov-May •Jasna +421 44 5478 8889 www.jasna.sk

Donovaly 65 B5 1360m 15 lifts Nov-May •Ruzomberok +421 48 4199 8812 www.parksnow.sk

Martinské Hole 65 A4 1456m 7 lifts Nov-May •Zilina +421 41 500 3429 www.martinskehole.sk

Plejsy 65 B6 912m 8 lifts Nov-May •Krompachy +421 53 447 1121 www.plejsy.com

Strbske Pleso 65 A6 1915m 8 lifts Nov-May •Poprad +421 52 449 2343 www.parksnow.sk

Rohace 65 A5 1450m 4 lifts Nov-May •Liptovsky Mikulas +421 43 5395481

Slovenia

Julijske Alpe

Kanin 72 B3 2289m 6 lifts Dec-May •Bovec +386 5 3841 919 www.bovec.si

Kobla 72 B3 1480m 6 lifts Dec-Apr •Bohinjska Bistrica +386 4 5747 100 www.bohinj.si/kobla

Kranjska Gora 72 B3 1620m 20 lifts Dec-Apr •Kranjska Gora +386 4 588 1768 www.kranjska-gora.si

Vogel 72 B3 1800m 9 lifts Dec-Apr •Bohinjska Bistrica +386 4 5724 236 www.bohinj.si/vogel

Kawiniske Savinjske Alpe

Krvavec 73 B4 1970m 13 lifts Dec-May •Kranj +386 4 2525 930 www.rtc-krvavec.si

Pohorje

Rogla 73 B5 1517m 11 lifts Dec-May •Slovenska Bistrica +386 3 757 6000 www.unior.si/slo/turizem

Spain

Baqueira/Beret 90 A3 1500m 24 lifts Dec-Apr •Viella (15km) +34 973 644455 www.baqueira.es Roads normally clear but keep chains accessible. Snowfone tel +34 973 645025. Near Salardú.

Sistema Penibetico

Sierra Nevada 100 B2 2102m 21 lifts Dec-May •Granada (32km) +34 958 249100 www.sierranevadaski.com Access road designed to be avalanche safe and is snow cleared. Snowfone +34 958 249119.

Sweden

Idre Fjäll 2 F20 710m 30 lifts Oct-May •Mora (140km) +46 253 41000 www.idrefjall.se Be prepared for extreme weather conditions.

Sälen 2 F20 360m 101 lifts Nov-Apr •Malung (70km) +46 280 88000 www.salen.se, www.salenfjallen.se Be prepared for extreme weather conditions.

Switzerland

Adelboden 70 B2 1353m 50 lifts Dec-Apr •Frutigen (15km) +41 33 673 80 80 www.adelboden.ch

Arosa 71 B4 1800m 16 lifts Dec-Apr •Chur (30km) +41 81 378 70 20 www.arosa.ch Roads cleared but keep chains accessible because of high altitude (1800m).

Crans Montana 70 B2 1500m 35 lifts Dec-Apr, Jul-Oct •Sierre (15km) +41 27 485 04 04 www.crans-montana.ch Roads normally cleared, however keep chains accessible for ascent from Sierre.

Davos 71 B4 1560m 54 lifts Nov-Apr •Davos +41 81 415 21 21 www.davos.ch

Engelberg 70 B3 1000m 26 lifts Nov-Jun •Luzern (39km) +41 41 639 77 77 www.engelberg.ch Straight access road normally cleared.

Flums (Flumserberg) 71 A4 1400m 17 lifts Dec-Apr •Buchs (25km) +41 81 720 18 18 www.flumserberg.com Roads normally cleared, but 1000-metre vertical ascent; keep chains accessible.

Grindelwald 1034m 30 lifts Dec-Apr •Interlaken (20km) +41 33 854 12 12 www.grindelwald.ch

Gstaad – Saanenland 1050m 66 lifts Dec-Apr •Gstaad +41 33 748 81 81 www.gstaad.ch

Klosters 71 B4 1191m 61 lifts Dec-Apr •Davos (10km) +41 81 410 20 20 www.klosters.ch

Leysin 1263m 19 lifts Dec-Apr •Aigle (6km) +41 24 494 22 44 www.leysin.ch

Mürren 1650m 37 lifts Dec-Apr •Interlaken (18km) +41 33 856 86 86 www.wengen-muerren.ch No road access. Park in Strechelberg (1500 free places) and take the two-stage cable car.

Nendaz 1365m 91 lifts Nov-Apr •Sion (16km) +41 27 289 55 89 www.nendaz.ch Roads normally cleared, however keep chains accessible for ascent from Sion. Near Vex.

Saas-Fee 1800m 25 lifts Jan-Dec •Brig (35km) +41 27 958 18 58 www.saas-fee.ch Roads normally cleared but keep chains accessible because of altitude.

St Moritz 71 B4 1856m 58 lifts Nov-May •Chur (89km) +41 81 837 33 33 www.stmoritz.ch Roads normally cleared but keep chains accessible because of altitude.

Samnaun 71 B5 1846m 42 lifts Dec-May •Scuol (30km) +41 81 868 58 58 www.samnaun.ch Roads normally cleared but keep chains accessible.

Verbier 1500m 95 lifts Nov-May, Jun-Jul •Martigny (27km) +41 27 775 38 88 www.verbier.ch Roads normally cleared.

Villars 1253m 37 lifts Nov-Apr, Jun-Jul •Montreux (35km) +41 24 495 32 32 www.villars.ch Roads normally cleared but keep chains accessible for ascent from N9. Near Bex.

Wengen 1270m 37 lifts Dec-Apr •Interlaken (12km) +41 33 855 14 14 www.wengen-muerren.ch No road access. Park at Lauterbrunnen and take mountain railway.

Zermatt 1620m 73 lifts all year •Brig (42km) +41 27 966 81 00 www.zermatt.ch Cars not permitted in resort, park in Täsch (3km) and take shuttle train.

Turkey

North Anatolian Mountains

Uludag 114 B4 2543m 14 lifts Dec-March •Bursa (36km) +90 224 254 22 74 www.goski.com/rtur/uludag.htm

To the best of the Publisher's knowledge the information in this table was correct at the time of going to press. No responsibility can be accepted for any errors or their consequences.

300 greatest sights of Europe

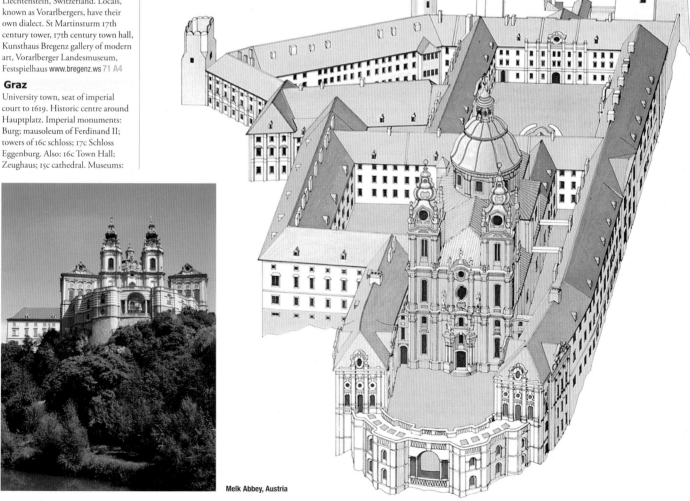

Maholicahaus, Vienna, Austria

Albania Shquipëria

www.albanian.com

Berat
Fascinating old town with picturesque Ottoman Empire buildings and traditional Balkan domestic architecture. 105 C5

Tirana Tiranë
Capital of Albania. Skanderbeg Square has main historic buildings. Also: 18c Haxhi Ethem Bey Mosque; Art Gallery (Albanian); National Museum of History. Nearby: medieval Krujë; Roman monuments. 105 B5

Austria Österreich

www.austria-tourism.at

Bregenz
Lakeside town bordering Germany, Liechtenstein, Switzerland. Locals, known as Vorarlbergers, have their own dialect. St Martinsturm 17th century tower, 17th century town hall, Kunsthaus Bregenz gallery of modern art, Vorarlberger Landesmuseum, Festspielhaus www.bregenz.ws 71 A4

Graz
University town, seat of imperial court to 1619. Historic centre around Hauptplatz. Imperial monuments: Burg; mausoleum of Ferdinand II; towers of 16c schloss; 17c Schloss Eggenburg. Also: 16c Town Hall; Zeughaus; 15c cathedral. Museums: Old Gallery (Gothic, Flemish); New Gallery (good 19–20c). www.graztourismus.at 73 A5

Innsbruck
Old town is reached by Maria-Theresien-Strasse with famous views. Buildings: Goldenes Dachl (1490s); 18c cathedral; remains of Hofburg imperial residence; 16c Hofkirche (tomb of Maximilian I). www.innsbruck.info 71 A6

Krems
On a hill above the Danube, medieval quarter has Renaissance mansions. Also: Gothic Piaristenkirche; Wienstadt Museum. www.krems.at 63 B6

Linz
Port on the Danube. Historic buildings are concentrated on Hauptplatz below the imperial 15c schloss. Notable: Baroque Old Cathedral; 16c Town Hall; New Gallery. www.linz.at 63 B5

Melk
Set on a rocky hill above the Danube, the fortified abbey is the greatest Baroque achievement in Austria – particularly the Grand Library and abbey church. www.stiftmelk.at 63 B6

Salzburg
Set in subalpine scenery, the town was associated with powerful 16-17c prince-archbishops. The 17c cathedral has a complex of archiepiscopal buildings: the Residence and its gallery (excellent 16–19c); the 13c Franciscan Church (notable altar). Other sights: Mozart's birthplace; the Hohensalzburg fortress; the Collegiate Church of St Peter (cemetery, catacombs); scenic views from Mönchsberg and Hettwer Bastei. The Grosse Festspielhaus runs the Salzburg festival. www2.salzburg.info 62 C4

Salzkammergut
Natural beauty with 76 lakes (Wolfgangersee, Altersee, Gosausee, Traunsee, Grundlsee) in mountain scenery. Attractive villages (St Wolfgang) and towns (Bad Ischl, Gmunden) include Hallstatt, famous for Celtic remains. www.salzkammergut.at 63 C4

Vienna Wien
Capital of Austria. The historic centre lies within the Ring. Churches: Gothic St Stephen's Cathedral; 17c Imperial Vault; 14c Augustine Church; 14c Church of the Teutonic Order (treasure); 18c Baroque churches (Jesuit Church, Franciscan Church, St Peter, St Charles). Imperial residences: Hofburg; Schönbrunn. Architecture of Historicism on Ringstrasse (from 1857). Art Nouveau: Station Pavilions, Postsparkasse, Looshaus, Majolicahaus. Exceptional museums: Art History Museum (antiquities, old masters); Cathedral and Diocesan Museum (15c); Academy of Fine Arts (Flemish); Belvedere (Gothic, Baroque, 19–20c). www.wien.gv.at 64 B2

Belgium Belgique

www.visitbelgium.com

Antwerp Antwerpen
City with many tall gabled Flemish houses on the river. Heart of the city is Great Market with 16–17c guild-houses and Town Hall. 14–16c Gothic cathedral has Rubens paintings. Rubens also at the Rubens House and his burial place in St Jacob's Church. Excellent museums: Mayer van den Berg Museum (applied arts); Koninklijk Museum of Fine Arts (Flemish, Belgian). www.visitantwerp.be 49 B5

Bruges Brugge
Well-preserved medieval town with narrow streets and canals. Main squares: the Market with 13c Belfort and covered market; the Burg with Basilica of the Holy Blood and Town Hall. The Groeninge Museum and Memling museum in St Jans Hospital show 15c Flemish masters. The Onze Lieve Vrouwekerk has a famous *Madonna and Child* by Michelangelo www.brugge.be 49 B4

Brussels Bruxelles
Capital of Belgium. The Lower Town is centred on the enormous Grand Place with Hôtel de Ville and rebuilt guildhouses. Symbols of the city include the 'Manneken Pis' and Atomium (giant model of a molecule). The 13c Notre Dame de la Chapelle is the oldest church. The Upper Town contains: Gothic cathedral; Neoclassical Place Royale; 18c King's Palace; Royal Museums of Fine Arts (old and modern masters). Also: much Art Nouveau (Victor Horta Museum, Hôtel Tassel, Hôtel Solvay); Place du Petit Sablon and Place du Grand Sablon; 19c Palais de Justice. www.brusselsinternational.be 49 C5

Ghent Gent
Medieval town built on islands surrounded by canals and rivers. Views from Pont St-Michel. The Graslei and Koornlei quays have Flemish guild houses. The Gothic cathedral has famous Van Eyck altarpiece. Also: Belfort; Cloth Market; Gothic Town

Melk Abbey, Austria

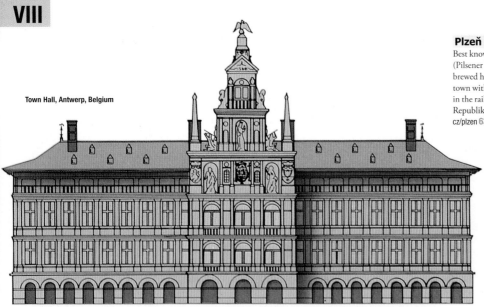
Town Hall, Antwerp, Belgium

Hall; Gravensteen. Museums: Bijloke Museum in beautiful abbey (provincial and applied art); Museum of Fine Arts (old masters). www.gent.be **49 B4**

Namur
Reconstructed medieval citadel is the major sight of Namur, which also has a cathedral and provincial museums. www.namur.be **49 C5**

Tournai
The Romanesque-Gothic cathedral is Belgium's finest (much excellent art). Fine Arts Museum has a good collection (15–20c). www.tournai.be **49 C4**

Bulgaria Bulgariya
www.bulgariatravel.org

Black Sea Coast
Beautiful unspoiled beaches (Zlatni Pyasŭtsi). The delightful resort Varna is popular. Nesebuˇr is famous for Byzantine churches. Also: Danube Delta in Hungary. **11 E9**

Koprivshtitsa
Beautiful village known both for its half-timbered houses and links with the April Rising of 1876. Six house museums amongst which the Lyutov House and the Oslekov House, plus the birthplaces of Georgi Benkovski, Dimcho Debelyanov, Todor Kableshkov, and Lyuben Karavelov.

Plovdiv
City set spectacularly on three hills. The old town has buildings from many periods: 2c Roman stadium and amphitheatre; 14c Dzumaiya Mosque; 19c Koyumdjioglu House and Museum (traditional objects). Nearby: Bačkovo Monastery (frescoes). www.plovdiv.org **11 E8**

Rila
Bulgaria's finest monastery, set in the most beautiful scenery of the Rila mountains. The church is richly decorated with frescoes.

Sofia Sofiya
Capital of Bulgaria. Sights: exceptional neo-Byzantine cathedral; Church of St Sofia; 4c rotunda of St George (frescoes); Byzantine Boyana Church (frescoes) on panoramic Mount Vitoša. Museums: National Historical Museum (particularly for Thracian artefacts); National Art Gallery (icons, Bulgarian art). www.sofia.bg/en **11 E7**

Veliko Tŭrnovo
Medieval capital with narrow streets. Notable buildings: House of the Little

Monkey; Hadji Nicoli Inn; ruins of medieval citadel; Baudouin Tower; churches of the Forty Martyrs and of SS Peter and Paul (frescoes); 14c Monastery of the Transfiguration. www.veliko-tarnovo.net **11 E8**

Croatia Hrvatska
www.croatia.hr

Dalmatia Dalmacija
Exceptionally beautiful coast along the Adriatic. Among its 1185 islands, those of the Kornati Archipelago and Brijuni Islands are perhaps the most spectacular. Along the coast are several attractive medieval and Renaissance towns, most notably Dubrovnik, Split, Šibenik, Trogir, Zadar. www.dalmacija.net **83 B4**

Dubrovnik
Surrounded by medieval and Renaissance walls, the city's architecture dates principally from 15–16c. Sights: many churches and monasteries including Church of St Vlah and Dominican monastery (art collection); promenade street of Stradun, Dubrovnik Museums; Renaissance Rector's Palace; Onofrio's fountain; Sponza Palace. The surrounding area has some 80 16c noblemen's summer villas. www.dubrovnik-online.com **105 A4**

Islands of Croatia
There are over 1,000 islands off the coast of Croatia among which there is Brač, known for its white marble and the beautiful beaches of Bol (www.bol.hr); Hvar (www.hvar.hr) is beautifully green with fields of lavender, marjoram, rosemary, sage and thyme; Vis (www.tz-vis.hr) has the beautiful towns of Komiža and Vis Town, with the Blue Cave on nearby Biševo. **83–84**

Istria Istra
Peninsula with a number of ancient coastal towns (Rovinj, Poreč, Pula, Piran in Slovene Istria) and medieval hill-top towns (Motovun). Pula has Roman monuments (exceptional 1c amphitheatre). Poreč has narrow old streets; the mosaics in 6c Byzantine basilica of St Euphrasius are exceptional. See also Slovenia. www.istra.com **82 A2**

Plitvička Jezera
Outstandingly beautiful world of water and woodlands with 16 lakes and 92 waterfalls interwoven by canyons. www.np-plitvicka-jezera.hr **83 B4**

Split
Most notable for the exceptional 4c palace of Roman Emperor Diocletian, elements of which are incorporated into the streets and buildings of the town itself. The town also has a cathedral (11c baptistry) and a Franciscan monastery. www.split.hr **83 C5**

Trogir
The 13–15c town centre is surrounded by medieval city walls. Romanesque-Gothic cathedral includes the chapel of Ivan the Blessed. Dominican and Benedictine monasteries house art collections. www.trogir-online.com **83 C5**

Zagreb
Capital city of Croatia with cathedral and Archbishop's Palace in Kaptol and to the west Gradec with Baroque palaces. Donji Grad is home to the Archaeological Museum, Art Pavilion, Museum of Arts and Crafts, Ethnographic Museum, Mimara Museum and National Theatre. www.zagreb-touristinfo.hr **73 C5**

Czech Republic Česka Republica
www.czech.cz

Brno
Capital of Moravia. Sights: Vegetable Market and Old Town Hall; Capuchin crypt decorated with bones of dead monks; hill of St Peter with Gothic cathedral; Mies van der Rohe's buildings (Bata, Avion Hotel, Togendhat House). Museums: UPM (modern applied arts); Pražáků Palace (19c Czech art). www.brno.cz **64 A2**

České Budějovice
Famous for Budvar beer, the medieval town is centred on náměsti Přemysla Otokara II. The Black Tower gives fine views. Nearby: medieval Český Krumlov. www.c-budejovice.cz **63 B5**

Kutná Hora
A town with strong silver mining heritage shown in the magnificent Cathedral of sv Barbara which was built by the miners. See also the ossuary with 40,000 complete sets of bones moulded into sculptures and decorations. www.kutnohorsko.cz **53 D5**

Olomouc
Well-preserved medieval university town of squares and fountains. The Upper Square has the Town Hall. Also: 18c Holy Trinity; Baroque Church of St Michael. www.olomoucko.cz **64 A3**

Plzeň
Best known for Plzeňský Prazdroj (Pilsener Urquell), beer has been brewed here since 1295. An industrial town with eclectic architecture shown in the railway stations and the namesti Republiky (main square). www.zcu.cz/plzen **63 A3**

Prague Praha
Capital of Czech Republic and Bohemia. The Castle Quarter has a complex of buildings behind the walls (Royal Castle; Royal Palace; cathedral). The Basilica of St George has a fine Romanesque interior. The Belvedere is the best example of Renaissance architecture. Hradčani Square has aristocratic palaces and the National Gallery. The Little Quarter has many Renaissance (Wallenstein Palace) and Baroque mansions and the Baroque Church of St Nicholas. The Old Town has its centre at the Old Town Square with the Old Town Hall (astronomical clock), Art Nouveau Jan Hus monument and Gothic Týn church. The Jewish quarter has 14c Staranova Synagogue and Old Jewish Cemetery. The Charles Bridge is famous. The medieval New Town has many Art Nouveau buildings and is centred on Wenceslas Square. www.prague.cz **53 C4**

Spas of Bohemia
Spa towns of Karlovy Vary (Carlsbad), Márianske Lázně (Marienbad) and Frantiskovy Lázně (Franzenbad). **52 C2**

Denmark Danmark
www.visitdenmark.com

Århus
Second largest city in Denmark with a mixture of old and new architecture that blends well, Århus has been dubbed the culture capital of Denmark with the Gothic Domkirke; Latin Quarter; 13th Century Vor Frue Kirke; Den Gamle By, open air museum of traditional Danish life; ARoS, Århus Art Museum. www.visitaarhus.com **39 C3**

Copenhagen København
Capital of Denmark. Old centre has fine early 20c Town Hall. Latin Quarter has 19c cathedral. 18c Kastellet has statue of the Little Mermaid nearby. The 17c Rosenborg Castle was a royal residence, as was the Christianborg (now government offices). Other popular sights: Nyhavn canal; Tivoli Gardens. Excellent art collections: Ny Carlsberg Glypotek; State Art Museum; National Museum. www.visitcopenhagen.dk **41 D2**

Hillerød
Frederiksborg is a fine red-brick Renaissance castle set among three lakes. **41 D2**

Roskilde
Ancient capital of Denmark. The marvellous cathedral is a burial place of the Danish monarchy. www.visitroskilde.com **39 D5**

Estonia Eesti
www.visitestonia.com

Kuressaare
Main town on the island of Saaremaa with the 14c Kuressaare Kindlus. www.kuressaare.ee **6 B7**

Pärnu
Sea resort with an old town centre. Sights: 15c Red Tower; neoclassical Town Hall; St Catherine's Church. www.parnu.ee **6 B8**

Tallinn
Capital of Estonia. The old town is centred on the Town Hall Square. Sights: 15c Town Hall; Toompea Castle; Three Sisters houses. Churches: Gothic St Nicholas; 14c Church of the Holy Spirit; St Olaf's Church. www.tallinn.ee **6 B8**

Tartu
Historic town with 19c university. The Town Hall Square is surrounded by neoclassical buildings. Also: remains of 13c cathedral; Estonian National Museum. www.tartu.ee **7 B9**

Finland Suomi
www.virtualfinland.fi

Finnish Lakes
Area of outstanding natural beauty covering about one third of the country with thousands of lakes, of which Päijänne and Saimaa are the most important. Tampere, industrial centre of the region, has numerous museums, including the Sara Hildén Art Museum (modern). Savonlinna has the medieval Olavinlinna Castle. Kuopio has the Orthodox and Regional Museums. **3 E27**

Helsinki
Capital of Finland. The 19c neoclassical town planning between the Esplanade and Senate Square includes the Lutheran cathedral. There is also a Russian Orthodox cathedral. The Constructivist Stockmann Department Store is the largest in Europe. The main railway station is Art Nouveau. Gracious 20c buildings in Mannerheimintie avenue include Finlandiatalo by Alvar Aalto. Many good museums: Art Museum of the Ateneum (19–20c); National Museum; Museum of Applied Arts; Helsinki City Art Museum (modern Finnish); Open Air Museum (vernacular architecture); 18c fortress of Suomenlinna has several museums. www.hel.fi **7 A8**

Lappland (Finnish)
Vast unspoiled rural area. Lappland is home to thousands of nomadic Sámi living in a traditional way. The capital, Rovaniemi, was rebuilt after WWII; museums show Sámi history and culture. Nearby is the Arctic Circle with the famous Santa Claus Village. Inari is a centre of Sámi culture. See also Norway and Sweden. www.laplandfinland.com **3 C26**

France
www.franceguide.com

Albi
Old town with rosy brick architecture. The vast Cathédrale Ste-Cécile (begun 13c) holds some good art. The Berbie Palace houses the Toulouse-Lautrec museum. www.mairie-albi.fr **77 C5**

Alps
Grenoble, capital of the French Alps, has a good 20c collection in the Museum of Painting and Sculpture. The Vanoise Massif has the greatest number of resorts (Val d'Isère, Courchevel). Chamonix has spectacular views on Mont Blanc, France's and Europe's highest peak. www.thealps.com **69 C5**

Amiens
France's largest Gothic cathedral has beautiful decoration. The Museum of Picardy has unique 16c panel paintings. www.amiens.fr 58 A3

Arles
Ancient, picturesque town with Roman relics (1c amphitheatre), 11c cathedral, Archaeological Museum (Roman art). www.ville-arles.fr 78 C3

Avignon
Medieval papal capital (1309–77) with 14c walls and many ecclesiastical buildings. Vast Palace of the Popes has stunning frescoes. The Little Palace has fine Italian Renaissance painting. The 12–13c Bridge of St Bénézet is famous. www.ot-avignon.fr 78 C3

Bourges
The Gothic Cathedral of St Etienne, one of the finest in France, has a superb sculptured choir. Also notable is the House of Jacques Coeur. www.bourgestourisme.com 68 A2

Burgundy Bourgogne
Rural wine region with a rich Romanesque, Gothic and Renaissance heritage. The 12c cathedral in Autun and 12c basilica in Vézelay have fine Romanesque sculpture. Monasteries include 11c L'Abbaye de Cluny (ruins) and L'Abbaye de Fontenay. Beaune has beautiful Gothic Hôtel-Dieu and 15c Nicolas Rolin hospices. www.burgundy-tourism.com 69 B4

Brittany Bretagne
Brittany is famous for cliffs, sandy beaches and wild landscape. It is also renowned for megalithic monuments (Carnac) and Celtic culture. Its capital, Rennes, has the Palais de Justice and good collections in the Museum of Brittany (history) and Museum of Fine Arts. Also: Nantes; St-Malo. www.brittany-bretagne.com 56–57

Caen
City with two beautiful Romanesque buildings: Abbaye aux Hommes; Abbaye aux Dames. The château has two museums (15–20c painting; history). The *Bayeux Tapestry* is displayed in nearby Bayeux. www.ville-caen.fr 57 A5

Carcassonne
Unusual double-walled fortified town of narrow streets with an inner fortress. The fine Romanesque Church of St Nazaire has superb stained glass. www.carcassonne.org 77 C5

Chartres
The 12–13c cathedral is an exceptionally fine example of Gothic architecture (Royal Doorway, stained glass, choir screen). The Fine Arts Museum has a good collection. www.chartres.com 58 B2

Loire Valley
The Loire Valley has many 15–16c châteaux built amid beautiful scenery by French monarchs and members of their courts. Among the most splendid are Azay-le-Rideau, Chenonceaux and Loches. Also: Abbaye de Fontévraud. www.lvo.com 67 A5

Clermont-Ferrand
The old centre contains the cathedral built out of lava and Romanesque basilica. The Puy de Dôme and Puy de Sancy give spectacular views over some 60 extinct volcanic peaks (puys). www.ville-clermont-ferrand.fr 68 C3

Colmar
Town characterised by Alsatian half-timbered houses. The Unterlinden Museum has excellent German religious art including the famous Isenheim altarpiece. The Dominican church also has a fine altarpiece. www.ot-colmar.fr 60 B3

Corsica Corse
Corsica has a beautiful rocky coast and mountainous interior. Napoleon's birthplace of Ajaccio has: Fesch Museum with Imperial Chapel and a large collection of Italian art; Maison Bonaparte; cathedral. Bonifacio, a medieval town, is spectacularly set on a rock over the sea. www.visit-corsica.com 102

Côte d'Azur
The French Riviera is best known for its coastline and glamorous resorts. There are many relics of artists who worked here: St-Tropez has Musée de l'Annonciade; Antibes has 12c Château Grimaldi with the Picasso Museum; Cagnes has the Renoir House and Mediterranean Museum of Modern Art; St-Paul-de-Vence has the excellent Maeght Foundation and Matisse's Chapelle du Rosaire. Cannes is famous for its film festival. Also: Marseille, Monaco, Nice. www.cote.azur.fr 79 C6

Dijon
Great 15c cultural centre. The Palais des Ducs et des Etats is the most notable monument and contains the Museum of Fine Arts. Also: the Charterhouse of Champmol. www.dijon-tourism.com 69 A5

Disneyland Paris
Europe's largest theme park follows in the footsteps of its famous predecessors in the United States. www.disneylandparis.com 59 B3

Le Puy-en-Velay
Medieval town bizarrely set on the peaks of dead volcanoes. It is dominated by the Romanesque cathedral (cloisters). The Romanesque chapel of St-Michel is dramatically situated on the highest rock. www.ot-lepuyenvelay.fr 78 A2

Lyon
France's third largest city has an old centre and many museums including the Museum of the History of Textiles and the Museum of Fine Arts (old masters). www.lyon-france.com 69 C4

Marseilles
Marseille
Second largest city in France. Spectacular views from the 19c Notre-Dame-de-la-Garde. The Old Port has 11-12c Basilique St Victor (crypt, catacombs). Cantini Museum has major collection of 20c French art. Château d'If was the setting of Dumas' *The Count of Monte Cristo*. www.marseille-tourisme.com 79 C4

Mont-St-Michel
Gothic pilgrim abbey (11–12c) set dramatically on a steep rock island rising from mud flats and connected to the land by a road covered by the tide. The abbey is made up of a complex of buildings. www.e-mont-saint-michel.com 57 B4

Nancy
A centre of Art Nouveau. The 18c Place Stanislas was constructed by dethroned Polish king Stanislas. Museums: School of Nancy Museum (Art Nouveau furniture); Fine Arts Museum. www.ot-nancy.fr 60 B2

Nantes
Former capital of Brittany, with the 15c Château des ducs de Bretagne. The cathedral has a striking interior. www.nantes-tourisme.com 66 A3

Nice
Capital of the Côte d'Azur, the old town is centred on the old castle on the hill. The seafront includes the famous 19c Promenade des Anglais. The aristocratic quarter of the Cimiez Hill has the Marc Chagall Museum and the Matisse Museum. Also: Museum of Modern and Contemporary Art (especially neo-Realism and Pop Art). www.nicetourism.com 79 C6

Paris
Capital of France, one of Europe's most interesting cities. The Île de la Cité area, an island in the River Seine has the 12–13c Gothic Notre Dame (wonderful stained glass) and La Sainte-Chapelle (1240–48), one of the jewels of Gothic art. The Left Bank area: Latin Quarter with the famous Sorbonne university; Museum of Cluny housing medieval art; the Panthéon; Luxembourg Palace and Gardens; Montparnasse, interwar artistic and literary centre; Eiffel Tower; Hôtel des Invalides with Napoleon's tomb. Right Bank: the great boulevards (Avenue des Champs-Élysées joining the Arc de Triomphe and Place de la Concorde); 19c Opéra Quarter; Marais, former aristocratic quarter of elegant mansions (Place des Vosges); Bois de Boulogne, the largest park in Paris; Montmartre, centre of 19c bohemianism, with the Basilique Sacré-Coeur.

The Church of St Denis is the first gothic church and the mausoleum of the French monarchy. Paris has three of the world's greatest art collections: The Louvre (to 19c, *Mona Lisa*), Musée d'Orsay (19–20c) and National Modern Art Museum in the Pompidou Centre. Other major museums include: Orangery Museum; Paris Museum of Modern Art; Rodin Museum; Picasso Museum. Notable cemeteries with graves of the famous: Père-Lachaise, Montmartre, Montparnasse. Near Paris are the royal residences of Fontainebleau and Versailles. www.paris.fr 58 B3

Pyrenees
Beautiful unspoiled mountain range. Towns include: delightful sea resorts of St-Jean-de-Luz and Biarritz; Pau, with access to the Pyrenees National Park; pilgrimage centre Lourdes. www.pyrenees-online.fr 76-77

Reims
Together with nearby Epernay, the centre of champagne production. The 13c Gothic cathedral is one of the greatest architectural achievements in France (stained glass by Chagall). Other sights: Palais du Tau with cathedral sculpture, 11c Basilica of St Rémi; cellars on Place St-Niçaise and Place des Droits-des-Hommes. www.reims-tourisme.com 59 A5

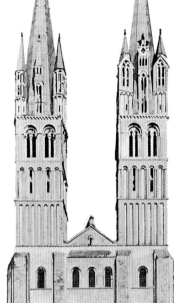
Abbaye aux Hommes, Caen, France

Rouen
Old centre with many half-timbered houses and 12–13c Gothic cathedral and the Gothic Church of St Maclou with its fascinating remains of a dance macabre on the former cemetery of Aître St-Maclou. The Fine Arts Museum has a good collection. www.mairie-rouen.fr 58 A2

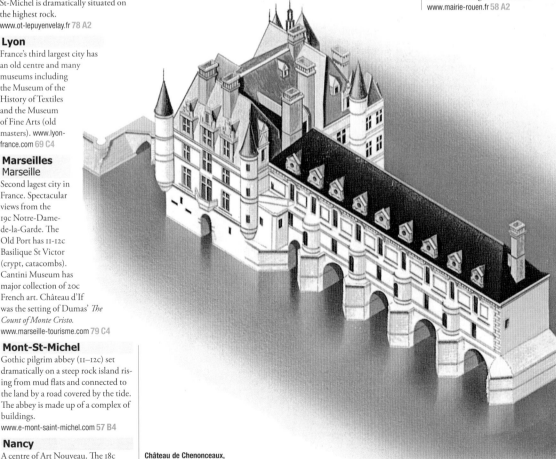
Château de Chenonceaux, Châteaux of the Loire, France

St-Malo

Fortified town (much rebuilt) in a fine coastal setting. There is a magnificent boat trip along the river Rance to Dinan, a splendid well-preserved medieval town. www.saint-malo.fr **57 B3**

Strasbourg

Town whose historic centre includes a well-preserved quarter of medieval half-timbered Alsatian houses, many of them set on the canal. The cathedral is one of the best in France. The Palais Rohan contains several museums. www.strasbourg.fr **60 B3**

Toulouse

Medieval university town characterised by flat pink brick (Hôtel Assézat). The Basilique St Sernin, the largest Romanesque church in France, has many art treasures. Marvellous Church of the Jacobins holds the body of St Thomas Aquinas. www.ot-toulouse.fr **77 C4**

Tours

Historic town centred on Place Plumereau. Good collections in the Guilds Museum and Fine Arts Museum. www.tours.fr **67 A5**

Versailles

Vast royal palace built for Louis XIV, primarily by Mansart, set in large formal gardens with magnificent fountains. The extensive and much-imitated state apartments include the famous Hall of Mirrors and the exceptional Baroque chapel. www.chateauversailles.fr **58 B3**

Vézère Valley Caves

A number of prehistoric sites, most notably the cave paintings of Lascaux (some 17,000 years old), now only seen in a duplicate cave, and the cave of Font de Gaume. The National Museum of Prehistory is in Les Eyzies. www.leseyzies.com **77 B4**

Germany Deutschland

www.germany-tourism.de

Northern Germany

Aachen

Once capital of the Holy Roman Empire. Old town around the Münsterplatz with magnificent cathedral. An exceptionally rich treasure is in the Schatzkammer. The Town Hall is on the medieval Market. www.aachen.de **50 C2**

Berlin

Capital of Germany. Sights include: the Kurfürstendamm avenue; Brandenburg Gate, former symbol of the division between East and West Germany; Tiergarten; Unter den Linden; 19c Reichstag. Berlin has many excellent art and history collections. Museum Island includes: Pergamon Museum (classical antiquity, Near and Far East, Islam); Bode Museum (Egyptian, Early Christian, Byzantine and European); Old National Gallery (19–20c German). Dahlem Museums: Picture Gallery (13–18c); Sculpture Collection (13–19c); Prints and Drawings Collection; Die Brücke Museum (German Expressionism). Tiergarten Museums: New National Gallery (19–20c); Decorative Arts Museum; Bauhaus Archive. In the Kreuzberg area: Berlin Museum; Grupius Building with Jewish Museum and Berlin Gallery; remains of Berlin Wall and Checkpoint Charlie House. Schloss Charlottenburg houses a number of collections including the National Gallery's Romantic Gallery; the Egyptian Museum is nearby. www.berlin-tourist-information.de **45 C5**

Cologne Köln

Ancient city with 13–19c cathedral (rich display of art). In the old town are the Town Hall and many Romanesque churches (Gross St Martin, St Maria im Kapitol, St Maria im Lyskirchen, St Ursula, St Georg, St Severin, St Pantaleon, St Apostolen). Museums: Diocesan Museum (religious art); Roman-German Museum (ancient history); Wallraf-Richartz/Ludwig Museum (14–20c art). www.koeln.de **50 C2**

German Alpine Road Deutsche Alpenstrasse

German Alpine Road in the Bavarian Alps, from Lindau on Bodensee to Berchtesgaden. The setting for 19c fairy-tale follies of Ludwig II of Bavaria (Linderhof, Hohenschwangau, Neuschwanstein), charming old villages (Oberammergau) and Baroque churches (Weiss, Ottobeuren). Garmisch-Partenkirchen has views on Germany's highest peak, the Zugspitze. www.deutsche-alpenstrasse.de **62 C2**

Dresden

Historic centre with a rich display of Baroque architecture. Major buildings: Castle of the Electors of Saxony; 18c Hofkirche; Zwinger Palace with fountains and pavilions (excellent old masters); Albertinum with excellent Gallery of New Masters; treasury of Grünes Gewölbe. The Baroque-planned New Town contains the Japanese Palace and Schloss Pillnitz. www.dresden.de **53 B3**

Frankfurt

Financial capital of Germany. The historic centre around the Römerberg Square has 13–15c cathedral, 15c Town Hall, Gothic St Nicholas Church, Saalhof (12c chapel). Museums: Museum of Modern Art (post-war); State Art Institute. www.frankfurt.de **51 C4**

Hamburg

Port city with many parks, lakes and canals. The Kunsthalle has Old Masters and 19-20c German art. Buildings: 19c Town Hall; Baroque St Michael's Church. www.hamburg-tourismus.de **44 B2**

Hildesheim

City of Romanesque architecture (much destroyed). Principal sights: St Michael's Church; cathedral (11c interior, sculptured doors, St Anne's Chapel); superb 15c Tempelhaus on the Market Place. www.hildesheim.de **51 A5**

Lübeck

Beautiful old town built on an island and characterised by Gothic brick architecture. Sights: 15c Holsten Gate; Market with the Town Hall and Gothic brick St Mary's Church; 12–13c cathedral; St Ann Museum. www.luebeck-tourism.de **44 B2**

Mainz

The Electoral Palatinate schloss and Market fountain are Renaissance. Churches: 12c Romanesque cathedral; Gothic St Steven's (with stained glass by Marc Chagall). www.mainz.de **50 C4**

Marburg

Medieval university town with the Market Place and Town Hall, St Elizabeth's Church (frescoes, statues, 13c shrine); 15–16c schloss. www.marburg.de **51 C4**

Münster

Historic city with well-preserved Gothic and Renaissance buildings: 14c Town Hall; Romanesque-Gothic cathedral. The Westphalian Museum holds regional art. www.munster.de **50 B3**

Potsdam

Beautiful Sanssouci Park contains several 18–19c buildings including: Schloss Sanssouci; Gallery (European masters); Orangery; New Palace; Chinese Teahouse. www.potsdam.de **45 C5**

Rhein Valley Rheintal

Beautiful 80km gorge of the Rhein Valley between Mainz and Koblenz with rocks (Loreley), vineyards (Bacharach, Rüdesheim), white medieval towns (Rhens, Oberwesel) and castles. Some castles are medieval (Marksburg, Rheinfels, island fortress Pfalzgrafenstein) others were built or rebuilt in the 19c (Stolzenfels, Rheinstein). www.rheintal.de **50 C3**

Weimar

The Neoclassical schloss, once an important seat of government, now houses a good art collection. Church

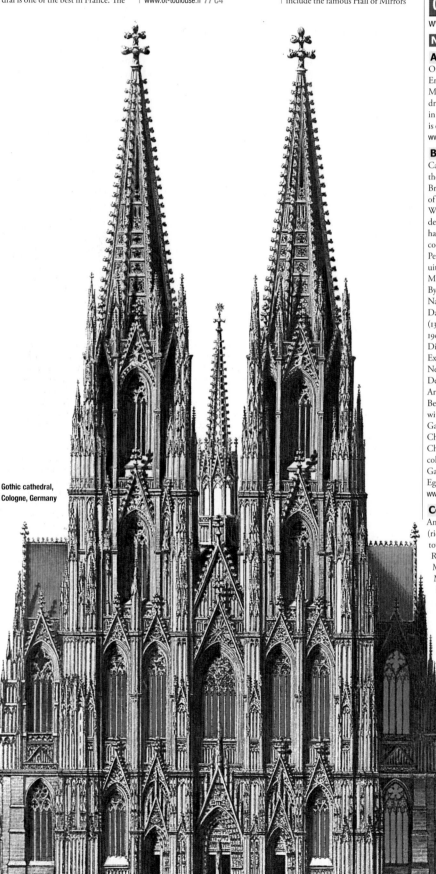

Gothic cathedral, Cologne, Germany

of SS Peter and Paul has a Cranach masterpiece. Houses of famous people: Goethe, Schiller, Liszt. The famous Bauhaus was founded at the School of Architecture and Engineering. www.weimar.de 52 C1

Southern Germany

Augsburg
Attractive old city. The Town Hall is one of Germany's finest Renaissance buildings. Maximilianstrasse has several Renaissance houses and Rococo Schaezler Palace (good art collection). Churches: Romanesque-Gothic cathedral; Renaissance St Anne's Church. The Fuggerei, founded 1519 as an estate for the poor, is still in use. www.augsburg.de 62 B1

Bamberg
Well-preserved medieval town. The island, connected by two bridges, has the Town Hall and views of Klein Venedig. Romanesque-Gothic cathedral (good art) is on an exceptional square of Gothic, Renaissance and Baroque buildings – Alte Hofhalttung; Neue Residenz with State Gallery (German masters); Ratstube. www.bamberg.info 62 A1

Black Forest Schwarzwald
Hilly region between Basel and Karlsruhe, the largest and most picturesque woodland in Germany, with the highest summit, Feldberg, lake resorts (Titisee), health resorts (Baden-Baden) and clock craft (Triberg). Freiburg is regional capital. www.schwarzwald.de 61 B4

Freiburg
Old university town with system of streams running through the streets. The Gothic Minster is surrounded by the town's finest buildings. Two towers remain of the medieval walls. The Augustine Museum has a good collection. www.freiburg.de 60 C3

Heidelberg
Germany's oldest university town, majestically set on the banks of the river and romantically dominated by the ruined schloss. The Gothic Church of the Holy Spirit is on the Market Place with the Baroque Town Hall. Other sights include the 16c Knight's House and the Baroque Morass Palace with a museum of Gothic art. www.heidelberg.de 61 A4

Lake Constance Bodensee
Lake Constance, with many pleasant lake resorts. Lindau, on an island, has numerous gabled houses. Birnau has an 18c Rococo church. Konstanz (Swiss side) has the Minster set above the Old Town. www.bodensee.de 61 C5

Munich München
Old town centred on the Marienplatz with 15c Old Town Hall and 19c New Town Hall. Many richly decorated churches: St Peter's (14c tower); Gothic red-brick cathedral; Renaissance St Michael's (royal portraits on the façade); Rococo St Asam's. The Residenz palace consists of seven splendid buildings holding many art objects. Schloss Nymphenburg has a palace, park, botanical gardens and four beautiful pavilions. Superb museums: Old Gallery (old masters), New Gallery (18–19c), Lenbachhaus (modern German). Many famous beer gardens. www.muenchen.de 62 B2

Nuremberg Nürnberg
Beautiful medieval walled city dominated by the 12c Kaiserburg. Romanesque-Gothic St Sebaldus

Church and Gothic St Laurence Church are rich in art. On Hauptmarkt is the famous 14c Schöner Brunnen. Also notable is 15c Dürer House. The German National Museum has excellent German medieval and Renaissance art. www.nuernberg.de 62 A2

Regensburg
Medieval city set majestically on the Danube. Views from 12c Steinerne Brücke. Churches: Gothic cathedral; Romanesque St Jacob's; Gothic St Blaisius; Baroque St Emmeram. Other sights: Old Town Hall (museum); Haidplatz; Schloss Thurn und Taxis; State Museum. www.regensburg.de 62 A3

Romantic Road
Romantische Strasse
Romantic route between Aschaffenburg and Füssen, leading through picturesque towns and villages of medieval Germany. The most popular section is the section between Würzburg and Augsburg, centred on Rothenburg ob der Tauber, an attractive medieval walled town. Also notable are Nördlingen, Harburg Castle, Dinkelsbühl, Creglingen. www.romantischestrasse.de 61 A6

Rothenburg ob der Tauber
Attractive medieval walled town with tall gabled and half-timbered houses on narrow cobbled streets. The Market Place has Gothic-Renaissance Town Hall, Rattrinke-stubbe and Gothic St Jacob's Church (altarpiece). www.rothenburg.de 61 A6

Speyer
11c cathedral is one of the largest and best Romanesque buildings in Germany. 12c Jewish Baths are well-preserved. www.speyer.de 61 A4

Stuttgart
Largely modern city with old centre around the Old Schloss, Renaissance Alte Kanzlei, 15c Collegiate Church and Baroque New Schloss. Museums: Regional Museum; post-modern State Gallery (old masters, 20c German). The 1930s Weissenhofsiedlung is by several famous architects. www.stuttgart.de 61 B5

Trier
Superb Roman monuments: Porta Nigra; Aula Palatina (now a church); Imperial Baths; amphitheatre. The Regional Museum has Roman artefacts. Also, Gothic Church of Our Lady; Romanesque cathedral. www.trier.de 60 A2

Ulm
Old town with half-timbered gabled houses set on a canal. Gothic 14–19c minster has tallest spire in the world (161m). www.tourismus.ulm.de 61 B5

Würzburg
Set among vineyard hills, the medieval town is centred on the Market Place with the Rococo House of the Falcon. The 18c episcopal princes' residence (frescoes) is magnificent. The cathedral is rich in art. Work of the great local Gothic sculptor, Riemenschneider, is in Gothic St Mary's Chapel, Baroque New Minster, and the Mainfränkisches Museum. www.wuerzburg.de 61 A5

Great Britain
www.visitbritain.com

England

Bath
Elegant spa town with notable 18c architecture: Circus, Royal Crescent, Pulteney Bridge, Assembly Rooms; Pump Room. Also: well-preserved Roman baths; superb Perpendicular Gothic Bath Abbey. Nearby: Elizabethan Longleat House; exceptional 18c landscaped gardens at Stourhead. www.visitbath.co.uk 29 B5

Brighton
Resort with a sea-front of Georgian, Regency and Victorian buildings with the Palace Pier, and an old town of narrow lanes. The main sight is the 19c Royal Pavilion in Oriental styles. www.brighton.co.uk 31 D3

Bristol
Old port city with the fascinating Floating Harbour. Major sights include Gothic 13–14c Church of St Mary Redcliffe and 19c Clifton Suspension Bridge. www.visitbristol.co.uk 29 B5

Cambridge
City with university founded in the early 13c. Peterhouse (1284) is the oldest college. Most famous colleges were founded in 14–16c: Queen's, King's (with the superb Perpendicular Gothic 15–16c King's College Chapel), St John's (with famous 19c Bridge of Sighs), Trinity, Clare, Gonville and Caius, Magdalene. Museums: excellent Fitzwilliam Museum (classical, medieval, old masters). Kettle's Yard (20c British). www.visitcambridge.org 30 B4

Canterbury
Medieval city and old centre of Christianity. The Norman-Gothic cathedral has many sights and was a major medieval pilgrimage site (as related in Chaucer's Canterbury Tales). St Augustine, sent to convert the English in 597, founded St Augustine's Abbey, now in ruins. www.canterbury.co.uk 31 C5

Chatsworth
One of the richest aristocratic country houses in England (largely 17c) set in a large landscaped park. The palatial interior has some 175 richly furnished rooms and a major art collection. www.chatsworth-house.co.uk 27 B4

Chester
Charming medieval city with complete walls. The Norman-Gothic cathedral has several abbey buildings. www.visitchester.co.uk 26 B3

Cornish Coast
Scenic landscape of cliffs and sandy beaches (the north coast being a popular surfing destination) with picturesque villages (Fowey, Mevagissey). St Ives has the Tate Gallery with work of the St Ives Group. The island of St Michael's Mount holds a priory. www.cornwalltouristboard.co.uk 28 C2

Dartmoor
Beautiful wilderness area in Devon with tors and its own breed of wild pony as well as free-ranging cattle and sheep. www.dartmoor-npa.gov.uk 28 C4

Durham
Historic city with England's finest Norman cathedral and a castle, both placed majestically on a rock above the river. www.durham.gov.uk 27 A4

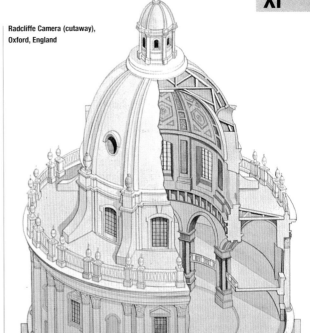
Radcliffe Camera (cutaway), Oxford, England

Eden Project
Centre showing the diversity of plant life on the planet, built in a disused clay pit. Two biomes, one with Mediterranean and Southern African focus and the larger featuring a waterfall, river and tropical trees plants and flowers. Outdoors also features plantations including bamboo and tea. www.edenproject.com 28 C3

Hadrian's Wall
Built to protect the northernmost border of the Roman Empire in the 2c AD, the walls originally extended some 120km with castles every mile and 16 forts. Best-preserved walls around Hexam; forts at Housesteads and Chesters. www.hadrians-wall.org 25 C5

Lake District
Beautiful landscape of lakes (Windermere, Coniston) and England's high peaks (Scafell Pike, Skiddaw, Old Man), famous for its poets, particularly Wordsworth. www.lake-district.gov.uk 26 A2

Leeds Castle
One of the oldest and most romantic English castles, standing in the middle of a lake. Most of the present appearance dates from 19c. www.leeds-castle.com 31 C4

Lincoln
Old city perched on a hill with narrow streets, majestically dominated by the Norman-Gothic cathedral and castle. www.visitlincolnshire.com 27 B5

Liverpool
City on site of port founded in 1207 and focused around 1846 Albert Dock, now a heritage attraction. Croxteth Hall and Country Park; Speke Hall; Sudley House; Royal Liver Buiolding; Liverpool Cathedral; Walker Art Gallery; University of Liverpool Art Gallery. www.visitliverpool.com 26 B3

London
Capital of UK and Europe's largest city. To the east of the medieval heart of the city – now the largely modern financial district and known as the City of London – is the Tower of London (11c White Tower, Crown Jewels) and 1880s Tower Bridge. The popular heart of the city and its entertainment is the West End, around Piccadilly Circus, Leicester Square and Trafalgar Square (Nelson's Column). Many sights of political and royal power: Whitehall (Banqueting House, 10 Downing Street, Horse Guards); Neo-Gothic Palace of Westminster (Houses of Parliament) with Big Ben; The Mall leading to Buckingham Palace (royal residence, famous ceremony of the Changing of the Guard). Numerous churches include: 13–16c Gothic Westminster Abbey (many tombs, Henry VII's Chapel); Wren's Baroque St Paul's Cathedral, St Mary-le-Bow, spire of St Bride's, St Stephen Walbrook. Museums of world fame: British Museum (prehistory, oriental and classical antiquity, medieval); Victoria and Albert Museum (decorative arts); National Gallery (old masters to 19c); National Portrait Gallery (historic and current British portraiture); Tate – Britain and Modern; Science Museum; Natural History Museum. Madame Tussaud's waxworks museum is hugely popular. Other sights include: Kensington Palace; Greenwich with Old Royal Observatory (Greenwich meridian), Baroque Royal Naval College, Palladian Queen's House; Tudor Hampton Court Palace; Syon House. Nearby: Windsor Castle (art collection, St George's Chapel). www.visitlondon.com 31 C3

Longleat
One of the earliest and finest Elizabethan palaces in England. The

palace is richly decorated. Some of the grounds have been turned into a pleasure park, with the Safari Park, the first of its kind outside Africa. www.longleat.co.uk **29 B5**

Manchester
Founded on a Roman settlement of 79AD and a main player in the Industrial Revolution. Victorian Gothic Town Hall; Royal Exchange; Cathedral. Many museums including Imperial War Museum North, Lowry Centre and Manchester Art Gallery. www.visitmanchester.com **26 B3**

Newcastle
A key player in the Industrial Revolution with 12th century cathedral and many museums as well as strong railway heritage. www.visitnewcastle.co.uk **25 D6**

Norwich
Medieval quarter has half-timbered houses. 15c castle keep houses a museum and gallery. Many medieval churches include the Norman-Gothic cathedral. www.visitnorwich.co.uk **30 B5**

Oxford
Old university city. Earliest colleges date from 13c: University College; Balliol; Merton. 14–16c colleges include: New College; Magdalen; Christ Church (perhaps the finest). Other buildings: Bodleian Library; Radcliffe Camera; Sheldonian Theatre; cathedral. Good museums: Ashmolean Museum (antiquity to 20c); Museum of Modern Art; Christ Church Picture Gallery (14–17c). Nearby: outstanding 18c Blenheim Palace. www.visitoxford.org **31 C2**

Petworth
House (17c) with one of the finest country-house art collections (old masters), set in a huge landscaped park. www.nationaltrust.org.uk **31 D3**

Salisbury
Pleasant old city with a magnificent 13c cathedral built in an unusually unified Gothic style. Nearby: Wilton House. www.visitsalisburyuk.com **29 B6**

Stonehenge
Some 4000 years old, one of the most famous and haunting Neolithic monuments in Europe. Many other Neolithic sites are nearby. www.english-heritage.org.uk **29 B6**

Stourhead
Early 18c palace famous for its grounds, one of the finest examples of neoclassical landscaped gardening,

consisting of a lake surrounded by numerous temples. www.nationaltrust.org.uk **29 B5**

Stratford-upon-Avon
Old town of Tudor and Jacobean half-timbered houses, famed as the birth and burial place of William Shakespeare. Nearby: Warwick Castle. www.shakespeare-country.co.uk **29 A6**

Wells
Charming city with beautiful 12–16c cathedral (west facade, scissor arches, chapter house, medieval clock). Also Bishop's Palace; Vicar's Close. **29 B5**

Winchester
Historic city with 11–16c cathedral (tombs of early English kings). Also: 13c Great Hall; Winchester College; St Cross almshouses. www.visitwinchester.co.uk **29 B6**

York
Attractive medieval city surrounded by well-preserved walls with magnificent Gothic 13–15c Minster. Museums: York City Art Gallery (14–19c); Jorvik Viking Centre. Nearby: Castle Howard. www.york-tourism.co.uk **27 B4**

Scotland

Edinburgh
Capital of Scotland, built on volcanic hills. The medieval Old Town is dominated by the castle set high on a volcanic rock (Norman St Margaret's Chapel, state apartments, Crown Room). Holyrood House (15c and 17c) has lavishly decorated state apartments and the ruins of Holyrood Abbey (remains of Scottish monarchs). The 15c cathedral has the Crown Spire and Thistle Chapel. The New Town has good Georgian architecture (Charlotte Square, Georgian House). Excellent museums: Scottish National Portrait Gallery, National Gallery of Scotland; Scottish National Gallery of Modern Art. www.edinburgh.org **25 C4**

Glamis Castle
In beautiful, almost flat landscaped grounds, 14c fortress, rebuilt 17c, gives a fairy-tale impression. www.glamis-castle.co.uk **25 B5**

Glasgow
Scotland's largest city, with centre around George Square and 13–15c Gothic cathedral. The Glasgow School of Art is the masterpiece of Charles Rennie Mackintosh. Fine art collections: Glasgow Museum

and Art Gallery; Hunterian Gallery; Burrell Collection. www.seeglasgow.com **24 C3**

Loch Ness
In the heart of the Highlands, the lake forms part of the scenic Great Glen running from Inverness to Fort William. Famous as home of the fabled Loch Ness Monster (exhibition at Drumnadrochit). Nearby: ruins of 14–16c Urquhart Castle. www.loch-ness-scotland.com **23 D4**

Wales

Caernarfon
Town dominated by a magnificent 13c castle, one of a series built by Edward I in Wales (others include Harlech, Conwy, Beaumaris, Caerphilly). www.visitcaernarfon.com **26 B1**

Cardiff
Capital of Wales, most famous for its medieval castle, restored 19c in Greek, Gothic and Oriental styles. Also: National Museum and Gallery. www.visitcardiff.info **29 B4**

Greece Ellas
www.gnto.gr

Athens Athínai
Capital of Greece. The Acropolis, with 5c BC sanctuary complex (Parthenon, Propylaia, Erechtheion, Temple of Athena Nike), is the greatest architectural achievement of antiquity in Europe. The Agora was a public meeting place in ancient Athens. Pláka has narrow streets and small Byzantine churches (Kapnikaréa). The Olympeum was the largest temple in Greece. Also: Olympic Stadium; excellent collections of ancient artefacts (Museum of Cycladic and Ancient Greek Art; Acropolis

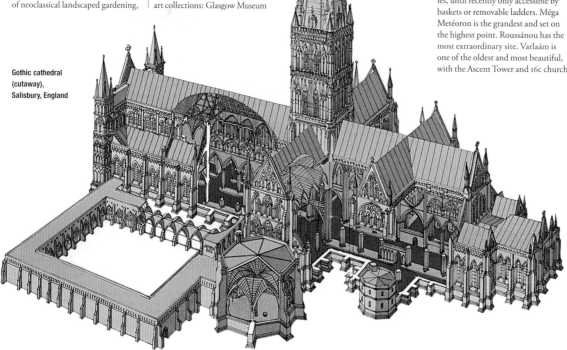

Gothic cathedral (cutaway), Salisbury, England

Museum; National Archeological Museum; Benáki Museum). www.athens.gr **113 E5**

Corinth Kórinthos
Ancient Corinth (ruins), with 5c BC Temple of Apollo, was in 44 BC made capital of Roman Greece by Julius Caesar. Set above the city, the Greek-built acropolis hill of Acrocorinth became the Roman and Byzantine citadel (ruins). **113 E4**

Crete Kríti
Largest Greek island, Crete was home to the great Minoan civilization (2800–1100 BC). The main relics are the ruined Palace of Knossós and Mália. Gortys was capital of the Roman province. Picturesque Réthimno has narrow medieval streets, a Venetian fortress and a former Turkish mosque. Mátala has beautiful beaches and famous caves cut into cliffs. Iráklio (Heraklion), the capital, has a good Archeological Museum. **113 G7**

Delphí
At the foot of the Mount Parnassós, Delphi was the seat of the Delphic Oracle of Apollo, the most important oracle in Ancient Greece. Delphi was also a political meeting place and the site of the Pythian Games. The Sanctuary of Apollo consists of: Temple of Apollo, led to by the Sacred Way; Theatre; Stadium. The museum has a display of objects from the site (5c BC Charioteer). www.delphi.gr **112 D4**

Epídavros
Formerly a spa and religious centre focused on the Sanctuary of Asclepius (ruins). The enormous 4c BC theatre is probably the finest of all ancient theatres. www.ancientepidavros.org **113 E5**

Greek Islands
Popular islands with some of the most beautiful and spectacular beaches in Europe. The many islands are divided into various groups and individual islands: The major groups are the Kikládhes and Dhodhekanisos in the Aegean Sea, the largest islands are Kérkira (Corfu) in the Ionian Sea and Kríti. **112-113**

Metéora
The tops of bizarre vertical cylinders of rock and towering cliffs are the setting for 14c Cenobitic monasteries, until recently only accessible by baskets or removable ladders. Méga Metéoron is the grandest and set on the highest point. Roussánou has the most extraordinary site. Varlaám is one of the oldest and most beautiful, with the Ascent Tower and 16c church

with frescoes. Áyiou Nikólaou also has good frescoes. **112 C3**

Mistrás
Set in a beautiful landscape, Mystra is the site of a Byzantine city, now in ruins, with palaces, frescoed churches, monasteries and houses. **113 E4**

Mount Olympus Óros Ólimpos
Mount Olympus, mythical seat of the Greek gods, is the highest, most dramatic peak in Greece. **112 B4**

Mycenae Mykenai
The citadel of Mycenae prospered between 1950 bc and 1100 bc and consists of the royal complex of Agamemnon: Lion Gate, royal burial site, Royal Palace, South House, Great Court. **113 E4**

Olympia
In a stunning setting, the Panhellenic Games were held here for a millennium. Ruins of the sanctuary of Olympia consist of the Doric temples of Zeus and Hera and the vast Stadium. There is also a museum (4c BC figure of Hermes). **113 E3**

Rhodes Ródhos
One of the most attractive islands with wonderful sandy beaches. The city of Rhodes has a well-preserved medieval centre with the Palace of the Grand Masters and the Turkish Süleymaniye Mosque. **16 C4**

Salonica Thessaloníki
Largely modern city with Byzantine walls and many fine churches: 8c Ayía Sofía; 11c Panayía Halkéon; 14c Dhódheka Apóstoli; 14c Áyios Nikólaos Orfanós; 5c Áyios Dhimítrios (largest in Greece, 7c Mosaics). www.thessalonikicity.gr **112 B4**

Hungary Magyarország
www.hungarytourism.hu

Balaton
The 'Hungarian sea', famous for its holiday resorts: Balatonfüred, Tihany, Badasconytomaj, Keszthely. www.balaton.hu **74 B2**

Budapest
Capital of Hungary on River Danube, with historic area centring on the Castle Hill of Buda district. Sights include: Matthias church; Pest district with late 19c architecture, centred on Ferenciek tere; neo-Gothic Parliament Building on river; Millennium Monument. The Royal Castle houses a number of museums: Hungarian National Gallery, Budapest History Museum; Ludwig Collection. Other museums: National Museum of Fine Arts (excellent Old and Modern masters); Hungarian National Museum (Hungarian history). Famous for public thermal baths: Király and Rudas baths, both made under Turkish rule; Gellért baths, the most visited. www.budapestinfo.hu **75 A4**

Esztergom
Medieval capital of Hungary set in scenic landscape. Sights: Hungary's largest basilica (completed 1856); royal palace ruins. www.esztergom.hu **65 C4**

Pécs
Attractive old town with Europe's fifth oldest university (founded 1367). Famous for Turkish architecture (Mosque of Gazi Kasim Pasha, Jakovali Hassan Mosque). www.pecs.hu **74 B3**

Sopron

Beautiful walled town with many Gothic and Renaissance houses. Nearby: Fertöd with the marvellous Eszergázy Palace. www.sopron.hu **64 C2**

Ireland

www.ireland.travel.ie
www.discovernorthernireland.com

Northern Ireland

Antrim Coast

Spectacular coast with diverse scenery of glens (Glenarm, Glenariff), cliffs (Murlough Bay) and the famous Giant's Causeway, consisting of some 40,000 basalt columns. Carrickefergus Castle is the largest and best-preserved Norman castle in Ireland. www.northantrim.com **19 A5**

Belfast

Capital of Northern Ireland. Sights: Donegall Square with 18c Town Hall; neo-Romanesque Protestant cathedral; University Square; Ulster Museum (European painting). www.gotobelfast.com **19 B6**

Giant's Causeway

Spectacular and unique rock formations in the North Antrim coast, formed by volcanic activity 50–60 million years ago. World Heritage Site. www.northantrim.com **19 A5**

Republic of Ireland

Aran Islands

Islands with spectacular cliffs and notable pre-Christian and Christian sights, especially on Inishmore. www.visitaranislands.com **18 B3**

Cashel

Town dominated by the Rock of Cashel (61m) topped by ecclesiastical ruins including 13c cathedral; 15c Halls of the Vicars; beautiful Romanesque 12c Cormac's Chapel (fine carvings). www.connemar-tourism.org **21 B4**

Connemara

Beautiful wild landscape of mountains, lakes, peninsulas and beaches. Clifden is the capital. www.connemar-tourism.org **18 C1**

Cork

Pleasant city with its centre along St Patrick's Street and Grand Parade lined with fine 18c buildings. Churches: Georgian St Anne's Shandon (bell tower); 19c cathedral. www.corkcorp.ie **20 C3**

County Donegal

Rich scenic landscape of mystical lakes and glens and seascape of cliffs (Slieve League cliffs are the highest in Europe). The town of Donegal has a finely preserved Jacobean castle. www.donegaldirect.ie **18 B3**

Dublin

Capital of Ireland. City of elegant 18c neoclassical and Georgian architecture with gardens and parks (St Stephen's Green, Merrion Square with Leinster House – now seat of Irish parliament). City's main landmark, Trinity College (founded 1591), houses in its Old Library fine Irish manuscripts (7c Book of Durrow, 8c Book of Kells). Two Norman cathedrals: Christ Church; St Patrick's. Other buildings: originally medieval Dublin Castle with State Apartments; James Gandon's masterpieces: Custom House; Four Courts. Museums: National Museum (Irish history); National Gallery (old masters, Impressionists, Irish painting);

Il Redentore, Venice, Italy

Neville Morgan / Alamy

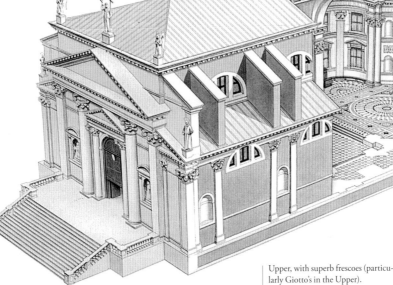

Guinness Brewery Museum; Dublin Writers' Museum (Joyce, Wilde, Yeats and others). www.visitdublin.com **19 C5**

Glendalough

Impressive ruins of an important early Celtic (6c) monastery with 9c cathedral, 12c St Kevin's Cross, oratory of St Kevin's Church. www.wicklow.com/glendalough **21 A5**

Kilkenny

Charming medieval town, with narrow streets dominated by 12c castle (restored 19c). The 13c Gothic cathedral has notable tomb monuments. www.kilkenny.ie **21 B4**

Newgrange

One of the best passage graves in Europe, the massive 4500-year-old tomb has stones richly decorated with patterns. www.knowth.com/newgrange **19 C5**

Ring of Kerry

Route around the Iveragh peninsula with beautiful lakes (Lough Leane), peaks overlooking the coastline and islands (Valencia Island, Skelling). Also: Killarney; ruins of 15c Muckross Abbey. www.ringofkerrytourism.com **20 B2**

Italy Italia

www.enit.it

Northern Italy

Alps

Wonderful stretch of the Alps running from the Swiss and French borders to Austria. The region of Valle d'Aosta is one of the most popular ski regions, bordered by the highest peaks of the Alps. www.thealps.com **70–71**

Arezzo

Beautiful old town set on a hill dominated by 13c cathedral. Piazza Grande is surrounded by medieval and Renaissance palaces. Main sight: Piero della Francesca's frescoes in the choir of San Francesco. www.arezzocitta.com **81 C5**

Assisi

Hill-top town that attracts crowds of pilgrims to the shrine of St Francis of Assisi at the Basilica di San Francesco, consisting of two churches, Lower and Upper, with superb frescoes (particularly Giotto's in the Upper). www.assisi.com **82 C1**

Bologna

Elegant city with oldest university in Italy. Historical centre around Piazza Maggiore and Piazza del Nettuno with the Town Hall, Palazzo del Podestà, Basilica di San Petronio. Other churches: San Domenico; San Giacomo Maggiore. The two towers (one incomplete) are symbols of the city. Good collection in the National Gallery (Bolognese). www.commune.bologna.it/bolognaturismo **81 B5**

Dolomites Dolomiti

Part of the Alps, this mountain range spreads over the region of Trentino-Alto Adige, with the most picturesque scenery between Bolzano and Cortina d'Ampezzo. www.dolomiti.it **72 B1**

Ferrara

Old town centre around Romanesque-Gothic cathedral and Palazzo Communale. Also: Castello Estense; Palazzo Schifanoia (frescoes); Palazzo dei Diamanti housing Pinacoteca Nazionale. www.ferraraturismo.it **81 B5**

Florence Firenze

City with exceptionally rich medieval

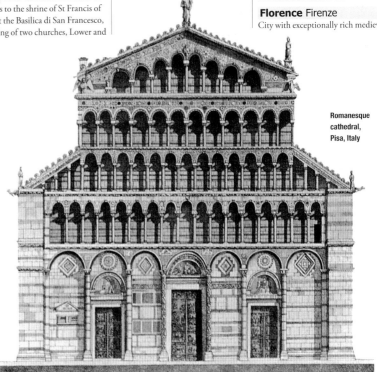
Romanesque cathedral, Pisa, Italy

and Renaissance heritage. Piazza del Duomo has: 13–15c cathedral (first dome since antiquity); 14c campanile; 11c baptistry (bronze doors). Piazza della Signoria has: 14c Palazzo Vecchio (frescoes); Loggia della Signoria (sculpture); 16c Uffizi Gallery with one of the world's greatest collections (13–18c). Other great paintings: Museo di San Marco; Palatine Gallery in 15–16c Pitti Palace surrounded by Boboli Gardens. Sculpture: Cathedral Works Museum; Bargello Museum; Academy Gallery (Michelangelo's *David*). Among many other Renaissance palaces: Medici-Riccardi; Rucellai; Strozzi. The 15c church of San Lorenzo has Michelangelo's tombs of the Medici. Many churches have richly frescoed chapels: Santa Maria Novella, Santa Croce, Santa Maria del Carmine. The 13c Ponte Vecchio is one of the most famous sights. www.firenzeturismo.it **81 C5**

Italian Lakes
Beautiful district at the foot of the Alps, most of the lakes with holiday resorts. Many lakes are surrounded by aristocratic villas (Maggiore, Como, Garda). **70-71**

Mántova
Attractive city surrounded by three lakes. Two exceptional palaces: Palazzo Ducale (Sala del Pisanello; Camera degli Sposi, Castello San Giorgio); luxurious Palazzo Tè (brilliant frescoes). Also: 15c Church of Sant'Andrea; 13c law courts. www.mantova.com **71 C5**

Milan Milano
Modern city, Italy's fashion and design capital (Corso and Galleria Vittoro Emmanuelle II). Churches include: Gothic cathedral (1386–1813), the world's largest (4c baptistry); Romanesque St Ambrose; 15c San Satiro; Santa Maria delle Grazie with Leonardo da Vinci's *Last Supper* in the convent refectory. Great art collections, Brera Gallery, Ambrosian Library, Museum of Contemporary Art. Castello Sforzesco (15c, 19c) also has a gallery. The famous La Scala theatre founded in 1778. Nearby: monastery at Pavia. www.milaninfotourist.com **71 C4**

Pádova
Pleasant old town with arcaded streets. Basilica del Santo is a place of pilgrimage to the tomb of St Anthony. Giotto's frescoes in the Scrovegni chapel are exceptional. Also: Piazza dei Signori with Palazzo del Capitano; vast Palazzo della Ragione; church of the Eremitani (frescoes). www.turismopadova.it **72 C1**

Parma
Attractive city centre, famous for Correggio's frescoes in the Romanesque cathedral and church of St John the Evangelist, and Parmigianino's frescoes in the church of Madonna della Steccata. Their works are also in the National Gallery. www.commune.parma.it **81 B4**

Perúgia
Hill-top town centred around Piazza Quattro Novembre with the cathedral, Fontana Maggiore and Palazzo dei Priori. Also: Collegio di Cambio (frescoes); National Gallery of Umbria; many churches. www.perugiaonline.it **82 C1**

Pisa
Medieval town centred on the Piazza dei Miracoli. Sights: famous Romanesque Leaning Tower, Romanesque cathedral (excellent façade, Gothic pulpit); 12–13c Baptistry; 13c Camposanto cloistered cemetery (fascinating 14c frescoes). www.commune.pisa.it **81 C4**

Ravenna
Ancient town with exceptionally well-preserved Byzantine mosaics. The finest are in 5c Mausoleo di Galla Placidia and 6c Basilica di San Vitale. Good mosaics also in the basilicas of Sant'Apollinare in Classe and Sant'Apollinare Nuovo. www.turismo.ravenna.it **82 B1**

Sienna Siena
Outstanding 13–14c medieval town centred on beautiful Piazza del Campo with Gothic Palazzo Publico (frescoes of secular life). Delightful Romanesque-Gothic Duomo (Libreria Piccolomini, baptistry, art works). Many other richly decorated churches. Fine Sienese painting in Pinacoteca Nazionale and Museo dell'Opera del Duomo. www.terresiena.it **81 C5**

Turin Torino
City centre has 17–18c Baroque layout dominated by twin Baroque churches. Also: 15c cathedral (holds Turin Shroud); Palazzo Reale; 18c Superga Basilica; Academy of Science with two museums (Egyptian antiquities; European painting). www.commune.torino.it **80 A1**

Urbino
Set in beautiful hilly landscape, Urbino's heritage is mainly due to the 15c court of Federico da Montefeltro at the magnificent Ducal Palace (notable Studiolo), now also a gallery. www.turismo.pesaurbino.it **82 C1**

Venice Venezia
Stunning old city built on islands in a lagoon, with some 150 canals. The Grand Canal is crossed by the famous 16c Rialto Bridge and is lined with elegant palaces (Gothic Ca'd'Oro and Ca'Foscari, Renaissance Palazzo Grimani, Baroque Rezzonico). The district of San Marco has the core of the best known sights and is centred on Piazza San Marco with 11c Basilica di San Marco (bronze horses, 13c mosaics); Campanille (exceptional views) and Ducal Palace (connected with the prison by the famous Bridge of Sighs). Many churches (Santa Maria Gloriosa dei Frari, Santa Maria della Salute, Redentore, San Giorgio Maggiore, San Giovanni e Paolo) and scuole (Scuola di San Rocco, Scuola di San Giorgio degli Schiavoni) have excellent works of art. The Gallery of the Academy houses superb 14–18c Venetian art. The Guggenheim Museum holds 20c art. http://english.comune.venezia.it **72 C2**

Verona
Old town with remains of 1c Roman Arena and medieval sights including the Palazzo degli Scaligeri; Arche Scaligere; Romanesque Santa Maria Antica; Castelvecchio; Ponte Scaliger. The famous 14c House of Juliet has associations with *Romeo and Juliet*. Many churches with fine art works (cathedral; Sant'Anastasia; basilica di San Zeno Maggiore). www.tourism.verona.it **71 C6**

Vicenza
Beautiful town, famous for the architecture of Palladio, including the Olympic Theatre (extraordinary stage), Corso Palladio with many of his palaces, and Palazzo Chiericati. Nearby: Villa Rotonda, the most influential of all Palladian buildings. www.vicenzae.org **71 C6**

Southern Italy

Naples Napoli
Historical centre around Gothic cathedral (crypt). Spaccanapoli area has numerous churches (bizarre Cappella Sansevero; Gesù Nuovo, Gothic Santa Chiara with fabulous tombs). Buildings: 13c Castello Nuovo; 13c Castel dell'Ovo; 15c Palazzo Cuomo. Museums: National Archeological Museum (artefacts from Pompeii and Herculaneum); National Museum of Capodimonte (Renaissance painting). Nearby: spectacular coast around Amalfi; Pompeii; Herculaneum. www.inaples.it **103 C7**

Orvieto
Medieval hill-top town with a number of monuments including the Romanesque-Gothic cathedral (façade, frescoes). www.commune.orvieto.tr.it **82 D1**

Rome Roma
Capital of Italy, exceptionally rich in sights from many eras. Ancient sights: Colosseum; Arch of Constantine; Trajan's Column; Roman and Imperial fora; hills of Palatino and Campidoglio (Capitoline Museum shows antiquities); Pantheon; Castel Sant'Angelo; Baths of Caracalla). Early Christian sights: catacombs (San Calisto, San Sebastiano, Domitilla); basilicas (San Giovanni in Laterano, Santa Maria Maggiore, San Paolo Fuori le Mura). Rome is known for richly decorated Baroque churches: il Gesù, Sant'Ignazio, Santa Maria della Vittoria, Chiesa Nuova. Other churches, often with art treasures: Romanesque Santa Maria in Cosmadin, Gothic Santa Maria Sopra Minevra, Renaissance Santa Maria del Popolo, San Pietro in Vincoli. Several Renaissance and Baroque palaces and villas house superb art collections (Palazzo Barberini, Palazzo Doria Pamphilj, Palazzo Spada, Palazzo Corsini, Villa Giulia, Galleria Borghese) and are beautifully frescoed (Villa Farnesina). Fine Baroque public spaces with fountains: Piazza Navona; Piazza di Spagna with the Spanish Steps, Trevi Fountain). Nearby: Tivoli; Villa Adriana. Rome also contains the Vatican City (Città del Vaticano). www.romaturismo.com **102 B5**

Volcanic Region
Region from Naples to Sicily. Mount Etna is one of the most famous European volcanoes. Vesuvius dominates the Bay of Naples and has at its foot two of Italy's finest Roman sites, Pompeii and Herculaneum, both destroyed by its eruption in 79AD. Stromboli is one of the beautiful Aeolian Islands.

Sardinia Sardegna
Sardinia has some of the most beautiful beaches in Italy (Alghero). Unique are the nuraghi, some 7000 stone constructions (Su Nuraxi, Serra Orios), the remains of an old civilization (1500–400 BC). Old towns include Cagliari and Sássari. www.sardi.it **110**

Sicily Sicilia
Surrounded by beautiful beaches and full of monuments of many periods, Sicily is the largest island in the Mediterranean. Taormina with its Greek theatre has one of the most spectacular beaches, lying under the mildly active volcano Mount Etna. Also: Agrigento; Palermo; Siracusa. www.regione.sicilia.it/turismo/web_turismo **108-109**

Agrigento
Set on a hill above the sea and famed for the Valley of the Temples. The nine originally 5c Doric temples are Sicily's best-preserved Greek remains. www.agrigento-sicilia.it **108 B2**

Palermo
City with Moorish, Norman and Baroque architecture, especially around the main squares (Quattro Canti, Piazza Pretoria, Piazza Bellini). Sights: remains of Norman palace (12c Palatine Chapel); Norman cathedral; Regional Gallery (medieval); some 8000 preserved bodies in the catacombs of the Cappuchin Convent. Nearby: 12c Norman Duomo di Monreale. www.commune.palermo.it **108 A2**

Syracuse Siracusa
Built on an island connected to the mainland by a bridge, the old town has a 7c cathedral, ruins of the Temple of Apollo; Fountain of Arethusa; archaeological museum. On the mainland: 5c BC Greek theatre with seats cut out of rock; Greek fortress of Euralus; 2c Roman amphitheatre; 5–6c Catacombs of St John. www.apt-siracusa.it **109 B4**

Palazzo Publico, Siena, Italy

Latvia Latvija
www.lv

Riga
Well-preserved medieval town centre around the cathedral. Sights: Riga Castle; medieval Hanseatic houses; Great Guild Hall; Gothic Church of St Peter; Art Nouveau buildings in the New Town. Nearby: Baroque Rundale Castle. www.riga.lv **6 C8**

Lithuania Lietuva
www.tourism.lt

Vilnius
Baroque old town with fine architecture including: cathedral; Gediminas Tower; university complex; Archbishop's Palace; Church of St Anne. Also: remains of Jewish life; Vilnius Picture Gallery (16–19c regional); Lithuanian National Museum. www.vilnius.lt **7 D8**

Luxembourg
www.ont.lu

Luxembourg
Capital of Luxembourg, built on a rock with fine views. Old town is around the Place d'Armes. Buildings: Grand Ducal Palace; fortifications of Rocher du Bock; cathedral. Museum of History and Art holds an excellent regional collection. www.ont.lu **60 A2**

Macedonia Makedonija

www.macedonia.org

Skopje
Historic town with Turkish citadel, fine 15c mosques, oriental bazaar, ancient bridge. Superb Byzantine churches nearby.
www.skopjeonline.com.mk 10 E6

Ohrid
Old town, beautifully set by a lake, with houses of wood and brick, remains of a Turkish citadel, many churches (two cathedrals; St Naum south of the lake). www.ohrid.org.mk 112 A2

Malta

www.visitmalta.com

Valletta
Capital of Malta. Historic walled city, founded in 16c by the Maltese Knights, with 16c Grand Master's Palace and a richly decorated cathedral. 107 C5

Monaco

www.visitmonaco.com

Monaco
Major resort area in a beautiful location. Sights include: Monte Carlo casino; Prince's Palace at Monaco-Ville; 19c cathedral; oceanographic museum. www.visitmonaco.com 80 C1

The Netherlands
Nederland

www.visitholland.com

Amsterdam
Capital of the Netherlands. Old centre has picturesque canals lined with distinctive elegant 17–18c merchants' houses. Dam Square has 15c New Church and Royal Palace. Other churches include Westerkerk. The Museumplein has three world-famous museums: Rijksmuseum (several art collections including 15–17c painting); Van Gogh Museum; Municipal Museum (art from 1850 on). Other museums: Anne Frank House; Jewish Historical Museum; Rembrandt House. www.visitamsterdam.nl 42 C1

Westerkerk, Amsterdam, Netherlands

Delft
Well-preserved old Dutch town with gabled red-roofed houses along canals. Gothic churches: New Church; Old Church. Famous for Delftware (two museums). www.delft.nl 49 A5

The Hague Den Haag
Seat of Government and of the royal house of the Netherlands. The 17c Mauritshuis houses the Royal Picture Gallery (excellent 15–18c Flemish and Dutch). Other good collections: Prince William V Gallery; Hesdag Museum; Municipal Museum www.denhaag.nl 49 A5

Haarlem
Many medieval gabled houses centred on the Great Market with 14c Town Hall and 15c Church of St Bavon. Museums: Frans Hals Museum; Teylers Museum. www.haarlem.nl 42 C1

Het Loo
Former royal palace and gardens set in a vast landscape (commissioned by future Queen of England, Mary Stuart). www.paleishetloo.nl 50 A1

Keukenhof
Landscaped gardens, planted with bulbs of many varieties, are the largest flower gardens in the world. www.keukenhof.nl 49 A5

Leiden
University town of beautiful gabled houses set along canals. The Rijksmuseum Van Oudheden is Holland's most important home to archaeological artefacts from the Antiquity. The 16c Hortus Botanicus is one of the oldest botanical gardens in Europe. The Cloth Hall with van Leyden's *Last Judgement* . www.leidenpromotie.nl 49 A5

Rotterdam
The largest port in the world. The Boymans-van Beuningen Museum has a huge and excellent decorative and fine art collection (old and modern). Nearby: 18c Kinderdijk with 19 windmills. www.rotterdam.nl 49 B5

Utrecht
Delightful old town centre along canals with the Netherlands' oldest university and Gothic cathedral. Good art collections: Central Museum; National Museum. www.utrecht.nl 49 A6

Norway Norge

www.norway.no

Bergen
Norway's second city in a scenic setting. The Quay has many painted wooden medieval buildings. Sights: 12c Romanesque St Mary's Church; Bergenhus fortress with 13c Haakon's Hall; Rosenkrantztårnet; Grieghallen; Rasmus Meyer Collection (Norwegian art); Bryggens Museum. www.visitbergen.com 32 A2

Lappland (Norwegian)
Vast land of Finnmark is home to the Sámi. Nordkapp is the northern point of Europe. Also Finland, Sweden. www.lappland.no 3 B25

Norwegian Fjords
Beautiful and majestic landscape of deep glacial valleys filled by the sea. The most thrilling fjords are between Bergen and Ålesund. www.fjords.com 2 F16

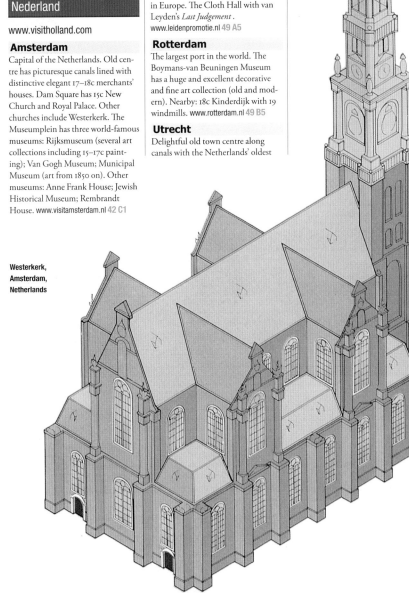

Oslo
Capital of Norway with a modern centre. Buildings: 17c cathedral; 19c city hall, 19c royal palace; 19c Stortinget (housing parliament); 19c University; 13c Akershus (castle); 12c Akerskirke (church). Museums: National Gallery; Munch Museum; Viking Ship Museum; Folk Museum (reconstructed buildings). www.visitoslo.com 34 B2

Stavkirker
Wooden medieval stave churches of bizarre pyramidal structure, carved with images from Nordic mythology. Best preserved in southern Norway.

Tromsø
Main arctic city of Norway with a university and two cathedrals. www.destinasjontromso.no 3 B23

Trondheim
Set on the edge of a fjord, a modern city with the superb Nidaros cathedral (rebuilt 19c). Also: Stiftsgaard (royal residence); Applied Arts Museum. www.trondheim.com 2 E19

Poland Polska

www.poland.pl

Częstochowa
Centre of Polish Catholicism, with the 14c monastery of Jasna Góra a pilgrimage site to the icon of the Black Madonna for six centuries. 55 C4

Gdańsk
Medieval centre with: 14c Town Hall (state rooms); Gothic brick St Mary's Church, Poland's largest; Long Market has fine buildings (Artus Court); National Art Museum. www.gdansk.pl 47 A4

Kraków
Old university city, rich in architecture, centred on superb 16c Marketplace with Gothic-Renaissance Cloth Hall containing the Art Gallery (19c Polish), Clock Tower, Gothic redbrick St Mary's Church (altarpiece). Czartoryski Palace has city's finest art collection. Wawel Hill has the Gothic cathedral and splendid Renaissance Royal Palace. The former Jewish ghetto in Kazimierz district has 16c Old Synagogue, now a museum. www.krakow.pl 55 C4

Poznań
Town centred on the Old Square with Renaissance Town Hall and Baroque mansions. Also: medieval castle; Gothic cathedral; National Museum (European masters). www.plot.poznan.pl 46 C2

Tatry
One of Europe's most delightful mountain ranges with many beautiful ski resorts (Zakopane). Also in Slovakia. 65 A5

Warsaw Warszawa
Capital of Poland, with many historic monuments in the Old Town with the Royal Castle (museum) and Old Town Square surrounded by reconstructed 17–18c merchants' houses. Several churches including: Gothic cathedral; Baroque Church of the Nuns of Visitation. Richly decorated royal palaces and gardens: Neoclassical Łazienki Palace; Baroque palace in Wilanów. The National Museum has Polish and European art. www.warsawtour.pl 55 A5

Wrocław
Historic town centred on the Market Square with 15c Town Hall and man-

sions. Churches: Baroque cathedral; St Elizabeth; St Adalbert. National Museum displays fine art. Vast painting of Battle of Racławice is specially housed. www.wroclaw.pl 54 B2

Portugal

www.visitportugal.pt

Alcobaça
Monastery of Santa Maria, one of the best examples of a Cistercian abbey, founded in 1147 (exterior 17–18c). The church is Portugal's largest (14c tombs). 92 B1

Algarve
Modern seaside resorts among picturesque sandy beaches and rocky coves (Praia da Rocha). Old towns: Lagos; Faro. www.rtalgarve.pt 98 B2

Batalha
Abbey is one of the masterpieces of French Gothic and Manueline architecture, English Perpendicular chapel, unfinished pantheon). 92 B2

Braga
Historic town with cathedral and large Archbishop's Palace. www.cm-braga.com.pt 87 C2

Coimbra
Old town with narrow streets set on a hill. The Romanesque cathedral is particularly fine (portal). The university (founded 1290) has a fascinating Baroque library. Also: Museum of Machado de Castro; many monasteries and convents. 92 A2

Évora
Centre of the town, surrounded by walls, has narrow streets of Moorish character and medieval and Renaissance architecture. Churches: 12–13c Gothic cathedral; São Francisco with a chapel decorated with bones of some 5000 monks; 15c Convent of Dos Lóis. The Jesuit university was founded in 1559. Museum of Évora holds fine art (particularly Flemish and Portugese). 92 C3

Guimarães
Old town with a castle with seven towers on a vast keep. Churches: Romanesque chapel of São Miguel; São Francisco. Alberto Sampaio Museum and Martins Sarmento Museum are excellent. 87 C2

Lisbon Lisboa
Capital of Portugal. Baixa is the Neoclassical heart of Lisbon with the Praça do Comércio and Rossío squares. São Jorge castle (Visigothic, Moorish, Romanesque) is surrounded by the medieval quarters. Bairro Alto is famous for *fado* (songs). Monastery of Jerónimos is exceptional. Churches: 12c cathedral; São Vicente de Fora; São Roque (tiled chapels); Torre de Belém; Convento da Madre de Deus. Museums: Gulbenkian Museum (ancient, oriental, European), National Museum of Antique Art (old masters), Modern Art Centre; Azulejo Museum (decorative tiles). Nearby: palatial monastic complex Mafra; royal resort Sintra. www.cm-lisboa.pt 92 C1

Porto
Historic centre with narrow streets. Views from Clérigos Tower. Churches: São Francisco; cathedral. Soares dos Reis Museum holds fine and decorative arts (18–19c). The suburb of Vila Nova de Gaia is the centre for port wine. www.portoturismo.pt 87 C2

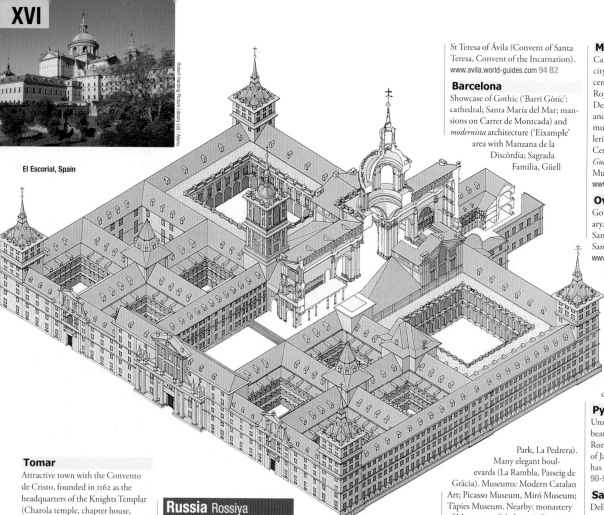

El Escorial, Spain

Tomar

Attractive town with the Convento de Cristo, founded in 1162 as the headquarters of the Knights Templar (Charola temple, chapter house, Renaissance cloisters). **92 B2**

Romania

www.turism.ro

Bucovina

Beautiful region in northern Romanian Moldova renowned for a number of 15–16c monasteries and their fresco cycles. Of particular note are Moldovita, Voroneţ and Suceviţa. **11 C8**

Bucharest Bucureşti

Capital of Romania with the majority of sites along the Calea Victoriei and centring on Piaţa Revoluţei with 19c Romanian Athenaeum and 1930s Royal Palace housing the National Art Gallery. The infamous 1980s Civic Centre with People's Palace is a symbol of dictatorial aggrandisement. www.bucuresti.ro **11 D9**

Carpathian Mountains Carpaţii

The beautiful Carpathian Mountains have several ski resorts (Sinaia) and peaks noted for first-rate mountaineering (Făgă raşuiui, Rodnei).Danube Delta Europe's largest marshland, a spectacular nature reserve. Travel in the area is by boat, with Tulcea the starting point for visitors. The Romanian Black Sea Coast has a stretch of resorts (Mamaia, Eforie) between Constanţaţ and the border, and well-preserved Roman remains in Histria. **11 C8**

Transylvania Transilvania

Beautiful and fascinating scenic region of medieval citadels (Timişoara, Sibiu) provides a setting for the haunting image of the legendary Dracula (Sighişoara, Braşov, Bran Castle). Cluj-Napoca is the main town. **11 C7**

Russia Rossiya

www.russia.com

Moscow Moskva

Capital of Russia, with many monuments. Within the Kremlin's red walls are: 15c Cathedral of the Dormition; 16c Cathedral of the Archangel; Cathedral of the Annunciation (icons), Armour Palace. Outside the walls, Red Square has the Lenin Mausoleum and 16c St Basil's Cathedral. There are a number of monasteries (16c Novodevichi). Two superb museums: Tretiakov Art Gallery (Russian); Pushkin Museum of Fine Art (European). Kolomenskoe, once a royal summer retreat, has the Church of the Ascension. The VDNKh is a symbol of the Stalinist era. www.moscow-guide.ru **7 D14**

Novgorod

One of Russia's oldest towns, centred on 15c Kremlin with St Sophia Cathedral (iconostasis, west door). Two other cathedrals: St Nicholas; St George. Museum of History, Architecture and Art has notable icons and other artefacts. www.novgorod.ru **7 B11**

Petrodvorets

Grand palace with numerous pavilions (Monplaisir) set in beautiful parkland interwoven by a system of fountains, cascades and waterways connected to the sea. www.petrodvorets.ru **7 B10**

Pushkin

(Tsarskoye Selo) Birthplace of Alexander Pushkin, with the vast Baroque Catherine Palace – splendid state apartments, beautiful gardens and lakes. www.pushkin-town.net **7 B11**

Saint Petersburg Sankt Peterburg

Founded in 1703 with the SS Peter and Paul Fortress and its cathedral by Peter the Great, and functioning as seat of court and government until 1918. Many of the most famous sights are around elegant Nevski Prospekt. The Hermitage, one of the world's largest and finest art collections is housed in five buildings including the Baroque Winter and Summer palaces. The Mikhailovsky Palace houses the Russian Museum (Russian art). Other sights: neoclassical Admiralty; 19c St Isaac's Cathedral and St Kazan Cathedral; Vasilievsky Island with 18c Menshikov Palace; Alexander Nevsky Monastery; 18c Smolny Convent. www.spb.ru **7 B11**

Sergiev Posad

(Zagorsk) Trinity St Sergius monastery with 15c cathedral. www.musobl.divo.ru **7 C15**

Serbia & Montenegro Srbija i Crna Gora

www.serbia-tourism.org;
www.visit-montenegro.com

Belgrade Beograd

Capital of Serbia & Montenegro. The largely modern city is set between the Danube and Sava rivers. The National Museum holds European art. To the south there are numerous fascinating medieval monasteries, richly embellished with frescoes. www.belgradetourism.org.yu **85 B5**

Spain España

www.spaintour.com

Ávila

Medieval town with 2km-long 11c walls. Pilgrimage site to shrines to St Teresa of Ávila (Convent of Santa Teresa, Convent of the Incarnation). www.avila.world-guides.com **94 B2**

Barcelona

Showcase of Gothic ('Barri Gòtic': cathedral; Santa María del Mar; mansions on Carrer de Montcada) and *modernista* architecture ('Eixample' area with Manzana de la Discòrdia; Sagrada Familia, Güell Park, La Pedrera). Many elegant boulevards (La Rambla, Passeig de Gràcia). Museums: Modern Catalan Art; Picasso Museum, Miró Museum; Tàpies Museum. Nearby: monastery of Montserrat (Madonna); Figueres (Dali Museum). www.barcelonaturisme.com **91 B5**

Burgos

Medieval town with Gothic cathedral, Moorish-Gothic Royal Monastery and Charterhouse of Miraflores. www.burgos.es **88 B3**

Cáceres

Medieval town surrounded by originally Moorish walls and with several aristocratic palaces with solars. www.caceres.es **93 B4**

Córdoba

Capital of Moorish Spain with a labyrinth of streets and houses with tile-decorated patios. The 8–10c Mezquita is the finest mosque in Spain. A 16c cathedral was added at the centre of the building and a 17c tower replaced the minaret. The old Jewish quarter has 14c synagogue. www.cordoba.es **100 B1**

El Escorial

Immense Renaissance complex of palatial and monastic buildings and mausoleum of the Spanish monarchs. www.patrimonionacional.es/escorial/escorial.htm **94 B2**

Granada

The Alhambra was hill-top palace-fortress of the rulers of the last Moorish kingdom and is the most splendid example of Moorish art and architecture in Spain. The complex has three principal parts: Alcazaba fortress (11c); Casa Real palace (14c, with later Palace of Carlos V); Generalife gardens. Also: Moorish quarter; gypsy quarter; Royal Chapel with good art in the sacristy. www.granadatur.com **100 B2**

León

Gothic cathedral has notable stained glass. Royal Pantheon commemorates early kings of Castile and León. **88 B1**

Madrid

Capital of Spain, a mainly modern city with 17–19c architecture at its centre around Plaza Mayor. Sights: Royal Palace with lavish apartments; Descalzas Reales Convent (tapestries and other works); Royal Armoury museum. Spain's three leading galleries: Prado (15–18c); Queen Sofia Centre (20c Spanish, Picasso's *Guernica*); Thyssen-Bornemisza Museum (medieval to modern). www.munimadrid.es **94 B3**

Oviedo

Gothic cathedral with 12c sanctuary. Three Visigoth (9c) churches: Santullano, Santa María del Naranco, San Miguel de Lillo. www.ayto-oviedo.es **88 A1**

Palma

Situated on Mallorca, the largest and most beautiful of the Balearic islands, with an impressive Gothic cathedral. www.a-palma.es **97 B2**

Picos de Europa

Mountain range with river gorges and peaks topped by Visigothic and Romanesque churches. **88 A2**

Pyrenees

Unspoiled mountain range with beautiful landscape and villages full of Romanesque architecture (cathedral of Jaca). The Ordesa National Park has many waterfalls and canyons. **90-91**

Salamanca

Delightful old city with some uniquely Spanish architecture: Renaissance Plateresque is famously seen on 16c portal of the university (founded 1215); Baroque Churrigueresque on 18c Plaza Mayo; both styles at the Convent of San Esteban. Also: Romanesque Old Cathedral; Gothic-Plateresque New Cathedral; House of Shells. www.salamanca.com **94 B1**

Santiago di Compostella

Medieval city with many churches and religious institutions. The famous pilgrimage to the shrine of St James the Apostle ends here in the magnificent cathedral, originally Romanesque with many later elements (18c Baroque façade). www.santiagoturismo.com **86 B2**

Segovia

Old town set on a rock with a 1c Roman aqueduct. Also: 16c Gothic cathedral; Alcázar (14–15c, rebuilt 19c); 12-sided 13c Templar church of Vera Cruz. www.viasegovia.com **94 B2**

Seville Sevilla

City noted for festivals and flamenco. The world's largest Gothic cathedral (15c) retains the Orange Court and minaret of a mosque. The Alcazar is a fine example of Moorish architecture. The massive 18c tobacco factory, now part of the university, was the setting for Bizet's *Carmen*. Barrio de Santa Cruz is the old Jewish quarter with narrow streets and white houses. Casa de Pilatos (15–16c) has a fine domestic patio. Hospital de la Caridad has good Spanish painting. Nearby: Roman Italica with amphitheatre. www.sevilla.org **99 B5**

Tarragona

The city and its surroundings have some of the best-preserved Roman heritage in Spain. Also: Gothic cathedral (cloister); Archaeological Museum. www.tarragona.es **91 B4**

Robert Harding Picture Library Ltd / Alamy

Toledo

Historic city with Moorish, Jewish and Christian sights. The small 11c mosque of El Cristo de la Luz is one of the earliest in Spain. Two synagogues have been preserved: Santa María la Blanca; El Tránsito. Churches: San Juan de los Reyes; Gothic cathedral (good artworks). El Greco's *Burial of the Count of Orgaz* is in the Church of Santo Tomé. More of his works are in the El Greco house and, with other art, in Hospital de Santa Cruz. www.toledo.es **94 C2**

Valencia

The old town has houses and palaces with elaborate façades. Also: Gothic cathedral and Lonja de la Seda church. www.comunitatvalenciana.com **96 B2**

Zaragoza

Town notable for Moorish architecture (11c Aljafería Palace). The Basilica de Nuestra Señora del Pilar, one of two cathedrals, is highly venerated. www.zaragoza-ciudad.com **90 B2**

Slovenia Slovenija
www.slovenia-tourism.si

Istria Istra
Two town centres, Koper and Piran, with medieval and Renaissance squares and Baroque palaces. See also Croatia. www.slo-istra.com **72 C3**

Julian Alps Julijske Alpe
Wonderfully scenic section of the Alps with lakes (Bled, Bohinj), deep valleys (Planica, Vrata) and ski resorts (Kranjska Gora, Bohinjska Bistrica). **72 B3**

Karst Caves
Numerous caves with huge galleries, extraordinary stalactites and stalagmites, and underground rivers. The most spectacular are Postojna (the most famous, with Predjamski Castle nearby) and Škocjan. www.postojnska-jama.si **73 C4**

Ljubljana
Capital of Slovenia. The old town, dominated by the castle (good views), is principally between Prešeren Square and Town Hall (15c, 18c), with the Three Bridges and colonnaded market. Many Baroque churches (cathedral, St Jacob, St Francis, Ursuline) and palaces (Bishop's Palace, Seminary, Gruber Palace). Also: 17c Križanke church and monastery complex; National Gallery and Modern Gallery show Slovene art. www.ljubljana.si **73 B4**

Slovakia
Slovenska Republika

www.slovenska-republika.com

Bratislava
Capital of Slovakia, dominated by the castle (Slovak National Museum, good views). Old Town centred on the Main Square with Old Town Hall and Jesuit Church. Many 18–19c palaces (Mirbach Palace, Pálffy Palace, Primate's Palace), churches (Gothic cathedral, Corpus Christi Chapel) and museums (Slovak National Gallery). www.bratislava.sk **64 B3**

Košice
Charming old town with many Baroque and neoclassical buildings and Gothic cathedral. www.kosice.sk **10 B6**

Spišské Podhradie
Region, east of the Tatry, full of picturesque medieval towns (Levoča, Kežmarok, Prešov) and architectural monuments (Spišský Castle). **65 A6**

Tatry
Beautiful mountain region. Poprad is an old town with 19c villas. Starý Smokovec is a popular ski resort. See also Poland. www.tatry.sk **65 A5**

Sweden Sverige
www.sweden.se

Abisko
Popular resort in the Swedish part of Lapland set in an inspiring landscape of lakes and mountains. www.abisko.nu **3 B23**

Gothenburg Göteborg
Largest port in Sweden, the historic centre has 17–18c Dutch architectural character (Kronhuset). The Art Museum has interesting Swedish works. www.goteborg.com **35 D3**

Gotland
Island with Sweden's most popular beach resorts (Ljugarn) and unspoiled countryside with churches in Baltic Gothic style (Dahlem, Bunge). Visby is a pleasant walled medieval town. www.gotland.se **37 D5**

Lappland (Swedish)
Swedish part of Lappland with 18c Arvidsjaur the oldest preserved Sámi village. Jokkmokk is a Sámi cultural centre, Abisko a popular resort in fine scenery. Also Finland, Norway. www.lappland.se **3 B23**

Lund
Charming university city with medieval centre and a fine 12c Romanesque cathedral (14c astronomical clock, carved tombs). www.lund.se **41 D3**

Malmö
Old town centre set among canals and parks dominated by a red-brick castle (museums) and a vast market square with Town Hall and Gothic Church of St Peter. www.malmo.se **41 D3**

Mora
Delightful village on the shores of Siljan Lake in the heart of the Dalarna region, home to folklore and traditional crafts. www.mora.se **2 F21**

Stockholm
Capital of Sweden built on a number of islands. The Old Town is largely on three islands with 17–18c houses, Baroque Royal Castle (apartments and museums), Gothic cathedral, parliament. Riddarholms church has tombs of the monarchy. Museums include: Modern Gallery (one of world's best modern collections); Nordiska Museet (cultural history); open-air Skansen (Swedish houses). Baroque Drottningholm Castle is the residence of the monarchy. www.stockholm.se **36 B5**

Swedish Lakes
Beautiful region around the Vättern and Vänern Lakes. Siljan Lake is in the Dalarna region where folklore and crafts are preserved (Leksand, Mora, Rättvik). **35 C5**

Uppsala
Appealing university town with a medieval centre around the massive Gothic cathedral. www.uppsala.se **36 B4**

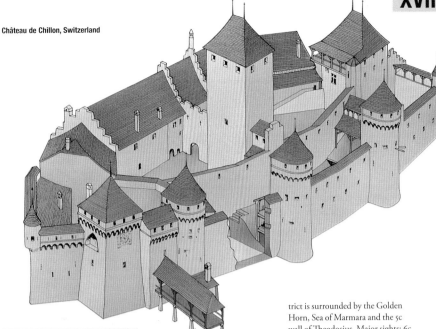

Château de Chillon, Switzerland

Switzerland Schweiz
www.myswitzerland.com

Alps
The most popular Alpine region is the Berner Oberland with the town of Interlaken a starting point for exploring the large number of picturesque peaks (Jungfrau). The valleys of the Graubünden have famous ski resorts (Davos, St Moritz). Zermatt lies below the highest and most recognizable Swiss peak, the Matterhorn. www.thealps.com **70 B2**

Basel
Medieval university town with Romanesque-Gothic cathedral (tomb of Erasmus). Superb collections: Art Museum; Museum of Contemporary Art. www.baseltourismus.ch **70 A2**

Bern
Capital of Switzerland. Medieval centre has fountains, characteristic streets (Spitalgasse) and tower-gates. The Bärengraben is famed for its bears. Also: Gothic cathedral; good Fine Arts Museum. www.berne.ch **70 B2**

Geneva Genève
Wonderfully situated on the lake with the world's highest fountain. The historic area is centred on the Romanesque cathedral and Place du Bourg du Four. Excellent collections: Art and History Museum; Museum of Modern Art in 19c Petit Palais. On the lake shore: splendid medieval Château de Chillon. www.geneva-tourism.ch **69 B6**

Interlaken
Starting point for excursions to the most delightful part of the Swiss Alps, the Bernese Oberland, with Grindelwald and Lauterbrunnen – one of the most thrilling valleys leading up to the ski resort of Wengen with views on the Jungfrau. www.interlakentourism.ch **70 B2**

Lucerne Luzern
On the beautiful shores of Vierwaldstättersee, a charming medieval town of white houses on narrow streets and of wooden bridges (Kapellbrücke, Spreuerbrücke). It is centred on the Kornmarkt with the Renaissance Old Town Hall and Am Rhyn-Haus (Picasso collection). www.luzern.org **70 A3**

Zürich
Set on Zürichsee, the old quarter is around Niederdorf with 15c cathedral. Gothic Fraumünster has stained glass by Chagall. Museums: Swiss National Museum (history); Art Museum (old and modern masters); Bührle Foundation (Impressionists, Post-impressionists). www.zuerich.com **70 A3**

Turkey Türkiye
www.tourismturkey.org

Istanbul
Divided by the spectcular Bosphorus, the stretch of water that separates Europe from Asia, the historic district is surrounded by the Golden Horn, Sea of Marmara and the 5c wall of Theodosius. Major sights: 6c Byzantine church of St Sophia (converted first to a mosque in 1453 and then a museum in 1934); 15c Topkapi Palace; treasury and Archaeological Museum; 17c Blue Mosque; 19c Bazaar; 16c Süleymaniye Mosque; 12c Kariye Camii; European district with Galata Tower and 19c Dolmabahçe Palace. www.istanbul.com **114 A3**

Ukraine Ukraina
www.ukraine.com

Kiev Kyïv
Capital of Ukraine, known for its cathedral (11c, 17c) with Byzantine frescoes and mosaics. The Monastery of the Caves has churches, monastic buildings and catacombs. www.uazone.net/kiev **11 A11**

Vatican City
Città del Vaticano

www.vatican.va

Vatican City
Città del Vaticano
Independent state within Rome. On Piazza San Pietro is the 15–16c Renaissance-Baroque Basilica San Pietro (Michelangelo's dome and *Pietà*, the world's most important Roman Catholic church. The Vatican Palace contains the Vatican Museums with many fine art treasures including Michelangelo's frescoes in the Sistine Chapel. www.vatican.va **102 B5**

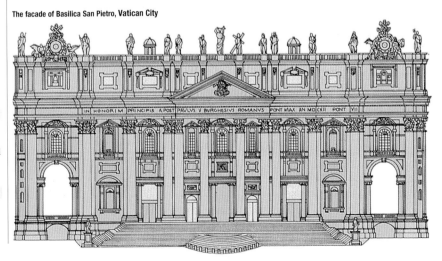

The facade of Basilica San Pietro, Vatican City

History and culture of Europe

The following definitions describe some of the key terms in the timeline below.

Aegean civilization Bronze Age cultures, chiefly Minoan (on Crete, at its height c.1700BC–c.1100BC) and Mycenaean (at its height c.1580BC–c.1120BC).

Baroque Style of art and architecture which at its best was a blend of light, colour, and movement calculated to overwhelm through emotional appeal. Buildings were heavily decorated with ornament and free-standing sculpture. Baroque became increasingly complex and florid. The term is often used to describe the period in history as well as the style.

Byzantine Empire Christian, Greek-speaking, Eastern Roman Empire that outlasted the Western Empire by nearly 1000 years. The area of the Byzantine Empire varied greatly, and its history from c.600 was marked by continual military crisis and recovery.

Carolingian period Cultural revival in France and Italy beginning under the encouragement of Charlemagne, who gathered notable educators and artists to his court at Aachen.

Counter-Reformation Revival of the Roman Catholic Church in Europe, beginning as a reaction to the Reformation. The reforms were largely conservative, trying to remove many of the abuses of the late medieval church and win new prestige for the papacy. The Council of Trent (1545-63) generated many of the key decisions and doctrines.

Dark Ages Term that at one time historians used to imply cultural and economic backwardness, but now is used mainly to indicate our ignorance of the period due to lack of historical evidence.

Enlightenment (Age of Reason) Philosophical movement that influenced many aspects of 18th-century society. It was inspired by the scientific and philosophical revolutions of the late 17th century and stressed the use of reason and the rational side of human nature.

Gothic Architecture and painting characterized by the pointed arch and ribbed vault. Religious in inspiration, its greatest expression was the cathedral. Gothic sculpture was elegant and more realistic than Romanesque. The Gothic style was also well expressed in manuscript illumination.

High Renaissance Brief period regarded as the height of Italian (particularly Roman) Renaissance art, brought to an end by the sack of Rome by the troops of Charles V.

Historicism, 19th-century Revival of past architectural styles. Ancient Greek and Gothic forms predominated, though buildings were constructed in a wide range of styles, including Renaissance, Romanesque and baroque.

Holy Roman Empire Empire centred on Germany, which aimed to echo ancient Rome. It was founded when Otto I was crowned in Rome (some date it from the coronation of Charlemagne). The Emperor claimed to be the worldly sovereign of Christendom ruling in co-operation with

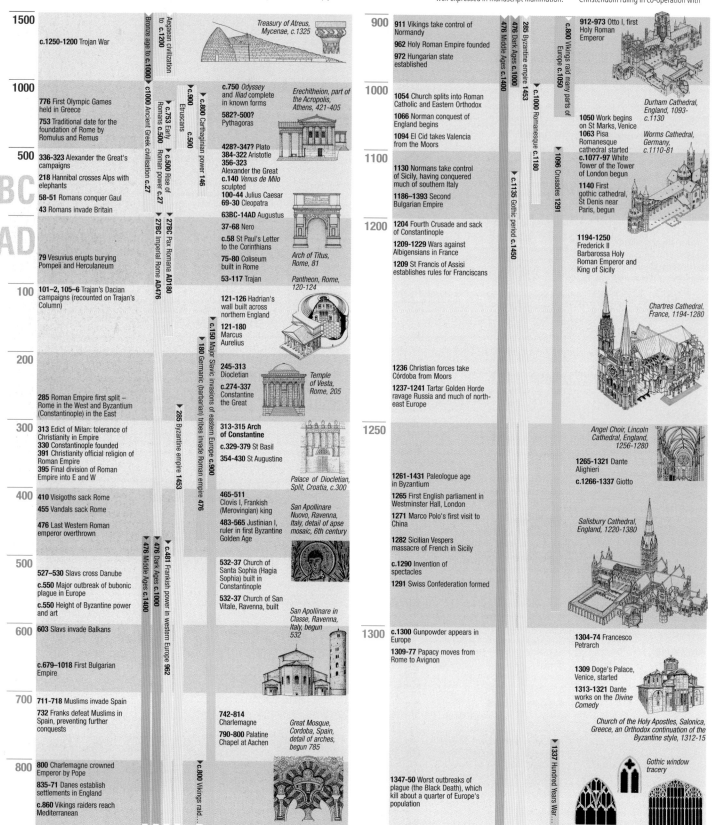

1500

c.1250-1200 Trojan War

Bronze age to c.1000 | Aegean civilization to c.1200

Treasury of Atreus, Mycenae, c.1325

1000

776 First Olympic Games held in Greece

753 Traditional date for the foundation of Rome by Romulus and Remus

c1000 Ancient Greek civilisation c.27 | c.900 Etruscans | c.800 Carthaginian power 146 | c.753 Early Romans c.500 | c.500 Rise of Roman power c.27

c.750 *Odyssey* and *Iliad* complete in known forms

582?-500? Pythagoras

Erechitheion, part of the Acropolis, Athens, 421-405

500

336-323 Alexander the Great's campaigns

218 Hannibal crosses Alps with elephants

58-51 Romans conquer Gaul

43 Romans invade Britain

BC

AD

428?-347? Plato
384-322 Aristotle
356-323 Alexander the Great
c.140 *Venus de Milo* sculpted
100-44 Julius Caesar
69-30 Cleopatra

63BC-14AD Augustus

37-68 Nero

c.58 St Paul's Letter to the Corinthians

75-80 Coliseum built in Rome

53-117 Trajan

278C Imperial Rome AD476 | 278C Pax Romana AD180

Arch of Titus, Rome, 81

Pantheon, Rome, 120-124

79 Vesuvius erupts burying Pompeii and Herculaneum

100

101–2, 105–6 Trajan's Dacian campaigns (recounted on Trajan's Column)

121-126 Hadrian's wall built across northern England

121-180 Marcus Aurelius

c.150 Major Slavic invasions of eastern Europe c.900 | 180 Germanic (barbarian) tribes invade Roman empire 476

200

285 Roman Empire first split – Rome in the West and Byzantium (Constantinople) in the East

245-313 Diocletian

c.274-337 Constantine the Great

Temple of Vesta, Rome, 205

285 Byzantine empire 1453

300

313 Edict of Milan: tolerance of Christianity in Empire
330 Constantinople founded
391 Christianity official religion of Roman Empire
395 Final division of Roman Empire into E and W

313-315 Arch of Constantine

c.329-379 St Basil
354-430 St Augustine

Palace of Diocletian, Split, Croatia, c.300

400

410 Visigoths sack Rome

455 Vandals sack Rome

476 Last Western Roman emperor overthrown

465-511 Clovis I, Frankish (Merovingian) king

483-565 Justinian I, ruler in first Byzantine Golden Age

San Apollinare Nuovo, Ravenna, Italy, detail of apse mosaic, 6th century

476 Dark Ages c.1000 | 476 Middle Ages c.1400 | c.481 Frankish power in western Europe 962

500

527–530 Slavs cross Danube

c.550 Major outbreak of bubonic plague in Europe

c.550 Height of Byzantine power and art

532-37 Church of Santa Sophia (Hagia Sophia) built in Constantinople

532-37 Church of San Vitale, Ravenna, built

San Apollinare in Classe, Ravenna, Italy, begun 532

600

603 Slavs invade Balkans

c.679–1018 First Bulgarian Empire

700

711-718 Muslims invade Spain

732 Franks defeat Muslims in Spain, preventing further conquests

c.860 Vikings raiders reach Mediterranean

742-814 Charlemagne

790-800 Palatine Chapel at Aachen

Great Mosque, Cordoba, Spain, detail of arches, begun 785

800

800 Charlemagne crowned Emperor by Pope

835-71 Danes establish settlements in England

c.800 Vikings raid....

900

911 Vikings take control of Normandy

962 Holy Roman Empire founded

972 Hungarian state established

476 Middle Ages c.1000 | 476 Dark Ages c.1000 | 285 Byzantine empire 1453 | c.1000 Romanesque c.1180 | c.800 Vikings raid many parts of Europe c.1050

1000

1054 Church splits into Roman Catholic and Eastern Orthodox

1066 Norman conquest of England begins

1094 El Cid takes Valencia from the Moors

Durham Cathedral, England, 1093-c.1130

1050 Work begins on St Marks, Venice
1063 Pisa Romanesque cathedral started

c.1077-97 White Tower of the Tower of London begun

1140 First gothic cathedral, St Denis near Paris, begun

Worms Cathedral, Germany, c.1110-81

1100

1130 Normans take control of Sicily, having conquered much of southern Italy

1186–1393 Second Bulgarian Empire

c.1135 Gothic period c.1450 | c.1096 Crusades 1291

1194-1250 Frederick II Barbarossa Holy Roman Emperor and King of Sicily

1200

1204 Fourth Crusade and sack of Constantinople

1209-1229 Wars against Albigensians in France

1209 St Francis of Assisi establishes rules for Franciscans

Chartres Cathedral, France, 1194-1280

1236 Christian forces take Córdoba from Moors

1237-1241 Tartar Golden Horde ravage Russia and much of north-east Europe

1250

Angel Choir, Lincoln Cathedral, England, 1256-1280

1265-1321 Dante Alighieri

c.1266-1337 Giotto

1261-1431 Paleologue age in Byzantium

1265 First English parliament in Westminster Hall, London

1271 Marco Polo's first visit to China

1282 Sicilian Vespers massacre of French in Sicily

c.1290 Invention of spectacles

1291 Swiss Confederation formed

Salisbury Cathedral, England, 1220-1380

1300

c.1300 Gunpowder appears in Europe

1309-77 Papacy moves from Rome to Avignon

1304-74 Francesco Petrarch

1309 Doge's Palace, Venice, started

1313-1321 Dante works on the *Divine Comedy*

Church of the Holy Apostles, Salonica, Greece, an Orthodox continuation of the Byzantine style, 1312-15

1347-50 Worst outbreaks of plague (the Black Death), which kill about a quarter of Europe's population

1337 Hundred Years War....

Gothic window tracery

the Pope. After 1648 the Empire became a loose confederation, containing hundreds of virtually independent states. It was abolished by Napoleon I.

Imperial Rome Period of Roman history starting when Augustus declared himself emperor, ending the Roman republic. Most of the empire had already been conquered.

International Gothic Style of painting characterized by naturalistic detail, elegant elongated figures and jewel-like colour.

Mannerism Loose term applied to the art and architecture of Italy between the High Renaissance and the Baroque. A self-conscious style, it aimed to exceed earlier work in emotional impact. Painting is characterized by elongated figures in distorted poses, often using lurid colours.

Middle Ages Period between the disintegration of the Roman Empire and the Renaissance. The Middle Ages were, above all, the age of the Christian church and of the social structure known as the feudal system.

Modern art Loose term that describes painting and sculpture that breaks from traditions going back to the Renaissance. There have been many movements, including fauvism, cubism, surrealism and expressionism.

Neoclassicism Movement in art and architecture that grew out of the Enlightenment. Exponents admired and imitated the order and clarity of ancient Greek and Roman art.

Pax Romana Period when ancient Rome was so powerful that its authority could not be challenged by outside forces and peace was maintained in the empire.

Reformation Sixteenth-century movement that sought reform of the Catholic Church and resulted in the development of Protestantism. The starting date is often given as 1517, when Martin Luther nailed his 95 theses to the door of the Schlosskirche in Wittenburg, Germany, protesting against abuses of the clergy. In Zurich, the Reformation was led by Ulrich Zwingli and then by John Calvin.

Renaissance Period of rapid cultural and economic development. An important element in this was humanism, which involved a revival of interest in classical learning and emphasis on the philosophical and moral importance of the human individual. There was a great flowering of all the arts. Architectural and artistic style emerged in Italy and was heavily influenced by Greek and Roman models and by humanism. There was development of perspective, increasing use of secular and pagan subjects, a rise of portraiture, constant experimentation, and growing concern for the expression of the individual artist. The ideas spread and were emulated with national variations.

Rococo Playful, light style of art, architecture and decoration that developed from baroque. Rococo brought to interior decoration swirls, scrolls, shells and arabesques. It was also applied to furniture, porcelain and silverware.

Romanesque Medieval architectural style preceding gothic. It was characterized by heavy round arches and massive walls, often decorated with carving or, originally, painted scenes.

Romanticism Movement that valued individual experience and intuition, rather than the orderly, structured universe of neoclassicism. An emphasis on nature was also a characteristic. In music, the term refers to the rather later period from c.1800–1910.

1350

1353 First Ottoman (Turkish) invasion of Europe

1378-81 War of Chioggia – Venice takes control of Mediterranean

1378-1417 Great Schism in the Papacy between Rome and Avignon

1389 Battle of Kosovo - Turks gain firm foothold in the Balkans

476 Middle Ages c.1400

c.1135 Gothic period c.1450

285 Byzantine empire 1453

c.1370 International Gothic style c.1450

1337 Hundred Years War between England and Franc 1453

1353 Giovanni Boccaccio writes the *Decameron*

1377-1446 Filippo Brunelleschi

1378-1455 Lorenzo Ghiberti

1386-1466 Donatello

1387/1400-55 Fra Angelico

c.1390-1441 Jan van Eyck

1386-1400 Geoffrey Chaucer's *Canterbury Tales*

Church of the Holy Cross, Schwabisch-Gemund, Germany, begun c.1350

1400

c.1400 onward Full plate armour begins to be used instead of chain main

1414 Discovery of Vitruvius' ancient treatise on architecture

1415 Introduction of oil paints by Jan and Hubert van Eyck in the Netherlands

1434-94 Medici family gain power in Florence

1431 Joan of Arc executed at Rouen

c.1440 Gutenberg invents moveable type allowing large-scale printing

c.1400 Renaissance c.1600

c.1400-1464 Roger van der Weyden

1401-c1428 Masaccio

1404-72 Leon Battista Alberti

1415-92 Piero della Francesca

c.1420 Work begins on dome of Florence Cathedral

1434 Van Eyck paints the *Arnolfini Marriage*

c.1445-1510 Sandro Botticelli

Foundling Hospital, Florence, Italy, from 1429

Town Hall, Louvain, Belgium, 1448-63

1450

1453 Turks capture Constantinople

1479 Aragon and Castile unite to become Spain

1479 Start of Spanish Inquisition

1492 Christopher Columbus reaches the Americas; Spanish and Portuguese colonization begins

1494 Spanish take Granada, the last Moorish stronghold

1499 Portuguese discover sea route to India

c.1450 Late Gothic period c.1550

c.1480 Great age of European discovery c.1580

c.1450-1516 Hieronymus Bosch

1452-1519 Leonardo da Vinci

1466?-1536 Erasmus of Rotterdam

1471-1528 Albrecht Dürer

1475-1564 Michelangelo Buonarotti

1473-1543 Nicolaus Copernicus

1483-1512 Raphael Sanzio

c.1487-1576 Titian

1492/9-1546 Giuliano Romano

1497/8-1543 Hans Holbein the Younger

c.1480 Botticelli paints *The Birth of Venus*

St Georges Chapel, Windsor Castle, England, 1481-1528

St Maria Novella, Florence, Italy, from 1458

1500

1506 Antique statue of the Laocöon discovered near Rome, sparking increased interest in the forms of Hellenistic sculpture

1517 Martin Luther publishes his 95 Theses in Wittenberg

1522 Magellan's expedition completes circumnavigation of the globe

1527 Sack of Rome by Imperial troops

1541 John Calvin founds church in Geneva

1543 Copernicus publishes idea that Earth revolves around the Sun

1495 High Renaissance 1527

1517 Reformation c.1600

c.1520 Mannerism c.1610

1500 Bosch paints *The Garden of Earthly Delights*

1503 Leonardo da Vinci paints *Mona Lisa*

1504 Michelangelo sculpts *David*

1506 St Peter's, Rome, begun on Boromini's plan

1508-1512 Michelangelo paints Sistine Chapel

1508-80 Andrea Palladio

1513 Machiavelli's *The Prince*

1541-1614 El Greco

1547 Ivan IV (the Terrible) Tsar of Russia

Palazzo Strozzi, Florence, Italy, from 1490

Bibliotecha Laurenziana, door to library, Florence, Italy, from 1524

1550

1545-63 Council of Trent

1562 Netherlands revolt against Spanish rule

1562-98 Wars of Religion in France; end with religious tolerance under Edict of Nantes

1557-82 Livonia War between Sweden and its Baltic neighbours

1571 Ottoman Turk navy defeated by Holy League at Battle of Lepanto

1572 St Bartholomew's Day Massacre in Paris

1572-1648 Dutch revolt against Spanish rule

1581 Independence of United Provinces (Netherlands)

1588 English fleet defeats Spanish Armada

c.1400 Renaissance c.1600

1545 Counter Reformation 1648

c.1520 Mannerism c.1610

c.1480 Great age of European discovery c.1580

1558-1603 Elizabeth I Queen of England

1564-1616 William Shakespeare

1571-1610 Michelangelo Merisi da Caravaggio

1573-1652 Inigo Jones

1577-1640 Peter Paul Rubens

1581/5-1666 Frans Hals

1594-1665 Nicolas Poussin

1598-1680 Gianlorenzo Bernini

1599-1660 Diego Velazquez

1599-1641 Sir Anthony Van Dyck

1598-1666 Françcois Mansart

Palace of Charles V, Granada, Spain, detail, begun 1526

S. Georgio Maggiore, Venice,

1600

1607 First English colony in North America at Jamestown

1618 Defenestration of Prague starts Thirty Years' War

1630 Sweden enters Thirty Year's War

1635 Peace of Prague ends German involvement in Thirty Years' War

1635 France enters Thirty Years' War

1642-5 English Civil War

1648 Treaty of Westphalia ends Thirty Years' War

1649 Execution of Charles I of England

c.1600 Baroque c.1750

1618 Thirty Years' War 1648

1600-92 Claude Lorraine

1603 *Hamlet* written by Shakespeare

1606-69 Rembrandt van Rijn

1624 Frans Hals paints *The Laughing Cavalier*

1624 Palace of Versailles started

1627-1725 Peter I, the Great, of Russia

1632-75 Jan Vermeer

1632-1723 Sir Christopher Wren

1633 Galileo tried for heresy

1642 Rembrandt paints *The Night Watch*

Mauritzhuis, The Hague, Netherlands, c.1633

1650

1652-3, 1665-7, 1672-4 1st, 2nd and 3rd Anglo-Dutch wars

1660 Restoration of English monarchy

1666 Great Fire of London

1671 Spain and United Provinces ally against France

1671 Hungarian Revolt and Reign of Terror

1682 Spain and Holy Roman Empire ally against France

1683 Turks besiege Vienna

1685 Edict of Nantes revoked and Huguenots leave France

1689 English Parliament passes Bill of Rights

1699 Habsburgs recover Hungary from Turks

1661 Louis XIV takes power in France

1667 John Milton, *Paradise Lost*

1667-70 Main façade of Louvre

1687 Isaac Newton publishes *Principia Mathematica*

1696 Peter I, the Great, becomes Tsar of Russia

1696-1770 Giovanni Battista Tiepolo

S. Carlo alle Quatro Fontane, Rome, Italy, detail, begun 1633

Troja Palace, Prague, Czech Republic, 1679-96

1700

1700-21 Great Northern War between Sweden and Russia and its allies

1702-1713 War of Spanish Succession (ends with Peace of Utrecht)

1703 St Petersburg founded

1704 "Grand Alliance" of Holland, England and Austria defeat France at Blenheim

1707 Act of Union between England and Scotland

1730 Methodism founded by John and Charles Wesley

1740-86 Prussia under Frederick the Great

1740-8 War of Austrian Succession

c.1700 Rococo c.1750

c.1700 Age of Enlightenment 1789

c.1730 Gothic Revival c.1780

1719 Daniel Defoe, *Robinson Crusoe*

1720 J.S.Bach *Brandenburg Concertos*

1726 Jonathan Swift, *Gulliver's Travels*

1728-92 Robert Adam

1742 Handel's *Messiah*

1746-1828 Goya

1748-1825 Jacques-Louis David

1749-1832 Johann Wolfgang von Goethe

Baroque interior, St John Nepomuk, Munich, Germany 1732-46

Amalienburg Palace, near Munich, Rococo detail and decoration, 1734

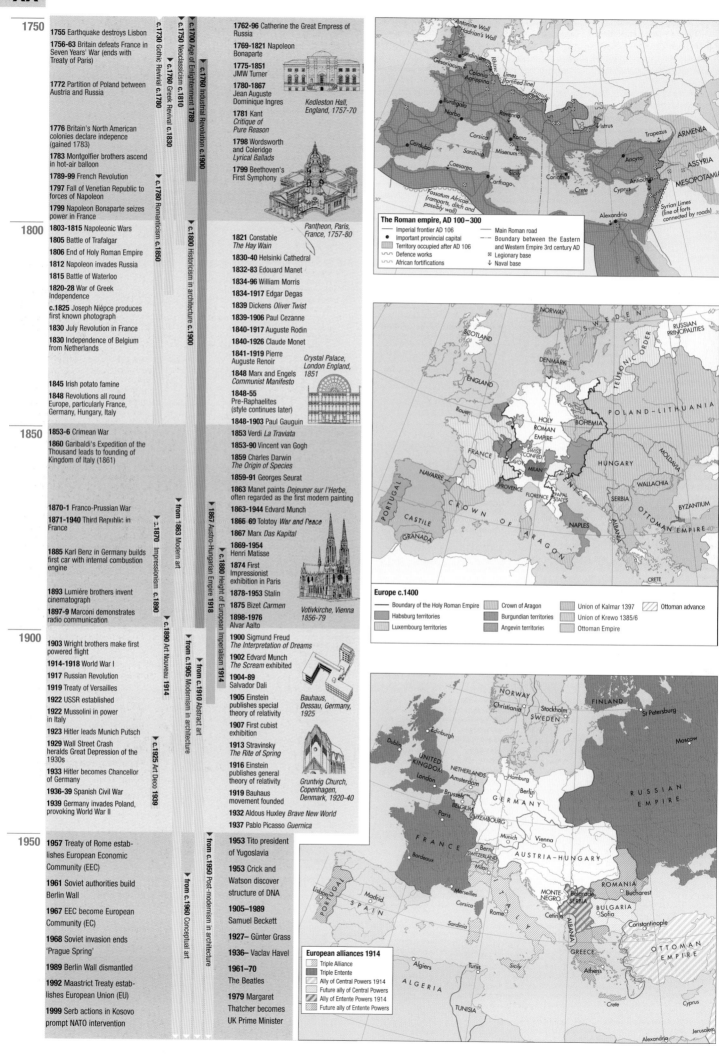

1750

1755 Earthquake destroys Lisbon

1756-63 Britain defeats France in Seven Years' War (ends with Treaty of Paris)

1772 Partition of Poland between Austria and Russia

1776 Britain's North American colonies declare indepence (gained 1783)

1783 Montgolfier brothers ascend in hot-air balloon

1789-99 French Revolution

1797 Fall of Venetian Republic to forces of Napoleon

1799 Napoleon Bonaparte seizes power in France

1800

1803-1815 Napoleonic Wars

1805 Battle of Trafalgar

1806 End of Holy Roman Empire

1812 Napoleon invades Russia

1815 Battle of Waterloo

1820-28 War of Greek Independence

c.1825 Joseph Niépce produces first known photograph

1830 July Revolution in France

1830 Independence of Belgium from Netherlands

1845 Irish potato famine

1848 Revolutions all round Europe, particularly France, Germany, Hungary, Italy

1850

1853-6 Crimean War

1860 Garibaldi's Expedition of the Thousand leads to founding of Kingdom of Italy (1861)

1870-1 Franco-Prussian War

1871-1940 Third Republic in France

1885 Karl Benz in Germany builds first car with internal combustion engine

1893 Lumière brothers invent cinematograph

1897-9 Marconi demonstrates radio communication

1900

1903 Wright brothers make first powered flight

1914-1918 World War I

1917 Russian Revolution

1919 Treaty of Versailles

1922 USSR established

1922 Mussolini in power in Italy

1923 Hitler leads Munich Putsch

1929 Wall Street Crash heralds Great Depression of the 1930s

1933 Hitler becomes Chancellor of Germany

1936-39 Spanish Civil War

1939 Germany invades Poland, provoking World War II

1950

1957 Treaty of Rome establishes European Economic Community (EEC)

1961 Soviet authorities build Berlin Wall

1967 EEC become European Community (EC)

1968 Soviet invasion ends 'Prague Spring'

1989 Berlin Wall dismantled

1992 Maastrict Treaty establishes European Union (EU)

1999 Serb actions in Kosovo prompt NATO intervention

(vertical movement labels)

c.1730 Gothic Revival c.1780

c.1760 Greek Revival c.1830

c.1750 Neoclassicism c.1810

c.1760 Age of Enlightenment 1789

c.1700 Industrial Revolution c.1900

c.1780 Romanticism c.1850

c.1800 Historicism in architecture c.1900

1867 Austro-Hungarian Empire 1918

c.1880 Height of European Imperialism 1914

from 1863 Modern art

c.1870 Impressionism c.1890

c.1890 Art Nouveau 1914

from c.1905 Modernism in architecture

from c.1910 Abstract art

c.1925 Art Deco 1939

from c.1950 Post-modernism in architecture

from c.1960 Conceptual art

(cultural / scientific column)

1762-96 Catherine the Great Empress of Russia

1769-1821 Napoleon Bonaparte

1775-1851 JMW Turner

1780-1867 Jean Auguste Dominique Ingres

1781 Kant *Critique of Pure Reason*

1798 Wordsworth and Coleridge *Lyrical Ballads*

1799 Beethoven's First Symphony

1821 Constable *The Hay Wain*

1830-40 Helsinki Cathedral

1832-83 Edouard Manet

1834-96 William Morris

1834-1917 Edgar Degas

1839 Dickens *Oliver Twist*

1839-1906 Paul Cezanne

1840-1917 Auguste Rodin

1840-1926 Claude Monet

1841-1919 Pierre Auguste Renoir

1848 Marx and Engels *Communist Manifesto*

1848-55 Pre-Raphaelites (style continues later)

1848-1903 Paul Gauguin

1853 Verdi *La Traviata*

1853-90 Vincent van Gogh

1859 Charles Darwin *The Origin of Species*

1859-91 Georges Seurat

1863 Manet paints *Dejeuner sur l'Herbe*, often regarded as the first modern painting

1863-1944 Edvard Munch

1866-69 Tolstoy *War and Peace*

1867 Marx *Das Kapital*

1869-1954 Henri Matisse

1874 First Impressionist exhibition in Paris

1878-1953 Stalin

1875 Bizet *Carmen*

1898-1976 Alvar Aalto

1900 Sigmund Freud *The Interpretation of Dreams*

1902 Edvard Munch *The Scream* exhibited

1904-89 Salvador Dali

1905 Einstein publishes special theory of relativity

1907 First cubist exhibition

1913 Stravinsky *The Rite of Spring*

1916 Einstein publishes general theory of relativity

1919 Bauhaus movement founded

1932 Aldous Huxley *Brave New World*

1937 Pablo Picasso *Guernica*

1953 Tito president of Yugoslavia

1953 Crick and Watson discover structure of DNA

1905–1989 Samuel Beckett

1927– Günter Grass

1936– Vaclav Havel

1961–70 The Beatles

1979 Margaret Thatcher becomes UK Prime Minister

(image captions)

Kedleston Hall, England, 1757-70

Pantheon, Paris, France, 1757-80

Crystal Palace, London England, 1851

Votivkirche, Vienna 1856-79

Bauhaus, Dessau, Germany, 1925

Gruntvig Church, Copenhagen, Denmark, 1920-40

The Roman empire, AD 100–300
- Imperial frontier AD 106
- Important provincial capital
- Territory occupied after AD 106
- Defence works
- African fortifications
- Main Roman road
- Boundary between the Eastern and Western Empire 3rd century AD
- Legionary base
- Naval base

Europe c.1400
- Boundary of the Holy Roman Empire
- Habsburg territories
- Luxembourg territories
- Crown of Aragon
- Burgundian territories
- Angevin territories
- Union of Kalmar 1397
- Union of Krewo 1385/6
- Ottoman Empire
- Ottoman advance

European alliances 1914
- Triple Alliance
- Triple Entente
- Ally of Central Powers 1914
- Future ally of Central Powers
- Ally of Entente Powers 1914
- Future ally of Entente Powers

European politics and economics

EUROPEAN UNION MEMBERSHIP

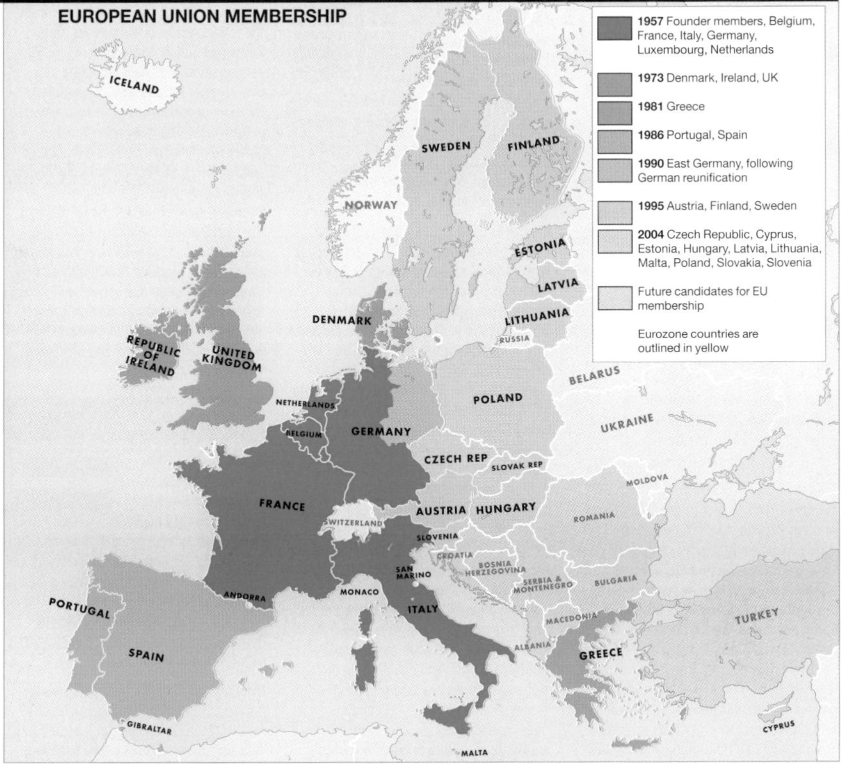
1957 Founder members, Belgium, France, Italy, Germany, Luxembourg, Netherlands
1973 Denmark, Ireland, UK
1981 Greece
1986 Portugal, Spain
1990 East Germany, following German reunification
1995 Austria, Finland, Sweden
2004 Czech Republic, Cyprus, Estonia, Hungary, Latvia, Lithuania, Malta, Poland, Slovakia, Slovenia
Future candidates for EU membership
Eurozone countries are outlined in yellow
ICELAND
NORWAY
SWEDEN
FINLAND
ESTONIA
LATVIA
LITHUANIA
RUSSIA
DENMARK
REPUBLIC OF IRELAND
UNITED KINGDOM
NETHERLANDS
BELGIUM
GERMANY
POLAND
BELARUS
UKRAINE
CZECH REP
SLOVAK REP
MOLDOVA
FRANCE
AUSTRIA
HUNGARY
ROMANIA
SWITZERLAND
SLOVENIA
CROATIA
BOSNIA HERZEGOVINA
SAN MARINO
SERBIA & MONTENEGRO
BULGARIA
ANDORRA
MONACO
ITALY
MACEDONIA
ALBANIA
GREECE
TURKEY
PORTUGAL
SPAIN
GIBRALTAR
MALTA
CYPRUS

Albania *Shquipëria*

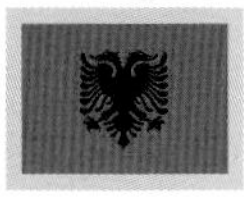

Area 28,748 sq km (11,100 sq miles) **Population** 3,582,205 **Capital** Tirana / Tiranë (300,000) **Languages** Albanian (official), Greek **GDP** 2002 US$4,400 **Currency** Lek = 100 Quindars **Government** multiparty republic **Head of state** President Alfred Moisiu, 2002 **Head of government** Prime Minister Fatos Nano, Socialist Party, 2002

Events Government wishes to sign an association accord with the EU but has been told that political and economic reforms must progress further before this can happen. Living standards still poor and there were protests and calls for the resignation of Nano is February 2004 as a result of this dissatisfaction.
Economy 56% of the workforce are engaged in agriculture. Private ownership of land has been encouraged since 1991. Crops include fruits, maize, olives, potatoes, sugar beet, vegetables, and wheat. Livestock farming is also important. Chromite, copper, and nickel are exported. Other resources include oil, brown coal, and hydroelectricity.
Website www.parlament.al

Andorra *Principat d'Andorra*

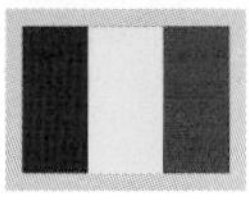

Area 468 sq km (181 sq miles) **Population** 69,150 **Capital** Andorra la Vella (22,000) **Languages** Catalan (official), French, Spanish **GDP** 2002 US$19,000 **Currency** Euro = 100 cents **Government** independent state and co-principality **Head of state** co-princes: Joan Enric Vives Sicilia, Bishop of Urgell, 2003 and Jacques Chirac (see France), 1995 **Head of government** Head of government Chief Executive Marc Forné Molné, 1994

Events In 1993 a new democratic constitution was adopted that reduced the roles of the President of France and the Bishop of Urgell to purely constitutional figureheads.
Economy The main sources of income include agriculture; the sale of water and hydroelectricity to Catalonia; tourism, particularly skiing.
Website www.andorra.ad

Austria *Österreich*

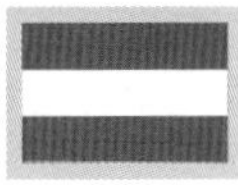

Area 83,859 sq km (32,377 sq miles) **Population** 8,188,000 **Capital** Vienna / Wien (1,560,000) **Languages** German (official) **GDP** 2002 US$27,900 **Currency** Euro = 100 cents **Government** federal republic **Head of state** President Heinz Fischer, Social Democrats, 2004 **Head of government** Federal Chancellor Wolfgang Schüssel, People's Party, 2000

Events In general elections in 1999, the extreme right Freedom Party, under Jörg Haider, made gains at the expense of the Social Democrats. He subsequently resigned as leader. People's Party electoral win in 2002 wasn't sufficient to form a government so a new government coalition was formed with the Freedom Party after failure of talks with the Social Democrats and the Greens. As a result Chancellor Schüssel is widely deemed to have moved to the right having introduced the toughest asylum laws in Europe. Freedom Party suffered heavy losses in the European elections of June 2004. In July 2004 President Fischer's predecessor Thomas Klestil died of a heart attack one day before Heinz Fischer was due to take his place.
Economy Austria is a wealthy nation which, despite plenty of hydroelectric power, is dependent on the import of fossil fuels. Austria's leading economic activity is the manufacture of metals. Dairy and livestock farming are the principal agricultural activities. Tourism is an important industry.
Website www.austria.gv.at/e/

Belarus

Area 207,600 sq km (80,154 sq miles) **Population** 10,322,151 **Capital** Minsk (1,677,000) **Languages** Belarussian, Russian (both official) **GDP** 2002 US$8,700 **Currency** Belarussian rouble = 100 kopek **Government** Republic **Head of state** President Alexander Lukashenko, 1994 **Head of government** Prime Minister Sergei Sidorsky, 2003

Events Belarus was very badly contaminated by the Chernobyl disaster in April 1986, lying as it does just to the north of the reactor. Belarus is a founder member of the CIS, of which Minsk is the administrative centre. In 1997, despite opposition from nationalists, Belarus signed a Union Treaty with Russia, committing it to integration with Russia. Currency union scheduled for 2008. As a result of a referendum in 1996 the president increased his power at the expense of parliament. He was re-elected in 2001 though the elections were widely deemed undemocratic by western observers and his rule is seen as a dictatorship. Belarus has been heavily criticised for the restrictions it places on press freedom.
Economy Belarus has faced problems in the transition to a free-market economy. In 1995 an agreement with Russia enabled Belarus to receive subsidised fuel. Agriculture, especially meat and dairy farming, is important.
Website http://government.by/eng/sovmin/index.htm

Belgium *Belgique*

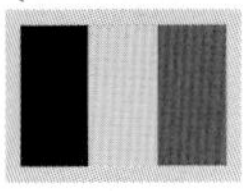

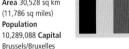

Area 30,528 sq km (11,786 sq miles) **Population** 10,289,088 **Capital** Brussels/Bruxelles (136,000) **Languages** Dutch, French, German (all official) **GDP** 2002 US$29,200 **Currency** Euro = 100 cents **Government** federal constitutional monarchy **Head of state** King Albert II, 1993 **Head of government** Prime Minister Guy Verhofstadt, Flemish Liberal Democrats, 1999

Events In 1993 Belgium adopted a federal system of government, each of the regions having its own parliament. The socialist and liberal parties have two thirds of the seats in parliament, each main party is split into two – one half for the Flemish and one half for the Walloons.
Economy Belgium is a major trading nation. The leading activity is manufacturing and products include steel and chemicals. Agriculture employs only 3% of the workforce, but the country is mostly self-sufficient. Barley and wheat are the chief crops, but the most valuable activities are dairy farming and livestock rearing.
Website www.belgium.be

Bosnia-Herzegovina *Bosna i Hercegovina*

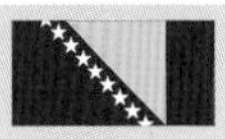

Area 51,197 sq km (19,767 sq miles) **Population** 3,989,000 **Capital** Sarajevo (529,000) **Languages** Serbian/Croatian **GDP** 2002 US$1,900 **Currency** Convertible Marka = 100 convertible pfenniga **Government** federal republic **Head of state** Chairman of the Presidency Sulejman Tihic, Muslim Party of Democratic Action, 2004 **Head of government** Chairman of the Council of Ministers Adnan Terzic, Muslim Party of Democratic Action, 2002

Events In 1992 a referendum approved independence from the Yugoslav federation. The Bosnian Serb population was against independence and in the resulting war occupied over two-thirds of the land. Croat forces seized other parts of the country. The 1995 Dayton Peace Accord ended the war and set up the Bosnian Muslim/Croat Federation and the Bosnian Serb Republic, each with their own president, government, parliament, military and police, there is also a central Bosnian government and rotating presidency the other members of which are Dragan Covic (Croatian Democratic Union) and Borislav Paravac (Serb Democratic Party). The office of the High Representative has power to impose decisions where the authorities are unable to agree or where political or economic interests are affected. NATO troops remain as a peace-keeping force.
Economy Excluding Macedonia, Bosnia was the least developed of the former republics of Yugoslavia. Currently receiving substantial aid, though this will be reduced.
Website www.fbihvlada.gov.ba

Bulgaria *Bulgariya*

Area 110,912 sq km (42,822 sq miles) **Population** 7,537,929 **Capital** Sofia (1,139,000) **Languages** Bulgarian (official), Turkish **GDP** 2002 US$6,500 **Currency** Lev = 100 stotinki **Government** multiparty republic **Head of state** President Georgi Purvanov, Bulgarian Socialist Party, 2002 **Head of government** Prime Minister Simeon Saxe-Coburg-Gotha, National Movement for Simeon II, 2001

Events In 1990 the first non-communist president for 40 years, Zhelyu Zhelev, was elected. A new constitution in 1991 saw the adoption of free-market reforms. Former king Simeon Saxe-Coburg-Gotha was the first ex-monarch in post-communist eastern Europe to return to power. He leads a coalition government, has gained membership of Nato for Bulgaria and also hopes to join the EU. He has supported the US-led campaign in Iraq and has sent more than 400 troops to the join the peace-keeping force.
Economy Bulgaria is a lower-middle-income developing country, faced with a difficult transition to a market economy. Manufacturing is the leading economic activity but has outdated technology. The main products are chemicals, metals, machinery and textiles. Mineral reserves include molybdenum. Wheat and maize are the main crops. The valleys of the Maritsa are ideal for winemaking, plums and tobacco. Tourism is increasing rapidly.
Website www.president.bg/en

Croatia *Hrvatska*

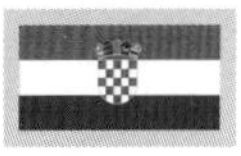

Area 56,538 sq km (21,829 sq miles) **Population** 4,422,000 **Capital** Zagreb (779,000) **Languages** Croatian **GDP** 2002 US$ 9,800 **Currency** Kuna = 100 lipas **Government** multiparty republic **Head of state** President Stjepan Mesic, 2000 **Head of government** Prime Minister Ivo Sanader, Croatian Democratic Union, 2003

Events A 1991 referendum voted overwhelmingly in favour of independence. Serb-dominated areas took up arms to remain in the federation. Serbia armed Croatian Serbs, war broke out between Serbia and Croatia, and Croatia lost much territory. In 1992 United Nations peacekeeping troops were deployed. In 1995 Croatian government forces occupied Krajina and 150,000 Serbs fled. Following the Dayton Peace Accord of 1995, Croatia and Yugoslavia established diplomatic relations. An agreement between the Croatian government and Croatian Serbs provided for the eventual reintegration of Krajina into Croatia in 1998. PM Sanader leads a minority government with the support of many smaller parties. Croatia is now actively co-operating with the international tribunal at the Hague.
Economy The wars have badly disrupted Croatia's relatively prosperous economy. Croatia has a wide range of manufacturing industries, such as steel, chemicals, oil refining, and wood products. Agriculture is the principal employer. Crops include maize, soya beans, sugar beet and wheat.
Website www.croatia.hr

Czech Republic *Česka Republica*

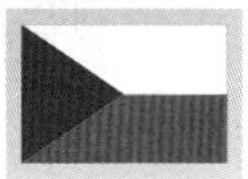

Area 78,864 sq km (30,449 sq miles) **Population** 10,249,000 **Capital** Prague/Praha (1,193,000) **Languages** Czech (official), Moravian **GDP** 2002 US$15,300 **Currency** Czech Koruna = 100 haler **Government** multiparty republic **Head of state** President Václav Klaus, 2003 **Head of government** Prime Minister Stanislav Gross, Czech Social Democratic Party, 2004

Events Free elections were held in 1990, resulting in the re-election of Vaclav Havel. In 1992 the government agreed to the secession of the Slovak Republic, and on 1 January 1993 the Czech Republic was created. The Czech Republic was granted full membership of Nato in 1999 and joined the EU in May 2004. The coalition government has a small majority and is formed of Social Democrats and an alliance of Christian Democrats and Freedom Union. The country still experiences problems of discrimination against the Roma. The opposition Civic Democratic Party with their agenda of not ceding too much power to the EU were the winners in the European elections of June 2004, as a result of which Prime Minister Vladimir Spidla resigned, to be replaced by Stanislav Gross.
Economy The country has deposits of coal, uranium, iron ore, magnesite, tin and zinc. Industries include chemicals, beer, iron and steel, and machinery. Private ownership of land is gradually being restored. Agriculture employs 12% of the workforce. Livestock raising is important. Crops include grains, fruit, and hops for brewing. Prague is now a major tourist destination.
Website www.czech.cz

Denmark *Danmark*

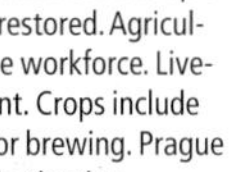

Area 43,094 sq km (16,638 sq miles) **Population** 5,384,000 **Capital** Copenhagen / København (499,000) **Languages** Danish (official) **GDP** 2002 US$28,900 **Currency** Krone = 100 øre **Government** parliamentary monarchy **Head of state** Queen Margrethe II, 1972 **Head of government** Prime Minister Anders Fogh Rasmussen, Venstre (Left) Party, 2001

Events In 1992 Denmark rejected the Maastricht Treaty, but reversed the decision in a 1993 referendum. In 1998 the Amsterdam Treaty was ratified by a further referendum. Currency pegged to Euro but still independent. The government is a coalition formed with the Conservative Party. Anti-immigration policies are backed by the well-supported far-right Danish People's Party. Rasmussen wants a second referendum on the Euro. The opposition Social Democrats were clear winners in the European elections of June 2004, though this

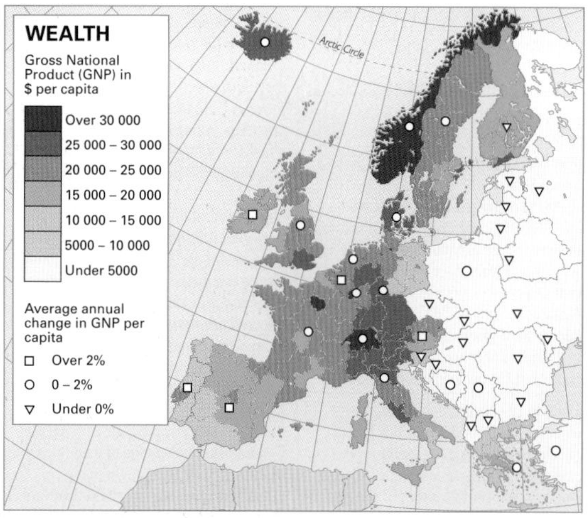
WEALTH
Gross National Product (GNP) in $ per capita
Over 30 000
25 000 – 30 000
20 000 – 25 000
15 000 – 20 000
10 000 – 15 000
5000 – 10 000
Under 5000
Average annual change in GNP per capita
Over 2%
0 – 2%
Under 0%
Arctic Circle

could be down to opposition to the government's support for the war in Iraq.
Economy Danes enjoy a high standard of living. Denmark is self-sufficient in oil and natural gas. Products include furniture, electrical goods and textiles. Services, including tourism, form the largest sector (63% of GDP). Farming employs only 4% of the workforce but is highly productive. Fishing is also important.
Website www.denmark.dk

Estonia *Eesti*

Area 45,100 sq km (17,413 sq miles) **Population** 1,408,556 **Capital** Tallinn (418,000) **Languages** Estonian (official), Russian **GDP** 2002 US$11,000 **Currency** Kroon = 100 sents **Government** multiparty republic **Head of state** President Arnold Rüütel, Estonian People's Union, 2001 **Head of government** Prime Minister Juhan Parts, Res Publica, 2003

Events In 1992 Estonia adopted a new constitution and multiparty elections were held. Estonia joined Nato in March 2004 and the EU in May 2004. In June 2004 the value of the Kroon was fixed against the Euro with a view to joining in 2007. Many of the populace are without citizenship as many Russian speakers brought in during the Soviet era have failed to learn the language, knowledge of which is now a criterion for citizenship. The government is formed of a coalition between Res Publica and a partnership of the centre-right Reform Party and centre-left People's Union. The pro-EU Social Democratic Party won three out of six seats in the European elections of June 2004.
Economy Privatisation and free-trade reforms have increased foreign investment and trade with the EU. Chief natural resources are oil shale and forests. Manufactures include petrochemicals, fertilisers and textiles. Agriculture and fishing are important. Barley, potatoes and oats are major crops.
Website www.riik.ee/en

Finland *Suomi*

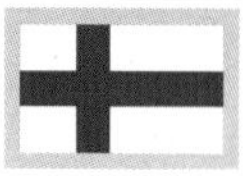

Area 338,145 sq km (130,557 sq miles) **Population** 5,190,000 **Capital** Helsinki (549,000) **Languages** Finnish, Swedish (both official) **GDP** 2002 US$25,800 **Currency** Euro = 100 cents **Government** multiparty republic **Head of state** President Tarja Kaarina Halonen, 2000 **Head of government** Prime Minister Matti Vanhanen, Centre Party, 2003

Events In 1986 Finland became a member of EFTA, and in 1995 joined the EU. A new constitution was established in March 2000. A coalition was set up between the Social Democrats and the Swedish Peoples' Party after a close election result in 2003.
Economy Forests are Finland's most valuable resource, with wood and paper products accounting for 35% of exports. Engineering, shipbuilding and textile industries have grown. Also a leading light in the telecoms industry. Farming employs 9% of the workforce. Livestock and dairy farming are the chief activities.
Website www.government.fi

France

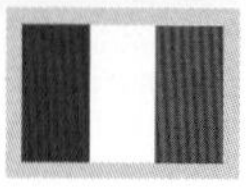

Area 551,500 sq km (212,934 sq miles) **Population** 60,181,000 **Capital** Paris (2,152,000) **Languages** French (official), Breton, Occitan **GDP** 2002 US$26,000 **Currency** Euro = 100 cents **Government** multiparty republic **Head of state** President Jacques Chirac, Assembly for the Republic, 1995 **Head of government** Prime Minister Jean-Pierre Raffarin, Democratie Liberale, 2002

Events In 2002 voter apathy led to FN leader Jean-Marie Le Pen reaching second round of voting in presidential elections above Lionel Jospin, who resigned as PM after the presidential elections which Jacques Chirac won with 82% of the vote. As a result of their opposition to the 2003 war in Iraq France and Germany have forged closer ties while relations with the UK and the US have been put under some strain. The US believes that France is being ungrateful for their assistance in WWII some 60 years before. The opposition Socialist Party were clear victors in the European elections of June 2004.
Economy France is a leading industrial nation. It is the world's fourth-largest manufacturer of cars. Industries include chemicals and steel. It is the leading producer of farm products in western Europe. Livestock and dairy farming are vital sectors. It is the world's second-largest producer of cheese and wine. Tourism is a major industry.
Website www.elysee.fr

Germany *Deutschland*

Area 357,022 sq km (137,846 sq miles) **Population** 82,398,000 **Capital** Berlin (3,387,000) **Languages** German (official) **GDP** 2002 US$26,200 **Currency** Euro = 100 cents **Government** federal multiparty republic **Head of state** President Horst Köhler, Christian Democratic Union, 2004 **Head of government** Chancellor Gerhard Schröder, Social Democratic Party, 1998

Events Germany is a major supporter of the European Union, and former chancellor Helmut Köhl was the driving force behind the creation of the Euro. During 2002, state elections in the former German Democratic Republic saw massive losses for the Social Democrats. As a result of their opposition to the 2003 war in Iraq Germany and France have forged closer ties. Economy not as strong as before as the many still heading West from the East exacerbate the imbalance. The Social Democrats suffered terrible results in the European elections of June 2004.
Economy Germany is one of the world's greatest economic powers. Services form the largest economic sector. Machinery and transport equipment account for 50% of exports. It is the world's third-largest car producer. Other major products: ships, iron, steel, petroleum, tyres. It has the world's second-largest lignite mining industry. Other minerals: copper, potash, lead, salt, zinc, aluminium. Germany is the world's second-largest producer of hops and beer, and fifth-largest of wine. Other products: cheese and milk, barley, rye, pork.
Website www.deutschland.de

Greece *Ellas*

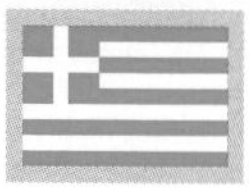

Area 131,957 sq km (50,948 sq miles) **Population** 10,665,000 **Capital** Athens / Athinai (772,000) **Languages** Greek (official) **GDP** 2002 US$19,100 **Currency** Euro = 100 cents **Government** multiparty republic **Head of state** President Konstantinos Stephanopoulos, Political Spring Party, 1995 **Head of government** Prime Minister Costas Karamanlis, New Democracy Party, 2004

Events In 1981 Greece joined the EU and Andreas Papandreou became Greece's first socialist prime minister, 1981-89 and 1993-96. Konstantinos Stephanopoulos became president in 1995. PM Costas Karamanlis is the nephew of former Greek president Constantine Karamanlis. The issue of Cyprus is still contentious in Greece's relations with Turkey, with the southern two-thirds still being Greek Cypriot and no agreement on unification yet reached. In July 2004 Greece unexpectedly won the European football championships. The 28th Olympiad took place in Greece in August 2004.
Economy Greece is one of the poorest members of the European Union. Manufacturing is important. Products: textiles, cement, chemicals, metallurgy. Minerals: lignite, bauxite, chromite. Farmland covers 33% of Greece, grazing land 40%. Major crops: tobacco, olives, grapes, cotton, wheat. Livestock are raised. Shipping and tourism are also major sectors.
Website www.greece.gr

Hungary *Magyarorszàg*

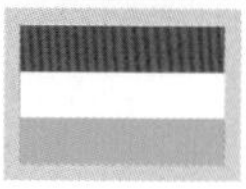

Area 93,032 sq km (35,919 sq miles) **Population** 10,045,000 **Capital** Budapest (1,825,000) **Languages** Hungarian (official) **GDP** 2002 US$13,300 **Currency** Forint = 100 filler **Government** multiparty republic **Head of state** President Ferenc Madl, 2000 **Head of government** Prime Minister Peter Medgyessy, 2002

Events In 1990 multiparty elections were won by the conservative Democratic Forum. Current PM Medgyessy is not a member of any political party but was selected by the Socialists in 2001. Narrowly avoided having to resign in 2002 when he admitted to having worked for the secret services in the late 70s / early 80s, but denied working for the KGB. Hungary joined Nato in March 2004 and the EU in May 2004. The PM is pro-Euro. Hungary still has problems with discrimination against the Roma community, though in the European elections of June 2004 a member of this ethnic group was elected for the first time.
Economy Since the early 1990s, Hungary has adopted market reforms and privatisation programmes. The economy has suffered from the collapse in exports to the former Soviet Union and Yugoslavia. The manufacture of machinery and transport is the most valuable sector. Hungary's resources include bauxite, coal and natural gas. Major crops include grapes for wine-making, maize, potatoes, sugar beet and wheat. Tourism is a growing sector.
Website www.magyarorszag.hu/angol

Iceland *Island*

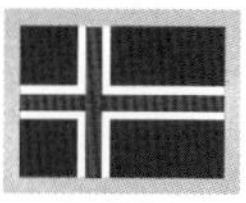

Area 103,000 sq km (39,768 sq miles) **Population** 280,798 **Capital** Reykjavik (108,000) **Languages** Icelandic **GDP** 2002 US$30,200 **Currency** Krona = 100 aurar **Government** multiparty republic **Head of state** President Olafur Ragnar Grimsson, 1996 **Head of government** Prime Minister Halldor Asgrimsson, Progressive Party, 2004

Events In 1944, a referendum decisively voted to sever links with Denmark, and Iceland became a fully independent republic. In 1946 it joined NATO. The USA maintained military bases on Iceland after WWII. In 1970 Iceland joined the European Free Trade Association. The extension of Iceland's fishing limits in 1958 and 1972 precipitated the "Cod War" with the UK. In 1977, the UK agreed not to fish within Iceland's 370km fishing limits. The continuing US military presence remains a political issue. David Oddson leader of the Independence Party stood down as PM in September 2004 and the leader of coalition partner the Progressive Party Halldor Asgrimsson took over the premiership.
Economy Fishing and fish processing are major industries, accounting for 80% of Iceland's exports. Barely 1% of the land is used to grow crops, and 23% is used for grazing sheep and cattle. Iceland is self-sufficient in meat and dairy products. Vegetables and fruits are grown in greenhouses. Manufacturing – aluminium, cement, electrical equipment and fertilizers. Geothermal power is an important energy source. Overfishing is an economic problem.
Website http://government.is

Ireland, Republic of *Eire*

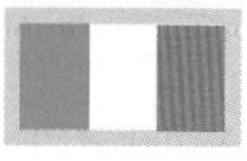

Area 70,273 sq km (27,132 sq miles) **Population** 3,924,000 **Capital** Dublin (482,000) **Languages** Irish, English (both official) **GDP** 2002 US$29,300 **Currency** Euro = 100 cents **Government** multiparty republic **Head of state** President Mary McAleese, 1997 **Head of government** Taoiseach Bertie Ahern, 1997 (Fianna Fáil)

Events The Anglo-Irish Agreement (1985) gave Ireland a consultative role in the affairs of Northern Ireland. Following a 1995 referendum, divorce was legalised. Abortion remains a contentious political issue. In 1997 elections Bertie Ahern became taoiseach and Mary McAleese became president. In the Good Friday Agreement of 1998 the Irish Republic gave up its constitutional claim to Northern Ireland and a North-South Ministerial Council was established. Sinn Fein got its first seats in the European elections of June 2004.
Economy Ireland has benefited greatly from its membership of the European Union. Grants have enabled the modernisation of farming, which employs 14% of the workforce. Major products include cereals, cattle and dairy products, sheep, sugar beet and potatoes. Fishing is important. Traditional sectors, such as brewing, distilling and textiles, have been supplemented by high-tech industries, such as electronics. Tourism is the most important component of the service industry.
Website www.irlgov.ie

Italy *Italia*

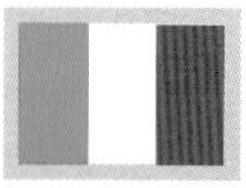

Area 301,318 sq km (116,338 sq miles) **Population** 57,998,000 **Capital** Rome / Roma (2,460,000) **Languages** Italian (official) **GDP** 2002 US$25,100 **Currency** Euro = 100 cents **Government** multiparty republic **Head of state** President Carlo Ciampi, 1997 **Head of government** Silvio Berlusconi, Casa della Libertà coalition, 2001

Events In 2001 Silvio BerluOsconi won the general election as leader of the Casa della Libertà coalition. In 2003 he was tried for matters relating to his business affairs in the 1980s, however the trial was halted when parliament approved a law giving serving prime ministers immunity from prosecution. This law was subsequently thrown out and Berlusconi's trial restarted in April 2004. The close relationship between media and politics is a point of contention due to Berlusconi's ownership of a media empire.
Economy Italy's main industrial region is the north-western triangle of Milan, Turin and Genoa. It is the world's eighth-largest car and steel producer. Machinery and transport equipment account for 37% of exports. Agricultural production is important. Italy is the world's largest producer of wine. Tourism is a vital economic sector.
Website www.enit.it

Latvia *Latvija*

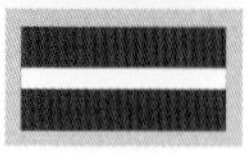

Area 64,589 sq km (24,942 sq miles) **Population** 2,349,000 **Capital** Riga (793,000) **Languages** Latvian (official), Russian **GDP** 2002 US$8,900 **Currency** Lats = 100 santimi **Government** multiparty republic **Head of state** President Vaira Vike-Freiberga, 1999 **Head of government** Prime Minister Indulis Emsis, Greens and Farmers Union, 2004

Events In 1993 Latvia held its first multiparty elections. President Vaira Vike-Freiberga was re-elected for a second four-year term in June 2003. Latvia became a member of Nato in March 2004 and of the EU in May 2004. People applying for citizenship are now required to pass a Latvian language test, which has caused much upset amongst the one third of the population who are Russian speakers. As a result many are without citizenship, much like their compatriots in Estonia. PM Indulis Emsis was chosen as a result of the resignation of his predecessor just before Latvia's accession to the EU. Only one party in the three-party governing coalition won a seat in the European elections of June 2004, but the turnout was low, as across all countries.
Economy Latvia is a lower-middle-income country. The country has to import many of the materials needed for manufacturing. Latvia produces only 10% of the electricity it needs, and the rest has to be imported from Belarus, Russia and Ukraine. Manufactures include electronic goods, farm machinery and fertiliser. Farm exports include beef, dairy products and pork.
Website www.lv

Liechtenstein

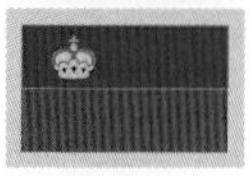

Area 157 sq km (61 sq miles) **Population** 33,000 **Capital** Vaduz (5,000) **Languages** German (official) **GDP** 2002 US$25,000 **Currency** Swiss franc = 100 centimes **Government** independent principality **Head of state** Prince Alois, 2004 **Head of government** Prime Minister Otmar Hasler, Progressive Citizens Party, 2001

Events Independent principality in western central Europe in a currency and customs union with Switzerland. Women finally got the vote in 1984. The principality joined the UN in 1990. In 2003 the people voted in a referendum to give Prince Hans Adam II new political powers thus rendering the country Europe's only absolute monarchy with the prince having power of veto over the government. Its status as a tax haven has been criticised as it has been alleged that many billions are laundered there each year, the law has therefore been reformed to ensure that anonymity is no longer permitted when opening a bank account. In August 2004 Prince Hans Adam II transferred the day-to-day running of the country to his son Prince Alois, though he did not abdicate.
Economy Liechtenstein is the fourth-smallest country in the world and one of the richest per capita. Since 1945 it has rapidly

developed a specialised manufacturing base. The major part of state revenue is derived from international companies attracted by low taxation rates. Tourism is increasingly important.
Website www.liechtenstein.li

Lithuania *Lietuva*

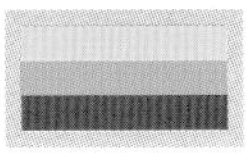

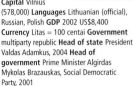

Area 65,200 sq km (25,173 sq miles) **Population** 3,593,000 **Capital** Vilnius (578,000) **Languages** Lithuanian (official), Russian, Polish **GDP** 2002 US$8,400 **Currency** Litas = 100 centai **Government** multiparty republic **Head of state** President Valdas Adamkus, 2004 **Head of government** Prime Minister Algirdas Mykolas Brazauskas, Social Democratic Party, 2001

Events The Soviet Union recognised Lithuania as independent in September 1991. In 1993 Soviet troops completed their withdrawal. Rolandas Paksas was impeached in April 2004 after being found guilty of leaking classified material and unlawfully granting citizenship to a Russian businessman who had funded his election campaign. His successor was also his predecessor. Lithuania joined Nato in March 2004 and the EU in May 2004. In June 2004 Lithuania fixed the value of the Litas against the Euro with a view to joining in 2007.
Economy Lithuania is a developing country. It is dependent on Russian raw materials. Manufacturing is the most valuable export sector: major products include chemicals, electronic goods and machine tools. Dairy and meat farming and fishing are also important activities.
Website www.lithuania.lt

Luxembourg

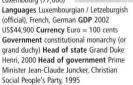

Area 2,586 sq km (998 sq miles) **Population** 454,000 **Capital** Luxembourg (77,000) **Languages** Luxembourgian / Letzeburgish (official), French, German **GDP** 2002 US$44,900 **Currency** Euro = 100 cents **Government** constitutional monarchy (or grand duchy) **Head of state** Grand Duke Henri, 2000 **Head of government** Prime Minister Jean-Claude Juncker, Christian Social People's Party, 1995

Events Following 1994 elections, the Christian Social People's Party (CD) and the Luxembourg Socialist Workers' Party (SOC) formed a coalition government. Jean-Claude Juncker (CD) became prime minister. Grand Duke Jean abdicated in favour of his son Prince Henri in October 2000.
Economy There are rich deposits of iron ore, and Luxembourg is a major producer of iron and steel. Other industries include chemicals, textiles, tourism, banking and electronics. Farmers raise cattle and pigs. Major crops include cereals, fruits and grapes for winemaking. The city of Luxembourg is a major centre of European administration and finance. Its strict laws on secrecy in banking have meant that tax evasion and fraud are prevalent.
Website www.luxembourg.lu

Former Yugoslav Republic of Macedonia *Makedonija*

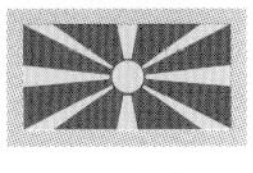

Area 25,713 sq km (9,927 sq miles) **Population** 2,063,000 **Capital** Skopje (430,000) **Languages** Macedonian (official), Albanian **GDP** 2002 US$5,100 **Currency** Denar = 100 deni **Government** multiparty republic **Head of state** President Branko Crvenkovski, Social Democrat Union, 2004 **Head of government** Prime Minister Hari Kostov, Social Democrat Union, 2004

Events In 1993 the UN accepted the new republic as a member. In 2001 there was an uprising of rebels demanding greater rights for the ethnic Albanian population. A peace deal was eventually brokered by the late president Boris Trajkovski leading to a new constitution acknowledging the rights of ethnic Albanians. Still retains the FYR prefix due to Greek fears that the names implies territorial ambitions towards the Greek region named Macedonia. President Branko Crvenovski was elected in April 2004 as a result of the death in a plane crash of Boris Trajkovski. He aims to continue the improvement of the country with EU membership as the goal. The government is a coalition of Social Democrat Union and Democratic Union for Integration (Albanian community).
Economy Macedonia is a developing country. The poorest of the six former republics of Yugoslavia, its economy was devastated by UN trade damaged by sanctions against Yugoslavia and by the Greek embargo. The GDP is increasing each year and successful privatisation in 2000 boosted the country's reserves to over $700 Million. Manufactures, especially metals, dominate exports. Agriculture employs 17% of the workforce. Major crops include cotton, fruits, maize, tobacco and wheat.
Website www.gov.mk/english

Malta

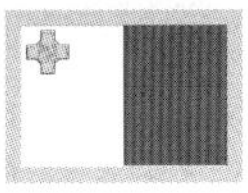

Area 316 sq km (122 sq miles) **Population** 400,420 **Capital** Valetta (9,000) **Languages** Maltese, English (both official) **GDP** 2002 US$17,200 **Currency** Maltese lira = 100 cents **Government** multiparty republic **Head of state** President Edward Fenech Adami, Christian Democratic Nationalist Party, 2004 **Head of government** Prime Minister Lawrence Gonzi, Christian Democratic Nationalist Party, 2004

Events In 1990 Malta applied to join the EU. In 1997 the newly elected Malta Labour Party pledged to rescind the application. The Christian Democratic Nationalist Party, led by the pro-European Edward Fenech Adami, regained power in 1998 elections. Malta joined the EU in May 2004.
Economy Malta is an upper-middle-income developing country. Machinery and transport equipment account for more than 50% of exports. Malta's historic naval dockyards are now used for commercial shipbuilding and repair. The state-owned Malta Drydocks is Malta's leading industry. Manufactures include chemicals, electronic equipment and textiles. The largest sector is services, especially tourism. The main crops are barley, fruits, vegetables and wheat. Privatisation of state-controlled companies and liberalisation of markets is still a contentious issue.
Website www.gov.mt

Moldova

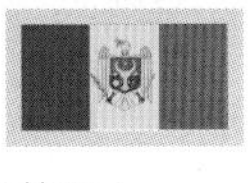

Area 33,851 sq km (13,069 sq miles) **Population** 4,439,000 **Capital** Chisinau (658,000) **Languages** Moldovan / Romanian (official) **GDP** 2002 US$2,600 **Currency** Leu = 100 bani **Government** multiparty republic **Head of state** President Vladimir Voronin, Communist Party, 2001 **Head of government** Prime Minister Vasile Tarlev, Communist Party, 2001

Events In 1994 a referendum rejected reunification with Romania and Parliament voted to join the CIS. A new constitution established a presidential parliamentary republic. In 2001 Vladimir Voronin was elected president. The Transnistria region mainly inhabited by Russian and Ukrainian speakers declared independence from Moldova in 1990 fearing the impact of closer ties with Romania, this independence has never been recognised. Withdrawal of Russian troops from Transnistria still planned but repeatedly falters. Moldova still wishes to have ties with Russia.
Economy Moldova is a lower-middle-income developing economy. Agriculture is important and major products include fruits and grapes for wine-making. Farmers also raise livestock, including dairy cattle and pigs. Moldova has to import materials and fuels for its industries. Major manufactures include agricultural machinery and consumer goods. Exports include food, wine, tobacco, textiles and footwear.
Website www.parliament.md/en.html

Monaco

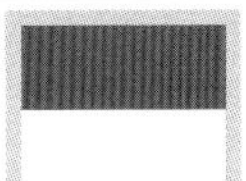

Area 1.5 sq km (0.6 sq miles) **Population** 30,000 **Capital** Monaco-Ville **Languages** French (official), Italian, Monegasque **GDP** 2002 US$27,000 **Currency** Euro = 100 cents **Government** principality **Head of state** Prince Rainier III, 1949 **Head of government** Minister of State Patrick Leclerque, 2000

Events Monaco has been ruled by the Grimaldi family since the end of the 13th century and been under the protection of France since 1860.
Economy The chief source of income is tourism, attracted by the casinos of Monte Carlo. There is some light industry, including printing, textiles and postage stamps. Also a major banking centre, residents live tax free. The state has been accused of tolerating money laundering.
Website www.monaco.gouv.mc

The Netherlands *Nederland*

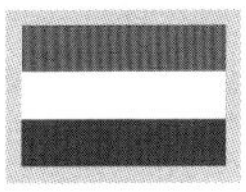

Area 41,526 sq km (16,033 sq miles) **Population** 16,151,000 **Capital** Amsterdam (729,000); administrative capital 's-Gravenhage (The Hague) (440,000) **Languages** Dutch (official), Frisian **GDP** 2002 US$ 27,200 **Currency** Euro = 100 cents **Government** constitutional monarchy **Head of state** Queen Beatrix, 1980 **Head of government** Prime Minister Jan Pieter Balkenende, Christian Democrats, 2002

Events In 2002 Pim Fortuyn, leader of right wing anti-immigrant party Lijst Pim Fortuyn was assassinated. Subsequently Wim Kok lost power to Jan Peter Balkenende who formed a coalition cabinet with the Democrats-66 and VVD (Peoples' Party for Freedom and Democracy).
Economy The Netherlands has prospered through its close European ties. Private enterprise has successfully combined with progressive social policies. It is highly industrialised. Products include aircraft, chemicals, electronics and machinery. Natural resources include natural gas. Agriculture is intensive and mechanised, employing only 5% of the workforce. Dairy farming is the leading agricultural activity. Major products are cheese, barley, flowers and bulbs.
Website www.holland.com

Norway *Norge*

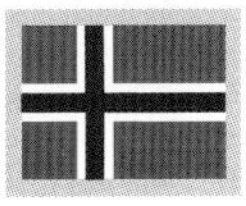

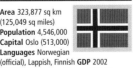

Area 323,877 sq km (125,049 sq miles) **Population** 4,546,000 **Capital** Oslo (513,000) **Languages** Norwegian (official), Lappish, Finnish **GDP** 2002 US$33,000 **Currency** Krone = 100 øre **Government** constitutional monarchy **Head of state** King Harald V, 1991 **Head of government** Prime Minister Kjell Magne Bondevik (Christian People's Party), 2001

Events In referenda in 1972 and 1994 Norway rejected joining the EU. A centre-right coalition of Christian People's Party, Conservative Party and Liberal Party rules with a minority.
Economy Norway has one of the world's highest standards of living. Its chief exports are oil and natural gas. Norway is the world's eighth-largest producer of crude oil. Per capita, Norway is the world's largest producer of hydroelectricity. Major manufactures include petroleum products, chemicals, aluminium, wood pulp and paper. The chief farming activities are dairy and meat production, but Norway has to import food. Norway has the largest fish catch in Europe after Russia and continues with whaling despite opposition and the fact that it contravenes the International Whaling Commission ban on whaling.
Website www.norge.no

Poland *Polska*

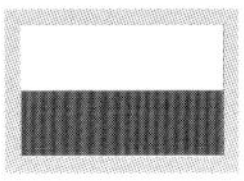

Area 323,250 sq km (124,807 sq miles) **Population** 38,623,000 **Capital** Warsaw / Warszawa (1,615,000) **Languages** Polish (official) **GDP** 2002 US$9,700 **Currency** Zloty = 100 groszy **Government** multiparty republic **Head of state** President Aleksander Kwasniewski, Alliance of the Democratic Left (SdRP / SLD), 1995 **Head of government** Prime Minister Marek Belka, Alliance of the Democratic Left (SdRP / SLD), 2004

Events In 1996 Poland joined the OECD. Poland joined Nato in 1999 and the EU in May 2004. Marek Belka took over as PM on the resignation of Leszek Miller, but then suffered a vote of no-confidence, which he managed to overturn in a subsequent second vote. Poland sent about 2,000 troops to Iraq in support of the US. In the European elections of June 2004 the ruling party came fifth in a very low turnout of only 20%.
Economy Of the workforce, 27% is employed in agriculture and 37% in industry. Poland is the world's fifth-largest producer of lignite and seventh-largest producer of bituminous coal. Copper ore is also a vital resource. Manufacturing accounts for 24% of exports. Poland is the world's fifth-largest producer of ships. Agriculture remains important. Major crops include barley, potatoes and wheat. Economic growth is slowly returning.
Website www.poland.pl

Portugal

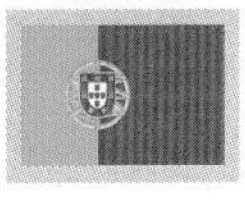

Area 88,797 sq km (34,284 sq miles) **Population** 10,102,000 **Capital** Lisbon / Lisboa (663,000) **Languages** Portuguese (official) **GDP** 2002 US$19,400 **Currency** Euro = 100 cents **Government** multiparty republic **Head of state** President Jorge Sampaio, Socialist Party, 1996 **Head of government** Prime Minister Pedro Santana Lopes, Social Democrat Party, 2004

Events In 1986 Portugal joined the EU. In 2002 the Social Democrat Party won the election and formed a coalition government with the Popular Party. The opposition Socialist Party were clear victors in European elections of June 2004, a result attributed in part to the ruling party's support for the war in Iraq. Portugal hosted the Euro 2004 football championships in summer 2004. PM Barroso was chosen as president of EU Commission in July 2004 and consequently resigned his premiership. President Sampaio chose Lisbon mayor Pedro Santana Lopes to succeed him. The leader of the Socialists Eduardo Ferro Rodrigues then resigned in protest saying Sampaio should have ordered elections.
Economy Portugal's commitment to the EU has seen the economy emerge from recession. Manufacturing accounts for 33% of exports. Textiles, footwear and clothing are major exports. Portugal is the world's fifth-largest producer of tungsten and eighth-largest producer of wine. Olives, potatoes and wheat are also grown. Tourism is very important.
Website www.portugal.gov.pt

Romania

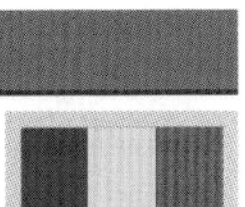

Area 238,391 sq km (92,042 sq miles) **Population** 22,272,000 **Capital** Bucharest / Bucuresti (2,016,000) **Languages** Romanian (official), Hungarian **GDP** 2002 U$7,600 **Currency** Romanian leu = 100 bani **Government** multiparty republic **Head of state** President Ion Iliescu, Social Democratic Party of Romania, 2000 **Head of government** Prime Minister Adrian Nastase, Social Democratic Party of Romania, 2000

Events A new constitution was introduced in 1991. Ion Iliescu, a former communist official, was re-elected in 2000. Romania joined Nato in March 2004 and could join the EU in 2007 if it continues with current reforms. The Romany minority still suffer from discrimination.
Economy Industry accounts for 40% of GDP. Oil, natural gas and antimony are the main mineral resources. Agriculture employs 29% of the workforce. Romania is the world's second-largest producer of plums (after China) and ninth-largest producer of wine. Other major crops include maize and cabbages. Economic reform is slow.
Website www.gov.ro/engleza/index.php

Russia *Rossiya*

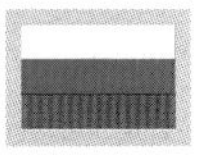

Area 17,075,000 sq km (6,592,800 sq miles) **Population** 144,526,000 **Capital** Moscow / Moskva (9,700,000) **Languages** Russian (official), and many others **GDP** 2002 US$8,297 **Currency** Russian rouble = 100 kopeks **Government** federal multiparty republic **Head of state** President Vladimir Putin, 2000 **Head of government** Prime Minister Mikail Fradkov, 2003

Events In 1992 the Russian Federation became a co-founder of the CIS. A new Federal Treaty was signed between the central government and the autonomous republics within the Russian Federation, Chechnya refused to sign and declared independence. In December 1993 a new democratic constitution was adopted. From 1994 to 1996, Russia fought a costly civil war in Chechnya which flared up again in 1999. Having supported the US-led campaign against terrorism in 2002 a Nato-Russian Council was formed with an eye on terrorism policy. Russia did not support the war in Iraq of 2003. Now reliant on world oil prices to keep its economy from crashing. Tycoons who have capitalised on the change to a capitalist system find themselves under criminal investigation. Putin re-elected March 2004, much criticism in the west of media bias towards him that left opponents little opportunity to broadcast their views, this also applied to parliamentary elections of December 2003. Putin has a very high level of control over parliament and appointed the PM Mikhail Fradkov. The only privately owned national television station was closed in 2003. Moscow-backed Chechen president Akhmet Kadryov assassinated in May 2004. In September 2004 Chechen separatists stormed a school in North Ossetia taking over 1000 children and adults hostage. Hundreds died when bombs were set off and a gun battle ensued.
Economy In 1993 mass privatisation began. By 1996, 80% of the Russian economy was in private hands. A major problem remains the size of Russia's foreign debt. Industry employs 46% of the workforce and contributes 48% of GDP. Mining is the most valuable activity. Russia is the world's leading producer of natural gas and nickel, the second largest producer of aluminium and phosphates. and the third-largest of crude oil, lignite and brown coal. Light industries are growing in importance. Most farmland is still government-owned or run as collectives, with important products barley, oats, rye, potatoes, beef and veal.
Website http://president.kremlin.ru/eng/

San Marino

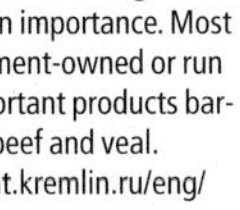

Area 61 sq km (24 sq miles) **Population** 28,119 **Capital** San Marino (5,000) **Languages** Italian (official) **GDP** 2002 US$34,600 **Currency** Euro = 100 cents **Government** multiparty republic **Head of state** co-Captains Regent: Giovanni Lonternini, Valeria Ciavatta

Events World's smallest republic and per-

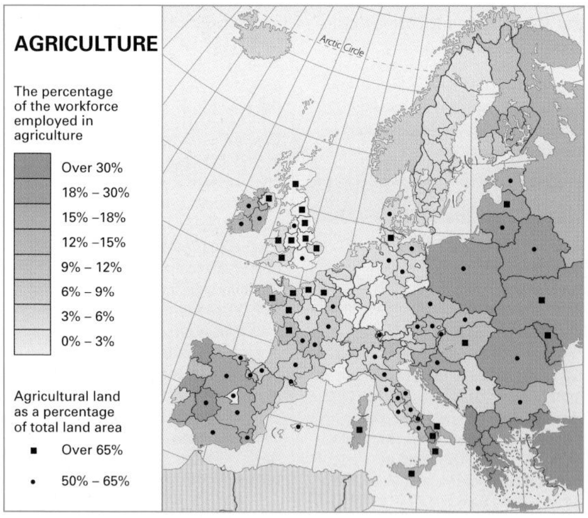
AGRICULTURE
The percentage of the workforce employed in agriculture
Over 30%
18% – 30%
15% –18%
12% –15%
9% – 12%
6% – 9%
3% – 6%
0% – 3%
Agricultural land as a percentage of total land area
Over 65%
50% – 65%
Arctic Circle

haps Europe's oldest state, San Marino's links with Italy led to the adoption of the Euro. Its 60-member Great and General Council is elected every five years and headed by two captains-regent, who are elected by the council every six months.
Economy The economy is largely agricultural. Tourism is vital to the state's income. Also a tax haven used by many non-residents. Income also from stamps and coins.
Website www.omniway.sm

Serbia & Montenegro *Srbija i Crna Gora*

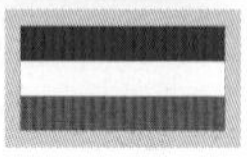

Area 102,173 sq km (39,449 sq miles) **Population** 10,656,000 **Capital** Belgrade / Beograd (1,594,000) **Languages** Serbian (official), Albanian **GDP** 2002 US$2,200 **Currency** Dinar = 100 paras (Serbia), Euro = 100 cents (Montenegro) **Government** federal republic **Head of state** President of Serbia & Montenegro Svetozvar Marovic, Democratic Party of Socialists, 2003; President of Serbia Boris Tadic, Democratic Party, 2004; President of Montenegro Filip Vujanovic, 2003 **Head of government** Prime Minister of Serbia Vojislav Kostunica, Democratic Party of Serbia, 2004; Prime Minister of Montenegro Milo Djukanovic, Democratic Party of Socialists, 2002

Events In 1989 Slobodan Milosević became president of Serbia and called for the creation of a "Greater Serbia". Serbian attempts to dominate the Yugoslav federation led to the secession of Slovenia and Croatia (with whom Serbia fought a brief war) in 1991 and to Bosnia-Herzegovina's declaration of independence in March 1992. In April 1992 Serbia and Montenegro announced the formation of a new Yugoslav federation and invited Serbs in Croatia and Bosnia-Herzegovina to join. Serbian aid to the Bosnian Serb campaign of "ethnic cleansing" in the civil war in Bosnia led the UN to impose sanctions on Serbia, Milosević severed support for the Bosnian Serbs. In 1995 Milosević signed the Dayton Peace Accord, which ended the Bosnian war. In 1997 Milosević became president of Yugoslavia. In 1998 fighting erupted in Kosovo between Albanian nationalists and Serbian security forces. In 1999, following the forced expulsion of Albanians from Kosovo, NATO bombed Yugoslavia, forcing withdrawal of Serbian forces from Kosovo. Kostunica won the elections of September 2000, but Milosević refused to hand over power. After a week of civil unrest and increased support for Kostunica, Milosević was finally ousted. A constitutional charter for the union of Serbia and Montenegro was agreed in December 2002. There is a federal presidency with federal foreign and defence ministries, but the two republics are semi-independent states in charge of their own economies. This arrangement will remain for a minimum of three years. Kosovo is legally part of Serbia, but is an international protectorate. The position of president in Serbia was left vacant between January 2003 and June 2004 after Milan Milutinovic surrendered to the war crimes tribunal in The Hague. The Serbian government must govern in coalition with small parties as well as relying on the support of Slobodan Milosović's Socialist Party. Although no longer controlled by Milosović, such co-operation could impact on the continuing extradition of war crimes suspects to The Hague.
Economy The lower-middle income economy was devastated by war and economic sanctions. Industrial production collapsed. Natural resources include bauxite, coal and copper. There is some oil and natural gas. Manufacturing includes aluminium, cars, machinery, plastics, steel and textiles. Agriculture is important.
Website www.info.gov.yu; www.serbia-tourism.org; www.montenegro.yu

Slovakia *Slovenska Republika*

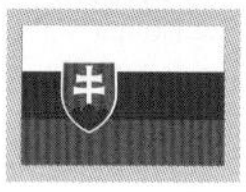

Area 49,012 sq km (18,923 sq miles) **Population** 5,430,000 **Capital** Bratislava (449,000) **Languages** Slovak (official), Hungarian **GDP** 2002 US$12,400 **Currency** Koruna = 100 halierov **Government** multiparty republic **Head of state** President Ivan Gasparovic, 2004 **Head of government** Prime Minister Mikulás Dzurinda, Democratic & Christian Union, 1998

Events In 1993 the Slovak Republic became a sovereign state, breaking peaceably from the Czech Republic, with whom it maintains close relations. In 1996 the Slovak Republic and Hungary ratified a treaty confirming their borders and stipulating basic rights for the 560,000 Hungarians in Slovakia. Mikulás Dzurinda of Democratic & Christian Union heads centre right coalition made up of ethnic Hungarians – Magyar Koalicio Partja, Christian Democrats and ANO – Allianca Noveno Obcana (New Citizens' Alliance). Slovakia joined Nato in March 2004 and the EU in May 2004. There is still a problem with the Romany population being deprived. The 17% turn-out for the European elections in June 2004 was the lowest of all 25 members.
Economy The transition from communism to private ownership has been painful with industrial output falling, unemployment and inflation rising. In 1995 the privatisation programme was suspended. Manufacturing employs 33% of the workforce. Bratislava and Hošice are the chief industrial cities. Major products include ceramics, machinery and steel. Farming employs 12% of the workforce. Crops include barley and grapes. Tourism is growing.
Website www.slovakia.org

Slovenia *Slovenija*

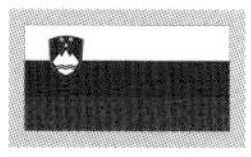

Area 20,256 sq km (7,820 sq miles) **Population** 1,936,000 **Capital** Ljubljana (264,000) **Languages** Slovene **GDP** 2002 US$19,200 **Currency** Tolar = 100 stotin **Government** multiparty republic **Head of state** President Janez Drnovsek, Liberal Democrats of Slovenia, 2002 **Head of government** Prime Minister Anton Rop, Liberal Democrats of Slovenia, 2002

Events In 1990 Slovenia declared itself independent, which led to brief fighting between Slovenes and the federal army. In 1992 the EU recognised Slovenia's independence. Janez Drnovsek was elected president in December 2002 and immediately stepped down as prime minister. Slovenia joined Nato in March 2004 and the EU in May 2004. In June 2004 the value of the Tolar was fixed against the Euro with a view to joining in 2007. Their reputation as a liberal nation has been somewhat scarred by the recent referendum overturning a parliamentary bill that restored citizenship of Slovenia to resident nationals of other former Yugoslav countries.
Economy The transformation of a centrally planned economy and the fighting in other parts of former Yugoslavia have caused problems for Slovenia. Manufacturing is the leading activity. Major manufactures include chemicals, machinery, transport equipment, metal goods and textiles. Major crops include maize, fruit, potatoes and wheat.
Website www.gov.si

Spain *España*

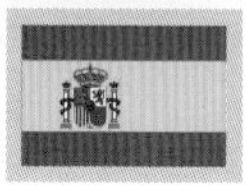

Area 497,548 sq km (192,103 sq miles) **Population** 40,217,000 **Capital** Madrid (2,939,000) **Languages** Castilian Spanish (official), Catalan, Galician, Basque **GDP** 2002 US$21,200 **Currency** Euro = 100 cents **Government** constitutional monarchy **Head of state** King Juan Carlos, 1975 **Head of government** Prime Minister Jose Luis Rodriguez Zapatero, Socialist Party, 2004

Events From 1959 the militant Basque organization ETA waged a campaign of terror but announced a ceasefire in 1998. Basque separatist party Batasuna was permanently banned in 2003 as it is thought to be the political wing of ETA. In March 2004 terrorist bombs exploded in Madrid killing 191 people, this was deemed to be the work of al Qaeda, though the then government were keen to persuade the public that it was the work of ETA. The country went to the polls three days later and voted Aznar out, largely seen as a reaction to his support of the US in Iraq and the sending of troops which was to blame for the bombing some three days earlier. The new PM subsequently withdrew all troops from Iraq. Although the ruling Socialist Party are short of a majority, Zapatero has pledged to govern through dialogue with others rather than form a coalition.
Economy Spain has rapidly transformed from a largely poor, agrarian society into a prosperous industrial nation. Agriculture now employs only 10% of the workforce. Spain is the world's third-largest wine producer. Other crops include citrus fruits, tomatoes and olives. Industries: cars, ships, chemicals, electronics, metal goods, steel, textiles.
Website www.la-moncloa.es/

Switzerland *Schweiz*

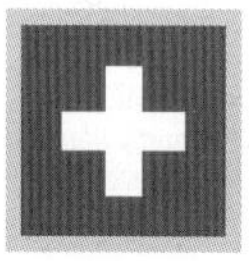

Area 41,284 sq km (15,939 sq miles) **Population** 7,319,000 **Capital** Bern (124,000) **Languages** French, German, Italian, Romansch (all official) **GDP** 2002 US$32,000 **Currency** Swiss Franc = 100 centimes **Government** federal republic **Head of state** President Joseph Deiss, 2004

Events A referendum in 1986 rejected Swiss membership of the UN to avoid compromising its neutrality. EU membership was similarly rejected in 1992. The federal council is made up of seven federal ministers from whom the president is chosen on an annual basis. Prior to 2003 the allocation of posts was fixed between Free Democrats (2), Social Democrats (2), Christian Democrats (2) and Swiss People's Party (SVP) (1), however this changed after the elections of 2003 when the SVP increased their share of the vote to 28%, thereby becoming the largest party. The allocation was subsequently changed (after much debate) with the SVP taking an extra seat and the Christian Democrats losing one.
Economy Switzerland is wealthy and industrialised. Manufactures include chemicals, electrical equipment, machinery, precision instruments, watches and textiles. Livestock raising, notably dairy farming, is the chief agricultural activity. Tourism is important, and Swiss banks attract worldwide investment.
Website www.gov.ch

Sweden *Sverige*

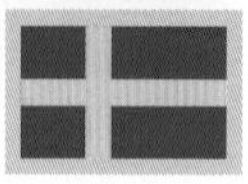

Area 449,964 sq km (173,731 sq miles) **Population** Population 8,878,000 **Capital** Stockholm (744,000) **Languages** Swedish (official), Finnish **GDP** 2002 US$26,000 **Currency** Swedish krona = 100 ore **Government** constitutional monarchy **Head of state** King Carl XVI Gustaf, 1973 **Head of government** Prime Minister Göran Persson, Social Democratic Workers' Party (SSA), 1996

Events In 1995 Sweden joined the European Union. Göran Persson was re-elected in 2002. The cost of maintaining Sweden's extensive welfare services has become a major political issue. In September 2003 Sweden was shocked by the murder of popular minister Anna Lindh (a pro-Euro campaigner), thus reigniting discussion over the relaxed attitude to security. Days later Sweden said no to the Euro. Brand new Euro-sceptic party Junilistan (June List) came third in the European elections, exceeding all expectations and underlining Swedish ambivalence towards Europe.
Economy Sweden is a highly developed industrial country. It has rich iron ore deposits, but other industrial materials are imported. Steel is a major product, used to manufacture aircraft, cars, machinery and ships. Forestry and fishing are important. Livestock and dairy farming are valuable activities; crops include barley and oats.
Website www.sweden.gov.se

Turkey *Türkiye*

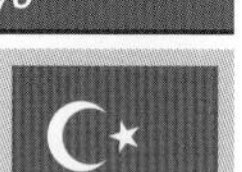

Area 774,815 sq km (299,156 sq miles) **Population** 68,109,000 **Capital** Ankara (2,984,000) **Languages** Turkish (official), Kurdish **GDP** 2002 US$7,300 **Currency** Turkish lira = 100 kurus **Government** multiparty republic **Head of state** President Ahmet Necdet Sezer, 2000 **Head of government** Prime Minister Recep Tayyip Erdogan, Justice and Development Party (AK), 2002

Events Civil unrest between Turkish forces and the Kurdistan Workers Party (PKK) in the 1980s and 1990s. In 1999 the PKK leader Ocalan was sentenced to death, since commuted to life imprisonment on the abolition of the death penalty. The PKK changed their name to Congress for Freedom and Democracy in Kurdistan (KADEK) and say they want to campaign peacefully for Kurdish rights, but in September 2003 they ended a four year ceasefire with the aim of increasing pressure on the government to listen to Kurdish demands. Membership of the EU is an aim but Turkey's record on human rights needs to improve before this can happen, along with a resolution to the Cyprus issue. The president is interested in greater freedom of expression. The PM is leader of the Islamist Justice & Development Party, though claims to be committed to secularism.
Economy Turkey is a lower-middle income developing country. Agriculture employs 47% of the workforce. Turkey is a leading producer of citrus fruits, barley, cotton, wheat, tobacco and tea. It is a major producer of chromium and phosphate fertilisers. Tourism is a vital source of foreign exchange.
Website www.tourismturkey.org

Ukraine *Ukraina*

Area 603,700 sq km (233,088 sq miles) **Population** 48,055,000 **Capital** Kiev / Kyviv (2,590,000) **Languages** Ukrainian (official), Russian **GDP** 2002 US$4,500 **Currency** Hryvna = 100 kopiykas **Government** multiparty republic **Head of state** President Leonid Kuchma, 1994 **Head of government** Prime Minister Viktor Yanukovych, 2002

Events The Chernobyl disaster of 1986 contaminated large areas of Ukraine. Leonid Kuchma was elected president in 1994. He continued the policy of establishing closer ties with the West and sped up the pace of privatisation. There are continuing disputes over the the powers of the Crimean legislature. Ukraine is pushing for membership of Nato though reforms are required before this can happen. There are 1,500 Ukranian peacekeepers in Iraq as part of the Polish force. Much external pressure on the country to ensure that the next elections are free and fair. Press freedom in Ukraine is at times restricted with opposition papers being closed and the mysterious disappearance of several journalists.
Economy Ukraine is a lower-middle-income economy. Agriculture is important. It is the world's leading producer of sugar beet, the second-largest producer of barley, and a major producer of wheat. Ukraine has extensive raw materials, including coal (though many mines are exhausted), iron ore and manganese ore. Ukraine is reliant on oil and natural gas imports. Ukraine's debt to Russia has been partly offset by allowing Russian firms majority shares in many Ukrainian industries.
Website www.mfa.gov.ua/eng/

United Kingdom

Area 241,857 sq km (93,381 sq miles) **Population** 60,095,000 **Capital** London (8,089,000) **Languages** English (official), Welsh (also official in Wales), Gaelic **GDP** 2002 US$25,500 **Currency** Sterling (pound) = 100 pence **Government** constitutional monarchy **Head of state** Queen Elizabeth II, 1952 **Head of government** Prime Minister Tony Blair, Labour Party, 1997

Events The United Kingdom of Great Britain and Northern Ireland is a union of four countries – England, Northern Ireland, Scotland and Wales. In 1997 referenda on devolution saw Scotland and Wales gain their own legislative assemblies. The Scottish assembly was given tax-varying power. The Good Friday Agreement of 1998 offered the best chance of peace in Northern Ireland for a generation. Tony Blair controversially gave full support to Bush over the war in Iraq in 2003. In the European elections of June 2004 the Euro-sceptic UK Independence Party came third, showing that many of the English electorate are against the European Union (though the turnout was only 38%).
Economy The UK is a major industrial and trading nation. The economy has become more service-centred and high-technology industries have grown in importance. A producer of oil, petroleum products, natural gas, potash, salt and lead. Agriculture employs only 2% of the workforce. Financial services and tourism are the leading service industries.
Website www.parliament.uk

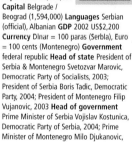

1:4 250 000 map pages

Calais

548	**Dublin**				Dublin ▶ Göteborg = 477 km
726	346	**Edinburgh**			
575	1123	1301	**Frankfurt**		
1342	477	176	1067	**Göteborg**	
760	477	1486	485	582	**Hamburg**

000 = [ferry symbol]

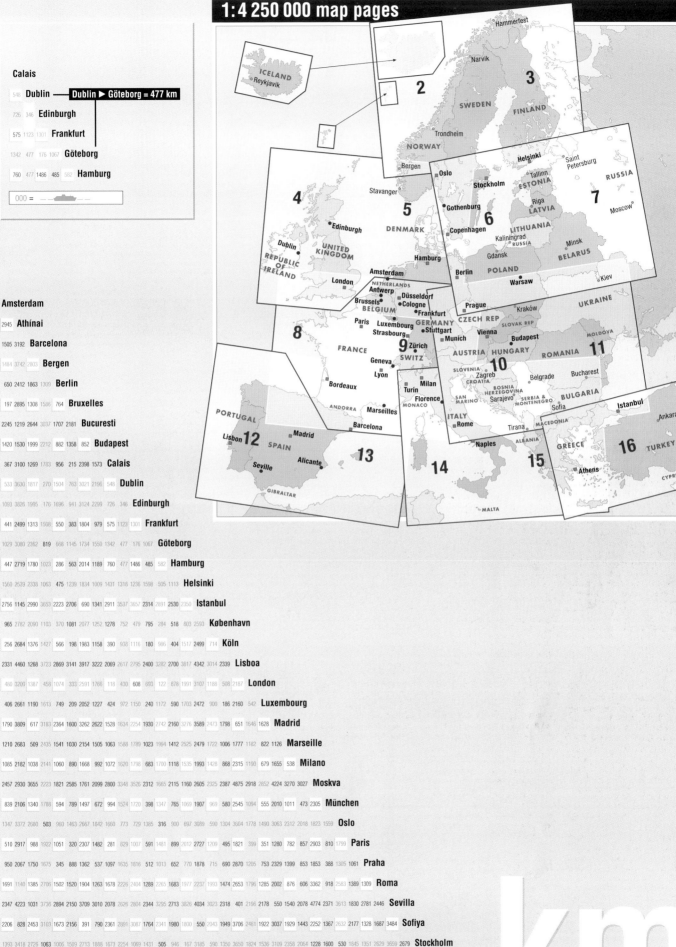

Amsterdam
2945 **Athínai**
1505 3192 **Barcelona**
1484 3742 2803 **Bergen**
650 2412 1863 1309 **Berlin**
197 2895 1308 1586 764 **Bruxelles**
2245 1219 2644 3037 1707 2181 **Bucuresti**
1420 1530 1999 2212 882 1358 852 **Budapest**
367 3100 1269 1783 956 215 2398 1573 **Calais**
533 3630 1817 270 1504 763 3021 2196 548 **Dublin**
1093 3826 1995 176 1696 941 3124 2299 726 346 **Edinburgh**
441 2499 1313 1508 550 383 1804 979 575 1123 1301 **Frankfurt**
1029 3080 2362 819 668 1145 1734 1550 1342 477 176 1067 **Göteborg**
447 2719 1780 1023 286 563 2014 1189 760 477 1486 485 582 **Hamburg**
1560 2539 2338 1063 475 1239 1834 1009 1431 1318 1236 1598 505 1113 **Helsinki**
2756 1145 2990 3653 2223 2706 690 1341 2911 3537 3657 2314 2891 2530 2350 **Istanbul**
965 2782 2090 1103 370 1081 2077 1252 1278 752 479 795 284 518 803 2593 **København**
256 2684 1376 1427 566 198 1983 1158 390 938 1116 180 986 404 1517 2499 714 **Köln**
2331 4460 1268 3723 2869 3141 3917 3222 2069 2617 2795 2400 3282 2700 3817 4342 3014 2339 **Lisboa**
480 3200 1387 458 1074 333 2591 1766 118 430 608 693 122 878 1991 3107 1188 508 2187 **London**
406 2661 1190 1613 749 209 2052 1227 424 972 1150 240 1172 590 1703 2472 900 186 2160 542 **Luxembourg**
1790 3809 617 3183 2364 1690 3262 2622 1528 1634 2254 1930 2742 2160 3276 3589 2473 1798 651 1646 1628 **Madrid**
1210 2683 509 2435 1541 1030 2154 1505 1063 1588 1789 1023 1994 1412 2525 2479 1722 1006 1777 1162 822 1126 **Marseille**
1085 2182 1038 2141 1060 890 1668 992 1072 1620 1798 683 1700 1118 1535 1993 1428 868 2315 1190 679 1655 538 **Milano**
2457 2930 3655 2223 1821 2585 1761 2099 2800 3348 3526 2312 1665 2115 1160 2605 2325 2387 4875 2918 2852 4224 3270 3027 **Moskva**
839 2106 1340 1788 594 789 1497 672 994 1524 1720 398 1347 765 1069 1907 969 580 2545 1094 555 2010 1011 473 2305 **München**
1347 3372 2680 503 960 1463 2667 1842 1660 773 729 1385 316 900 697 3089 590 1304 3604 1778 1490 3063 2312 2018 1823 1559 **Oslo**
510 2917 988 1922 1051 320 2307 1482 281 829 1007 591 1481 899 2012 2727 1209 495 1821 399 351 1280 782 857 2903 810 1799 **Paris**
950 2067 1750 1675 345 888 1362 537 1097 1635 1816 512 1013 652 770 1878 715 690 2870 1205 753 2329 1399 853 1853 388 1305 1061 **Praha**
1691 1140 1385 2706 1502 1520 1904 1263 1678 2226 2404 1289 2265 1683 1977 2237 1993 1474 2653 1796 1285 2002 876 606 3362 918 2583 1389 1309 **Roma**
2347 4223 1031 3736 2894 2150 3709 3010 2078 2626 2804 2344 3295 2713 3826 4034 3023 2318 401 2196 2178 550 1540 2078 4774 2371 3613 1830 2781 2446 **Sevilla**
2206 828 2453 3103 1673 2156 391 790 2361 2891 3087 1764 2341 1980 1800 550 2043 1949 3706 2461 1922 3037 1929 1443 2252 1367 2632 2177 1328 1687 3484 **Sofiya**
1393 3418 2726 1063 1006 1509 2713 1888 1673 2254 1069 1431 505 946 167 3185 590 1350 3650 1824 1536 3109 2358 2064 1228 1600 530 1851 1351 2629 3659 2679 **Stockholm**
1256 2128 2366 1909 606 1350 1473 648 1542 2110 2268 1136 1274 886 361 1989 956 1152 3480 1680 1345 2960 2015 1469 1245 996 1506 1677 616 1853 3397 1439 1612 **Warszawa**
1168 1772 1856 1970 640 1114 1067 242 1308 1954 2034 731 1308 947 1088 1583 1010 916 3100 1524 993 2473 1353 818 2137 430 1600 1240 295 1126 2876 1033 1646 727 **Wien**
816 2426 1030 1938 863 619 1810 985 804 1352 1530 464 1497 915 2164 2323 1433 589 2296 922 410 1647 699 292 2552 303 1815 592 691 898 2061 1173 1861 1307 743 **Zürich**

km

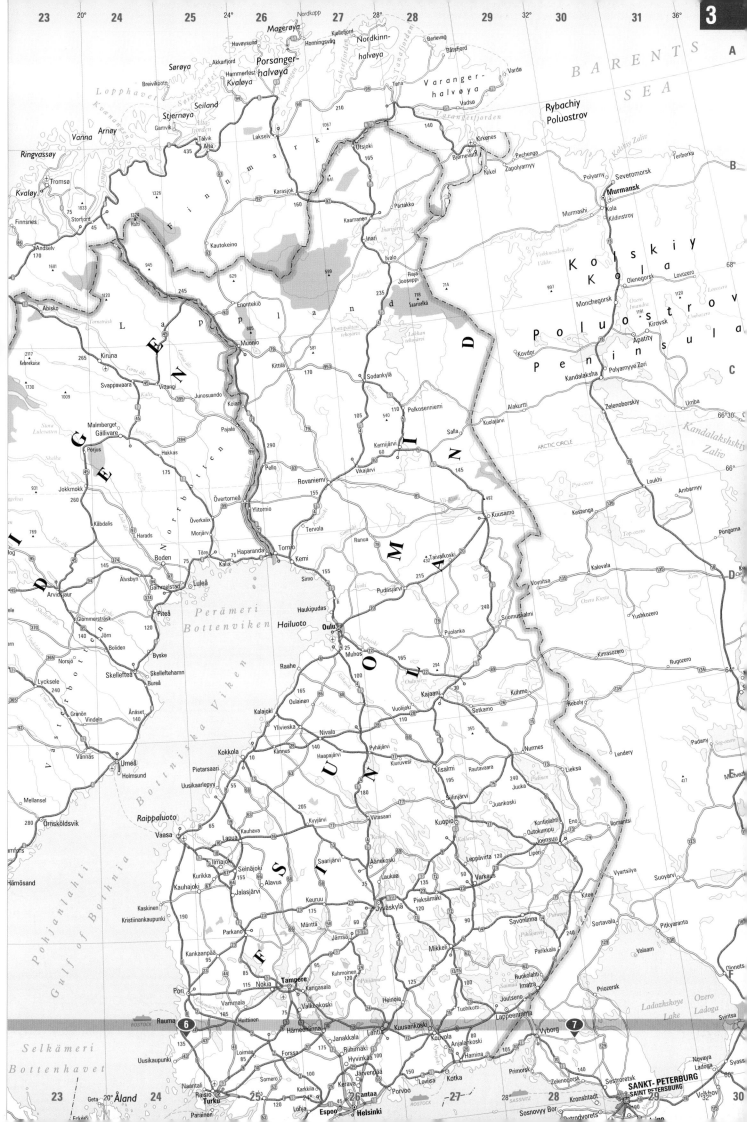

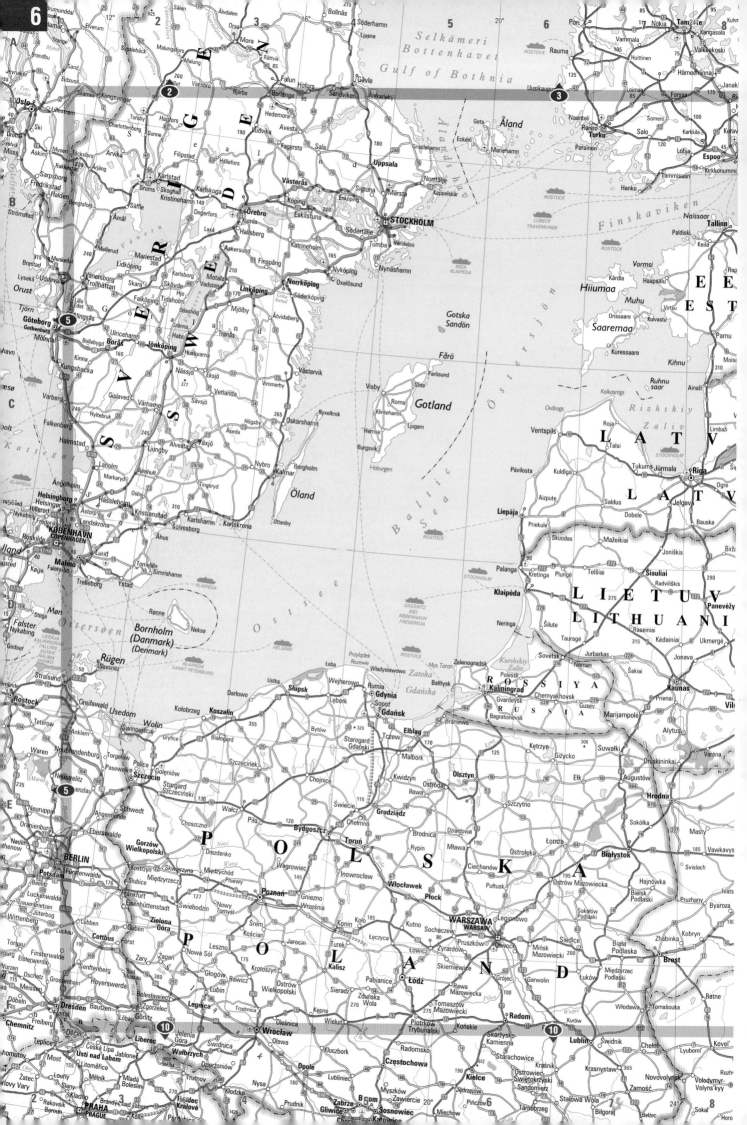

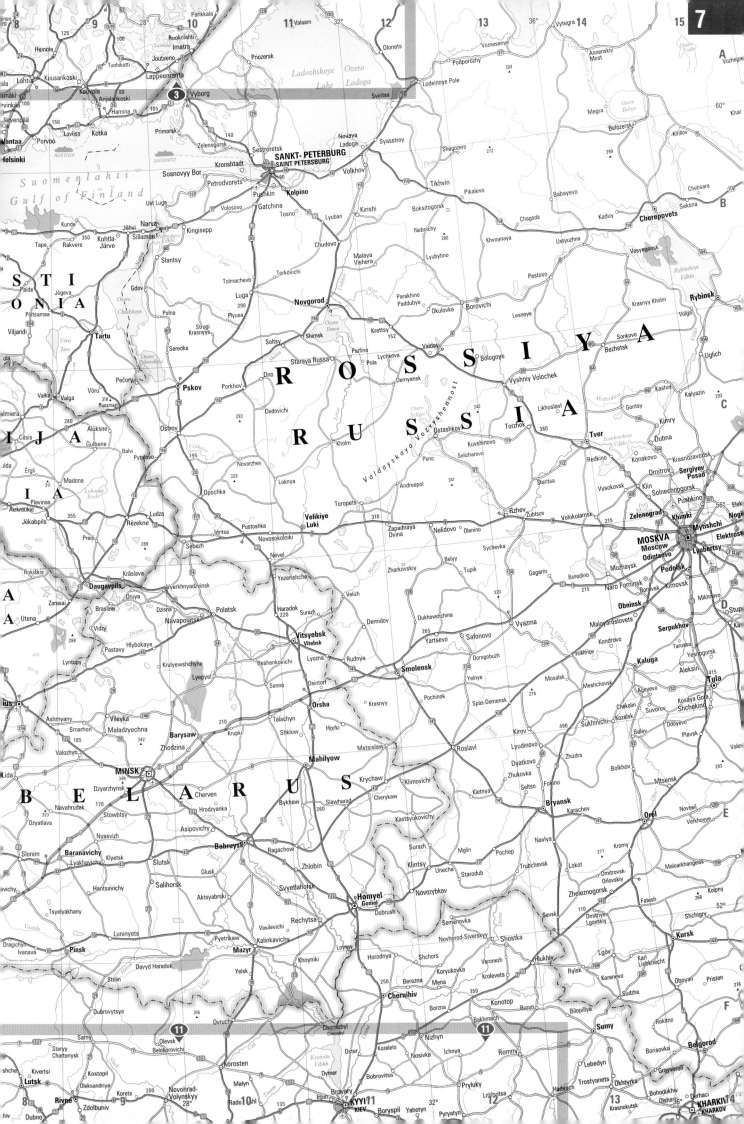

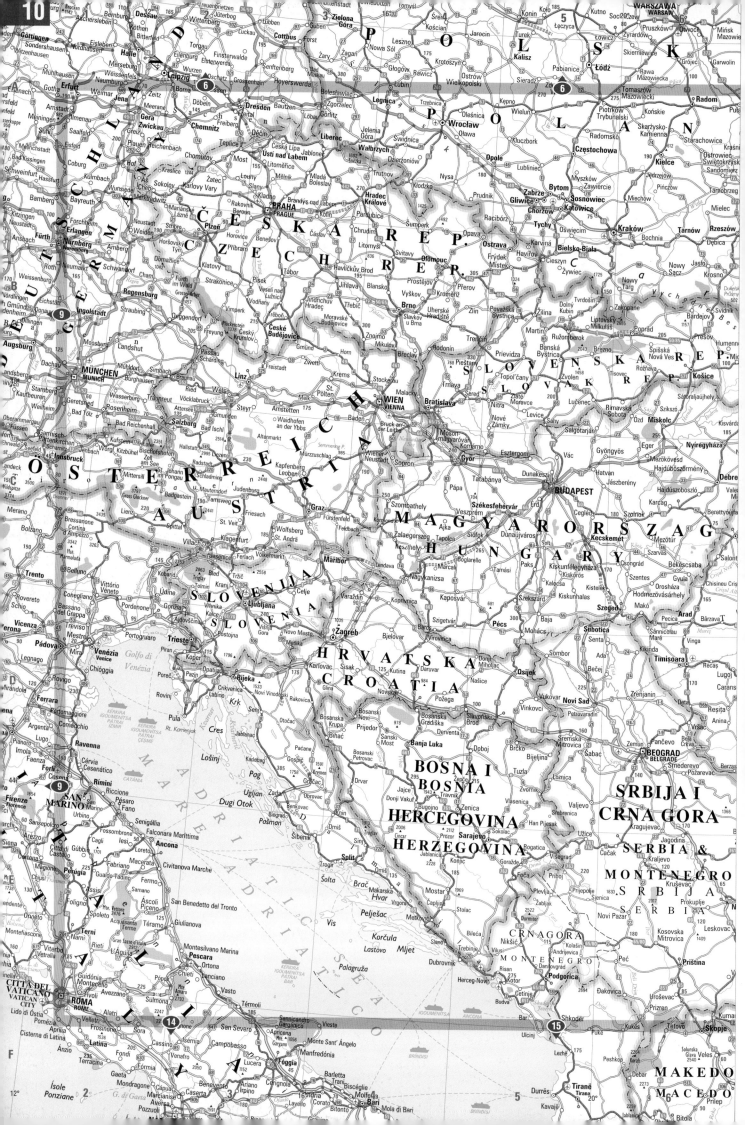

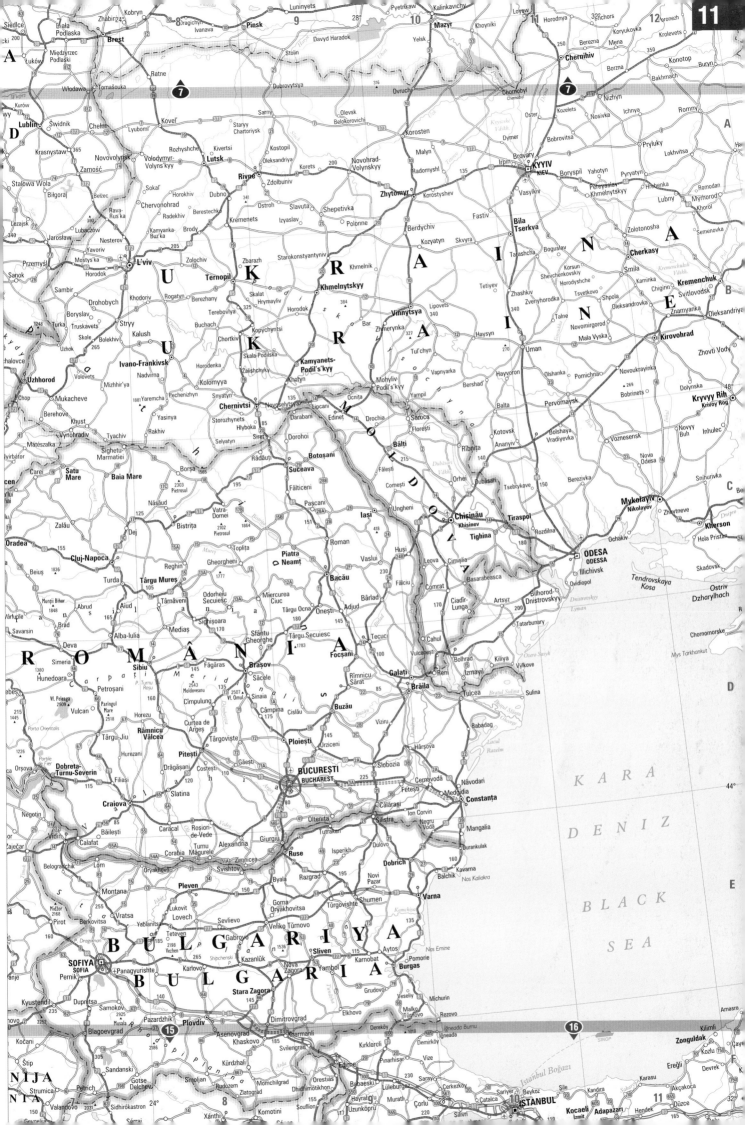

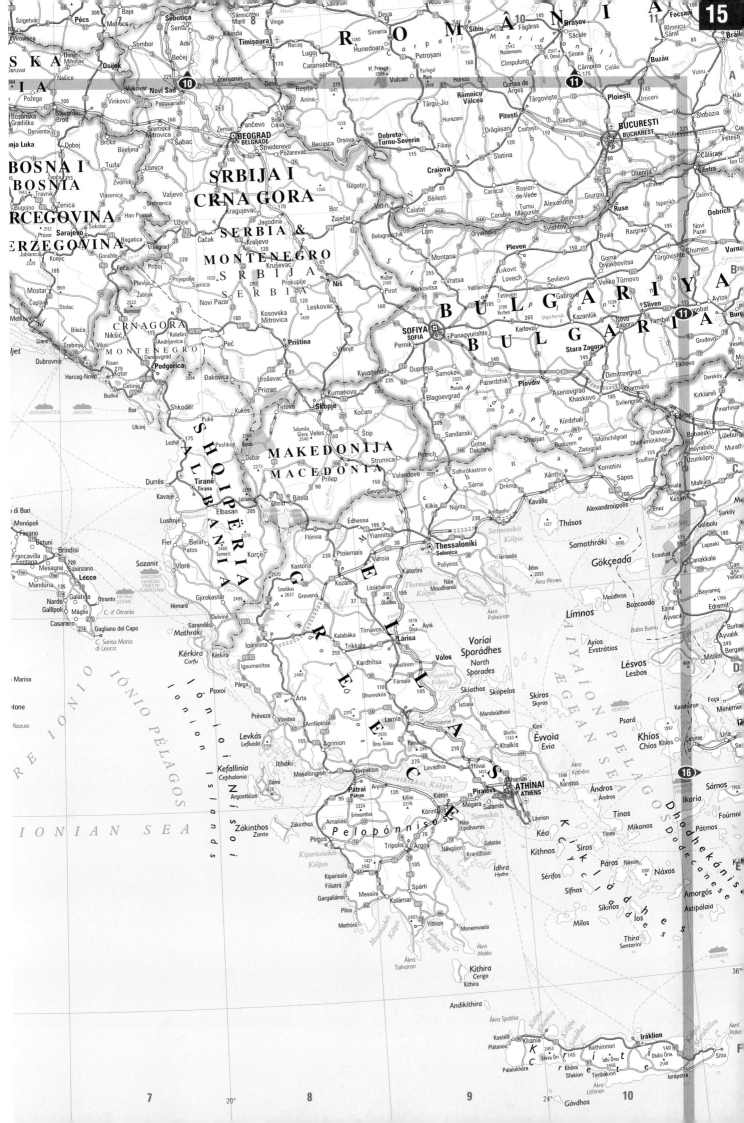

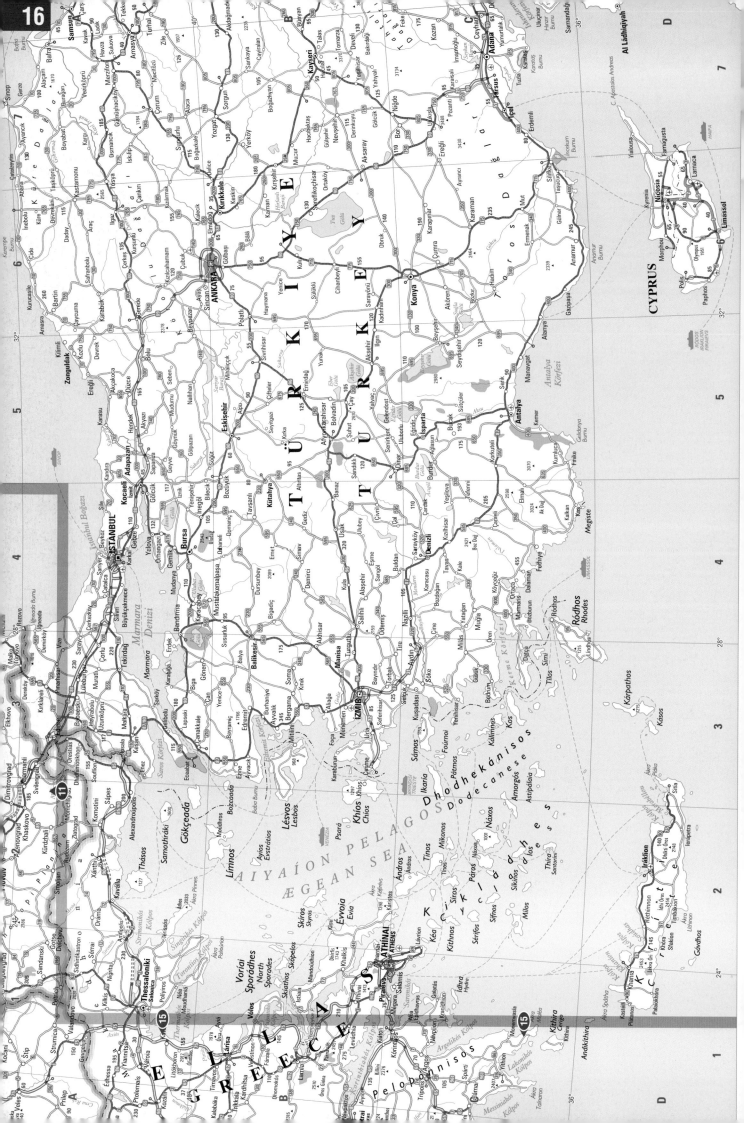

Key to 1:1000000 map pages

● Florence **City plan**
Firenze

□ Istanbul **City approach map**

▣ Milan **City plan and approach map**
Milano

See pages 115–138 for city plans and approach maps

97 Map pages at 1:1 000 000

114 Map pages at 1:2 000 000

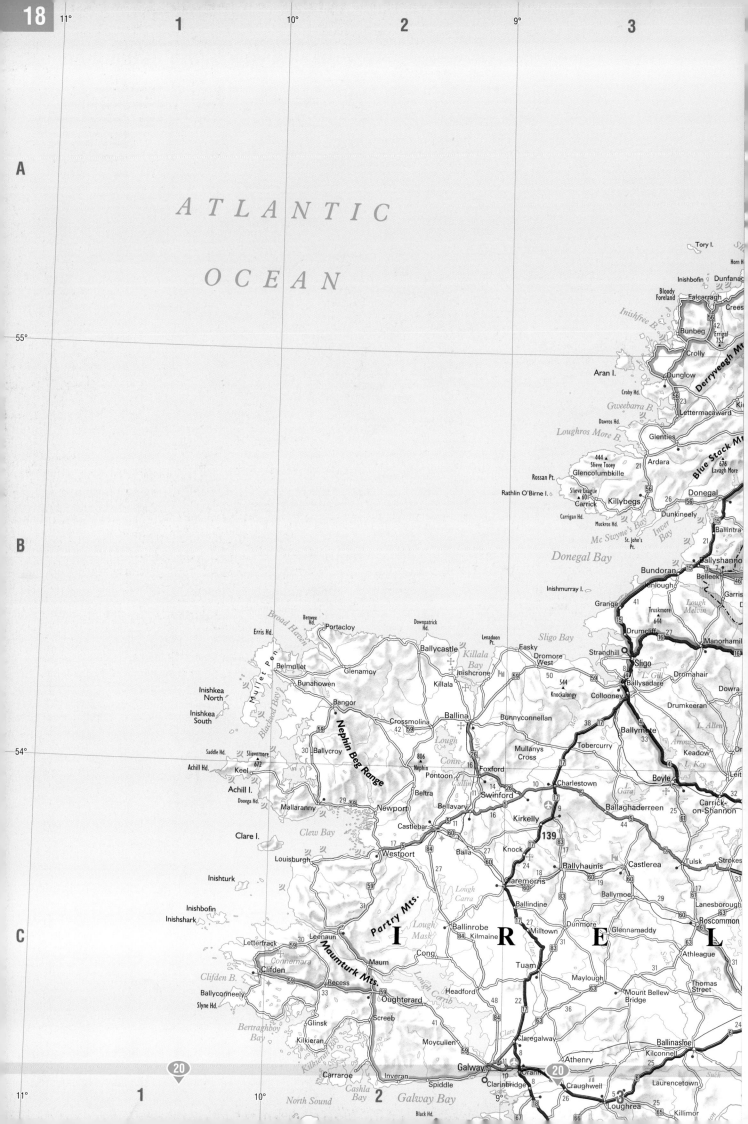

A

ATLANTIC

OCEAN

Tory I.

Inishbofin Dunfana
Bloody
Foreland Falcarragh Crees
56
Bunbeg
Errigal 752
Crolly Ki

Aran I. Dunglow
Crohy Hd. 56 23
Gweebarra B. Lettermacaward
Dawros Hd.
Loughros More B. Glenties

444 Slieve Tooey Ardara Blue Stack M
21
Rossan Pt. Glencolumbkille 676
Lavagh More
Slieve League
Rathlin O'Birne I. 601 Carrick 26 Donegal
Killybegs 56
Carrigan Hd. Dunkineely
Muckros Hd. Ballintra
Mc Swyne's Bay St. John's *Inver* 21 Ballyshanno
Pt. *Bay*

B *Donegal Bay* Bundoran 15 Belleek 46
Kinlough Garris
Inishmurray I. Grange 41 Truskmore *Lough*
644 *Melvin*
Benwee *Sligo Bay* Drumcliff 27
Hd. Manorhamil
Erris Hd. *Broad Haven* Portacloy Downpatrick Lenadoon Easky Strandhill Sligo 16
Hd. Pt. Dromore
Ballycastle *Killala* West 50 Ballysadare
Bay Inishcrone 59 Dromahair
Belmullet Glenamoy Killala 544 Collooney Dowra
Bunahowen Knockalongy 59
Bangor Crossmolina Ballina Bunnyconnellan 38 17 Ballymote *L. Allen*
42 59 33 *L.*
Inishkea *Lough* Mullanys Tobercurry Keadow *Arrow*
North 30 Ballycroy *Conn* 26 Cross 17 4 *L. Key*
Inishkea 806 16 Foxford Charlestown Boyle
South Nephin 10 5 32
Saddle Hd. Slievemore Pontoon 14 26 *L.* Carrick-
Achill Hd. 672 *Gutting* Swinford *Gara* on-Shannon
Keel Beltra 11 *Nephin Beg Range* Bellavary 16 Kirkelly Ballaghaderreen 61 Leit
Dooega Hd. 29 Newport 11 9 139 44
Achill I. Mallaranny Castlebar 60 Knock 17 Tulsk Strokes
Clare I. 11 Balla 27 24 Ballyhaunis Castlerea 33
Clew Bay 60 60 19
Westport 84 Claremorris 83 Ballymoe Lanesborough
Louisburgh 27 60 Ballindine Dunmore 29 60 Roscommon
Inishturk 31 Glennamaddy 61
Ballinrobe 17 27 Milltown 31 Athleague 31
Inishbofin *Lough* Kilmaine 84 Maylough Thomas
Inishshark Leenaun *Mask* Cong Tuam 63 Mount Bellew Street
C 30 Letterfrack 59 I Maum R E Bridge L
Connemara *Partry Mts.* *Lough Corrib* 48 36
Clifden *Maumturk Mts.* Headford 84 22
Clifden B. Recess 59 Oughterard 63 Ballinasloe
Ballyconneely 33 Screeb 41 Claregalway Kilconnell
Slyne Hd. Glinsk Moycullen 59 Athenry 25 24
Bertraghboy Kilkieran *Clare* 18
Bay Galway 10 Oranmore Craughwell Laurencetown Suck
20 Carraroe Inveran Spiddle Clarinbridge 8 20 26 Loughrea 65 Killimor
North Sound *Cashla* 9° 67 66
Bay *Galway Bay*
Black Hd.

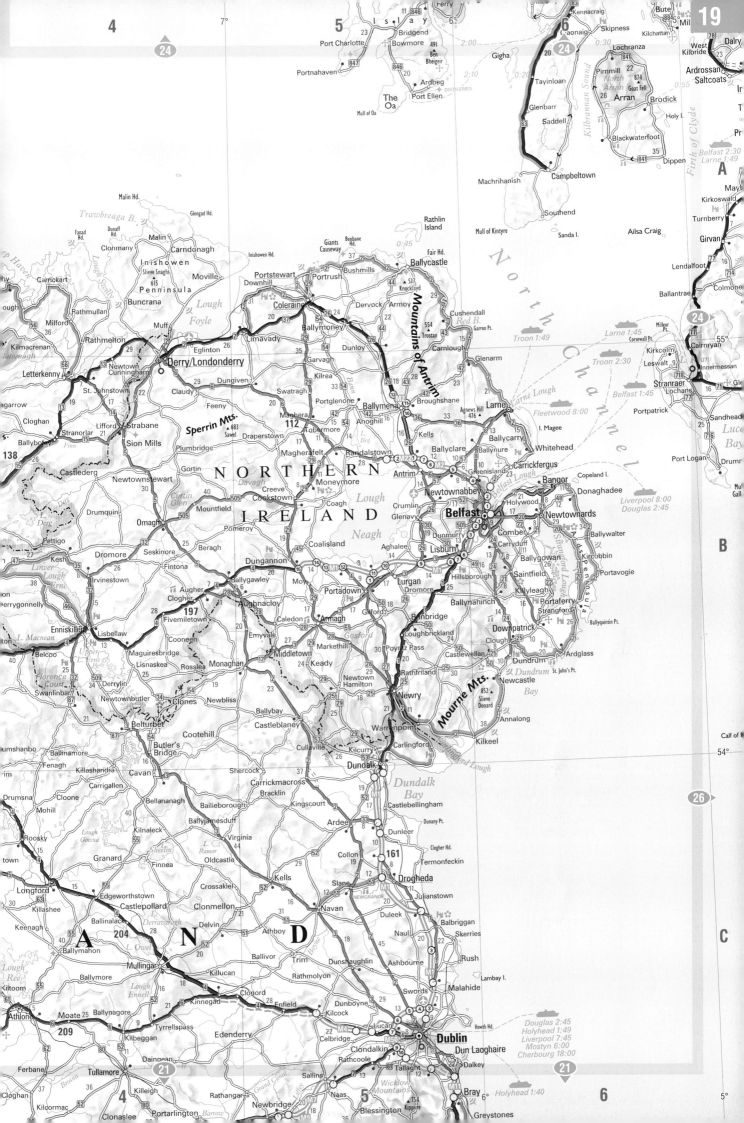

22

7   8   2   6   3   5°

Shetland Islands

Norwick
Baltasound
Haroldswick
Balta
Cullivoe
Unst
968
Gutcher
Belmont
Pt. of Fethaland
Isbister
26
Fetlar
Mid Yell
968
Funzie
Ronas Hill
970
450
Yell
Ulsta
Burravoe
Esha Ness
6   15
Hillswick
20
St. Magnus Bay
Muckle Roe
Lunna Ness
Out Skerries
Brae
15   968
Vidlin
1:30
Papa Stour
Voe
Whalsay
Sandness
Aith
23
Neap
Symbister
Dale
971
Walls
29
Easter Skeld
970
Bressay
Shetland
Scalloway
Lerwick
I. of Noss
Hamnavoe
West Burra
42
Helli Ness
Bard Hd.

Aberdeen 14:00
Bergen 12:00
Kirkwall 6:00
Seydisfjördur 30:00
Torshavn 12:30

Northpunds
Scousburgh
970
Boddam
Toloi
Sumburgh
Sumburgh Hd.

Foula

C

Butt of Lewis
Dail bho Dheas
Port Nis
857
24
Barabhas
Tolastadh bho Thuath
Tolsta Hd.
Siabost
857
Bac
Broad Bay
Carlabhagh
858
292
Tiumpan Hd.
Gallan Hd.
Ben Mholach
Great Berriera
Newmarket
Port Nan Giuran
Timspearraidh
Calanais
51
Stornoway
574
856
866
Mealisval
Lewis
Mealabost
Giosla
Chicken Hd.
Scarp
48
859
Crosbost
Kintarvie
Husinish
Leumrabhagh
Grabhair
799
572
Kebock Hd.
Clisham
Beinn Mhor
Taransay
Ardhasig
West L. Tarber
Aird Asaig
Shiant Is.
Tairbeart
Harris
Scalpay
Sgarasta Mhor
East L. Tarber
Toe Hd.
An t-Ob
Roghadal
1:45
Renish Pt.

Fair Isle

Rona

North West Sutherland
C. Wrath
Durness
29
838
Kinlochbervie
L. Inchard
Rhiconich
908
Foinaven
Laxford Bridge
Scourie
894
L. More
838
Eddrachillis Bay
Drumbeg
34
Kylestrome
Kinloch
Pt. of Stoer
Stoer
18
837
Inchnadamph
Enard B.
998
Lochinver
L. Assynt
Ben More Assynt
Rubha Coigeach
Assynt-Colgath
111
Achiltibuie
837
Ledmore
L. Lurgainn
Elphin
L. Broom
835
Strathkanaird
2:40
Oykel Bridge
Rosehall
Ullapool
25
26
Greenstone Pt.
Gruinard B.
62
Ardessie
Ardcharnich
17
835
Cove
Aultbea
1062
Ben Dearg
Melvaig
832
An Teallach
1081
Braemore
Poolewe
Fionn Loch
832
Longa I.
Gairloch
L. Maree
Wester
1110
Garve
Port Henderson
Kerrysdale
Sgurr Mor
835
Red Point
Talladale
29
832
Ross
L. Fannich
Kinlochewe
24
890
15
Achnasheen
25
Strath
Torridon
L. Torridon
Scardroy
Mui
Shieldaig
27
890
Glen Strathfarrar
28
Applecross
896
Achnashellach
Monar Lodge
Struy
Coulags
L. Monar
Ardarroch
27
Carron
Liatrie
Cannich
831
Lochcarron
890
Drumn
Stromeferry
20
Loch Mullardoch
Glen Affric
19
Kyle of Lochalsh
8
Auchtertyre
Affric Lodge
Glen Affric
Dornie
87
Kintail
10
Kyleakin
12
L. Alsh
Glen Affric
Broadford
28
Kylerhea
Glenelg
Shiel Bridge
Invermoriston
851
30
887
27
82
21
Fort Augustus
20
87
Teangue
Sd. of Sleat
L. Hourn
22
Tomdoun
Invergarry
Armadale
Knoydart
L. Quoich
Glen
L. Garry
Laggan
Mallaig
Pt. of Sleat
0:25
L. Nevis
L. Arkaig
Gairlochy
Arisaig
26
830
Murlaggan
Spean Bridge
18
Glenfinnan
830
18
Lochailort
882
Glen
861
Rhois-Bheinn
Corpach
1344
Fort William

Cuillin Hills

Rubha Hunish
855
Staffin
Trotternish
51
Uig
Vaternish Pt.
87   23
The Storr
Geary
719
Stein
Carbost
L. Snizort
850
32
Dunvegan Hd.
855
Lephin
Dunvegan
Roskhill
863
34
Portree
Bracadale
15
Sound of Raasay
Rona
Inner Sound
Raasay
Clachan
Scalpay
Carbost
Drynoch
Sconser
Kyle of Lochalsh
L. Carron
Cuillin Hills
Glenbrittle
The Cuillin Hills
Soay
Elgol
L. Eishort
Sd. of Sleat
L. Hourn

North Uist
865
Loch nam Madadh
865
867
Clachan na Luib
Baleshare
Ronay
Benbecula
Creag Ghoraidh
Wiay
865
Tobha Mor
53
South Uist
South
Uist
Machair
865
Dalabrog
Loch Baghasdail
Pol a Charra
Sound of Barra
Eriskay
0:50
1:45
Barra
888
Bagh a Chaisteil
18
Vatersay
Sandray
Mingulay

Monach Is.
Sound of Monach
48
1:10
Sd. of Pabbay
Pabbay
Berneray
Solas
Harris
Sound of Harris

L. Bracadale
L. Bracadale

North Minch
Little Minch
The Minch
Inner Hebrides
Outer Hebrides
South Lewis, Harris & North Uist

24

Oban
Muck
Eigg
Galmisdale
Morar, Moidart &
Shona I.
Rùm
Kinloch
Canna
Sanday
Sound of Rùm
The Small Isles
Glen
L. Shiel
L. Morar

1   2   3

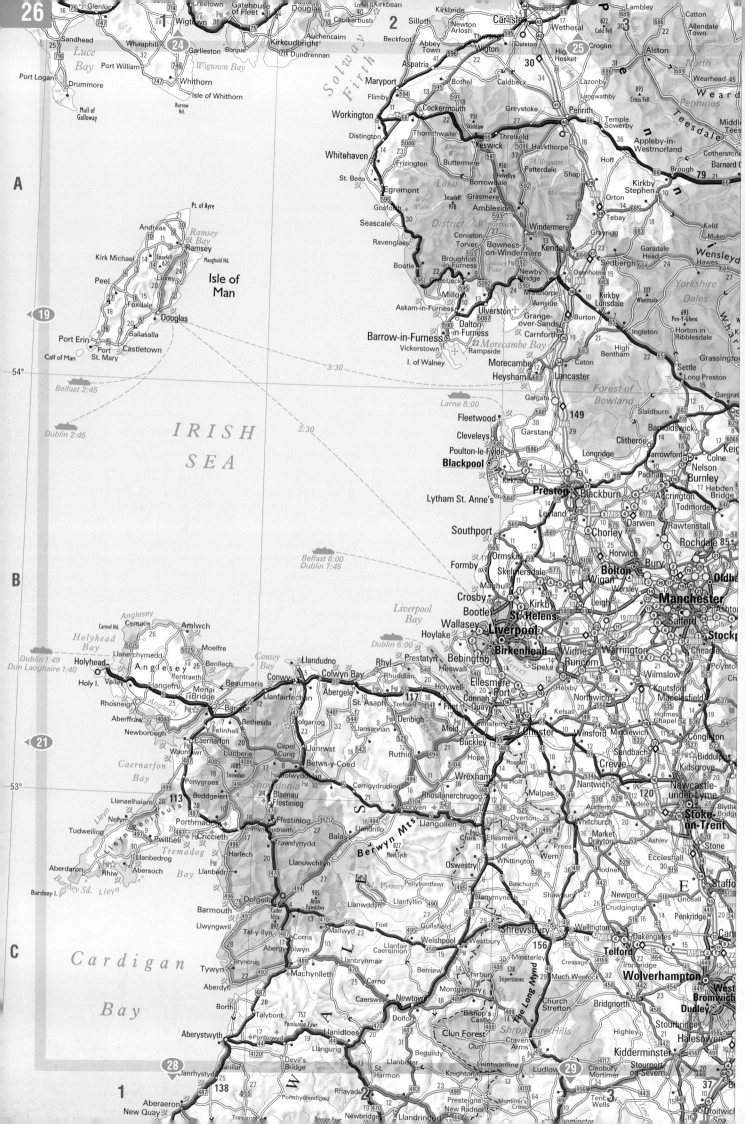

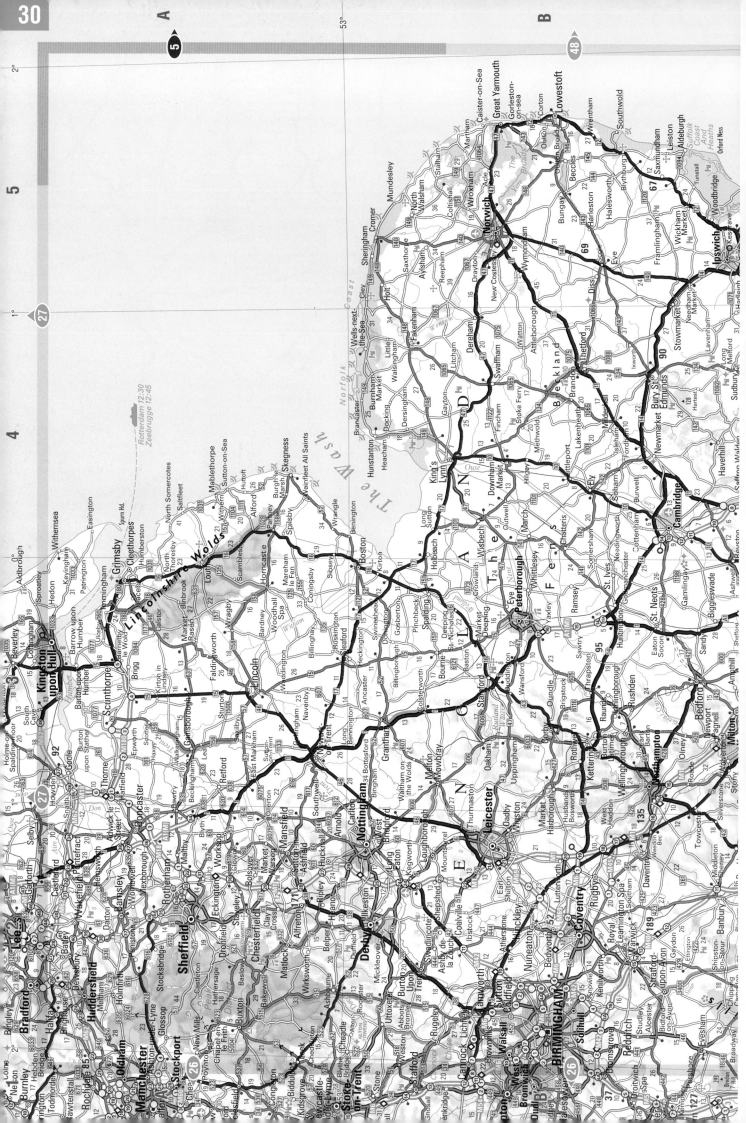

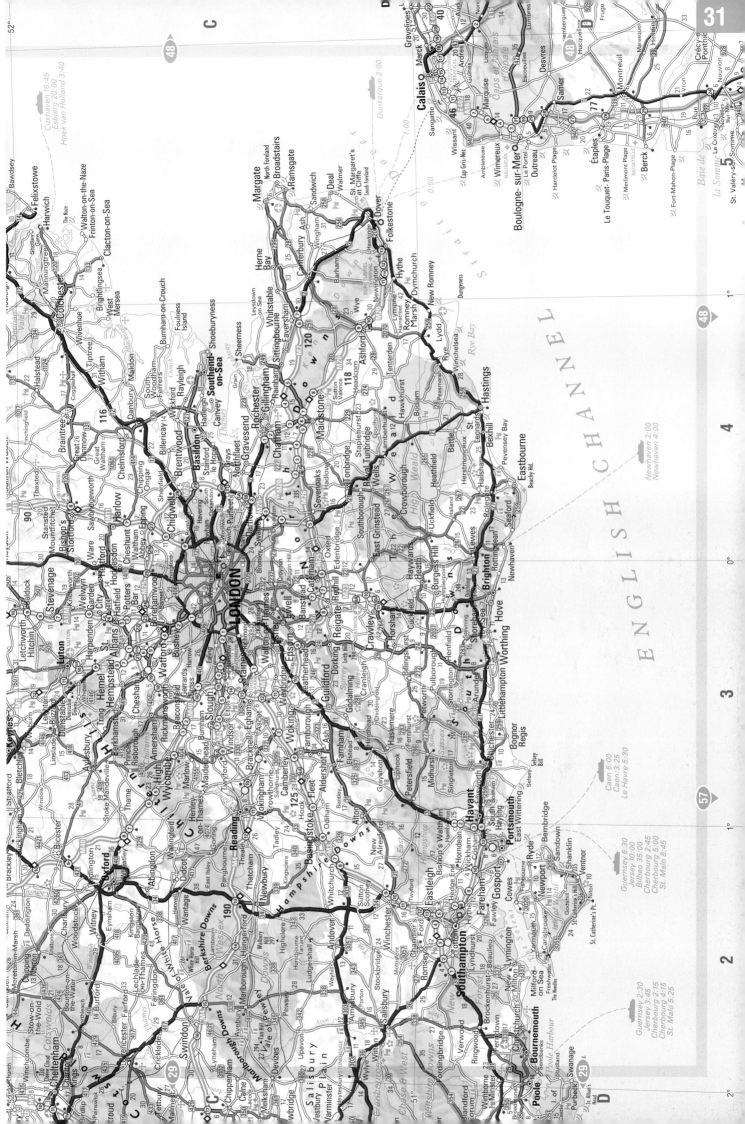

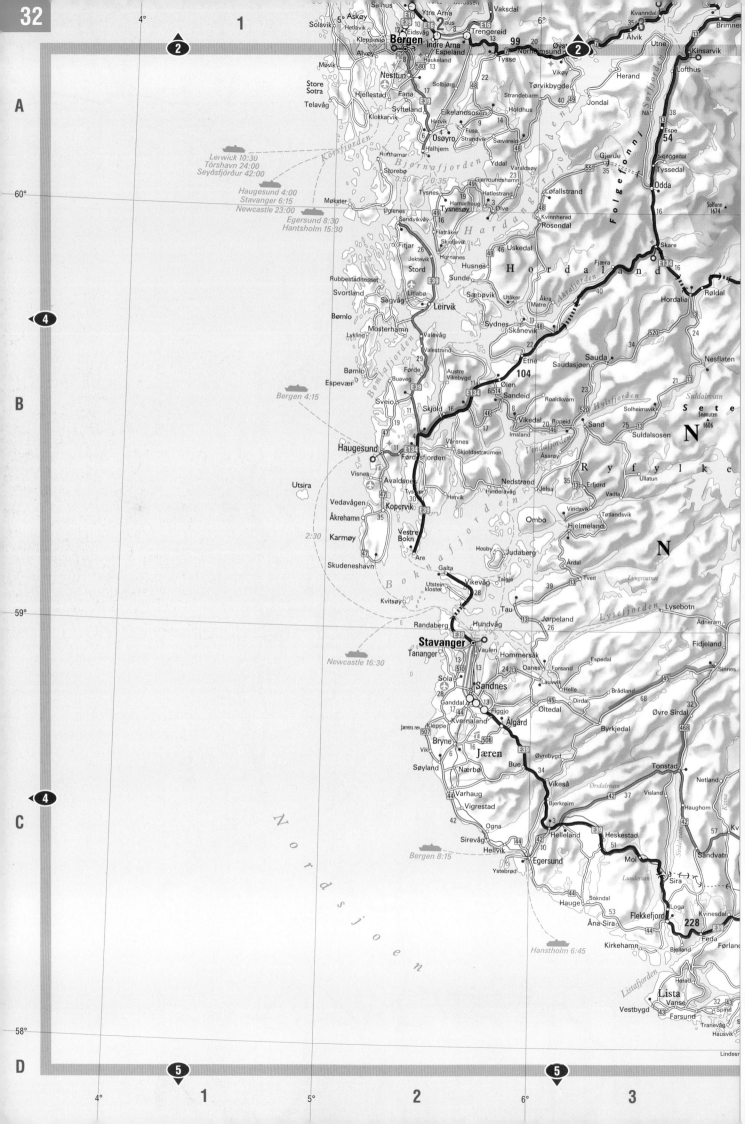

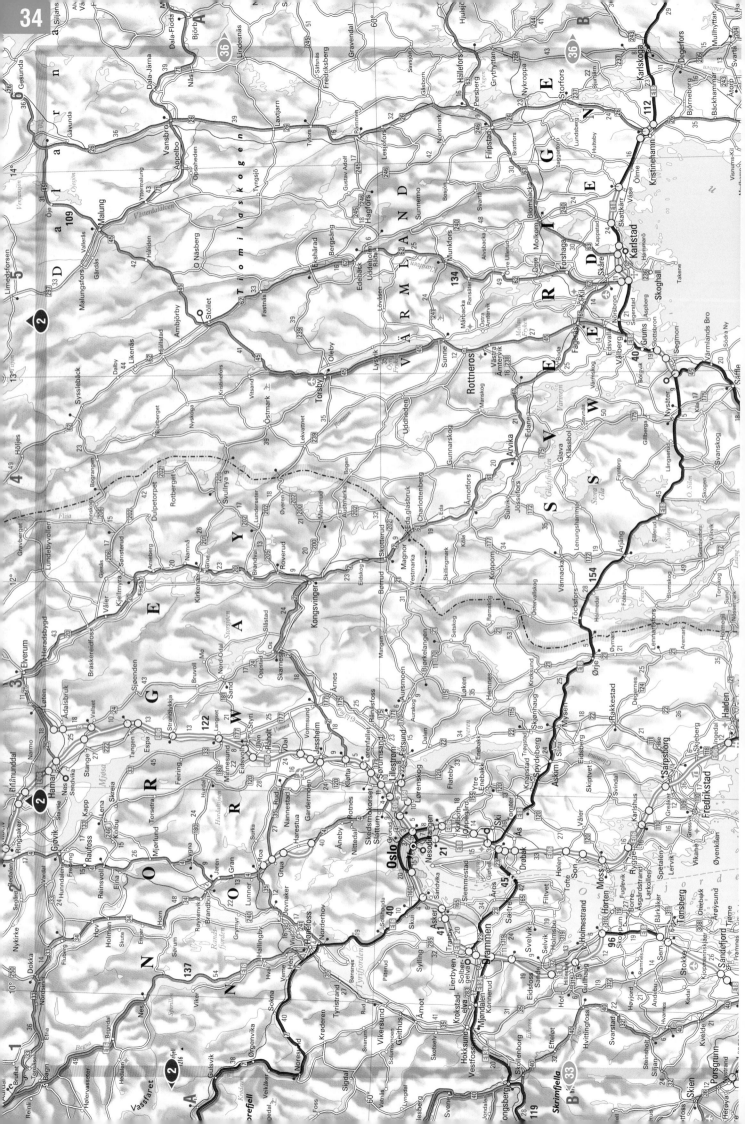

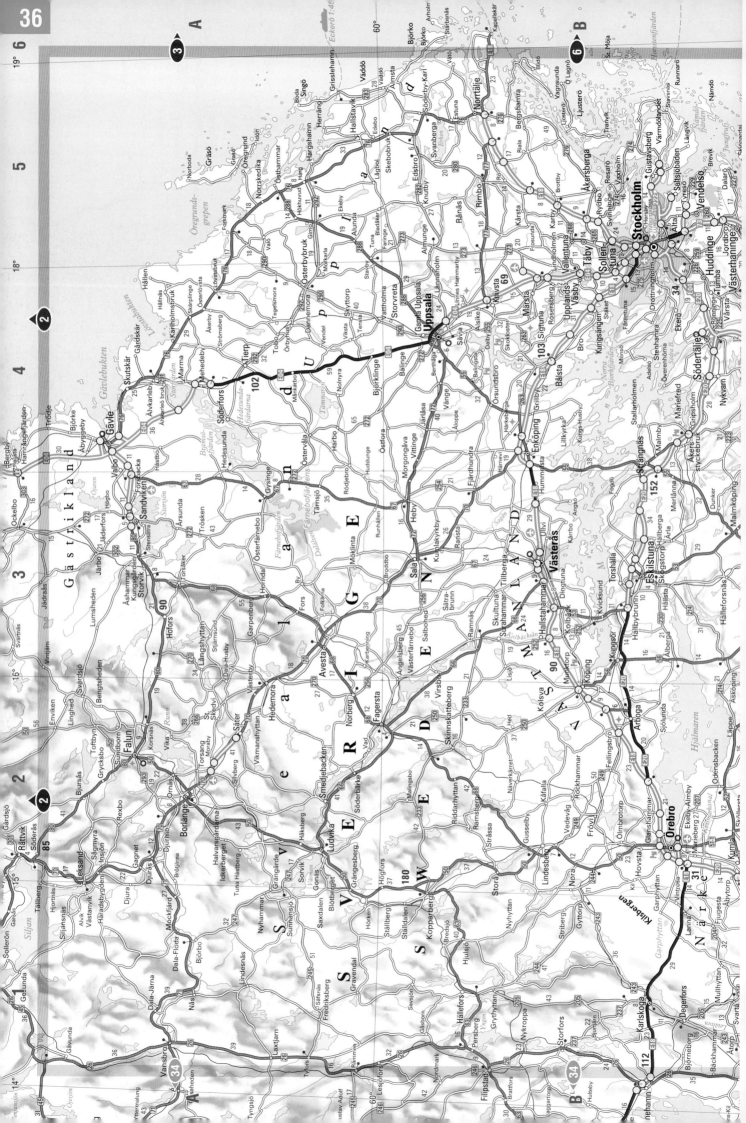

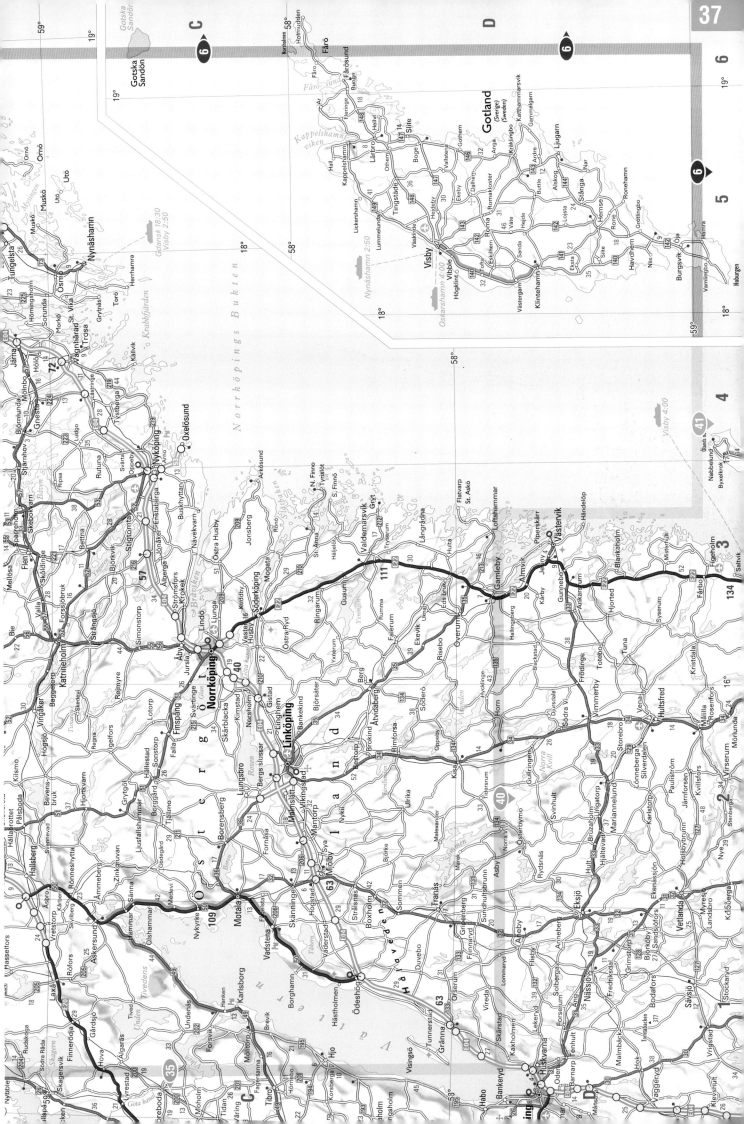

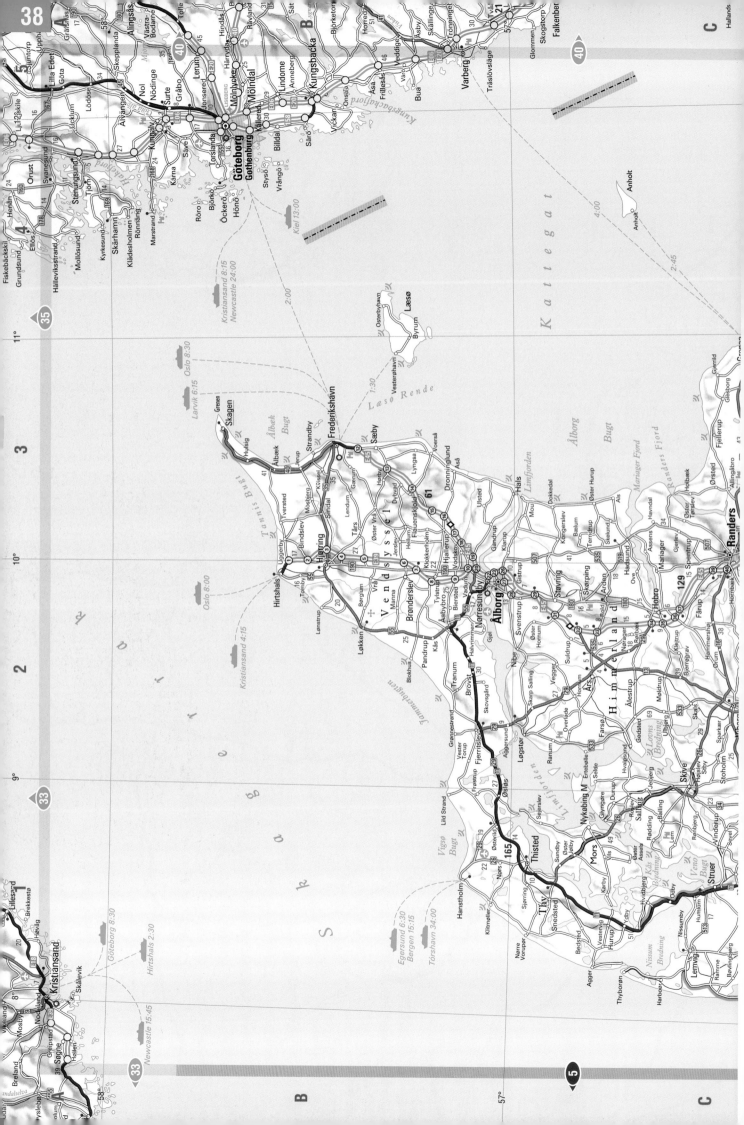

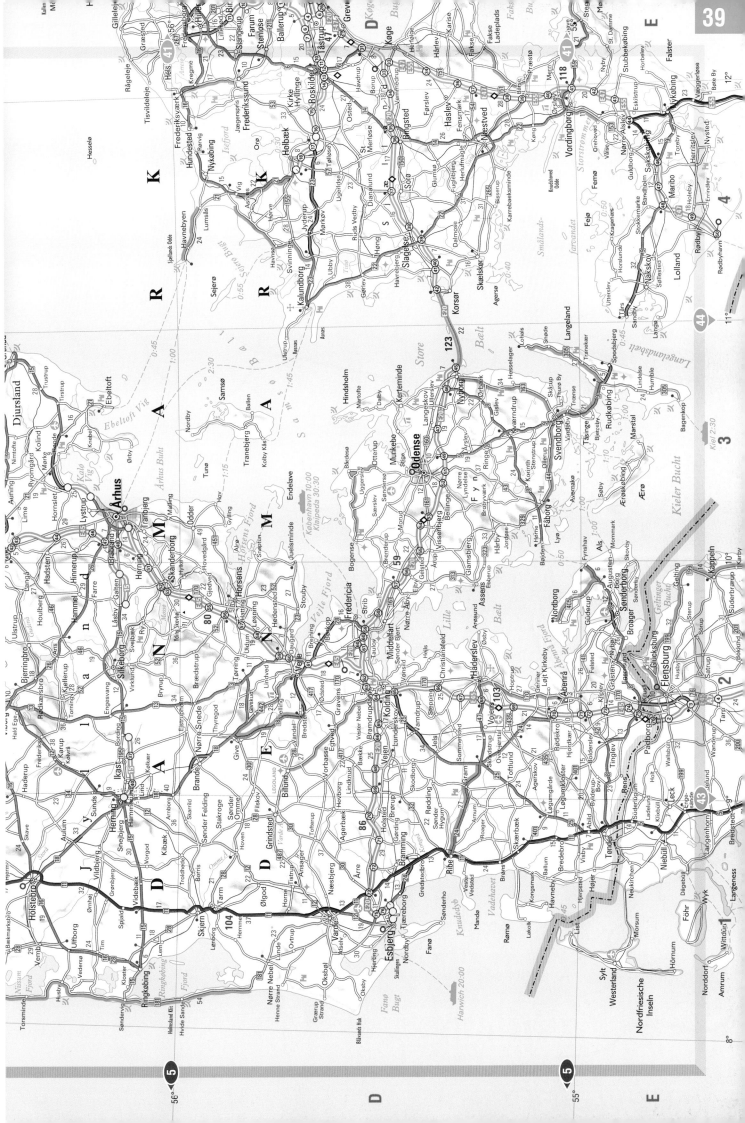

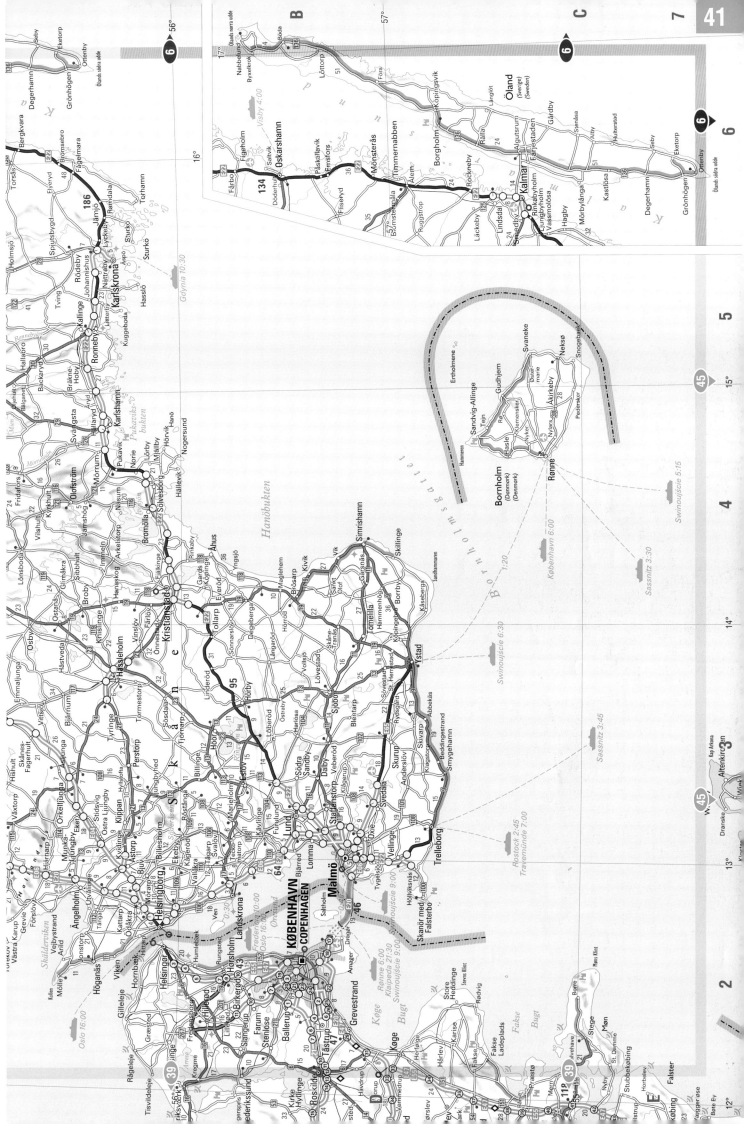

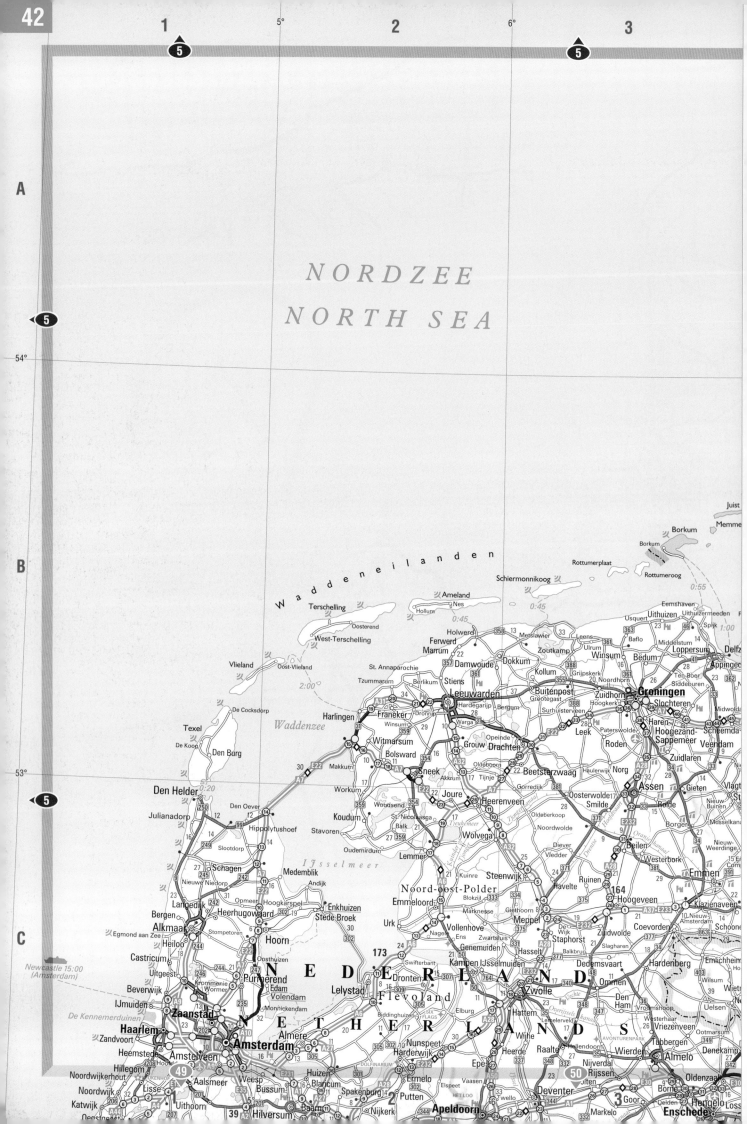

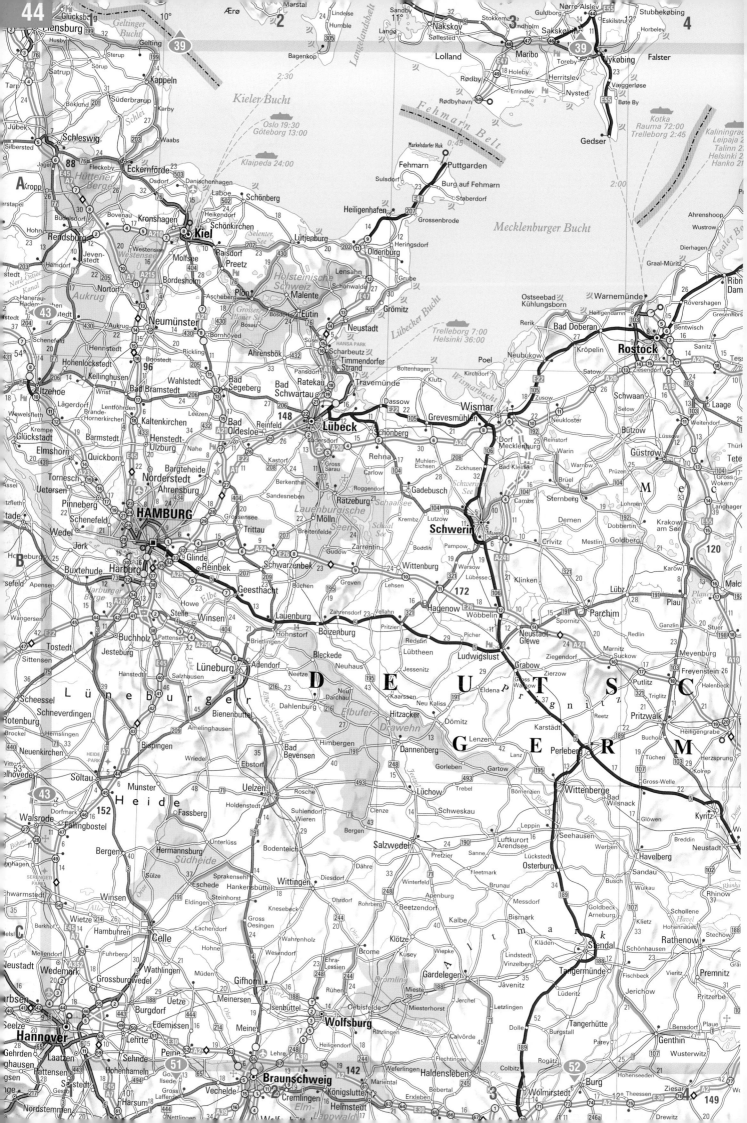

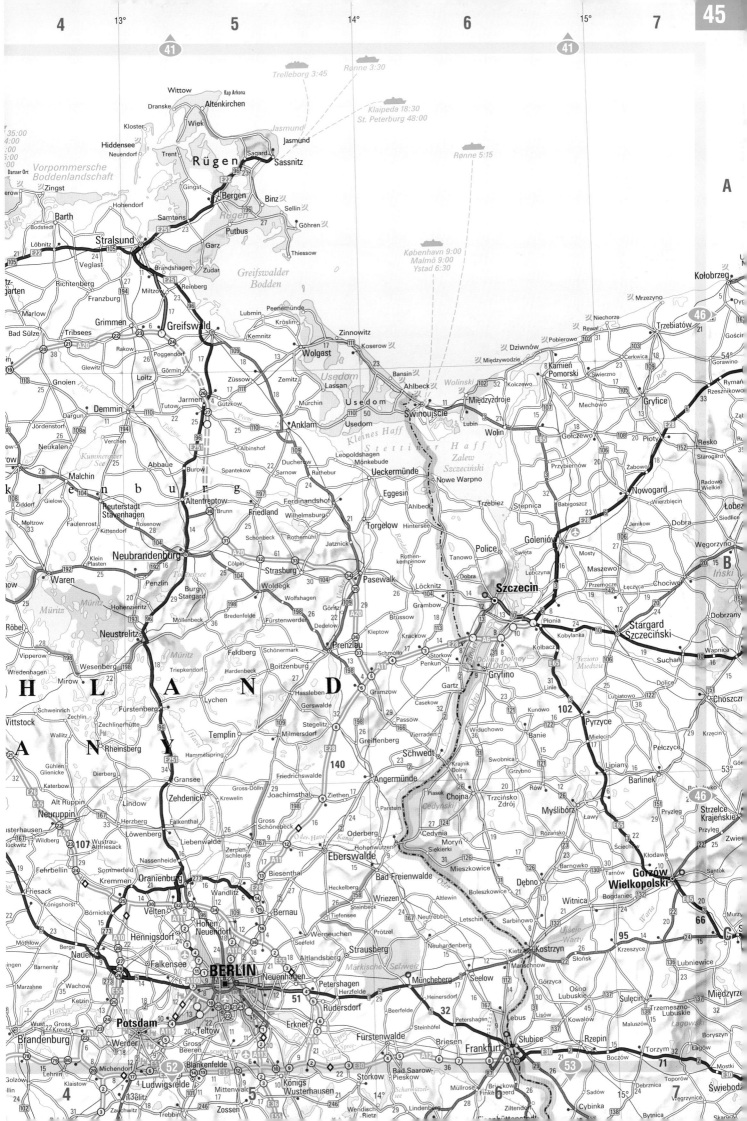

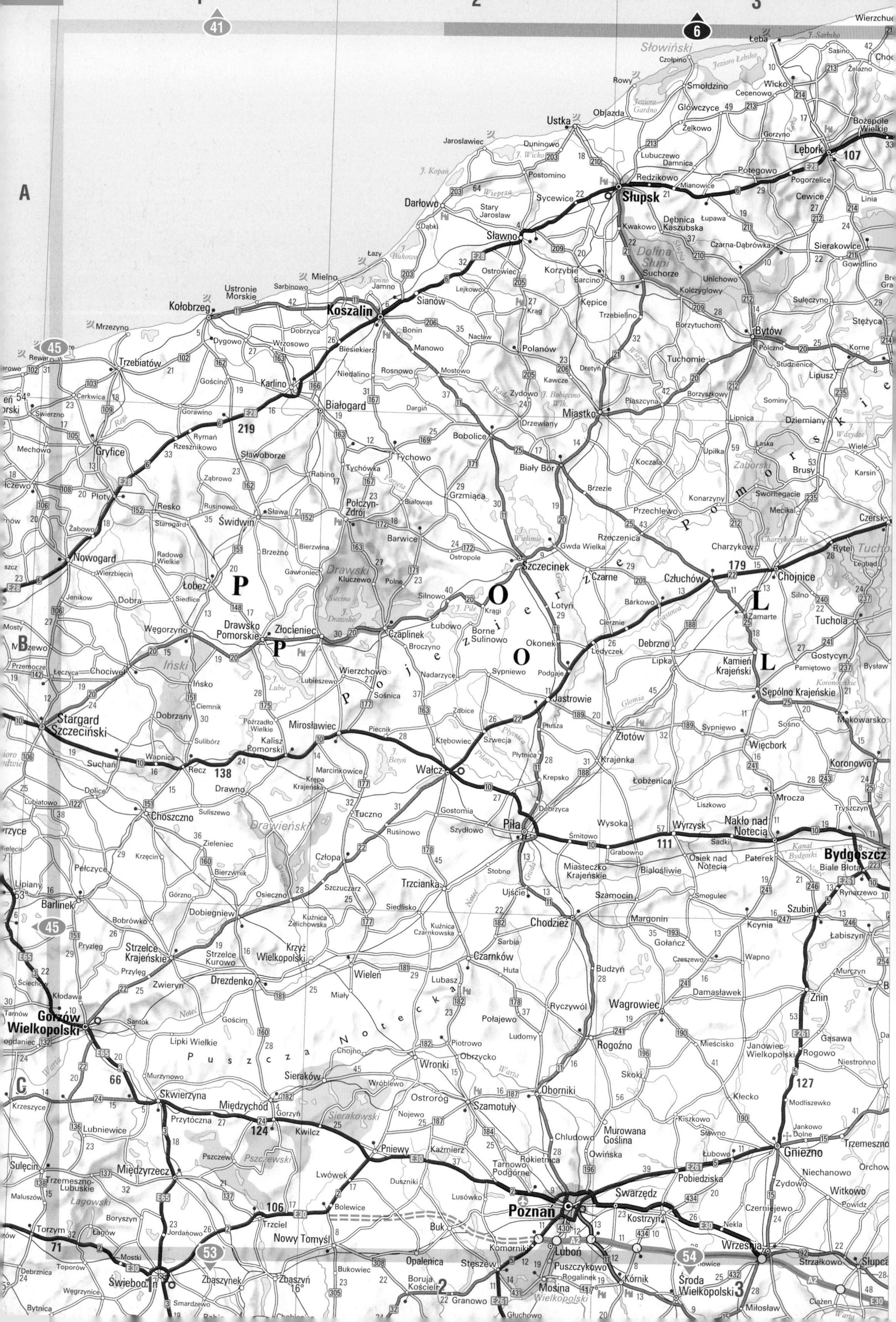

1   16°   2   17°   3

41   6

A

B

C

Słowiński

Wierzchuc

Łeba   J. Sarbsko   Sasino   Żelazno

Czołpino   Jezioro Łebsko   Żarnowiec

Rowy   Smołdzino   Wicko   Cecenowo   214

Jezioro   Główczyce   49   213   Bożepole Wielkie

Objazda   Gardno   Żelkowo   Gorzyno   Gra

Ustka   Żelkowo   Lębork   107   33

Jarosławiec   Duninowo   Lubuczewo   Pogorzelice   E28   Cewice

J. Wicka   203   Damnica   Potęgowo   Linia

Darłowo   203   Sycewice   Słupsk   21   6   29   212   214

Stary Jarosław   210   Redzikowo   Mianowice   Sierakowice   211

Sławno   209   Korzybie   Kwakowo   Debnica Kaszubska   Łupawa   Czarna-Dąbrówka   37   Gowidlino

Łazy   Ostrowiec   Barcino   Suchorze   Unichowo   Sulęczyno

Mielno   E28   Lejkowo   Kępice   Kolczygłowy   Bytów   Stężyca

Ustronie Morskie   Sianów   Nacław   Trzebielino   Borzytuchom   Połczno   Korne

Kołobrzeg   Koszalin   Bonin   Polanów   Kawcze   Studzienice   Lipusz

Dygowo   Dobrzyca   Biesiekierz   Manowo   Zydowo   Miastko   Piaszczyna   Dziemiany

Trzebiatów   Karlino   Niedalino   Rosnowo   Mostowo   Drzewiany   Lipnica   Sominy

Gościno   Białogard   Dargiń   Zabartowo   Bobolice   Upiłka

Gorawino   E28   Tychowo   Biały Bór   Koczała   Laska

Gryfice   Rymań   Sławoborze   Tychówka   Grzmiąca   Brzezie   Konarzyny   Brusy

Płoty   Rabino   Białowąs   Rzeczenica   Przechlewo   Swornegacie

Resko   Rusinowo   Połczyn-Zdrój   Barwice   Gwda Wielka   Charzykowy   Czersk

Nowogard   Świdwin   Brzeźno   Bierzwina   Ostropole   Szczecinek   Człuchów   179   Chojnice   Rytel

Łobez   Drawsko Pomorskie   Złocieniec   Czaplinek   Łubowo   Czarne   Barkowo   Silno   Tuchola

Węgorzyno   Broczyno   Borne Sulinowo   Okonek   Cierznie   Zamarte

Iński   Ińsko   Wierzchowo   Nadarzyce   Sypniewo   Lędyczek   Debrzno   Kamień Krajeński   Gostycyn

Dobrzany   Lubieszewo   Sośnica   Jastrowie   Lipka   Sępólno Krajeńskie

Stargard Szczeciński   Recz   138   Mirosławiec   Zdbice   Złotów   Sypniewo   Sośno   Makowarsko

Suchań   Marcinkowice   Kłębowiec   Szwecja   Krajenka   Więcbork   Koronowo

Wapnica   Piecnik   Płytnica   Łobżenica   Mrocza

Dolice   Drawno   Tuczno   Wałcz   Dobrzyca   Krepsko   Liszkowo   Tryszczyn

Choszczno   Suliszewo   Rusinowo   Gostomia   Wysoka   Wyrzysk   Nakło nad Notecią   Bydgoszcz

Drawieński   Zieleniec   Człopa   Szydłowo   Piła   Śmitowo   111   Sadki   Osiek nad Notecią   Paterek

Krzęcin   Bierzwnik   Szczuczarz   Trzcianka   Miasteczko Krajeńskie   Białośliwie   Szubin

Pełczyce   Górzno   Osieczno   Siedlisko   Ujście   Szamocin   Smogulec   Kcynia

Barlinek   45   Dobiegniew   Kuźnica Żelichowska   Kuźnica Czarnkowska   Chodzież   Margonin   Łabiszyn

Lipiany   Bobrówko   Krzyż Wielkopolski   Sarbia   Gołańcz   Wapno

Przyłęg   Strzelce Krajeńskie   Strzelce Kurowo   Czarnków   Huta   Czeszewo   Żnin

Kłodawa   Zwierzyn   Drezdenko   Wieleń   Lubasz   Ryczywół   Wągrowiec   Damasławek

Gorzów Wielkopolski   Santok   Gościm   Miały   Połajewo   Ludomy   Rogoźno   Mieścisko   Janowiec Wielkopolski   Gąsawa

Lipki Wielkie   Sieraków   Chojno   Piotrowo   Obrzycko   Budzyń   Skoki   Kłecko   Rogowo

Murzynowo   Sierakowski   Wronki   Ostroróg   Oborniki   Kiszkowo   Sławno   127

Skwierzyna   Międzychód   Wróblewo   Szamotuły   Murowana Goślina   Łubowo   Gniezno

Przytoczna   124   Kwilcz   Nojewo   Chludowo   Owińska   Modliszewko   Jankowo Dolne   Trzemeszno

Lubniewice   Pszczew   Pniewy   Kaźmierz   Rokietnica   Pobiedziska   Niechanowo   Orchowo

Sulęcin   Międzyrzecz   Pszczewski   Lwówek   Duszniki   Tarnowo Podgórne   Swarzędz   Zydowo   Witkowo   Powidz

Trzemeszno-Lubuskie   106   E30   Lusówko   Poznań   Kostrzyn   Nekla   Czerniejewo

Łagowski   Trzciel   Bolewice   Buk   A2   434   Środa Wielkopolski   Strzałkowo

Boryszyn   Nowy Tomyśl   Komorniki   Luboń   Puszczykowo   Kórnik   Wrześnią   Słupc

Torzym   Łagów   Jordanowo   Opalenica   Steszew   Mosina   Rogalinek   432   Środa Wielkopolski

Świebodzin   Zbąszynek   Zbąszyń   Bukowiec   Boruja Kościelna   Granowo   E30   Nowice

71   53   2   54   3

Dębrznica   Węgrzynice   Smardzewo   Chobienice   Granowo   Głuchowo   Ciążeń   Miłosław

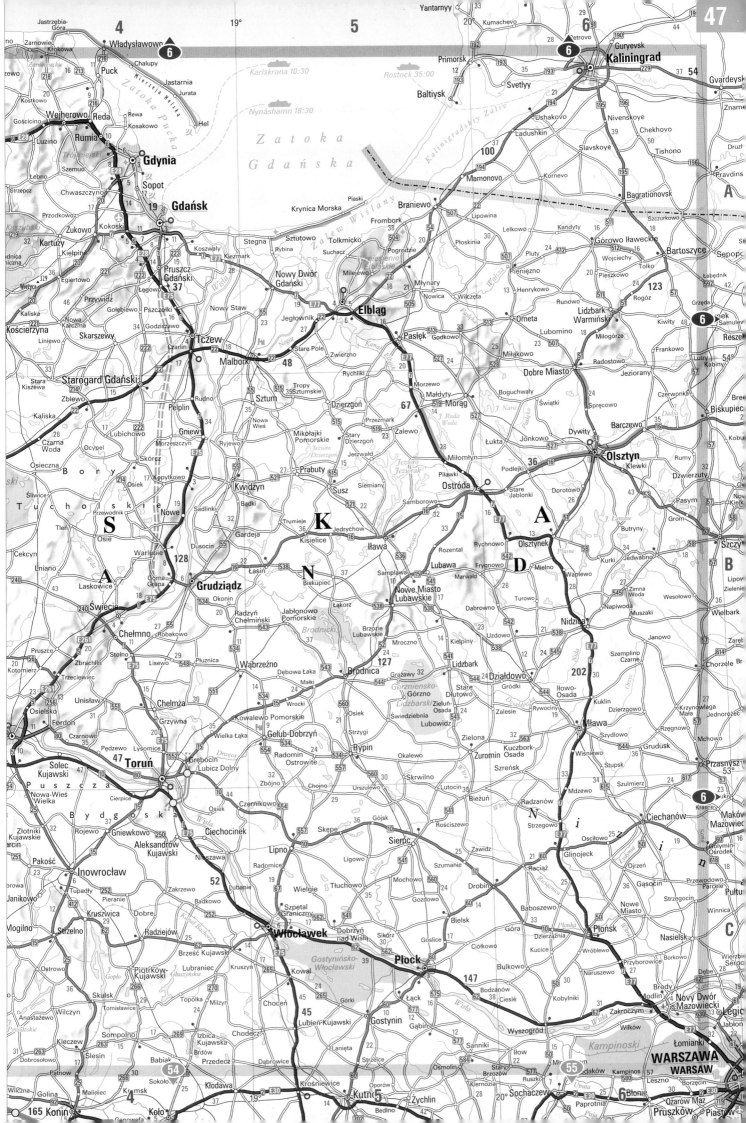

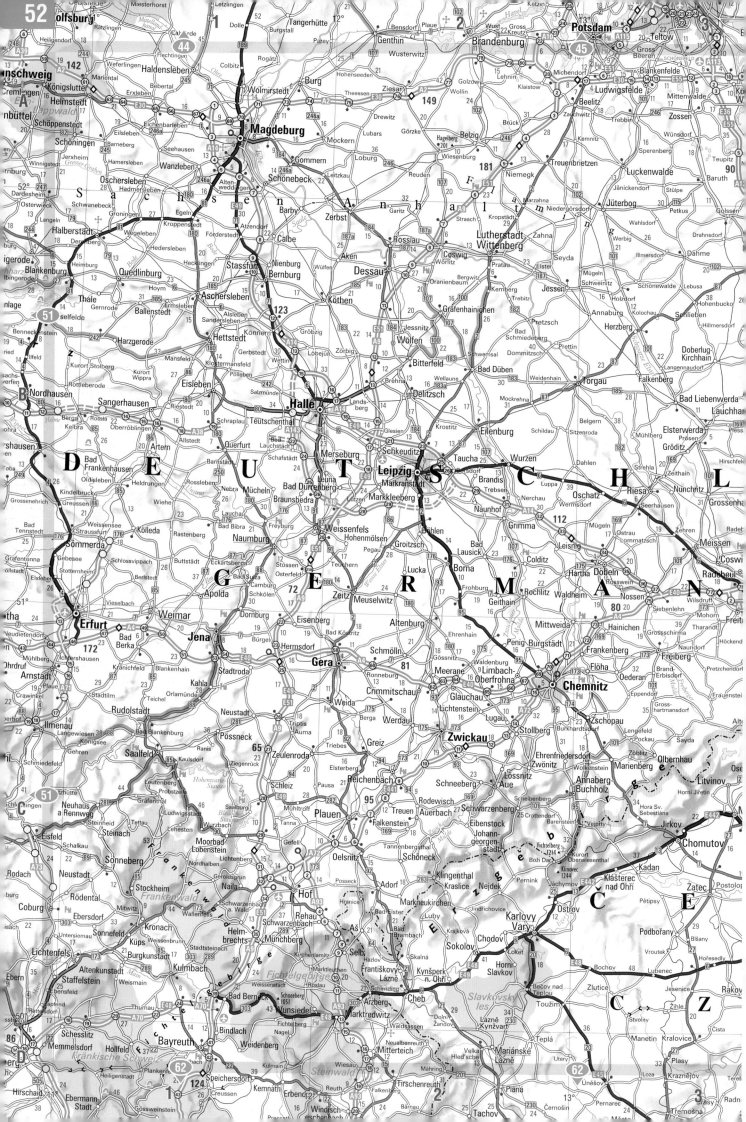

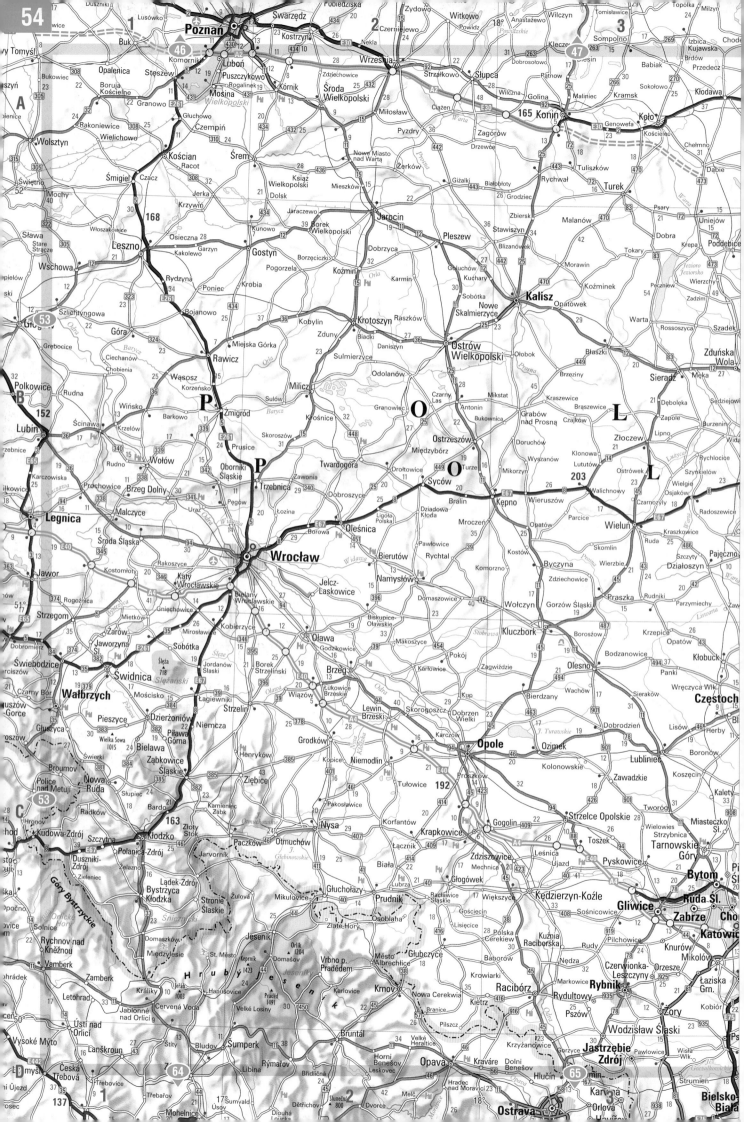

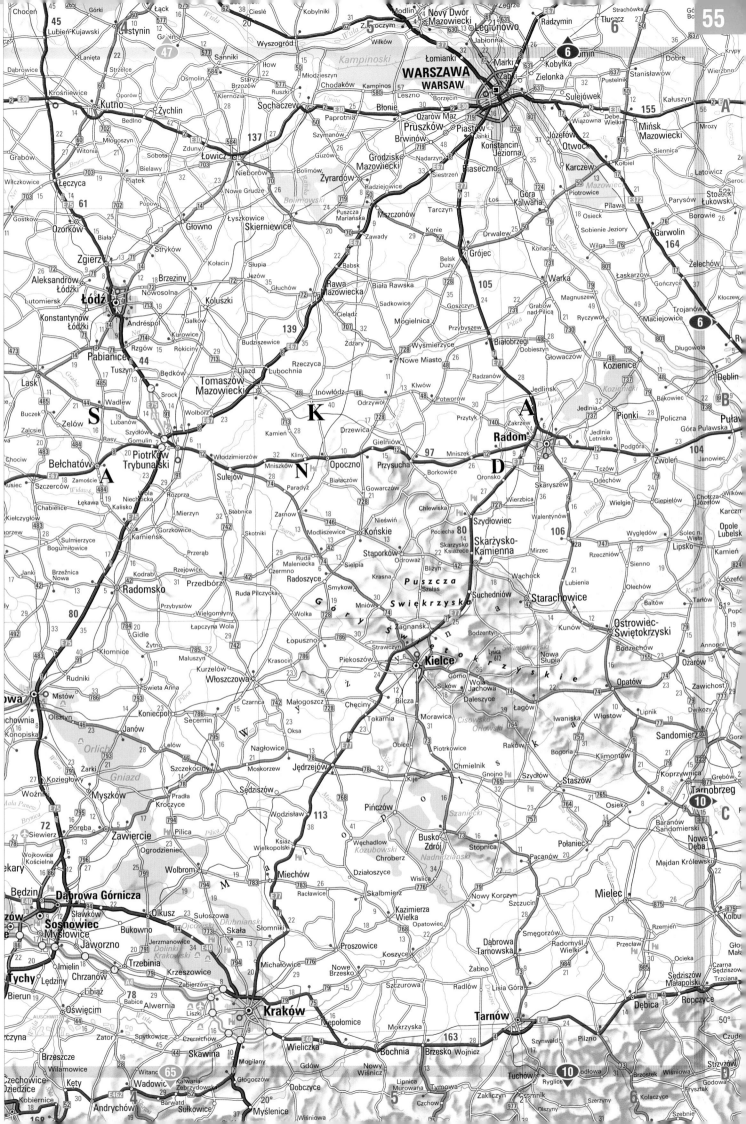

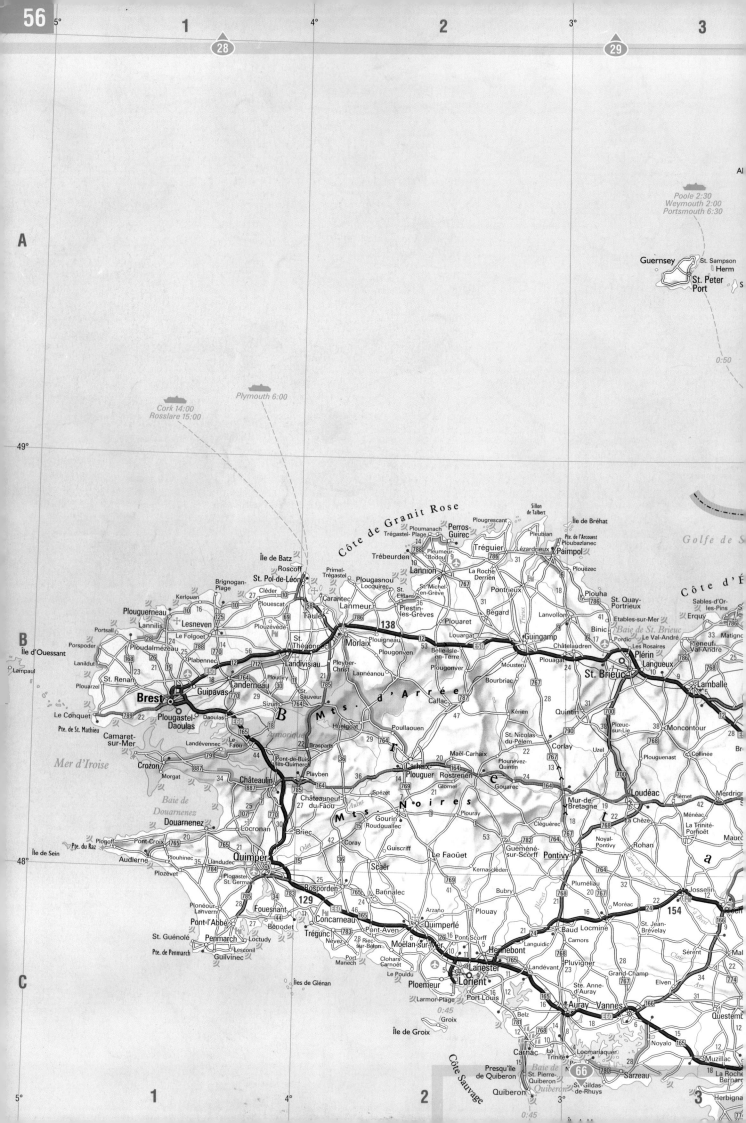

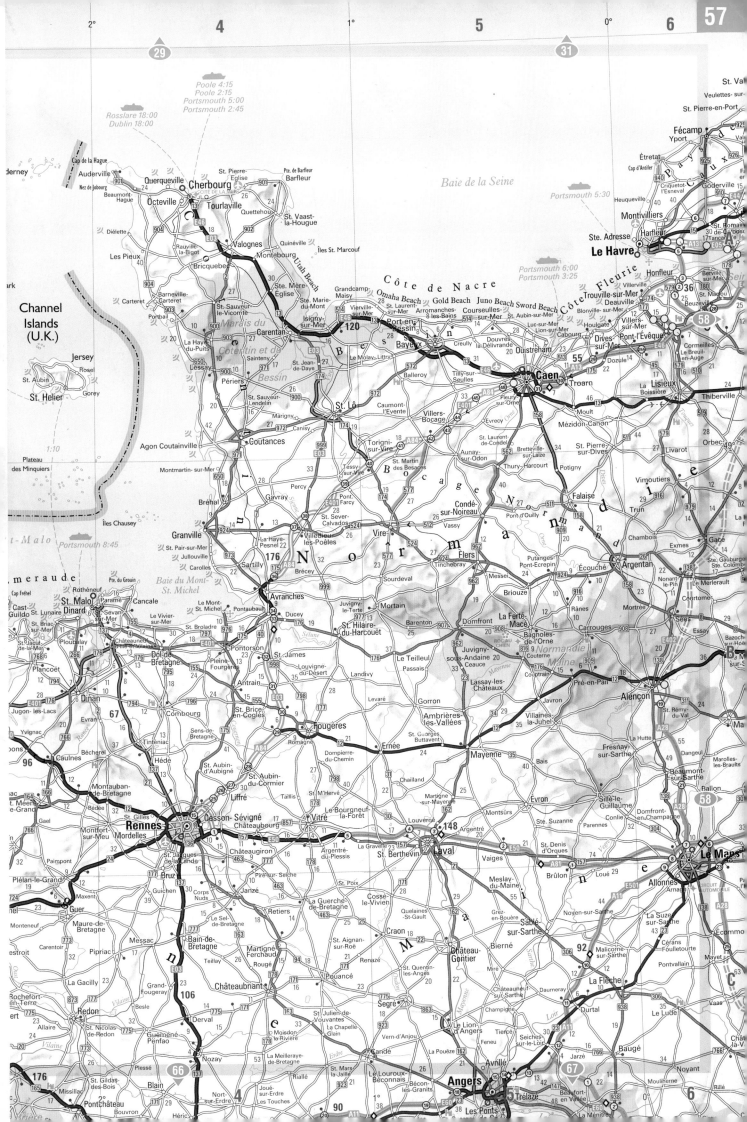

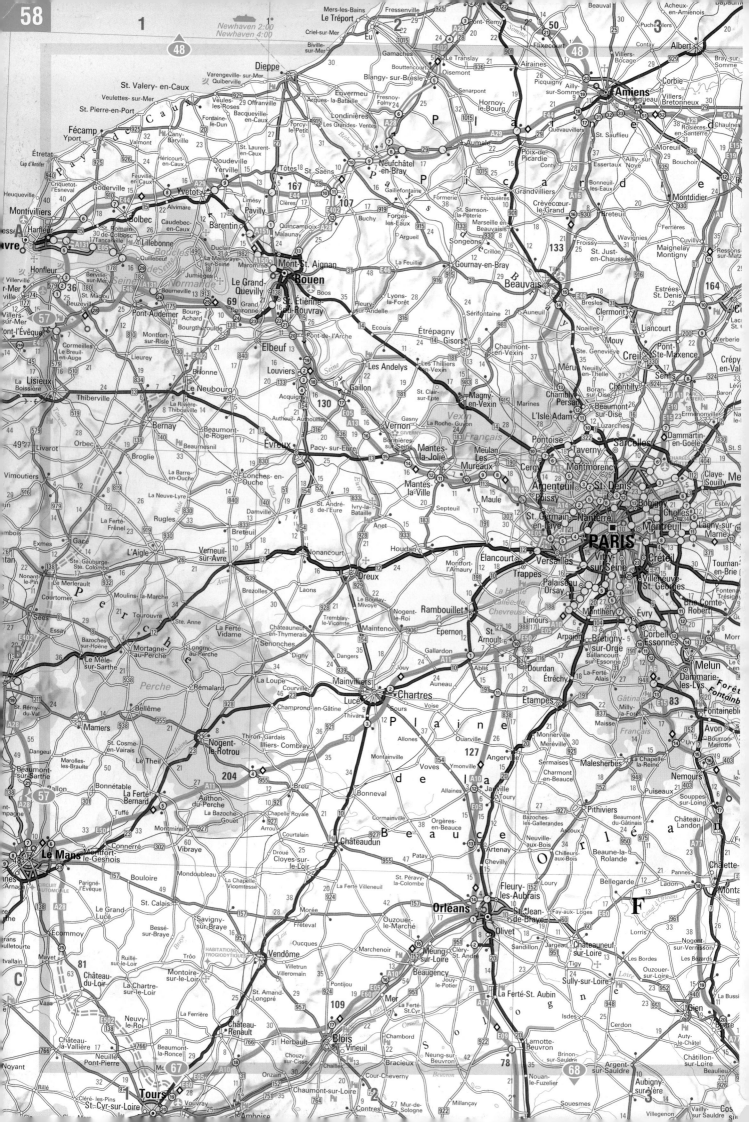

4   5 Couvin   6   St. Hubert

Bertincourt   Walincourt   Landrecies   Trélon   Chimay   Bailleux   Vireux   Wellin   803
Gouzeaucourt   Étroeungt   Fourmies   Macon   Hargnies   Haut-Fays   Freux   Morhet
Prémont   Le Nouvion-en-Thiérache   Rienne   Gedinne   Libramont
Fresnoy-le-Grand   La Capelle   Hirson   Rocroi   Revin   Bièvre   Recogne   Vaux-sur-Sûre
Hargicourt   Guise   Étréaupont   Signy-le-Petit   Les Mazures   Monthermé   Sugny   Corbion   Bouillon   Herbeumont   Léglise
Péronne   Vervins   Maubert-Fontaine   Rimogne   Nouzonville   Vrigne-aux-Bois   St. Menges   Bertrix   Neufchâteau   Martelange
St. Quentin   Ribemont   Rumigny   Charleville-Mézières   Flize   Sedan   Florenville   Rossignol   Jamoigne   Tintigny   Etalle
Origny-Ste Benoîte   Sains   Marle   Liart   Signy-l'Abbaye   Poix-Terron   Douzy   Carignan   Mouzon   Virton   St. Leger
Ham   Crécy-sur-Serre   Montcornet   Chaumont-Porcien   Chemery-sur-Bar   Raucourt-et-Flaba   Margut   Montmédy   Avioth

Thiérache   Vendeuil   Pierrepont   Dizy-le-Gros   Seraincourt   Novion-Porcien   Beaumont-en-Argonne   Stenay   Longuyon
La Fère   Crépy   Athies-sous-Laon   Sévigny   Château-Porcien   Rethel   Tannay-en-Argonne   Lanneuville-sur-Meuse   Marville
Chauny   Laon   Sissonne   Lor   Novy-Chevrières   Attigny   Le Chesne   Buzancy   Dun-sur-Meuse   Damvillers
Noyon   St. Gobain   Festieux   Tagnon   Neuflize   Vouziers   Grandpré   Montfaucon-d'Argonne   Côtes de Meuse
Anizy-le-Château   Chavignon   Corbeny   Juniville   Machault   Monthois   Varennes-en-Argonne   Verdun
Coucy-le-Château-Auffrique   Vailly-sur-Aisne   Craonne   Neufchâtel-sur-Aisne   Bourgogne   Béthenville   Sommepy-Tahure   Clermont-en-Argonne   179
Compiègne   Soissons   Braine   Hermonville   Witry-les-Reims   Pontfaverger-Moronvilliers   Souain   Argonne
Pierrefonds   Fismes   Joncheray-sur-Vesle   Reims   Beine-Nauroy   Ville-sur-Tourbe   Ste-Ménéhould
Villers-Cotterêts   Courville   Mourmelon-le-Grand   Suippes   Souilly
Neuilly-St. Front   Fère-Tardenois   Verzy   Livry-Louvercy   Somme-Tourbe   Dieue-sur-Meuse
La Ferté-Milon   Oulchy-le-Château   131   Montagne de Reims   Louvois   La Cheppe   Châlons-en-Champagne   Tilloy Bellay
Belleau   Verneuil   Châtillon-sur-Marne   Condé-sur-Marne   Triaucourt-en-Argonne
Château-Thierry   Ay   Épernay   Chouilly   Jâlons   Givry-en-Argonne   Rembercourt-aux-Pots
Montreuil-aux-Lions   Dormans   St. Martin-d'Ablois   Fagnières   Marson   Chaumont-sur-Aire
La Ferté-sous-Jouarre   Condé-en-Brie   Avize   Le Mesnil-sur-Oger   Coupéville   Vanault-les-Dames   St. Mihiel
Crécy-la-Chapelle   Montmirail   Champaubert   Vertus   Thibie   Pogny   La Chaussée-sur-Marne   Revigny-sur-Ornain   Apremont
Montmort-Lucy   Bergères-lès-Vertus   Soudron   Vatry   Fontaine   Pargny-sur-Saulx   Rumont
Coulommiers   La Ferté-Gaucher   Fère-Champenoise   Coole   Blacy   Sermaize-les-Bains   Bar-le-Duc   Commercy
Provins   Sézanne   Connantre   Sommesous   Vitry-le-François   Thiéblemont-Farémont   Ligny-en-Barrois
Nangis   Esternay   Pleurs   Mailly-le-Camp   Sompuis   Stainville   Ancerville   St. Aubin-sur-Aire
Nogent-sur-Seine   Barbonne-Fayel   Villiers-St. Georges   St. Remy-en-Bouzemont   Brillon-en-Barrois   Vaucouleurs
Montereau-Fault-Yonne   Villenauxe-la-Grande   Anglure   Plancy-l'Abbaye   Herbisse   Lhuître   St. Dizier   Éclaron   Morley   Houdelaincourt
Marcilly-sur-Seine   Margerie-Hancourt   Giffaumont-Champaubert   Rachécourt-sur-Marne   Chevillon   Gondrecourt-le-Château
Romilly-sur-Seine   Méry-sur-Seine   Vinets   Chavanges   Wassy   Thonnance-lès-Joinville   Pancey   Poissons
Nogent-sur-Seine   Châtres   Arcis-sur-Aube   Chaudrey   Ramerupt   Montier-en-Der   Joinville   Germay
Bray-sur-Seine   Voué   Lesmont   Doulevant-le-Château   Dommartin-le-Franc   Trampot
Bercenay-le-Château   Brienne-le-Château   Soulaines-Dhuys   Vignory   Doulaincourt
La Chapelle-St. Luc   Piney   Forêt d'Orient   Géraudot   Lusigny-sur-Barse   Bar-sur-Aube   Colombey-les-deux-Églises   Andelot   St. Blin
Troyes   Ste-Savine   Bucheres   Vendeuvre-sur-Barse   Dolancourt   Briaucourt   Bologne   St. Thiébault
Sens   Estissac   Villemaur-sur-Vanne   Bar-sur-Seine   Bayel   Juzennecourt   Longchamp-sur-Aujon   Chaumont   Clefmont
Villeneuve-l'Archevêque   Aix-en-Othe   Bouilly   Fouchères   Eguilly-sous-Bois   Ville-sous-la-Ferté   Nogent
Villeneuve-sur-Yonne   St. Mards-en-Othe   Landreville   Essoyes   Châteauvillain   180   Richebourg   Montigny-le-Roi
Courtenay   Cerisiers   Forêt d'Othe   Chailley   Neuvy-Santour   Ervy-le-Châtel   Chaource   Gyé-sur-Seine   Mussy-sur-Seine   Montigny-sur-Aube   Auberive   Langres
Joigny   Migennes   St. Florentin   Chessy-lès-Prés   Les Riceys   Arc-en-Barrois   Chalindrey
Châteaurenard   Bassou   Ligny-le-Châtel   Flogny-la-Chapelle   Channes   Villon   Boudreville   Neuilly-l'Évêque
Charny   Pontigny   Tonnerre   Laignes   Châtillon-sur-Seine   Leuglay   Grancey-le-Château
Monéteau   Chablis   Ancy-le-Franc   Lézinnes   Aisey-sur-Seine   Recey-sur-Ource   Prauthoy
Auxerre   St. Bris-le-Vineux   Lichères-près-Aigremont   Nuits   Coulmier-le-Sec   Aignay-le-Duc   Coublanc
Pourrain   Champs-sur-Yonne   219   Vermenton   Noyers   Aisy-sur-Armançon   Chassigny
Toucy   Coulanges-la-Vineuse   Joux-la-Ville   Arcy-sur-Cure   Baigneux-les-Juifs   Selongey
Bléneau   Mézilles   Ouanne   Courson-les-Carrières   Montbard   Venarey-les-Laumes   Fontaine-Française
Collines de la Puisaye   Mailly-le-Château   Nitry   Barjon   Is-sur-Tille
Clamecy   Vézelay   Avallon   Cussy-les-Forges   Semur-en-Auxois   Verrey-sous-Salmaise   Til-Châtel
St. Amand-en-Puisaye   Châtel-Censoir   Époisses   Vitteaux   Val-Suzon   Mirebeau-sur-Bèze

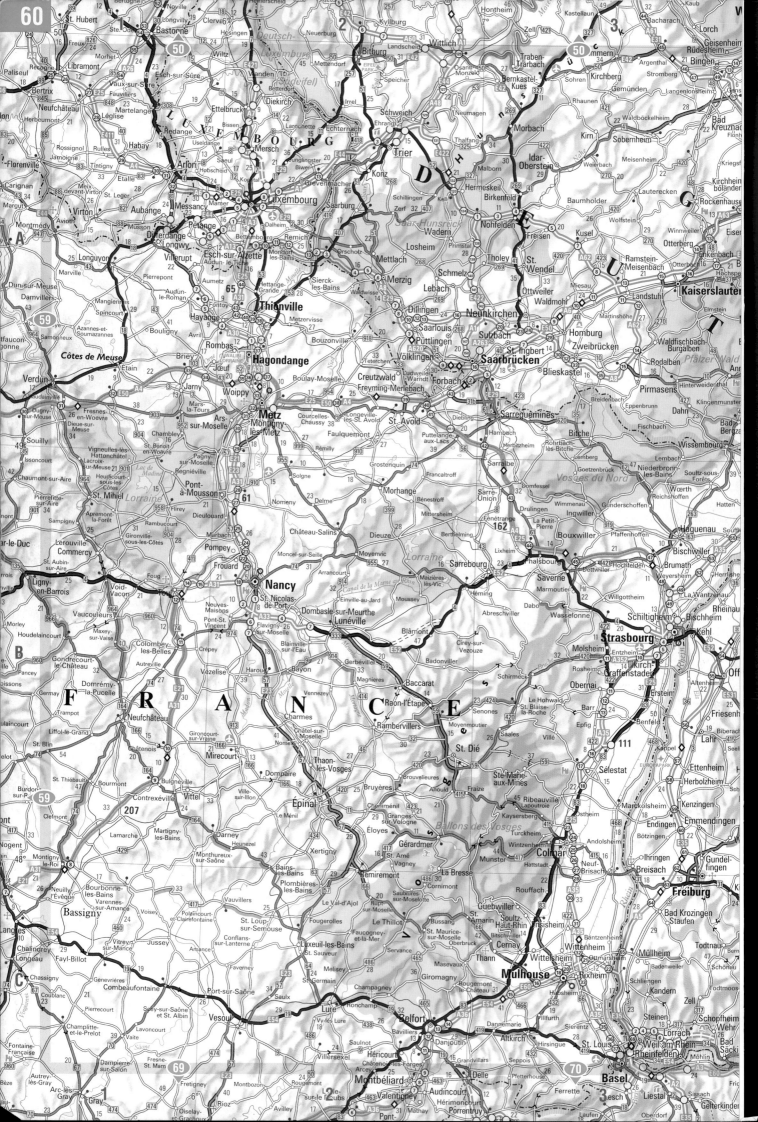

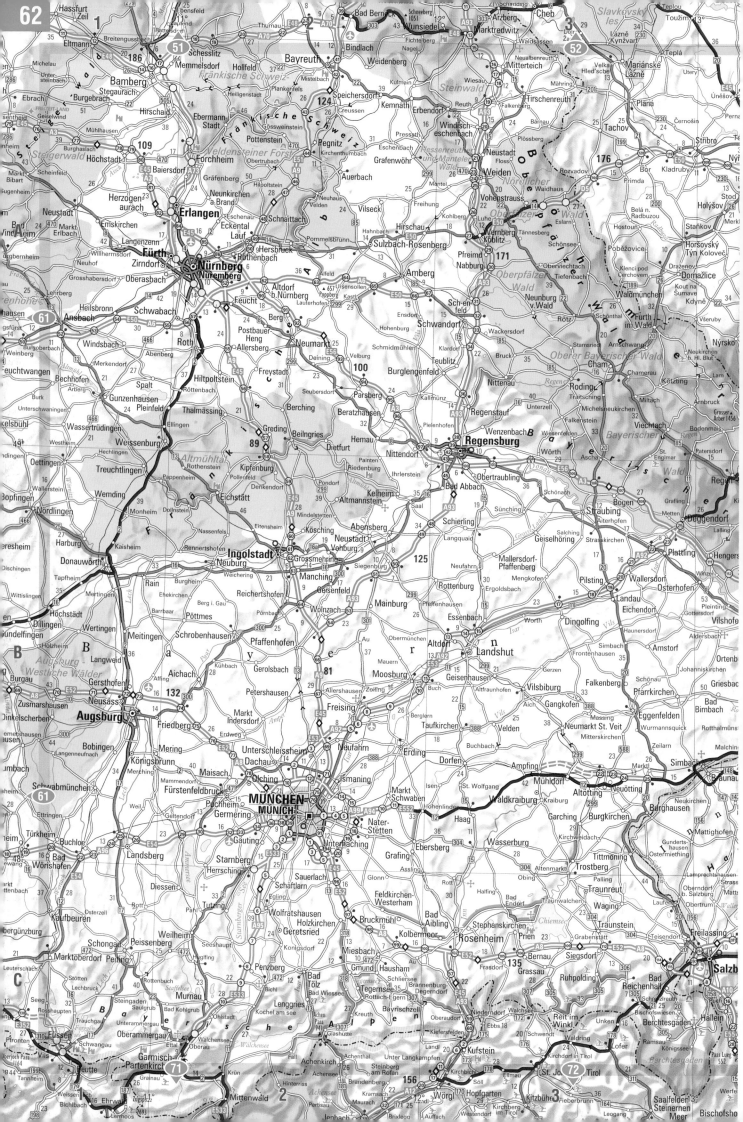

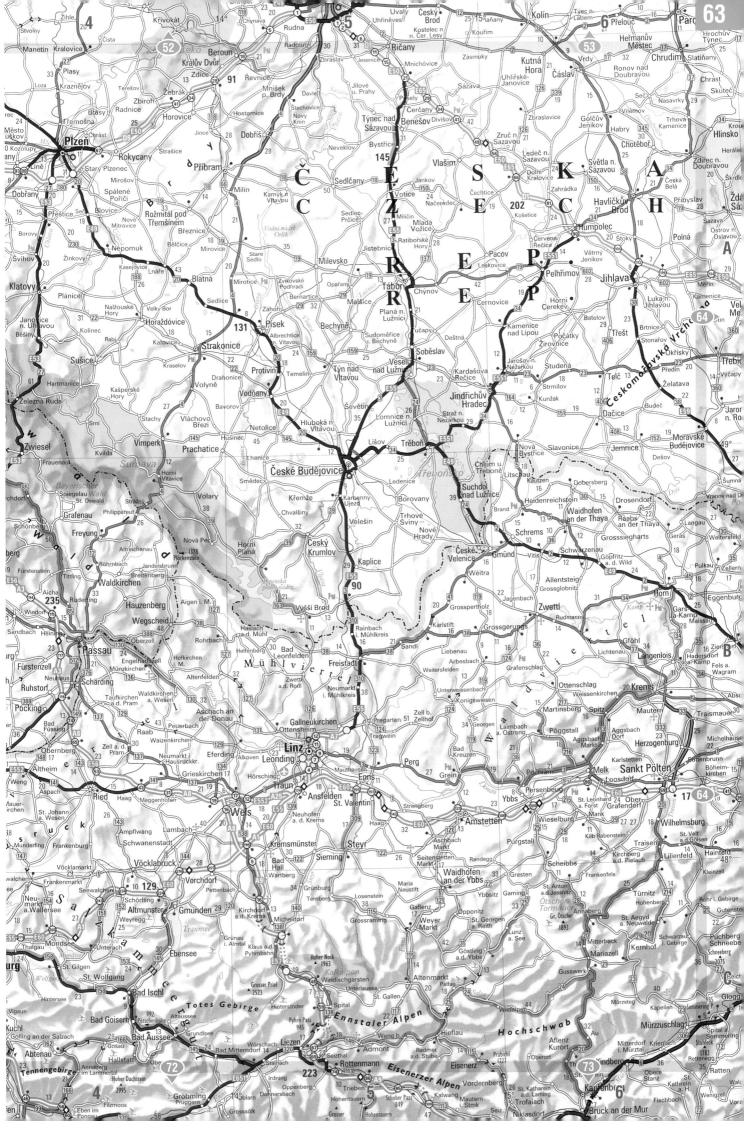

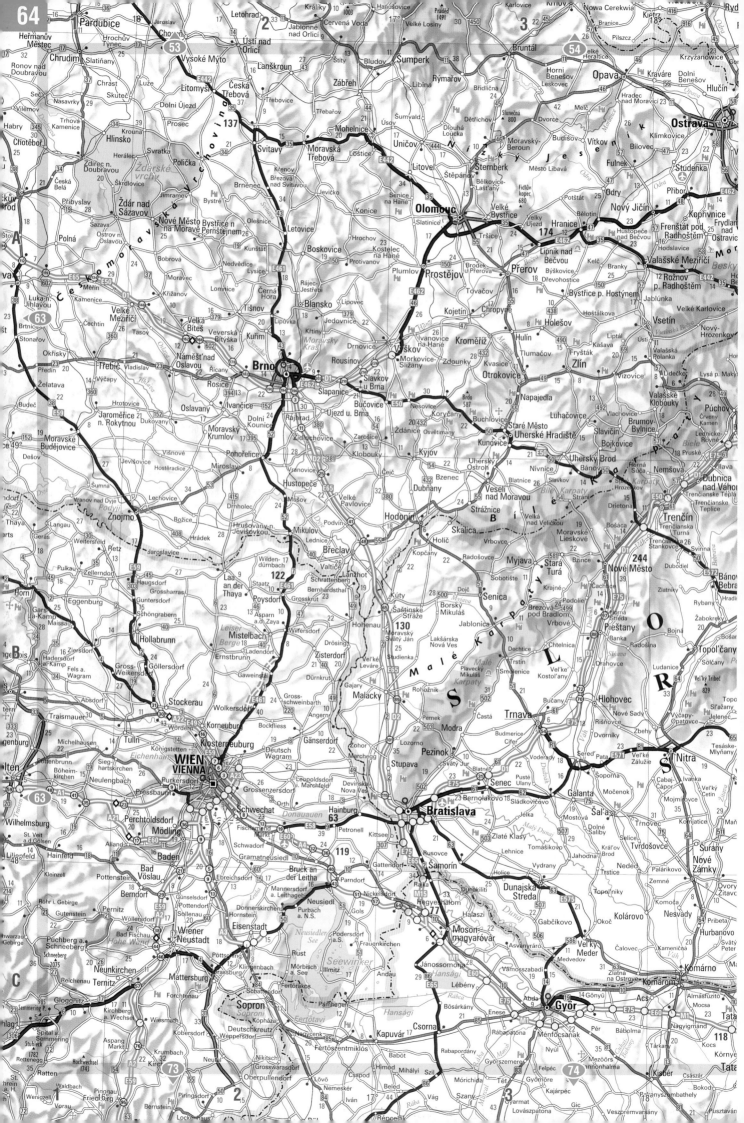

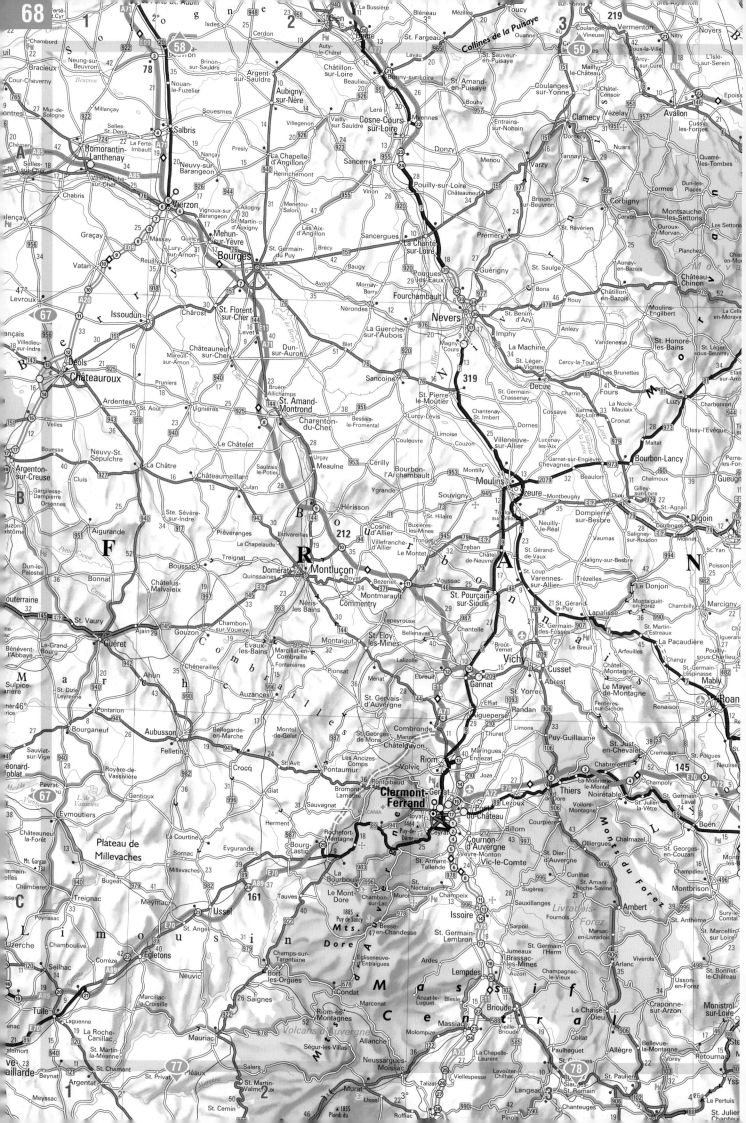

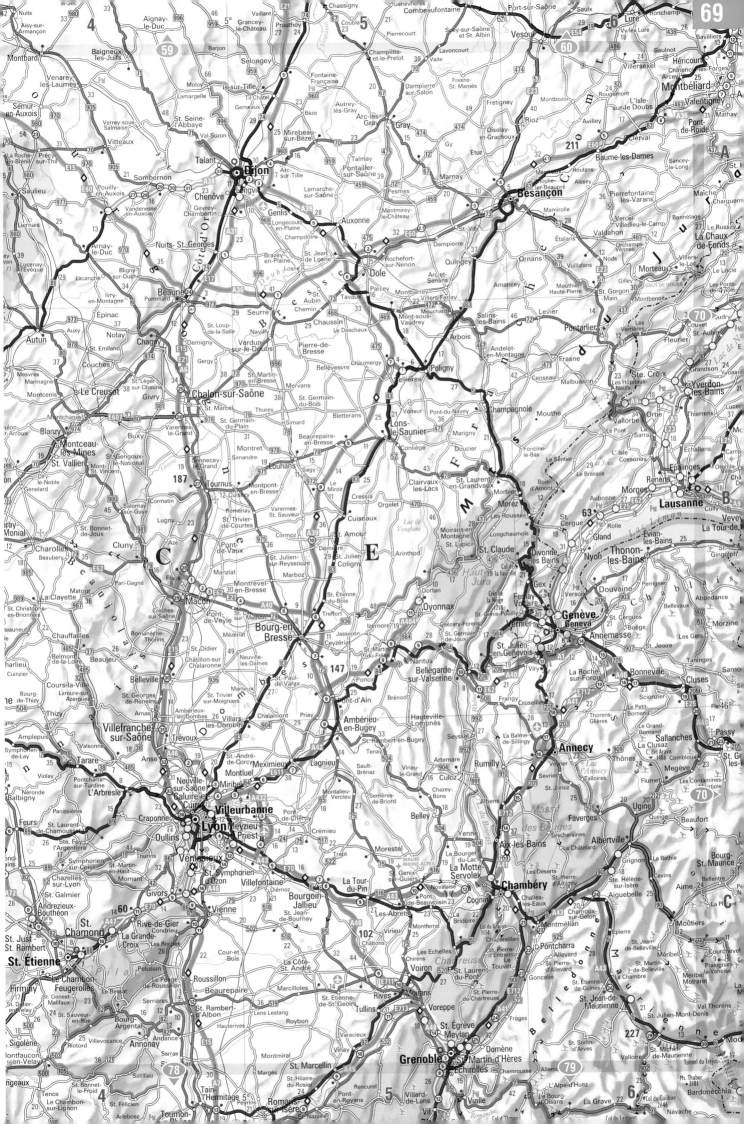

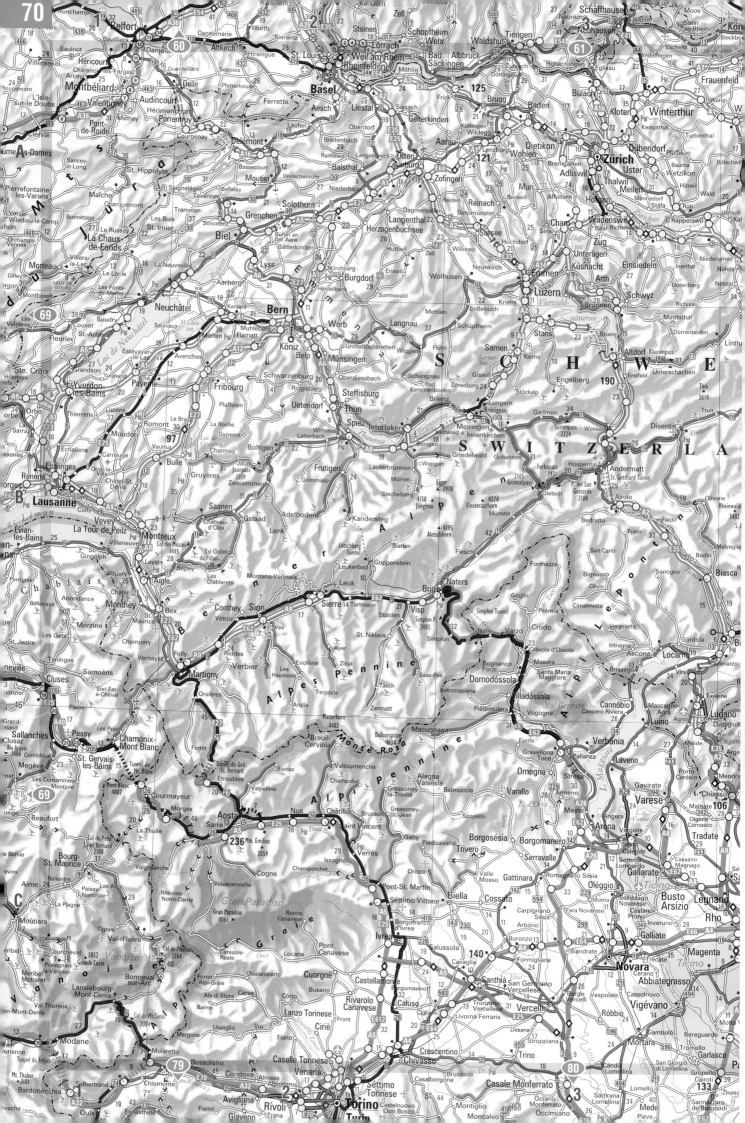

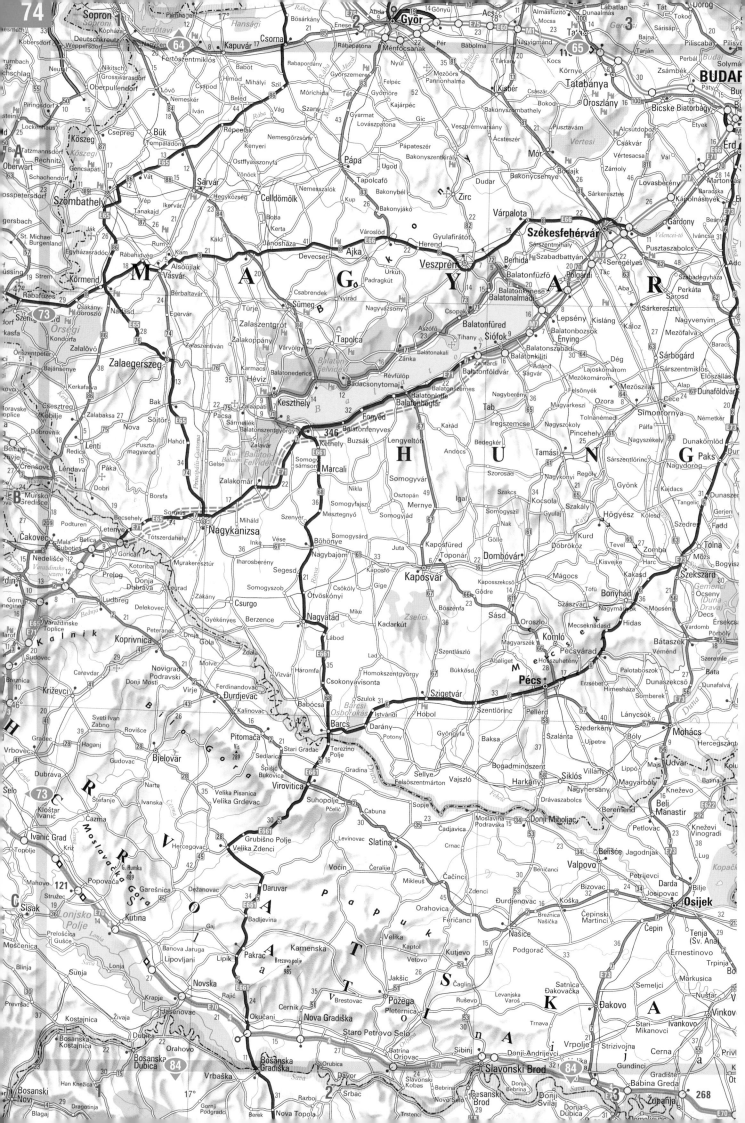

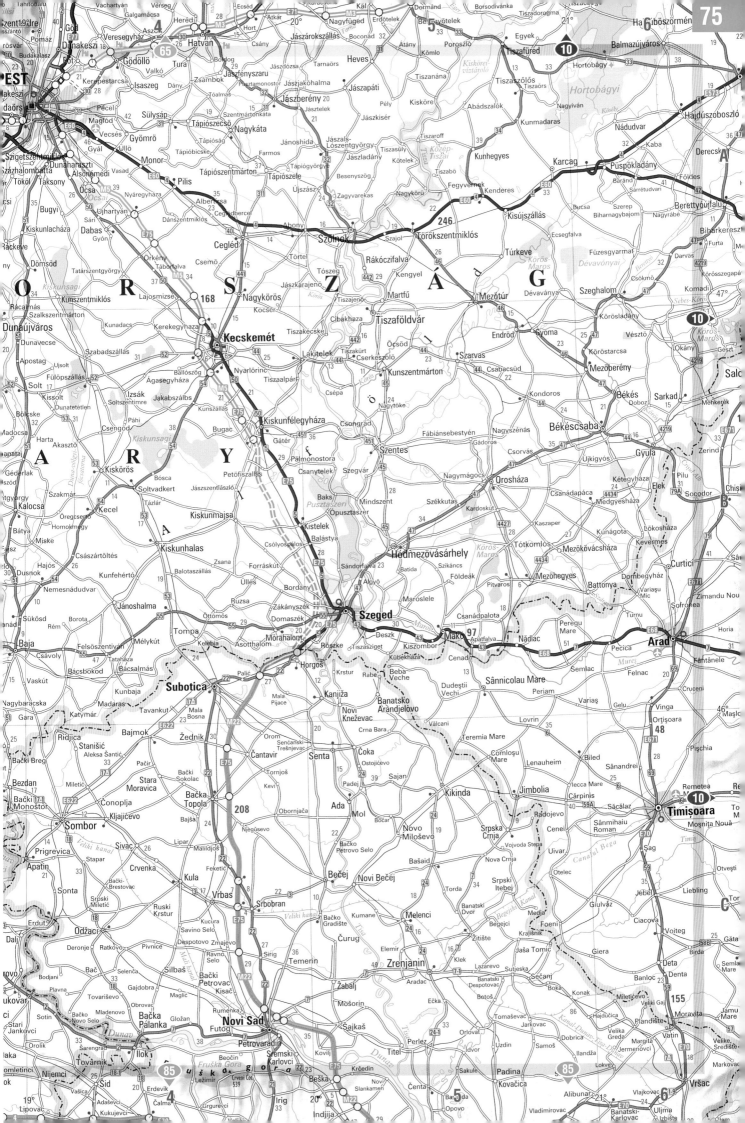

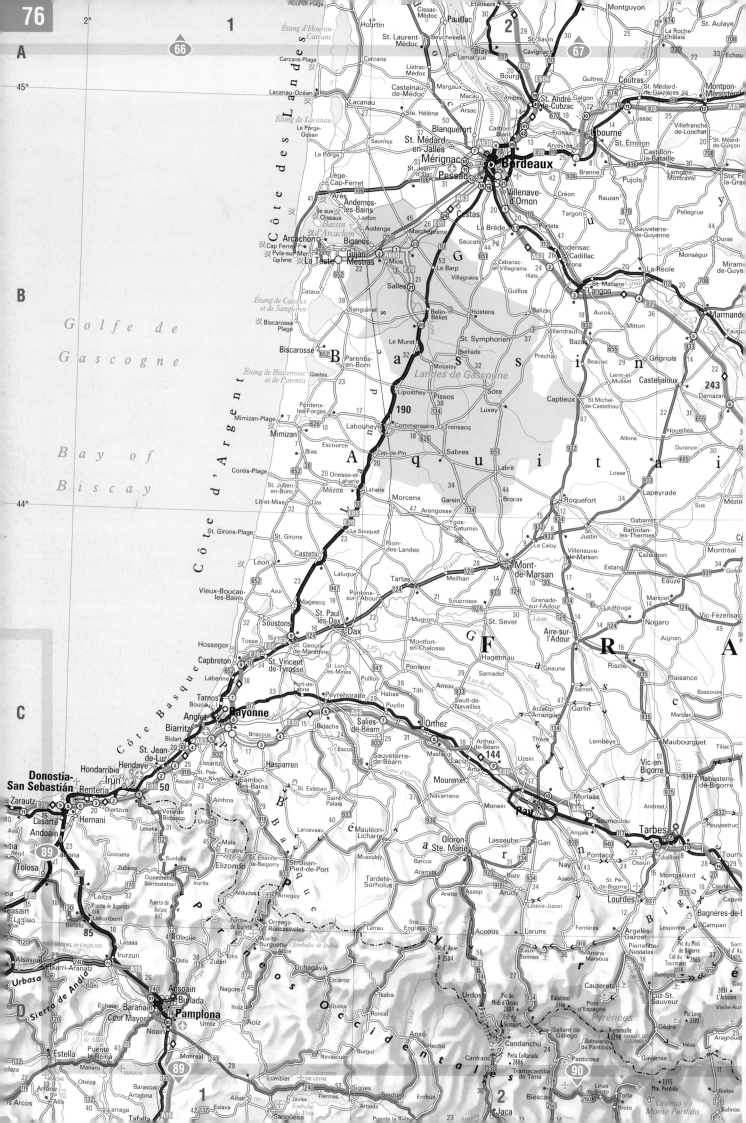

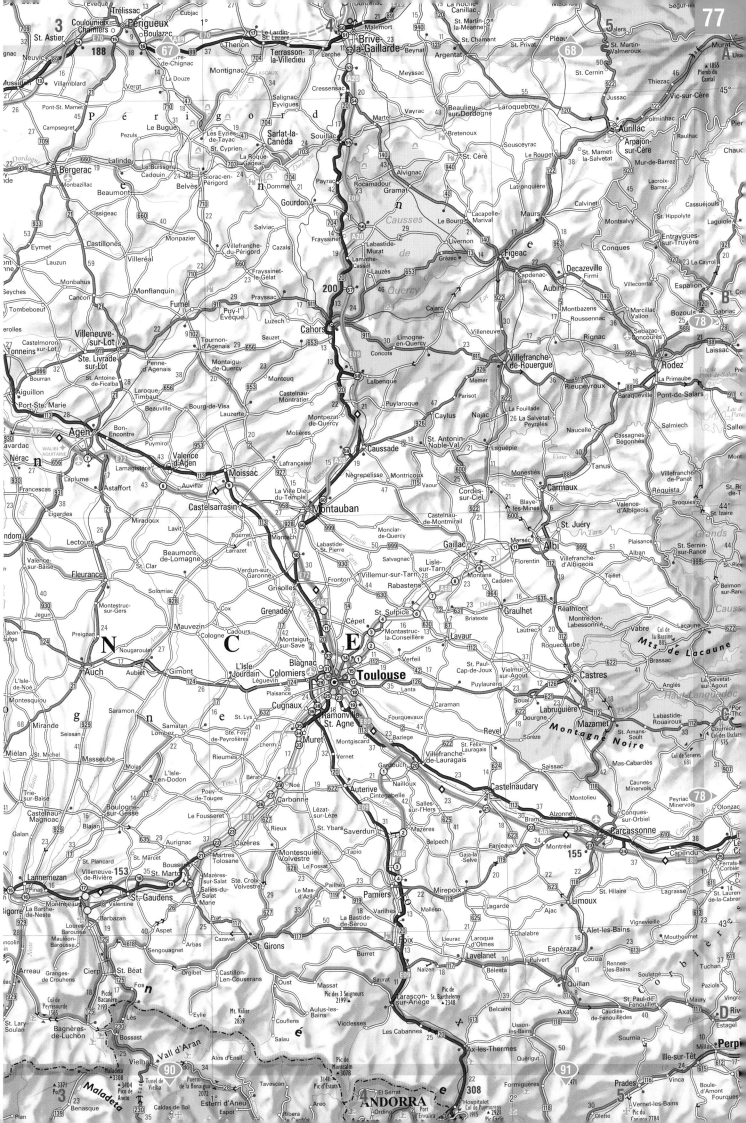

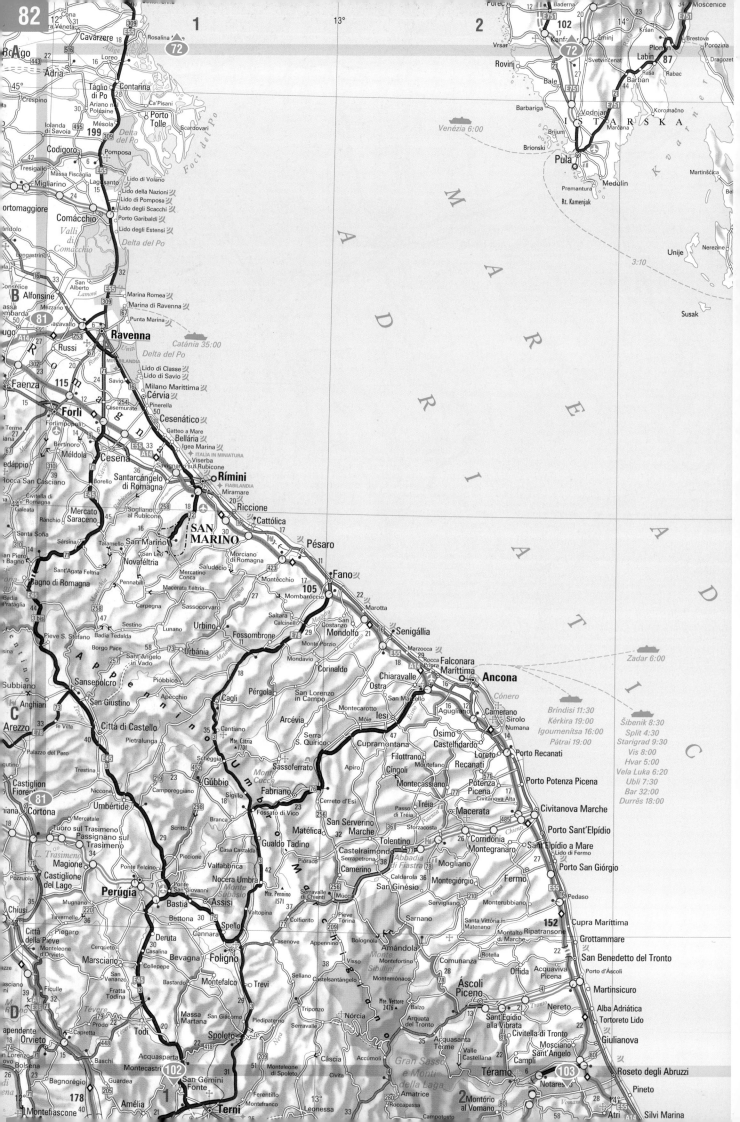

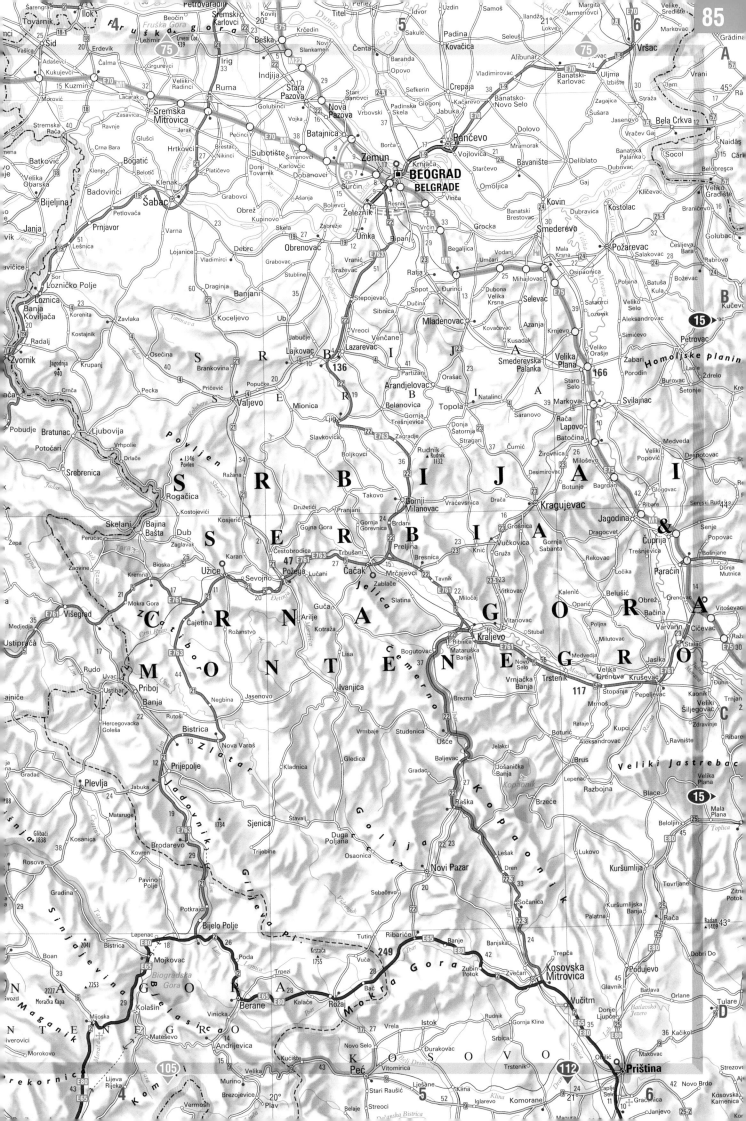

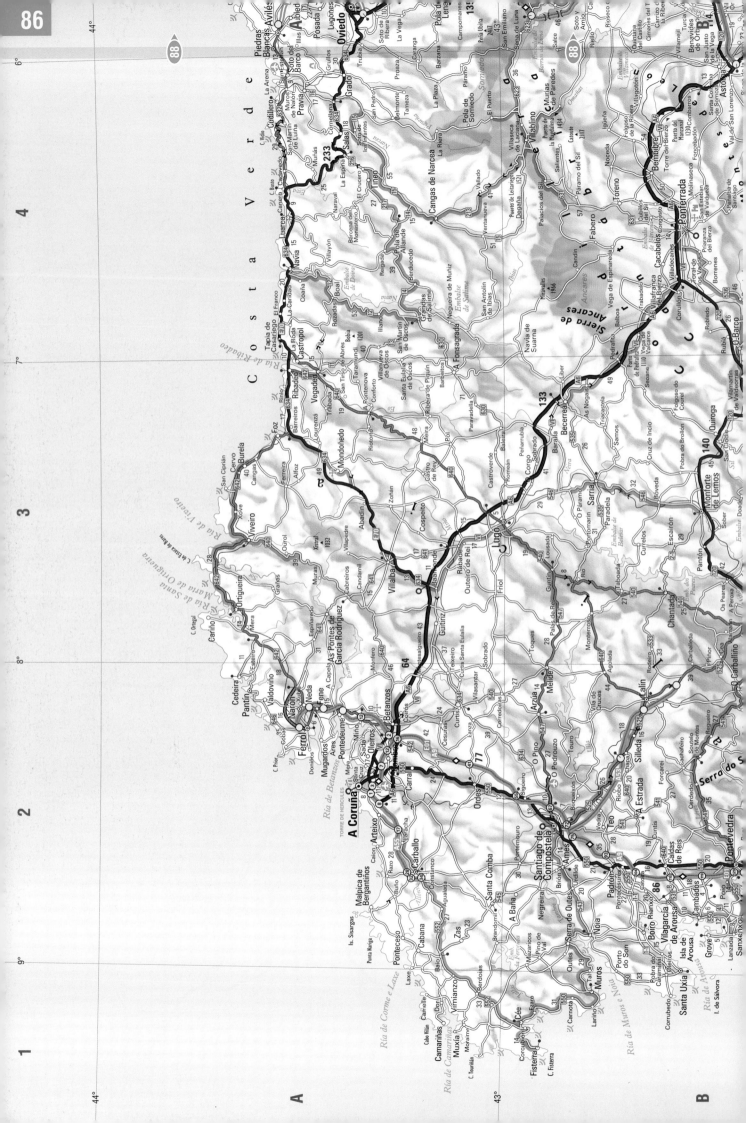

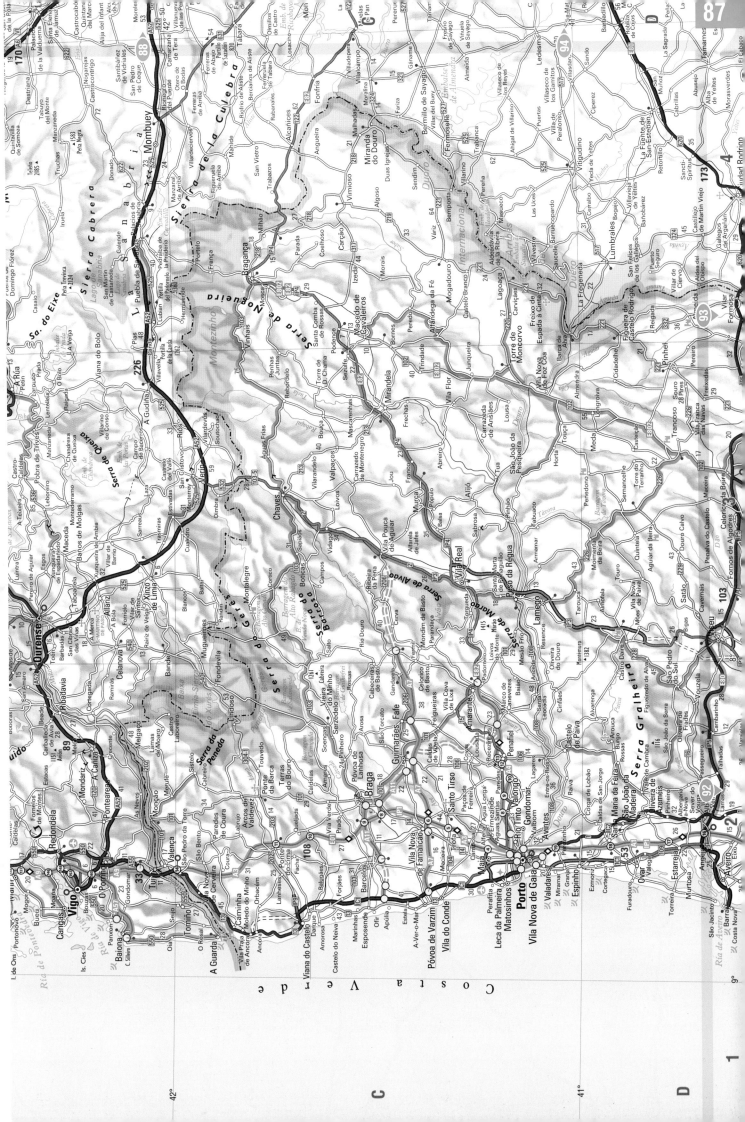

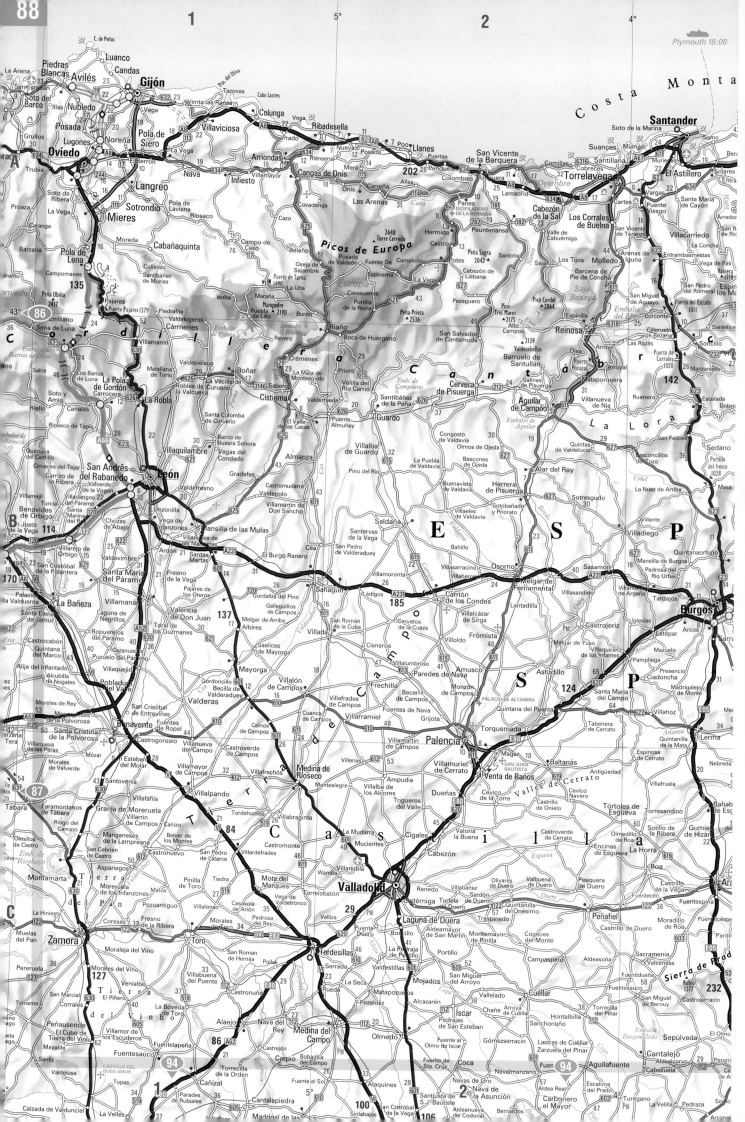

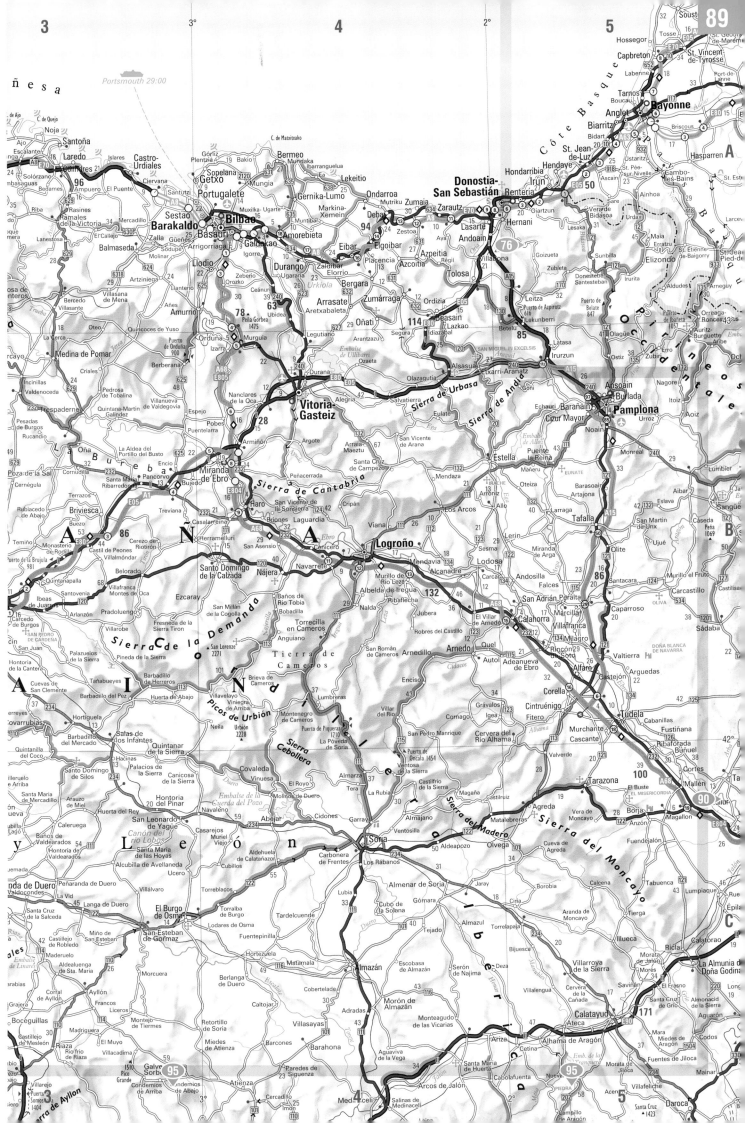

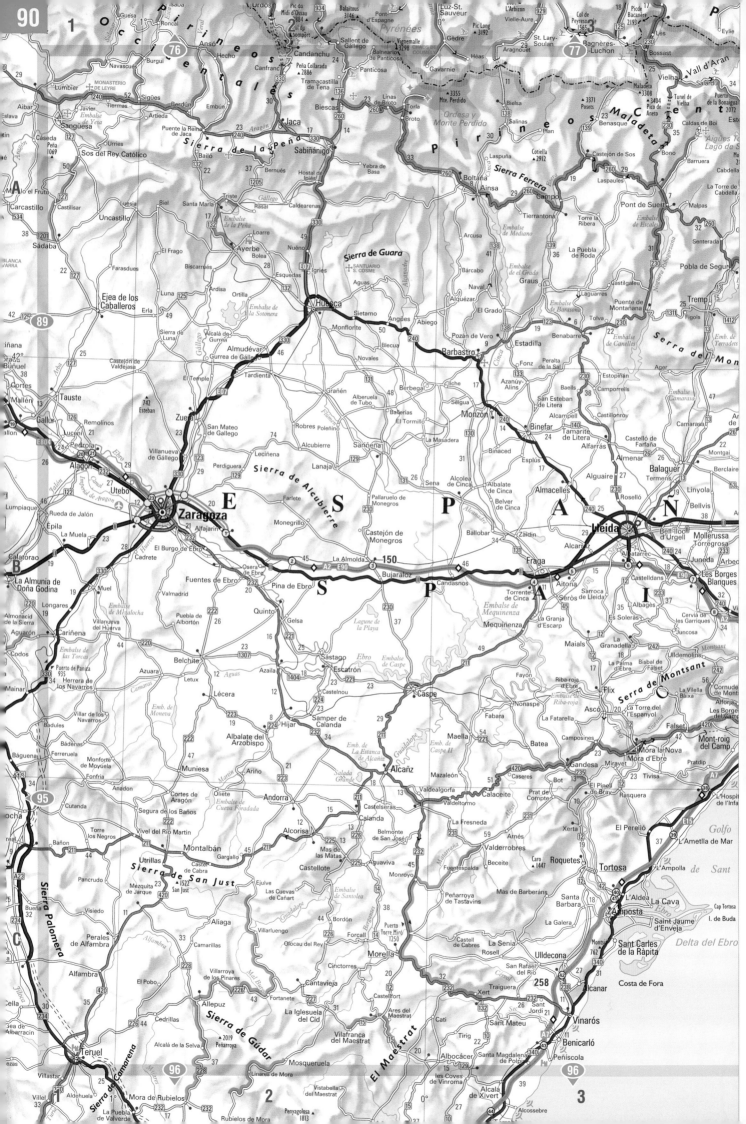

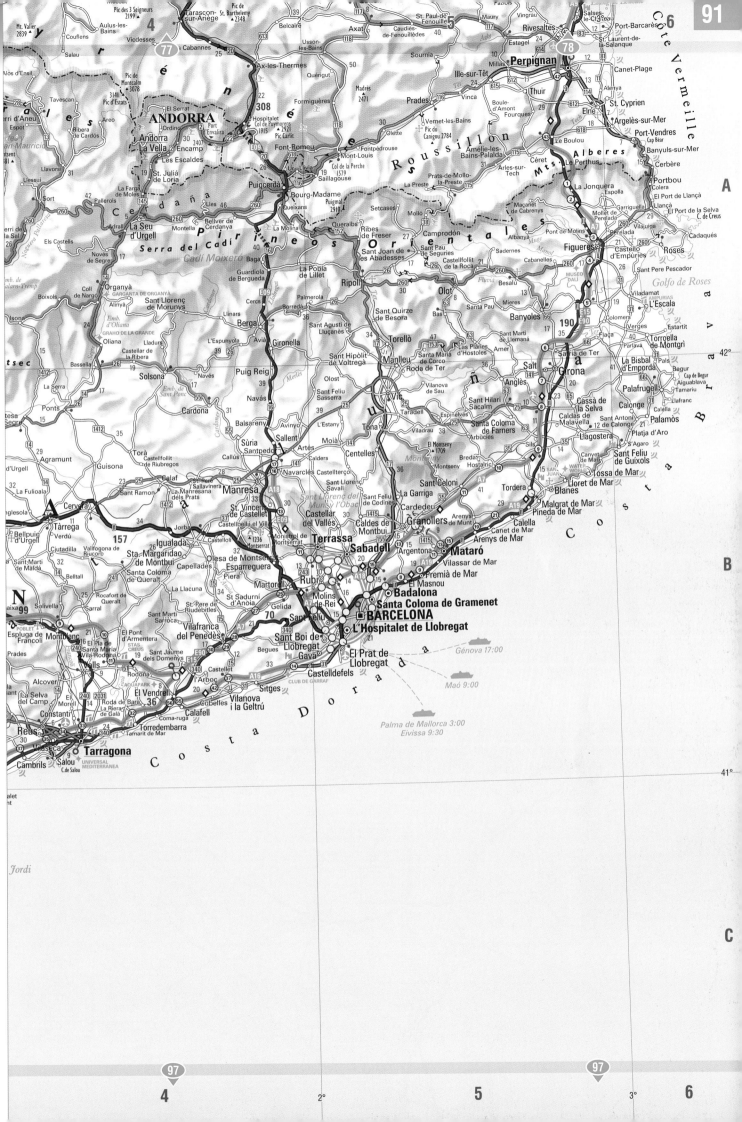

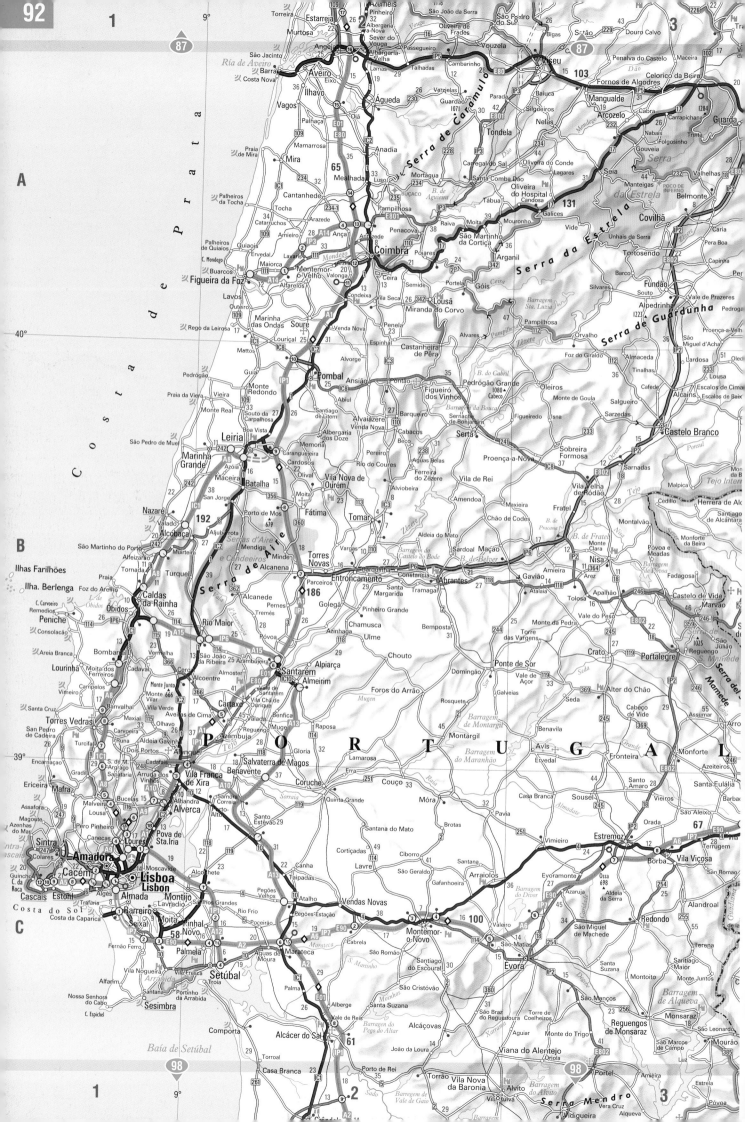

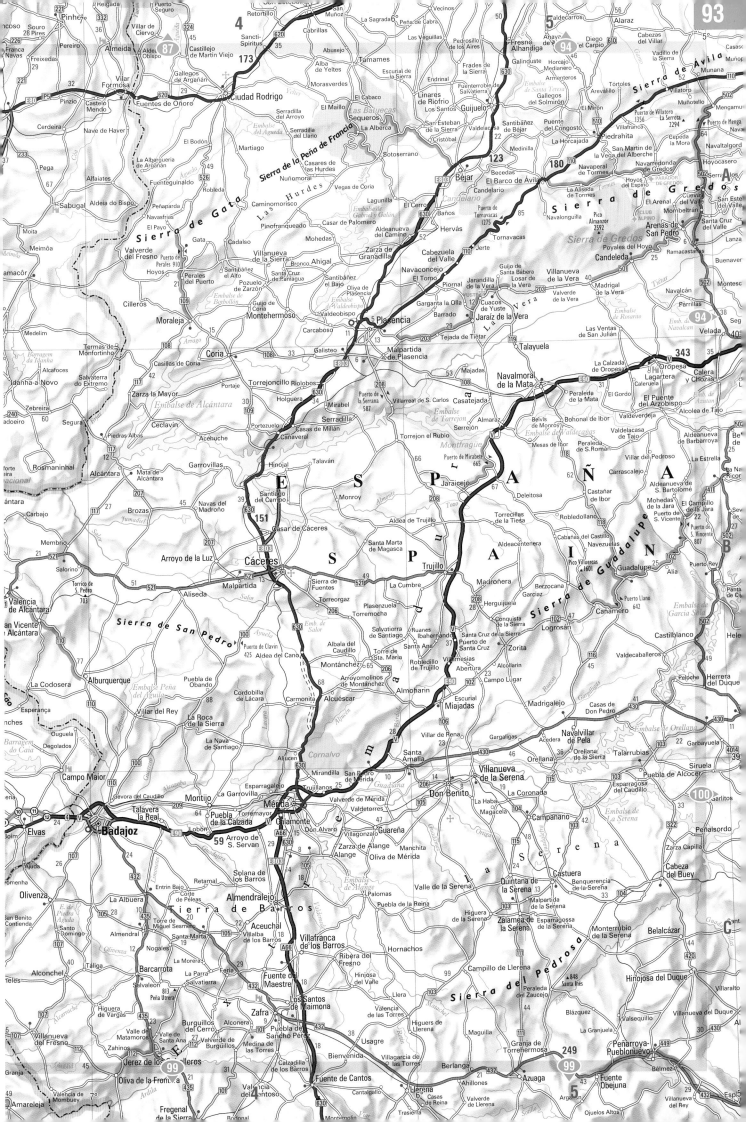

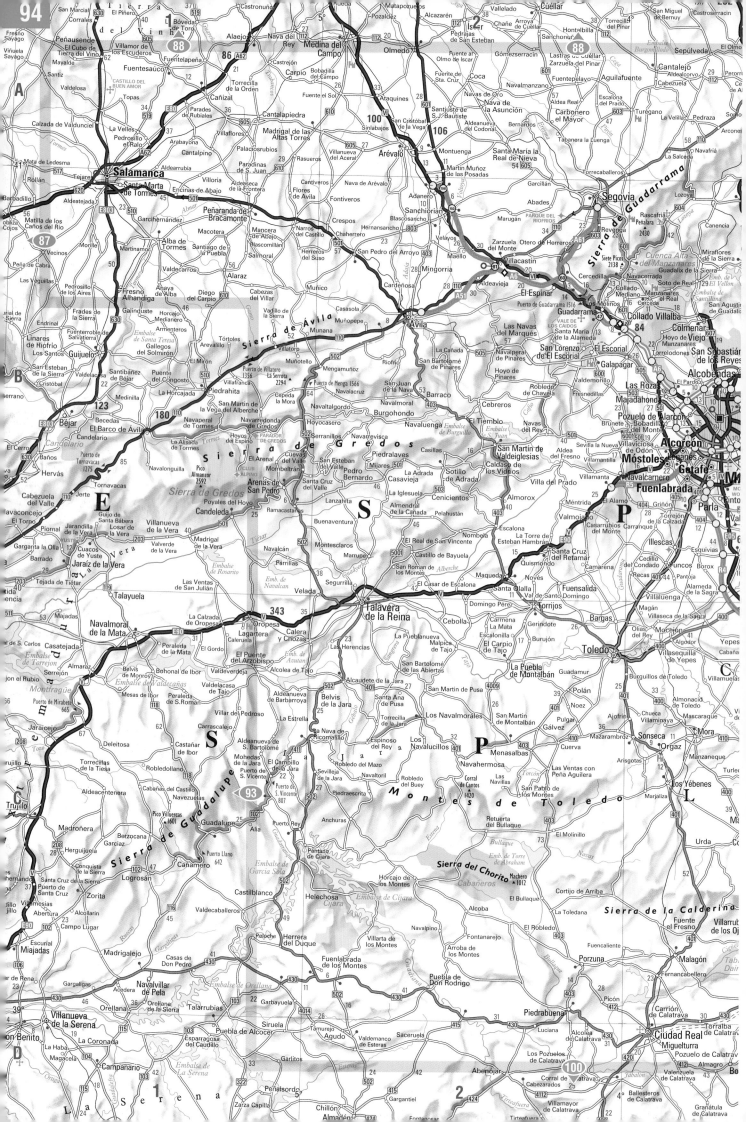

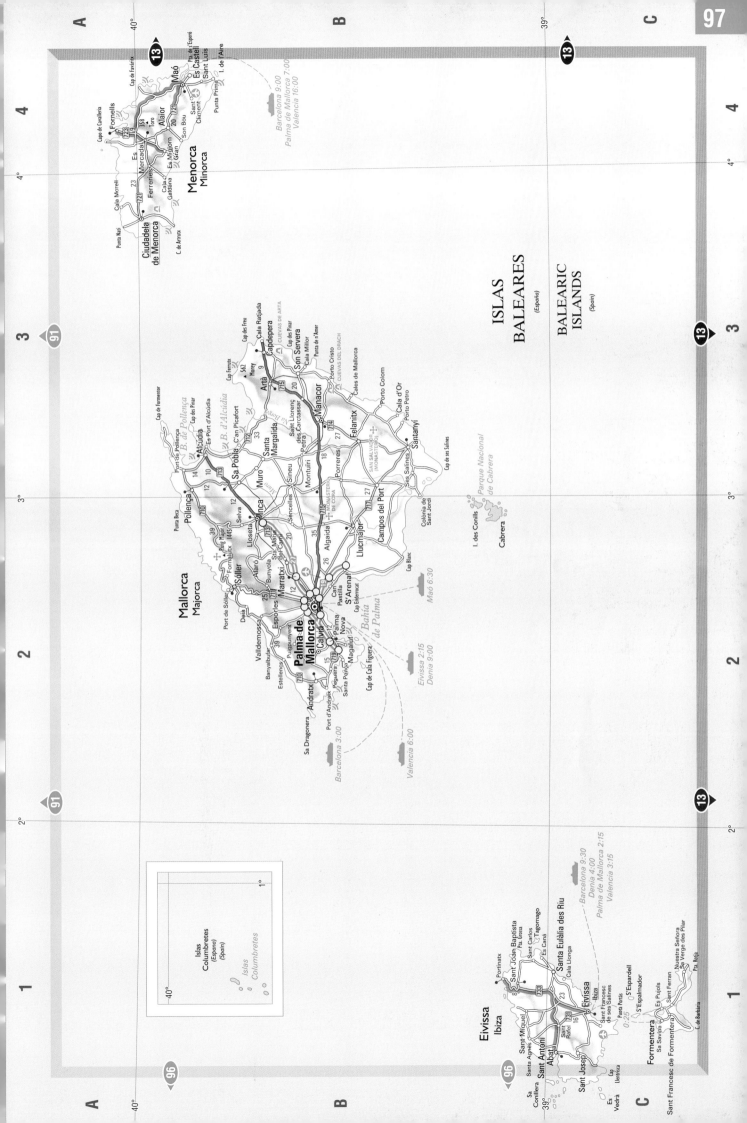

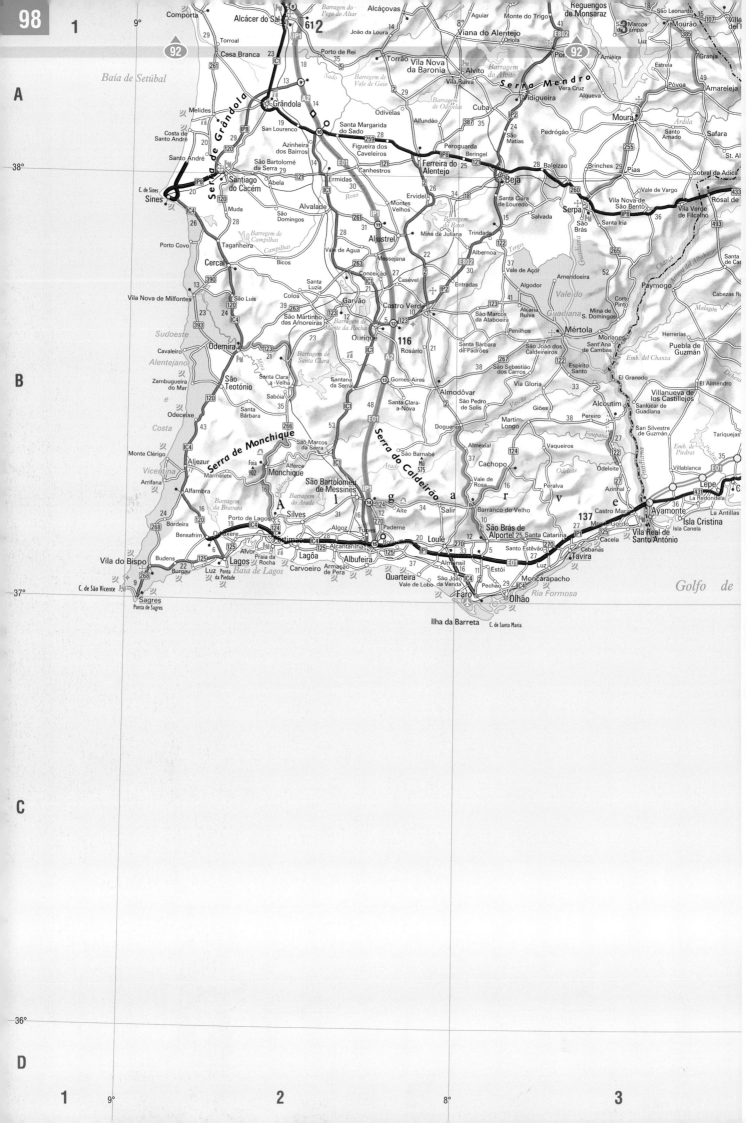

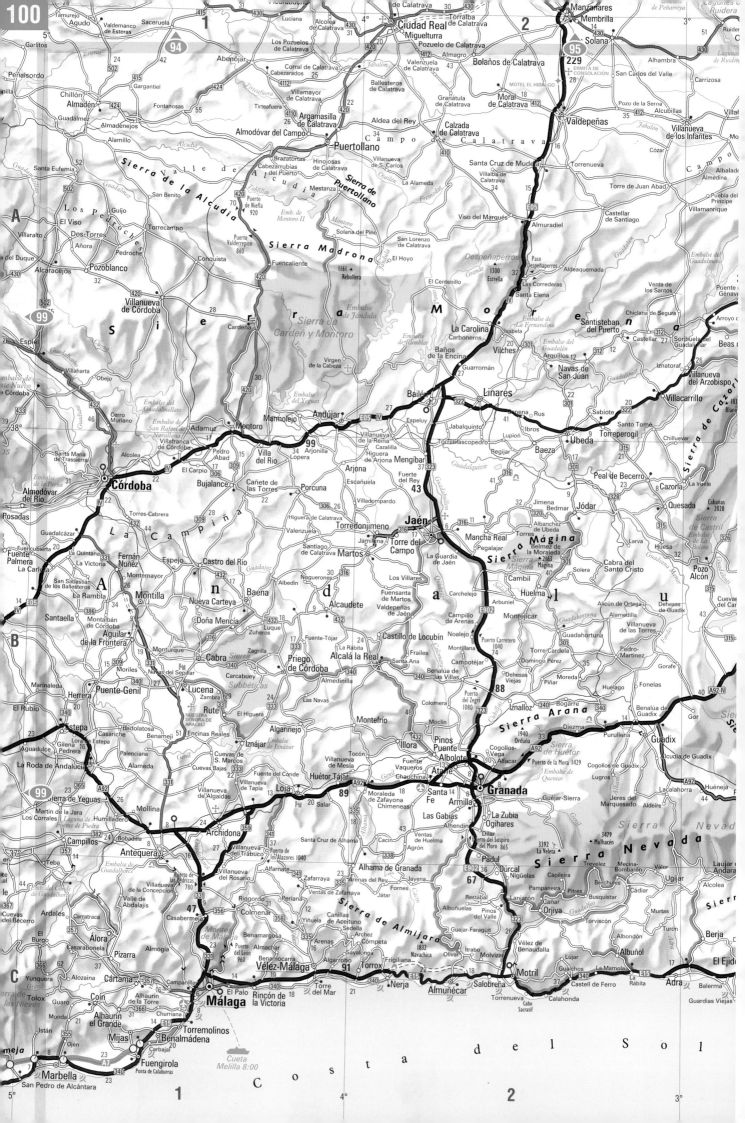

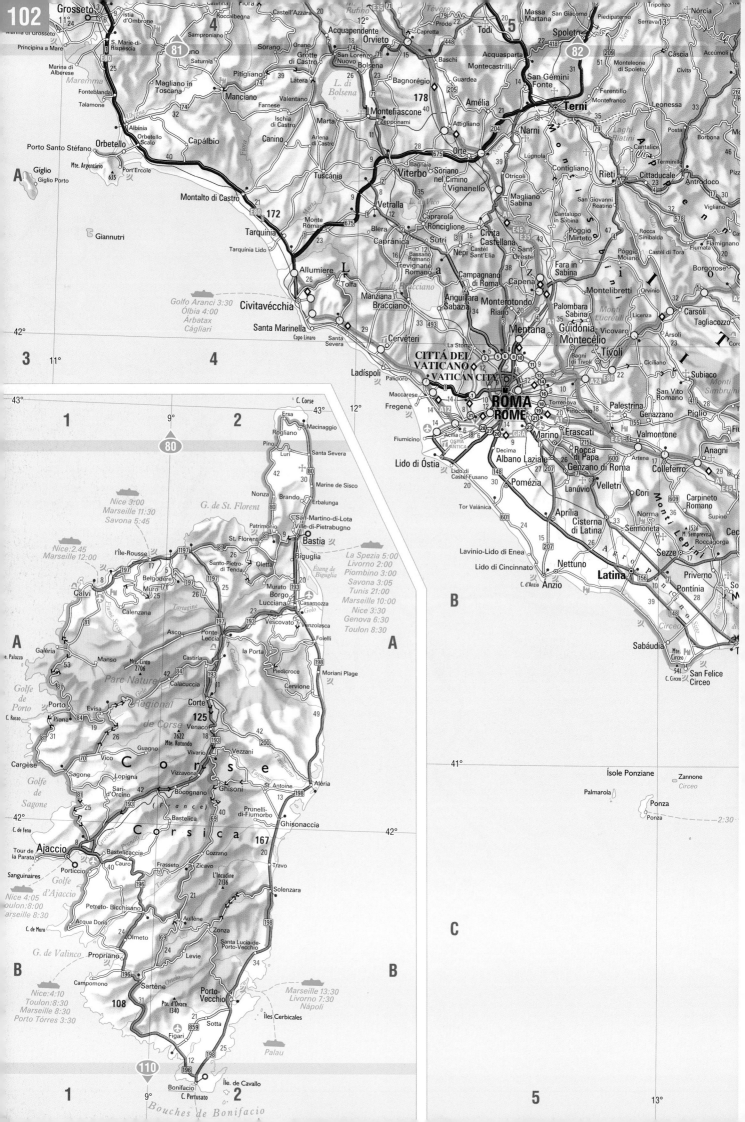

A

B

C

D

5

4

5

17°

18°

19°

40°

39°

38°

Map labels

Lido di Metaponto
Marina di Ginosa
Talsano
Pulsano
Lizzano
24
Sava
San Pancrazio Salentino
Guagnano
Trepuzzi
Surbo
Lecce
San Cataldo
Manduria
Torricella
Avetrana
Marúggio
29
Salice Salentino
Véglie
Campi Salentina
Monteroni di Lecce
San Cesário di Lecce
Vérnole
543
12
611
San Foca
Silvana
104
Leverano
174
Copertino
Léquile
101
Melendugno
Torre dell'Orso
34
105
di Scanzano
no Jónico
Golfo
Porto Cesáreo
20
Galatina
664
30
Calimera
Martano
Policoro
di
Nardò
Galátone
Cutrofiano
Soleto
Otranto
16
15
C. d'Otranto
Táranto
Santa Maria al Bagno
101
14
Máglie
Uggiano la Chiesa
ina
Gallípoli
Alézio
Collepasso
Poggiardo
lara
Sant'Andrea
Parábita
Casarano
Diso
Nociglia
275
Santa Cesárea Terme
40°
24
Ruffano
38
173
Castro
Taviano
Rácale
Miggiano
43
Ugento
274
Taurisano
Tricase
24
Presicce
Alessano
Marina di Nováglie
Castrignano del Capo
Gagliano del Capo
C. Santa Maria di Léuca
Marina di Léuca

C. Trionto
106
Crosia
13
E90
21
oriccio
383
Cariati
108
24
Pta. Fiume Nicá
Campana
Crúcoli
Pta. Alice
42
Cirò
Ciró Marina
Umbriático
San Nicola dell'Alto
Giovanni in Fiore
E90
106
Strôngoli
ri
Vitravo
31
Neto
23
107
Cotronei
Santa Severina
Roccabernarda
ro
20
Scandale
9
Crotone
Mesoraca
109
12
C. Colonna
Petronà
109
Cutro
Crópani
9
E90
25
Ísola di Capo Rizzuto
Botricello
106
C. Rizzuto
rina
olfo di
illace

Sea labels

Golfo
di
Táranto

MARE
IONIO
IONIAN
SEA

Malta inset

14° 30'
Gozo
Catánia 11:00
Reggio di Calábria 15:00
San Dimitri Pt
194
Victoria (Rabat)
6
Mgarr
Comino
36°
0:30
36°
San Pawl il-Bahar
Mellieha
Mosta
20
Sliema
240
Valletta
Rabat
Birkirkara
Paola
MALTA
253
Birzebbugia
Filfla
Benghisa Pt
14° 30'

112

113

15

15

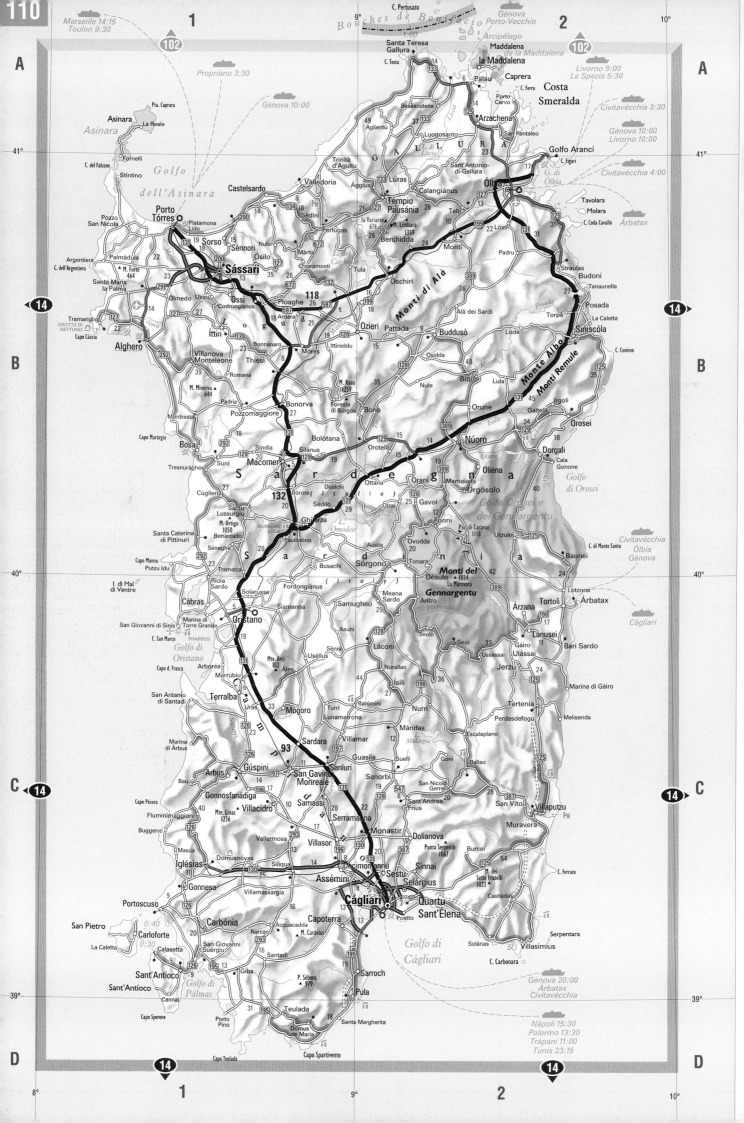

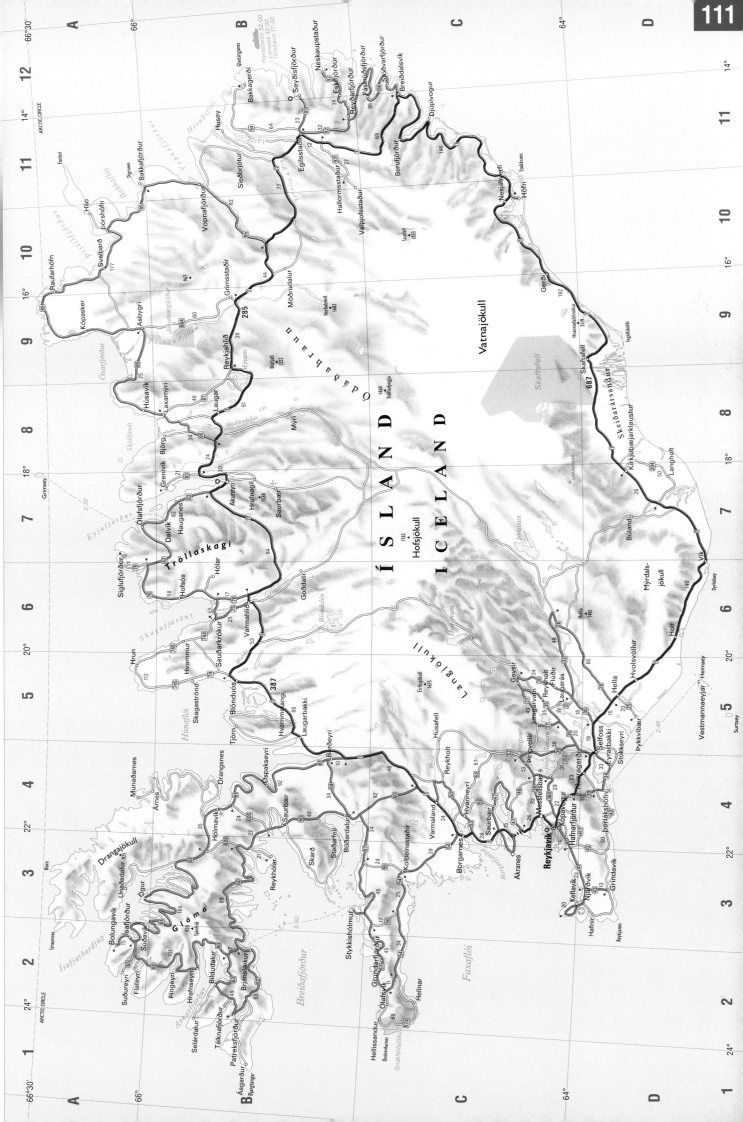

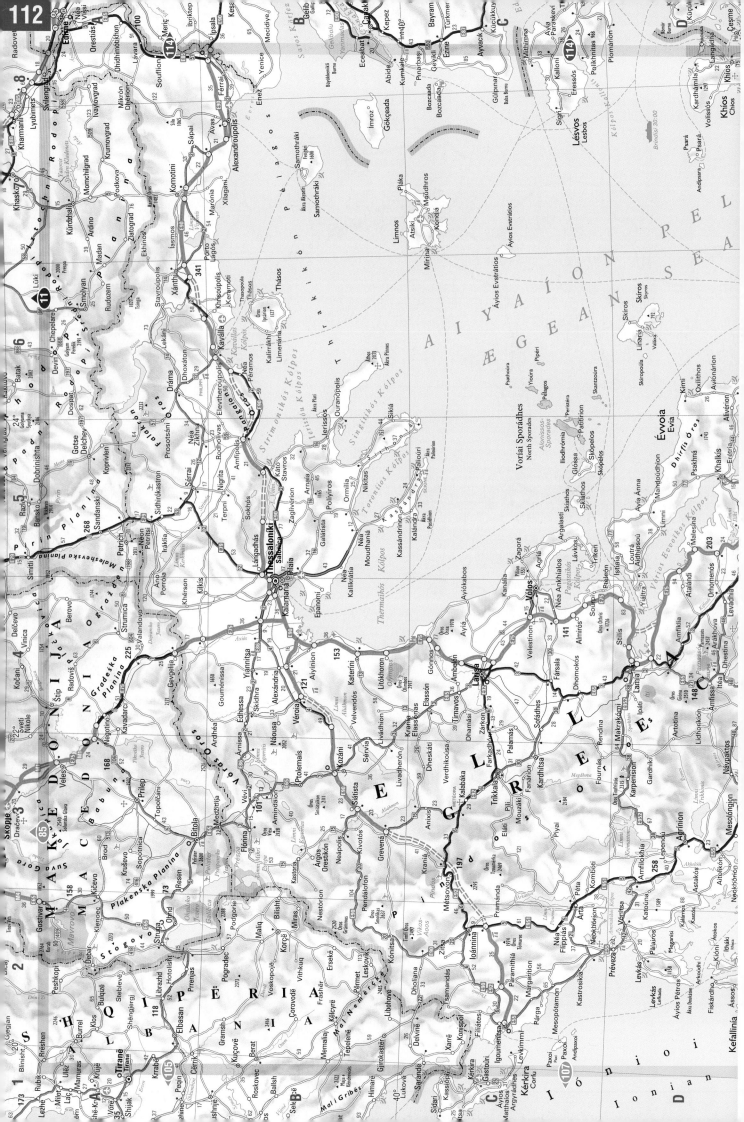

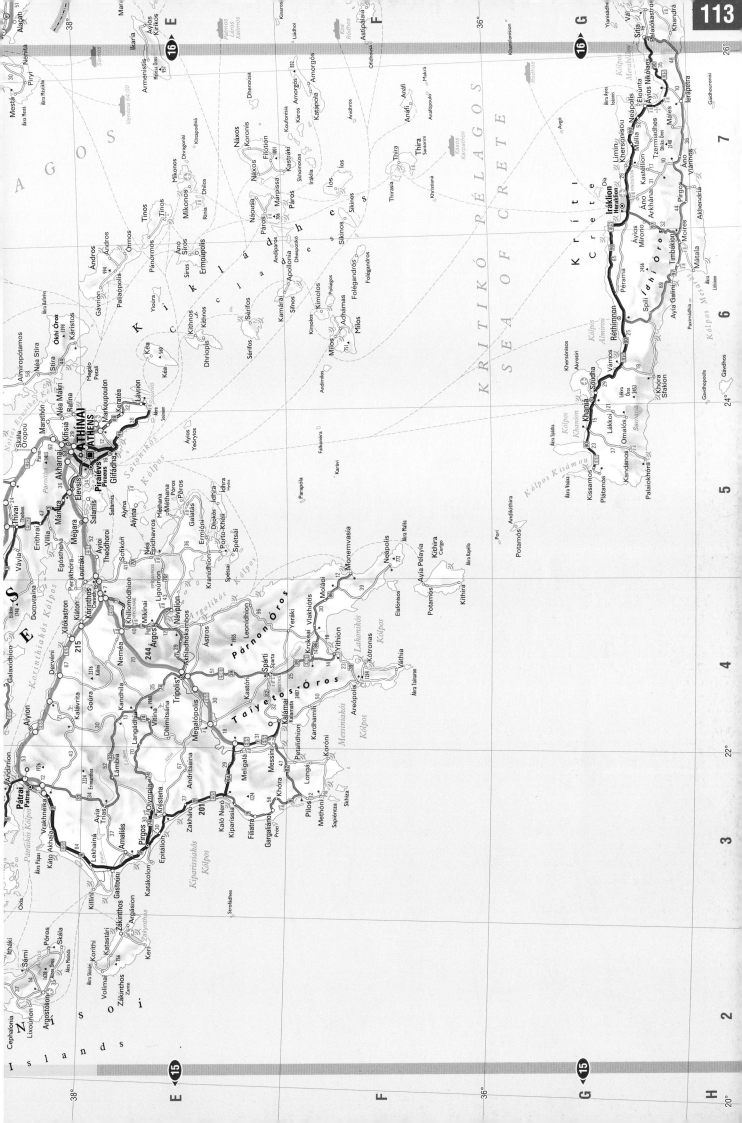

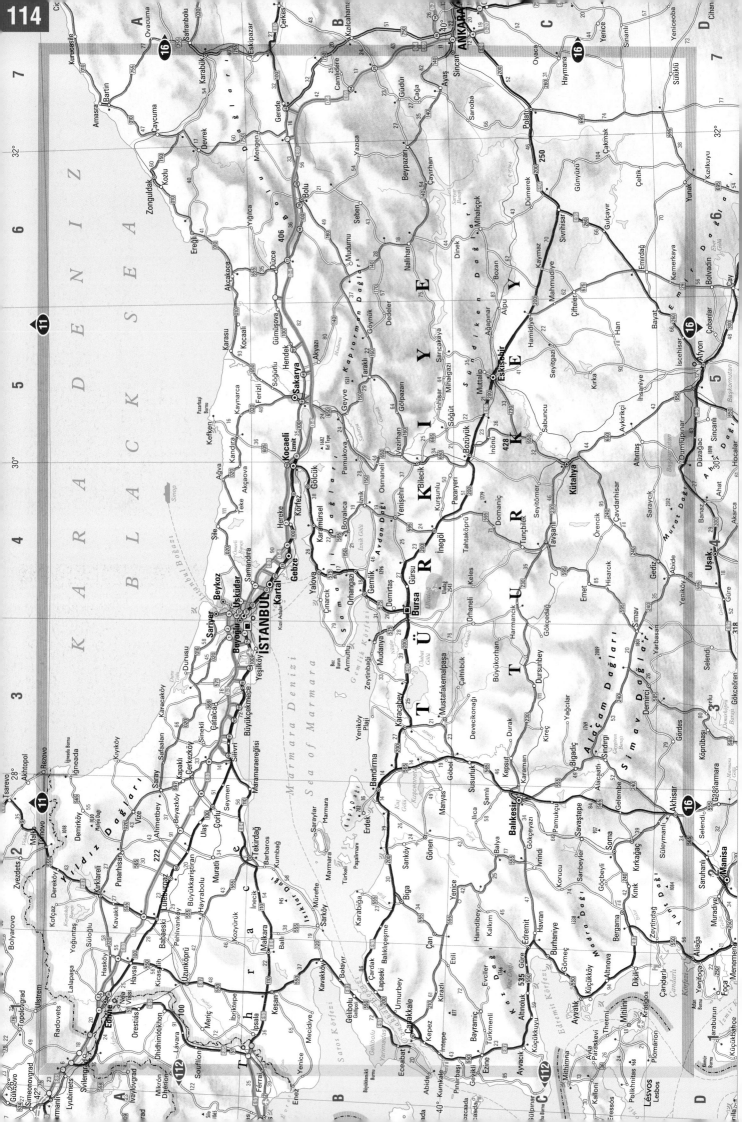

City plans • Plans de villes
Stadtpläne • Piante di città

Motorway	Autoroute		Autobahn	Autostrada
Major through route	Route principale majeur		Hauptstrecke	Strada di grande communicazione
Through route	Route principale		Schnellstrasse	Strada d'importanza regionale
Secondary road	Route secondaire		Nebenstrasse	Strada d'interesse locale
Dual carriageway	Chaussées séparées		Zweispurig Schnellstrasse	Strada a carreggiate doppie
Other road	Autre route		Nebenstrecke	Altra strada
Tunnel	Tunnel		Tunnel	Galleria stradale
Limited access / pedestrian road	Rue réglementée / rue piétonne		Beschränkter Zugang/ Fussgängerzone	Strada pedonale / a accesso limitato
One-way street	Sens unique		Einbahnstrasse	Senso unico
Parking	Parc de stationnement		Parkplatz	Parcheggio
Motorway number A7	Numéro d'autoroute		Autobahnnummer A7	Numero di autostrada
National road number 447	Numéro de route nationale		Nationalstrassen-nummer 447	Numero di strada nazionale
European road number E45	Numéro de route européenne		Europäische Strassennummer E45	Numero di strada europea
Destination GENT	Destination		Ziel GENT	Destinazione
Car ferry	Bac passant les autos		Autofähre	Traghetto automobili
Railway	Chemin de fer		Eisenbahn	Ferrovia
Rail/bus station	Gare / gare routière		Bahnhof / Busstation	Stazione ferrovia / pullman
Underground, metro station	Station de métro		U-Bahnstation	Metropolitano
Cable car	Téléférique		Drahtseilbahn	Funivia
Abbey, cathedral †	Abbaye, cathédrale		Abtei, Kloster, Kathedrale †	Abbazia, duomo
Church of interest †	Église intéressante		Interessante Kirche †	Chiesa da vedere
Synagogue ✡	Synagogue		Synagoge ✡	Sinagoga
Hospital	Hôpital		Krankenhaus	Ospedale
Police station POL	Police		Polizeiwache POL	Polizia
Post office	Bureau de poste		Postamt	Ufficio postale
Tourist information i	Office de tourisme		Informationsbüro i	Ufficio informazioni turistiche
Place of interest Theatre	Autre curiosité		Sonstige Sehenswürdigkeit Theatre	Luogo da vedere

Approach maps • Agglomérations
Carte régionale • Regionalkarte

Toll motorway – with motorway number A10	Autoroute – avec numéro d'autoroute		Gebührenpflichtige Autobahn – mit Autobahnnummer A10	Autostrada a pedaggio – con numero
Toll-free motorway with European road number E51	Autoroute avec numéro de route européenne		Gebührenfreie Autobahn – Europäische Strassennummer E51	Autostrada – con numero di strada europea
Motorway services	Aire de service		Autobahnservice	Area di servizio autostradale
Motorway junction 24	Échangeur d'autoroute		Autobahnkreuz 24	Raccordi autostradali
Under construction	En construction		Im Bau	In construzione
Tunnel	Tunnel		Tunnel	Galleria stradale
Major route dual carriageway 14 single carriageway 14	Route principale chausées séparées chausée sans séparation		Hauptstrecke zweispurige 14 Schnellstrasse 14	Strada di grande communicazione carreggiata doppia carreggiata unica
Secondary route dual carriageway 96 single carriageway 96	Route secondaire chaussées séparées chausée sans séparation		Nebenstrasse zweispurige 96 Schnellstrasse 96	Strada d'interesse locale carreggiata doppia carreggiata unica
Other road	Autre route		Nebenstrecke	Altra strada
Car ferry	Bac passant les autos		Autofähre	Traghetto automobili
Destination GIRONA	Destination		Ziel GIRONA	Destinazione
Railway	Chemin de fer		Eisenbahn	Ferrovia
Railway station Estación Central	Gare		Hauptbahnhof Estación Central	Stazione ferrovia
Height above sea level – in metres 234	Altitude – en mètres		Höhe über dem Meeresspiegel 234	Altezza in metri
Airport	Aéroport principal		Flughafen	Aeroporto
Airfield	Autre aéroport		Flugplatz	Aerodromo/campo d'aviazione
City plan coverage area	Région de plan de ville		Vom Stadtplan abgedecktes Gebiet	Area della pianta della città

Alicante
0 — km — 0.5

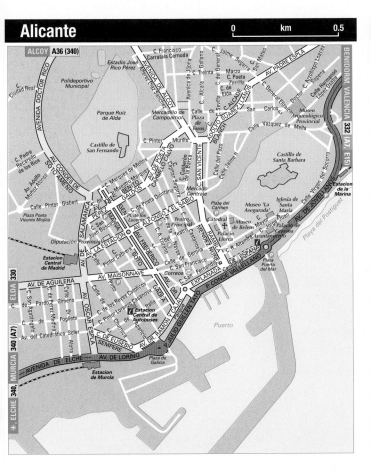

Antwerpen Antwerp
0 — km — 1

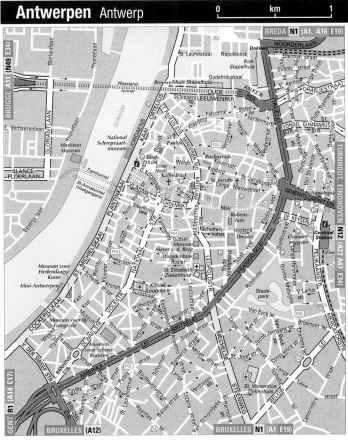

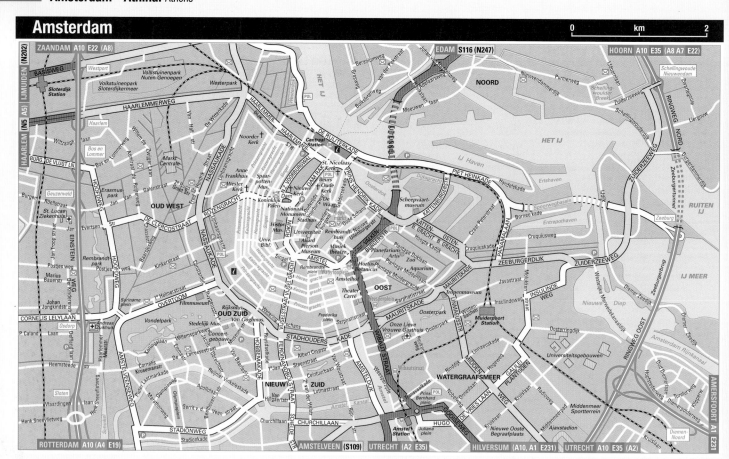

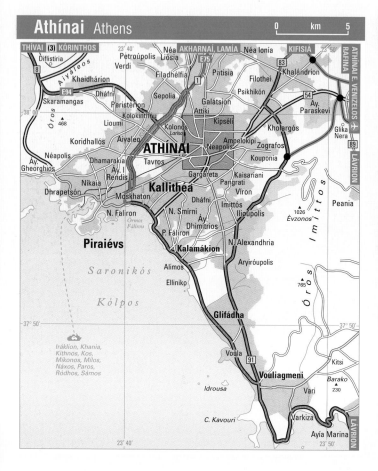

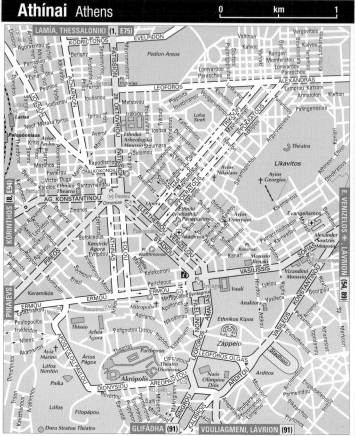

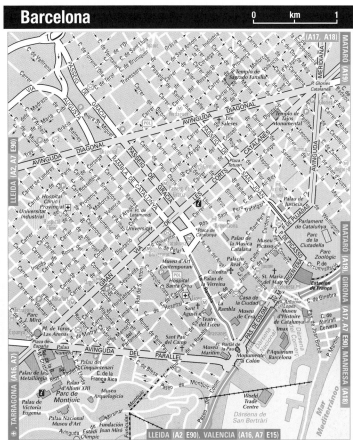

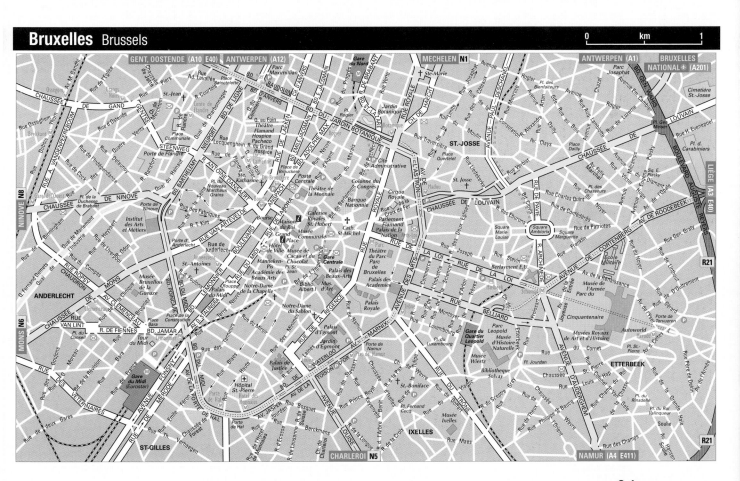

For **Cologne** see page 125
For **Copenhagen** see page 124

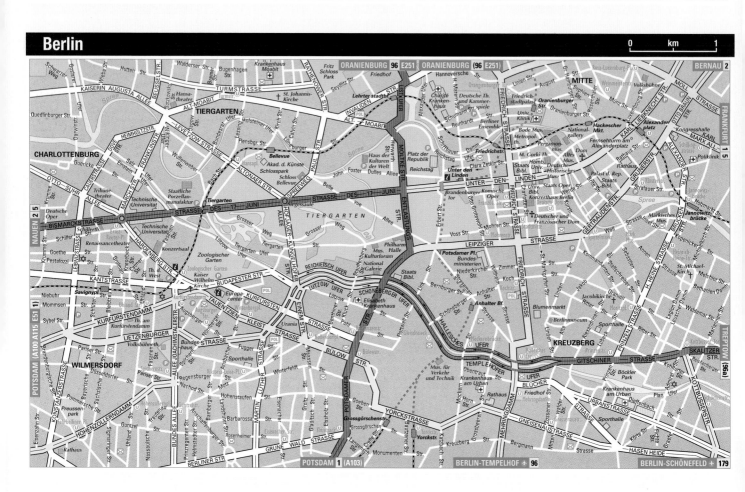

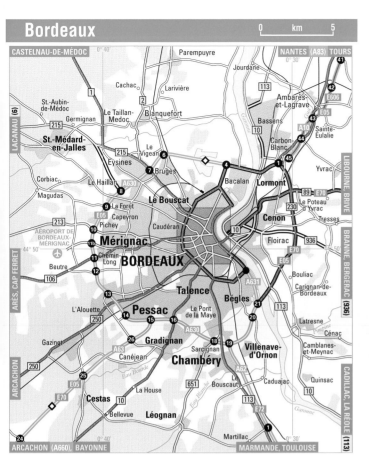

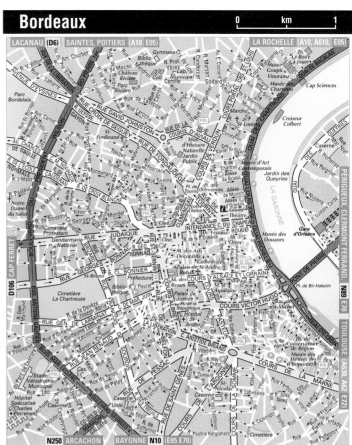

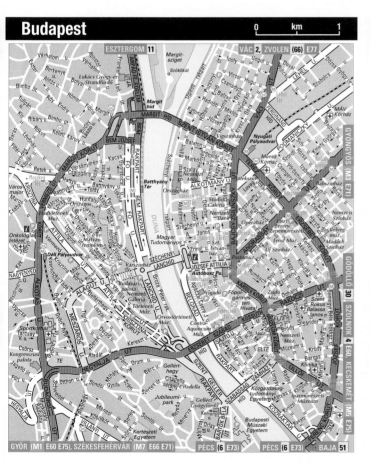

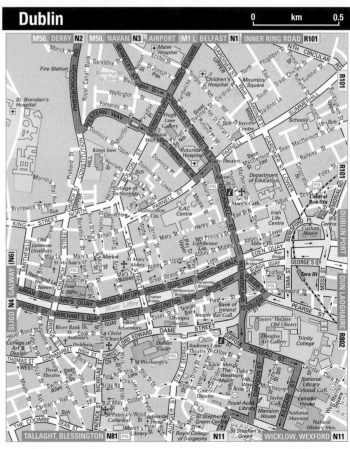

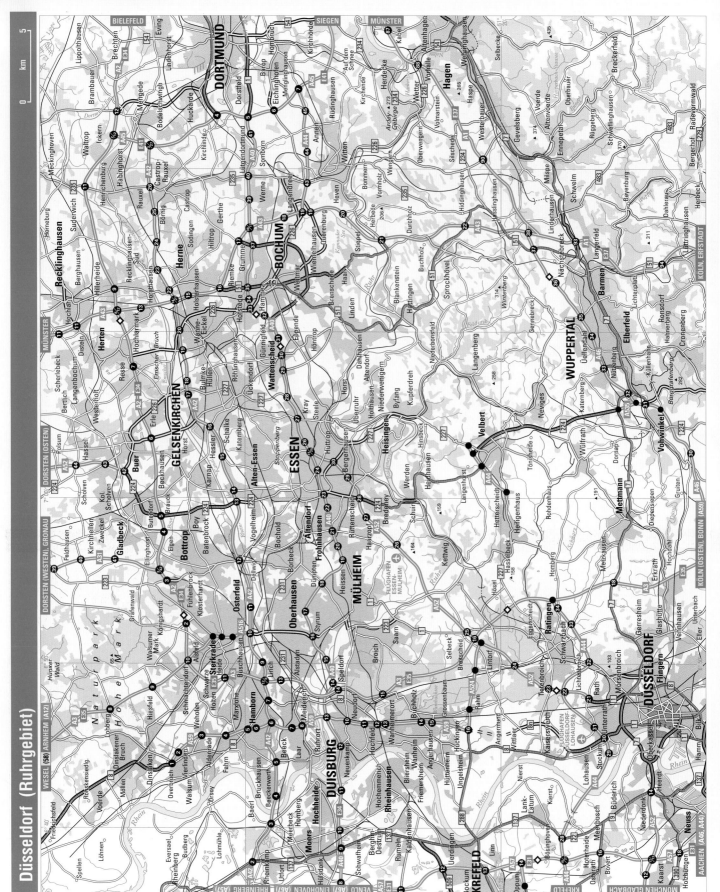

Düsseldorf

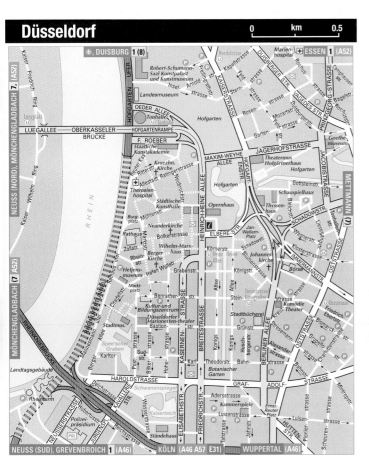

Edinburgh

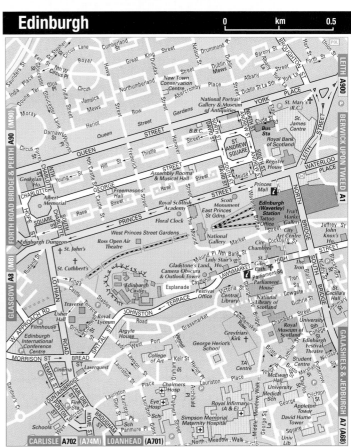

Firenze Florence

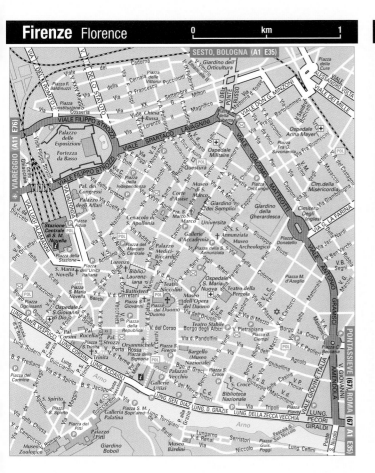

Frankfurt

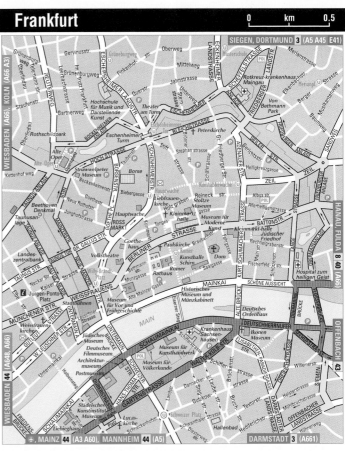

Genève Geneva

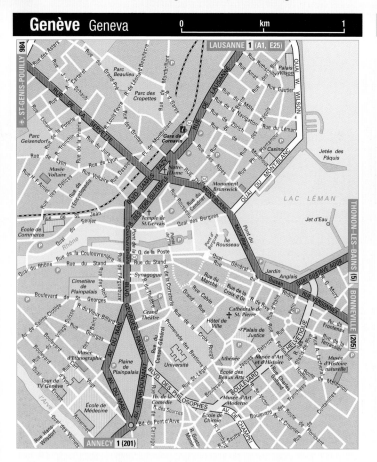

Göteborg Gothenburg

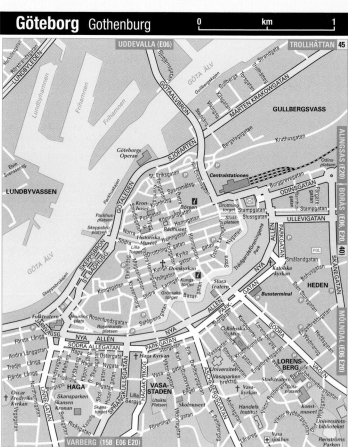

Hamburg

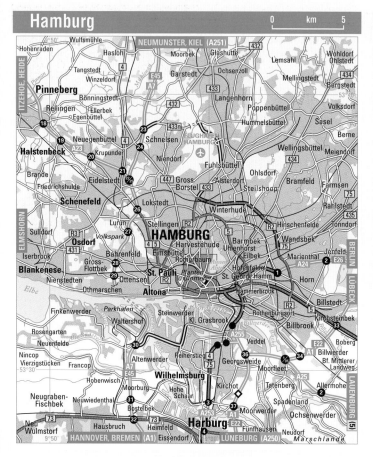

Hamburg

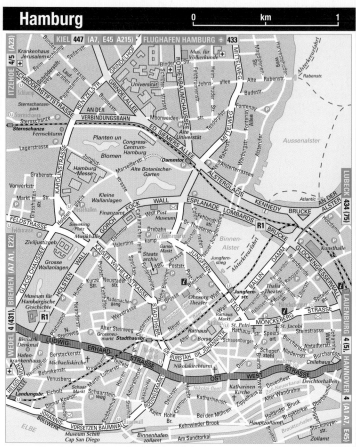

Helsinki

0 km 10

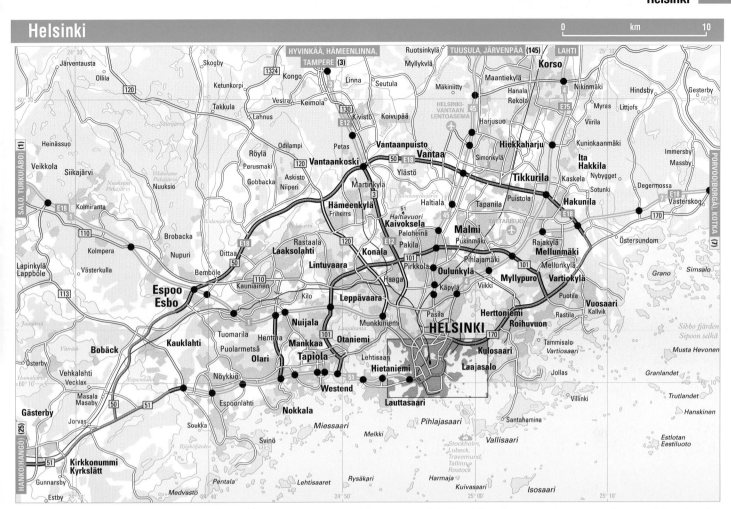

Helsinki

0 km 1

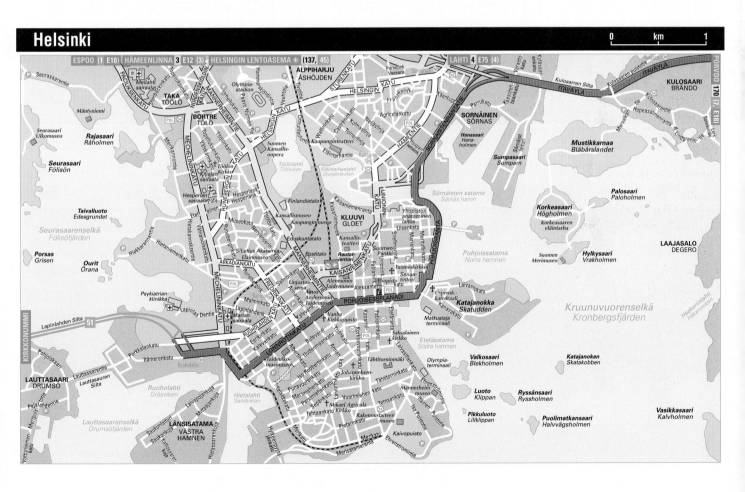

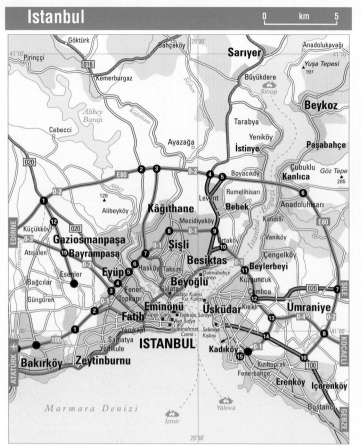

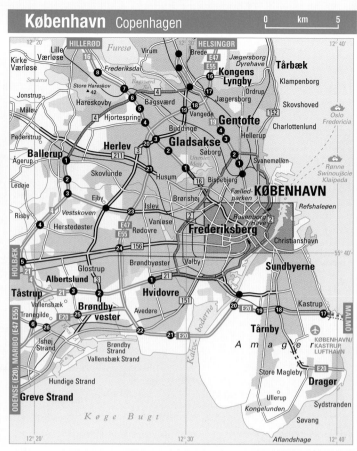

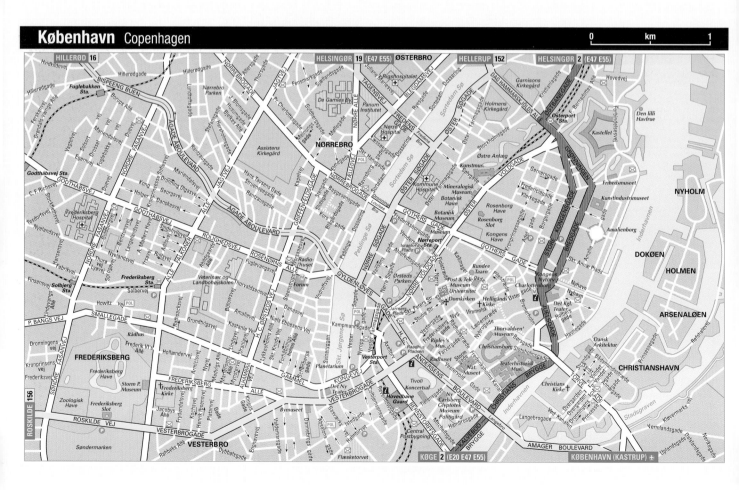

Köln Cologne

0 — km — 1

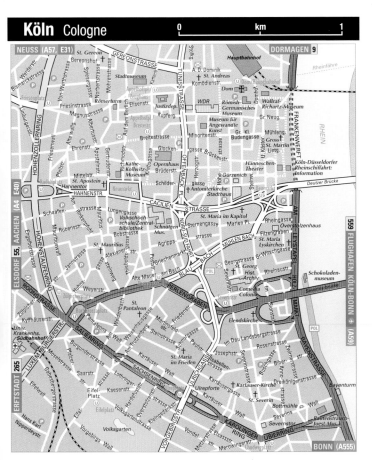

Luxembourg

0 — km — 0.5

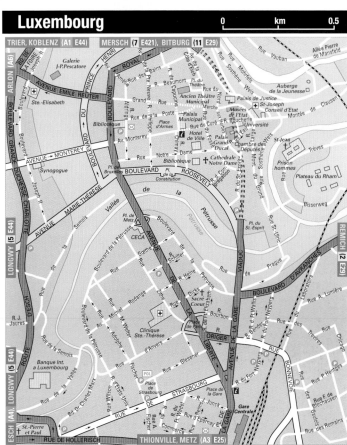

Lisboa Lisbon

0 — km — 5

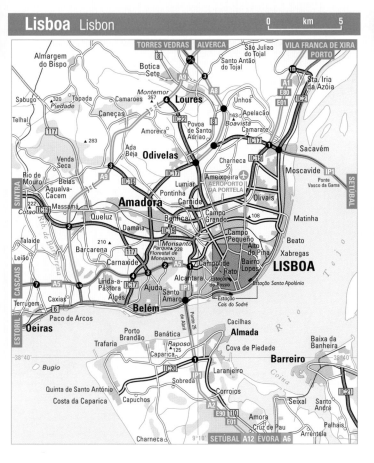

Lisboa Lisbon

0 — km — 1

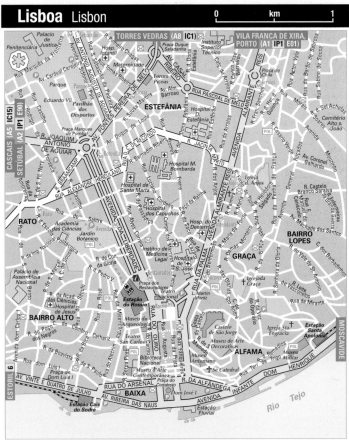

0 km 10

London

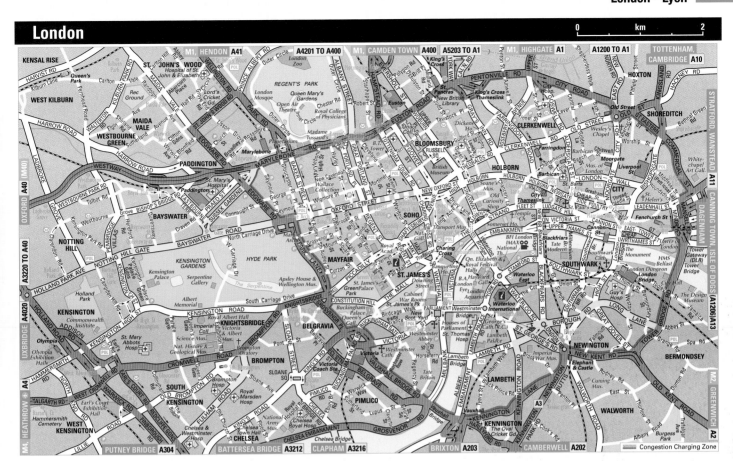

Lyon

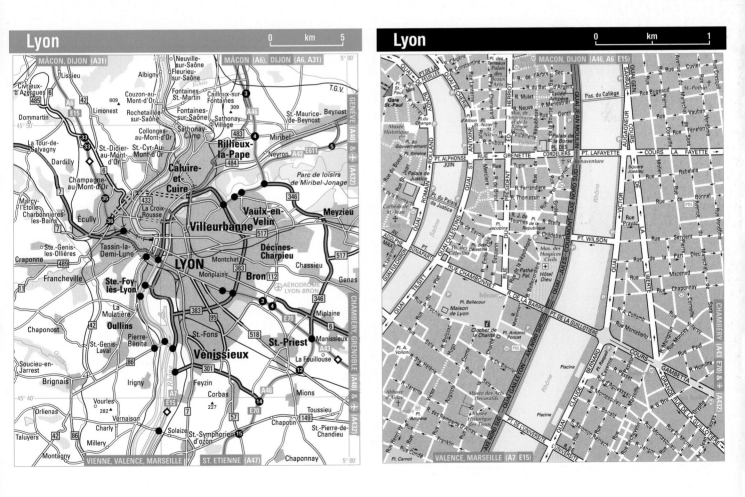

Madrid

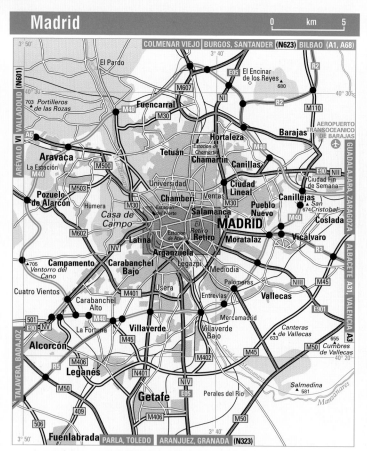

Marseille Marseilles

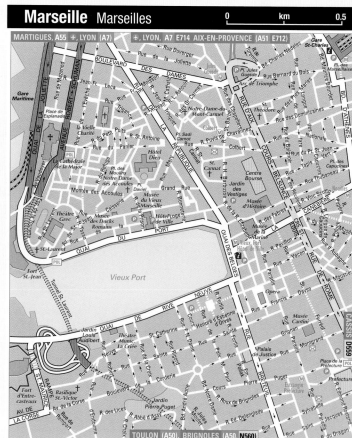

Madrid

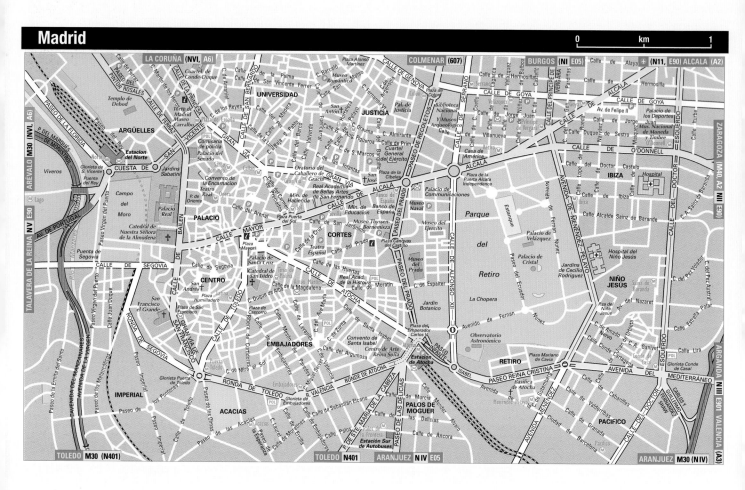

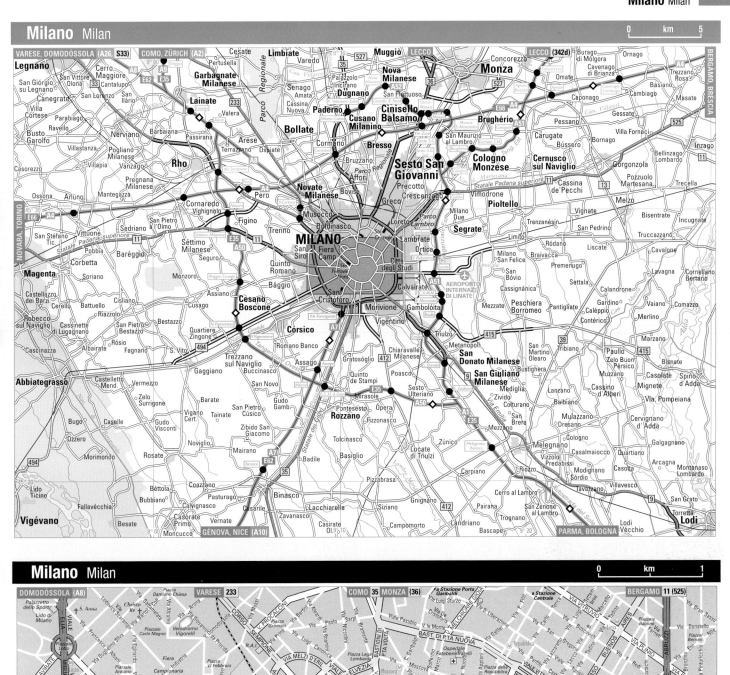

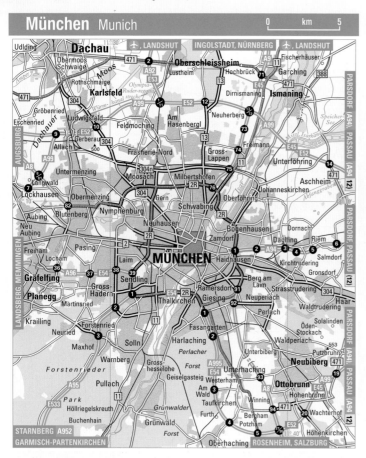

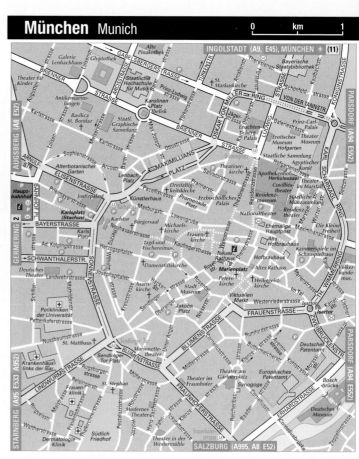

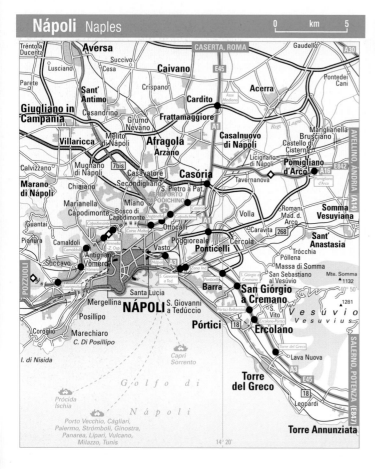

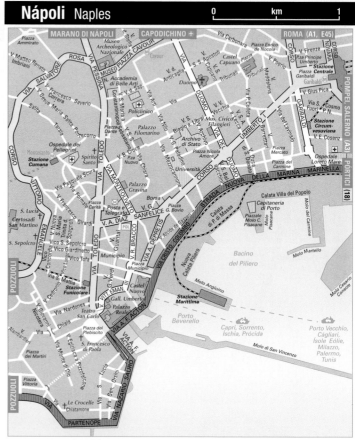

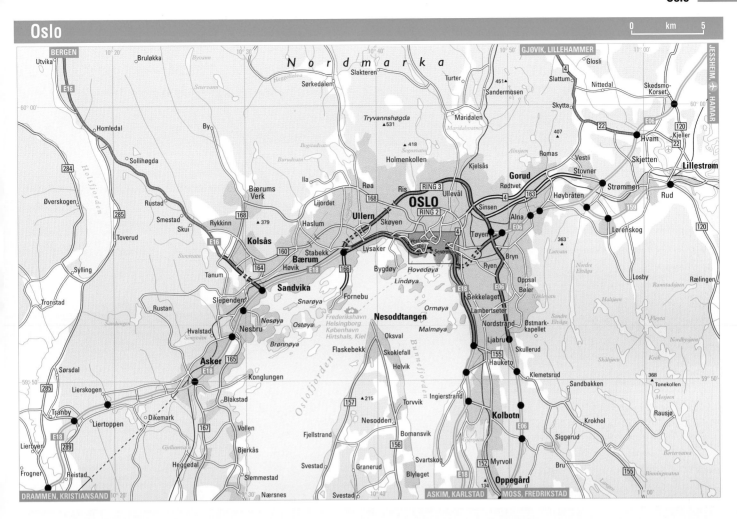

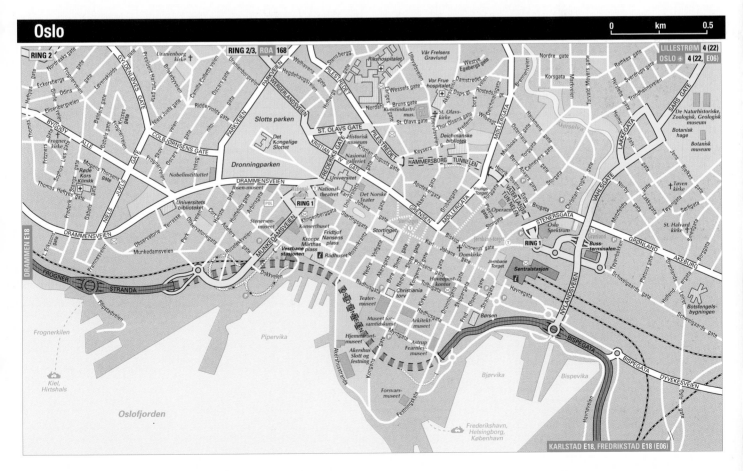

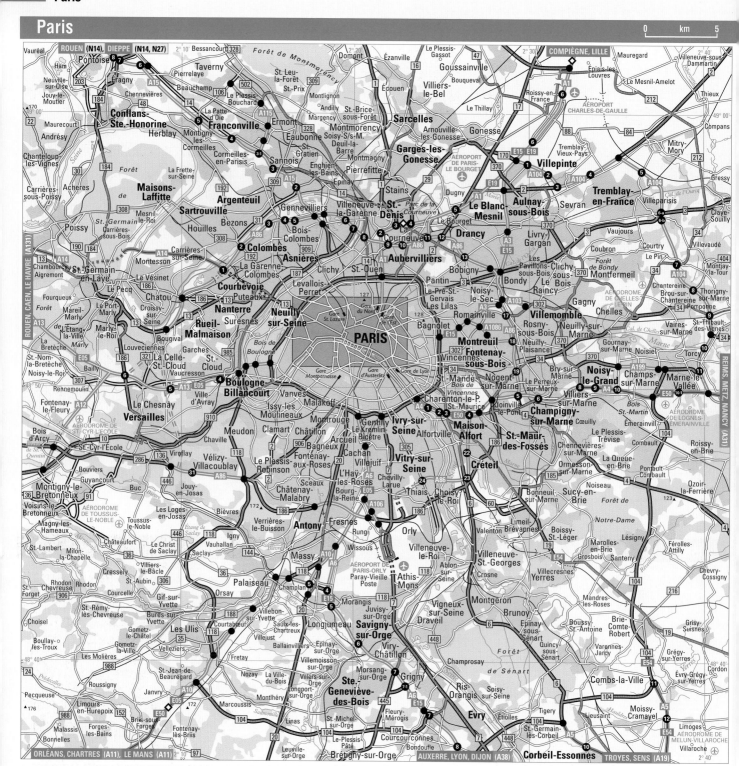

Paris

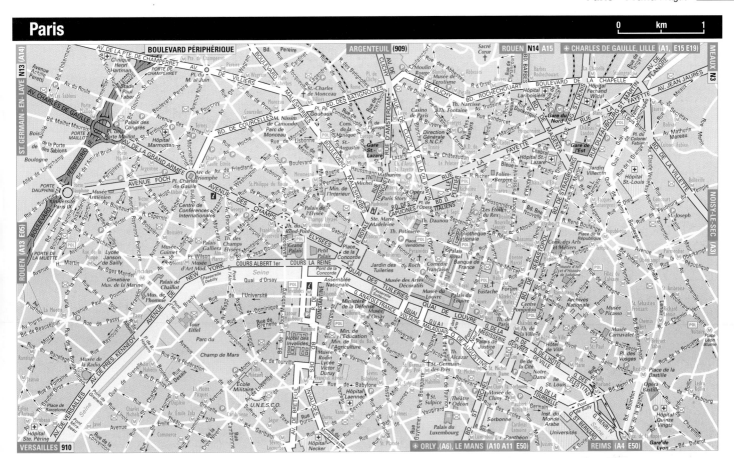

Praha Prague

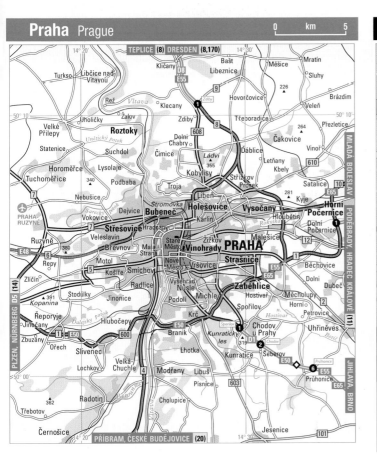

Praha Prague

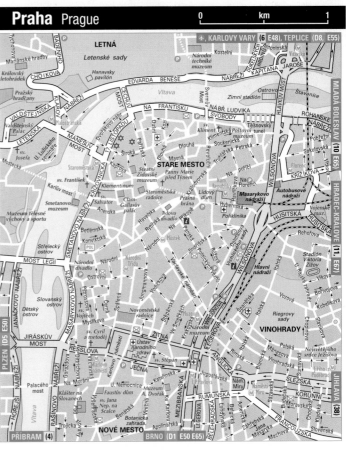

Roma Rome

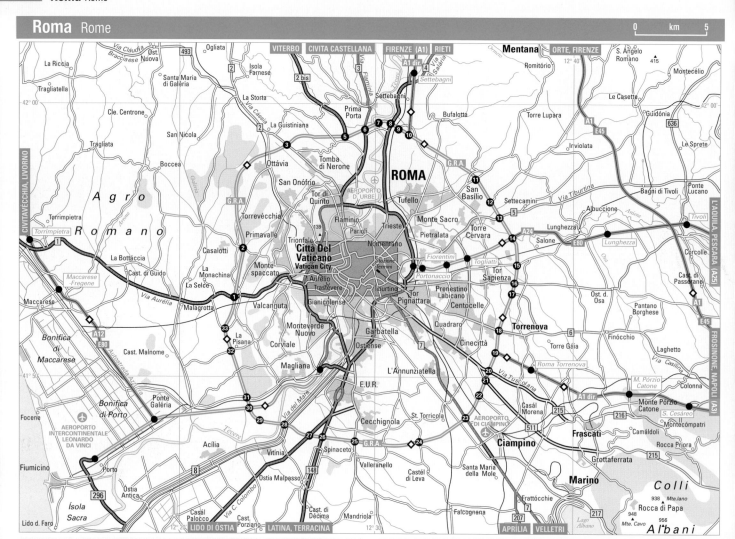

Roma Rome

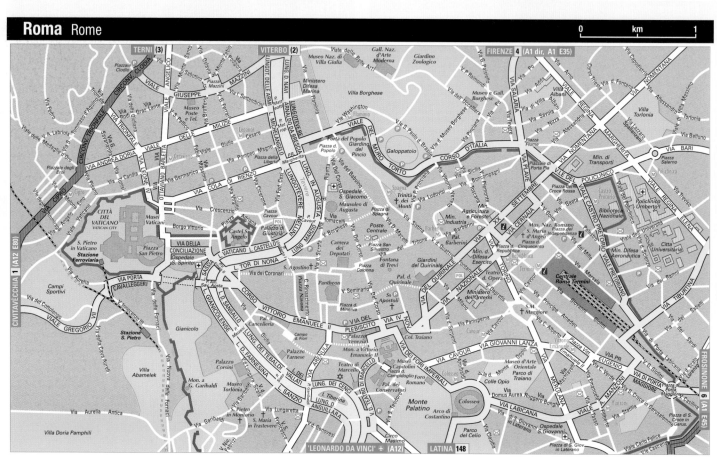

Stockholm

0 km 5

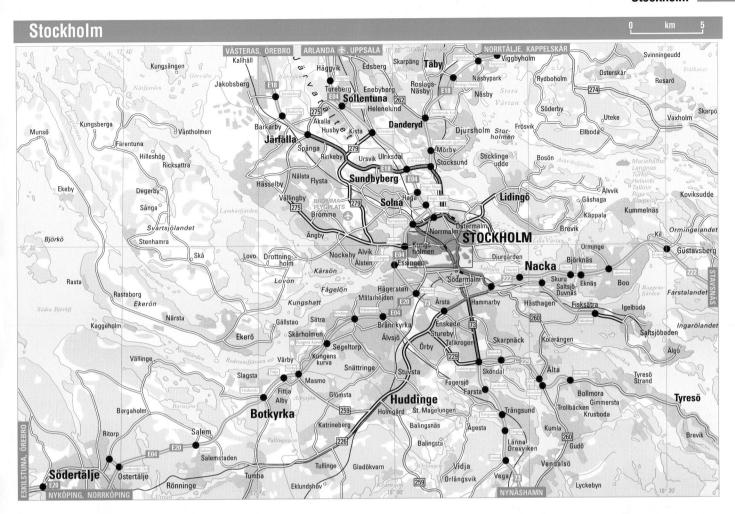

Stockholm

0 km 1

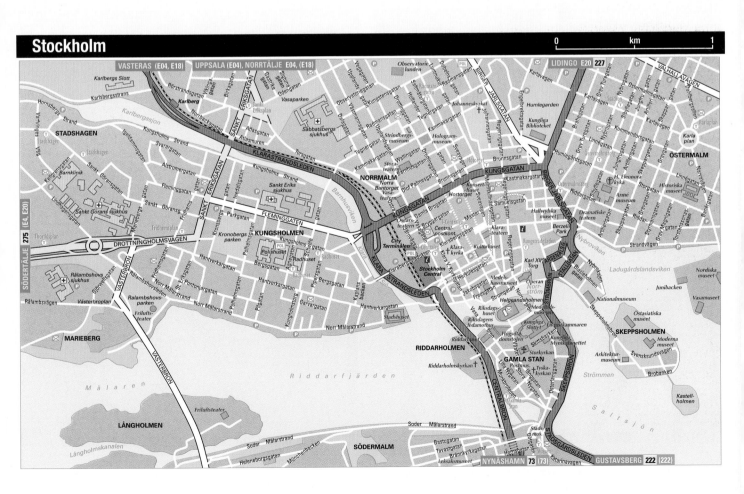

Strasbourg
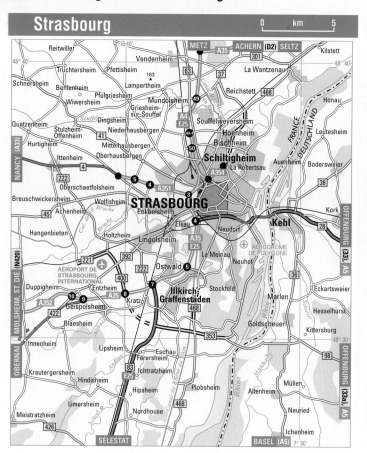

Strasbourg
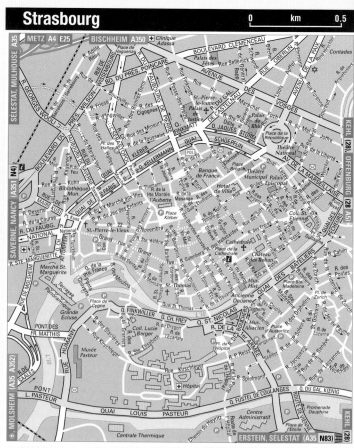

Sevilla Seville
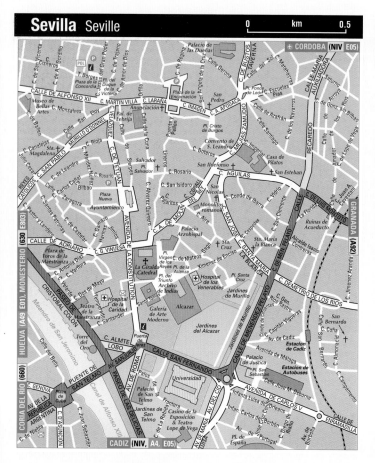

Stuttgart
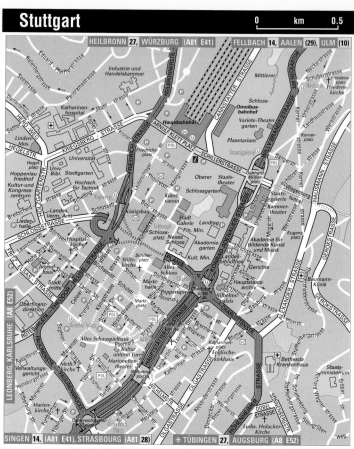

Torino Turin

0 km 5

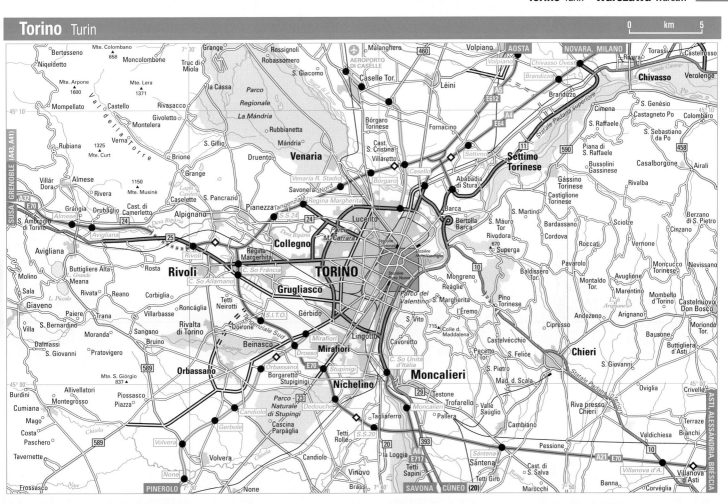

Torino Turin

0 km 1

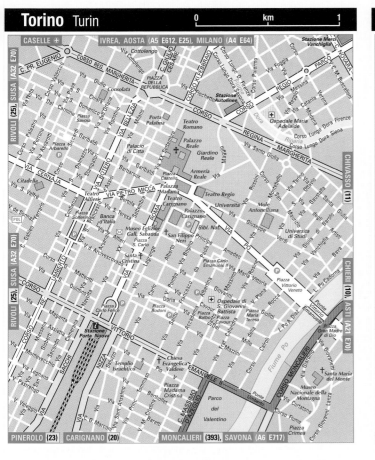

Warszawa Warsaw

0 km 1

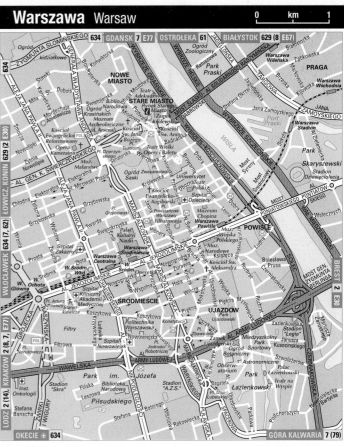

For **Vienna** see page 138

Wien Vienna

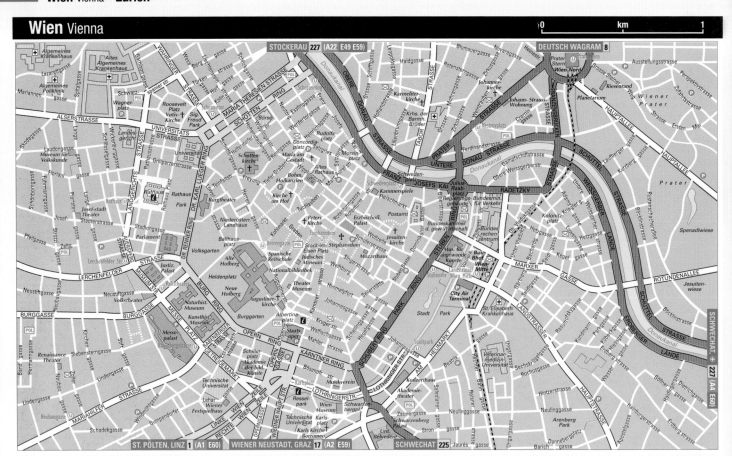

Wien Vienna

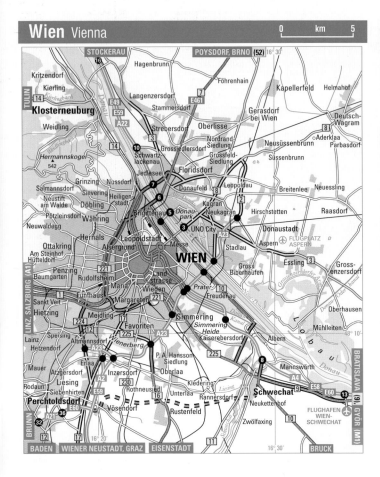

Zürich

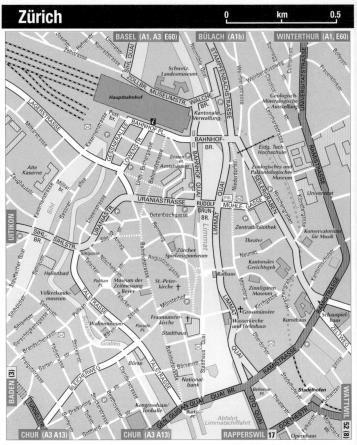

GB	F		D	I
Austria	Autriche	A	Österreich	Austria
Albania	Albanie	AL	Albanien	Albania
Andorra	Andorre	AND	Andorra	Andorra
Belgium	Belgique	B	Belgien	Belgio
Bulgaria	Bulgarie	BG	Bulgarien	Bulgaria
Bosnia-Hercegovina	Bosnia-Herzegovine	BIH	Bosnien-Herzegowina	Bosnia-Herzogovina
Belarus	Belarus	BY	Weissrussland	Bielorussia
Switzerland	Suisse	CH	Schweiz	Svizzera
Cyprus	Chypre	CY	Zypern	Cipro
Czech Republic	République Tchèque	CZ	Tschechische Republik	Repubblica Ceca
Germany	Allemagne	D	Deutschland	Germania
Denmark	Danemark	DK	Dänemark	Danimarca
Spain	Espagne	E	Spanien	Spagna
Estonia	Estonie	EST	Estland	Estonia
France	France	F	Frankreich	Francia
Finland	Finlande	FIN	Finnland	Finlandia
Liechtenstein	Liechtenstein	FL	Liechtenstein	Liechtenstein
Faeroe Islands	Îles Féroé	FO	Färoër-Inseln	Isole Faroe
United Kingdom	Royaume Uni	GB	Grossbritannien und Nordirland	Regno Unito
Gibraltar	Gibraltar	GBZ	Gibraltar	Gibilterra
Greece	Grèce	GR	Greichenland	Grecia
Hungary	Hongrie	H	Ungarn	Ungheria
Croatia	Croatie	HR	Kroatien	Croazia
Italy	Italie	I	Italien	Italia
Ireland	Irlande	IRL	Irland	Irlanda
Iceland	Islande	IS	Island	Islanda
Luxembourg	Luxembourg	L	Luxemburg	Lussemburgo
Lithuania	Lituanie	LT	Litauen	Lituania
Latvia	Lettonie	LV	Lettland	Lettonia
Malta	Malte	M	Malta	Malta
Monaco	Monaco	MC	Monaco	Monaco
Moldova	Moldavie	MD	Moldawien	Moldavia
Macedonia	Macédoine	MK	Makedonien	Macedonia
Norway	Norvège	N	Norwegen	Norvegia
Netherlands	Pays-Bas	NL	Niederlande	Paesi Bassi
Portugal	Portugal	P	Portugal	Portogallo
Poland	Pologne	PL	Polen	Polonia
Romania	Roumanie	RO	Rumanien	Romania
San Marino	Saint-Marin	RSM	San Marino	San Marino
Russia	Russie	RUS	Russland	Russia
Sweden	Suède	S	Schweden	Svezia
Slovak Republic	République Slovaque	SK	Slowak Republik	Repubblica Slovacca
Slovenia	Slovénie	SLO	Slowenien	Slovenia
Turkey	Turquie	TR	Türkei	Turchia
Ukraine	Ukraine	UA	Ukraine	Ucraina
Serbia and Montenegro	Serbie et Monténégro	YU	Serbien und Montenegro	Serbia e Montenegro

A

A Baña E 86 B2
A Bola E 87 B3
A Cañiza E 87 B2
A Capela E 86 A2
A Coruña E 86 A2
A Estrada E 86 B2
A Fonsagrada E 86 A3
A Guarda E 87 C2
A Gudiña E 87 B3
A Merca E 87 B3
A Peroxa E 86 B3
A Pontenova E 86 A3
A Rúa E 87 B3
A Teixeira E 87 B3
A Veiga E 87 B3
A-Ver-o-Mar P 87 C2
Aabybro DK 38 B2
Aach D 71 A4
Aachen D 50 C2
Aalen D 61 B6
Aalsmeer NL 49 A5
Aalst B 49 C5
Aalten NL 50 B2
Aalter B 49 B4
Äänekoski FIN 3 E26
Aarau CH 70 A3
Aarberg CH 70 A2
Aarburg CH 70 A2
Aardenburg NL 49 B4
Aarschot B 49 C5
Aba H 74 A3
Abádanes E 95 B4
Abades E 94 B2
Abadin E 86 A3
Abádszalók H 75 A5
Abaliget H 74 B3
Abana TR 16 A7
Abanilla E 101 A4
Abano Terme I 72 C1
Abarán E 101 A4
Abasár H 65 C6
Abbadia San Salvatore I 81 D5
Abbehausen D 43 B5
Abbekås S 41 D3
Abbeville F 48 C2
Abbey IRL 20 A3
Abbey Town GB 25 D4
Abbeydorney IRL 20 B2
Abbeyfeale IRL 20 B2
Abbeyleix IRL 21 B4
Abbiategrasso I 70 C3
Abbots Bromley GB 27 C4
Abbotsbury GB 29 C5
Abda H 64 C3
Abejar E 89 C4
Abela P 98 B2
Abenberg D 62 A1
Abenójar E 100 A1
Åbenrå DK 39 D2
Abensberg D 62 B2
Aberaeron GB 28 A3
Abercarn GB 29 B4
Aberchirder GB 23 D6
Aberdare GB 29 B4
Aberdaron GB 26 C1
Aberdeen GB 23 D6
Aberdulais GB 28 B4
Aberdyfi GB 26 C1
Aberfeldy GB 25 B4
Aberffraw GB 26 B1
Aberfoyle GB 24 B3
Abergavenny GB 29 B4
Abergele GB 26 B2
Abergynolwyn GB 26 C2
Aberporth GB 28 A3
Abersoch GB 26 C1
Abertillery GB 29 B4
Abertura E 93 B5
Aberystwyth GB 26 C1
Abetone I 81 B4
Abfaltersbach A 72 B2
Abide, *Çanakkale* TR 114 B1
Abide, *Kütahya* TR 114 D4
Abiego E 90 A2
Abild DK 39 E1
Abingdon GB 31 C2
Abington GB 25 C4
Abisko S 3 B23
Abiul P 92 B2
Abla E 101 B3
Ablis F 58 B2
Abondance F 70 B1
Abony H 75 A5
Aboyne GB 23 D6
Abrantes P 92 B2
Abrest F 68 B3
Abriès F 79 B5
Abrud RO 11 C7
Absdorf A 64 B1
Abtenau A 72 A3
Abtsgmünd D 61 B5
Abusejo E 93 A4
Åby, *Kronoberg* S 40 B4
Åby, *Östergötland* S 37 C3
Åbytorp S 36 B2
Acate I 109 B3
Accadia I 103 B8
Accéglio I 79 B5
Accettura I 104 C2
Acciaroli I 106 A2
Accous F 76 D2
Accrington GB 26 B3
Accúmoli I 82 D2
Acedera E 93 B5
Acehuche E 93 B4
Acered E 95 A5
Acerenza I 104 C1
Acerno I 103 C8
Acerra I 103 C7
Aceuchal E 93 C4
Acharacle GB 24 B2
Achavanich GB 23 C5
Achene B 49 C6
Achenkirch A 72 A1
Achensee A 72 A1
Achenthal A 72 A1
Achern D 61 B4
Acheux-en-Amienois F 48 C3
Achiltibuie GB 22 C3
Achim D 43 B6
Achnasheen GB 22 D3
Achnashellach GB 22 D3
Achosnich GB 24 B1
Aci Castello I 109 B4
Aci Catena I 109 B4
Acilia I 102 B5
Acireale I 109 B4
Acle GB 30 B5
Acquacadda I 110 C1
Acquanegra sul Chiese I 71 C5
Acquapendente I 81 D5
Acquasanta Terme I 82 D2
Acquasparta I 102 A5
Acquaviva I 81 C5
Acquaviva delle Fonti I 104 C2
Acquaviva Picena I 82 D2
Ácqui Terme I 80 B2
Acquigny F 58 A2
Acri I 106 B3
Acs H 64 C4
Acsa H 65 C5
Ácsteszér H 74 A2
Acy-en-Multien F 59 A3
Ada YU 75 C5
Adamuz E 100 A1
Adana TR 16 C7
Ádánd H 74 B3
Adanero E 94 B2
Adare IRL 20 B3
Adaševci YU 85 A4
Adeanueva de Ebro E 89 B5
Adelboden CH 70 B2
Adelebsen D 51 B5
Adélfia I 104 B2
Adelmannsfelden D 61 B6
Adelsheim D 61 A5
Adelsö S 36 B4
Ademuz E 96 A1
Adenau D 50 C2
Adendorf D 44 B2
Adhámas GR 113 F6
Adinkerke B 48 B3
Adjud RO 11 C9
Adliswil CH 70 A3
Admont A 63 C5
Ådneram N 32 B3
Adony H 74 A3
Adorf, *Hessen* D 51 B4
Adorf, *Sachsen* D 52 C2
Adra E 100 C2
Adradas E 89 C4
Adrall E 91 A4
Adrano I 109 B3
Ádria I 82 A1
Adrigole IRL 20 C2
Adwick le Street GB 27 B4
Adzaneta E 96 A2
Ærøskøbing DK 39 E3
Aesch CH 70 A2
Affing D 62 B1
Affoltern CH 70 A3
Affric Lodge GB 22 D3
Åfjord N 2 E19
Aflenz Kurort A 73 A5
Afragóla I 103 C7
Afritz A 72 B3
Afyonkarahisar TR 16 B5
Ağapınar TR 114 C5
Ágasegyháza H 75 B4
Agay F 79 C5
Agazzano I 80 B3
Agde F 78 C2
Agen F 77 B3
Ager E 90 B3
Agerbæk DK 39 D1
Agerskov DK 39 D2
Ageyevo RUS 7 D14
Agger DK 38 C1
Aggersund DK 38 B2
Àggius I 110 B2
Aggsbach Dorf A 63 B6
Aggsbach Markt A 63 B6
Aggtelek H 65 B6
Aghalee GB 19 B5
Agiči BIH 83 B5
Agira I 109 B3
Ağlasun TR 16 C5
Aglientu I 110 A2
Agnières F 79 B4
Agno CH 70 C3
Agnone I 103 B7
Agolada E 86 B2
Agon Coutainville F 57 A4
Ágordo I 72 B2
Agost E 96 C2
Agramón E 101 A4
Agramunt E 91 B4
Agreda E 89 C5
Agriá GR 112 C5
Agrigento I 108 B2
Agrinion GR 112 D3
Agrón E 100 B2
Agrópoli I 103 C7
Agua Longa P 87 C2
Aguadulce, *Almería* E 101 C3
Aguadulce, *Sevilla* E 100 B1
Agualada E 86 A2
Aguarón E 89 C5
Aguas E 90 A2
Aguas Belas P 92 B2
Aguas de Busot E 96 C2
Aguas de Moura P 92 C2
Águas Frias P 87 C3
Aguas Santas P 87 C2
Aguaviva E 90 C2
Aguaviva de la Vega E 89 C4
Agudo E 94 D2
Águeda P 92 A2
Aguessac F 78 B2
Agugliano I 82 C2
Aguiar P 92 C3
Aguiàr da Beira P 87 D3
Aguilafuente E 94 A2
Aguilar de Campóo E 88 B2
Aguilar de la Frontera E 100 B1
Aguilas E 101 B4
Ağva TR 114 A4
Ahaus D 50 A2
Ahigal E 93 A4
Ahigal de Villarino E 87 C4
Ahillones E 99 A5
Ahlbeck, *Mecklenburg-Vorpommern* D 45 B6
Ahlbeck, *Mecklenburg-Vorpommern* D 45 B6
Ahlen D 50 B3
Ahlhorn D 43 C5
Ahmetbey TR 114 A2
Ahoghill GB 19 B5
Ahrensbök D 44 A2
Ahrensburg D 44 B2
Ahrenshoop D 44 A4
Ahun F 68 B2
Åhus S 41 D4
Aibar E 89 B5
Aich D 62 B3
Aicha D 63 B4
Aichach D 62 B2
Aidone I 109 B3
Aiello Cálabro I 106 B3
Aigen im Mühlkreis A 63 B4
Aigle CH 70 B1
Aignan F 76 C3
Aignay-le-Duc F 59 C5
Aigre F 67 C5
Aigrefeuille-d'Aunis F 66 B4
Aigrefeuille-sur-Maine F 66 A3
Aiguablava E 91 B6
Aiguebelle F 69 C6
Aigueperse F 68 B3
Aigues-Mortes F 78 C3
Aigues-Vives F 78 C1
Aiguilles F 79 B5
Aiguillon F 77 B3
Aigurande F 68 B1
Ailefroide F 79 B5
Aillant-sur-Tholon F 59 C4
Ailly-sur-Noye F 58 A3
Ailly-sur-Somme F 58 A3
Aimargues F 78 C3
Aime F 69 C6
Ainaži LV 6 C8
Ainet A 72 B2
Ainhoa F 76 C1
Ainsa E 90 A3
Airaines F 48 D2
Aird GB 24 B2
Aird Asaig Tairbeart GB 22 D2
Airdrie GB 25 C4
Aire-sur-la-Lys F 48 C3
Aire-sur-l'Adour F 76 C2
Airole I 80 C1
Airolo CH 70 B3
Airvault F 67 B4
Aisey-sur-Seine F 59 C5
Aïssey F 69 A6
Aisy-sur-Armançon F 59 C5
Aiterhofen D 62 B3
Aith, *Orkney* GB 23 B6
Aith, *Shetland* GB 22 A7
Aitolikón GR 112 D3
Aitona E 90 B3
Aitrach D 61 C6
Aiud RO 11 C7
Aix-en-Othe F 59 B4
Aix-en-Provence F 79 C4
Aix-les-Bains F 69 C5
Aixe-sur-Vienne F 67 C6
Aiyina GR 113 E5
Aiyinion GR 112 B4
Aiyion GR 113 D4
Aizenay F 66 B3
Aizkraukle LV 7 C8
Aizpute LV 6 C6
Ajaccio F 102 B1
Ajain F 68 B1
Ajdovščina SLO 72 C3
Ajka H 74 A2
Ajo E 89 A3
Ajofrin E 94 C3
Ajuda P 93 C3
Akasztó H 75 B4
Akçakoca TR 114 A6
Akçaova TR 114 A4
Aken D 52 B2
Åkerby S 36 A4
Åkernes N 33 C4
Åkers styckebruk S 36 B4
Åkersberga S 36 B5
Akharnaí GR 113 D5
Akhendriá GR 113 H7
Akhisar TR 114 D2
Akhladhókambos GR 113 E4
Åkirkeby DK 41 D4
Akkarfjord N 3 A25
Akkrum NL 42 B2
Akören TR 16 C6
Åkra N 32 B3
Akranes IS 111 C3
Åkrehamn N 32 B2
Aksaray TR 16 B7
Akşehir TR 16 B5
Aktsyabrski BY 7 E10
Akureyri IS 111 B7
Åkvåg N 33 C6
Akyazı TR 114 B5
Ala I 71 C6
Alà dei Sardi I 110 B2
Ala di Stura I 70 C2
Alaca TR 16 A7
Alacaatlı TR 114 C3
Alaçam TR 16 A7
Alaejos E 88 C1
Alagna Valsésia I 70 C2
Alagón E 90 B1
Alaior E 97 B4
Alájar E 99 B4
Alakurtti RUS 3 C29
Alameda E 100 B1
Alameda de la Sagra E 94 B3
Alamedilla E 100 B2
Alamillo E 100 A1
Alaminos E 95 B4
Alandroal P 92 C3
Alange E 93 C4
Alanís E 99 B5
Alanno I 103 A6
Alanya TR 16 C6
Alap H 74 B3
Alaquáso E 96 B2
Alar del Rey E 88 B2
Alaraz E 94 B1
Alarcón E 95 C4
Alaró E 97 B2
Alaşehir TR 16 B4
Alássio I 80 B2
Alatoz E 96 B1
Alatri I 103 B6
Alavus FIN 3 E25
Alba E 95 B5
Alba I 80 B2
Alba Adriática I 82 D2
Alba de Tormes E 94 B1
Alba de Yeltes E 93 A4
Alba-Iulia RO 11 C7
Albacete E 95 D5
Ålbæk DK 38 B3
Albaida E 96 C2
Albala del Caudillo E 93 B4
Albaladejo E 101 A3
Albalat E 96 B2
Albalate de Cinca E 90 B3
Albalate de las Nogueras E 95 B4
Albalate del Arzobispo E 90 B2
Albalete de Zorita E 95 B4
Alban F 77 C5
Albánchez E 101 B3
Albanchez de Ubeda E 100 B2
Albano Laziale I 102 B5
Albanyà E 91 A5
Albaredo d'Adige I 71 C6
Albares E 95 B3
Albarracín E 95 B5
Albatana E 101 A4
Albatarrec E 90 B3
Albatera E 101 A5
Albbruck D 61 C4
Albedin E 100 B1
Albelda de Iregua E 89 B4
Albenga I 80 B2
Albens F 69 C5
Ålberga, *Södermanland* S 36 B3
Ålberga, *Södermanland* S 37 C3
Albergaria-a-Nova P 87 D2
Albergaria-a-Velha P 92 A2
Albergaria dos Doze P 92 B2
Alberge P 92 C2
Alberic E 96 B2
Albernoa P 98 B3
Alberobello I 104 C3
Alberoni I 72 C2
Albersdorf D 43 A6
Albersloh D 50 B3
Albert F 48 C3
Albertirsa H 75 A4
Albertville F 69 C6
Alberuela de Tubo E 90 B2
Albi F 77 C5
Albidona I 106 B3
Albinia I 102 A4
Albino I 71 C4
Albires E 88 B1
Albisola Marina I 80 B2
Albocácer E 90 C3
Albolote E 100 B2
Albondón E 100 C2
Alborea E 96 B1
Ålborg DK 38 B2
Albox E 101 B3
Albrechtice nad Vitavou CZ 63 A5
Albstadt D 61 B5
Albufeira P 98 B2
Albuñol E 100 C2
Albuñuelas E 100 C2
Alburquerque E 93 B3
Alby S 41 C6
Alcácer do Sal P 92 C2
Alcáçovas P 92 C2
Alcadozo E 101 A4
Alcafoces P 93 B3
Alcains P 92 B3
Alcalá de Guadaira E 99 B5
Alcalá de Gurrea E 90 A2
Alcalá de Henares E 95 B3
Alcalá de la Selva E 90 C2
Alcalá de los Gazules E 99 C5
Alcalá de Xivert E 90 C3
Alcalá del Júcar E 96 B1
Alcalá del Río E 99 B5
Alcalá del Valle E 99 C5
Alcalá la Real E 100 B2
Álcamo I 108 B1
Alcampell E 90 B3
Alcanadre E 89 B4
Alcanar E 90 C3
Alcanede P 92 B2
Alcanena P 92 B2
Alcañices E 87 C4
Alcántara E 93 B4
Alcantarilha P 98 B2
Alcantarilla E 101 B4
Alcañiz E 90 B2
Alcara il Fusi I 109 A3
Alcaracejos E 100 A1
Alcaraz E 101 A3
Alcaria Ruiva P 98 B3
Alcarraz E 90 B3
Alcaudete E 100 B1
Alcaudete de la Jara E 94 C2
Alcázar de San Juan E 95 C3
Alcazarén E 88 C2
Alcester GB 29 A6
Alcoba E 94 C2
Alcobaça P 92 B1
Alcobendas E 94 B3
Alcocer E 95 B4
Alcochete P 92 C2
Alcoentre P 92 B2
Alcolea, *Almería* E 100 B2
Alcolea, *Córdoba* E 100 B1
Alcolea de Calatrava E 94 D2
Alcolea de Cinca E 90 B3
Alcolea de Tajo E 93 B5
Alcolea del Pinar E 95 A4
Alcolea del Rio E 99 B5
Alcollarin E 93 B5
Alconchel E 93 C3
Alconera E 93 C4
Alcontar E 101 B3
Alcora E 96 A2
Alcorcón E 94 B3
Alcorisa E 90 C2
Alcossebre E 96 A3
Alcoutim P 98 B3
Alcover E 91 B4
Alcoy E 96 C2
Alcsútdoboz H 74 A3
Alcubierre E 90 B2
Alcubilla de Avellaneda E 89 C3
Alcubilla de Nogales E 88 B1
Alcubillas E 100 A2
Alcublas E 96 B2
Alcúdia E 97 B3
Alcudia de Guadix E 100 B2
Alcuéscar E 93 B4
Aldbrough GB 27 B5
Aldea de Trujillo E 93 B5
Aldea del Cano E 93 B4
Aldea del Fresno E 94 B2
Aldea del Obispo E 87 D4
Aldea del Rey E 100 A2
Aldea Real E 94 A2
Aldeacentenera E 93 B5
Aldeadávila de la Ribera E 87 C4
Aldealcorvo E 94 A3
Aldealuenga de Santa Maria E 89 C3
Aldeamayor de San Martin E 88 C2
Aldeanueva de Barbarroya E 94 C1
Aldeanueva de San Bartolomé E 94 C1
Aldeanueva del Camino E 93 A5
Aldeanueva del Codonal E 94 A2
Aldeapozo E 89 C4
Aldeaquemada E 100 A2
Aldearrubia E 94 A1
Aldeaseca de la Frontera E 94 B1
Aldeasoña E 88 C2
Aldeatejada E 94 B1
Aldeavieja E 94 B2
Aldeburgh GB 30 B5
Aldehuela E 96 A1
Aldehuela de Calatañazor E 89 C4
Aldeia da Serra P 92 C3
Aldeia do Bispo P 93 A4
Aldeia do Mato P 92 B2
Aldeia Gavinha P 92 B1
Aldeire E 100 B2
Aldenhoven D 50 C2
Aldersbach D 62 B4
Aldershot GB 31 C3
Aldudes F 76 C1
Åled S 40 C2
Aledo E 101 B4
Alegria E 89 B4
Aleksa Šantić YU 75 C4
Aleksandrovac, *Srbija* YU 85 B6
Aleksandrovac, *Srbija* YU 85 C6
Aleksandrów Kujawski PL 47 C4
Aleksandrów Łódźki PL 55 B4
Aleksin RUS 7 D14
Ålem S 40 C6
Alençon F 57 B6
Alenquer P 92 B1
Alenya F 91 A5
Aléria F 102 A2
Alès F 78 B3
Áles I 110 C1
Alessándria I 80 B2
Alessándria della Rocca I 108 B2
Alessano I 107 B5
Ålestrup DK 38 C2
Ålesund N 2 E17
Alet-les-Bains F 77 D5
Alexandria GB 24 C3
Alexándria GR 112 B4
Alexandria RO 11 E8
Alexandroúpolis GR 112 B7
Alézio I 107 A5
Alfacar E 100 B2
Alfaiates P 93 A4
Alfajarin E 90 B2
Alfambra E 90 C1
Alfambra P 98 B2
Alfândega da Fé P 87 C4
Alfarela de Jafes P 87 C3
Alfarelos P 92 A2
Alfarim P 92 C1
Alfarnate E 100 C1
Alfaro E 89 B5
Alfarrás E 90 B3
Alfaz del Pi E 96 C2
Alfedena I 103 B7
Alfeizarão P 92 B1
Alfeld, *Bayern* D 62 A2
Alfeld, *Niedersachsen* D 51 B5
Alfena P 87 C2
Alferce P 98 B2
Alfhausen D 43 C4
Alfonsine I 81 B6
Alford, *Aberdeenshire* GB 23 D6
Alford, *Lincolnshire* GB 27 B6
Alforja E 90 B3
Alfoz E 86 A3
Alfreton GB 27 B4
Alfundão P 98 A2
Algaida E 97 B2
Algar E 99 C5
Älgarås S 35 C6
Ålgård N 32 C2
Algarinejo E 100 B1
Algarrobo E 100 C1
Algatocin E 99 C5
Algeciras E 99 C5
Algemesí E 96 B2
Algés P 92 C1
Algete E 95 B3
Alghero I 110 B1
Älghult S 40 B5
Alginet E 96 B2
Algodonales E 99 C5
Algodor E 94 C3
Algodor P 98 B3
Algora E 95 B4
Algoz P 98 B2
Alguaire E 90 B3
Alguazas E 101 A4
Algutsrum S 41 C6
Algyö H 75 B5
Alhama de Almería E 101 C3
Alhama de Aragón E 89 C5
Alhama de Granada E 100 C2
Alhama de Murcia E 101 B4
Alhambra E 100 A2
Alhandra P 92 C1
Alhaurin de la Torre E 100 C1
Alhaurín el Grande E 100 C1
Alhendin E 100 B2
Alhóndiga E 95 B4
Ali Terme I 109 A4
Alia E 93 B5
Ália I 108 B2
Aliaga E 90 C2

Aliağa TR 114 D1
Alibunar YU 85 A5
Alicante E 96 C2
Alicún de Ortega E 100 B2
Alife I 103 B7
Alija del Infantado E 88 B1
Alijó P 87 C3
Alimena I 109 B3
Alingsås S 40 B2
Alinyà E 91 A4
Aliseda E 93 B4
Alivérion GR 112 D6
Alixan F 79 B4
Aljaraque E 99 B3
Aljezur P 98 B2
Aljorra E 101 B4
Aljubarrota P 92 B2
Aljucen E 93 B4
Aljustrel P 98 B2
Alken B 49 C6
Alkmaar NL 42 C1
Alkoven A 63 B5
Allaines F 58 B2
Allaire F 57 C3
Allanche F 68 C2
Alland A 64 B2
Allariz E 87 B3
Allassac F 67 C6
Allauch F 79 C4
Alleen N 33 C4
Allègre F 68 C3
Allemont F 69 C6
Allendale Town GB 25 D5
Allendorf D 51 C4
Allentsteig A 63 B6
Allepuz E 90 C2
Allersberg D 62 A2
Allershausen D 62 B2
Alles E 88 A2
Allevard F 69 C6
Allihies IRL 20 C1
Allingåbro DK 38 C3
Allmannsdorf D 61 C5
Allo E 89 B4
Alloa GB 25 B4
Allogny F 68 A2
Allones, *Eure et Loire* F 58 B2
Allones, *Maine-et-Loire* F 67 A5
Allonnes F 57 C6
Allons F 76 B2
Allos F 79 B5
Allstedt D 52 B1
Alltwalis GB 28 B3
Allumiere I 102 A4
Almaceda P 92 B3
Almacelles E 90 B3
Almachar E 100 C1
Almada P 92 C1
Almadén E 100 A1
Almadén de la Plata E 99 B4
Almadenejos E 100 A1
Almadrones E 95 B4
Almagro E 100 A2
Almajano E 89 C4
Almansa E 96 C1
Almansil P 98 B2
Almanza E 88 B1
Almaraz E 93 B5
Almargen E 99 C5
Almarza E 89 C4
Almásfüzitő H 64 C4
Almassora E 96 B2
Almazán E 89 C4
Almazul E 89 C4
Alme D 51 B4
Almedina E 100 A3
Almedinilla E 100 B1
Almeida E 87 C4
Almeida P 93 A4
Almeirim P 92 B2
Almelo NL 42 C3
Almenar E 90 B3
Almenar de Soria E 89 C4
Almenara E 96 B2
Almendra P 87 D3
Almendral E 93 C4
Almendral de la Cañada E 94 B2
Almendralejo E 93 C4
Almenno San Bartolomeo I 71 C4
Almere NL 42 C2
Almería E 101 C3
Almerimar E 101 C3
Almese I 70 C2
Almexial P 98 B3
Älmhult S 40 C4
Almiropótamos GR 113 D6
Almirós GR 112 C4
Almodôvar P 98 B2
Almodóvar del Campo E 100 A1
Almodóvar del Pinar E 95 C5
Almodóvar del Río E 99 B5
Almofala P 87 D3
Almogia E 100 C1
Almoharin E 93 B4
Almonacid de la Sierra E 89 C5
Almonacid de Toledo E 94 C3
Almonaster la Real E 99 B4
Almondsbury GB 29 B5
Almonte E 99 B4
Almoradí E 101 A5
Almoraima E 99 C5
Almorox E 94 B2
Almoster P 92 B2
Älmsta S 36 B5
Almudena E 101 A4
Almudévar E 90 A2
Almuñécar E 100 C2
Almunge S 36 B5
Almuradiel E 100 A2
Almussafes E 96 B2
Alness GB 23 D4
Alnmouth GB 25 C6
Alnwick GB 25 C6
Álora E 100 C1
Alos d'Ensil E 91 A4
Alosno E 99 B3
Alozaina E 100 C1
Alpbach A 72 A1
Alpedrete de la Sierra E 95 B3
Alpedrinha P 92 A3
Alpen D 50 B2
Alpera E 96 C1
Alphen aan de Rijn NL 49 A5
Alpiarça P 92 B2
Alpignano I 70 C2
Alpirsbach D 61 B4
Alpu TR 114 C5
Alpuente E 96 B1
Alqueva P 98 A3
Alquézar E 90 A3
Als DK 38 C3
Alsasua E 89 B4
Alsdorf D 50 C2
Alselv DK 39 D1
Alsfeld D 51 C5
Alsike S 36 B4
Alskog S 37 D5
Alsleben D 52 B1
Alsónémedi H 75 A4
Alsótold H 65 C5
Alsóújlak H 74 A1
Alstätte D 50 A2
Alsterbro S 40 C5
Alstermo S 40 C5
Alston GB 25 D5
Alt Ruppin D 45 C4
Alta N 3 B25
Älta S 36 B5
Altamura I 104 C2
Altarejos E 95 C4
Altaussee A 63 C4
Altavilla Irpina I 103 B7
Altavilla Silentina I 103 C8
Altdöbern D 53 B4
Altdorf CH 70 B3
Altdorf D 62 B3
Altdorf bei Nürnberg D 62 A2
Alte P 98 B2
Altea E 96 C2
Altedo I 81 B5
Alten-weddingen D 52 A1
Altena D 50 B3
Altenau D 51 B6
Altenberg D 53 C3
Altenberge D 50 A3
Altenbruch D 43 B5
Altenburg D 52 C2
Altenfelden A 63 B4
Altengronau D 51 C5
Altenheim D 60 B3
Altenhundem D 50 B4
Altenkirchen, *Mecklenburg-Vorpommern* D 45 A5
Altenkirchen, *Radom* D 50 C3
Altenkunstadt D 52 C1
Altenmarkt A 63 C5
Altenmarkt D 62 B3
Altenmarkt im Pongall A 72 A3
Altensteig D 61 B4
Altentreptow D 45 B5
Altenwalde D 43 B5
Alter do Chão P 92 B3
Altfraunhofen D 62 B3
Altheim A 63 B4
Altheim D 61 A5
Althofen A 73 B4
Altinoluk TR 114 C1
Altinova TR 114 C1
Altıntaş TR 114 C5
Altkirch F 60 C3
Altlandsberg D 45 C5
Altlewin D 45 C6
Altmannstein D 62 B2
Altmorschen D 51 B5
Altmunster A 63 C4
Altnaharra GB 23 C4
Alto Campoó E 88 A2
Altofonte I 108 A2
Altomonte I 106 B3
Alton, *Hampshire* GB 31 C3
Alton, *Staffordshire* GB 27 C4
Altopáscio I 81 C4
Altötting D 62 B3
Altreichenau D 63 B4
Altshausen D 61 C5
Altstätten CH 71 A4
Altura E 96 B2
Altusried D 61 C6
Alūksne LV 7 C9
Alunda S 36 A5
Alustante E 95 B5
Alva GB 25 B4
Alvaiázere P 92 B2
Alvalade P 98 B2
Älvängen S 38 B5
Alvarenga P 87 D2
Alvares P 92 A2
Alvdal N 2 E19
Älvdalen S 2 F21
Alverca P 92 C1
Alvesta S 40 C4
Alvignac F 77 B4
Alvignano I 103 B7
Alvimare F 58 A1
Alviobeira P 92 B2
Alvito P 98 A3
Älvkarleby S 36 A4
Älvkarleö bruk S 36 A4
Alvor P 98 B2
Alvorge P 92 B2
Alvøy N 32 A2
Älvsbacka S 34 B5
Älvsbyn S 3 D24
Älvsered S 40 B2
Alwernia PL 55 C4
Alwinton GB 25 C5
Alyth GB 25 B4
Alytus LT 6 D8
Alzénau D 51 C5
Alzey D 61 A4
Alzira E 96 B2
Alzonne F 77 C5
Amadora P 92 C1
Åmål S 35 B4
Amalfi I 103 C7
Amaliás GR 113 E3
Amance F 60 C2
Amancey F 69 A6
Amándola I 82 D2
Amantea I 106 B3
Amarante P 87 C2
Amareleja P 98 A3
Amares P 87 C2
Amaseno I 103 B6
Amasra TR 114 A7
Amasya TR 16 A7
Amatrice I 103 A6
Amay B 49 C6
Ambarnyy RUS 3 D30
Ambazac F 67 C6
Ambelón GR 112 C4
Amberg D 62 A2
Ambérieu-en-Bugey F 69 C5
Ambérieux-en-Dombes F 69 B4
Ambert F 68 C3
Ambés F 76 A2
Ambjörby S 34 A5
Ambjörnarp S 40 B3
Amble GB 25 C6
Ambleside GB 26 A3
Ambleteuse F 48 C2
Amboise F 67 A5
Ambrières-les-Vallées F 57 B5
Amden CH 71 A4
Amel B 50 C2
Amélia I 102 A5
Amélie-les-Bains-Palalda F 91 A5
Amelinghausen D 44 B2
Amendoa P 92 B2
Amendoeira P 98 B3
Amendolara I 106 B3
Amer E 91 A5
Amerongen NL 49 A6
Amersfoort NL 49 A6
Amersham GB 31 C3
Ames E 86 B2
Amesbury GB 29 B6
Amfíklia GR 112 D4
Amfilokhía GR 112 D3
Amfípolis GR 112 B5
Ámfissa GR 112 D4
Amièira, *Évora* P 98 A3
Amieira, *Portalegre* P 92 B3
Amieiro P 92 A2
Amiens F 58 A3
Amindaion GR 112 B3
Åminne S 40 B3
Åmli N 33 C5
Amlwch GB 26 B1
Ammanford GB 28 B4
Åmmeberg S 37 C1
Amorbach D 61 A5
Amorebieta E 89 A4
Amorgós GR 113 F7
Amorosa P 87 C2
Amorosi I 103 B7
Åmot, *Buskerud* N 33 B6
Åmot, *Telemark* N 33 B4
Åmotfors S 34 B4
Åmotsdal N 33 B5
Amou F 76 C2
Ampezzo I 72 B2
Ampfing D 62 B3
Ampflwang A 63 B4
Amplepuis F 69 C4
Amposta E 90 C3
Ampthill GB 30 B3
Ampudia E 88 C2
Ampuero E 89 A3
Amriswil CH 71 A4
Amstelveen NL 49 A5
Amsterdam NL 42 C1
Amstetten A 63 B5
Amtzell D 61 C5
Amulree GB 25 B4
Amurrio E 89 A4
Amusco E 88 B2
An t-Ob GB 22 D1
Åna-Sira N 32 C3
Anacapri I 103 C7
Anadia P 92 A2
Anadon E 90 C1
Anáfi GR 113 F7
Anagni I 102 B6
Anamur TR 16 C6
Ananyiv UA 11 C10
Anascaul IRL 20 B1
Ånäset S 3 D24
Anastażewo PL 47 C4
Anaya de Alba E 94 B1
Ança P 92 A2
Ancaster GB 27 C5
Ancede P 87 C2
Ancenis F 66 A3
Ancerville F 59 B6
Anchuras E 94 C2
Ancona I 82 C2
Ancora P 87 C2
Ancrum GB 25 C5
Ancy-le-Franc F 59 C5
Andalo I 71 B5
Åndalsnes N 2 E17
Andance F 69 C4
Andau A 64 C3
Andebu N 34 B2
Andeer CH 71 B4
Andelfingen CH 61 C4
Andelot F 59 B6
Andelot-en-Montagne F 69 B5
Andenes N 2 B22
Andenne B 49 C6
Anderlues B 49 C5
Andermatt CH 70 B3
Andernach D 50 C3
Andernos-les-Bains F 76 B1
Anderslöv S 41 D3
Anderstorp S 40 B3
Andijk NL 42 C2
Andirrion GR 113 D3
Andoain E 89 A4
Andocs H 74 B2
Andolsheim F 60 B3
Andorra E 90 C2
Andorra La Vella AND 91 A4
Andosilla E 89 B5
Andover GB 31 C2
Andratx E 97 B2
Andreapol RUS 7 C12
Andreas GB 26 A1
Andréspol PL 55 B4
Andrest F 76 C3
Andretta I 103 C8
Andrezieux-Bouthéon F 69 C4
Ándria I 104 B2
Andrijevica YU 85 D4
Andrítsaina GR 113 E3
Ándros GR 113 E6
Andrychów PL 65 A5
Andselv N 3 B23
Andújar E 100 A1
Anduze F 78 B2
Åneby N 34 A2
Åneby S 40 B4
Añes E 89 A3
Anet F 58 B2
Anfo I 71 C5
Ang S 40 B4
Anga S 37 D5
Angaïs F 76 C2
Ånge S 2 E21
Angeja P 92 A2
Ängelholm S 41 C2
Ängelsberg S 36 B3
Anger A 73 A5
Angera I 70 C3
Angermünde D 45 B6
Angern A 64 B2
Angers F 67 A4
Angerville F 58 B3
Anghiari I 82 C1
Angle GB 28 B2
Anglès E 91 B5
Anglés, *Tarn* F 77 C5
Angles, *Vendée* F 66 B3
Angles sur l'Anglin F 67 B5
Anglesola E 91 B4
Anglet F 76 C1
Anglure F 59 B4
Angoulême F 67 C5
Angoulins F 66 B3
Angsö S 36 B3
Angües E 90 A2
Anguiano E 89 B4
Anguillara Sabazia I 102 A5
Anguillara Véneta I 72 C1
Anhée B 49 C5
Anholt DK 38 C4
Aniane F 78 C2
Aniche F 49 C4
Ånimskog S 35 C4
Anina RO 10 D6
Anixis GR 112 C3
Anizy-le-Château F 59 A4
Anjalankoski FIN 3 F27
Ankara TR 114 C7
Ankaran SLO 72 C3
Ankarsrum S 40 B6
Anklam D 45 B5
Ankum D 43 C4
Anlauftal A 72 A3
Annaberg A 63 C6
Annaberg-Buchholz D 52 C3
Annaberg im Lammertal A 72 A3
Annaburg D 52 B3
Annahütte D 53 B3
Annalong GB 19 B6
Annan GB 25 D4
Anneberg, *Halland* S 38 B5
Anneberg, *Jönköping* S 40 B4
Annecy F 69 C6
Annelund S 40 B3
Annemasse F 69 B6
Annenskiy Most RUS 7 A14
Annerstad S 40 C3
Annestown IRL 21 B4
Annevoie-Rouillon B 49 C5
Annonay F 69 C4
Annot F 79 C5
Annweiler D 60 A3
Áno Arkhánai GR 113 G7
Áno Porróia GR 112 A5
Áno Síros GR 113 E6
Áno Viánnos GR 113 G7
Añora E 100 A1
Anould F 60 B2
Anquela del Ducado E 95 B4
Anröchte D 51 B4
Ans DK 39 C2
Ansager DK 39 D1
Ansbach D 62 A1
Anse F 69 C4
Anserœul B 49 C4
Ansfelden A 63 B5
Ansião P 92 B2
Ansó E 76 D2
Ansoain E 76 D1
Anstruther GB 25 B5
Antalya TR 16 C5
Antas E 101 B4
Antegnate I 71 C4
Antequera E 100 B1
Anterselva di Mezzo I 72 B2
Antibes F 79 C6
Antigüedad E 88 C2
Antillo I 109 B4
Antoing B 49 C4
Antonin PL 54 B2
Antrain F 57 B4
Antrim GB 19 B5
Antrodoco I 102 A6
Antronapiana I 70 B3
Antuzede P 92 A2
Antwerp = Antwerpen B 49 B5
Antwerpen = Antwerp B 49 B5
Anversa d'Abruzzi I 103 B6
Anvin F 48 C3
Anzat-le-Luguet F 68 C3
Anzi I 104 C1
Ánzio I 102 B5
Anzola d'Emilia I 81 B5
Anzón E 89 C5
Aoiz E 76 D1
Aosta I 70 C2
Apalhão P 92 B3
Apátfalva H 75 B5
Apatin YU 75 C4
Apatity RUS 3 C30
Apc H 65 C5
Apécchio I 82 C1
Apeldoorn NL 50 A1
Apen D 43 B4
Apenburg D 44 C3
Apensen D 43 B6
Apiro I 82 C2
Apolda D 52 B1
Apollonia GR 113 F6
Apostag H 75 B3
Äppelbo S 34 A6
Appennino I 82 D2
Appenzell CH 71 A4
Appiano I 71 B6
Appingedam NL 42 B3
Appleby-in-Westmorland GB 26 A3
Applecross GB 22 D3
Appledore GB 28 B3
Appoigny F 59 C4
Apremont-la-Forêt F 60 B1
Aprica I 71 B5
Apricena I 103 B8
Aprigliano I 106 B3
Aprília I 102 B5
Apt F 79 C4
Apúlia P 87 C2
Aquiléia I 72 C3
Aquilónia I 103 C8
Aquino I 103 B6
Ar S 37 D5
Arabayona E 94 A1
Arabba I 72 B1
Araç TR 16 A6
Aracena E 99 B4
Arad RO 75 B6
Aradac YU 75 C5
Aragona I 108 B2
Arákhova GR 112 D4
Aramits F 76 C2
Aramon F 78 C3
Aranda de Duero E 88 C3
Aranda de Moncayo E 89 C5
Arandjelovac YU 85 B5
Aranjuez E 95 B3
Arantzazu E 89 B4
Aranzueque E 95 B3
Aras de Alpuente E 96 B1
Arauzo de Miel E 89 C3
Arazede P 92 A2
Arbas F 77 D3
Árbatax I 110 C2
Arbeca E 90 B3
Arberg D 62 A1
Arbesbach A 63 B5
Arboga S 36 B2
Arbois F 69 B5
Arbon CH 71 A4
Arboréa I 110 C1
Arbório I 70 C3
Arbroath GB 25 B5
Arbùcies E 91 B5
Arbuniel E 100 B2
Arbus I 110 C1
Arc-en-Barrois F 59 C5
Arc-et-Senans F 69 A5
Arc-lès-Gray F 69 A5
Arc-sur-Tille F 69 A5
Arcachon F 76 B1
Arce I 103 B6
Arcen NL 50 B2
Arces-Dilo F 59 B4
Arcévia I 82 C1
Archena E 101 A4
Archez E 100 C2
Archiac F 67 C4
Archidona E 100 B1
Archiestown GB 23 D5
Archivel E 101 A4
Arcidosso I 81 D5
Arcille I 81 D5
Arcis-sur-Aube F 59 B5
Arco I 71 C5
Arcones E 94 A3
Arcos E 88 B3
Arcos de Jalón E 95 A4
Arcos de la Frontera E 99 C5
Arcos de la Sierra E 95 B4
Arcos de las Salinas E 96 B1
Arcos de Valdevez P 87 C2
Arcozelo P 92 A3
Arcusa E 90 A3
Arcy-sur-Cure F 59 C4
Ardagh IRL 20 B2
Årdal N 32 B3
Ardala S 35 C5
Ardales E 100 C1
Ardara I 110 B1
Ardara IRL 18 B3
Ardarroch GB 22 D3
Ardbeg GB 24 C1
Ardcharnich GB 22 D3
Ardchyle GB 24 B3
Ardee IRL 19 C5
Arden DK 38 C2
Ardentes F 68 B1
Ardenza I 81 C4
Ardersier GB 23 D4
Ardes F 68 C3
Ardessie GB 22 D3
Ardez CH 71 B5
Ardfert IRL 20 B2
Ardgay GB 23 D4
Ardglass GB 19 B6
Ardgroom IRL 20 C2
Ardhasig GB 22 D2
Ardhéa GR 112 B4
Ardino BG 112 A7
Ardisa E 90 A2
Ardkearagh IRL 20 C1
Ardlui GB 24 B3
Ardlussa GB 24 B2
Ardón E 88 B1
Ardooie B 49 C4
Ardore I 106 C3
Ardre S 37 D5
Ardres F 48 C2
Ardrishaig GB 24 B2
Ardrossan GB 24 C3
Are N 32 B2
Åre S 2 E20
Areia Branca P 92 B1
Aremark N 34 B3
Arenales de San Gregorio E 95 C3
Arenas E 100 C1
Arenas de Iguña E 88 A2
Arenas de San Juan E 95 C3
Arenas de San Pedro E 94 B1
Arenas del Rey E 100 C2
Arendal N 33 C5
Arendonk B 49 B6
Arengosse F 76 B2
Arentorp S 35 C4
Arenys de Mar E 91 B5
Arenys de Munt E 91 B5
Arenzano I 80 B2
Areo E 91 A4
Areópolis GR 113 F4
Ares E 86 A2
Arès F 76 B1
Ares del Maestrat E 90 C2
Arette F 76 C2
Aretxabaleta E 89 A4
Arevalillo E 93 A5
Arévalo E 94 A2
Arez P 92 B3
Arezzo I 81 C5
Arfeuilles F 68 B3
Argalastí GR 112 C5
Argallón E 99 A5
Argamasilla de Alba E 95 C3
Argamasilla de Calatrava E 100 A1
Arganda E 95 B3
Arganil P 92 A2
Argásion GR 113 E2
Argegno I 71 C4
Argelès-Gazost F 76 C2
Argelès-sur-Mer F 91 A6
Argent-sur-Sauldre F 68 A2
Argenta I 81 B5
Argentan F 57 B5
Argentat F 77 A4
Argentera I 79 B5
Argenteuil F 58 B3
Argenthal D 50 D3
Argentiera I 110 B1
Argenton-Château F 67 B4
Argenton-sur-Creuse F 67 B6
Argentona E 91 B5
Argentré F 57 B5
Argentré-du-Plessis F 57 B4
Árgos GR 113 E4
Árgos Orestikón GR 112 B3
Argostólion GR 113 D2
Argote E 89 B4
Arguedas E 89 B5
Argueil F 58 A2
Argyrádhes GR 112 C1
Arholma S 36 B6
Århus DK 39 C3
Ariano Irpino I 103 B8
Ariano nel Polésine I 82 B1
Aribe E 76 D1
Arienzo I 103 B7
Arild S 41 C2
Arileod GB 24 B1
Arilje YU 85 C5
Arinagour GB 24 B1
Ariño E 90 B2
Arinthod F 69 B5
Arisaig GB 24 B2
Arisgotas E 94 C3
Aritzo I 110 C2
Ariza E 89 C4
Årjäng S 34 B4
Arjeplog S 3 C23
Arjona E 100 B1
Arjonilla E 100 B1
Arkelstorp S 41 C4
Arklow IRL 21 B5
Arkösund S 37 C3
Ärla S 36 B3
Arlanc F 68 C3
Arlanzón E 89 B3
Arlebosc F 78 A3
Arlena di Castro I 102 A4
Arles F 78 C3
Arles-sur-Tech F 91 A5
Arló H 65 B6
Arlon B 60 A1
Armação de Pera P 98 B2
Armadale, *Highland* GB 22 D3
Armadale, *West Lothian* GB 25 C4
Armagh GB 19 B5
Armamar P 87 C3
Armenistís GR 113 E8
Armeno I 70 C3
Armenteros E 93 A5
Armentières F 48 C3
Armilla E 100 B2
Armiñón E 89 B4
Armoy GB 19 A5
Armuña de Tajuña E 95 B3
Armutlu TR 114 B3
Arnac-Pompadour F 67 C6
Arnage F 57 C6
Arnaia GR 112 B5
Arnas F 69 B4
Årnäs S 35 C5
Arnay-le-Duc F 69 A4
Arnborg DK 39 C2
Arnbruck D 62 A3
Arneburg D 44 C4
Arnedillo E 89 B4
Arnedo E 89 B4
Arneguy F 76 C1
Arnés E 90 C3
Árnes IS 111 A4
Årnes N 34 A3
Arnfels A 73 B5
Arnhem NL 50 B1
Arnissa GR 112 B3
Arno S 37 C4
Arnold GB 27 B4
Arnoldstein A 72 B3
Arnsberg D 50 B4
Arnschwang D 62 A3
Arnsdorf D 53 B3
Arnside GB 26 A3
Arnstadt D 51 C6
Arnstein D 51 D5
Arnstorf D 62 B3
Arnum DK 39 D1
Aroche E 99 B4
Arolla CH 70 B2
Arolsen D 51 B5
Arona I 70 C3
Åros N 34 B2
Arosa CH 71 B4
Arosa P 87 C2
Arøsund DK 39 D2
Arouca P 87 D2
Årøysund N 34 B2
Arpajon F 58 B3
Arpajon-sur-Cère F 77 B5
Arpino I 103 B6
Arquata del Tronto I 82 D2
Arques F 48 C3
Arques-la-Bataille F 58 A2
Arquillos E 100 A2
Arraia-Maeztu E 89 B4
Arraiolos P 92 C2
Arrancourt F 60 B2
Arras F 48 C3
Arrasate E 89 A4
Arreau F 77 D3
Arredondo E 89 A3
Arrens-Marsous F 76 D2
Arriate E 99 C5
Arrifana P 98 B2
Arrigorriaga E 89 A4
Arriondas E 88 A1
Arroba de los Montes E 94 C2
Arrochar GB 24 B3
Arromanches-les-Bains F 57 A5
Arronches P 92 B3
Arroniz E 89 B4
Arrou F 58 B2
Arroya E 88 B2
Arroya de Cuéllar E 88 C2
Arroyal E 88 B2
Arroyo de la Luz E 93 B4
Arroyo de San Servan E 93 C4
Arroyo del Ojanco E 100 A3
Arroyomolinos de Leon E 99 A4
Arroyomolinos de Montánchez E 93 B4
Arruda dos Vinhos P 92 C1
Års DK 38 C2
Ars-en-Ré F 66 B3
Ars-sur-Moselle F 60 A2
Arsac F 76 B2
Arsiè I 72 C1
Arsiero I 71 C6
Årslev DK 39 D3
Arsoli I 102 A6
Ärsunda S 36 A3
Artà E 97 B3
Árta GR 112 C3
Artajona E 89 B5
Artegna I 72 B3
Arteixo E 86 A2
Artemare F 69 C5
Arten I 72 B1
Artena I 102 B5
Artenay F 58 B2
Artern D 52 B1
Artés E 91 B4
Artesa de Segre E 91 B4
Arth CH 70 A3
Arthez-de-Béarn F 76 C2
Arthon-en-Retz F 66 A3
Arthurstown IRL 21 B5
Artieda E 90 A2
Artix F 76 C2
Artotína GR 112 D4
Artsyz UA 11 C10
Artziniega E 89 A3
Arudy F 76 C2
Arundel GB 31 D3
Årup DK 39 D3
Arveyres F 76 B2
Arvidsjaur S 3 D23
Arvieux F 79 B5
Arvika S 34 B4
Åryd, *Blekinge* S 41 C5
Åryd, *Kronoberg* S 40 C4
Arzachena I 110 A2
Arzacq-Arraziguet F 76 C2
Arzano F 56 C2
Aržano HR 84 C1
Arzberg D 52 C2
Arzignano I 71 C6
Arzila P 92 A2
Arzl im Pitztal A 71 A5
Arzúa E 86 B2
As B 49 B6
Aš CZ 52 C2
Ås N 34 B2
As Neves E 87 B2
As Nogaís E 86 B3
As Pontes de García Rodríguez E 86 A3
Aså DK 38 B3
Åsa S 40 B2
Ašanja YU 85 B5
Åsarna S 2 E21
Åsarp S 35 C5
Asasp F 76 C2
Åsbro S 37 B2
Asby S 40 B5
Asbygri IS 111 A9
Ascain F 76 C1
Ascea I 106 A2
Ascha D 62 A3
Aschach an der Donau A 63 B5
Aschaffenburg D 51 D5
Aschbach Markt A 63 B5
Ascheberg, *Nordrhein-Westfalen* D 50 B3
Ascheberg, *Schleswig-Holstein* D 44 A2
Aschendorf D 43 B4
Aschersleben D 52 B1
Asciano I 81 C5
Ascó E 90 B3
Áscoli Piceno I 82 D2
Áscoli Satriano I 104 B1

Ascona CH 70 B3
Ascot GB 31 C3
Ascoux F 58 B3
Åseda S 40 B5
Asendorf D 43 C6
Asenovgrad BG 11 E8
Åsensbruk S 35 C4
Åseral N 33 C4
Asfeld F 59 A5
Ásgarður IS 111 B1
Åsgårdstrand N 34 B2
Ash, *Kent* GB 31 C5
Ash, *Surrey* GB 31 C3
Åshammar S 36 A3
Ashbourne GB 27 B4
Ashbourne IRL 21 A5
Ashburton GB 28 C4
Ashby de-la-Zouch GB 27 C4
Ashchurch GB 29 B5
Ashford GB 31 C4
Ashington GB 25 C6
Ashley GB 26 C3
Ashmyany BY 7 D8
Ashton Under Lyne GB 26 B3
Ashwell GB 30 B3
Asiago I 71 C6
Asipovichy BY 7 E10
Askam-in-Furness GB 26 A2
Askeaton IRL 20 B3
Asker N 34 B2
Askersund S 37 C1
Askim N 34 B3
Askland N 33 C5
Äsköping S 36 B3
Askøy N 2 F16
Åsljunga S 41 C3
Asnæs DK 39 D4
Asola I 71 C5
Asolo I 72 C1
Asotthalom H 75 B4
Aspach A 63 B4
Aspang Markt A 64 C2
Aspariegos E 88 C1
Asparn an der Zaya A 64 B2
Aspatria GB 26 A2
Aspberg S 34 B5
Aspe E 101 A5
Aspet F 77 C3
Äspö S 41 C5
Aspres-sur-Buëch F 79 B4
Assafora P 92 C1
Asse B 49 C5
Assel D 43 B6
Asselborn L 50 C1
Assémini I 110 C1
Assen NL 42 C3
Assenede B 49 B4
Assens, *Aarhus Amt.* DK 38 C3
Assens, *Fyns Amt.* DK 39 D2
Assesse B 49 C6
Assisi I 82 C1
Assling D 62 C3
Asso I 71 C4
Åssoro I 109 B3
Assos GR 112 D2
Assumar P 92 B3
Astaffort F 77 B3
Astakós GR 112 D3
Asten NL 50 B1
Asti I 80 B2
Astorga E 86 B4
Åstorp S 41 C2
Ástros GR 113 E4
Astudillo E 88 B2
Asuni I 110 C1
Asványráró H 64 C3
Aszód H 65 C5
Aszófő H 74 B2
Atalaia P 92 B3
Atalándi GR 112 D4
Atalho P 92 C2
Átány H 65 C6
Atanzón E 95 B3
Ataquines E 94 A2
Atarfe E 100 B2
Ateca E 89 C5
Atella I 104 C1
Atessa I 103 A7
Ath B 49 C4
Athboy IRL 19 C5
Athea IRL 20 B2
Athenry IRL 20 A3
Athens = Athínai GR 113 E5
Atherstone GB 27 C4
Athies F 59 A3
Athies-sous-Laon F 59 A4
Athínai = Athens GR 113 E5
Athleague IRL 20 A3
Athlone IRL 21 A4
Athy IRL 21 B5
Atienza E 95 A4
Atina I 103 B6
Atkár H 65 C5
Åtorp S 36 B1
Åtrå N 33 B5
Åtran S 40 B2
Atri I 103 A6
Atripalda I 103 C7
Atsikí GR 112 C7
Attendorn D 50 B3
Attichy F 59 A4
Attigliano I 102 A5
Attigny F 59 A5
Attleborough GB 30 B5
Åtvidaberg S 37 C2
Atzendorf D 52 B1
Au, *Steiermark* A 63 C6
Au, *Vorarlberg* A 71 A4
Au, *Bayern* D 62 B2
Au, *Bayern* D 62 C2
Aub D 61 A6
Aubagne F 79 C4
Aubange B 60 A1
Aubel B 50 C1
Aubenas F 78 B3
Aubenton F 59 A5
Auberive F 59 C6
Aubeterre-sur-Dronne F 67 C5
Aubiet F 77 C3
Aubigné F 67 B4
Aubigny F 66 B3
Aubigny-au-Bac F 49 C4
Aubigny-en-Artois F 48 C3
Aubigny-sur-Nère F 68 A2
Aubin F 77 B5
Aubonne CH 69 B6
Aubrac F 78 B1
Aubusson F 68 C2
Auch F 77 C3
Auchencairn GB 25 D4
Auchinleck GB 24 C3
Auchterarder GB 25 B4
Auchtermuchty GB 25 B4
Auchtertyre GB 22 D3
Audenge F 76 B1
Auderville F 57 A4
Audierne F 56 B1
Audincourt F 70 A1
Audlem GB 26 C3
Audruicq F 48 C3
Audun-le-Roman F 60 A1
Audun-le-Tiche F 60 A1
Aue, *Nordrhein-Westfalen* D 50 B4
Aue, *Sachsen* D 52 C2
Auerbach, *Bayern* D 62 A2
Auerbach, *Sachsen* D 52 C2
Auffach A 72 A2
Augher GB 19 B5
Aughnacloy GB 19 B5
Aughrim IRL 21 B5
Augignac F 67 C5
Augsburg D 62 B1
Augusta I 109 B4
Augusten-borg DK 39 E2
Augustfehn D 43 B4
Augustów PL 6 E7
Aukrug D 44 A1
Auldearn GB 23 D5
Aulendorf D 61 C5
Auletta I 103 C8
Aulla I 81 B3
Aullène F 102 B2
Aulnay F 67 B4
Aulnoye-Aymeries F 49 C4
Ault F 48 C2
Aultbea GB 22 D3
Aulum DK 39 C1
Aulus-les-Bains F 77 D4
Auma D 52 C1
Aumale F 58 A2
Aumetz F 60 A1
Aumont-Aubrac F 78 B2
Aunay-en-Bazois F 68 A3
Aunay-sur-Odon F 57 A5
Auneau F 58 B2
Auneuil F 58 A2
Auning DK 39 C3
Aups F 79 C5
Aura D 51 C5
Auray F 56 C3
Aurich D 43 B4
Aurignac F 77 C3
Aurillac F 77 B5
Auriol F 79 C4
Auritz-Burguette E 76 D1
Auronzo di Cadore I 72 B2
Auros F 76 B2
Auroux F 78 B2
Aurskog N 34 B3
Aursmoen N 34 B3
Ausónia I 103 B6
Ausservillgraton A 72 B2
Austad N 33 C4
Austbygda N 33 A5
Aústis I 110 B2
Austmarka N 34 A4
Austre Moland N 33 C5
Austre Vikebygd N 32 B2
Auterive F 77 C4
Autheuil-Authouillet F 58 A2
Authon F 79 B5
Authon-du-Perche F 58 B1
Autol E 89 B5
Autreville F 60 B1
Autrey-lès-Gray F 69 A5
Autun F 69 B4
Auty-le-Châtel F 58 C3
Auvelais B 49 C5
Auvillar F 77 B3
Auxerre F 59 C4
Auxi-le-Château F 48 C3
Auxon F 59 B4
Auxonne F 69 A5
Auxy F 69 B4
Auzances F 68 B2
Auzon F 68 C3
Availles-Limouzine F 67 B5
Avaldsnes N 32 B2
Avallon F 68 A3
Ávas GR 112 B7
Avebury GB 29 B6
Aveiras de Cima P 92 B2
Aveiro P 92 A2
Avelgem B 49 C4
Avellino I 103 C7
Avenches CH 70 B2
Aversa I 103 C7
Avesnes-le-Comte F 48 C3
Avesnes-sur-Helpe F 49 C4
Avesta S 36 A3
Avetrana I 105 C3
Avezzano I 103 A6
Avià E 91 A4
Aviano I 72 B2
Aviemore GB 23 D5
Avigliana I 80 A1
Avigliano I 104 C1
Avignon F 78 C3
Ávila E 94 B2
Avilés E 88 A1
Avintes P 87 C2
Avinyo E 91 B4
Àvio I 71 C5
Avionárion GR 112 D6
Avioth F 59 A6
Avis P 92 B3
Avize F 59 B5
Ávola I 109 C4
Avon F 58 B3
Avonmouth GB 29 B5
Avord F 68 A2
Avranches F 57 B4
Avril F 60 A1
Avrillé F 67 A4
Avtovac BIH 84 C3
Awans B 49 C6
Ax-les-Thermes F 77 D4
Axams A 71 A6
Axat F 77 D5
Axbridge GB 29 B5
Axel NL 49 B4
Axminster GB 29 C4
Axvall S 35 C5
Ay F 59 A4
Aya E 89 A4
Ayamonte E 98 B3
Ayancık TR 16 A7
Ayaş TR 114 B7
Aydın TR 16 C3
Ayelo de Malferit E 96 C2
Ayer CH 70 B2
Ayerbe E 90 A2
Ayette F 48 C3
Ayiá GR 112 C4
Ayía Ánna GR 112 D5
Ayía Galíni GR 113 G6
Ayía Paraskeví GR 114 C1
Ayía Pelayía GR 113 F4
Ayia Trías GR 113 E3
Áyioi Theódhoroi GR 113 E5
Ayiókabos GR 112 C4
Áyios Evstrátios GR 112 C6
Áyios Matthaíos GR 112 C1
Áyios Mírono GR 113 G7
Áyios Nikólaos GR 113 G7
Áyios Pétros GR 112 D2
Aykirikçi TR 114 C5
Aylesbury GB 31 C3
Ayllón E 89 C3
Aylsham GB 30 B5
Ayna E 101 A3
Ayódar E 96 B2
Ayora E 96 B1
Ayr GB 24 C3
Ayrancı TR 16 C6
Ayron F 67 B5
Aysgarth GB 27 A4
Ayton GB 25 C5
Aytos BG 11 E9
Ayvacık TR 114 C1
Ayvalık TR 114 C1
Aywaille B 49 C6
Azaila E 90 B2
Azambuja P 92 B2
Azambujeira P 92 B2
Azanja YU 85 B5
Azannes-et-Soumazannes F 60 A1
Azanúy-Alins E 90 B3
Azaruja P 92 C3
Azay-le-Ferron F 67 B6
Azay-le-Rideau F 67 A5
Azcoitia E 89 A4
Azé F 69 B4
Azeiteiros P 92 B3
Azenhas do Mar P 92 C1
Azinhaga P 92 B2
Azinhal P 98 B3
Azinheira dos Bairros P 98 A2
Aznalcázar E 99 B4
Aznalcóllar E 99 B4
Azóia P 92 B2
Azpeitia E 89 A4
Azuaga E 99 A5
Azuara E 90 B2
Azuqueca de Henares E 95 B3
Azur F 76 C1
Azzano Décimo I 72 C2

B

Baad A 71 A5
Baamonde E 86 A3
Baar CH 70 A3
Baarle-Nassau B 49 B5
Baarn NL 49 A6
Babadag RO 11 D10
Babaeski TR 114 A2
Babayevo RUS 7 B13
Babenhausen, *Bayern* D 61 B6
Babenhausen, *Hessen* D 51 D4
Babiak PL 54 A3
Babice PL 55 C4
Babigoszcz PL 45 B6
Babimost PL 53 A5
Babina Greda HR 84 A3
Babócsa H 74 B2
Bábolma H 64 C3
Baborów PL 54 C2
Babót H 64 C3
Babruysk BY 7 E10
Babsk PL 55 B5
Bac GB 22 C2
Bač, *Crna Gora* YU 85 D5
Bač, *Vojvodina* YU 75 C4
Bacares E 101 B3
Bacău RO 11 C9
Baccarat F 60 B2
Bacharach D 50 C3
Bačina YU 85 C6
Bačka Palanka YU 75 C4
Bačka Topola YU 75 C4
Backaryd S 41 C5
Bäckebo S 40 C6
Bäckefors S 35 C4
Bäckhammar S 34 B6
Bački Breg YU 75 C3
Bački-Brestovac YU 75 C4
Bački Monoštor YU 75 C3
Bački Petrovac YU 75 C4
Bački Sokolac YU 75 C4
Backnang D 61 B5
Bačko Gradište YU 75 C5
Bačko Novo Selo YU 75 C4
Bačko Petrovo Selo YU 75 C5
Bácoli I 103 C7
Bacqueville-en-Caux F 58 A2
Bácsalmás H 75 B4
Bácsbokod H 75 B4
Bad Abbach D 62 B3
Bad Aibling D 62 C3
Bad Aussee A 63 C4
Bad Bederkesa D 43 B5
Bad Bentheim D 50 A3
Bad Bergzabern D 60 A3
Bad Berka D 52 C1
Bad Berleburg D 51 B4
Bad Berneck D 52 C1
Bad Bevensen D 44 B2
Bad Bibra D 52 B1
Bad Birnbach D 62 B4
Bad Blankenburg D 52 C1
Bad Bleiberg A 72 B3
Bad Brambach D 52 C2
Bad Bramstedt D 44 B1
Bad Breisig D 50 C3
Bad Brückenau D 51 C5
Bad Buchau D 61 B5
Bad Camberg D 50 C4
Bad Doberan D 44 A3
Bad Driburg D 51 B5
Bad Düben D 52 B2
Bad Dürkheim D 61 A4
Bad Dürrenberg D 52 B2
Bad Dürrheim D 61 B4
Bad Elster D 52 C2
Bad Ems D 50 C3
Bad Endorf D 62 C3
Bad Essen D 50 A4
Bad Fischau A 64 C2
Bad Frankenhausen D 52 B1
Bad Freienwalde D 45 C6
Bad Friedrichshall D 61 A5
Bad Füssing D 63 B4
Bad Gandersheim D 51 B6
Bad Gleichenberg A 73 B5
Bad Goisern A 63 C4
Bad Gottleuba D 53 C3
Bad Grund D 51 B6
Bad Hall A 63 B5
Bad Harzburg D 51 B6
Bad Herrenalb D 61 B4
Bad Hersfeld D 51 C5
Bad Hofgastein A 72 A3
Bad Homburg D 51 C4
Bad Honnef D 50 C3
Bad Hönningen D 50 C3
Bad Iburg D 50 A4
Bad Inner-laterns A 71 A4
Bad Ischl A 63 C4
Bad Karlshafen D 51 B5
Bad Kemmeriboden CH 70 B2
Bad Kissingen D 51 C6
Bad Kleinen D 44 B3
Bad Kohlgrub D 62 C2
Bad König D 61 A5
Bad Königshofen D 51 C6
Bad Köstritz D 52 C2
Bad Kreuzen A 63 B5
Bad Kreuznach D 60 A3
Bad Krozingen D 60 C3
Bad Laasphe D 51 C4
Bad Langensalza D 51 B6
Bad Lauchstädt D 52 B1
Bad Lausick D 52 B2
Bad Lauterberg D 51 B6
Bad Leonfelden A 63 B5
Bad Liebenwerda D 52 B3
Bad Liebenzell D 61 B4
Bad Lippspringe D 51 B4
Bad Meinberg D 51 B4
Bad Mergentheim D 61 A5
Bad Mitterndorf A 72 A3
Bad Münder D 51 A5
Bad Münstereifel D 50 C2
Bad Muskau D 53 B4
Bad Nauheim D 51 C4
Bad Nenndorf D 43 C6
Bad Neuenahr-Ahrweiler D 50 C3
Bad Neustadt D 51 C6
Bad Oeynhausen D 51 A4
Bad Oldesloe D 44 B2
Bad Orb D 51 C5
Bad Peterstal D 61 B4
Bad Pyrmont D 51 B5
Bad Radkersburg A 73 B5
Bad Ragaz CH 71 B4
Bad Rappenau D 61 A5
Bad Reichenhall D 62 C3
Bad Saarow-Pieskow D 53 A4
Bad Sachsa D 51 B6
Bad Säckingen D 70 A2
Bad Salzdetfurth D 51 A6
Bad Salzig D 50 C3
Bad Salzuflen D 51 A4
Bad Salzungen D 51 C6
Bad Sankt Leonhard A 73 B4
Bad Sassendorf D 50 B4
Bad Schandau D 53 C4
Bad Schmiedeberg D 52 B2
Bad Schönborn D 61 A4
Bad Schussenried D 61 B5
Bad Schwalbach D 50 C4
Bad Schwartau D 44 B2
Bad Segeberg D 44 B2
Bad Soden D 51 C4
Bad Soden-Salmünster D 51 C5
Bad Sooden-Allendorf D 51 B5
Bad Sulza D 52 B1
Bad Sülze D 45 A4
Bad Tatzmannsdorf A 73 A6
Bad Tennstedt D 51 B6
Bad Tölz D 62 C2
Bad Urach D 61 B5
Bad Vellach A 73 B4
Bad Vilbel D 51 C4
Bad Vöslau A 64 C2
Bad Waldsee D 61 C5
Bad Wiessee D 62 C2
Bad Wildungen D 51 B5
Bad Wilsnack D 44 C3
Bad Windsheim D 61 A6
Bad Wörishafen D 62 B1
Bad Wurzach D 61 C5
Bad Zwesten D 51 B5
Bad Zwischenahn D 43 B5
Badacsonytomaj H 74 B2
Badajoz E 93 C4
Badalona E 91 B5
Badalucco I 80 C1
Baden A 64 B2
Baden CH 70 A3
Baden-Baden D 61 B4
Bádenas E 90 B1
Badenweiler D 60 C3
Baderna HR 72 C3
Badgastein A 72 A3
Badia Calavena I 71 C6
Badia Polésine I 81 A5
Badia Pratáglia I 81 C5
Badia Tedalda I 82 C1
Bądki PL 47 B4
Badljevina HR 74 C2
Badolato I 106 C3
Badolatosa E 100 B1
Badonviller F 60 B2
Badovinci YU 85 B4
Badules E 90 B1
Bække DK 39 D2
Bækmarksbro DK 39 C1
Baells E 90 B3
Bælum DK 38 C3
Baena E 100 B1
Baesweiler D 50 C2
Baeza E 100 B2
Baflo NL 42 B3
Bafra TR 16 A7
Baga E 91 A4
Bagaladi I 106 C2
Bagenkop DK 39 E3
Baggetorp S 37 B3
Bagh a Chaisteil GB 22 E1
Bagheria I 108 A2
Bagnacavallo I 81 B5
Bagnáia I 102 A5
Bagnara Cálabra I 106 C2
Bagnasco I 80 B2
Bagnères-de-Bigorre F 76 C3
Bagnères-de-Luchon F 77 D3
Bagni del Másino I 71 B4
Bagni di Lucca I 81 B4
Bagni di Rabbi I 71 B5
Bagni di Tivoli I 102 B5
Bagno di Romagna I 81 C5
Bagnoles-de-l'Orne F 57 B5
Bagnoli dei Trigno I 103 B7
Bagnoli di Sopra I 72 C1
Bagnoli Irpino I 103 C8
Bagnolo Mella I 71 C5
Bagnols-en-Forêt F 79 C5
Bagnols-sur-Cèze F 78 B3
Bagnorégio I 102 A5
Bagolino I 71 C5
Bagrationovsk RUS 47 A6
Bagrdan YU 85 B6
Báguena E 95 A5
Bahabón de Esgueva E 88 C3
Bahillo E 88 B2
Báia delle Zágare I 104 B2
Báia Domizia I 103 B6
Baia Mare RO 11 C7
Baiano I 103 C7
Baião P 87 C2
Baiersbronn D 61 B4
Baiersdorf D 62 A2
Baignes-Ste. Radegonde F 67 C4
Baigneux-les-Juifs F 59 C5
Baildon GB 27 B4
Bailén E 100 A2
Băileşti RO 11 D7
Baileux B 49 C5
Bailieborough IRL 19 C5
Bailleul F 48 C3
Baillonville B 49 C6
Bailó E 90 A2
Bain-de-Bretagne F 57 C4
Bains F 78 A2
Bains-les-Bains F 60 B2
Bainton GB 27 B5
Baio E 86 A2
Baiona E 87 B2
Bais F 57 B5
Baiso I 81 B4
Baiuca P 92 A3
Baja H 75 B3
Bajánsenye H 73 B6
Bajina Bašta YU 85 C4
Bajmok YU 75 C4
Bajna H 65 C4
Bajovo Polje YU 84 C3
Bajša YU 75 C4
Bak H 74 B1
Bakar HR 73 C4
Bakewell GB 27 B4
Bakhmach UA 7 F12
Bakio E 89 A4
Bakırdağı TR 16 B7
Bakkafjörður IS 111 A11
Bakkagerði IS 111 B12
Bakonybél H 74 A2
Bakonycsernye H 74 A3
Bakonyjákó H 74 A2
Bakonyszentkirály H 74 A2
Bakonyszombathely H 74 A2
Bakov nad Jizerou CZ 53 C4
Bąkowiec PL 55 B6
Baks H 75 B5
Baksa H 74 C3
Bakum D 43 C5
Bala GB 26 C2
Bâlâ TR 16 B6
Balaguer E 90 B3
Balassagyarmat H 65 B5
Balástya H 75 B5
Balatonakali H 74 B2
Balatonalmádi H 74 A3
Balatonboglár H 74 B2
Balatonbozsok H 74 B3
Balatonederics H 74 B2
Balatonfenyves H 74 B2
Balatonföldvár H 74 B2
Balatonfüred H 74 B2
Balatonfűzfő H 74 A3
Balatonkenese H 74 A3
Balatonkiliti H 74 B3
Balatonlelle H 74 B2
Balatonszabadi H 74 B3
Balatonszemes H 74 B2
Balatonszentgyörgy H 74 B2
Balazote E 101 A3
Balbeggie GB 25 B4
Balbigny F 69 C4
Balboa E 86 B4
Balbriggan IRL 19 C5
Balchik BG 11 E10
Baldock GB 31 C3
Bale HR 82 A2
Baleira E 86 A3
Baleizao P 98 A3
Balen B 49 B6
Balerma E 100 C3
Balestrand N 2 F17
Balestrate I 108 A2
Balfour GB 23 B6
Bälganet S 41 C5
Balıkesir TR 114 C2
Balıklıçeşme TR 114 B2
Bälinge S 36 B4
Balingen D 61 B4
Balingsta S 36 B4
Balintore GB 23 D5
Baljevac YU 85 C5
Balk NL 42 C2
Balkbrug NL 42 C3
Balla IRL 18 C2
Ballachulish GB 24 B2
Ballaghaderreen IRL 18 C3
Ballancourt-sur-Essonne F 58 B3
Ballantrae GB 24 C3
Ballao I 110 C2
Ballasalla GB 26 A1
Ballater GB 23 D5
Ballen DK 39 D3
Ballenstedt D 52 B1
Ballerias E 90 B2
Balleroy F 57 A5
Ballerup DK 41 D2
Ballesteros de Calatrava E 100 A2
Ballı TR 114 B2
Ballina IRL 18 C2
Ballinalack IRL 19 C4
Ballinamore IRL 19 B4
Ballinascarty IRL 20 C3
Ballinasloe IRL 20 A3
Ballindine IRL 18 C3
Balling DK 38 C1
Ballingarry, *Limerick* IRL 20 B3
Ballingarry, *Tipperary* IRL 21 B4
Ballingeary IRL 20 C2
Ballinhassig IRL 20 C3
Ballinluig GB 25 B4
Ballino I 71 C5
Ballinrobe IRL 18 C2
Ballinskellings IRL 20 C1
Ballinspittle IRL 20 C3
Ballintra IRL 18 B3
Ballivor IRL 21 A5
Ballobar E 90 B3
Ballon F 58 B1
Ballon IRL 21 B5
Ballószög H 75 B4
Ballum DK 39 D1
Ballybay IRL 19 B5
Ballybofey IRL 19 B4
Ballybunion IRL 20 B2
Ballycanew IRL 21 B5
Ballycarry GB 19 B6
Ballycastle GB 19 A5
Ballycastle IRL 18 B2
Ballyclare GB 19 B6
Ballyconneely IRL 18 C1
Ballycotton IRL 20 C3
Ballycroy IRL 18 B2
Ballydehob IRL 20 C2
Ballyferriter IRL 20 B1
Ballygawley GB 19 B4
Ballygowan GB 19 B6
Ballyhaunis IRL 18 C3
Ballyheige IRL 20 B2
Ballyjamesduff IRL 19 C4
Ballylanders IRL 20 B3
Ballylynan IRL 21 B4
Ballymahon IRL 21 A4
Ballymena GB 19 B5
Ballymoe IRL 18 C3
Ballymoney GB 19 A5
Ballymore IRL 21 A4
Ballymote IRL 18 B3
Ballynacorra IRL 20 C3
Ballynagore IRL 21 A4
Ballynahinch GB 19 B6
Ballynure GB 19 B6
Ballyragget IRL 21 B4
Ballysadare IRL 18 B3
Ballyshannon IRL 18 B3
Ballyvaghan IRL 20 A2
Ballyvourney IRL 20 C2
Ballywalter GB 19 B6
Balmaclellan GB 24 C3
Balmaseda E 89 A3
Balme I 70 C2
Balmedie GB 23 D6
Balmuccia I 70 C3
Balna-paling GB 23 D4
Balneario de Panticosa E 76 D2
Balotaszállás H 75 B4
Balsa P 87 C3
Balsareny E 91 B4
Balsorano-Nuovo I 103 B6
Bålsta S 36 B4
Balsthal CH 70 A2
Balta UA 11 B10
Baltanás E 88 C2
Baltar E 87 C3
Baltasound GB 22 A8
Bălţi MD 11 C9
Baltimore IRL 20 C2
Baltinglass IRL 21 B5
Baltiysk RUS 47 A5
Bałtów PL 55 B6
Balugães P 87 C2
Balve D 50 B3
Balvi LV 7 C9
Balvicar GB 24 B2
Balya TR 114 C2
Balzo I 82 D2
Bamberg D 62 A1
Bamburgh GB 25 C6
Banatska Palanka YU 85 B6
Banatski Brestovac YU 85 B5
Banatski Despotovac YU 75 C5
Banatski Dvor YU 75 C5
Banatski-Karlovac YU 85 A6
Banatsko Arandjelovo YU 75 B5
Banatsko-Novo Selo YU 85 B5
Banaz TR 16 B4
Banbridge GB 19 B5
Banbury GB 30 B2
Banchory GB 23 D6
Bande B 49 C6
Bande E 87 B3
Bandholm DK 39 E4
Bandırma TR 114 B2
Bandol F 79 C4
Bandon IRL 20 C3
Bañeres E 96 C2
Banff GB 23 D6
Bangor F 66 A1
Bangor, *Down* GB 19 B6
Bangor, *Gwynedd* GB 26 B1
Bangor IRL 18 B2
Banie PL 45 B6
Banja YU 85 C4
Banja Koviljača YU 85 B4
Banja Luka BIH 84 B2
Banja Vručica BIH 84 B2
Banjaloka SLO 73 C4
Banjani YU 85 B4
Banje YU 85 D5
Banjska YU 85 D5
Banka SK 64 B3
Bankekind S 37 C2
Bankend GB 25 C4
Bankeryd S 40 B4
Bankfoot GB 25 B4
Banloc RO 75 C6
Bannalec F 56 C2
Bannes F 59 B4
Bannockburn GB 25 B4
Bañobárez E 87 D4
Bañon E 90 C1
Banon F 79 B4
Baños E 93 A5
Baños de Gigonza E 99 C5
Baños de la Encina E 100 A2
Baños de Molgas E 87 B3
Baños de Rio Tobia E 89 B4
Baños de Valdearados E 89 C3
Bánov CZ 64 B3
Banova Jaruga HR 74 C1
Bánovce nad Bebravou SK 64 B4
Banoviči BIH 84 B3
Banoviči Selo BIH 84 B3
Bánréve H 65 B6
Bansin D 45 B6
Banská Belá SK 65 B4
Banská Bystrica SK 65 B5
Banská Štiavnica SK 65 B4
Banstead GB 31 C3
Banteer IRL 20 B3
Bantry IRL 20 C2
Bantzenheim F 60 C3
Banyalbufar E 97 B2
Banyoles E 91 A5
Banyuls-sur-Mer F 91 A6
Bapaume F 48 C3
Bar UA 11 B9
Bar YU 105 A5
Bar-le-Duc F 59 B6
Bar-sur-Aube F 59 B5
Bar-sur-Seine F 59 B5
Barabhas GB 22 C2
Barači BIH 84 B1
Baracs H 74 B3
Baracska H 74 A3
Barahona E 89 C4
Barajes de Melo E 95 B4
Barakaldo E 89 A4
Baralla E 86 B3
Barañain E 76 D1
Baranavichy BY 7 E9
Baránd H 75 A6
Baranda YU 85 A5
Baranello I 103 B7
Baranów Sandomierski PL 55 C6
Baraqueville F 77 B5
Barasoain E 89 B5
Barbacena P 92 C3
Barbadás E 87 B3
Barbadillo E 94 B1
Barbadillo de Herreros E 89 B3
Barbadillo del Mercado E 89 B3
Barbadillo del Pez E 89 B3
Barban HR 82 A3
Barbarano Vicento I 71 C6
Barbariga HR 82 B2
Barbaros TR 114 B2
Barbastro E 90 A3
Barbate de Franco E 99 C5
Barbatona E 95 A4
Barbâtre F 66 B2
Barbazan F 77 C3
Barbeitos E 86 A3
Barbentane F 78 C3
Barberino di Mugello I 81 B5
Barbezieux-St. Hilaire F 67 C4
Barbonne-Fayel F 59 B4
Barbotan-les-Thermes F 76 C2
Barby D 52 B1

Barca de Alva P 87 C4
Bárcabo E 90 A3
Barcarrota E 93 C4
Barcellona-Pozzo di Gotto I 109 A4
Barcelona E 91 B5
Barcelonette F 79 B5
Barcelos P 87 C2
Barcena de Pie de Concha E 88 A2
Bárcena del Monasterio E 86 A4
Barchfeld D 51 C6
Barcin PL 46 C3
Barcino PL 46 A2
Bárcis I 72 B2
Barco P 92 A3
Barcones E 89 C4
Barcs H 74 C2
Barcus F 76 C2
Barczewo PL 47 B6
Bardejov SK 10 B6
Bårdesø DK 39 D3
Bardi I 81 B3
Bardney GB 27 B5
Bardo PL 54 C1
Bardolino I 71 C5
Bardonécchia I 79 A5
Bardoňovo SK 65 B4
Barèges F 76 D3
Barenstein D 52 C3
Barentin F 58 A1
Barenton F 57 B5
Barevo BIH 84 B2
Barfleur F 57 A4
Barga I 81 B4
Bargas E 94 C2
Barge I 79 B6
Bargemon F 79 C5
Barghe I 71 C5
Bargoed GB 29 B4
Bargrennan GB 24 C3
Bargteheide D 44 B2
Barham GB 31 C5
Bari I 104 B2
Bari Sardo I 110 C2
Barič Draga HR 83 B4
Barilović HR 73 C5
Barisciano I 103 A6
Barjac F 78 B3
Barjols F 79 C4
Bårkåker N 34 B2
Barkowo, *Dolnośląskie* PL 54 B1
Barkowo, *Pomorskie* PL 46 B3
Bârlad RO 11 C9
Barles F 79 B5
Barletta I 104 B2
Barlinek PL 45 C7
Barmouth GB 26 C1
Barmstedt D 43 B6
Barnard Castle GB 27 A4
Barnarp S 40 B4
Bärnau D 62 A3
Bärnbach A 73 A5
Barneberg D 52 A1
Barnenitz D 45 C4
Barnet GB 31 C3
Barnetby le Wold GB 27 B5
Barneveld NL 49 A6
Barneville-Carteret F 57 A4
Barnoldswick GB 26 B3
Barnowko PL 45 C6
Barnsley GB 27 B4
Barnstädt D 52 B1
Barnstaple GB 28 B3
Barnstorf D 43 C5
Barntrup D 51 B5
Baron F 58 A3
Baronissi I 103 C7
Barqueiro P 92 B2
Barquinha P 92 B2
Barr F 60 B3
Barr GB 24 C3
Barra P 92 A2
Barracas E 96 A2
Barraco E 94 B2
Barrado E 93 A5
Barrafranca I 109 B3
Barranco do Velho P 98 B3
Barrancos P 99 A4
Barrax E 95 C4
Barrbaar D 62 B1
Barre-des-Cevennes F 78 B2
Barreiro P 92 C1
Barreiros E 86 A3
Barrême F 79 C5
Barret-le-Bas F 79 B4
Barrhead GB 24 C3
Barrhill GB 24 C3
Barrio de Nuesra Señora E 88 B1
Barrow-in-Furness GB 26 A2
Barrow upon Humber GB 27 B5
Barrowford GB 26 B3
Barruecopardo E 87 C4
Barruelo de Santullán E 88 B2
Barruera E 90 A3
Barry GB 29 B4
Bårse DK 39 D4
Barsinghausen D 51 A5
Barssel D 43 B4
Barth D 45 A4
Bartholomä D 61 B5
Bartin TR 114 A7
Barton upon Humber GB 27 B5
Bartoszyce PL 47 A6
Barúmini I 110 C1
Baruth D 52 A3
Barvaux B 49 C6
Barver D 43 C5
Barwałd PL 65 A5
Barwice PL 46 B2
Barysaw BY 7 D10
Barzana E 88 A1
Bârzava RO 10 C6
Bárzio I 71 C4
Bas E 91 A5
Bašaid YU 75 C5
Basaluzzo I 80 B2
Basarabeasca MD 11 C10
Basauri E 89 A4
Baschi I 82 D1
Baschurch GB 26 C3
Basconcillos del Tozo E 88 B3
Bascones de Ojeda E 88 B2
Basécles B 49 C4
Basel CH 70 A2
Basélice I 103 B7
Basildon GB 31 C4
Basingstoke GB 31 C2
Baška CZ 65 A4
Baška HR 83 B3
Baška Voda HR 84 C1
Baslow GB 27 B4
Basovizza I 72 C3
Bassacutena I 110 A2
Bassano del Grappa I 72 C1
Bassano Romano I 102 A5
Bassecourt CH 70 A2
Bassella E 91 A4
Bassou F 59 C4
Bassoues F 76 C3
Bassum D 43 C5
Båstad S 40 C2
Bastardo I 82 D1
Bastelica F 102 A2
Bastelicaccia F 102 B1
Bastia F 102 A2
Bastia I 82 C1
Bastogne B 50 C1
Baston GB 30 B3
Bata H 74 B3
Batajnica YU 85 B5
Batalha P 92 B2
Bátaszék H 74 B3
Batea E 90 B3
Batelov CZ 63 A6
Bath GB 29 B5
Bathgate GB 25 C4
Batida H 75 B5
Batignano I 81 D5
Batina HR 74 C3
Bátka SK 65 B6
Batković BIH 85 B4
Batlava YU 85 D6
Batley GB 27 B4
Batočina YU 85 B6
Bátonyterenye H 65 C5
Batrina HR 74 C2
Båtsfjord N 3 A28
Battaglia Terme I 72 C1
Bätterkinden CH 70 A2
Battice B 50 C1
Battipáglia I 103 C7
Battle GB 31 D4
Battonya H 75 B6
Batuša YU 85 B6
Bátya H 75 B3
Baud F 56 C2
Baudour B 49 C4
Baugé F 67 A4
Baugy F 68 A2
Bauma CH 70 A3
Baume-les-Dames F 69 A6
Baumholder D 60 A3
Baunatal D 51 B5
Baunei I 110 B2
Bauska LV 6 C8
Bautzen D 53 B4
Bavanište YU 85 B5
Bavay F 49 C4
Bavilliers F 60 C2
Bavorov CZ 63 A5
Bawdsey GB 31 B5
Bawinkel D 43 C4
Bawtry GB 27 B4
Bayat TR 114 D5
Bayel F 59 B5
Bayeux F 57 A5
Bayındır TR 16 B3
Bayon F 60 B2
Bayonne F 76 C1
Bayons F 79 B5
Bayramiç TR 114 C1
Bayreuth D 52 D1
Bayrischzell D 62 C3
Baza E 101 B3
Bazas F 76 B2
Baziege F 77 C4
Bazoches-les-Gallerandes F 58 B3
Bazoches-sur-Hoëne F 58 B1
Bazzano I 81 B5
Beaconsfield GB 31 C3
Beade E 87 B2
Beadnell GB 25 C6
Beaminster GB 29 C5
Bearsden GB 24 C3
Beas E 99 B4
Beas de Segura E 100 A3
Beasain E 89 A4
Beattock GB 25 C4
Beaubery F 69 B4
Beaucaire F 78 C3
Beaufort F 69 C6
Beaufort IRL 20 B2
Beaufort-en Vallée F 67 A4
Beaugency F 58 C2
Beaujeu, *Alpes-de-Haute-Provence* F 79 B5
Beaujeu, *Rhône* F 69 B4
Beaulac F 76 B2
Beaulieu F 68 A2
Beaulieu GB 31 D2
Beaulieu-sous-la-Roche F 66 B3
Beaulieu-sur-Dordogne F 77 B4
Beaulieu-sur-Mer F 80 C1
Beaulon F 68 B3
Beauly GB 23 D4
Beaumaris GB 26 B1
Beaumesnil F 58 A1
Beaumetz-lès-Loges F 48 C3
Beaumont B 49 C5
Beaumont F 77 B3
Beaumont-de-Lomagne F 77 C3
Beaumont-du-Gâtinais F 58 B3
Beaumont-en-Argonne F 59 A6
Beaumont-Hague F 57 A4
Beaumont-la-Ronce F 58 C1
Beaumont-le-Roger F 58 A1
Beaumont-sur-Oise F 58 A3
Beaumont-sur-Sarthe F 57 B6
Beaune F 69 A4
Beaune-la-Rolande F 58 B3
Beaupréau F 66 A4
Beauraing B 49 C5
Beaurepaire F 69 C5
Beaurepaire-en-Bresse F 69 B5
Beaurières F 79 B4
Beauvais F 58 A3
Beauval F 48 C3
Beauville F 77 B3
Beauvoir-sur-Mer F 66 B2
Beauvoir-sur-Niort F 67 B4
Beba Veche RO 75 B5
Bebertal D 52 A1
Bebington GB 26 B2
Bebra D 51 C5
Bebrina HR 84 A2
Beccles GB 30 B5
Becedas E 93 A5
Beceite E 90 C3
Bečej YU 75 C5
Becerreá E 86 B3
Becerril de Campos E 88 B2
Bécherel F 57 B4
Bechhofen D 61 A6
Bechyně CZ 63 A5
Becilla de Valderaduey E 88 B1
Beckfoot GB 25 D4
Beckingham GB 27 B5
Beckum D 50 B4
Beco P 92 B2
Bécon-les-Granits F 66 A4
Bečov nad Teplou CZ 52 C2
Becsehely H 74 B1
Bedale GB 27 A4
Bedames E 89 A3
Bédar E 101 B4
Bédarieux F 78 C2
Bédarrides F 78 B3
Bedburg D 50 C2
Beddgelert GB 26 B1
Beddingestrand S 41 D3
Bédée F 57 B4
Bedegkér H 74 B3
Bedford GB 30 B3
Będków PL 55 B4
Bedlington GB 25 C6
Bedlno PL 55 A4
Bedmar E 100 B2
Bédoin F 79 B4
Bedónia I 80 B3
Bedretto CH 70 B3
Bedsted DK 38 C1
Bedum NL 42 B3
Bedwas GB 29 B4
Bedworth GB 30 B2
Będzin PL 55 C4
Beek en Donk NL 49 B6
Beekbergen NL 50 A1
Beelen D 50 B4
Beelitz D 52 A2
Beer GB 29 C4
Beerfelde D 45 C6
Beerfelden D 61 A4
Beernem B 49 B4
Beeskow D 53 A4
Beetsterzwaag NL 42 B3
Beetzendorf D 44 C3
Beflelay CH 70 A2
Begaljica YU 85 B5
Bégard F 56 B2
Begejci YU 75 C5
Begijar E 100 B2
Begijnendijk B 49 B5
Begues E 91 B4
Beguildy GB 26 C2
Begur E 91 B6
Beho B 50 C1
Behringen D 51 B6
Beilen NL 42 C3
Beilngries D 62 A2
Beine-Nauroy F 59 A5
Beinwil CH 70 A3
Beiseförth D 51 B5
Beith GB 24 C3
Beiuș RO 11 C7
Beja P 98 A3
Béjar E 93 A5
Békés H 75 B6
Békéscsaba H 75 B6
Bela SK 65 A4
Bela Crkva YU 85 B6
Belá nad Radbuzou CZ 62 A3
Bělá pod Bezdězem CZ 53 C4
Belâbre F 67 B6
Belalcázar E 93 C5
Belanovica YU 85 B5
Bélapátfalva H 65 B6
Belcaire F 77 D4
Bełchatów PL 55 B4
Belchite E 90 B2
Bělčice CZ 63 A4
Belcoo GB 19 B4
Belecke D 51 B4
Beled H 74 A2
Belej HR 83 B3
Beleño E 88 A1
Bélesta F 77 D4
Belev RUS 7 E14
Belfast GB 19 B6
Belford GB 25 C6
Belfort F 60 C2
Belgentier F 79 C4
Belgern D 52 B3
Belgioioso I 71 C4
Belgodère F 102 A2
Belgooly IRL 20 C3
Belgorod RUS 7 F14
Belgrade = Beograd YU 85 B5
Belhade F 76 B2
Beli Manastir HR 74 C3
Belica HR 74 B1
Belin-Bèliet F 76 B2
Belinchón E 95 B3
Belišće HR 74 C3
Bělkovice-Lašťany CZ 64 A3
Bell-lloc d'Urgell E 90 B3
Bella I 104 C1
Bellac F 67 B6
Bellágio I 71 C4
Bellananagh IRL 19 C4
Bellano I 71 B4
Bellária I 82 B1
Bellavary IRL 18 C2
Belle-Isle-en-Terre F 56 B2
Belleau F 59 A4
Belleek GB 18 B3
Bellegarde, *Gard* F 78 C3
Bellegarde, *Loiret* F 58 C3
Bellegarde-en-Diois F 79 B4
Bellegarde-en-Marche F 68 C2
Bellegarde-sur-Valserine F 69 B5
Bellême F 58 B1
Bellenaves F 68 B3
Bellentre F 70 C1
Bellevaux F 69 B6
Belleville F 69 B4
Belleville-sur-Vie F 66 B3
Bellevue-la-Montagne F 68 C3
Belley F 69 C5
Bellheim D 61 A4
Bellinge DK 39 D3
Bellingham GB 25 C5
Bellinzago Novarese I 70 C3
Bellinzona CH 70 B4
Bello E 95 B5
Bellpuig d'Urgell E 91 B4
Bellreguart E 96 C2
Bellsbank GB 24 C3
Belltall E 91 B4
Belluno I 72 B2
Bellver de Cerdanya E 91 A4
Bellvis E 90 B3
Bélmez E 93 C5
Belmez de la Moraleda E 100 B2
Belmont GB 22 A8
Belmont-de-la-Loire F 69 B4
Belmont-sur-Rance F 78 C1
Belmonte, *Asturias* E 86 A4
Belmonte, *Cuenca* E 95 C4
Belmonte P 92 A3
Belmonte de San José E 90 C2
Belmonte de Tajo E 95 B3
Belmullet IRL 18 B2
Belœil B 49 C4
Belogradchik BG 11 E7
Belokorovichi UA 11 A10
Beloljin YU 85 C6
Belorado E 89 B3
Belotič YU 85 B4
Bělotín CZ 64 A3
Belozersk RUS 7 B14
Belp CH 70 B2
Belpasso I 109 B3
Belpech F 77 C4
Belper GB 27 B4
Belsay GB 25 C6
Belsk Duzy PL 55 B5
Beltinci SLO 73 B6
Beltra IRL 18 C2
Belturbet IRL 19 B4
Beluša SK 64 A4
Belušić YU 85 C6
Belvedere Maríttimo I 106 B2
Belver de Cinca E 90 B3
Belver de los Montes E 88 C1
Belvès F 77 B3
Belvezet F 78 B2
Belvis de la Jara E 94 C2
Belvis de Monroy E 93 B5
Belyy RUS 7 D12
Belz F 56 C2
Bełżec PL 11 A7
Belzig D 52 A2
Bembibre E 86 B4
Bembridge GB 31 D2
Bemmel NL 50 B1
Bemposta, *Bragança* P 87 C4
Bemposta, *Santarém* P 92 B2
Benabarre E 90 A3
Benacazón E 99 B4
Benaguacil E 96 B2
Benahadux E 101 C3
Benalmádena E 100 C1
Benalúa de Guadix E 100 B2
Benalúa de las Villas E 100 B2
Benalup E 99 C5
Benamargosa E 100 C1
Benamaurel E 101 B3
Benameji E 100 B1
Benamocarra E 100 C1
Benaocaz E 99 C5
Benaoján E 99 C5
Benarrabá E 99 C5
Benasque E 90 A3
Benátky nad Jizerou CZ 53 C4
Benavente E 88 B1
Benavente P 92 C2
Benavides de Órbigo E 88 B1
Benavila P 92 B3
Bendorf D 50 C3
Bene Vagienna I 80 B1
Benedikt SLO 73 B5
Benejama E 101 A5
Benejúzar E 101 A5
Benešov CZ 63 A5
Bénestroff F 60 B2
Benet F 67 B4
Bénévent-l'Abbaye F 67 B6
Benevento I 103 B7
Benfeld F 60 B3
Benfica P 92 B2
Bengtsfors S 35 B4
Beničanci HR 74 C3
Benicarló E 90 C3
Benicássim E 96 A3
Benidorm E 96 C2
Benifaió E 96 B2
Beniganim E 96 C2
Benington GB 27 B6
Benisa E 96 C3
Benkovac HR 83 B4
Benllech GB 26 B1
Benneckenstein D 51 B6
Bénodet F 56 C1
Benquerencia de la Serena E 93 C5
Bensafrim P 98 B2
Bensdorf D 44 C4
Benshausen D 51 C6
Bensheim D 61 A4
Bentley GB 31 C3
Bentwisch D 44 A4
Beočin YU 75 C4
Beograd = Belgrade YU 85 B5
Beragh GB 19 B4
Berane YU 85 D4
Beranga E 89 A3
Berat AL 105 C5
Bérat F 77 C4
Beratzhausen D 62 A2
Bérbaltavár H 74 A1
Berbegal E 90 B2
Berbenno di Valtellina I 71 B4
Berberana E 89 B3
Bercedo E 89 A3
Bercel H 65 C5
Bercenay-le-Hayer F 59 B4
Berceto I 81 B3
Berchem B 49 C4
Berchidda I 110 B2
Berching D 62 A2
Berchtesgaden D 62 C4
Bérchules E 100 C2
Bercianos de Aliste E 87 C4
Berck F 48 C2
Berclaire d'Urgell E 90 B3
Berdoias E 86 A1
Berducedo E 86 A4
Berdún E 90 A2
Berdychiv UA 11 B10
Bere Alston GB 28 C3
Bere Regis GB 29 C5
Bereguardo I 70 C4
Berehove UA 11 B7
Berek BIH 84 A2
Beremend H 74 C3
Berestechko UA 11 A8
Berettyóújfalu H 10 C6
Berezhany UA 11 B8
Berezivka UA 11 C11
Berezna UA 7 F11
Berg D 62 A2
Berg S 37 C3
Berg im Gau D 62 B2
Berga, *Sachsen-Anhalt* D 51 B7
Berga, *Thüringen* D 52 C2
Berga E 91 A4
Berga S 40 B6
Bergama TR 114 C2
Bérgamo I 71 C4
Bergara E 89 A4
Berge, *Brandenburg* D 45 C4
Berge, *Niedersachsen* D 43 C4
Berge, *Telemark* N 33 B5
Berge, *Telemark* N 33 B5
Bergen, *Mecklenburg-Vorpommern* D 45 A5
Bergen, *Niedersachsen* D 44 C1
Bergen, *Niedersachsen* D 44 C2
Bergen N 32 A2
Bergen NL 42 C1
Bergen op Zoom NL 49 B5
Bergerac F 77 B3
Bergères-lés-Vertus F 59 B5
Bergeyk NL 49 B6
Berghausen D 61 B4
Bergheim D 50 C2
Berghem S 40 B2
Bergisch Gladbach D 50 C3
Bergkamen D 50 B3
Bergkvara S 41 C6
Berglern D 62 B2
Bergneustadt D 50 B3
Bergs slussar S 37 C2
Bergshamra S 36 B5
Bergtheim D 61 A6
Bergues F 48 C3
Bergum NL 42 B2
Bergün Bravuogn CH 71 B4
Bergwitz D 52 B2
Berhida H 74 A3
Beringel P 98 A3
Beringen B 49 B6
Berja E 100 C3
Berkeley GB 29 B5
Berkenthin D 44 B2
Berkhamsted GB 31 C3
Berkheim D 61 B6
Berkhof D 43 C6
Berkovići BIH 84 C3
Berkovitsa BG 11 E7
Berlanga E 99 A5
Berlanga de Duero E 89 C4
Berlevag N 3 A28
Berlikum NL 42 B2
Berlin D 45 C5
Berlstedt D 52 B1
Bermeo E 89 A4
Bermillo de Sayago E 87 C4
Bern CH 70 B2
Bernalda I 104 C2
Bernardos E 94 A2
Bernartice, *Jihočeský* CZ 63 A5
Bernartice, *Východočeský* CZ 53 C5
Bernau, *Baden-Württemberg* D 61 C4
Bernau, *Bayern* D 62 C3
Bernau, *Brandenburg* D 45 C5
Bernaville F 48 C3
Bernay F 58 A1
Bernburg D 52 B1
Berndorf A 64 C2
Berne D 43 B5
Bernecebarati H 65 B4
Bernhardsthal A 64 B2
Bernkastel-Kues D 60 A3
Bernolakovo SK 64 B3
Bernsdorf D 53 B4
Bernstadt D 53 B4
Bernstein A 73 A6
Bernués E 90 A2
Beromünster CH 70 A3
Beroun CZ 53 D4
Berovo MK 112 A4
Berre-l'Etang F 79 C4
Berriedale GB 23 C5
Berriew GB 26 C2
Berrocal E 99 B4
Bersenbrück D 43 C4
Bershad' UA 11 B10
Berthåga S 36 B4
Berthelming F 60 B2
Bertincourt F 48 C3
Bertinoro I 82 B1
Bertogne B 49 C6
Bertrix B 59 A6
Berufjörður IS 111 C11
Berville-sur-Mer F 58 A1
Berwick-Upon-Tweed GB 25 C5
Berzasca RO 10 D6
Berzence H 74 B2
Berzocana E 93 B5
Besalú E 91 A5
Besançon F 69 A6
Besenfeld D 61 B4
Besenyötelek H 65 C6
Besenyszög H 75 A5
Beshenkovichi BY 7 D10
Besigheim D 61 B5
Běšiny CZ 63 A4
Beška YU 75 C5
Besle F 57 C4
Besnyő H 74 A3
Bessais-le-Fromental F 68 B2
Bessan F 78 C2
Besse-en-Chandesse F 68 C2
Bessé-sur-Braye F 58 C1
Bessèges F 78 B3
Bessines-sur-Gartempe F 67 B6
Best NL 49 B6
Bestorp S 37 C2
Betanzos E 86 A2
Betelu E 76 C1
Bétera E 96 B2
Beteta E 95 B4
Béthenville F 59 A5
Bethesda GB 26 B1
Béthune F 48 C3
Beton-Bazoches F 59 B4
Bettembourg L 60 A2
Betterdorf L 60 A2
Bettna S 37 C3
Béttola I 80 B3
Bettona I 82 C1
Bettyhill GB 23 C4
Betws-y-Coed GB 26 B2
Betxi E 96 B2
Betz F 59 A3
Betzdorf D 50 C3
Beuil F 79 B5
Beulah GB 29 A4
Beuzeville F 58 A1
Bevagna I 82 D1
Bevens-bruk S 37 B2
Beveren B 49 B5
Beverley GB 27 B5
Bevern D 51 B5
Beverstedt D 43 B5
Beverungen D 51 B5
Beverwijk NL 42 C1
Bex CH 70 B2
Bexhill GB 31 D4
Beyazköy TR 114 A2
Beychevelle F 76 A2
Beykoz TR 114 A4
Beynat F 68 C1
Beyoğlu TR 114 A4
Beypazarı TR 114 B6
Beyşehir TR 16 C5
Bezas E 95 B5
Bezau A 71 A4
Bezdan YU 75 C3
Bèze F 69 A5
Bezenet F 68 B2
Bezhetsk RUS 7 C14
Béziers F 78 C2
Bezzecca I 71 C5
Biadki PL 54 B2
Biała, *Łódzkie* PL 55 B4
Biała, *Opolskie* PL 54 C2
Biała Podlaska PL 6 E7
Biała Rawska PL 55 B5
Białaczów PL 55 B5
Biale Błota PL 46 B3
Białobłoty PL 54 A2
Białobrzegi PL 55 B5
Białogard PL 46 B1
Białośliwie PL 46 B3
Biały Bór PL 46 B2
Białystok PL 6 E7
Biancavilla I 109 B3
Bianco I 106 C3
Biandrate I 70 C3
Biar E 101 A5
Biarritz F 76 C1
Bias F 76 B1
Biasca CH 70 B3
Biatorbágy H 74 A3
Bibbiena I 81 C5
Bibbona I 81 C4
Biberach, *Baden-Württemberg* D 61 B4
Biberach, *Baden-Württemberg* D 61 B5
Bibinje HR 83 B4
Bibione I 72 C3
Biblis D 61 A4
Bibury GB 29 B6
Biccari I 103 B8
Bicester GB 31 C2
Bichl D 62 C2
Bichlbach A 71 A5
Bicorp E 96 B2
Bicske H 74 A3
Bidache F 76 C1
Bidart F 76 C1
Biddinghuizen NL 42 C2
Biddulph GB 26 B3
Bideford GB 28 B3
Bidford-on-Avon GB 29 A6
Bie S 37 B3
Bieber D 51 C5
Biebersdorf D 53 B3
Biedenkopf D 51 C4
Biel CH 70 A2
Biel E 90 A2
Bielany Wroclawskie PL 54 B1
Bielawa PL 54 C1
Bielawy PL 55 A4
Bielefeld D 51 A4
Biella I 70 C3
Bielsa E 90 A3
Bielsk PL 47 C5
Bielsk Podlaski PL 6 E7
Bielsko-Biała PL 65 A5
Bienenbuttel D 44 B2
Bieniow PL 53 B5
Bienservida E 101 A3
Bienvenida E 93 C4
Bierdzany PL 54 C3
Bierné F 57 C5
Biersted DK 38 B2
Bierun PL 55 C4
Bierutów PL 54 B2
Bierwart B 49 C6
Bierzwina PL 46 B1
Bierzwnik PL 46 B1
Biescas E 90 A2
Biesenthal D 45 C5
Biesiekierz PL 46 A2
Bietigheim-Bissingen D 61 B5
Bièvre B 49 D6
Bieżuń PL 47 C5
Biga TR 114 B2
Bigadiç TR 114 C3
Biganos F 76 B2
Bigas P 87 D3
Bigastro E 101 A5
Bigbury GB 28 C4
Biggar GB 25 C4
Biggin Hill GB 31 C4
Biggleswade GB 30 B3
Bignasco CH 70 B3
Biguglia F 102 A2
Bihać BIH 83 B4
Biharnagybajom H 75 A6
Bijeljani BIH 84 C3
Bijeljina BIH 85 B4
Bijelo Polje YU 85 C4
Bijuesca E 89 C5
Bila Tserkva UA 11 B11
Bilaj HR 83 B4
Bilbao E 89 A4
Bilcza PL 55 C5
Bildudalur IS 111 B2
Bileća BIH 84 D3
Bilecik TR 114 B4
Biled RO 75 C5
Biłgoraj PL 11 A7
Bilhorod-Dnistrovskyy UA 11 C11
Bílina CZ 53 C3
Bilisht AL 112 B2
Bilje HR 74 C3
Billdal S 38 B4
Billerbeck D 50 B3
Billericay GB 31 C4
Billesholm S 41 C2
Billingborough GB 30 B3
Billinge S 41 D3
Billingham GB 27 A4
Billinghay GB 27 B5
Billingsfors S 35 C4
Billingshurst GB 31 C3
Billom F 68 C3
Billund DK 39 D2
Bilopillya UA 7 F13
Bílovec CZ 64 A4
Bilstein D 50 B4
Bilthoven NL 49 A6
Bilzen B 49 C6
Biňa SK 65 C4
Binaced E 90 B3
Binasco I 71 C4
Binbrook GB 27 B5
Binche B 49 C5
Bindlach D 52 D1
Bindslev DK 38 B3
Binefar E 90 B3
Bingen D 50 D3
Bingham GB 27 C5
Bingley GB 27 B4
Binic F 56 B3
Binz D 45 A5
Biograd na Moru HR 83 C4
Bionaz I 70 C2
Bioska YU 85 C4
Birda RO 75 C6
Birdlip GB 29 B5
Birkeland N 33 C5
Birkenfeld, *Baden-Württemberg* D 61 B4
Birkenfeld, *Rheinland-Pfalz* D 60 A3
Birkenhead GB 26 B2
Birkerød DK 41 D2
Birkfeld A 73 A5
Birkirkara M 107 C5
Birmingham GB 27 C4
Birr IRL 21 A4
Birresborn D 50 C2
Birstein D 51 C5
Biržai LT 6 C8
Birzebbugia M 107 C5

Bisáccia I 103 B8
Bisacquino I 108 B2
Bisbal de Falset E 90 B3
Biscarosse F 76 B1
Biscarosse Plage F 76 B1
Biscarrués E 90 A2
Biscéglie I 104 B2
Bischheim F 60 B3
Bischofsheim D 51 C5
Bischofshofen A 72 A3
Bischofswerda D 53 B4
Bischofswiesen D 62 C3
Bischofszell CH 71 A4
Bischwiller F 60 B3
Bisenti I 103 A6
Bishop Auckland GB 27 A4
Bishop's Castle GB 26 C3
Bishops Lydeard GB 29 B4
Bishop's Stortford GB 31 C4
Bishop's Waltham GB 31 D2
Bisignano I 106 B3
Bisingen D 61 B4
Biskupice-Oławskie PL 54 B2
Biskupiec PL 47 B5
Bismark D 44 C3
Bispingen D 44 B1
Bissen L 60 A2
Bissendorf D 50 A4
Bisserup DK 39 D4
Bistango I 80 B2
Bistarac Donje BIH 84 B3
Bistrica BIH 84 B2
Bistrica, *Crna Gora* YU 85 D4
Bistrica, *Srbija* YU 85 C4
Bistrica ob Sotli SLO 73 B5
Bistriţa RO 11 C8
Bisztynek PL 47 A6
Bitburg D 50 D2
Bitche F 60 A3
Bitetto I 104 B2
Bitola MK 112 A3
Bitonto I 104 B2
Bitschwiller F 60 C3
Bitterfeld D 52 B2
Bitti I 110 B2
Biville-sur-Mer F 48 D2
Bivona I 108 B2
Biwer L 60 A2
Bizeljsko SLO 73 B5
Bizovac HR 74 C3
Bjåen N 33 B4
Bjärnum S 41 C3
Bjärred S 41 D3
Bjelland, *Vest-Agder* N 32 C3
Bjelland, *Vest-Agder* N 33 C4
Bjelovar HR 74 C1
Bjerkreim N 32 C3
Bjerreby DK 39 E3
Bjerringbro DK 39 C2
Björbo S 36 A1
Björg IS 111 B8
Bjørkelangen N 34 B3
Björketorp S 40 B2
Björklinge S 36 A4
Björko, *Stockholm* S 36 B6
Björkö, *Västra Götaland* S 38 B4
Björköby S 40 B4
Björkvik S 37 C3
Björneborg S 34 B6
Björnerod S 35 B3
Bjørnevatn N 3 B28
Björnlunda S 37 B4
Björsäter S 37 C3
Bjurtjärn S 34 B6
Bjuv S 41 C2
Blace YU 85 C6
Blachownia PL 54 C3
Blackburn GB 26 B3
Blackpool GB 26 B2
Blackstad S 40 B6
Blackwater IRL 21 B5
Blackwaterfoot GB 24 C2
Blacy F 59 B5
Bladåker S 36 A5
Blaenau Ffestiniog GB 26 C2
Blaenavon GB 29 B4
Blaengarw GB 29 B4
Blagaj BIH 83 A5
Blagaj BIH 84 C2
Blagdon GB 29 B5
Blagnac F 77 C4
Blagoevgrad BG 11 E7
Blaichach D 61 C6
Blain F 66 A3
Blainville-sur-l'Eau F 60 B2
Blair Atholl GB 25 B4
Blairgowrie GB 25 B4
Blajan F 77 C3
Blakeney GB 29 B5
Blakstad N 33 C5
Blâmont F 60 B2
Blanca E 101 A4
Blancos E 87 C3
Blandford Forum GB 29 C5
Blanes E 91 B5
Blangy-sur-Bresle F 58 A2
Blankaholm S 40 B6
Blankenberge B 49 B4
Blankenburg D 51 B6
Blankenfelde D 45 C5
Blankenhain D 52 C1
Blankenheim D 50 C2
Blanquefort F 76 B2
Blansko CZ 64 A2
Blanzac F 67 C5
Blanzy F 69 B4
Blaricum NL 49 A6
Blarney IRL 20 C3
Blascomillán E 94 B1
Blascosancho E 94 B2
Błaszki PL 54 B3
Blatná CZ 63 A4
Blatné SK 64 B3
Blatnice CZ 64 B3
Blatnika BIH 84 B2
Blato HR 84 D1
Blato na Cetini HR 84 C1
Blatten CH 70 B2
Blatzheim D 50 C2
Blaubeuren D 61 B5
Blaufelden D 61 A5
Blaustein D 61 B5
Blaydon GB 25 D6
Blaye F 76 A2
Blaye-les-Mines F 77 B5
Blázquez E 93 C5
Bleckede D 44 B2
Blecua E 90 A2
Bled SLO 73 B4
Bleiburg A 73 B4
Bleichenbach D 51 C5
Bleicherode D 51 B6
Bléneau F 59 C3
Blera I 102 A5
Blérancourt F 59 A4
Bléré F 67 A5
Blesle F 68 C3
Blessington IRL 21 A5
Blet F 68 B2
Bletchley GB 31 C3
Bletterans F 69 B5
Blidö S 36 B5
Blidsberg S 40 B3
Blieskastel D 60 A3
Bligny-sur-Ouche F 69 A4
Blikstorp S 35 C6
Blinja HR 73 C6
Blizanówek PL 54 B3
Bliżyn PL 55 B5
Blois F 58 C2
Blokhus DK 38 B2
Blokzijl NL 42 C2
Blombacka S 34 B5
Blomberg D 51 B5
Blomskog S 34 B4
Blomstermåla S 40 C6
Blönduós IS 111 B5
Błonie PL 55 A5
Blonville-sur-Mer F 57 A6
Blötberget S 36 A2
Blovice CZ 63 A4
Bloxham GB 31 B2
Blšany CZ 52 C3
Bludenz A 71 A4
Bludov CZ 64 A2
Blumberg D 61 C4
Blyth, *Northumberland* GB 25 C6
Blyth, *Nottinghamshire* GB 27 B4
Blyth Bridge GB 25 C4
Blythburgh GB 30 B5
Blythe Bridge GB 26 C3
Bø N 33 B6
Boa Vista P 92 B2
Boal E 86 A4
Boan YU 85 D4
Boario Terme I 71 C5
Boat of Garten GB 23 D5
Boba H 74 A2
Bobadilla, *Logroño* E 89 B4
Bobadilla, *Málaga* E 100 B1
Bobadilla del Campo E 94 A1
Bobadilla del Monte E 94 B3
Bóbbio I 80 B3
Bóbbio Pellice I 79 B6
Bobigny F 58 B3
Bobingen D 62 B1
Böblingen D 61 B5
Bobolice PL 46 B2
Boboras E 87 B2
Bobowa PL 65 A6
Bobrinets UA 11 B12
Bobrová CZ 64 A2
Bobrovitsa UA 11 A11
Bobrowice PL 53 B5
Bobrówko PL 46 C1
Boca de Huérgano E 88 B2
Bocairent E 96 C2
Bočar YU 75 C5
Bocchigliero I 106 B3
Boceguillas E 89 C3
Bochnia PL 55 D5
Bocholt B 49 B6
Bocholt D 50 B2
Bochov CZ 52 C3
Bochum D 50 B3
Bockara S 40 B6
Bockenem D 51 A6
Bockfliess A 64 B2
Bockhorn D 43 B5
Bočna SLO 73 B4
Bocognano F 102 A2
Boconád H 65 C6
Boczów PL 45 C6
Böda, *Öland* S 41 B7
Boda, *Stockholm* S 36 A5
Boda, *Värmland* S 34 B5
Boda Glasbruk S 40 C5
Bodafors S 40 B4
Bodajk H 74 A3
Boddam, *Aberdeenshire* GB 23 D7
Boddam, *Shetland* GB 22 B7
Boddin D 44 B3
Bödefeld-Freiheit D 51 B4
Boden S 3 D24
Bodenmais D 62 A4
Bodenteich D 44 C2
Bodenwerder D 51 B5
Bodiam GB 31 C4
Bodinnick GB 28 C3
Bodio CH 70 B3
Bodjani YU 75 C4
Bodmin GB 28 C3
Bodø N 2 C21
Bodonal de la Sierra E 99 A4
Bodrum TR 16 C3
Bodzanów PL 47 C6
Bodzanowice PL 54 C3
Bodzechów PL 55 C6
Bodzentyn PL 55 C5
Boecillo E 88 C2
Boëge F 69 B6
Boën F 68 C4
Bogács H 65 C6
Bogadmindszent H 74 C3
Bogajo E 87 D4
Bogarra E 101 A3
Bogarre E 100 B2
Bogatić YU 85 B4
Bogatynia PL 53 C4
Boğazkale TR 16 A7
Boğazlıyan TR 16 B7
Bogdaniec PL 45 C7
Boge S 37 D5
Bogen D 62 B3
Bogen S 34 A4
Bogense DK 39 D3
Bognanco Fonti I 70 B3
Bognes N 2 B22
Bogno CH 70 B4
Bognor Regis GB 31 D3
Bogoria PL 55 C6
Boguchwały PL 47 B6
Bogumiłowice PL 55 B4
Boguslav UA 11 B11
Boguszów-Gorce PL 53 C6
Bogutovac YU 85 C5
Bogyiszló H 74 B3
Bohain-en-Vermandois F 49 D4
Böheimkirchen A 64 B1
Bohinjska Bistrica SLO 72 B3
Böhlen D 52 B2
Böhmenkirch D 61 B5
Bohmte D 43 C5
Bohonal de Ibor E 93 B5
Böhönye H 74 B2
Bohumin CZ 65 A4
Boiro E 86 B2
Bois-d'Amont F 69 B6
Boisseron F 78 C3
Boitzenburg D 45 B5
Boixols E 91 A4
Boizenburg D 44 B2
Bojadła PL 53 B5
Bojano I 103 B7
Bojanowo PL 54 B1
Bøjden DK 39 D3
Bojkovice CZ 64 A3
Bojná SK 64 B4
Bojnice SK 65 B4
Boka YU 75 C5
Böklund D 43 A6
Bokod H 74 A3
Böksholm S 40 B4
Boksitogorsk RUS 7 B12
Bol HR 83 C5
Bolaños de Calatrava E 100 A2
Bolayır TR 114 B1
Bolbec F 58 A1
Bölcske H 75 B3
Bolderslev DK 39 E2
Boldog H 65 C5
Boldva H 65 B6
Bolea E 90 A2
Bolekhiv UA 11 B7
Bolesławiec PL 53 B5
Boleszkowice PL 45 C6
Bolewice PL 46 C2
Bólgheri I 81 C4
Bolhrad UA 11 D10
Boliden S 3 D24
Bolimów PL 55 A5
Boliqueime P 98 B2
Boljevci YU 85 B5
Boljkovci YU 85 B5
Bolkhov RUS 7 E14
Bolków PL 53 C6
Bollebygd S 40 B2
Bollène F 78 B3
Bólliga E 95 B4
Bollnäs S 2 F22
Bollullos E 99 B4
Bollullos par del Condado E 99 B4
Bologna I 81 B5
Bologne F 59 B6
Bolognetta I 108 B2
Bolognola I 82 D2
Bologoye RUS 7 C13
Bolótana I 110 B1
Bolsena I 102 A4
Bolshaya Vradiyevka UA 11 C11
Bolsover GB 27 B4
Bolstad S 35 C4
Bolsward NL 42 B2
Boltaña E 90 A3
Boltenhagen D 44 B3
Boltigen CH 70 B2
Bolton GB 26 B3
Bolu TR 114 B6
Bolungavík IS 111 A2
Bolvadin TR 16 B5
Bóly H 74 C3
Bolzaneto I 80 B2
Bolzano I 71 B6
Bomba I 103 A7
Bombarral P 92 B1
Bömenzien D 44 C3
Bomlitz D 43 C6
Bømlo N 32 B2
Bøn N 34 A3
Bon-Encontre F 77 B3
Bonaduz CH 71 B4
Bonanza E 99 C4
Boñar E 88 B1
Bonarbridge GB 23 D4
Bonárcado I 110 B1
Bonares E 99 B4
Bonassola I 80 B3
Bonawe GB 24 B2
Bondal N 33 B5
Bondeno I 81 B5
Bondorf D 61 B4
Bondstorp S 40 B3
Bo'ness GB 25 B4
Bonete E 101 A4
Bonifacio F 102 B2
Bonigen CH 70 B2
Bonin PL 46 A2
Bonn D 50 C3
Bonnánaro I 110 B1
Bonnat F 68 B1
Bonndorf D 61 C4
Bonnétable F 58 B1
Bonnétage F 70 A1
Bonneuil-les-Eaux F 58 A3
Bonneuil-Matours F 67 B5
Bonneval F 58 B2
Bonneval-sur-Arc F 70 C2
Bonneville F 69 B6
Bonnières-sur-Seine F 58 A2
Bonnieux F 79 C4
Bönnigheim D 61 A5
Bonny-sur-Loire F 68 A2
Bonnyrigg GB 25 C4
Bono E 90 A3
Bono I 110 B2
Bonorva I 110 B1
Bønsnes N 34 A2
Bonyhád H 74 B3
Boom B 49 B5
Boos F 58 A2
Boostedt D 44 A2
Bootle, *Cumbria* GB 26 A2
Bootle, *Merseyside* GB 26 B2
Bopfingen D 61 B6
Boppard D 50 C3
Boqueixón E 86 B2
Bor CZ 62 A3
Bor S 40 B4
Bor TR 16 C7
Bor YU 11 D7
Boran-sur-Oise F 58 A3
Borås S 40 B2
Borba P 92 C3
Borbona I 102 A6
Borča YU 85 B5
Borci BIH 84 C3
Borculo NL 50 A2
Bordány H 75 B4
Bordeaux F 76 B2
Bordeira P 98 B2
Bordesholm D 44 A2
Borðeyri IS 111 B4
Bordighera I 80 C1
Bording DK 39 C2
Bordón E 90 C2
Bore I 81 B3
Borehamwood GB 31 C3
Borek Strzeliński PL 54 C2
Borek Wielkopolski PL 54 B2
Boreland GB 25 C4
Borello I 82 B1
Borensberg S 37 C2
Borgarnes IS 111 C4
Borgentreich D 51 B5
Börger D 43 C4
Borger NL 42 C3
Borggård S 37 C2
Borghamn S 37 C1
Borghetta di Vara I 81 B3
Borghetto d'Arróscia I 80 B1
Borghetto Santo Spirito I 80 B2
Borgholm S 41 C6
Borghorst D 50 A3
Bórgia I 106 C3
Borgloon B 49 C6
Børglum DK 38 B2
Borgo F 102 A2
Borgo a Mozzano I 81 C4
Borgo alla Collina I 81 C5
Borgo Pace I 82 C1
Borgo San Dalmazzo I 80 B1
Borgo San Lorenzo I 81 C5
Borgo Val di Taro I 81 B3
Borgo Valsugana I 71 B6
Borgo Vercelli I 70 C3
Borgoforte I 81 A4
Borgofranco d'Ivrea I 70 C2
Borgomanero I 70 C3
Borgomasino I 70 C2
Borgonovo Val Tidone I 80 A3
Borgorose I 102 A6
Borgosésia I 70 C3
Borgstena S 40 B3
Borgue GB 24 D3
Borgvik S 34 B4
Borisovka RUS 7 F14
Borja E 89 C5
Bork D 50 B3
Borken D 50 B2
Børkop DK 39 D2
Borkowice PL 55 B5
Borkowo PL 47 C6
Borkum D 42 B3
Borlänge S 36 A2
Bormes-les-Mimosas F 79 C5
Bórmio I 71 B5
Bormujos E 99 B4
Borna D 52 B2
Borne NL 50 A2
Borne Sulinowo PL 46 B2
Bornes P 87 C3
Bornheim D 50 C2
Bornhöved D 44 A2
Börnicke D 45 C4
Bornos E 99 C5
Borobia E 89 C5
Borodino RUS 7 D13
Borohrádek CZ 53 C6
Boronów PL 54 C3
Bórore I 110 B1
Boroszów PL 54 C3
Borota H 75 B4
Boroughbridge GB 27 A4
Borovany CZ 63 B5
Borovichi RUS 7 B12
Borovnica SLO 73 C4
Borovo HR 75 C3
Borovsk RUS 7 D14
Borovy CZ 63 A4
Borowa PL 54 B2
Borowie PL 55 B6
Borox E 94 B3
Borrby S 41 D4
Borre DK 41 E2
Borre N 34 B2
Borredá E 91 A4
Borrenes E 86 B4
Borriol E 96 A2
Borris DK 39 D1
Borris IRL 21 B5
Borris-in-Ossory IRL 21 B4
Borrisokane IRL 20 B3
Borrisoleigh IRL 21 B4
Borrowdale GB 26 A2
Borşa RO 11 C8
Borsdorf D 52 B2
Borsfa H 74 B1
Borský Mikuláš SK 64 B3
Borsodivánka H 65 C6
Borsodnádasd H 65 B6
Bort-les-Orgues F 68 C2
Börte N 33 B4
Borth GB 26 C1
Boruja Kościelne PL 54 A1
Borup DK 39 D4
Boryslav UA 11 B7
Boryspil UA 11 A11
Boryszyn PL 46 C1
Borzęciczki PL 54 B2
Borzęcin PL 55 A5
Borzna UA 7 F12
Borzonasca I 80 B3
Borzyszkowy PL 46 A3
Borzytuchom PL 46 A3
Bosa I 110 B1
Bošáca SK 64 B3
Bosanci HR 73 C5
Bosanska Dubica BIH 74 C1
Bosanska Gradiška BIH 74 C2
Bosanska Kostajnica BIH 74 C1
Bosanska Krupa BIH 83 B5
Bosanski Brod BIH 84 A2
Bosanski Novi BIH 83 A5
Bosanski Petrovac BIH 83 B5
Bosanski Šamac BIH 84 A3
Bosansko Grahovo BIH 83 B5
Bošany SK 64 B4
Bösárkány H 64 C3
Bosau D 44 A2
Bósca H 75 B4
Boscastle GB 28 C3
Bosco Chiesanuova I 71 C6
Bösdorf D 44 A2
Bösel D 43 B4
Bosham GB 31 D3
Bösingfeld D 51 A5
Boskoop NL 49 A5
Boskovice CZ 64 A2
Bošnjaci HR 84 A3
Bossast E 77 D3
Bossolasco I 80 B2
Boštanj SLO 73 B5
Boston GB 27 C5
Bostrak N 33 B5
Böszénfa H 74 B2
Bot E 90 B3
Botajica BIH 84 B3
Bøte By DK 44 A3
Bothel GB 26 A2
Boticas P 87 C3
Botilsäter S 35 B5
Botoš YU 75 C5
Botoşani RO 11 C9
Botricello I 107 C3
Bottendorf D 51 B4
Bottesford GB 27 C5
Bottnaryd S 40 B3
Bottrop D 50 B2
Botunje YU 85 B6
Boturić YU 85 C5
Bötzingen D 60 B3
Bouaye F 66 A3
Bouça P 87 C3
Boucau F 76 C1
Bouchain F 49 C4
Bouchoir F 58 A3
Boudreville F 59 C5
Boudry CH 70 B1
Bouesse F 67 B6
Bouguenais F 66 A3
Bouhy F 68 A3
Bouillargues F 78 C3
Bouillon B 59 A6
Bouilly F 59 B4
Bouin F 66 B3
Boulay-Moselle F 60 A2
Boulazac F 67 C5
Boule-d'Amont F 91 A5
Bouligny F 60 A1
Boulogne-sur-Gesse F 77 C3
Boulogne-sur-Mer F 48 C2
Bouloire F 58 C1
Bouquemaison F 48 C3
Bourbon-Lancy F 68 B3
Bourbon-l'Archambault F 68 B3
Bourbonne-les-Bains F 60 C1
Bourbourg F 48 C3
Bourbriac F 56 B2
Bourcefranc-le-Chapus F 66 C3
Bourdeaux F 79 B4
Bouresse F 67 B5
Bourg F 76 A2
Bourg-Achard F 58 A1
Bourg-Argental F 69 C4
Bourg-de-Péage F 79 A4
Bourg-de-Thizy F 69 B4
Bourg-de-Visa F 77 B3
Bourg-en-Bresse F 69 B5
Bourg-et-Comin F 59 A4
Bourg-Lastic F 68 C2
Bourg-Madame F 91 A4
Bourg-St. Andéol F 78 B3
Bourg-St. Maurice F 70 C1
Bourganeuf F 68 C1
Bourges F 68 A2
Bourgneuf-en-Retz F 66 A3
Bourgogne F 59 A5
Bourgoin-Jallieu F 69 C5
Bourgtheroulde F 58 A1
Bourgueil F 67 A5
Bourmont F 60 B1
Bourne GB 30 B3
Bournemouth GB 29 C6
Bourneville F 58 A1
Bournezeau F 66 B3
Bourran F 77 B3
Bourret F 77 C4
Bourron-Marlotte F 58 B3
Bourton-on-The-Water GB 29 B6
Boussac F 68 B2
Boussens F 77 C3
Boutersem B 49 C5
Bouttencourt F 48 D2
Bouvières F 79 B4
Bouvron F 66 A3
Bouxwiller F 60 B3
Bouzas E 87 B2
Bouzonville F 60 A2
Bova I 106 D2
Bova Marina I 106 D2
Bovalino Marina I 106 C3
Bovallstrand S 35 C3
Bovec SLO 72 B3
Bóveda E 86 B3
Bóvegno I 71 C5
Bovenau D 44 A1
Bovenden D 51 B5
Bóves I 80 B1
Bovey Tracey GB 28 C4
Bovino I 103 B8
Bøvlingbjerg DK 38 C1
Bovolenta I 72 C1
Bovolone I 71 C6
Bowes GB 27 A4
Bowmore GB 24 C1
Bowness-on-Windermere GB 26 A3
Box GB 29 B5
Boxberg, *Baden-Württemberg* D 61 A5
Boxberg, *Sachsen* D 53 B4
Boxholm S 37 C2
Boxmeer NL 50 B1
Boxtel NL 49 B6
Boyabat TR 16 A7
Boyalıca TR 114 B4
Boyle IRL 18 C3
Bozan TR 114 C6
Božava HR 83 B3
Bozburun TR 16 C4
Bozcaada TR 112 C8
Bozdoğan TR 16 C4
Božepole Wielkie PL 46 A3
Boževac YU 85 B6
Boži Dar CZ 52 C2
Božice CZ 64 B2
Bozkır TR 16 C6
Bozouls F 78 B1
Bozüyük TR 114 C5
Bózzolo I 81 A4
Bra I 80 B1
Braås S 40 B5
Brabrand DK 39 C3
Bracadale GB 22 D2
Bracciano I 102 A5
Bracieux F 67 A6
Bräcke S 2 E21
Brackenheim D 61 A5
Brackley GB 30 B2
Bracklin IRL 19 C5
Bracknell GB 31 C3
Brackwede D 51 B4
Braco GB 25 B4
Brad RO 11 C7
Bradford GB 27 B4
Bradford on Avon GB 29 B5
Bradina BIH 84 C3
Brådland N 32 C3
Brae GB 22 A7
Brædstrup DK 39 D2
Braemar GB 23 D5
Braemore GB 22 D3
Braga P 87 C2
Bragança P 87 C4
Brăila RO 11 D9
Braine F 59 A4
Braine-le-Comte B 49 C5
Braintree GB 31 C4
Braives B 49 C6
Brake D 43 B5
Brakel B 49 C4
Brakel D 51 B5
Bräkne-Hoby S 41 C5
Brålanda S 35 C4
Bralin PL 54 B2
Brallo di Pregola I 80 B3
Bram F 77 C5
Bramafan F 79 C5
Bramberg am Wildkogel A 72 A2
Bramdrupdam DK 39 D2
Bramming DK 39 D1
Brampton GB 25 D5
Bramsche D 43 C4
Branca I 82 C1
Brancaleone Marina I 106 D3
Brancaster GB 30 B4
Brand, *Nieder Östereich* A 63 B6
Brand, *Vorarlberg* A 71 A4
Brand-Erbisdorf D 52 C3
Brandbu N 34 A2
Brande DK 39 D2
Brande-Hornerkirchen D 43 B6
Brandenberg A 72 A1
Brandenburg D 45 C4
Brandis D 52 B2
Brando F 102 A2
Brandomil E 86 A2
Brandon GB 30 B4
Brandshagen D 45 A5
Brandval N 34 A4
Brandýs nad Labem CZ 53 C4
Branice PL 54 C2
Braniewo PL 47 A5
Branik SLO 72 C3
Brankovina YU 85 B4
Branky CZ 64 A3
Branne F 76 B2
Brannenburg-Degerndorf D 62 C3
Brantôme F 67 C5
Branzi I 71 B4
Bras d'Asse F 79 C5
Braslaw BY 7 D9
Braşov RO 11 D8
Brasparts F 56 B2
Brassac, *Charente* F 67 C4
Brassac, *Tarn* F 77 C5
Brassac-les-Mines F 68 C3
Brasschaat B 49 B5
Brastad S 35 C3
Břasy CZ 63 A4
Brąszewice PL 54 B3
Bratislava SK 64 B3
Brattfors S 34 B6
Bratunac BIH 85 B4
Braubach D 50 C3
Braunau A 62 B4
Braunfels D 51 C4
Braunlage D 51 B6
Braunsbedra D 52 B1
Braunschweig D 51 A6
Bray IRL 21 A5
Bray Dunes F 48 B3
Bray-sur-Seine F 59 B4
Bray-sur-Somme F 48 D3
Brazatortas E 100 A1
Brazey-en-Plaine F 69 A5
Brbinj HR 83 B4
Brčko BIH 84 B3
Brdani YU 85 C5
Brdów PL 47 C4
Brea de Tajo E 95 B3
Brécey F 57 B4
Brechen D 50 C4
Brechin GB 25 B5
Brecht B 49 B5
Brecketfeld D 50 B3
Břeclav CZ 64 B2
Brecon GB 29 B4
Brécy F 68 A2
Breda E 91 B5
Breda NL 49 B5
Bredaryd S 40 B3
Breddin D 44 C4
Bredebro DK 39 D1
Bredelar D 51 B4
Bredenfelde D 45 B5
Bredsjö S 36 B1
Bredstedt D 43 A5
Bredsten DK 39 D2
Bree B 49 B6
Bregana HR 73 C5
Breganze I 72 C1
Bregenz A 71 A4
Bréhal F 57 B4
Brehna D 52 B2
Breidenbach F 60 A3
Breiðdalsvík IS 111 C11
Breil-sur-Roya F 80 C1
Breisach D 60 B3
Breitenbach CH 70 A2
Breitenbach D 51 C5
Breitenberg D 63 B4
Breitenfelde D 44 B2
Breitengussbach D 51 D6
Breivikbotn N 3 A25
Brejning DK 39 D2
Brekken N 2 E19
Brekkestø N 33 C5
Brekstad N 2 E18
Brem-sur-Mer F 66 B3
Bremen D 43 B5
Bremerhaven D 43 B5
Bremervörde D 43 B6
Bremgarten CH 70 A3
Brenderup DK 39 D2
Brenes E 99 B5
Brengova SLO 73 B5
Brenna PL 65 A4
Breno I 71 C5
Brénod F 69 B5
Brensbach D 61 A4
Brentwood GB 31 C4
Brescello I 81 B4
Bréscia I 71 C5
Breskens NL 49 B4
Bresles F 58 A3
Bresnica YU 85 C5
Bressana I 80 A3
Bressanone I 72 B1
Bressuire F 67 B4
Brest BY 6 E7
Brest F 56 B1
Brest HR 72 C3
Brestač YU 85 B4
Brestanica SLO 73 B5
Brestova HR 82 A3
Brestovac HR 74 C2
Bretenoux F 77 B4
Breteuil, *Eure* F 58 B1
Breteuil, *Oise* F 58 A3
Brétigny-sur-Orge F 58 B3
Bretten D 61 A4
Bretteville-sur-Laize F 57 A5
Brettheim D 61 A6
Breuil-Cervínia I 70 C2
Breukelen NL 49 A6
Brevik N 33 B6
Brevik S 36 B5
Breza BIH 84 B3
Brežice SLO 73 C5
Bréziers F 79 B5
Brezna YU 85 C5
Breznica HR 73 B6
Breznica Našička HR 74 C3
Březnice CZ 63 A4
Brezno SK 65 B5
Brezolles F 58 B2
Březová nad Svitavou CZ 64 A2
Brezová pod Bradlom SK 64 B3
Brezovica SK 65 A6
Brezovica SLO 73 B4
Brezovo Polje Selo BIH 84 B3
Briançon F 79 B5
Brianconnet F 79 C5
Briare F 58 C3
Briatexte F 77 C4
Briático I 106 C3
Briaucourt F 59 B6
Bribir HR 73 C4
Bricquebec F 57 A4
Bridge of Cally GB 25 B4
Bridge of Don GB 23 D6
Bridge of Earn GB 25 B4
Bridge of Orchy GB 24 B3
Bridgend, *Argyll & Bute* GB 24 C1
Bridgend, *Bridgend* GB 29 B4
Bridgnorth GB 26 C3
Bridgwater GB 29 B5
Břidličná CZ 64 A3
Bridlington GB 27 A5
Bridport GB 29 C5

Brie-Comte-Robert F 58 B3
Briec F 56 B1
Brienne-le-Château F 59 B5
Brienon-sur-Armançon F 59 C4
Brienz CH 70 B3
Brienza I 104 C1
Brieskow Finkenheerd D 53 A4
Brietlingen D 44 B2
Brieva de Cameros E 89 B4
Briey F 60 A1
Brig CH 70 B3
Brigg GB 27 B5
Brighouse GB 27 B4
Brightlingsea GB 31 C5
Brighton GB 31 D3
Brignogan-Plage F 56 B1
Brignoles F 79 C5
Brigstock GB 30 B3
Brihuega E 95 B4
Brijuni HR 82 B2
Brillon-en-Barrois F 59 B6
Brilon D 51 B4
Brinches P 98 A3
Bríndisi I 105 C3
Brinje HR 83 A4
Brinon-sur-Beuvron F 68 A3
Brinon-sur-Sauldre F 68 A2
Brinyan GB 23 B5
Brión E 86 B2
Briones E 89 B4
Brionne F 58 A1
Brioude F 68 C3
Brioux-sur-Boutonne F 67 B4
Briouze F 57 B5
Briscous F 76 C1
Brisighella I 81 B5
Brissac-Quincé F 67 A4
Brissago CH 70 B3
Bristol GB 29 B5
Brive-la-Gaillarde F 67 C6
Briviesca E 89 B3
Brixham GB 29 C4
Brixlegg A 72 A1
Brjánslækur IS 111 B2
Brka BIH 84 B3
Brnaze HR 83 C5
Brněnec CZ 64 A2
Brno CZ 64 A2
Bro S 36 B4
Broad Haven GB 28 B2
Broadclyst GB 29 C4
Broadford GB 22 D3
Broadford IRL 20 B3
Broadstairs GB 31 C5
Broadstone GB 29 C5
Broadway GB 29 A6
Broager DK 39 E2
Broaryd S 40 B3
Broby S 41 C4
Brobyværk DK 39 D3
Bročanac BIH 84 C2
Broćanac YU 84 D3
Brocas F 76 B2
Brock D 50 A3
Brockel D 43 B6
Brockenhurst GB 31 D2
Broczyno PL 46 B2
Brod MK 112 A3
Brod na Kupi HR 73 C4
Brodalen S 35 C3
Brodarevo YU 85 C4
Broddbo S 36 B3
Brodek u Přerova CZ 64 A3
Broden-bach D 50 C3
Brodick GB 24 C2
Brodnica PL 47 B5
Brodnica Graniczna PL 47 A4
Brody, *Lubuskie* PL 53 A5
Brody, *Lubuskie* PL 53 B4
Brody, *Mazowieckie* PL 47 C6
Brody UA 11 A8
Broglie F 58 B1
Brójce PL 53 A5
Brokind S 37 C2
Brolo I 109 A3
Brome D 44 C2
Bromley GB 31 C4
Bromölla S 41 C4
Bromont-Lamothe F 68 C2
Brömsebro S 41 C5
Bromsgrove GB 29 A5
Bromyard GB 29 A5
Bronchales E 95 B5
Bronco E 93 A4
Brønderslev DK 38 B2
Broni I 80 A3
Brønnøysund N 2 D20
Brøns DK 39 D1
Bronte I 109 B3
Bronzani Mejdan BIH 84 B1
Bronzolo I 71 B6
Broons F 57 B3
Broquies F 78 B1
Brora GB 23 C5
Brørup DK 39 D2
Brösarp S 41 D4
Brostrud N 33 A5
Brotas P 92 C2
Brötjärna S 36 A2
Broto E 90 A2
Brottby S 36 B5
Brou F 58 B2
Brouage F 66 C3
Brough GB 26 A3
Broughshane GB 19 B5
Broughton GB 25 C4
Broughton-in-Furness GB 26 A2
Broumov CZ 53 C6
Broût-Vernet F 68 B3
Brouvelieures F 60 B2
Brouwershaven NL 49 B4
Brovary UA 11 A11
Brovst DK 38 B2
Brownhills GB 27 C4
Brozas E 93 B4
Brozzo I 71 C5
Brtnice CZ 63 A6
Brtonigla HR 72 C3
Bruay-la-Buissière F 48 C3
Bruchhausen-Vilsen D 43 C6
Bruchsal D 61 A4
Bruck, *Bayern* D 62 A3
Brück, *Brandenburg* D 52 A2
Bruck an der Grossglocknerstrasse A 72 A2
Bruck an der Leitha A 64 B2
Bruck an der Mur A 73 A5
Brückl A 73 B4
Bruckmühl D 62 C2
Brue-Auriac F 79 C4
Brüel D 44 B3
Bruen CH 70 B3
Bruère-Allichamps F 68 B2
Bruff IRL 20 B3
Brugg CH 70 A3
Brugge B 49 B4
Brüggen D 50 B2
Brühl D 50 C2
Bruinisse NL 49 B5
Brûlon F 57 C5
Brumano I 71 C4
Brumath F 60 B3
Brummen NL 50 A2
Brumov-Bylnice CZ 64 A4
Brumunddal N 2 F19
Brunau D 44 C3
Brunehamel F 59 A5
Brünen D 50 B2
Brunete E 94 B2
Brunflo S 2 E21
Brunico I 72 B1
Brunkeberg N 33 B5
Brunn D 45 B5
Brunnen CH 70 B3
Brunsbüttel D 43 B6
Brunssum NL 50 C1
Bruntál CZ 54 D2
Brus YU 85 C6
Brušane HR 83 B4
Brusasco I 70 C3
Brusio CH 71 B5
Brusno SK 65 B5
Brusque F 78 C1
Brussels = Bruxelles B 49 C5
Brusson I 70 C2
Brüssow D 45 B6
Brusy PL 46 B3
Bruton GB 29 B5
Bruvno HR 83 B4
Bruvoll N 34 A3
Bruxelles = Brussels B 49 C5
Bruyères F 60 B2
Bruz F 57 B4
Bruzaholm S 40 B5
Brwinów PL 55 A5
Bryansk RUS 7 E13
Brynamman GB 28 B4
Bryncrug GB 26 C1
Bryne N 32 C2
Brynmawr GB 29 B4
Brzeće YU 85 C5
Brzeg PL 54 C2
Brzeg Dolny PL 54 B1
Brześć Kujawski PL 47 C4
Brzesko PL 55 D5
Brzeszcze PL 55 D4
Brzezie PL 46 B2
Brzeziny, *Łódzkie* PL 55 B4
Brzeziny, *Wielkopolskie* PL 54 B3
Brzeźnica Nowa PL 55 B4
Brzeżno PL 46 B1
Brzotín SK 65 B6
Brzozie Lubawskie PL 47 B5
Bua S 40 B2
Buarcos P 92 A2
Buaveg N 32 B2
Bubbio I 80 B2
Bubry F 56 C2
Bucak TR 16 C5
Bučany SK 64 B3
Buccheri I 109 B3
Buccino I 103 C8
Bucelas P 92 C1
Buch, *Bayern* D 61 B6
Buch, *Bayern* D 62 B3
Buchach UA 11 B8
Bucharest = Bucureşti RO 11 D9
Buchbach D 62 B3
Buchboden A 71 A4
Buchen, *Baden-Württemberg* D 61 A5
Büchen, *Schleswig-Holstein* D 44 B2
Buchenberg D 61 C6
Buchères F 59 B5
Buchholz D 44 B1
Buchloe D 62 B1
Buchlovice CZ 64 A3
Buchlyvie GB 24 B3
Bucholz D 44 B4
Buchs CH 71 A4
Buchy F 58 A2
Bückeburg D 51 A5
Buckfastleigh GB 28 C4
Buckhaven GB 25 B4
Buckie GB 23 D6
Buckingham GB 31 B3
Buckley GB 26 B2
Bückwitz D 44 C4
Bučovice CZ 64 A3
Bucsa H 75 A6
Bucureşti = Bucharest RO 11 D9
Bucy-lés-Pierreport F 59 A4
Buczek PL 55 B4
Budakalasz H 65 C5
Budakeszi H 75 A3
Budaörs H 75 A3
Budapest H 75 A4
Buddusò I 110 B2
Bude GB 28 C3
Budeč CZ 63 A6
Büdelsdorf D 43 A6
Budens P 98 B2
Búðardalur IS 111 B4
Budia E 95 B4
Budimlić-Japra BIH 83 B5
Büdingen D 51 C5
Budinšćina HR 73 B6
Budišov CZ 64 A3
Budleigh Salterton GB 29 C4
Budmerice SK 64 B3
Budoni I 110 B2
Búdrio I 81 B5
Budva YU 105 A4
Budyně nad Ohří CZ 53 C4
Budziszewice PL 55 B4
Budzyń PL 46 C2
Bue N 32 C2
Bueña E 95 B5
Buenache de Alarcón E 95 C4
Buenache de la Sierra E 95 B5
Buenaventura E 94 B2
Buenavista de Valdavia E 88 B2
Buendia E 95 B4
Bueu E 87 B2
Buezo E 89 B3
Bugac H 75 B4
Bugarra E 96 B2
Bugeat F 68 C1
Buggerru I 110 C1
Bugojno BIH 84 B2
Bugyi H 75 A4
Bühl, *Baden-Württemberg* D 61 B4
Bühl, *Bayern* D 61 C6
Bühlertal D 61 B4
Bühlertann D 61 A5
Buia I 72 B3
Builth Wells GB 29 A4
Buis-les-Baronnies F 79 B4
Buitenpost NL 42 B3
Buitrago del Lozoya E 94 B3
Bujalance E 100 B1
Bujaraloz E 90 B2
Buje HR 72 C3
Bujedo E 89 B3
Bük H 74 A1
Buk PL 46 C2
Bükkösd H 74 B2
Bükkszérc H 65 C6
Bukovci SLO 73 B5
Bukowiec PL 53 A6
Bukowina Tatrzańska PL 65 A6
Bukownica PL 54 B3
Bukowno PL 55 C4
Bülach CH 70 A3
Búland IS 111 D7
Buldan TR 16 B4
Bulgnéville F 60 B1
Bülkau D 43 B5
Bulkowo PL 47 C6
Bullas E 101 A4
Bulle CH 70 B2
Büllingen B 50 C2
Bulqizë AL 112 A2
Buna BIH 84 C2
Bunahowen IRL 18 B2
Bunbeg IRL 18 A3
Bunclody IRL 21 B5
Buncrana IRL 19 A4
Bunde, *Niedersachsen* D 43 B4
Bünde, *Nordrhein-Westfalen* D 51 A4
Bundoran IRL 18 B3
Bunessan GB 24 B1
Bungay GB 30 B5
Bunge S 37 D6
Bunić HR 83 B4
Bunmahon IRL 21 B4
Bunnyconnellan IRL 18 B2
Buño E 86 A2
Buñol E 96 B2
Bunratty IRL 20 B3
Bunsbeek B 49 C5
Buñuel E 89 C5
Bünyan TR 16 B7
Bunyola E 97 B2
Buonabitácolo I 104 C1
Buonalbergo I 103 B7
Buonconvento I 81 C5
Buonvicino I 106 B2
Burano I 72 C2
Burbach D 50 C4
Burcei I 110 C2
Burdur TR 16 C5
Bureå S 3 D24
Burela E 86 A3
Büren D 51 B4
Büren an der Aare CH 70 A2
Burford GB 29 B6
Burg, *Cottbus* D 53 B4
Burg, *Magdeburg* D 52 A1
Burg, *Schleswig-Holstein* D 43 B6
Burg auf Fehmarn D 44 A3
Burg Stargard D 45 B5
Burgas BG 11 E9
Burgau A 73 A6
Burgau D 61 B6
Burgau P 98 B2
Burgbernheim D 61 A6
Burgdorf CH 70 A2
Burgdorf D 44 C2
Burgebrach D 62 A1
Bürgel D 52 C1
Burgess Hill GB 31 D3
Burgh le Marsh GB 27 B6
Burghaslach D 61 A6
Burghausen D 62 B3
Burghead GB 23 D5
Burgheim D 62 B2
Búrgio I 108 B2
Burgkirchen D 62 B3
Burgkunstadt D 52 C1
Burglengenfeld D 62 A3
Burgo P 87 D2
Burgoberbach D 61 A6
Burgohondo E 94 B2
Burgos E 88 B3
Burgsinn D 51 C5
Burgstädt D 52 C2
Burgstall D 44 C3
Burgsvik S 37 D5
Burgui E 76 D2
Burguillos E 99 B5
Burguillos de Toledo E 94 C3
Burguillos del Cerro E 93 C4
Burhaniye TR 114 C1
Burhave D 43 B5
Burie F 67 C4
Burjassot E 96 B2
Burk D 61 A6
Burkhardtsdorf D 52 C2
Burlada E 76 D1
Burladingen D 61 B5
Burlage D 43 B4
Burness GB 23 B6
Burnham GB 31 C3
Burnham Market GB 30 B4
Burnham-on-Crouch GB 31 C4
Burnham-on-Sea GB 29 B5
Burniston GB 27 A5
Burnley GB 26 B3
Burntisland GB 25 B4
Burón E 88 A1
Buronzo I 70 C3
Burovac YU 85 B6
Burow D 45 B5
Burravoe GB 22 A7
Burret F 77 D4
Burriana E 96 B2
Burry Port GB 28 B3
Bürs A 71 A4
Bursa TR 114 B4
Burseryd S 40 B3
Bürstadt D 61 A4
Burton GB 26 A3
Burton Agnes GB 27 A5
Burton Bradstock GB 29 C5
Burton Latimer GB 30 B3
Burton upon Stather GB 27 B5
Burton Upon Trent GB 27 C4
Burujón E 94 C2
Burwell GB 30 B4
Burwick GB 23 C6
Bury GB 26 B3
Bury St. Edmunds GB 30 B4
Buryn UA 7 F12
Burzenin PL 54 B3
Busachi I 110 B1
Busalla I 80 B2
Busana I 81 B4
Busano I 70 C2
Busca I 80 B1
Busch D 44 C3
Buševec HR 73 C6
Bushey GB 31 C3
Bushmills GB 19 A5
Bušince SK 65 B5
Buskhyttan S 37 B3
Busko-Zdrój PL 55 C5
Busot E 96 C2
Busovača BIH 84 B2
Busquistar E 100 C2
Bussang F 60 C2
Busseto I 81 B4
Bussière-Badil F 67 C5
Bussière-Poitevine F 67 B5
Bussolengo I 71 C5
Bussoleno I 70 C2
Bussum NL 49 A6
Busto Arsízio I 70 C3
Büsum D 43 A5
Butera I 109 B3
Butgenbach B 50 C2
Butler's Bridge IRL 19 B4
Butryny PL 47 B6
Bütschwil CH 70 A4
Buttermere GB 26 A2
Buttevant IRL 20 B3
Buttle S 37 D5
Buttstädt D 52 B1
Butzbach D 51 C4
Bützfleth D 43 B6
Bützow D 44 B3
Buxières-les-Mines F 68 B2
Buxtehude D 43 B6
Buxton GB 27 B4
Buxy F 69 B4
Büyükçekmece TR 114 A3
Büyükkariştiran TR 114 A2
Büyükorhan TR 114 C3
Buzançais F 67 B6
Buzancy F 59 A5
Buzău RO 11 D9
Buzet HR 72 C3
Buzsák H 74 B2
Buzy F 76 C2
By S 36 A3
Byala BG 11 E8
Byaroza BY 6 E8
Byczyna PL 54 B3
Bydgoszcz PL 47 B4
Bygland N 33 C4
Byglandsfjord N 33 C4
Bykhaw BY 7 E11
Bykle N 33 B4
Bylderup-Bov DK 39 E2
Byrum DK 38 B3
Byšice CZ 53 C4
Byske S 3 D24
Býškovice CZ 64 A3
Bysław PL 46 B3
Bystré CZ 64 A2
Bystřice, *Středočeský* CZ 65 A4
Bystřice, *Středočeský* CZ 63 A5
Bystřice n Pernštejnem CZ 64 A2
Bystřice pod Hostýnem CZ 64 A3
Bystrzyca Kłodzka PL 54 C1
Bytča SK 65 A4
Bytom PL 54 C3
Bytom Odrzański PL 53 B5
Bytów PL 46 A3
Byxelkrok S 41 B7
Bzenec CZ 64 B3
Bzince SK 64 B3

C

Cabacos P 92 B2
Cabaj-Čápor SK 64 B4
Cabana E 86 A2
Cabanac-et-Villagrains F 76 B2
Cabañaquinta E 88 A1
Cabanas P 98 B3
Cabañas de Yepes E 95 C3
Cabañas del Castillo E 93 B5
Cabanelles E 91 A5
Cabanes E 96 A3
Cabanillas E 89 B5
Čabar HR 73 C4
Cabasse F 79 C5
Cabdella E 91 A4
Cabeceiras de Basto P 87 C2
Cabeço de Vide P 92 B3
Cabella Ligure I 80 B3
Cabeza del Buey E 93 C5
Cabeza la Vaca E 99 A4
Cabezamesada E 95 C3
Cabezarados E 100 A1
Cabezarrubias del Puerto E 100 A1
Cabezas del Villar E 94 B1
Cabezas Rubias E 98 B3
Cabezón E 88 C2
Cabezón de la Sal E 88 A2
Cabezón de Liébana E 88 A2
Cabezuela E 94 A3
Cabezuela del Valle E 93 A5
Cabo de Gata E 101 C3
Cabo de Palos E 101 B5
Cabolafuenta E 95 A4
Cabourg F 57 A5
Cabra E 100 B1
Cabra P 92 A3
Cabra del Santo Cristo E 100 B2
Cabrach GB 23 D5
Cábras I 110 C1
Cabreiro P 87 C2
Cabreiros E 86 A3
Cabrejas E 95 B4
Cabrela P 92 C2
Cabrillas E 87 D4
Cabuna HR 74 C2
Cacabelos E 86 B4
Čačak YU 85 C5
Cáccamo I 108 B2
Caccuri I 107 B3
Cacela P 98 B3
Cacém P 92 C1
Cáceres E 93 B4
Cachafeiro E 86 B2
Cachopo P 98 B3
Čachtice SK 64 B3
Cacin E 100 B2
Čačinci HR 74 C2
Cadafais P 92 C1
Cadalen F 77 C5
Cadalso E 93 A4
Cadaqués E 91 A6
Cadaval P 92 B1
Cadavedo E 86 A4
Čadavica BIH 84 B1
Čadca SK 65 A4
Cadéac F 77 D3
Cadelbosco di Sopra I 81 B4
Cadenazzo CH 70 B3
Cadenberge D 43 B6
Cadenet F 79 C4
Cadeuil F 66 C4
Cádiar E 100 C2
Cadillac F 76 B2
Cádiz E 99 C4
Čadjavica HR 74 C2
Cadouin F 77 B3
Cadours F 77 C4
Cadrete E 90 B2
Caen F 57 A5
Caerleon GB 29 B5
Caernarfon GB 26 B1
Caerphilly GB 29 B4
Caersws GB 26 C2
Cafede P 92 B3
Çağa TR 114 B7
Caggiano I 104 C1
Cagli I 82 C1
Cágliari I 110 C2
Čaglin HR 74 C2
Cagnano Varano I 104 B1
Cagnes-sur-Mer F 79 C6
Caher IRL 21 B4
Caherciveen IRL 20 C1
Caherdaniel IRL 20 C1
Cahors F 77 B4
Cahul MD 11 D10
Caiazzo I 103 B7
Caion E 86 A2
Cairndow GB 24 B3
Cairnryan GB 24 D2
Cairo Montenotte I 80 B2
Caister-on-Sea GB 30 B5
Caistor GB 27 B5
Caivano I 103 C7
Cajarc F 77 B4
Čajetina YU 85 C4
Čajniče BIH 84 C4
Çakmak TR 114 C6
Čakovec HR 73 B6
Çal TR 16 B4
Cala E 99 B4
Cala d'Or E 97 B3
Cala Galdana E 97 B3
Cala Gonone I 110 B2
Cala Llonga E 97 C1
Cala Millor E 97 B3
Cala Ratjada E 97 B3
Calabritto I 103 C8
Calaceite E 90 C3
Calacuccia F 102 A2
Calaf E 91 B4
Calafat RO 11 D7
Calafell E 91 B4
Calahonda E 100 C2
Calahorra E 89 B5
Calais F 48 C2
Calalzo di Cadore I 72 B2
Calamocha E 95 B5
Calamonte E 93 C4
Calanais GB 22 C2
Calañas E 99 B4
Calanda E 90 C2
Calangiánus I 110 B2
Călăraşi RO 11 D9
Calascibetta I 109 B3
Calasetta I 110 C1
Calasparra E 101 A4
Calatafimi I 108 B1
Calatayud E 89 C5
Calatorao E 89 C5
Calau D 53 B3
Calbe D 52 B1
Calcena E 89 C5
Calcinelli I 82 C1
Calco I 71 C4
Caldaro sulla strada del Vino I 71 B6
Caldarola I 82 C2
Caldas da Rainha P 92 B1
Caldas de Boì E 90 A3
Caldas de Malavella E 91 B5
Caldas de Reis E 86 B2
Caldas de San Jorge P 87 D2
Caldas de Vizela P 87 C2
Caldaso de los Vidrios E 94 B2
Caldbeck GB 26 A2
Caldearenas E 90 A2
Caldelas P 87 C2
Calders E 91 B4
Caldes de Montbui E 91 B5
Caldicot GB 29 B5
Caldirola I 80 B3
Caledon GB 19 B5
Calella, *Barcelona* E 91 B5
Calella, *Girona* E 91 B6
Calenzana F 102 A1
Calera de León E 99 A4
Calera y Chozas E 94 C2
Caleruega E 89 C3
Caleruela E 93 B5
Cales de Mallorca E 97 B3
Calestano I 81 B4
Calfsound GB 23 B6
Calgary GB 24 B1
Calimera I 105 C4
Calitri I 103 C8
Calizzano I 80 B2
Callac F 56 B2
Callan IRL 21 B4
Callander GB 24 B3
Callas F 79 C5
Calliano, *Piemonte* I 80 A2
Calliano, *Trentino Alto Adige* I 71 C6
Callington GB 28 C3
Callosa de Ensarriá E 96 C2
Callosa de Segura E 101 A5
Callús E 91 B4
Čalma YU 85 A4
Calmbach D 61 B4
Calne GB 29 B6
Calolziocorte I 71 C4
Calonge E 91 B6
Čalovec SK 64 C3
Calpe E 96 C3
Caltabellotta I 108 B2
Caltagirone I 109 B3
Caltanissetta I 109 B3
Caltavuturo I 108 B2
Çaltılıbük TR 114 C3
Caltojar E 89 C4
Caluire-et-Cuire F 69 C4
Caluso I 70 C2
Calvello I 104 C1
Calvi F 102 A1
Calviá E 97 B2
Calvisson F 78 C3
Calvörde D 44 C3
Calw D 61 B4
Calzada de Calatrava E 100 A2
Calzada de Valdunciel E 94 A1
Calzadilla de los Barros E 93 C4
Cam GB 29 B5
Camaiore I 81 C4
Camarasa E 90 B3
Camarena E 94 B2
Camarès F 78 C1
Camaret-sur-Aigues F 78 B3
Camaret-sur-Mer F 56 B1
Camarillas E 90 C2
Camariñas E 86 A1
Camarma E 95 B3
Camarzana de Tera E 87 B4
Camas E 99 B4
Camastra I 108 B2
Cambados E 86 B2
Cambarinho P 92 A2
Camberley GB 31 C3
Cambil E 100 B2
Cambo-les-Bains F 76 C1
Camborne GB 28 C2
Cambrai F 49 C4
Cambre E 86 A2
Cambridge GB 30 B4
Cambrils E 91 B4
Cambs D 44 B3
Camburg D 52 B1
Camden GB 31 C3
Cameleño E 88 A2
Camelford GB 28 C3
Çameli TR 16 C4
Camelle E 86 A1
Camerano I 82 C2
Camerino I 82 C2
Camerota I 106 A2
Camigliatello Silano I 106 B3
Caminha P 87 C2
Caminomorisco E 93 A4
Caminreal E 95 B5
Camisano Vicentino I 72 C1
Camlıdere TR 114 B7
Cammarata I 108 B2
Camogli I 80 B3
Camors F 56 C3
Camp IRL 20 B2
Campagna I 103 C8
Campagnano di Roma I 102 A5
Campagnático I 81 D5
Campan F 76 C3
Campana I 107 B3
Campanario E 93 C5
Campanillas E 100 C1
Campano E 99 C4
Campaspero E 88 C2
Campbeltown GB 24 C2
Campello E 96 C2
Campelos P 92 B1
Campi Bisénzio I 81 C5
Campi Salentina I 105 C4
Campico López E 101 B4
Campíglia Maríttima I 81 C4
Campillo de Altobuey E 95 C5
Campillo de Aragón E 95 A5
Campillo de Arenas E 100 B2
Campillo de Llerena E 93 C5
Campillos E 100 B1
Câmpina RO 11 D8
Campli I 82 D2
Campo E 90 A3
Campo de Bacerros E 87 B3
Campo de Caso E 88 A1
Campo de Criptana E 95 C3
Campo Ligure I 80 B2
Campo Lugar E 93 B5
Campo Maior P 93 B3
Campo Molino I 79 B6
Campo Real E 95 B3
Campo Túres I 72 B1
Campobasso I 103 B7
Campobello di Licata I 108 B2
Campobello di Mazara I 108 B1
Campodársego I 72 C1
Campodolcino I 71 B4
Campofelice di Roccella I 108 B2
Campofiorito I 108 B2
Campofórmido I 72 B3
Campofranco I 108 B2
Campofrio E 99 B4
Campogalliano I 81 B4
Campolongo I 72 B2
Campomanes E 88 A1
Campomarino I 103 B8
Camporeale I 108 B2
Camporeggiano I 82 C1
Camporrells E 90 B3
Camporrobles E 96 B1
Campos P 87 C3
Campos del Port E 97 B3
Camposa P 87 C2
Camposampiero I 72 C1
Camposanto I 81 B5
Camposines E 90 B3
Campotéjar E 100 B2
Campotosto I 103 A6
Camprodón E 91 A5
Campsegret F 77 B3
Camrose GB 28 B2
Camuñas E 95 C3
Çan TR 114 B2
Can Pastilla E 97 B2
C'an Picafort E 97 B3
Cana I 81 D5
Cañada del Hoyo E 95 C5
Cañada Rosal E 99 B5
Cañadajuncosa E 95 C4
Čanak HR 83 B4
Çanakkale TR 114 B1
Canal San Bovo I 72 B1
Canale I 80 B1
Canales, *Asturias* E 88 B1
Canales, *Castellón de la Plana* E 96 B2
Canals E 96 C2
Cañamares E 95 B4
Cañamero E 93 B5
Cañar E 100 C2
Cañate la Real E 99 C5
Cañaveral E 93 B4
Cañaveral de León E 99 A4
Cañaveras E 95 B4
Cañaveruelas E 95 B4
Canazei I 72 B1
Cancale F 57 B4
Cancellara I 104 C1
Cancello ed Arnone I 103 B7
Cancon F 77 B3
Canda E 87 B4
Candamil E 86 A3
Candanchu E 76 D2
Çandarlı TR 114 D1
Candas E 88 A1
Candasnos E 90 B3
Candé F 66 A3
Candela I 104 B1
Candelario E 93 A5
Candeleda E 93 A5
Cándia Lomellina I 70 C3
Candide Casamazzagno I 72 B2
Candin E 86 B4
Candosa P 92 A3
Canecas P 92 C1
Canelli I 80 B2
Canena E 100 A2
Canencia E 94 B3
Canero E 86 A4
Canet de Mar E 91 B5
Canet d'en Berenguer E 96 B2
Canet-Plage F 91 A6
Cañete E 95 B5

Cañete de las Torres E 100 B1
Canfranc E 76 D2
Cangas, *Lugo* E 86 A3
Cangas, *Pontevedra* E 87 B2
Cangas de Narcea E 86 A4
Cangas de Onís E 88 A1
Canha P 92 C2
Canhestros P 98 A2
Canicatti I 108 B2
Canicattini Bagni I 109 B4
Canicosa de la Sierra E 89 C3
Caniles E 101 B3
Canillas de Aceituno E 100 C1
Canino I 102 A4
Canisy F 57 A4
Cañizal E 94 A1
Cañizo E 88 C1
Canjáyar E 101 C3
Çankırı TR 16 A6
Cannara I 82 C1
Cánnero Riviera I 70 B3
Cannes F 79 C6
Canneto, *Sicilia* I 106 C1
Canneto, *Toscana* I 81 C4
Canneto sull'Oglio I 71 C5
Cannich GB 22 D4
Cannóbio I 70 B3
Cannock GB 26 C3
Canonbie GB 25 C5
Canosa di Púglia I 104 B2
Cantalapiedra E 94 A1
Cantalejo E 94 A3
Cantalgallo E 99 A4
Cantalice I 102 A5
Cantalpino E 94 A1
Cantalupo in Sabina I 102 A5
Cantanhede P 92 A2
Cantavieja E 90 C2
Čantavir YU 75 C4
Canterbury GB 31 C5
Cantiano I 82 C1
Cantillana E 99 B5
Cantiveros E 94 B2
Cantoria E 101 B3
Cantù I 71 C4
Canvey GB 31 C4
Cany-Barville F 58 A1
Canyet de Mar E 91 B5
Caol GB 24 B2
Cáorle I 72 C2
Caorso I 81 A3
Cap-de-Pin F 76 B2
Cap Ferret F 76 B1
Capáccio I 103 C8
Capaci I 108 A2
Capálbio I 102 A4
Capánnori I 81 C4
Caparde BIH 84 B3
Caparroso E 89 B5
Capbreton F 76 C1
Capdenac-Gare F 77 B5
Capdepera E 97 B3
Capel Curig GB 26 B2
Capellades E 91 B4
Capena I 102 A5
Capendu F 77 C5
Capestang F 78 C2
Capestrano I 103 A6
Capileira E 100 C2
Capinha P 92 A3
Ca'Pisani I 82 B1
Capistrello I 103 B6
Capizzi I 109 B3
Čaplje BIH 83 B5
Čapljina BIH 84 C2
Capo di Ponte I 71 B5
Caposile I 72 C2
Capoterra I 110 C1
Cappamore IRL 20 B3
Cappeln D 43 C5
Cappoquin IRL 21 B4
Capracotta I 103 B7
Capránica I 102 A5
Caprarola I 102 A5
Capretta I 82 D1
Capri I 103 C7
Capriati a Volturno I 103 B7
Caprino Veronese I 71 C5
Captieux F 76 B2
Cápua I 103 B7
Capurso I 104 B2
Capvern F 77 C3
Carabaña E 95 B3
Carabias E 88 C3
Caracal RO 11 D8
Caracenilla E 95 B4
Caráglio I 80 B1
Caraman F 77 C4
Caramánico Terme I 103 A7
Caranga E 86 A4
Caranguejeira P 92 B2
Caransebeş RO 11 D7
Carantec F 56 B2
Carapelle I 104 B1
Carasco I 80 B3
Carate Brianza I 71 C4
Caravaca de la Cruz E 101 A4
Caravággio I 71 C4
Carbajal E 100 C1
Carbajo E 93 B3
Carballeda E 86 B3
Carballeda de Avia E 87 B2
Carballo E 86 A2
Carbis Bay GB 28 C2
Carbon-Blanc F 76 B2
Carbonera de Frentes E 89 C4
Carboneras E 101 C4
Carboneras de Guadazaón E 95 C5
Carbonero el Mayor E 94 A2
Carboneros E 100 A2
Carbónia I 110 C1
Carbonin I 72 B2
Carbonne F 77 C4
Carbost, *Highland* GB 22 D2
Carbost, *Highland* GB 22 D2
Carcaboso E 93 A4
Carcabuey E 100 B1
Carcaixent E 96 B2
Carcans F 76 A1
Carcans-Plage F 76 A1
Carção P 87 C4
Carcar E 89 B5
Cárcare I 80 B2
Carcassonne F 77 C5
Carcastillo E 89 B5
Carcedo de Burgos E 89 B3
Carcelén E 96 B1
Carcès F 79 C5
Carchelejo E 100 B2
Çardak, *Çanakkale* TR 114 B1
Çardak, *Denizli* TR 16 C4
Cardedeu E 91 B5
Cardeña E 100 A1
Cardenete E 95 C5
Cardeñosa E 94 B2
Cardeto I 109 A4
Cardiff GB 29 B4
Cardigan GB 28 A3
Cardona E 91 B4
Cardosos P 92 B2
Carei RO 11 C7
Carentan F 57 A4
Carentoir F 57 C3
Careri I 106 C3
Carevdar HR 74 B1
Cargèse F 102 A1
Carhaix-Plouguer F 56 B2
Caria P 92 A3
Cariati I 107 B3
Carignan F 59 A6
Carignano I 80 B1
Cariñena E 90 B1
Carini I 108 A2
Cariño E 86 A3
Carinola I 103 B6
Carisbrooke GB 31 D2
Carlabhagh GB 22 C2
Carlepont F 59 A4
Carlet E 96 B2
Carlingford IRL 19 B5
Carlisle GB 25 D5
Carloforte I 110 C1
Carlópoli I 106 B3
Carlow D 44 B2
Carlow IRL 21 B5
Carlton GB 27 C4
Carluke GB 25 C4
Carmagnola I 80 B1
Carmarthen GB 28 B3
Carmaux F 77 B5
Carmena E 94 C2
Cármenes E 88 B1
Carmine I 80 B1
Carmona E 99 B5
Carmonita E 93 B4
Carmyllie GB 25 B5
Carnac F 56 C2
Carndonagh IRL 19 A4
Carnew IRL 21 B5
Carnforth GB 26 A3
Cárnia I 72 B3
Carnlough GB 19 B6
Carno GB 26 C2
Carnon Plage F 78 C2
Carnota E 86 B1
Carnoustie GB 25 B5
Carnwath GB 25 C4
Carolei I 106 B3
Carolinensiel D 43 B4
Carolles F 57 B4
Carona I 71 B4
Caronía I 109 A3
Carovigno I 104 C3
Carovilli I 103 B7
Carpaneto Piacentino I 81 B3
Carpegna I 82 C1
Carpenédolo I 71 C5
Carpentras F 79 B4
Carpi I 81 B4
Carpignano Sésia I 70 C3
Carpineti I 81 B4
Carpineto Romano I 102 B6
Cărpiniş RO 75 C5
Carpino I 104 B1
Carpinone I 103 B7
Carpio E 94 A1
Carquefou F 66 A3
Carqueiranne F 79 C5
Carral E 86 A2
Carranque E 94 B3
Carrapichana P 92 A3
Carrara I 81 B4
Carraroe IRL 20 A2
Carrascalejo E 93 B5
Carrascosa del Campo E 95 B4
Carratraca E 100 C1
Carrazeda de Ansiães P 87 C3
Carrazedo de Montenegro P 87 C3
Carrbridge GB 23 D5
Carregal do Sal P 92 A2
Carreña E 88 A2
Carrick IRL 18 B3
Carrick-on-Shannon IRL 18 C3
Carrick-on-Suir IRL 21 B4
Carrickart IRL 19 A4
Carrickfergus GB 19 B6
Carrickmacross IRL 19 C5
Carrigallen IRL 19 C4
Carrión E 99 B4
Carrión de Calatrava E 94 C3
Carrión de los Condes E 88 B2
Carrizo de la Ribera E 88 B1
Carrizosa E 100 A3
Carro F 79 C4
Carrocera E 88 B1
Carros F 79 C6
Carrouge CH 70 B1
Carrouges F 57 B5
Carrù I 80 B1
Carry-le-Rouet F 79 C4
Carryduff GB 19 B6
Carsòli I 102 A6
Carsphairn GB 24 C3
Cartagena E 101 B5
Cártama E 100 C1
Cartaxo P 92 B2
Cartaya E 98 B3
Carteret F 57 A4
Cartes E 88 A2
Carúnchio I 103 B7
Carviçais P 87 C4
Carvin F 48 C3
Carvoeira P 92 B1
Carvoeiro P 98 B2
Casa Branca, *Portalegre* P 92 C3
Casa Branca, *Setúbal* P 98 A2
Casa Castalda I 82 C1
Casa l'Abate I 105 C4
Casabermeja E 100 C1
Casacalenda I 103 B7
Casaio E 87 B4
Casàl di Principe I 103 B7
Casalarreina E 89 B4
Casalbordino I 103 A7
Casalborgone I 70 C2
Casalbuono I 104 C1
Casalbuttano ed Uniti I 71 C4
Casale Monferrato I 70 C3
Casalécchio di Reno I 81 B5
Casalina I 82 D1
Casalmaggiore I 81 B4
Casalnuovo Monterotaro I 103 B8
Casaloldo I 71 C5
Casalpusterlengo I 71 C4
Casamássima I 104 C2
Casamicciola Terme I 103 C6
Casamozza F 102 A2
Casar de Cáceres E 93 B4
Casar de Palomero E 93 A4
Casarabonela E 100 C1
Casarano I 107 A5
Casarejos E 89 C3
Casares E 99 C5
Casares de las Hurdes E 93 A4
Casariche E 100 B1
Casarrubios del Monte E 94 B2
Casas de Don Pedro E 93 B5
Casas de Fernando Alonso E 95 C4
Casas de Haro E 95 C4
Casas de Juan Gil E 96 B1
Casas de Millán E 93 B4
Casas de Reina E 99 A5
Casas de Ves E 96 B1
Casas del Juan Núñez E 95 C5
Casas del Puerto E 101 A4
Casas del Rio E 96 B1
Casas-Ibáñez E 96 B1
Casas Nuevas E 101 B4
Casasimarro E 95 C4
Casasola E 94 B2
Casasola de Arión E 88 C1
Casasuertes E 88 A2
Casatejada E 93 B5
Casavieja E 94 B2
Casazza I 71 C4
Cascais P 92 C1
Cascante E 89 C5
Cascante del Rio E 96 A1
Cáscia I 82 D2
Casciana Terme I 81 C4
Cáscina I 81 C4
Cáseda E 89 B5
Casekow D 45 B6
Casella I 80 B3
Caselle Torinese I 70 C2
Casemurate I 82 B1
Casenove I 82 D1
Caseres E 90 B3
Caserío Benali E 96 B2
Caserta I 103 B7
Casével P 98 B2
Cashel IRL 21 B4
Casillas E 94 B2
Casillas de Coria E 93 B4
Casina I 81 B4
Casinos E 96 B2
Čáslav CZ 63 A6
Cásola Valsénio I 81 B5
Cásole d'Elsa I 81 C5
Cásoli I 103 A7
Casória I 103 C7
Caspe E 90 B2
Cassà de la Selva E 91 B5
Cassagnas F 78 B2
Cassagnes-Bégonhès F 77 B5
Cassano allo Iónio I 106 B3
Cassano d'Adda I 71 C4
Cassano delle Murge I 104 C2
Cassano Magnago I 70 C3
Cassano Spinola I 80 B2
Cassel F 48 C3
Cassibile I 109 C4
Cassine I 80 B2
Cassino I 103 B6
Cassis F 79 C4
Cassolnovo I 70 C3
Cassuéjouls F 78 B1
Častá SK 64 B3
Castagnaro I 71 C6
Castagneto Carducci I 81 C4
Castagnola CH 70 B3
Castañar de Ibor E 93 B5
Castanheira de Pêra P 92 A2
Cástano Primo I 70 C3
Castasegna CH 71 B4
Castéggio I 80 A3
Casteição P 87 D3
Castejón E 89 B5
Castejón de Monegros E 90 B2
Castejón de Sos E 90 A3
Castejón de Valdejasa E 90 B2
Castèl Baronia I 103 B8
Castel Bolognese I 81 B5
Castel d'Aiano I 81 B4
Castel d'Ario I 71 C5
Castel de Cabra E 90 C2
Castél del Monte I 103 A6
Castel del Piano I 81 D5
Castel di Iúdica I 109 B3
Castel di Rio I 81 B5
Castèl di Sangro I 103 B7
Castél di Tora I 102 A5
Castèl Frentano I 103 A7
Castel San Gimignano I 81 C5
Castèl San Giovanni I 80 A3
Castèl San Pietro Terme I 81 B5
Castél Sant'Elia I 102 A5
Castél Volturno I 103 B6
Castelbuono I 109 B3
Casteldáccia I 108 A2
Casteldelfino I 79 B6
Castelfidardo I 82 C2
Castelfiorentino I 81 C4
Castelforte I 103 B6
Castelfranco Emília I 81 B5
Castelfranco in Miscano I 103 B8
Castelfranco Véneto I 72 C1
Casteljaloux F 76 B3
Castell Arquato I 81 B3
Castell de Cabres E 90 C3
Castell de Castells E 96 C2
Castell de Ferro E 100 C2
Castellabate I 103 C7
Castellammare del Golfo I 108 A1
Castellammare di Stábia I 103 C7
Castellamonte I 70 C2
Castellana Grotte I 104 C3
Castellane F 79 C5
Castellaneta I 104 C2
Castellaneta Marina I 104 C2
Castellar E 100 A2
Castellar de la Frontera E 99 C5
Castellar de la Ribera E 91 A4
Castellar de Santiago E 100 A2
Castellar del Vallés E 91 B5
Castellarano I 81 B4
Castell'Azzara I 81 D5
Castellbell i Villar E 91 B4
Castelldans E 90 B3
Castelldefels E 91 B4
Castelleone I 71 C4
Castellet E 91 B4
Castelletto di Brenzone I 71 C5
Castellfollit de la Roca E 91 A5
Castellfollit de Riubregos E 91 B4
Castellfort E 90 C2
Castellina in Chianti I 81 C5
Castellina Marittima I 81 C4
Castelló de Farfaña E 90 B3
Castelló de la Plana E 96 B2
Castello d'Empùries E 91 A6
Castello di Fiemme I 71 B6
Castello Tesino I 72 B1
Castelloli E 91 B4
Castellón de Rugat E 96 C2
Castellote E 90 C2
Castellterçol E 91 B5
Castellúcchio I 71 C5
Castellúccio de'Sàuri I 103 B8
Castelluccio Inferiore I 106 B2
Castelmassa I 81 A5
Castelmáuro I 103 B7
Castelmoron-sur-Lot F 77 B3
Castelnau-de-Médoc F 76 A2
Castelnau-de-Montmirail F 77 C4
Castelnau-Magnoac F 77 C3
Castelnau-Montratier F 77 B4
Castelnaudary F 77 C4
Castelnou E 90 B2
Castelnovo ne'Monti I 81 B4
Castelnuovo Berardenga I 81 C5
Castelnuovo della Dáunia I 103 B8
Castelnuovo di Garfagnana I 81 B4
Castelnuovo di Val di Cécina I 81 C4
Castelnuovo Don Bosco I 80 A1
Castelnuovo Scrivia I 80 B2
Castelo Branco, *Bragança* P 87 C4
Castelo Branco, *Castelo Branco* P 92 B3
Castelo de Paiva P 87 C2
Castelo de Vide P 92 B3
Castelo do Neiva P 87 C2
Castelo Mendo P 93 A4
Castelraimondo I 82 C2
Castelsantángelo I 82 D2
Castelsaraceno I 106 A2
Castelsardo I 110 B1
Castelsarrasin F 77 B4
Castelserás E 90 C2
Casteltérmini I 108 B2
Castelvecchio Subéquo I 103 A6
Castelvetrano I 108 B1
Castenédolo I 71 C5
Castets F 76 C1
Castiádas I 110 C2
Castiglion Fibocchi I 81 C5
Castiglion Fiorentino I 81 C5
Castiglioncello I 81 C4
Castiglione I 102 A6
Castiglione Chiavarese I 80 B3
Castiglione d'Adda I 71 C4
Castiglione dei Pepoli I 81 B5
Castiglione del Lago I 81 C6
Castiglione della Pescáia I 81 D4
Castiglione delle Stiviere I 71 C5
Castiglione di Sicilia I 109 B4
Castiglione d'Órcia I 81 C5
Castiglione Messer Marino I 103 B7
Castiglione Messer Raimondo I 103 A6
Castil de Peones E 89 B3
Castilblanco E 94 C1
Castilblanco de los Arroyos E 99 B5
Castilfrío de la Sierra E 89 C4
Castilgaleu E 90 A3
Castilisar E 90 A1
Castilleja E 99 B4
Castillejar E 101 B3
Castillejo de Martin Viejo E 93 A4
Castillejo de Mesleón E 89 C3
Castillejo de Robledo E 89 C3
Castillo de Bayuela E 94 B2
Castillo de Locubín E 100 B2
Castillon-la-Bataille F 76 B2
Castillon-Len-Couserans F 77 D4
Castillonès F 77 B3
Castillonroy E 90 B3
Castilruiz E 89 C4
Castione CH 70 B4
Castions di Strada I 72 C3
Castirla F 102 A2
Castle Cary GB 29 B5
Castle Douglas GB 25 D4
Castlebar IRL 18 C2
Castlebellingham IRL 19 C5
Castleblaney IRL 19 B5
Castlebridge IRL 21 B5
Castlecomer IRL 21 B4
Castlederg GB 19 B4
Castledermot IRL 21 B5
Castleford GB 27 B4
Castleisland IRL 20 B2
Castlemaine IRL 20 B2
Castlemartyr IRL 20 C3
Castlepollard IRL 19 C4
Castlerea IRL 18 C3
Castleton GB 27 B4
Castletown, *Highland* GB 23 C5
Castletown, *Isle of Man* GB 26 A1
Castletown Bearhaven IRL 20 C2
Castletownroche IRL 20 B3
Castlewellan GB 19 B6
Casto I 71 C5
Castrejón E 88 C1
Castrelo del Valle E 87 C3
Castres F 77 C5
Castricum NL 42 C1
Castries F 78 C2
Castrignano del Capo I 107 B5
Castril E 101 B3
Castrillo de Duero E 88 C3
Castrillo de la Vega E 88 C3
Castrillo de Onielo E 88 C2
Castro E 88 A2
Castro I 107 A5
Castro-Caldelas E 87 B3
Castro Daire P 87 D3
Castro de Rey E 86 A3
Castro dei Volsci I 103 B6
Castro del Río E 100 B1
Castro Laboreiro P 87 B2
Castro Marim P 98 B3
Castro-Urdiales E 89 A3
Castro Verde P 98 B2
Castrocabón E 88 B1
Castrocaro Terme I 81 B5
Castrocontrigo E 87 B4
Castrofilippo I 108 B2
Castrogonzaio E 88 B1
Castrojeriz E 88 B2
Castromonte E 88 C1
Castromudarra E 88 B1
Castronuevo E 88 C1
Castronuño E 88 C1
Castropol E 86 A3
Castroreale I 109 A4
Castroserracin E 88 C3
Castroverde E 86 A3
Castroverde de Campos E 88 C1
Castroverde de Cerrato E 88 C2
Castrovillari I 106 B3
Castuera E 93 C5
Catadau E 96 B2
Cataéggio I 71 B4
Çatalca TR 114 A3
Çatalzeytin TR 16 A7
Catánia I 109 B4
Catanzaro I 106 C3
Catanzaro Marina I 106 C3
Catarroja E 96 B2
Catarruchos P 92 A2
Catcleugh GB 25 C5
Catenanuova I 109 B3
Caterham GB 31 C3
Cati E 90 C3
Čatići BIH 84 B3
Catignano I 103 A6
Catillon F 49 C4
Catoira E 86 B2
Caton GB 26 A3
Catral E 101 A5
Catterick GB 27 A4
Cattólica I 82 C1
Cattólica Eraclea I 108 B2
Catton GB 25 D5
Caudebec-en-Caux F 58 A1
Caudete E 101 A5
Caudete de las Fuentes E 96 B1
Caudiel E 96 B2
Caudiès-de-Fenouillèdes F 77 D5
Caudry F 49 C4
Caulkerbush GB 25 D4
Caulnes F 57 B3
Caulónia I 106 C3
Caumont-l'Evente F 57 A5
Caunes-Minervois F 77 C5
Cauro F 102 B1
Caussade F 77 B4
Causse-de-la-Selle F 78 C2
Cauterets F 76 D2
Cava de Tirreni I 103 C7
Cavaglia I 70 C3
Cavaillon F 79 C4
Cavalaire-sur-Mer F 79 C5
Cavaleiro P 98 B2
Cavalese I 71 B6
Cavallermaggiore I 80 B1
Cavallino I 72 C2
Cavan IRL 19 C4
Cavárzere I 72 C2
Çavdarhisar TR 114 C4
Cavernais P 87 D3
Cavezzo I 81 B5
Cavignac F 76 A2
Čavle HR 73 C4
Cavo I 81 D4
Cavour I 80 B1
Cawdor GB 23 D5
Çay TR 16 B5
Çaycuma TR 114 A7
Cayeux-sur-Mer F 48 C2
Cayiralan TR 16 B7
Çayırhan TR 114 B6
Caylus F 77 B4
Cayres F 78 B2
Cazalilla E 100 B2
Cazalla de la Sierra E 99 B5
Cazals F 77 B4
Cazanuecos E 88 B1
Cazaubon F 76 C2
Cazaux F 76 B1
Cazères F 77 C4
Cazin BIH 83 B4
Cazis CH 71 B4
Čazma HR 74 C1
Cazo E 88 A1
Cazorla E 100 B3
Cazouls-lès-Béziers F 78 C2
Cea, *León* E 88 B1
Cea, *Orense* E 86 B3
Ceánuri E 89 A4
Ceauce F 57 B5
Cebolla E 94 C2
Čebovce SK 65 B5
Cebreros E 94 B2
Čečava BIH 84 B2
Ceccano I 103 B6
Cece H 74 B3
Cecenowo PL 46 A3
Čechtice CZ 63 A6
Čechtin CZ 64 A1
Cécina I 81 C4
Ceclavín E 93 B4
Cedégolo I 71 B5
Cedeira E 86 A2
Cedillo E 92 B3
Cedillo del Condado E 94 B3
Cedrillas E 90 C2
Cedynia PL 45 C6
Cée E 86 B1
Cefalù I 109 A3
Céggia I 72 C2
Cegléd H 75 A4
Ceglédbercel H 75 A4
Céglie Messápica I 104 C3
Cehegín E 101 A4
Ceilhes-et-Rocozels F 78 C2
Ceinos de Campos E 88 B1
Ceira P 92 A2
Čejč CZ 64 B2
Cela BIH 83 B5
Čelákovice CZ 53 C4
Celano I 103 A6
Celanova E 87 B3
Celbridge IRL 21 A5
Čelebić BIH 83 C5
Celenza Valfortore I 103 B7
Čelić BIH 84 B3
Čelinac BIH 84 B2
Celje SLO 73 B5
Cella E 95 B5
Celldömölk H 74 A2
Celle D 44 C2
Celle Ligure I 80 B2
Celles B 49 C5
Celles-sur-Belle F 67 B4
Cellino San Marco I 105 C3
Celorico da Beira P 92 A3
Celorico de Basto P 87 C2
Çeltik TR 114 C6
Cemaes GB 26 B1
Cembra I 71 B6
Čemerno BIH 84 C3
Cenad RO 75 B5
Cencenighe Agordino I 72 B1
Cenei RO 75 C5
Ceneselli I 81 A5
Cenicero E 89 B4
Cenicientos E 94 B2
Censeau F 69 B6
Čenta YU 85 A5
Centallo I 80 B1
Centelles E 91 B5
Cento I 81 B5
Centúripe I 109 B3
Cepeda la Mora E 94 B1
Čepin HR 74 C3
Čepinski Martinci HR 74 C3
Cepovan SLO 72 B3
Ceprano I 103 B6
Čeralije HR 74 C2
Cerami I 109 B3
Cerano I 70 C3
Cérans Foulletourte F 57 C6
Ceraso I 106 A2
Cerbaia I 81 C5
Cerbère F 91 A6
Cercadillo E 95 A4
Cercal, *Lisboa* P 92 B1
Cercal, *Setúbal* P 98 B2
Čerčany CZ 63 A5
Cerceda E 94 B3
Cercedilla E 94 B2
Cercemaggiore I 103 B7
Cercs E 91 A4
Cercy-la-Tour F 68 B3
Cerda I 108 B2
Cerdedo E 86 B2
Cerdeira P 93 A3
Cerdon F 58 C3
Cerea I 71 C6
Ceres GB 25 B5
Ceres I 70 C2
Cerese I 81 A4
Ceresole-Reale I 70 C2
Cereste F 79 C4
Céret F 91 A5
Cerezo de Abajo E 95 A3
Cerezo de Riotirón E 89 B3
Cerfontaine B 49 C5
Cergy F 58 A3
Cerignola I 104 B1
Cérilly F 68 B2
Cerisiers F 59 B4
Cerizay F 67 B4
Çerkeş TR 16 A6
Çerkezköy TR 114 A3
Cerkije SLO 73 B4
Cerknica SLO 73 C4
Cerkno SLO 72 B3
Cerkwica PL 45 A7
Cerna HR 74 C3
Černá Hora CZ 64 A2
Cernavodă RO 11 D10
Cernay F 60 C3
Cerne Abbas GB 29 C5
Cernégula E 89 B3
Cernik HR 74 C2
Cernóbbio I 70 C4
Černošin CZ 62 A3
Cernovice CZ 63 A5
Cérons F 76 B2
Cerovlje HR 73 C4
Cerovo SK 65 B5
Cerqueto I 82 D1
Cerralbo E 87 D4
Cerreto d'Esi I 82 C1
Cerreto Sannita I 103 B7
Cerrigydrudion GB 26 B2
Cerro Muriano E 100 A1
Certaldo I 81 C5
Certosa di Pésio I 80 B1
Cerva P 87 C3
Cervaro I 103 B6
Cervatos de la Cueza E 88 B2
Červena Řečice CZ 63 A6
Červená-Skala SK 65 B6
Cervená Voda CZ 54 C1
Cerveny Kostelec CZ 53 C6
Cervera E 91 B4
Cervera de la Cañada E 89 C5
Cervera de Pisuerga E 88 B2
Cervera del Llano E 95 C4
Cervera del Río Alhama E 89 B5
Cervéteri I 102 B5
Cérvia I 82 B1
Cerviá de les Garriques E 90 B3
Cervignano del Friuli I 72 C3
Cervinara I 103 B7
Cervione F 102 A2
Cervo E 86 A3
Cervon F 68 A3
Cesana Torinese I 79 B5
Cesarica HR 83 B4
Cesarò I 109 B3
Cesena I 82 B1
Cesenático I 82 B1
Cēsis LV 7 C8
Česká Belá CZ 63 A6
Česká Kamenice CZ 53 C4
Česká Lípa CZ 53 C4
Česká Skalice CZ 53 C6
Česká Třebová CZ 64 A2

České Budějovice CZ 63 B5
České Velenice CZ 63 B5
Český Brod CZ 53 C4
Český Krumlov CZ 63 B5
Český Těšin CZ 65 A4
Češljeva Bara YU 85 B6
Çeşme TR 16 B3
Cessenon F 78 C2
Cesson-Sévigné F 57 B4
Cestas F 76 B2
Čestobrodica YU 85 C5
Cesuras E 86 A2
Cetin Grad HR 73 C5
Cetina E 89 C5
Cetinje YU 105 A4
Cetraro I 106 B2
Ceuta E 99 D5
Ceuti E 101 A4
Ceva I 80 B2
Cevico de la Torre E 88 C2
Cevico Navero E 88 C2
Cevins F 69 C6
Cévio CH 70 B3
Cewice PL 46 A3
Ceyhan TR 16 C7
Ceyrat F 68 C3
Ceyzériat F 69 B5
Chaam NL 49 B5
Chabanais F 67 C5
Chabeuil F 79 B4
Chabielice PL 55 B4
Chablis F 59 C4
Châbons F 69 C5
Chabówka PL 65 A5
Chabreloche F 68 C3
Chabris F 67 A6
Chagford GB 28 C4
Chagny F 69 B4
Chagoda RUS 7 B13
Chaherrero E 94 B2
Chailland F 57 B5
Chaillé-les-Marais F 66 B3
Chailles F 67 A6
Chailley F 59 B4
Chalabre F 77 D5
Chalais F 67 C5
Chalamont F 69 C5
Châlette-sur-Loing F 58 B3
Chalindrey F 59 C6
Challacombe GB 28 B4
Challans F 66 B3
Challes-les-Eaux F 69 C5
Chalmazel F 68 C4
Chalmoux F 68 B3
Chalon-sur-Saône F 69 B4
Chalonnes-sur-Loire F 66 A4
Châlons-en-Champagne F 59 B5
Chalupy PL 47 A4
Châlus F 67 C5
Cham CH 70 A3
Cham D 62 A3
Chamberet F 68 C1
Chambéry F 69 C5
Chambilly F 68 B4
Chambley F 60 A1
Chambly F 58 A3
Chambon-sur-Lac F 68 C2
Chambon-sur-Voueize F 68 B2
Chambord F 58 C2
Chamborigaud F 78 B2
Chamboulive F 68 C1
Chamerau D 62 A3
Chamonix-Mont Blanc F 70 C1
Chamoux-sur-Gelon F 69 C6
Champagnac-le-Vieux F 68 C3
Champagney F 60 C2
Champagnole F 69 B5
Champagny-Mouton F 67 B5
Champaubert F 59 B4
Champdeniers-St. Denis F 67 B4
Champdieu F 68 C4
Champdôtre F 69 A5
Champeix F 68 C3
Champéry CH 70 B1
Champigne F 57 C5
Champignelles F 59 C4
Champigny-sur-Veude F 67 A5
Champlitte-et-le-Prelot F 60 C1
Champoluc I 70 C2
Champoly F 68 C3
Champorcher I 70 C2
Champrond-en-Gâtine F 58 B2
Champs-sur-Tarentaine F 68 C2
Champs-sur-Yonne F 59 C4
Champtoceaux F 66 A3
Chamrousse F 69 C5
Chamusca P 92 B2
Chanac F 78 B2
Chanaleilles F 78 B2
Chandler's Ford GB 31 D2
Chandrexa de Queixa E 87 B3
Chañe E 88 C2
Changy F 68 B3
Chantada E 86 B3
Chantelle F 68 B3
Chantenay-St. Imbert F 68 B3
Chanteuges F 78 A2
Chantilly F 58 A3
Chantonnay F 66 B3
Chão de Codes P 92 B2
Chaource F 59 B5
Chapa E 86 B2
Chapareillan F 69 C5
Chapel en le Frith GB 27 B4
Chapelle Royale F 58 B2
Chapelle-St. Laurent F 67 B4
Chard GB 29 C5
Charenton-du-Cher F 68 B2
Charlbury GB 31 C2
Charleroi B 49 C5
Charlestown IRL 18 C3
Charlestown of Aberlour GB 23 D5
Charleville IRL 20 B3
Charleville-Mézières F 59 A5
Charlieu F 68 B4
Charlottenberg S 34 B4
Charlton Kings GB 29 B5
Charly F 59 B4
Charmes F 60 B2
Charmes-sur-Rhône F 78 B3
Charmey CH 70 B2
Charminster GB 29 C5
Charny F 59 C4
Charolles F 69 B4
Chârost F 68 B2
Charquemont F 70 A1
Charrin F 68 B3
Charroux F 67 B5
Chartres F 58 B2
Charzykow PL 46 B3
Chasseneuil-sur-Bonnieure F 67 C5
Chassigny F 59 C6
Château-Arnoux F 79 B5
Château-Chinon F 68 A3
Château-d'Oex CH 70 B2
Château-d'Olonne F 66 B3
Château-du-Loir F 58 C1
Château-Gontier F 57 C5
Château-la-Vallière F 67 A5
Château-Landon F 58 B3
Château-l'Evêque F 67 C5
Château-Porcien F 59 A5
Château-Renault F 58 C1
Château-Salins F 60 B2
Château-Thierry F 59 A4
Châteaubernard F 67 C4
Châteaubourg F 57 B4
Châteaubriant F 57 C4
Châteaudun F 58 B2
Châteaugiron F 57 B4
Châteaulin F 56 B1
Châteaumeillant F 68 B2
Châteauneuf, *Nièvre* F 68 A3
Châteauneuf, *Saône-et-Loire* F 69 B4
Châteauneuf-de-Randon F 78 B2
Châteauneuf-d'Ille-et-Vilaine F 57 B4
Châteauneuf-du-Faou F 56 B2
Châteauneuf-du-Pape F 78 B3
Châteauneuf-en-Thymerais F 58 B2
Châteauneuf la-Forêt F 67 C6
Châteauneuf-le-Rouge F 79 C4
Châteauneuf-sur-Charente F 67 C4
Châteauneuf-sur-Cher F 68 B2
Châteauneuf-sur-Loire F 58 C3
Châteauneuf-sur-Sarthe F 57 C5
Châteauponsac F 67 B6
Châteauredon F 79 B5
Châteaurenard, *Bouches du Rhône* F 78 C3
Châteaurenard, *Loiret* F 59 C3
Châteauroux F 68 B1
Châteauroux-les-Alpes F 79 B5
Châteauvillain F 59 B5
Châtel F 70 B1
Châtel-Censoir F 68 A3
Châtel-de-Neuvre F 68 B3
Châtel-Montagne F 68 B3
Châtel-St. Denis CH 70 B1
Châtel-sur-Moselle F 60 B2
Châtelaillon-Plage F 66 B3
Châtelaudren F 56 B3
Châtelet B 49 C5
Châtelguyon F 68 C3
Châtellerault F 67 B5
Châtelus-Malvaleix F 68 B2
Châtenois F 60 B1
Châtenois-les-Forges F 70 A1
Chatham GB 31 C4
Châtillon I 70 C2
Châtillon-Coligny F 59 C3
Châtillon-en-Bazois F 68 A3
Châtillon-en-Diois F 79 B4
Châtillon-sur Chalaronne F 69 B4
Châtillon-sur-Indre F 67 B6
Châtillon-sur-Loire F 58 C3
Châtillon-sur-Marne F 59 A4
Châtillon-sur-Seine F 59 C5
Châtres F 59 B4
Chatteris GB 30 B4
Chatton GB 25 C6
Chauchina E 100 B2
Chaudes-Aigues F 78 B2
Chaudrey F 59 B5
Chauffailles F 69 B4
Chaulnes F 58 A3
Chaument Gistoux B 49 C5
Chaumergy F 69 B5
Chaumont F 59 B6
Chaumont-en-Vexin F 58 A2
Chaumont-Porcien F 59 A5
Chaumont-sur-Aire F 59 B6
Chaumont-sur-Loire F 67 A6
Chaunay F 67 B5
Chauny F 59 A4
Chaussin F 69 B5
Chauvigny F 67 B5
Chavagnes-en-Paillers F 66 B3
Chavanges F 59 B5
Chaves P 87 C3
Chavignon F 59 A4
Chazelles-sur-Lyon F 69 C4
Chazey-Bons F 69 C5
Cheadle, *Greater Manchester* GB 26 B3
Cheadle, *Staffordshire* GB 27 C4
Cheb CZ 52 C2
Chebsara RUS 7 B15
Checa E 95 B5
Chęciny PL 55 C5
Cheddar GB 29 B5
Cheddleton GB 26 B3
Chef-Boutonne F 67 B4
Chekalin RUS 7 D14
Chekhovo RUS 47 A6
Cheles E 93 C3
Chella E 96 B2
Chelles F 58 B3
Chełm PL 11 A7
Chełmno, *Kujawsko-Pomorskie* PL 47 B4
Chełmno, *Wielkopolskie* PL 54 A3
Chelmsford GB 31 C4
Chełmża PL 47 B4
Cheltenham GB 29 B5
Chelva E 96 B1
Chémery F 67 A6
Chemery-sur-Bar F 59 A5
Chemillé F 67 A4
Chemin F 69 B5
Chemnitz D 52 C2
Chénerailles F 68 B2
Cheniménil F 60 B2
Chenonceaux F 67 A6
Chenôve F 69 A4
Chepelare BG 112 A6
Chepstow GB 29 B5
Chera E 96 B2
Cherasco I 80 B1
Cherbourg F 57 A4
Cherchiara di Calábria I 106 B3
Cherepovets RUS 7 B14
Cherkasy UA 11 B12
Chernihiv UA 7 F11
Chernivtsi UA 11 B8
Chernobyl = Chornobyl UA 7 F11
Chernyakhovsk RUS 6 D6
Chéroy F 59 B3
Cherven BY 7 E10
Chervonohrad UA 11 A8
Cherykaw BY 7 E11
Chesham GB 31 C3
Cheshunt GB 31 C3
Chessy-lès-Pres F 59 B4
Cheste E 96 B2
Chester GB 26 B3
Chester-le-Street GB 25 D6
Chesterfield GB 27 B4
Chevagnes F 68 B3
Chevanceaux F 67 C4
Chevillon F 59 B6
Chevilly F 58 B2
Chew Magna GB 29 B5
Chézery-Forens F 69 B5
Chialamberto I 70 C2
Chiampo I 71 C6
Chianale I 79 B6
Chianciano Terme I 81 C5
Chiaramonte Gulfi I 109 B3
Chiaramonti I 110 B1
Chiaravalle I 82 C2
Chiaravalle Centrale I 106 C3
Chiaréggio I 71 B4
Chiari I 71 C4
Chiaromonte I 106 A3
Chiasso CH 70 C4
Chiávari I 80 B3
Chiavenna I 71 B4
Chiché F 67 B4
Chichester GB 31 D3
Chiclana de la Frontera E 99 C4
Chiclana de Segura E 100 A2
Chiddingfold GB 31 C3
Chieri I 80 A1
Chiesa in Valmalenco I 71 B4
Chieti I 103 A7
Chieti Scalo I 103 A7
Chiéuti I 103 B8
Chigirin UA 11 B12
Chigwell GB 31 C4
Chillarón de Cuenca E 95 B4
Chillarón del Rey E 95 B4
Chilleurs-aux-Bois F 58 B3
Chillón E 100 A1
Chilluevar E 100 B2
Chiloeches E 95 B3
Chimay B 49 C5
Chimeneas E 100 B2
Chinchilla de Monte Aragón E 96 C1
Chinchón E 95 B3
Chingford GB 31 C4
Chinon F 67 A5
Chióggia I 72 C2
Chiomonte I 79 A5
Chipiona E 99 C4
Chippenham GB 29 B5
Chipping Campden GB 29 A6
Chipping Norton GB 31 C2
Chipping Ongar GB 31 C4
Chipping Sodbury GB 29 B5
Chirac F 78 B2
Chirbury GB 26 C2
Chirens F 69 C5
Chirivel E 101 B3
Chirk GB 26 C2
Chirnside GB 25 C5
Chişinău = Khisinev MD 11 C10
Chisineu Criş RO 10 C6
Chissey-en-Morvan F 69 A4
Chiusa I 71 B6
Chiusa di Pésio I 80 B1
Chiusa Scláfani I 108 B2
Chiusaforte I 72 B3
Chiusi I 81 C5
Chiva E 96 B2
Chivasso I 70 C2
Chlewiska PL 55 B5
Chludowo PL 46 C2
Chlum u Třeboně CZ 63 B5
Chlumec nad Cidlinou CZ 53 C5
Chmielnik PL 55 C5
Chobienice PL 53 A5
Choceň CZ 53 D6
Choceń PL 47 C5
Chochołow PL 65 A5
Chocianów PL 53 B5
Chociw PL 55 B4
Chociwel PL 46 B1
Choczewo PL 46 A3
Chodaków PL 55 A5
Chodecz PL 47 C5
Chodov CZ 52 C2
Chodzież PL 46 C2
Chojna PL 45 C6
Chojnice PL 46 B3
Chojno PL 46 C2
Chojnów PL 53 B5
Cholet F 66 A4
Chomérac F 78 B3
Chomutov CZ 52 C3
Chop UA 11 B7
Chorges F 79 B5
Chorley GB 26 B3
Chornobyl = Chernobyl UA 7 F11
Chortkiv UA 11 B8
Chorzew PL 54 B3
Chorzów PL 54 C3
Choszczno PL 46 B1
Chotcza-Józefów PL 55 B6
Chotěboř CZ 63 A6
Chouilly F 59 A5
Chouto P 92 B2
Chouzy-sur-Cisse F 67 A6
Chozas de Abajo E 88 B1
Chrast, *Vychodočeský* CZ 64 A1
Chrást, *Západočeský* CZ 63 A4
Chrastava CZ 53 C4
Chřibská CZ 53 C4
Christchurch GB 29 C6
Christiansfeld DK 39 D2
Chroberz PL 55 C5
Chropyně CZ 64 A3
Chrudim CZ 53 D5
Chrzanów PL 55 C4
Chtelnica SK 64 B3
Chudovo RUS 7 B11
Chueca E 94 C3
Chulmleigh GB 28 C4
Chur CH 71 B4
Church Stretton GB 26 C3
Churriana E 100 C1
Churwalden CH 71 B4
Chvalšiny CZ 63 B5
Chwaszczyno PL 47 A4
Chynava CZ 53 C4
Chýnov CZ 63 A5
Ciacova RO 75 C6
Ciadîr-Lunga MD 11 C10
Ciadoncha E 88 B3
Cianciana I 108 B2
Ciano d'Enza I 81 B4
Ciążen PL 54 A2
Cibakhaza H 75 B5
Ciborro P 92 C2
Cicagna I 80 B3
Cicciano I 103 C7
Cićevac YU 85 C6
Ciciliano I 102 B5
Cicognolo I 71 C5
Cidadelhe P 87 D3
Cide TR 16 A6
Cidones E 89 C4
Ciechanów PL 47 C6
Ciechocinek PL 47 C4
Cielądz PL 55 B5
Ciemnik PL 46 B1
Ciempozuelos E 95 B3
Ciepielów PL 55 B6
Čierny Balog SK 65 B5
Cierp F 77 D3
Cierpice PL 47 C4
Ciervana E 89 A3
Cierznie PL 46 B3
Cieslé PL 47 C6
Cieszyn PL 65 A4
Cieutat F 76 C3
Cieza E 101 A4
Cifer SK 64 B3
Çifteler TR 114 C6
Cifuentes E 95 B4
Cigales E 88 C2
Cigliano I 70 C3
Cihanbeyli TR 16 B6
Cillas E 95 B5
Cilleros E 93 A4
Cilleruelo de Arriba E 88 C3
Cilleruelo de Bezana E 88 B3
Cimalmotto CH 70 B3
Cimanes del Tejar E 88 B1
Ciminna I 108 B2
Cimişlia MD 11 C10
Cimoláis I 72 B2
Cîmpulung RO 11 D8
Çınarcık TR 114 B4
Cinctorres E 90 C2
Cinderford GB 29 B5
Çine TR 16 C4
Činěves CZ 53 C5
Ciney B 49 C6
Cinfães P 87 C2
Cingia de Botti I 81 A4
Cingoli I 82 C2
Cinigiano I 81 D5
Cinobaňa SK 65 B5
Cinq-Mars-la-Pile F 67 A5
Cinquefrondí I 106 C3
Cintegabelle F 77 C4
Cintruénigo E 89 B5
Ciółkowo PL 47 C5
Ciperez E 87 D4
Cirat E 96 A2
Cirella I 106 B2
Cirencester GB 29 B6
Cirey-sur-Vezouze F 60 B2
Ciria E 89 C5
Ciriè I 70 C2
Cirigliano I 104 C2
Cirò I 107 B4
Cirò Marina I 107 B4
Ciry-le-Noble F 69 B4
Cislău RO 11 D9
Cismon del Grappa I 72 C1
Cisneros E 88 B2
Cissac-Médoc F 66 C4
Čista CZ 52 C3
Cisterna di Latina I 102 B5
Cistérniga E 88 C2
Cisternino I 104 C3
Cistierna E 88 B1
Čitluk BIH 84 C2
Citov CZ 53 C4
Città della Pieve I 81 D5
Città di Castello I 82 C1
Città Sant'Angelo I 103 A7
Cittadella I 72 C1
Cittaducale I 102 A5
Cittanova I 106 C3
Ciudad Real E 94 D3
Ciudad Rodrigo E 93 A4
Ciudadela de Menorca E 97 B3
Cividale del Friuli I 72 B3
Civita I 102 A6
Civita Castellana I 102 A5
Civitanova Alta I 82 C2
Civitanova Marche I 82 C2
Civitavécchia I 102 A4
Civitella di Romagna I 81 B5
Civitella di Tronto I 82 D2
Civitella Roveto I 103 B6
Civray F 67 B5
Çivril TR 16 B4
Cizur Mayor E 76 D1
Cjutadilla E 91 B4
Clabhach GB 24 B1
Clachan GB 22 D2
Clachan na Luib GB 22 D1
Clacton-on-Sea GB 31 C5
Cladich GB 24 B2
Claggan GB 24 B2
Clairvaux-les-Lacs F 69 B5
Clamecy F 68 A3
Claonaig GB 24 C2
Clarecastle IRL 20 B3
Claregalway IRL 20 A3
Claremorris IRL 18 C2
Clarinbridge IRL 20 A3
Clashmore GB 23 D4
Clashmore IRL 21 B4
Claudy GB 19 B4
Clausthal-Zellerfeld D 51 B6
Cláut I 72 B2
Clay Cross GB 27 B4
Claye-Souilly F 58 B3
Cléder F 56 B1
Cleethorpes GB 27 B5
Clefmont F 60 B1
Cléguérec F 56 B2
Clelles F 79 B4
Clenze D 44 C2
Cleobury Mortimer GB 29 A5
Cléon-d'Andran F 78 B3
Cléré-les-Pins F 67 A5
Clères F 58 A2
Clermont F 58 A3
Clermont-en-Argonne F 59 A6
Clermont-Ferrand F 68 C3
Clermont-l'Hérault F 78 C2
Clerval F 69 A6
Clervaux L 50 C2
Cléry-St. André F 58 C2
Cles I 71 B6
Clevedon GB 29 B5
Cleveleys GB 26 B2
Cley GB 30 B5
Clifden IRL 18 C1
Clifford GB 29 A4
Clisson F 66 A3
Clitheroe GB 26 B3
Clogh IRL 21 B4
Cloghan, *Donegal* IRL 19 B4
Cloghan, *Offaly* IRL 21 A4
Clogheen IRL 21 B4
Clogher GB 19 B4
Cloghjordan IRL 20 B3
Clohars-Carnoët F 56 C2
Clonakilty IRL 20 C3
Clonaslee IRL 21 A4
Clondalkin IRL 21 A5
Clones IRL 19 B4
Clonmany IRL 19 A4
Clonmel IRL 21 B4
Clonmellon IRL 19 C4
Clonord IRL 21 A4
Clonroche IRL 21 B5
Cloone IRL 19 C4
Cloppenburg D 43 C5
Closeburn GB 25 C4
Clough GB 19 B6
Clova GB 25 B4
Clovelly GB 28 C3
Clowne GB 27 B4
Cloyes-sur-le-Loir F 58 C2
Cloyne IRL 20 C3
Cluis F 68 B1
Cluj-Napoca RO 11 C7
Clun GB 26 C2
Clunes GB 24 B3
Cluny F 69 B4
Cluses F 69 B6
Clusone I 71 C4
Clydach GB 28 B4
Clydebank GB 24 C3
Coachford IRL 20 C3
Coagh GB 19 B5
Coalisland GB 19 B5
Coalville GB 27 C4
Coaña E 86 A4
Cobas E 86 A2
Cobertelade E 89 C4
Cobeta E 95 B4
Cóbh IRL 20 C3
Cobreces E 88 A2
Coburg D 51 C6
Coca E 94 A2
Cocentaina E 96 C2
Cochem D 50 C3
Cockburnspath GB 25 C5
Cockermouth GB 26 A2
Codigoro I 82 B1
Codogno I 71 C4
Codos E 89 C5
Codróipo I 72 C2
Codrongianos I 110 B1
Coelhoso P 87 C4
Coesfeld D 50 B3
Coevorden NL 42 C3
Cofrentes E 96 B1
Cogeces del Monte E 88 C2
Coggeshall GB 31 C4
Cognac F 67 C4
Cogne I 70 C2
Cognin F 69 C5
Cogolin F 79 C5
Cogollos de Guadix E 100 B2
Cogollos-Vega E 100 B2
Cogolludo E 95 B3
Coimbra P 92 A2
Coín E 100 C1
Coirós E 86 A2
Čoka YU 75 C5
Col SLO 73 C4
Colares P 92 C1
Cölbe D 51 C4
Colbitz D 52 A1
Colchester GB 31 C4
Coldingham GB 25 C5
Colditz D 52 B2
Coldstream GB 25 C5
Colebrooke GB 28 C4
Colera E 91 A6
Coleraine GB 19 A5
Colfiorito I 82 C1
Cólico I 71 B4
Coligny F 69 B5
Colindres E 89 A3
Coll de Nargó E 91 A4
Collado-Mediano E 94 B2
Collado Villalba E 94 B3
Collagna I 81 B4
Collanzo E 88 A1
Collat F 68 C3
Colle di Val d'Elsa I 81 C5
Colle Isarco I 71 B6
Colle Sannita I 103 B7
Collécchio I 81 B4
Colledimezzo I 103 B7
Colleferro I 102 B6
Collelongo I 103 B6
Collepasso I 107 A5
Collepepe I 82 D1
Collesalvetti I 81 C4
Collesano I 108 B2
Colli a Volturno I 103 B7
Collin GB 25 C4
Collinée F 56 B3
Collingham, *Nottinghamshire* GB 27 B5
Collingham, *West Yorkshire* GB 27 B4
Collinghorst D 43 B4
Cóllio I 71 C5
Collobrières F 79 C5
Collon IRL 19 C5
Collooney IRL 18 B3
Colmar F 60 B3
Colmars F 79 B5
Colmenar E 100 C1
Colmenar de la Sierra E 95 A3
Colmenar de Oreja E 95 B3
Colmenar Viejo E 94 B3
Colmonel GB 24 C3
Colne GB 26 B3
Colobraro I 106 A3
Cologna Véneta I 71 C6
Cologne = Köln D 50 C2
Cologne F 77 C3
Cologne al Serio I 71 C4
Colombey-les-Belles F 60 B1
Colombey-les-deux-Églises F 59 B5
Colombres E 88 A2
Colomera E 100 B2
Colomers E 91 A5
Colomiers F 77 C4
Colònia de Sant Jordi E 97 B3
Colorno I 81 B4
Colos P 98 B2
Cölpin D 45 B5
Colpy GB 23 D6
Colsterworth GB 30 B3
Coltishall GB 30 B5
Colunga E 88 A1
Colwell GB 25 C5
Colwyn Bay GB 26 B2
Colyford GB 29 C4
Coma-ruga E 91 B4
Comácchio I 82 B1
Combarros E 86 B4
Combeaufontaine F 60 C1
Comber GB 19 B6
Comblain-au-Pont B 49 C6
Combloux F 70 C1
Combourg F 57 B4
Combronde F 68 C3
Comeglians I 72 B2
Comillas E 88 A2
Comines F 49 C4
Cómiso I 109 C3
Comloşu Mare RO 75 C5
Commensacq F 76 B2
Commentry F 68 B2
Commerau D 53 B4
Commercy F 60 B1
Como I 71 C4
Cómpeta E 100 C2
Compiègne F 58 A3
Comporta P 92 C2
Comps-sur-Artuby F 79 C5
Comrat MD 11 C10
Comrie GB 25 B4
Comunanza I 82 D2
Cona, *Emilia Romagna* I 81 B5
Cona, *Veneto* I 72 C2
Concarneau F 56 C2
Conceição P 98 B2
Conches-en-Ouche F 58 B1
Concordia Sagittária I 72 C2
Concordia sulla Sécchia I 81 B4
Concots F 77 B4
Condat F 68 C2
Condé-en-Brie F 59 B4
Condé-sur-l'Escaut F 49 C4
Conde-sur-Marne F 59 A5
Condé-sur-Noireau F 57 B5
Condeixa P 92 A2
Condemios de Abajo E 95 A3
Condemios de Arriba E 95 A3
Condino I 71 C5
Condom F 77 C3
Condove I 70 C2
Condrieu F 69 C4
Conegliano I 72 C2
Conflans-sur-Lanterne F 60 C2
Confolens F 67 B5
Conforto E 86 A3
Cong IRL 18 C2
Congleton GB 26 B3
Congosto E 86 B4
Congosto de Valdavia E 88 B2
Congostrina E 95 A3
Conil de la Frontera E 99 C4
Coningsby GB 27 B5
Coniston GB 26 A2
Conlie F 57 B5
Conliège F 69 B5
Conna IRL 20 B3
Connah's Quay GB 26 B2
Connantre F 59 B4
Connaugh IRL 20 B3
Connaux F 78 B3
Connel GB 24 B2
Connerré F 58 B1
Cononbridge GB 23 D4
Čonoplja YU 75 C4
Conques F 77 B5
Conques-sur-Orbiel F 77 C5
Conquista E 100 A1
Conquista de la Sierra E 93 B5
Consándolo I 81 B5
Consélice I 81 B5
Conselve I 72 C1
Consett GB 25 D6
Consolacão P 92 B1
Constancia P 92 B2
Constanco E 86 A2
Constanța RO 11 D10
Constanti E 91 B4
Constantina E 99 B5
Consuegra E 95 C3
Consuma I 81 C5
Contarina I 82 A1
Conthey CH 70 B2
Contigliano I 102 A5
Contis-Plage F 76 B1
Contrada I 103 C7
Contres F 67 A6
Contrexéville F 60 B1
Controne I 103 C8
Contursi Termi I 103 C8
Conty F 58 A3
Conversano I 104 C3
Conwy GB 26 B2
Cookstown GB 19 B5
Coole F 59 B5
Coolgreany IRL 21 B5
Cooneen GB 19 B4
Cootehill IRL 19 B4
Cope E 101 B4
Copenhagen = København DK 41 D2
Copertino I 105 C4
Copparo I 81 B5
Coppenbrugge D 51 A5
Corabia RO 11 E8
Córaci I 106 B3
Coralići BIH 83 B4
Corato I 104 B2
Coray F 56 B2
Corbeil-Essonnes F 58 B3
Corbeny F 59 A4
Corbera E 96 B2
Corbie F 58 A3
Corbigny F 68 A3
Corbion B 59 A5
Corbridge GB 25 D5
Corby GB 30 B3
Corconte E 88 A3
Corcubión E 86 B1
Corcumello I 103 A6
Cordenòns I 72 C2
Cordes-sur-Ciel F 77 B4
Córdoba E 100 B1

Cordobilla de Lácara E 93 B4
Cordovado I 72 C2
Corella E 89 B5
Coreses E 88 C1
Corfe Castle GB 29 C5
Corga de Lobão P 87 D2
Cori I 102 B5
Coria E 93 B4
Coria del Río E 99 B4
Corigliano Cálabro I 106 B3
Corinaldo I 82 C1
Corinth = Kórinthos GR 113 E4
Cório I 70 C2
Coripe E 99 C5
Cork IRL 20 C3
Corlay F 56 B2
Corleone I 108 B2
Corleto Monforte I 103 C8
Corleto Perticara I 104 C2
Çorlu TR 114 A2
Cormainville F 58 B2
Cormatin F 69 B4
Cormeilles F 58 A1
Cormery F 67 A5
Cormòns I 72 C3
Cormoz F 69 B5
Cornago E 89 B4
Cornberg D 51 B5
Cornellana E 86 A4
Corneşti MD 11 C10
Corniglio I 81 B4
Cornimont F 60 C2
Corniolo I 81 C5
Cornuda I 72 C2
Cornudella de Montsant E 90 B3
Cornudilla E 89 B3
Cornus F 78 C2
Çorovodë AL 112 B2
Corpach GB 24 B2
Corps F 79 B4
Corps Nuds F 57 C4
Corral de Almaguer E 95 C3
Corral de Ayllon E 89 C3
Corral de Calatrava E 100 A1
Corral-Rubio E 101 A4
Corrales E 88 C1
Corran GB 24 B2
Corredoiras E 86 A2
Corréggio I 81 B4
Corrèze F 68 C1
Corridónia I 82 C2
Corris GB 26 C2
Corrubedo E 86 B1
Córsico I 71 C4
Corsock GB 25 C4
Corte F 102 A2
Corte de Peleas E 93 C4
Corte Pinto P 98 B3
Corteconcepción E 99 B4
Cortegaca P 87 D2
Cortegada E 87 B2
Cortegana E 99 B4
Cortemaggiore I 81 B3
Cortemilia I 80 B2
Cortes E 89 C5
Cortes de Aragón E 90 C2
Cortes de Arenoso E 96 A2
Cortes de Baza E 101 B3
Cortes de la Frontera E 99 C5
Cortes de Pallás E 96 B2
Cortiçadas P 92 C2
Cortico P 87 C3
Cortijo de Arriba E 94 C2
Cortijos Nuevos E 101 A3
Cortina d'Ampezzo I 72 B2
Corton GB 30 B5
Cortona I 81 C5
Coruche P 92 C2
Corullón E 86 B4
Çorum TR 16 A7
Corvara in Badia I 72 B1
Corvera E 101 B4
Corwen GB 26 C2
Cosenza I 106 B3
Cosham GB 31 D2
Coslada E 95 B3
Cosne-Cours-sur-Loire F 68 A2
Cosne d'Allier F 68 B2
Cospeito E 86 A3
Cossato I 70 C3
Cossaye F 68 B3
Cossé-le-Vivien F 57 C5
Cossonay CH 69 B6
Costa da Caparica P 92 C1
Costa de Santo André P 98 A2
Costa Nova P 92 A2
Costalpino I 81 C5
Costaros F 78 B2
Costeşti RO 11 D8
Costigliole d'Asti I 80 B2
Costigliole Saluzzo I 80 B1
Coswig, *Sachsen-Anhalt* D 52 B2
Coswig, *Sachsen* D 52 B3
Cotherstone GB 27 A4
Cotronei I 107 B3
Cottbus D 53 B4
Cottenham GB 30 B4
Cottingham GB 27 B5
Coublanc F 60 C1
Couches F 69 B4
Couço P 92 C2
Coucouron F 78 B2
Coucy-le-Château-Auffrique F 59 A4
Couëron F 66 A3
Couhé F 67 B5
Couiza F 77 D5
Coulags GB 22 D3
Coulanges F 68 B3
Coulanges-la-Vineuse F 59 C4
Coulanges-sur-Yonne F 68 A3
Couleuvre F 68 B2
Coulmier-le-Sec F 59 C5
Coulommiers F 59 B4
Coulonges-sur-l'Autize F 67 B4
Coulounieix-Chamiers F 67 C5
Coulport GB 24 B3
Coupar Angus GB 25 B4
Coupéville F 59 B5
Couptrain F 57 B5
Cour-Cheverny F 67 A6
Coura P 87 C2
Courcelles B 49 C5
Courcelles-Chaussy F 60 A2
Courchevel F 70 C1
Courcôme F 67 C5
Courçon F 66 B4
Courgenay CH 70 A2
Courmayeur I 70 C1
Courniou F 78 C1
Cournon-d'Auvergne F 68 C3
Cournonterral F 78 C2
Courpière F 68 C3
Cours-la-Ville F 69 B4
Coursan F 78 C2
Courseulles-sur-Mer F 57 A5
Courson-les-Carrières F 59 C4
Courtalain F 58 B2
Courtenay F 59 B4
Courtomer F 58 B1
Courville F 58 B2
Coussac-Bonneval F 67 C6
Coutances F 57 A4
Couterne F 57 B5
Coutras F 76 A2
Couvet CH 70 B1
Couvin B 49 C5
Couzon F 68 B3
Covadonga E 88 A1
Covaleda E 89 C4
Covarrubias E 89 B3
Covas P 87 C2
Cove GB 22 D3
Coventry GB 30 B2
Coverack GB 28 C2
Covigliáio I 81 B5
Covilhã P 92 A3
Cowbridge GB 29 B4
Cowdenbeath GB 25 B4
Cowes GB 31 D2
Cox F 77 C4
Cózar E 100 A2
Cozes F 66 C4
Craco I 104 C2
Craibstone GB 23 D6
Craighouse GB 24 C2
Craignure GB 24 B2
Crail GB 25 B5
Crailsheim D 61 A6
Craiova RO 11 D7
Cramlington GB 25 C6
Cranleigh GB 31 C3
Craon F 57 C5
Craonne F 59 A4
Craponne F 69 C4
Craponne-sur-Arzon F 68 C3
Crathie GB 23 D5
Crato P 92 B3
Craughwell IRL 20 A3
Craven Arms GB 26 C3
Crawford GB 25 C4
Crawinkel D 51 C6
Crawley GB 31 C3
Creag Ghoraidh GB 22 D1
Crecente E 87 B2
Crèches-sur-Saône F 69 B4
Crécy-en-Ponthieu F 48 C2
Crécy-la-Chapelle F 59 B3
Crécy-sur-Serre F 59 A4
Crediton GB 29 C4
Creeslough IRL 19 A4
Creetown GB 24 D3
Creeve GB 19 B5
Creglingen D 61 A6
Creil F 58 A3
Creissels F 78 B2
Crema I 71 C4
Cremeaux F 68 C3
Crémenes E 88 B1
Crémieu F 69 C5
Cremlingen D 51 A6
Cremona I 81 A4
Creney F 59 B5
Črenšovci SLO 73 B6
Créon F 76 B2
Crepaja YU 85 A5
Crépy F 59 A4
Crépy-en-Valois F 59 A3
Cres HR 83 B3
Crescentino I 70 C3
Crespino I 81 B5
Crespos E 94 B2
Cressage GB 26 C3
Cressensac F 77 A4
Crest F 79 B4
Cresta CH 71 B4
Créteil F 58 B3
Creully F 57 A5
Creussen D 62 A2
Creutzwald F 60 A2
Creuzburg D 51 B6
Crevalcore I 81 B5
Crèvecœur-le-Grand F 58 A3
Crevillente E 101 A5
Crévola d'Ossola I 70 B3
Crewe GB 26 B3
Crewkerne GB 29 C5
Criales E 89 B3
Crianlarich GB 24 B3
Criccieth GB 26 C1
Crickhowell GB 29 B4
Cricklade GB 29 B6
Crieff GB 25 B4
Criel-sur-Mer F 48 C2
Crikvenica HR 73 C4
Crillon F 58 A2
Crimmitschau D 52 C2
Crimond GB 23 D7
Crinitz D 53 B3
Cripán E 89 B4
Criquetot-l'Esneval F 57 A6
Crispiano I 104 C3
Crissolo I 79 B6
Cristóbal E 93 A5
Crivitz D 44 B3
Črna SLO 73 B4
Crna Bara, *Srbija* YU 85 B4
Crna Bara, *Vojvodina* YU 75 C5
Crnac HR 74 C2
Crnča YU 85 B4
Crni Lug BIH 83 B5
Crni Lug HR 73 C4
Črni Vrh SLO 73 C4
Crnjelovo Donje BIH 85 B4
Črnomelj SLO 73 C5
Crocketford GB 25 C4
Crocq F 68 C2
Crodo I 70 B3
Croglin GB 25 D5
Crolly IRL 18 A3
Cromarty GB 23 D4
Cromer GB 30 B5
Cronat F 68 B3
Crookhaven IRL 20 C2
Crookstown IRL 20 C3
Croom IRL 20 B3
Cropalati I 106 B3
Crópani I 107 C3
Crosbost GB 22 C2
Crosby GB 26 B2
Crosía I 106 B3
Cross-Hands GB 28 B3
Crossakiel IRL 19 C4
Crosshaven IRL 20 C3
Crosshill GB 24 C3
Crossmolina IRL 18 B2
Crotone I 107 B4
Crottendorf D 52 C2
Crouy F 59 A4
Crowborough GB 31 C4
Crowland GB 30 B3
Crowthorne GB 31 C3
Croyde GB 28 B3
Croydon GB 31 C3
Crozon F 56 B1
Cruas F 78 B3
Cruceni RO 75 B6
Crúcoli I 107 B4
Cruden Bay GB 23 D7
Crudgington GB 26 C3
Cruis F 79 B4
Crumlin GB 19 B5
Cruseilles F 69 B6
Crusheen IRL 20 B3
Cruz de Incio E 86 B3
Crvenka YU 75 C4
Črveny Kamen SK 64 A4
Csabacsüd H 75 B5
Csabrendek H 74 A2
Csákvár H 74 A3
Csanádapáca H 75 B5
Csanádpalota H 75 B5
Csány H 65 C5
Csanytelek H 75 B5
Csapod H 74 A1
Császár H 74 A3
Császártöltés H 75 B4
Csávoly H 75 B4
Csemö H 75 A4
Csengöd H 75 B4
Csépa H 75 B5
Csepreg H 74 A1
Cserkeszölö H 75 B5
Csernely H 65 B6
Csökmö H 75 A6
Csököly H 74 B2
Csokonyavisonta H 74 B2
Csólyospálos H 75 B4
Csongrád H 75 B5
Csopak H 74 B2
Csorna H 64 C3
Csorvás H 75 B5
Csurgo H 74 B2
Cuacos de Yuste E 93 A5
Cualedro E 87 C3
Cuanca de Campos E 88 B1
Cuba P 98 A3
Cubel E 95 A5
Cubelles E 91 B4
Cubillos E 89 C4
Cubillos del Sil E 86 B4
Cubo de la Solana E 89 C4
Çubuk TR 16 A6
Cuckfield GB 31 C3
Cucuron F 79 C4
Cudillero E 86 A4
Cuéllar E 88 C2
Cuenca E 95 B4
Cuers F 79 C5
Cuerva E 94 C2
Cueva de Agreda E 89 C5
Cuevas Bajas E 100 B1
Cuevas de San Clemente E 89 B3
Cuevas de San Marcos E 100 B1
Cuevas del Almanzora E 101 B4
Cuevas del Becerro E 99 C5
Cuevas del Campo E 100 B3
Cuevas del Valle E 94 B1
Cuges-les-Pins F 79 C4
Cúglieri I 110 B1
Cugnaux F 77 C4
Cuijk NL 50 B1
Cuinzier F 69 B4
Cuiseaux F 69 B5
Cuisery F 69 B5
Culan F 68 B2
Culemborg NL 49 B6
Cúllar E 101 B3
Cullaville GB 19 B5
Cullera E 96 B2
Cullivoe GB 22 A7
Cullompton GB 29 C4
Cully CH 70 B1
Culoz F 69 C5
Cults GB 23 D6
Cumbernauld GB 25 C4
Cumbres de San Bartolomé E 99 A4
Cumbres Mayores E 99 A4
Cumiana I 80 B1
Ćumić YU 85 B5
Cumnock GB 24 C3
Çumra TR 16 C6
Cúneo I 80 B1
Cunlhat F 68 C3
Čunski HR 83 B3
Cuntis E 86 B2
Cuorgnè I 70 C2
Cupar GB 25 B4
Cupello I 103 A7
Cupra Maríttima I 82 C2
Cupramontana I 82 C2
Ćuprija YU 85 C6
Curinga I 106 C3
Currelos E 86 B3
Currie GB 25 C4
Curtea de Argeş RO 11 D8
Curtici RO 75 B6
Curtis E 86 A2
Curtis Santa Eulalia E 86 A2
Čurug YU 75 C5
Cusano Mutri I 103 B7
Cushendall GB 19 A5
Cusset F 68 B3
Cussy-les-Forges F 68 A4
Cutanda E 90 C1
Cutro I 107 B3
Cutrofiano I 107 A5
Cuts F 59 A4
Cuvilly F 58 A3
Cuxhaven D 43 B5
Cvikov CZ 53 C4
Cwmbran GB 29 B4
Cybinka PL 53 A4
Czacz PL 54 A1
Czajków PL 54 B3
Czaplinek PL 46 B2
Czarlin PL 47 A4
Czarna-Dąbrówka PL 46 A3
Czarna Woda PL 47 B4
Czarnca PL 55 C4
Czarne PL 46 B2
Czarnków PL 46 C2
Czarnowo PL 47 B4
Czarnozyly PL 54 B3
Czarny Bór PL 53 C6
Czarny-Dunajec PL 65 A5
Czarny Las PL 54 B2
Czchow PL 65 A6
Czechowice-Dziedzice PL 65 A4
Czempiń PL 54 A1
Czermno PL 55 B5
Czernichow PL 55 D4
Czerniejewo PL 46 C3
Czernikowo PL 47 C4
Czersk PL 46 B3
Czerwieńsk PL 53 A5
Czerwionka-Leszczyny PL 54 C3
Czerwonka PL 47 B6
Częstochowa PL 55 C4
Czeszewo PL 46 C3
Człopa PL 46 B2
Człuchów PL 46 B3

D

Daaden D 50 C3
Dabas H 75 A4
Dąbie PL 54 A3
Dąbki PL 46 A2
Dabo F 60 B3
Dabrowa PL 46 C3
Dąbrowa Górnicza PL 55 C4
Dąbrowa Tarnowska PL 55 C5
Dąbrowice PL 55 A4
Dabrowno PL 47 B6
Dachau D 62 B2
Dačice CZ 63 A6
Daday TR 16 A6
Dagebüll D 39 E1
Dagmersellen CH 70 A2
Dahlen D 52 B2
Dahlenburg D 44 B2
Dahme D 52 B3
Dahn D 60 A3
Dähre D 44 C2
Dail bho Dheas GB 22 C2
Dailly GB 24 C3
Daimiel E 95 C3
Daingean IRL 21 A4
Đakovica YU 10 E6
Đakovo HR 74 C3
Dal, *Akershus* N 34 A3
Dal, *Telemark* N 33 B5
Dala-Floda S 36 A1
Dala-Husby S 36 A2
Dala-Järna S 36 A1
Dalaas A 71 A5
Dalabrog GB 22 D1
Dalaman TR 16 C4
Dalarö S 36 B5
Dalbeattie GB 25 D4
Dalby DK 39 D3
Dalby, *Skåne* S 41 D3
Dalby, *Uppsala* S 36 B4
Dale, *Pembrokeshire* GB 28 B2
Dale, *Shetland* GB 22 A7
Dalen, *Akershus* N 34 B3
Dalen, *Telemark* N 33 B5
Daleszyce PL 55 C5
Dalhalvaig GB 23 C5
Dalheim L 60 A2
Dalhem S 37 D5
Dalias E 100 C3
Dalj HR 75 C3
Dalkeith GB 25 C4
Dalkey IRL 21 A5
Dalmally GB 24 B3
Dalmellington GB 24 C3
Dalry, *Dumfries & Galloway* GB 24 C3
Dalry, *North Ayrshire* GB 24 C3
Dalrymple GB 24 C3
Dals Långed S 35 C4
Dals Rostock S 35 C4
Dalsjöfors S 40 B3
Dalskog S 35 C4
Dalston GB 25 D5
Dalstorp S 40 B3
Dalton-in-Furness GB 26 A2
Daluis F 79 B5
Dalum D 43 C4
Dalum S 40 B3
Dalvík IS 111 B7
Dalwhinnie GB 24 B3
Damasławek PL 46 C3
Damazan F 76 B3
Dammarie-les-Lys F 58 B3
Dammartin-en-Goële F 58 A3
Damme D 43 C5
Damnica PL 46 A3
Dampierre F 69 A5
Dampierre-sur-Salon F 69 A5
Damüls A 71 A4
Damville F 58 B2
Damvillers F 59 A6
Damwoude NL 42 B2
Danbury GB 31 C4
Dangé-St. Romain F 67 B5
Dångebo S 40 C5
Dangers F 58 B2
Dangeul F 58 B1
Danilovgrad YU 105 A5
Danischenhagen D 44 A2
Daniszyn PL 54 B2
Danjoutin F 60 C2
Dannas S 40 B3
Dannemarie F 60 C3
Dannemora S 36 A4
Dannenberg D 44 B3
Dánszentmiklós H 75 A4
Dány H 75 A4
Daoulas F 56 B1
Darabani RO 11 B9
Darány H 74 C2
Darda HR 74 C3
Dardesheim D 51 B6
Darfeld D 50 A3
Darfo I 71 C5
Dargiń PL 46 A2
Dargun D 45 B4
Darlington GB 27 A4
Darłowo PL 46 A2
Darmstadt D 61 A4
Darney F 60 B2
Daroca E 95 A5
Darque P 87 C2
Darragh IRL 20 B2
Dartford GB 31 C4
Dartington GB 28 C4
Dartmouth GB 29 C4
Darton GB 27 B4
Daruvar HR 74 C2
Darvas H 75 A6
Darvel GB 24 C3
Darwen GB 26 B3
Dassel D 51 B5
Dassow D 44 B2
Datça TR 16 C3
Datteln D 50 B3
Dattenfeld D 50 C3
Daugard DK 39 D2
Daugavpils LV 7 D9
Daumeray F 57 C5
Daun D 50 C2
Daventry GB 30 B2
Davle CZ 63 A5
Davor HR 84 A2
Davos CH 71 B4
Davyd Haradok BY 7 E9
Dawlish GB 29 C4
Dax F 76 C1
De Haan B 49 B4
De Koog NL 42 B1
De Panne B 48 B3
De Wijk NL 42 C3
Deal GB 31 C5
Deauville F 57 A6
Deba E 89 A4
Debar MK 112 A2
Debe Wielkie PL 55 A6
Dębica PL 55 C6
Dębnica Kaszubska PL 46 A3
Dębno PL 45 C6
Dęboļęka PL 54 B3
Dębowa Łaka PL 47 B5
Debrc YU 85 B4
Debrecen H 10 C6
Debrznica PL 53 A5
Debrzno PL 46 B3
Debstedt D 43 B5
Decazeville F 77 B5
Dechtice SK 64 B3
Decima I 102 B5
Decimomannu I 110 C1
Děčín CZ 53 C4
Decize F 68 B3
Decollatura I 106 B3
Decs H 74 B3
Deddington GB 31 C2
Dedeler TR 114 B5
Dedelow D 45 B5
Dedemsvaart NL 42 C3
Dédestapolcsány H 65 B6
Dedovichi RUS 7 C10
Deeping St. Nicholas GB 30 B3
Dég H 74 B3
Degaña E 86 B4
Degeberga S 41 D4
Degerfors S 36 B1
Degerhamn S 41 C6
Degernes N 34 B3
Deggendorf D 62 B3
Deggingen D 61 B5
Dego I 80 B2
Degolados P 93 B3
Dehesas de Guadix E 100 B2
Dehesas Viejas E 100 B2
Deia E 97 B2
Deining D 62 A2
Deinze B 49 C4
Déiva Marina I 80 B3
Dej RO 11 C7
Deje S 34 B5
Delabole GB 28 C3
Delary S 40 C3
Delbrück D 51 B4
Delden NL 50 A2
Deleitosa E 93 B5
Delekovec HR 74 B1
Delémont CH 70 A2
Delft NL 49 A5
Delfzijl NL 42 B3
Délia I 108 B2
Delianuova I 106 C2
Deliblato YU 85 B6
Delice TR 16 B6
Deliceto I 103 B8
Delitzsch D 52 B2
Dellach A 72 B3
Delle F 70 A2
Delme F 60 B2
Delmen-horst D 43 B5
Delnice HR 73 C4
Delvin IRL 19 C4
Delvinë AL 112 C2
Demandice SK 65 B4
Demidov RUS 7 D11
Demigny F 69 B4
Demirci TR 114 C3
Demirköy TR 114 A2
Demirtaş TR 114 B4
Demmin D 45 B5
Demonte I 79 B6
Demyansk RUS 7 C12
Den Burg NL 42 B1
Den Ham NL 42 C3
Den Helder NL 42 C1
Den Oever NL 42 C2
Denain F 49 C4
Denbigh GB 26 B2
Dender-monde B 49 B5
Denekamp NL 42 C3
Denholm GB 25 C5
Denia E 96 C3
Denizli TR 16 C4
Denkendorf D 62 B2
Denklingen D 50 C3
Denny GB 25 B4
Denta RO 75 C6
Déols F 68 B1
Derby GB 27 C4
Dereköy TR 114 A2
Derenberg D 51 B6
Derinkuyu TR 16 B7
Dermbach D 51 C6
Dermulo I 71 B6
Deronje YU 75 C4
Derrygonnelly GB 19 B4
Derrylin GB 19 B4
Derry/Londonderry GB 19 B4
Dersingham GB 30 B4
Deruta I 82 D1
Dervaig GB 24 B1
Derval F 57 C4
Dervéni GR 113 D4
Derventa BIH 84 B2
Dervock GB 19 A5
Desana I 70 C3
Descartes F 67 B5
Desenzano del Garda I 71 C5
Deševa BIH 84 C3
Desimirovac YU 85 B5
Désio I 71 C4
Deskle SLO 72 B3
Desná CZ 53 C5
Dešov CZ 63 B6
Despotovac YU 85 B6
Despotovo YU 75 C4
Dessau D 52 B2
Deštná CZ 63 A5
Destriana E 87 B4
Désulo I 110 B2
Desvres F 48 C2
Deszk H 75 B5
Deta RO 75 C6
Detmold D 51 B4
Dětřichov CZ 64 A3
Dettelbach D 61 A6
Dettingen D 61 B5
Dettwiller F 60 B3
Detva SK 65 B5
Deurne NL 50 B1
Deutsch Wagram A 64 B2
Deutschkreutz A 64 C2
Deutschlandsberg A 73 B5
Deva RO 11 D7
Dévaványa H 75 A5
Devecikonağı TR 114 C3
Devecser H 74 A2
Develi TR 16 B7
Deventer NL 50 A2
Devil's Bridge GB 28 A4
Devin BG 112 A6
Devinska Nova Ves SK 64 B2
Devizes GB 29 B6
Devonport GB 28 C3
Devrek TR 114 A6
Devrekâni TR 16 A6
Đevrske HR 83 C4
Dewsbury GB 27 B4
Deza E 89 C4
Dežanovac HR 74 C2
Dezzo I 71 C5
Dhamási GR 112 C4
Dheskáti GR 112 C3
Dhestina GR 112 D4
Dhidhimótikhon GR 114 A1
Dhimitsána GR 113 E4
Dholiana GR 112 C2
Dhomokós GR 112 C4
Dhoxáton GR 112 A6
Dhriopís GR 113 E6
Diamante I 106 B2
Dianalund DK 39 D4
Diano d'Alba I 80 B2
Diano Marina I 80 C2
Dicomano I 81 C5
Didcot GB 31 C2
Die F 79 B4
Diebling F 60 A2
Dieburg D 61 A4
Diego del Carpio E 93 A5
Diekirch L 60 A2
Diélette F 57 A4
Diémoz F 69 C5
Dienten am Hochkönig A 72 A2
Diepenbeck B 49 C6
Diepholz D 43 C5
Dieppe F 58 A2
Dierberg D 45 B4
Dierdorf D 50 C3
Dieren NL 50 A2
Dierhagen D 44 A4
Diesdorf D 44 C2
Diessen D 62 C2
Diest B 49 C6
Dietenheim D 61 B6
Dietfurt D 62 A2
Dietikon CH 70 A3
Dietzenbach D 51 C4
Dieue-sur-Meuse F 60 A1
Dieulefit F 79 B4
Dieulouard F 60 B2
Dieuze F 60 B2
Diever NL 42 C3
Diez D 50 C4
Diezma E 100 B2
Differdange L 60 A1
Dignac F 67 C5
Dignano I 72 B2
Digne-les-Bains F 79 B5
Digny F 58 B2
Digoin F 68 B3
Dijon F 69 A5
Dikili TR 114 C1
Diksmuide B 48 B3
Dilar E 100 B2
Dillenburg D 50 C4
Dillingen, *Bayern* D 61 B6
Dillingen, *Saarland* D 60 A2
Dilsen B 50 B1
Dimaro I 71 B5
Dimitrovgrad BG 11 E8
Dinami I 106 C3
Dinan F 57 B3
Dinant B 49 C5
Dinar TR 16 B5
Dinard F 57 B3
Dinek TR 114 C6
Dingden D 50 B2
Dingelstädt D 51 B6
Dingle IRL 20 B1
Dingle S 35 C3
Dingolfing D 62 B3
Dingtuna S 36 B3
Dingwall GB 23 D4
Dinkelsbühl D 61 A6
Dinkelscherben D 62 B1
Dinklage D 43 C5
Dinslaken D 50 B2
Dinxperlo NL 50 B2
Diö S 40 C4
Diósgyör H 65 B6
Diósjeno H 65 C5
Diou F 68 B3
Dippen GB 24 C2
Dipperz D 51 C5
Dippoldiswalde D 53 C3
Dirdal N 32 C3
Dirksland NL 49 B5
Dirlewang D 61 C6
Dischingen D 61 B6
Disentis CH 70 B3
Diso I 107 A5
Diss GB 30 B5
Dissen D 50 A4
Distington GB 26 A2
Ditzingen D 61 B5
Ditzum D 43 B4
Divača SLO 72 C3
Dives-sur-Mer F 57 A5
Divín SK 65 B5
Divion F 48 C3
Divišov CZ 63 A5
Divonne les Bains F 69 B6
Dixmont F 59 B4
Dizy-le-Gros F 59 A5
Djúpivogur IS 111 C11
Djura S 36 A1
Djurås S 36 A2
Djurmo S 36 A2
Djursdala S 40 B5
Dlouhá Loucka CZ 64 A3
Długowola PL 55 B6
Dmitriyev Lgovskiy RUS 7 E13
Dmitrov RUS 7 C14
Dmitrovsk-Orlovskiy RUS 7 E13
Dno RUS 7 C10
Doade E 86 B3
Dobanovci YU 85 B5
Dobbertin D 44 B4
Dobbiaco I 72 B2
Dobczyce PL 65 A6
Dobele LV 6 C7
Döbeln D 52 B3
Doberlug-Kirchhain D 52 B3
Dobern D 53 B4
Dobersberg A 63 B6
Dobiegniew PL 46 C1
Dobieszyn PL 55 B6
Doboj BIH 84 B3
Dobošnica BIH 84 B3
Doboz H 75 B6
Dobrá CZ 65 A4
Dobra, *Wielkopolskie* PL 54 B3
Dobra, *Zachodnio-Pomorskie* PL 45 B6
Dobra, *Zachodnio-Pomorskie* PL 45 B7
Dobrá Niva SK 65 B5
Dobřany CZ 63 A4
Dobre PL 47 C4
Dobre Miasto PL 47 B6
Dobreta-Turnu-Severin RO 11 D7
Dobri H 74 B1
Dobri Do YU 85 D6
Dobrica YU 75 C5
Dobrich BG 11 E9
Dobříš CZ 63 A5
Dobro E 89 B3
Dobrodzień PL 54 C3
Döbrököz H 74 B3
Dobromierz PL 53 C6
Dobrosołowo PL 47 C4
Dobroszyce PL 54 B2
Dobrovnik SLO 73 B6
Dobrush BY 7 E11
Dobruška CZ 53 C6
Dobrzany PL 46 B1

Dobrzen Wielki PL 54 C2
Dobrzyca, *Wielkopolskie* PL 46 B2
Dobrzyca, *Wielkopolskie* PL 54 B2
Dobrzyca, *Zachodnio-Pomorskie* PL 46 A1
Dobrzyń nad Wisłą PL 47 C5
Dobšiná SK 65 B6
Dobwalls GB 28 C3
Dochamps B 49 C6
Docking GB 30 B4
Doddington GB 25 C5
Döderhult S 40 B6
Doesburg NL 50 A2
Doetinchem NL 50 B2
Dogliani I 80 B1
Dogueno P 98 B3
Dois Portos P 92 B1
Doische B 49 C5
Dojč SK 64 B3
Dokkedal DK 38 C3
Dokkum NL 42 B2
Doležovje SLO 73 B6
Doksy CZ 53 C4
Dol-de-Bretagne F 57 B4
Dolancourt F 59 B5
Dolceácqua I 80 C1
Dole F 69 A5
Dølemo N 33 C5
Dolenja vas SLO 73 C4
Dolenjske Toplice SLO 73 C5
Dolfor GB 26 C2
Dolgarrog GB 26 B2
Dolgellau GB 26 C2
Dolianova I 110 C2
Dolice PL 45 B7
Doljani HR 83 B5
Döllach im Mölltal A 72 B2
Dolle D 44 C3
Dollnstein D 62 B2
Dollot F 59 B4
Döllstadt D 51 B6
Dolná Strehová SK 65 B5
Dolné Saliby SK 64 B3
Dolni Benešov CZ 64 A4
Dolni Bousov CZ 53 C5
Dolni Kounice CZ 64 A2
Dolni Kralovice CZ 63 A6
Dolni Újezd CZ 64 A2
Dolni Žandov CZ 52 C2
Dolný Kubín SK 65 A5
Dolo I 72 C2
Dolores E 96 C2
Dolovo YU 85 B5
Dölsach A 72 B2
Dolsk PL 54 B2
Dolwyddelan GB 26 B2
Dolynska UA 11 B12
Domaljevac BIH 84 A3
Domaniç TR 114 C4
Domaniža SK 65 A4
Domanovići BIH 84 C2
Domašov CZ 54 C2
Domaszék H 75 B4
Domaszków PL 54 C1
Domaszowice PL 54 B2
Domat-Ems CH 71 B4
Domažlice CZ 62 A3
Dombås N 2 E18
Dombasle-sur-Meurthe F 60 B2
Dombegyház H 75 B6
Dombóvár H 74 B3
Domène F 69 C5
Domérat F 68 B2
Domfessel F 60 B3
Domfront F 57 B5
Domfront-en-Champagne F 57 B6
Domingão P 92 B2
Domingo Pérez, *Granada* E 100 B2
Domingo Pérez, *Toledo* E 94 C2
Dömitz D 44 B3
Dommartin F 59 B5
Dommartin-le-Franc F 59 B5
Domme F 77 B4
Dommitzsch D 52 B2
Domodóssola I 70 B3
Domoszló H 65 C6
Dompaire F 60 B2
Dompierre-du-Chemin F 57 B4
Dompierre-sur-Besbre F 68 B3
Dompierre-sur-Mer F 66 B3
Domrémy-la-Pucelle F 60 B1
Dömsöd H 75 A4
Domsure F 69 B5
Dómus de Maria I 110 D1
Domusnóvas I 110 C1
Domvraina GR 113 D4
Domžale SLO 73 B4
Don Alvaro E 93 C4
Don Benito E 93 C5
Doña Mencía E 100 B1
Donado E 87 B4
Donaghadee GB 19 B6
Donaueschingen D 61 C4
Donauwörth D 62 B1
Doncaster GB 27 B4
Donegal IRL 18 B3
Donestebe-Santesteban E 76 C1
Donges F 66 A2
Dongo I 71 B4
Donington GB 30 B3
Doniños E 86 A2
Donja Bebrina HR 84 A3
Donja Brela HR 84 C1
Donja Dubica BIH 84 A3
Donja Dubrava HR 74 B1
Donja Kupčina HR 73 C5
Donja Šatornja YU 85 B5
Donja Stubica HR 73 C5
Donje Brišnik BIH 84 C2
Donje Ljupče YU 85 D6
Donje Stative HR 73 C5
Donji-Andrijevci HR 74 C3
Donji Kazanci BIH 83 C5
Donji Koričáni BIH 84 B2
Donji Lapac HR 83 B4
Donji Malovan BIH 84 C2
Donji Miholjac HR 74 C3
Donji Mosti HR 74 B1
Donji Poloj HR 73 C5
Donji-Rujani BIH 83 C5
Donji Srb HR 83 B5
Donji Svilaj BIH 84 A3
Donji Tovarnik YU 85 B4
Donji Vakuf BIH 84 B2
Donnalucata I 109 C3
Donnemarie-Dontilly F 59 B4
Donnersbach A 73 A4
Donnersbachwald A 73 A4
Donnerskirchen A 64 C2
Donorático I 81 C4
Donostia-San Sebastián E 76 C1
Donovaly SK 65 B5
Donzenac F 67 C6
Donzère F 78 B3
Donzy F 68 A3
Doonbeg IRL 20 B2
Doorn NL 49 A6
Dor E 86 A1
Dorchester GB 29 C5
Dørdal N 33 C6
Dordrecht NL 49 B5
Dörenthe D 50 A3
Dores GB 23 D4
Dorf Mecklenburg D 44 B3
Dorfen D 62 B3
Dorfgastein A 72 A3
Dorfmark D 43 C6
Dorgali I 110 B2
Dorking GB 31 C3
Dormagen D 50 B2
Dormánd H 65 C6
Dormans F 59 A4
Dornava SLO 73 B5
Dornbirn A 71 A4
Dornburg D 52 B1
Dorndorf D 51 C6
Dornecy F 68 A3
Dornes F 68 B3
Dornhan D 61 B4
Dornie GB 22 D3
Dornoch GB 23 D4
Dornum D 43 B4
Dorog H 65 C4
Dorogobuzh RUS 7 D12
Dorohoi RO 11 C9
Dorotowo PL 47 B6
Dörpen D 43 C4
Dorsten D 50 B2
Dortan F 69 B5
Dortmund D 50 B3
Doruchów PL 54 B3
Dorum D 43 B5
Dörverden D 43 C6
Dörzbach D 61 A5
Dos Aguas E 96 B2
Dos Hermanas E 99 B5
Dos-Torres E 100 A3
Dosbarrios E 95 C3
Dospat BG 112 A6
Dötlingen D 43 C5
Dottignies B 49 C4
Döttingen CH 70 A3
Douai F 49 C4
Douarnenez F 56 B1
Douchy F 59 C4
Douchy-les-Mines F 49 C4
Doucier F 69 B5
Doudeville F 58 A1
Doué-la-Fontaine F 67 A4
Douglas, *Isle of Man* GB 26 A1
Douglas, *South Lanarkshire* GB 25 C4
Doulaincourt F 59 B6
Doulevant-le-Château F 59 B5
Doullens F 48 C3
Dounby GB 23 B5
Doune GB 24 B3
Dounreay GB 23 C5
Dour B 49 C4
Dourdan F 58 B3
Dourgne F 77 C5
Dournazac F 67 C5
Douro Calvo P 87 D3
Douvaine F 69 B6
Douvres-la-Délivrande F 57 A5
Douzy F 59 A6
Dover GB 31 C5
Dovje SLO 72 B3
Dovre N 2 F18
Downham Market GB 30 B4
Downhill GB 19 A5
Downpatrick GB 19 B6
Dowra IRL 18 B3
Doyet F 68 B2
Dozule F 57 A5
Drača YU 85 B5
Dračevo BIH 84 D3
Drachten NL 42 B3
Draga SLO 73 C4
Drăgășani RO 11 D8
Dragatuš SLO 73 C5
Dragichyn BY 7 E8
Draginja YU 85 B4
Dragocvet YU 85 C6
Dragolovci BIH 84 B2
Dragoni I 103 B7
Dragør DK 41 D2
Dragotina HR 73 C6
Dragotinja BIH 83 A5
Dragozetići HR 82 A3
Draguignan F 79 C5
Drahnsdorf D 52 B3
Drahonice CZ 63 A5
Drahovce SK 64 B3
Dráma GR 112 A6
Drammen N 34 B2
Drangedal N 33 B6
Drangsnes IS 111 B4
Dransfeld D 51 B5
Dranske D 45 A5
Draperstown GB 19 B5
Drassburg A 64 C2
Drávaszabolcs H 74 C3
Dravograd SLO 73 B5
Drawno PL 46 B1
Drawsko Pomorskie PL 46 B1
Drayton GB 30 B5
Draženov CZ 62 A3
Draževac YU 85 B5
Dražice HR 73 C4
Drebkau D 53 B4
Dreieich D 51 C4
Dreisen D 61 A4
Dren YU 85 C5
Drenovac YU 85 C6
Drenovci HR 84 B3
Drensteinfurt D 50 B3
Dresden D 53 B3
Dretyń PL 46 A2
Dreux F 58 B2
Dřevohostice CZ 64 A3
Drewitz D 52 A2
Drezdenko PL 46 C1
Drežnica HR 83 A4
Drežnik-Grad HR 83 B4
Drietona SK 64 B3
Driffield GB 27 A5
Drimnin GB 24 B2
Drimoleague IRL 20 C2
Dringenberg D 51 B5
Drinić BIH 83 B5
Drinjača BIH 85 B4
Drinovci BIH 84 C2
Drlače YU 85 B4
Drnholec CZ 64 B2
Drniš HR 83 C5
Drnje HR 74 B1
Drnovice CZ 64 A2
Dro I 71 C5
Drøbak N 34 B2
Drobin PL 47 C6
Drochia MD 11 B9
Drochtersen D 43 B6
Drogheda IRL 19 C5
Drohobych UA 11 B7
Droitwich Spa GB 29 A5
Drołtowice PL 54 B2
Dromahair IRL 18 B3
Dromcolliher IRL 20 B3
Dromore, *Down* GB 19 B5
Dromore, *Tyrone* GB 19 B4
Dromore West IRL 18 B3
Dronero I 79 B6
Dronfield GB 27 B4
Drongan GB 24 C3
Dronninglund DK 38 B3
Dronrijp NL 42 B2
Dronten NL 42 C2
Drosendorf A 63 B6
Drösing A 64 B2
Drottningholm S 36 B4
Droué F 58 B2
Drulingen F 60 B3
Drumbeg GB 22 C3
Drumcliff IRL 18 B3
Drumgask GB 23 D4
Drumkeeran IRL 18 B3
Drummore GB 24 D3
Drumnadrochit GB 23 D4
Drumquin GB 19 B4
Drumshanbo IRL 18 B3
Drumsna IRL 19 C4
Drunen NL 49 B6
Druskininkai LT 6 D7
Druten NL 49 B6
Druya BY 7 D9
Družetići YU 85 B5
Drvar BIH 83 B5
Drvenik HR 84 C2
Drwalew PL 55 B6
Drymen GB 24 B3
Drynoch GB 22 D2
Drzewce PL 54 A2
Drzewiany PL 46 B2
Drzewica PL 55 B5
Dualchi I 110 B1
Duas Igrejas P 87 C4
Dub YU 85 C4
Dubá CZ 53 C4
Dubăsari MD 11 C10
Duben D 53 B3
Dübendorf CH 70 A3
Dubi CZ 53 C3
Dubica HR 74 C1
Dublin IRL 21 A5
Dubna RUS 7 C14
Dubňany CZ 64 B3
Dubnica nad Váhom SK 64 B4
Dubnik SK 65 C4
Dubno UA 11 A8
Dubodiel SK 64 B4
Dubona YU 85 B5
Dubovac YU 85 B6
Dubovic BIH 83 B5
Dubranec HR 73 C5
Dubrava HR 74 C1
Dubrave BIH 84 B3
Dubravica HR 73 C5
Dubravica YU 85 B6
Dubrovnik HR 84 D3
Dubrovytsya UA 7 F9
Ducey F 57 B4
Duchcov CZ 53 C3
Ducherow D 45 B5
Dučina YU 85 B5
Duclair F 58 A1
Dudar H 74 A2
Duddington GB 30 B3
Duderstadt D 51 B6
Dudeștii Vechi RO 75 B5
Dudley GB 26 C3
Dueñas E 88 C2
Dueville I 72 C1
Duffel B 49 B5
Duffield GB 27 C4
Dufftown GB 23 D5
Duga Poljana YU 85 C5
Duga Resa HR 73 C5
Dugi Rat HR 83 C5
Dugny-sur-Meuse F 59 A6
Dugo Selo HR 73 C6
Dugopolje HR 83 C5
Duino I 72 C3
Duisburg D 50 B2
Dukhovshchina RUS 7 D12
Dukovany CZ 64 A2
Duleek IRL 19 C5
Dülken D 50 B2
Dülmen D 50 B3
Dulovo BG 11 E9
Dulverton GB 29 B4
Dumbarton GB 24 C3
Dümerek TR 114 C6
Dumfries GB 25 C4
Dumlupınar TR 114 D4
Dun Laoghaire IRL 21 A5
Dun-le-Palestel F 67 B6
Dun-les-Places F 68 A4
Dun-sur-Auron F 68 B2
Dun-sur-Meuse F 59 A6
Dunaalmás H 65 C4
Dunabogdány H 65 C5
Dunafalva H 74 B3
Dunaföldvár H 74 B3
Dunaharaszti H 75 A4
Dunajská Streda SK 64 C3
Dunakeszi H 65 C5
Dunakiliti H 64 C3
Dunakömlöd H 74 B3
Dunapataj H 75 B3
Dunaszekcső H 74 B3
Dunaszentgyorgy H 74 B3
Dunatetétlen H 75 B4
Dunaújváros H 74 B3
Dunavecse H 75 B3
Dunbar GB 25 B5
Dunbeath GB 23 C5
Dunblane GB 25 B4
Dunboyne IRL 21 A5
Dundalk IRL 19 B5
Dundee GB 25 B5
Dundrennan GB 25 D4
Dundrum GB 19 B6
Dunfanaghy IRL 19 A4
Dunfermline GB 25 B4
Dungannon GB 19 B5
Dungarvan IRL 21 B4
Dungiven GB 19 B5
Dunglow IRL 18 B3
Dungourney IRL 20 C3
Duninowo PL 46 A2
Dunkeld GB 25 B4
Dunker S 36 B3
Dunkerque = Dunkirk F 48 B3
Dunkineely IRL 18 B3
Dunkirk = Dunkerque F 48 B3
Dunlavin IRL 21 A5
Dunleer IRL 19 C5
Dunlop GB 24 C3
Dunloy GB 19 A5
Dunmanway IRL 20 C2
Dunmore IRL 18 C3
Dunmore East IRL 21 B5
Dunmurry GB 19 B5
Dunnet GB 23 C5
Dunningen D 61 B4
Dunoon GB 24 C3
Duns GB 25 C5
Dunscore GB 25 C4
Dunsford GB 28 C4
Dunshaughlin IRL 21 A5
Dunstable GB 31 C3
Dunster GB 29 B4
Dunvegan GB 22 D2
Duplek SLO 73 B5
Dupnitsa BG 11 E7
Durach D 61 C6
Durağan TR 16 A7
Durak TR 114 C3
Đurakovac YU 85 D5
Durana E 89 B4
Durance F 76 B3
Durango E 89 A4
Durankulak BG 11 E10
Duras F 76 B3
Durban-Corbières F 78 D1
Dürbheim D 61 B4
Durbuy B 49 C6
Dúrcal E 100 C2
Đurđenovac HR 74 C3
Đurđevac HR 74 B2
Đurđevik BIH 84 B3
Düren D 50 C2
Durham GB 25 D6
Ðurinci YU 85 B5
Durlach D 61 B4
Đurmanec HR 73 B5
Durness GB 22 C4
Dürnkrut A 64 B2
Dürrboden CH 71 B4
Dürrenboden CH 70 B3
Durrës AL 105 B5
Durrow IRL 21 B4
Durrus IRL 20 C2
Dursunbey TR 114 C3
Durtal F 57 C5
Durup DK 38 C1
Durusu TR 114 A3
Dusina BIH 84 C2
Dusnok H 75 B3
Dusocin PL 47 B4
Düsseldorf D 50 B2
Dusslingen D 61 B5
Duszniki PL 46 C2
Duszniki-Zdrój PL 54 C1
Dutovlje SLO 72 C3
Duved S 2 E20
Düzce TR 114 B6
Dvor HR 83 A5
Dvorce CZ 64 A3
Dvorníky SK 64 B3
Dvory nad Žitavou SK 64 C4
Dvůr Králové nad Labem CZ 53 C5
Dyatkovo RUS 7 E13
Dybvad DK 38 B3
Dyce GB 23 D6
Dygowo PL 46 A1
Dykehead GB 25 B4
Dymchurch GB 31 C5
Dymer UA 11 A11
Dywity PL 47 B6
Džanići BIH 84 C2
Dziadowa Kłoda PL 54 B2
Działdowo PL 47 B6
Działoszyce PL 55 C5
Działoszyn PL 54 B3
Dziemiany PL 46 A3
Dzierząźnia PL 47 C6
Dzierzgoń PL 47 B5
Dzierzgowo PL 47 B6
Dzierżoniów PL 54 C1
Dzisna BY 7 D10
Dziwnów PL 45 A6
Dzyarzhynsk BY 7 E9
Dzyatlava BY 7 E8

E

Ea E 89 A4
Eaglesfield GB 25 C4
Ealing GB 31 C3
Eardisley GB 29 A4
Earl Shilton GB 30 B2
Earls Barton GB 30 B3
Earlston GB 25 C5
Easington GB 27 B6
Easky IRL 18 B3
East Calder GB 25 C4
East Dereham GB 30 B4
East Grinstead GB 31 C4
East Ilsley GB 31 C2
East Kilbride GB 24 C3
East Linton GB 25 C5
East Markham GB 27 B5
East Wittering GB 31 D3
Eastbourne GB 31 D4
Easter Skeld GB 22 A7
Eastleigh GB 31 D2
Easton GB 29 C5
Eaton Socon GB 30 B3
Eaux-Bonnes F 76 D2
Eauze F 76 C3
Ebberup DK 39 D2
Ebbs A 62 C3
Ebbw Vale GB 29 B4
Ebeleben D 51 B6
Ebeltoft DK 39 C3
Eben im Pongau A 72 A3
Ebene Reichenau A 72 B3
Ebensee A 63 C4
Ebensfeld D 51 C6
Eberbach D 61 A4
Ebergötzen D 51 B6
Ebermann-Stadt D 62 A2
Ebern D 51 C6
Eberndorf A 73 B4
Ebersbach D 53 B4
Ebersberg D 62 B2
Ebersdorf, *Bayern* D 52 C1
Ebersdorf, *Niedersachsen* D 43 B6
Eberstein A 73 B4
Eberswalde D 45 C5
Ebnat-Kappel CH 71 A4
Éboli I 103 C8
Ebrach D 61 A6
Ebreichsdorf A 64 C2
Ebreuil F 68 B3
Ebstorf D 44 B2
Ecclefechan GB 25 C4
Eccleshall GB 26 C3
Eceabat TR 114 B1
Echallens CH 69 B6
Echauri E 76 D1
Echiré F 67 B4
Échirolles F 69 C5
Echourgnac F 76 A3
Echt NL 50 B1
Echte D 51 B6
Echternach L 60 A2
Ecija E 99 B5
Ečka YU 75 C5
Eckartsberga D 52 B1
Eckelshausen D 51 C4
Eckental D 62 A2
Eckernförde D 44 A1
Eckerö FIN 6 A5
Eckington GB 27 B4
Éclaron F 59 B5
Écommoy F 58 C1
Écouché F 57 B5
Ecouis F 58 A2
Ecséd H 65 C5
Ecsegfalva H 75 A5
Écueillé F 67 A6
Ed S 35 C3
Eda S 34 B4
Eda glasbruk S 34 B4
Edam NL 42 C2
Edane S 34 B4
Edderton GB 23 D4
Ede NL 49 A6
Edebäck S 34 A5
Edebo S 36 A5
Edelény H 65 B6
Edelschrott A 73 A5
Edemissen D 44 C2
Edenbridge GB 31 C4
Edenderry IRL 21 A4
Edenkoben D 61 A4
Edesheim D 61 A4
Edewecht D 43 B4
Edgeworthstown IRL 19 C4
Édhessa GR 112 B4
Edinburgh GB 25 C4
Edineț MD 11 B9
Edirne TR 114 A1
Edland N 33 B4
Edolo I 71 B5
Edremit TR 114 C2
Eds bruk S 37 C3
Edsbro S 36 B5
Edsleskog S 35 B4
Edsvalla S 34 B5
Eekloo B 49 B4
Eemshaven NL 42 B3
Eerbeek NL 50 A2
Eersel NL 49 B6
Eferding A 63 B5
Effiat F 68 B3
Efteløt N 33 B6
Egeln D 52 B1
Eger H 65 C6
Egerbakta H 65 C6
Egernsund DK 39 E2
Egersund N 32 C3
Egerszólát H 65 C6
Egervár H 74 B1
Egg A 71 A4
Egg D 61 B6
Eggedal N 33 A6
Eggenburg A 64 B1
Eggenfelden D 62 B3
Eggesin D 45 B6
Egham GB 31 C3
Éghezée B 49 C5
Egiertowo PL 47 A4
Egilsstaðir IS 111 B11
Égletons F 68 C2
Egling D 62 C2
Eglinton GB 19 A4
Eglisau CH 61 C4
Égliseneuve-d'Entraigues F 68 C2
Eglofs D 61 C5
Egmond aan Zee NL 42 C1
Egna I 71 B6
Egósthena GR 113 D5
Egremont GB 26 A2
Eğridir TR 16 C5
Egtved DK 39 D2
Eguilles F 79 C4
Eguilly-sous-Bois F 59 B5
Éguzon-Chantôme F 67 B6
Egyek H 65 C6
Egyházasrádóc H 74 A1
Ehekirchen D 62 B2
Ehingen D 61 B5
Ehra-Lessien D 44 C2
Ehrang D 60 A2
Ehrenfriedersdorf D 52 C2
Ehrenhain D 52 C2
Ehrenhausen A 73 B5
Ehringshausen D 51 C4
Ehrwald A 71 A5
Eibar E 89 A4
Eibelstadt D 61 A6
Eibenstock D 52 C2
Eibergen NL 50 A2
Eibiswald A 73 B5
Eichenbarleben D 52 A1
Eichendorf D 62 B3
Eichstätt D 62 B2
Eickelborn D 50 B4
Eidsberg N 34 B3
Eidsfoss N 34 B2
Eidskog N 34 A4
Eidsvoll N 34 A3
Eikefjord N 2 F16
Eikelandsosen N 32 A2
Eiken N 33 C4
Eikstrand N 33 B6
Eilenburg D 52 B2
Eilsleben D 52 A1
Eimbeck D 51 B5
Eindhoven NL 49 B6
Einsiedeln CH 70 A3
Einville-au-Jard F 60 B2
Eisenach D 51 C6
Eisenberg, *Rheinland-Pfalz* D 61 A4
Eisenberg, *Thüringen* D 52 C1
Eisenerz A 73 A4
Eisenhüttenstadt D 53 A4
Eisenkappel A 73 B4
Eisenstadt A 64 C2
Eisentratten A 72 B3
Eisfeld D 51 C6
Eisleben D 52 B1
Eislingen D 61 B5
Eitensheim D 62 B2
Eiterfeld D 51 C5
Eitorf D 50 C3
Eivissa = Ibiza E 97 C1
Eixo P 92 A2
Ejby DK 39 D2
Ejea de los Caballeros E 90 A1
Ejstrupholm DK 39 D2
Ejulve E 90 C2
Eke B 49 C4
Ekeby, *Gotland* S 37 D5
Ekeby, *Skåne* S 41 D2
Ekeby, *Uppsala* S 36 A5
Ekeby-Almby S 36 B2
Ekenäs S 35 C5
Ekenässjön S 40 B5
Ekerö S 36 B4
Eket S 41 C3
Eketorp S 41 C6
Ekhinos GR 112 A7
Ekshärad S 34 A5
Eksjö S 40 B4
Eksta S 37 D5
El Alamo, *Madrid* E 94 B3
El Alamo, *Sevilla* E 99 B4
El Algar E 101 B5
El Almendro E 98 B3
El Alquián E 101 C3
El Arahal E 99 B5
El Arenal E 94 B1
El Arguellite E 101 A3
El Astillero E 88 A3
El Ballestero E 101 A3
El Barco de Ávila E 93 A5
El Berrón E 88 A1
El Berrueco E 95 B3
El Bodón E 93 A4
El Bonillo E 95 D4
El Bosque E 99 C5
El Bullaque E 94 C2
El Burgo E 100 C1
El Burgo de Ebro E 90 B2
El Burgo de Osma E 89 C3
El Burgo Ranero E 88 B1
El Buste E 89 C5
El Cabaco E 93 A4
El Callejo E 89 A3
El Campillo E 99 B4
El Campillo de la Jara E 94 C1
El Cañavete E 95 C4
El Carpio E 100 B1
El Carpio de Tajo E 94 C2
El Casar E 95 B3
El Casar de Escalona E 94 B2
El Castillo de las Guardas E 99 B4
El Centenillo E 100 A2
El Cerro E 93 A5
El Cerro de Andévalo E 99 B4
El Comenar E 99 C5
El Coronil E 99 B5
El Crucero E 86 A4
El Cubo de Tierra del Vino E 88 C1
El Cuervo E 99 C4
El Ejido E 101 C3
El Escorial E 94 B2
El Espinar E 94 B2
El Frago E 90 A2
El Franco E 86 A4
El Frasno E 89 C5
El Garrobo E 99 B4
El Gastor E 99 C5
El Gordo E 93 B5
El Grado E 90 A3
El Granado E 98 B3
El Grao de Castelló E 96 B3
El Grau E 96 C2
El Higuera E 100 B1
El Hijate E 101 B3
El Hontanar E 96 A1
El Hoyo E 100 A2
El Madroño E 99 B4
El Maillo E 93 A4
El Masnou E 91 B5
El Mirón E 93 A5
El Molar E 95 B3
El Molinillo E 94 C2
El Morell E 91 B4
El Muyo E 89 C3
El Olmo E 88 C3
El Palo E 100 C1
El Pardo E 94 B3
El Payo E 93 A4
El Pedernoso E 95 C4
El Pedroso E 99 B5
El Peral E 95 C5
El Perelló, *Tarragona* E 90 C3
El Perelló, *Valencia* E 96 B2
El Picazo E 95 C4
El Pinell de Bray E 90 B3
El Piñero E 88 C1
El Pla de Santa Maria E 91 B4
El Pobo E 90 C2
El Pobo de Dueñas E 95 B5
El Pont d'Armentera E 91 B4
El Port de la Selva E 91 A6
El Port de Llançà E 91 A6
El Port de Sagunt E 96 B2
El Prat de Llobregat E 91 B5
El Provencio E 95 C4
El Puente E 89 A3
El Puente del Arzobispo E 93 B5
El Puerto E 86 A4
El Puerto de Santa María E 99 C4
El Real de la Jara E 99 B4
El Real de San Vincente E 94 B2
El Robledo E 94 C2
El Rocio E 99 B4
El Rompido E 99 B3
El Ronquillo E 99 B4
El Royo E 89 C4
El Rubio E 100 B1
El Sabinar E 101 A3
El Saler E 96 B2
El Salobral E 101 A4
El Saucejo E 99 B5
El Serrat AND 91 A4
El Temple E 90 B2
El Tiemblo E 94 B2
El Toboso E 95 C4
El Tormillo E 90 B2
El Torno E 93 A5
El Valle de las Casas E 88 B1
El Vellón E 95 B3
El Vendrell E 91 B4
El Villar de Arnedo E 89 B4
El Viso E 100 A1
El Viso del Alcor E 99 B5
Élancourt F 58 B2
Elassón GR 112 C4
Eláti GR 112 C3
Elbasan AL 112 A2
Elbeuf F 58 A1
Elbingerode D 51 B6
Elbląg PL 47 A5
Elburg NL 42 C2
Elche E 96 C2
Elche de la Sierra E 101 A3
Elchingen D 61 B6
Elda E 101 A5
Eldena D 44 B3
Eldingen D 44 C2
Elek H 75 B6
Elemir YU 75 C5
Elevsís GR 113 D5
Elevtheroúpolis GR 112 B6
Elgin GB 23 D5
Elgoibar E 89 A4
Elgol GB 22 D2
Elie GB 25 B5
Elizondo E 76 C1
Ełk PL 6 E7
Elkhovo BG 11 E9
Ellenberg D 61 A6
Ellesmere GB 26 C3
Ellesmere Port GB 26 B3
Ellezelles B 49 C4
Ellingen D 62 A1
Ellmau A 72 A2
Ellon GB 23 D6
Ellös S 35 C3
Ellrich D 51 B6
Ellwangen D 61 B6
Elm CH 71 B4
Elm D 43 B6
Elmadağ TR 16 B6
Elmalı TR 16 C4
Elmshorn D 43 B6
Elmstein D 60 A3
Elne F 91 A5
Elorrio E 89 A4
Előszállás H 74 B3
Eloúnta GR 113 G7
Éloyes F 60 B2
Elphin GB 22 C3
Els Castells E 91 A4
Elsdorf D 50 C2
Elsenfeld D 61 A5
Elsfleth D 43 B5
Elspeet NL 50 A1
Elst NL 50 B1
Elstead GB 31 C3
Elster D 52 B2
Elsterberg D 52 C2
Elsterwerda D 52 B3
Elstra D 53 B4
Eltmann D 51 D6

Eltville D 50 C4
Elvas P 93 C3
Elven F 56 C3
Elverum N 2 F19
Elvington GB 27 B5
Elxleben D 51 B6
Ely GB 30 B4
Elzach D 61 B4
Elze D 51 A5
Embleton GB 25 C6
Embrun F 79 B5
Embún E 90 A2
Emden D 43 B4
Emet TR 114 C4
Emirdağ TR 114 C6
Emlichheim D 42 C3
Emmaboda S 40 C5
Emmaljunga S 41 C3
Emmeloord NL 42 C2
Emmen CH 70 A3
Emmen NL 42 C3
Emmendingen D 60 B3
Emmer-Compascuum NL 43 C4
Emmerich D 50 B2
Emmern D 51 A5
Emöd H 65 C6
Émpoli I 81 C4
Emsbüren D 43 C4
Emsdetten D 50 A3
Emsfors S 40 B6
Emskirchen D 62 A1
Emstek D 43 C5
Emsworth GB 31 D3
Emyvale IRL 19 B5
Encamp AND 91 A4
Encarnaçao P 92 C1
Encinas de Abajo E 94 B1
Encinas de Esgueva E 88 C2
Encinas Reales E 100 B1
Encinasola E 99 A4
Encio E 89 B3
Enciso E 89 B4
Endingen D 60 B3
Endrinal E 93 A5
Endrőd H 75 B5
Enebakk N 34 B3
Eneryda S 40 C4
Enese H 64 C3
Enez TR 112 B8
Enfield IRL 21 A5
Eng A 72 A1
Enge-sande D 39 E1
Engelberg CH 70 B3
Engelhartszell A 63 B4
Engelskirchen D 50 C3
Engen D 61 C4
Engerdal N 2 F19
Engesvang DK 39 C2
Enghien B 49 C5
Engstingen D 61 B5
Engter D 43 C5
Enguera E 96 C2
Enguidanos E 95 C5
Enkenbach D 60 A3
Enkhuizen NL 42 C2
Enköping S 36 B4
Enna I 109 B3
Ennezat F 68 C3
Ennigerloh D 50 B4
Enningdal N 35 C3
Ennis IRL 20 B3
Enniscorthy IRL 21 B5
Enniskean IRL 20 C3
Enniskillen GB 19 B4
Ennistimon IRL 20 B2
Enns A 63 B5
Eno FIN 3 E29
Enontekiö FIN 3 B25
Ens NL 42 C2
Enschede NL 50 A2
Ensdorf D 62 A2
Ensisheim F 60 C3
Enstaberga S 37 C3
Enstone GB 31 C2
Entlebuch CH 70 A3
Entrácque I 80 B1
Entradas P 98 B2
Entrains-sur-Nohain F 68 A3
Entrambasaguas E 88 A3
Entrambasmestas E 88 A3
Entraygues-sur-Truyère F 77 B5
Entre-os-Rios P 87 C2
Entrevaux F 79 C5
Entrin Bajo E 93 C4
Entroncamento P 92 B2
Entzheim F 60 B3
Envermeu F 58 A2
Enying H 74 B3
Enzingerboden A 72 A2
Enzklösterle D 61 B4
Épagny F 59 A4
Epalinges CH 70 B1
Epannes F 67 B4
Epanomí GR 112 B4
Epe D 50 A3
Epe NL 42 C2
Épernay F 59 A4
Épernon F 58 B2
Epfig F 60 B3
Epierre F 69 C6
Épila E 90 B1
Épinac F 69 B4
Épinal F 60 B2
Episcopia I 106 A3
Epitálion GR 113 E3
Epoisses F 69 A4
Eppenbrunn D 60 A3
Eppendorf D 52 C3
Epping GB 31 C4
Eppingen D 61 A4
Epsom GB 31 C3
Epworth GB 27 B5
Eraclea I 72 C2
Eraclea Mare I 72 C2
Erba I 71 C4
Erbach, *Baden-Württemberg* D 61 B5
Erbach, *Hessen* D 61 A4
Erbalunga F 102 A2
Erbendorf D 62 A3
Érchie I 105 C3
Ercolano I 103 C7
Ercsi H 74 A3
Érd H 74 A3
Erdek TR 114 B2
Erdemli TR 16 C7
Erdevik YU 85 A4
Erding D 62 B2
Erdőtelek H 65 C6
Erdut HR 75 C4
Erdweg D 62 B2
Ereğli, *Konya* TR 16 C7
Ereğli, *Zonguldak* TR 114 A6
Eressós GR 112 C7
Erétria GR 112 D5
Erfde D 43 A6
Erfjord N 32 B3
Erfstadt D 50 C2
Erfurt D 52 C1
Ērgli LV 7 C8
Eriboll GB 22 C4
Érice I 108 A1
Ericeira P 92 C1
Eriksmåla S 40 C5
Eringsboda S 40 C5
Eriswil CH 70 A2
Erithraí GR 113 D5
Erkelenz D 50 B2
Erkner D 45 C5
Erkrath D 50 B2
Erla E 90 A2
Erlangen D 62 A2
Erli I 80 B2
Erlsbach A 72 B2
Ermelo NL 49 A6
Ermenak TR 16 C6
Ermenonville F 58 A1
Ermezinde P 87 C2
Ermidas P 98 A2
Ermióni GR 113 E5
Ermoúpolis GR 113 E6
Ermsleben D 52 B1
Erndtebrück D 50 C4
Ernée F 57 B5
Ernestinovo HR 74 C3
Ernstbrunn A 64 B2
Erolzheim D 61 B6
Erquelinnes B 49 C5
Erquy F 56 B3
Erra P 92 C2
Erratzu E 76 C1
Errindlev DK 44 A3
Erro E 76 D1
Ersa F 102 A2
Érsekcsanád H 75 B3
Ersekë AL 112 B2
Érsekvadkert H 65 C5
Erstein F 60 B3
Erstfeld CH 70 B3
Ertebølle DK 38 C2
Ertingen D 61 B5
Ervedal, *Coimbra* P 92 A2
Ervedal, *Portalegre* P 92 B3
Ervenik HR 83 B4
Ervidel P 98 B2
Ervy-le-Châtel F 59 B4
Erwitte D 51 B4
Erxleben D 52 A1
Erzsébet H 74 B3
Es Caná E 97 B1
Es Castell E 97 B4
Es Mercadal E 97 B4
Es Migjorn Gran E 97 B4
Es Port d'Alcúdia E 97 B3
Es Pujols E 97 C1
Es Soleràs E 90 B3
Esbjerg DK 39 D1
Esbly F 58 B3
Escacena del Campo E 99 B4
Escairón E 86 B3
Escalada E 88 B3
Escalante E 89 A3
Escalaplano I 110 C2
Escalona E 94 B2
Escalona del Prado E 94 A2
Escalonilla E 94 C2
Escalos de Baixo P 92 B3
Escalos de Cima P 92 B3
Escamilla E 95 B4
Escañuela E 100 B1
Escatrón E 90 B2
Esch-sur-Alzette L 60 A1
Eschach D 61 C5
Eschau D 61 A5
Eschede D 44 C2
Eschenau D 62 A2
Eschenbach D 62 A2
Eschenz CH 61 C4
Eschershausen D 51 B5
Eschwege D 51 B6
Eschweiler D 50 C2
Escobasa de Almazán E 89 C4
Escoeuilles F 48 C2
Escombreras E 101 B5
Escos F 76 C1
Escource F 76 B1
Escragnolles F 79 C5
Escrick GB 27 B4
Escurial E 93 B5
Escurial de la Sierra E 93 A5
Esens D 43 B4
Esgos E 87 B3
Esher GB 31 C3
Eskdalemuir GB 25 C4
Eskifjörður IS 111 B12
Eskilhem S 37 D5
Eskilsäter S 35 D5
Eskilstrup DK 39 E4
Eskilstuna S 36 B3
Eskipazar TR 114 B7
Eskişehir TR 114 C5
Eslarn D 62 A3
Eslava E 89 B5
Eslida E 96 B2
Eslohe D 50 B4
Eslöv S 41 D3
Eşme TR 16 B4
Espalion F 78 B1
Esparragalejo E 93 C4
Esparragosa del Caudillo E 93 C5
Esparragossa de la Serena E 93 C5
Esparreguera E 91 B4
Esparron F 79 C4
Espe N 32 B2
Espedal N 32 C3
Espejo, *Alava* E 89 B3
Espejo, *Córdoba* E 100 B1
Espelkamp D 43 C5
Espeluche F 78 B3
Espeluy E 100 A2
Espera E 99 C5
Esperança P 93 B3
Espéraza F 77 D5
Espéria I 103 B6
Espevær N 32 B2
Espiel E 99 A5
Espinama E 88 A2
Espiñaredo E 86 A3
Espinasses F 79 B5
Espinelves E 91 B5
Espinhal P 92 A2
Espinho P 87 C2
Espinilla E 88 A2
Espinosa de Cerrato E 88 C3
Espinosa de los Monteros E 89 A3
Espinoso del Rey E 94 C2
Espirito Santo P 98 B3
Espluga de Francolí E 91 B4
Esplús E 90 B3
Espolla E 91 A5
Espoo FIN 6 A8
Esporles E 97 B2
Esposende P 87 C2
Espot E 91 A4
Esquedas E 90 A2
Esquivias E 94 B3
Essen B 49 B5
Essen, *Niedersachsen* D 43 C4
Essen, *Nordrhein-Westfalen* D 50 B3
Essenbach D 62 B3
Essertaux F 58 A3
Essingen D 61 B6
Esslingen D 61 B5
Essoyes F 59 B5
Estacas E 87 B2
Estadilla E 90 A3
Estagel F 78 D1
Estaires F 48 C3
Estang F 76 C2
Estarreja P 87 D2
Estartit E 91 A6
Estavayer-le-Lac CH 70 B1
Este I 72 C1
Esteiro E 86 A2
Estela P 87 C2
Estella E 89 B4
Estellencs E 97 B2
Estepa E 100 B1
Estépar E 88 B3
Estepona E 99 C5
Esternay F 59 B4
Esterri d'Aneu E 91 A4
Esterwegen D 43 C4
Estissac F 59 B4
Estivadas E 87 B3
Estivareilles F 68 B2
Estivella E 96 B2
Estói P 98 B3
Estopiñán E 90 B3
Estoril P 92 C1
Estoublon F 79 C5
Estrée-Blanche F 48 C3
Estrées-St. Denis F 58 A3
Estrela P 98 A3
Estremera E 95 B3
Estremoz P 92 C3
Estuna S 36 B5
Esyres F 67 A5
Esztergom H 65 C4
Etables-sur-Mer F 56 B3
Étain F 60 A1
Étalans F 69 A6
Etalle B 60 A1
Étampes F 58 B3
Etang-sur-Arroux F 69 B4
Étaples F 48 C2
Etauliers F 67 C4
Etili TR 114 C1
Etne N 32 B2
Etoges F 59 B4
Eton GB 31 C3
Etréaupont F 59 A4
Étréchy F 58 B3
Étrépagny F 58 A2
Étretat F 57 A6
Étrœungt F 49 C4
Étroubles I 70 C2
Ettal D 62 C2
Ettelbruck L 60 A2
Etten NL 49 B5
Ettenheim D 60 B3
Ettington GB 29 A6
Ettlingen D 61 B4
Ettringen D 62 B1
Etxarri-Aranatz E 89 B4
Etyek H 74 A3
Eu F 48 C2
Euerdorf D 51 C6
Eulate E 89 B4
Eupen B 50 C2
Europoort NL 49 B5
Euskirchen D 50 C2
Eutin D 44 A2
Évaux-les-Bains F 68 B2
Evciler TR 114 C1
Evercreech GB 29 B5
Evergem B 49 B4
Everöd S 41 D4
Eversberg D 51 B4
Everswinkel D 50 B3
Evesham GB 29 A6
Évian-les-Bains F 69 B6
Evisa F 102 A1
Evje N 33 C4
Evolène CH 70 B2
Évora P 92 C3
Evoramonte P 92 C3
Evran F 57 B4
Evrecy F 57 A5
Évreux F 58 A2
Évron F 57 B5
Évry F 58 B3
Ewell GB 31 C3
Ewersbach D 50 C4
Excideuil F 67 C6
Exeter GB 29 C4
Exmes F 57 B6
Exminster GB 29 C4
Exmouth GB 29 C4
Eydehamn N 33 C5
Eye, *Peterborough* GB 30 B3
Eye, *Suffolk* GB 30 B5
Eyemouth GB 25 C5
Eyguians F 79 B4
Eyguières F 79 C4
Eygurande F 68 C2
Eylie F 77 D3
Eymet F 77 B3
Eymoutiers F 68 C1
Eynsham GB 31 C2
Eyrarbakki IS 111 D4
Eystrup D 43 C6
Ezaro E 86 B1
Ezcaray E 89 B4
Ezcároz E 76 D1
Ezine TR 114 C1
Ezmoriz P 87 D2

F

Fabara E 90 B3
Fábbrico I 81 B4
Fabero E 86 B4
Fábiánsebestyén H 75 B5
Fåborg DK 39 D3
Fabrègues F 78 C2
Fabriano I 82 C1
Fabrizia I 106 C3
Facha P 87 C2
Facinas E 99 C5
Fačkov SK 65 A4
Fadagosa P 92 B3
Fadd H 74 B3
Faédis I 72 B3
Faenza I 81 B5
Fafe P 87 C2
Fagagna I 72 B3
Făgăraş RO 11 D8
Fågelfors S 40 B5
Fågelmara S 41 C5
Fågelsta S 37 C2
Fagerhult S 40 B5
Fagernes N 2 F18
Fagersanna S 35 C6
Fagersta S 36 A2
Fåglavik S 35 C5
Fagnano Castello I 106 B3
Fagnières F 59 B5
Faido CH 70 B3
Fains F 59 B6
Fairford GB 29 B6
Fairlie GB 24 C3
Fajsz H 74 B3
Fakenham GB 30 B4
Fakse DK 39 D5
Fakse Ladeplads DK 41 D2
Falaise F 57 B5
Falcade I 72 B1
Falcarragh IRL 18 A3
Falces E 89 B5
Fălciu RO 11 C10
Falconara I 109 B3
Falconara Marittima I 82 C2
Falcone I 109 A4
Faldingworth GB 27 B5
Falerum S 37 C3
Făleşti MD 11 C9
Falkenberg, *Bayern* D 62 A3
Falkenberg, *Brandenburg* D 52 B3
Falkenberg S 40 C2
Falkensee D 45 C5
Falkenstein, *Bayern* D 62 A3
Falkenstein, *Sachsen* D 52 C2
Falkenthal D 45 C5
Falkirk GB 25 B4
Falkland GB 25 B4
Falköping S 35 C5
Fall D 62 C2
Falla S 37 C2
Fallingbostel D 43 C6
Falmouth GB 28 C2
Falset E 90 B3
Fălticeni RO 11 C9
Falun S 36 A2
Famagusta CY 16 D6
Fana N 32 A2
Fanano I 81 B4
Fanári GR 112 C3
Fanjeaux F 77 C5
Fano I 82 C2
Fântânele RO 75 B6
Fara in Sabina I 102 A5
Fara Novarese I 70 C3
Faramontanos de Tábara E 88 C1
Farasdues E 90 A1
Fårbo S 40 B6
Fareham GB 31 D2
Färentuna S 36 B4
Färgelanda S 35 C3
Faringdon GB 31 C2
Faringe S 36 B5
Farini I 80 B3
Fariza E 87 C4
Färjestaden S 41 C6
Farkadhón GR 112 C4
Farkasfa H 73 B6
Farlete E 90 B2
Färlöv S 41 C4
Farmos H 75 A4
Farnă SK 65 C4
Farnborough GB 31 C3
Farnese I 102 A4
Farnham GB 31 C3
Farnroda D 51 C6
Faro P 98 B3
Fåro S 37 D6
Fårösund S 37 D6
Farra d'Alpago I 72 B2
Farranfore IRL 20 B2
Fársala GR 112 C4
Farsø DK 38 C2
Farsund N 32 C3
Farum DK 41 D2
Fårup DK 38 C2
Fasana I 103 C8
Fasano I 104 C3
Fáskrúðsfjörður IS 111 C11
Fassberg D 44 C2
Fastiv UA 11 A10
Fatesh RUS 7 E13
Fátima P 92 B2
Faucogney-et-la-Mer F 60 C2
Fauguerolles F 76 B3
Faulenrost D 45 B4
Faulquemont F 60 A2
Fauquembergues F 48 C3
Fauske N 2 C21
Fauville-en-Caux F 58 A1
Fauvillers B 60 A1
Favara I 108 B2
Faverges F 69 C6
Faverney F 60 C2
Faversham GB 31 C4
Favignana I 108 B1
Fawley GB 31 D2
Fay-aux-Loges F 58 C3
Fayence F 79 C5
Fayet F 78 C1
Fayl-Billot F 60 C1
Fayón E 90 B3
Fearn GB 23 D5
Fécamp F 58 A1
Feda N 32 C3
Feeny GB 19 B4
Fegen S 40 B3
Fegyvernek H 75 A5
Fehrbellin D 45 C4
Fehring A 73 B6
Feichten A 71 A5
Feiring N 34 A3
Feistritz im Rosental A 73 B4
Feke TR 16 C7
Feketić YU 75 C4
Felanitx E 97 B3
Feld am See A 72 B3
Feldbach A 73 B5
Feldberg D 45 B5
Feldkirch A 71 A4
Feldkirchen in Kärnten A 73 B4
Feldkirchen-Westerham D 62 C2
Felgueiras P 87 C2
Felitto I 103 C8
Félix E 101 C3
Felixstowe GB 31 C5
Felizzano I 80 B2
Felletin F 68 C2
Fellingsbro S 36 B2
Felnac RO 75 B6
Felnémet H 65 C6
Felpéc H 74 A2
Fels am Wagram A 64 B1
Felsberg D 51 B5
Felsönyék H 74 B3
Felsöszentiván H 75 B4
Felsöszentmárton H 74 C2
Felsözsolca H 65 B6
Felsted DK 39 E2
Feltre I 72 B1
Femsjö S 40 C3
Fenagh IRL 19 B4
Fene E 86 A2
Fenestrelle I 79 A6
Fénétrange F 60 B3
Feneu F 57 C5
Fengersfors S 35 C4
Fenit IRL 20 B2
Fensmark DK 39 D4
Fenwick GB 24 C3
Feolin Ferry GB 24 C1
Ferbane IRL 21 A4
Ferdinandovac HR 74 B2
Ferdinandshof D 45 B5
Fère-Champenoise F 59 B4
Fère-en-Tardenois F 59 A4
Ferentillo I 102 A5
Ferentino I 103 B6
Feria E 93 C4
Feričanci HR 74 C2
Ferizli TR 114 B5
Ferla I 109 B3
Ferlach A 73 B4
Ferleiten A 72 A2
Fermil P 87 C3
Fermo I 82 C2
Fermoselle E 87 C4
Fermoy IRL 20 B3
Fernán Nuñéz E 100 B1
Fernán Peréz E 101 C3
Fernancaballero E 94 C3
Fernão Ferro P 92 C1
Fernay-Voltaire F 69 B6
Ferndown GB 29 C6
Ferness GB 23 D5
Fernhurst GB 31 C3
Ferns IRL 21 B5
Ferpècle CH 70 B2
Ferrai GR 112 B8
Ferrals-les-Corbières F 78 C1
Ferrandina I 104 C2
Ferrara I 81 B5
Ferrara di Monte Baldo I 71 C5
Ferreira E 86 A3
Ferreira do Alentejo P 98 A2
Ferreira do Zêzere P 92 B2
Ferreras de Abajo E 87 C4
Ferreras de Arriba E 87 C4
Ferreries E 97 B4
Ferreruela E 90 B1
Ferreruela de Tabara E 87 C4
Ferret CH 70 C2
Ferrette F 70 A2
Ferriere I 80 B3
Ferrière-la-Grande F 49 C4
Ferrières, *Loiret* F 58 B3
Ferrières, *Oise* F 58 A3
Ferrières-sur-Sichon F 68 B3
Ferrol E 86 A2
Ferryhill GB 27 A4
Fertörakos H 64 C2
Fertöszentmiklós H 64 C2
Ferwerd NL 42 B2
Festieux F 59 A4
Feteşti RO 11 D9
Fethard, *Tipperary* IRL 21 B4
Fethard, *Wexford* IRL 21 B5
Fethiye TR 16 C4
Fetsund N 34 B3
Fettercairn GB 25 B5
Feucht D 62 A2
Feuchtwangen D 61 A6
Feudingen D 50 C4
Feuges F 59 B5
Feuquières F 58 A2
Feurs F 69 C4
Fevik N 33 C5
Ffestiniog GB 26 C2
Fiamignano I 102 A6
Fiano I 70 C2
Ficarazzi I 108 A2
Ficarolo I 81 B5
Fichtelberg D 52 C1
Ficulle I 82 D1
Fidenza I 81 B4
Fidjeland N 32 C3
Fieberbrunn A 72 A2
Fier AL 105 C5
Fiera di Primiero I 72 B1
Fiesch CH 70 B3
Fiesso Umbertiano I 81 B5
Figari F 102 B2
Figeac F 77 B5
Figeholm S 40 B6
Figgjo N 32 C2
Figline Valdarno I 81 C5
Figols E 90 A3
Figueira da Foz P 92 A2
Figueira de Castelo Rodrigo P 87 D4
Figueira dos Caveleiros P 98 A2
Figueiredo P 92 B3
Figueiredo de Alva P 87 D3
Figueiró dos Vinhos P 92 B2
Figueres E 91 A5
Figueroles E 96 A2
Figueruela de Arriba E 87 C4
Filadélfia I 106 C3
Fil'akovo SK 65 B5
Filderstadt D 61 B5
Filey GB 27 A5
Filiaşi RO 11 D7
Filiátes GR 112 C2
Filiatrá GR 113 E3
Filipstad S 34 B6
Filisur CH 71 B4
Filótion GR 113 E7
Filottrano I 82 C2
Filskov DK 39 D2
Filton GB 29 B5
Filtvet N 34 B2
Filzmoos A 72 A3
Finale Emilia I 81 B5
Finale Lígure I 80 B2
Fiñana E 101 B3
Fincham GB 30 B4
Finchingfield GB 31 C4
Findhorn GB 23 D5
Findochty GB 23 D6
Finike TR 16 C5
Finkenberg A 72 A1
Finnea IRL 19 C4
Finnerödja S 35 C6
Finnsnes N 3 B23
Finócchio I 102 B5
Finsjö S 40 B6
Finsland N 33 C4
Finspång S 37 C2
Finsterwalde D 53 B3
Finsterwolde NL 43 B4
Finstown GB 23 B5
Fintona GB 19 B4
Fionnphort GB 24 B1
Fiorenzuola d'Arda I 81 B3
Firenze = Florence I 81 C5
Firenzuola I 81 B5
Firmi F 77 B5
Firminy F 69 C4
Firmo I 106 B3
Fischamend Markt A 64 B2
Fischbach A 73 A5
Fischbach D 60 A3
Fischbeck D 44 C4
Fischen D 71 A5
Fishbourne GB 31 D2
Fishguard GB 28 B3
Fiskárdho GR 112 D2
Fiskebäckskil S 35 C3
Fismes F 59 A4
Fisterra E 86 B1
Fitero E 89 B5
Fitjar N 32 B2
Fiuggi I 102 B6
Fiumata I 102 A6
Fiumefreddo Brúzio I 106 B3
Fiumefreddo di Sicília I 109 B4
Fiumicino I 102 B5
Fivemiletown GB 19 B4
Fivizzano I 81 B4
Fjæra N 32 B3
Fjälkinge S 41 C4
Fjällbacka S 35 C3
Fjärdhundra S 36 B3
Fjellerup DK 38 C3
Fjerritslev DK 38 B2
Fjugesta S 36 B1
Flåbygd N 33 B5
Flaça E 91 A5
Flace F 69 B4
Fladungen D 51 C6
Flåm N 2 F17
Flamatt CH 70 B2
Flamborough GB 27 A5
Flammersfeld D 50 C3
Flassans-sur-Issole F 79 C5
Flatdal N 33 B5
Flateby N 34 B3
Flateland N 33 B4
Flateyri IS 111 A2
Flatråker N 32 B2
Flattach A 72 B3
Flatvarp S 37 D3
Flavigny-sur-Moselle F 60 B2
Flavy-le-Martel F 59 A4
Flawil CH 71 A4
Flayosc F 79 C5
Flechtingen D 44 C3
Fleckeby D 44 A1
Fleet GB 31 C3
Fleetmark D 44 C3
Fleetwood GB 26 B2
Flehingen D 61 A4
Flekkefjord N 32 C3
Flen S 37 B3
Flensburg D 39 E2
Fleringe S 37 D5
Flerohopp S 40 C5
Flers F 57 B5
Flesberg N 33 B6
Fleurance F 77 C3
Fleuré F 67 B5
Fleurier CH 69 B6
Fleurus B 49 C5
Fleury, *Hérault* F 78 C2
Fleury, *Yonne* F 59 C4
Fleury-les-Aubrais F 58 C2
Fleury-sur-Andelle F 58 A2
Fleury-sur-Orne F 57 A5
Flieden D 51 C5
Flimby GB 26 A2
Flims CH 71 B4
Flines-lèz-Raches F 49 C4
Flint GB 26 B2
Flirey F 60 B1
Flirsch A 71 A5
Flisby S 40 B4
Fliseryd S 40 B6
Flix E 90 B3
Flixecourt F 48 C3
Flize F 59 A5
Flobecq B 49 C4
Floby S 35 C5
Floda S 40 B2
Flodden GB 25 C5
Flogny-la-Chapelle F 59 C4
Flöha D 52 C3
Flonheim D 61 A4
Florac F 78 B2
Floreffe B 49 C5
Florence = Firenze I 81 C5
Florennes B 49 C5
Florensac F 78 C2
Florentin F 77 C5
Florenville B 59 A6
Flores de Avila E 94 B1
Floresta I 109 B3
Floreşti MD 11 C10
Florídia I 109 B4
Flórina GR 112 B3
Florø N 2 F16
Flörsheim D 51 C4
Floss D 62 A3
Flúðir IS 111 C5
Flühli CH 70 B3
Flumet F 69 C6
Fluminimaggiore I 110 C1
Flums CH 71 A4
Flygsfors S 40 C5
Foča BIH 84 C3
Foça TR 16 B3
Fochabers GB 23 D5
Focşani RO 11 D9
Foel GB 26 C2
Foeni RO 75 C5
Fogdö S 36 B3
Fóggia I 104 B1
Foglianise I 103 B7
Fohnsdorf A 73 A4
Foiano della Chiana I 81 C5
Foix F 77 D4
Fojnica BIH 84 C2
Fojnica BIH 84 C3
Fokino RUS 7 E13
Földeák H 75 B5
Földes H 75 A6
Folégandros GR 113 F6
Folgaria I 71 C6
Folgosinho P 92 A3
Folgoso de la Ribera E 86 B4
Folgoso do Courel E 86 B3
Foligno I 82 D1
Folkärna S 36 A3
Folkestone GB 31 C5
Follafoss N 2 E19
Folldal N 2 E19
Follina I 72 C2
Follónica I 81 D4
Foncebadón E 86 B4
Foncine-le-Bas F 69 B6
Fondevila E 87 C2
Fondi I 103 B6
Fondo I 71 B6
Fonelas E 100 B2
Fonfría, *Teruel* E 90 C1
Fonfría, *Zamora* E 87 C4
Fonni I 110 B2
Font-Romeu F 91 A5
Fontaine de Vaucluse F 79 C4
Fontaine-Française F 69 A5
Fontaine-le-Dun F 58 A1
Fontainebleau F 58 B3
Fontan F 80 B1
Fontanarejo E 94 C2
Fontane I 80 B1
Fontanélice I 81 B5
Fontanières F 68 B2
Fontanosas E 100 A1
Fontebianda I 102 A4
Fontenay-le-Comte F 66 B4
Fontenay-Trésigny F 59 B3
Fontevrault-l'Abbaye F 67 A5
Fontiveros E 94 B2
Fontoy F 60 A1
Fontpédrouse F 91 A5
Fontstown IRL 21 A5
Fonyód H 74 B2
Fonz E 90 A3
Fonzaso I 72 B1

Fóppolo I 71 B4
Föra S 41 B6
Forbach D 61 B4
Forbach F 60 A2
Forcall E 90 C2
Forcalquier F 79 C4
Forcarei E 86 B2
Forchheim D 62 A2
Forchtenau A 64 C2
Forchtenberg D 61 A5
Ford GB 24 B2
Førde, *Hordaland* N 32 B2
Førde, *Sogn og Fjordane* N 2 F16
Förderstedt D 52 B1
Førdesfjorden N 32 B2
Fordham GB 30 B4
Fordingbridge GB 29 C6
Fordon PL 47 B4
Fordongiánus I 110 C1
Forenza I 104 C1
Foresta di Búrgos I 110 B1
Forfar GB 25 B5
Forges-les-Eaux F 58 A2
Foria I 106 A2
Forío I 103 C6
Forjães P 87 C2
Forli I 81 B6
Forlimpopoli I 82 B1
Formazza I 70 B3
Formby GB 26 B2
Formerie F 58 A2
Fórmia I 103 B6
Formígine I 81 B4
Formigliana I 70 C3
Formiguères F 91 A5
Fornalutx E 97 B2
Fornelli I 110 B1
Fornells E 97 A4
Fornelos de Montes E 87 B2
Fornes E 100 C2
Forni Avoltri I 72 B2
Forni di Sopra I 72 B2
Forni di Sotto I 72 B2
Forno, *Piemonte* I 70 C3
Forno, *Piemonte* I 79 A6
Forno Alpi-Gráie I 70 C2
Forno di Zoldo I 72 B2
Fornos de Algodres P 92 A3
Fornovo di Taro I 81 B4
Forráskút H 75 B4
Forres GB 23 D5
Forriolo E 87 B3
Fors S 36 A3
Forsand N 32 C3
Forsbacka S 36 A3
Forserum S 40 B4
Forshaga S 34 B5
Forsheda S 40 B3
Forsinain GB 23 C5
Förslöv S 41 C2
Forsmark S 36 A5
Forssa FIN 3 F25
Forssjöbruk S 37 C3
Forst D 53 B4
Forsvik S 37 C1
Fort Augustus GB 22 D4
Fort-Mahon-Plage F 48 C2
Fort William GB 24 B2
Fortanete E 90 C2
Forte dei Marmi I 81 C4
Fortezza I 72 B1
Forth GB 25 C4
Fortrie GB 23 D6
Fortrose GB 23 D4
Fortuna E 101 A4
Fortuneswell GB 29 C5
Fos F 77 D3
Fos-sur-Mer F 78 C3
Fosdinovo I 81 B4
Fosnavåg N 2 E16
Fossacésia I 103 A7
Fossano I 80 B1
Fossato di Vico I 82 C1
Fosse-la-Ville B 49 C5
Fossombrone I 82 C1
Fot H 65 C5
Fouchères F 59 B5
Fouesnant F 56 C1
Foug F 60 B1
Fougères F 57 B4
Fougerolles F 60 C2
Foulain F 59 B6
Fountainhall GB 25 C5
Fouras F 66 C3
Fourchambault F 68 A3
Fourmies F 49 C5
Fournás GR 112 C3
Fournels F 78 B2
Fournols F 68 C3
Fourques F 91 A5
Fourquevaux F 77 C4
Fours F 68 B3
Fowey GB 28 C3
Foxdale GB 26 A1
Foxford IRL 18 C2
Foyers GB 23 D4
Foynes IRL 20 B2
Foz E 86 A3
Foz do Arelho P 92 B1
Foz do Giraldo P 92 B3
Foza I 72 C1
Frabosa Soprana I 80 B1
Frades de la Sierra E 93 A5
Fraga E 90 B3
Fragagnano I 104 C3
Frailes E 100 B2
Fraire B 49 C5
Fraize F 60 B2
Framlingham GB 30 B5
Frammersbach D 51 C5
Framnes N 34 B2
França P 87 C4
Francaltroff F 60 B2
Francavilla al Mare I 103 A7
Francavilla di Sicília I 109 B4
Francavilla Fontana I 104 C3
Francavilla in Sinni I 106 A3
Francescas F 77 B3
Franco P 87 C3
Francofonte I 109 B3
Francos E 89 C3
Frändefors S 35 C4
Franeker NL 42 B2
Frangy F 69 B5
Frankenau D 51 B4
Frankenberg, *Hessen* D 51 B4
Frankenberg, *Sachsen* D 52 C3
Frankenburg A 63 B4
Frankenfels A 63 C6
Frankenmarkt A 63 C4
Frankenthal D 61 A4
Frankfurt, *Brandenburg* D 45 C6
Frankfurt, *Hessen* D 51 C4
Frankowo PL 47 A6
Františkovy Lázně CZ 52 C2
Franzburg D 45 A4
Frascati I 102 B5
Frasdorf D 62 C3
Fraserburgh GB 23 D6
Frashër AL 112 B2
Frasne F 69 B6
Frasnes-lez-Anvaing B 49 C4
Frasseto F 102 B2
Frastanz A 71 A4
Fratel P 92 B3
Fratta Todina I 82 D1
Frauenau D 63 B4
Frauenfeld CH 70 A3
Frauenkirchen A 64 C2
Frauenstein D 52 C3
Frauental A 73 B5
Frayssinet F 77 B4
Frayssinet-le-Gélat F 77 B4
Frechas P 87 C3
Frechen D 50 C2
Frechilla E 88 B2
Freckenhorst D 50 B3
Fredeburg D 50 B4
Fredelsloh D 51 B5
Fredensborg DK 41 D2
Fredericia DK 39 D2
Frederiks DK 39 C2
Frederikshavn DK 38 B3
Frederikssund DK 39 D5
Frederiksværk DK 39 D5
Fredrikberg S 34 A6
Fredriksdal S 40 B4
Fredrikstad N 34 B2
Fregenal de la Sierra E 99 A4
Fregene I 102 B5
Freiberg D 52 C3
Freiburg, *Baden-Württemberg* D 60 C3
Freiburg, *Niedersachsen* D 43 B6
Freienhagen D 51 B5
Freienhufen D 53 B3
Freihung D 62 A2
Freilassing D 62 C3
Freisen D 60 A3
Freising D 62 B2
Freistadt A 63 B5
Freital D 52 B3
Freixedas P 93 A3
Freixo de Espada à Cinta P 87 C4
Fréjus F 79 C5
Fremdingen D 61 B6
Frenštát pod Radhoštěm CZ 64 A4
Freren D 43 C4
Freshford IRL 21 B4
Freshwater GB 31 D2
Fresnay-sur-Sarthe F 57 B6
Fresne-St. Mamès F 69 A5
Fresneda de la Sierra E 95 B4
Fresneda de la Sierra Tiron E 89 B3
Fresnedillas E 94 B2
Fresnes-en-Woevre F 60 A1
Fresno Alhandiga E 94 B1
Fresno de la Ribera E 88 C1
Fresno de la Vega E 88 B1
Fresno de Sayago E 87 C5
Fresnoy-Folny F 58 A2
Fresnoy-le-Grand F 59 A4
Fressenville F 48 C2
Fréteval F 58 C2
Fretigney F 69 A5
Freudenberg, *Baden-Württemberg* D 61 A5
Freudenberg, *Nordrhein-Westfalen* D 50 C3
Freudenstadt D 61 B4
Freux B 49 D6
Frévent F 48 C3
Freyburg D 52 B1
Freyenstein D 44 B4
Freyming-Merlebach F 60 A2
Freystadt D 62 A2
Freyung D 63 B4
Frias de Albarracin E 95 B5
Fribourg CH 70 B2
Frick CH 70 A3
Fridafors S 41 C4
Fridaythorpe GB 27 A5
Friedberg A 73 A6
Friedberg, *Bayern* D 62 B1
Friedberg, *Hessen* D 51 C4
Friedeburg D 43 B4
Friedewald D 51 C5
Friedland, *Brandenburg* D 53 A4
Friedland, *Mecklenburg-Vorpommern* D 45 B5
Friedland, *Niedersachsen* D 51 B5
Friedrichroda D 51 C6
Friedrichsdorf D 51 C4
Friedrichshafen D 61 C5
Friedrichskoog D 43 A5
Friedrichstadt D 43 A6
Friedrichswalde D 45 B5
Friesach A 73 B4
Friesack D 45 C4
Friesenheim D 60 B3
Friesoythe D 43 B4
Frigiliana E 100 C2
Frillesås S 40 B2
Frinnaryd S 40 B4
Frinton-on-Sea GB 31 C5
Friockheim GB 25 B5
Friol E 86 A3
Fristad S 40 B2
Fritsla S 40 B2
Fritzlar D 51 B5
Frizington GB 26 A2
Frödinge S 40 B6
Froges F 69 C5
Frohburg D 52 B2
Frohnhausen D 50 C4
Frohnleiten A 73 A5
Froissy F 58 A3
Frombork PL 47 A5
Frome GB 29 B5
Frómista E 88 B2
Fröndenberg D 50 B3
Fronsac F 76 B2
Front I 70 C2
Fronteira P 92 B3
Frontenay-Rohan-Rohan F 67 B4
Frontenhausen D 62 B3
Frontignan F 78 C2
Fronton F 77 C4
Fröseke S 40 C5
Frosinone I 103 B6
Frosolone I 103 B7
Frøstrup DK 38 B1
Frosunda S 36 B5
Frouard F 60 B2
Frövi S 36 B2
Fruges F 48 C3
Frutigen CH 70 B2
Frýdek-Místek CZ 65 A4
Frýdlant CZ 53 C5
Frydlant nad Ostravicí CZ 65 A4
Frygnowo PL 47 B6
Fryšták CZ 64 A3
Fucécchio I 81 C4
Fuencaliente, *Ciudad Real* E 100 A1
Fuencaliente, *Ciudad Real* E 94 C3
Fuencemillán E 95 B3
Fuendejalón E 89 C5
Fuengirola E 100 C1
Fuenlabrada E 94 B3
Fuenlabrada de los Montes E 94 C2
Fuensalida E 94 B2
Fuensanta E 101 B4
Fuensanta de Martos E 100 B2
Fuente al Olmo de Iscar E 88 C2
Fuente-Álamo E 101 A4
Fuente-Álamo de Murcia E 101 B4
Fuente Dé E 88 A2
Fuente de Cantos E 99 A4
Fuente de Santa Cruz E 94 A2
Fuente del Arco E 99 A5
Fuente del Conde E 100 B1
Fuente del Maestre E 93 C4
Fuente el Fresno E 94 C3
Fuente el Saz de Jarama E 95 B3
Fuente el Sol E 94 A2
Fuente Obejuna E 99 A5
Fuente Palmera E 99 B5
Fuente-Tójar E 100 B1
Fuente Vaqueros E 100 B2
Fuentealbilla E 96 B1
Fuentecén E 88 C3
Fuenteguinaldo E 93 A4
Fuentelapeña E 88 C1
Fuentelcésped E 89 C3
Fuentelespino de Haro E 95 C4
Fuentelespino de Moya E 95 C5
Fuentenovilla E 95 B3
Fuentepelayo E 94 A2
Fuentepinilla E 89 C4
Fuenterroble de Salvatierra E 93 A5
Fuenterrobles E 96 B1
Fuentes E 95 C4
Fuentes de Andalucía E 99 B5
Fuentes de Ebro E 90 B2
Fuentes de Jiloca E 89 C5
Fuentes de la Alcarria E 95 B4
Fuentes de León E 99 A4
Fuentes de Nava E 88 B2
Fuentes de Oñoro E 93 A4
Fuentes de Ropel E 88 B1
Fuentesauco, *Segovia* E 88 C2
Fuentesaúco, *Zamora* E 94 A1
Fuentespalda E 90 C3
Fuentespina E 88 C3
Fuentidueña E 88 C3
Fuentidueña de Tajo E 95 B3
Fuerte del Rey E 100 B2
Fügen A 72 A1
Fuglebjerg DK 39 D4
Fuglevik N 34 B2
Fuhrberg D 44 C1
Fulda D 51 C5
Fulgatore I 108 B1
Fully CH 70 B2
Fulnek CZ 64 A3
Fülöpszállás H 75 B4
Fulpmes A 71 A6
Fumay F 49 D5
Fumel F 77 B3
Funäsdalen S 2 E20
Fundão P 92 A3
Funzie GB 22 A8
Furadouro P 87 D2
Fürstenau, *Niedersachsen* D 43 C4
Furstenau, *Nordrhein-Westfalen* D 51 B5
Fürstenberg D 45 B5
Fürstenfeld A 73 A6
Fürstenfeldbruck D 62 B2
Fürstenstein D 63 B4
Fürstenwalde D 45 C6
Fürstenwerder D 45 B5
Fürstenzell D 63 B4
Fürth, *Bayern* D 62 A1
Fürth, *Hessen* D 61 A4
Furth im Wald D 62 A3
Furtwangen D 61 B4
Furuby S 40 C5
Furulund S 41 D3
Furusjö S 40 B3
Fusa N 32 A2
Fuscaldo I 106 B3
Fusch an der Grossglocknerstrasse A 72 A2
Fusina I 72 C2
Fusio CH 70 B3
Füssen D 62 C1
Fustiñana E 89 B5
Futog YU 75 C4
Füzesabony H 65 C6
Füzesgyarmat H 75 A6
Fužine HR 73 C4
Fyllinge S 40 C2
Fynshav DK 39 E2
Fyresdal N 33 B5

G

Gaaldorf A 73 A4
Gabaldón E 95 C5
Gabarret F 76 C3
Gabčíkovo SK 64 C3
Gąbin PL 47 C5
Gabriac F 78 B1
Gabrovo BG 11 E8
Gaby I 70 C2
Gacé F 58 B1
Gacko BIH 84 C3
Gäddede S 2 D21
Gadebusch D 44 B3
Gadmen CH 70 B3
Gádor E 101 C3
Gádoros H 75 B5
Gael F 57 B3
Găeşti RO 11 D8
Gaeta I 103 B6
Gafanhoeira P 92 C2
Gaflenz A 63 C5
Gagarin RUS 7 D13
Gaggenau D 61 B4
Gagliano Castelferrato I 109 B3
Gagliano del Capo I 107 B5
Gagnet S 36 A2
Gaibanella I 81 B5
Gaildorf D 61 B5
Gaillac F 77 C4
Gaillefontaine F 58 A2
Gaillon F 58 A2
Gainsborough GB 27 B5
Gairloch GB 22 D3
Gairlochy GB 24 B3
Gáiro I 110 C2
Gaj HR 74 C2
Gaj YU 85 B6
Gajanejos E 95 B4
Gajary SK 64 B2
Gajdobra YU 75 C4
Galan F 77 C3
Galanta SK 64 B3
Galapagar E 94 B2
Galápagos E 95 B3
Galaroza E 99 B4
Galashiels GB 25 C5
Galatás GR 113 E5
Galaţi RO 11 D10
Galatina I 107 A5
Galátista GR 112 B5
Galátone I 107 A5
Galaxídhion GR 113 D4
Galdakao E 89 A4
Galeata I 81 C5
Galende E 87 B4
Galera E 101 B3
Galéria F 102 A1
Galgamácsa H 65 C5
Galgate GB 26 B3
Galgon F 76 B2
Galices P 92 A3
Galinduste E 93 A5
Galisteo E 93 B4
Galków PL 55 B4
Gallarate I 70 C3
Gallardon F 58 B2
Gallegos de Argañán E 93 A4
Gallegos del Solmirón E 93 A5
Galleguillos de Campos E 88 B1
Galleno I 81 C4
Galliate I 70 C3
Gallicano I 81 B4
Gállio I 72 C1
Gallipoli I 107 A4
Gallipoli = Gelibolu TR 114 B1
Gällivare S 3 C24
Gallizien A 73 B4
Gallneukirchen A 63 B5
Gallocanta E 95 B5
Gällstad S 40 B3
Gallur E 90 B1
Galmisdale GB 24 B1
Galmpton GB 29 C4
Galston GB 24 C3
Galta N 32 B2
Galtelli I 110 B2
Galten DK 39 C2
Galtür A 71 B5
Galve de Sorbe E 95 A3
Galveias P 92 B2
Gálvez E 94 C2
Galway IRL 20 A2
Gamaches F 48 D2
Gámbara I 71 C5
Gambárie I 106 C2
Gambassi Terme I 81 C4
Gambatesa I 103 B7
Gambolò I 70 C3
Gaming A 63 C6
Gamla Uppsala S 36 B4
Gamleby S 40 B6
Gamlingay GB 30 B3
Gammelgarn S 37 D5
Gammelstad S 3 D25
Gammertingen D 61 B5
Gams CH 71 A4
Gamvik N 3 A25
Gan F 76 C2
Gáname E 87 C4
Ganda di Martello I 71 B5
Gandarela P 87 C2
Ganddal N 32 C2
Ganderkesee D 43 B5
Gandesa E 90 B3
Gandía E 96 C2
Gandino I 71 C4
Gandrup DK 38 B3
Ganges F 78 C2
Gånghester S 40 B3
Gangi I 109 B3
Gangkofen D 62 B3
Gannat F 68 B3
Gannay-sur-Loire F 68 B3
Gänserdorf A 64 B2
Ganzlin D 44 B4
Gap F 79 B5
Gara H 75 B4
Garaballa E 96 B1
Garaguso I 104 C2
Garbayuela E 94 C1
Garbhallt GB 24 B2
Garbsen D 43 C6
Garching D 62 B3
Garciaz E 93 B5
Garcihernández E 94 B1
Garcillán E 94 B2
Garcinarro E 95 B4
Garda I 71 C5
Gardanne F 79 C4
Gårdby S 41 C6
Gardeja PL 47 B4
Gardelegen D 44 C3
Gardermoen N 34 A3
Gardhíki GR 112 D3
Garding D 43 A5
Gardone Riviera I 71 C5
Gardone Val Trómpia I 71 C5
Gárdony H 74 A3
Gardouch F 77 C4
Gards Köpinge S 41 D4
Gårdsjö S 35 C6
Gårdskär S 36 A4
Garein F 76 B2
Garelochhead GB 24 B3
Garéoult F 79 C5
Garešnica HR 74 C1
Garéssio I 80 B2
Garforth GB 27 B4
Gargaliánoi GR 113 E3
Gargaligas E 93 B5
Gargallo E 90 C2
Garganta la Olla E 93 A5
Gargantiel E 100 A1
Gargellen A 71 B4
Gargilesse-Dampierre F 67 B6
Gargnano I 71 C5
Gárgoles de Abajo E 95 B4
Gargrave GB 26 B3
Garitz D 52 B2
Garlasco I 70 C3
Garlieston GB 24 D3
Garlin F 76 C2
Garlitos E 94 D1
Garmisch-Partenkirchen D 71 A6
Garnat-sur-Engièvre F 68 B3
Garpenberg S 36 A3
Garphyttan S 36 B1
Garray E 89 C4
Garrel D 43 C5
Garriguella E 91 A6
Garrison GB 18 B3
Garrovillas E 93 B4
Garrucha E 101 B4
Gars-a-Kamp A 63 B6
Garsdale Head GB 26 A3
Gärsnäs S 41 D4
Garstang GB 26 B3
Gartow D 44 B3
Gartz D 45 B6
Garvagh GB 19 B5
Garvão P 98 B2
Garve GB 22 D4
Garwolin PL 55 B6
Garz D 45 A5
Garzyn PL 54 B1
Gąsawa PL 46 C3
Gåsborn S 34 B6
Gaschurn A 71 B5
Gascueña E 95 B4
Gasny F 58 A2
Gąsocin PL 47 C6
Gastes F 76 B1
Gastoúni GR 113 E3
Gastoúri GR 112 C1
Gata E 93 A4
Gata HR 83 C5
Gata de Gorgos E 96 C3
Gatchina RUS 7 B11
Gatehouse of Fleet GB 24 D3
Gátér H 75 B4
Gateshead GB 25 D6
Gátova E 96 B2
Gattendorf A 64 B2
Gatteo a Mare I 82 B1
Gattinara I 70 C3
Gattorna I 80 B3
Gaucín E 99 C5
Gauting D 62 B2
Gava E 91 B5
Gavardo I 71 C5
Gavarnie F 76 D2
Gavi I 80 B2
Gavião P 92 B3
Gavirate I 70 C3
Gävle S 36 A4
Gavoi I 110 B2
Gavorrano I 81 D4
Gavray F 57 B4
Gávrion GR 113 E6
Gaweinstal A 64 B2
Gawroniec PL 46 B2
Gaydon GB 30 B2
Gayton GB 30 B4
Gazipaşa TR 16 C6
Gazoldo degli Ippoliti I 71 C5
Gazzuolo I 81 A4
Gbelce SK 65 C4
Gdańsk PL 47 A4
Gdinj HR 84 C1
Gdov RUS 7 B9
Gdów PL 65 A6
Gdynia PL 47 A4
Gea de Albarracin E 95 B5
Geary GB 22 D2
Géaudot F 59 B5
Geaune F 76 C2
Gebesee D 51 B6
Gebze TR 114 B4
Géderlak H 75 B3
Gedern D 51 C5
Gedinne B 49 D5
Gediz TR 114 D4
Gèdre F 76 D3
Gedser DK 44 A3
Gedsted DK 38 C2
Geel B 49 B5
Geesthacht D 44 B2
Geetbets B 49 C6
Gefell D 52 C1
Gehrden D 51 A5
Gehren D 52 C1
Geilenkirchen D 50 C2
Geilo N 2 F18
Geinsheim D 61 A4
Geisa D 51 C5
Geiselhöring D 62 B3
Geiselwind D 61 A6
Geisenfeld D 62 B2
Geisenhausen D 62 B3
Geisenheim D 50 D4
Geising D 53 C3
Geisingen D 61 C4
Geislingen D 61 B5
Geistthal A 73 A5
Geithain D 52 B2
Geithus N 33 B6
Gela I 109 B3
Geldermalsen NL 49 B6
Geldern D 50 B2
Geldrop NL 49 B6
Geleen NL 50 C1
Gelembe TR 114 C2
Gelendost TR 16 B5
Gelibolu = Gallipoli TR 114 B1
Gelida E 91 B4
Gelnhausen D 51 C5
Gelnica SK 65 B6
Gelsa E 90 B2
Gelse H 74 B1
Gelsenkirchen D 50 B3
Gelsted DK 39 D2
Geltendorf D 62 B2
Gelterkinden CH 70 A2
Gelting D 39 E2
Gelu RO 75 B6
Gelves E 99 B4
Gembloux B 49 C5
Gemeaux F 69 A5
Gémenos F 79 C4
Gemerská Poloma SK 65 B6
Gemerská Ves SK 65 B6
Gemert NL 50 B1
Gemla S 40 C4
Gemlik TR 114 B4
Gemmenich B 50 C1
Gemona del Friuli I 72 B3
Gémozac F 67 C4
Gemund D 50 C2
Gemünden, *Bayern* D 51 C5
Gemünden, *Hessen* D 51 C4
Gemünden, *Rheinland-Pfalz* D 60 A3
Genappe B 49 C5
Génave E 101 A3
Genazzano I 102 B5
Gençay F 67 B5
Gencsapáti H 74 A1
Gendringen NL 50 B2
Genelard F 69 B4
Genemuiden NL 42 C3
Generalski Stol HR 73 C5
Geneva = Genève CH 69 B6
Genevad S 40 C3
Genève = Geneva CH 69 B6
Genevriéres F 60 C1
Gengenbach D 61 B4
Genillé F 67 A6
Genk B 49 C6
Genlis F 69 A5
Gennep NL 50 B1
Genner DK 39 D2
Gennes F 67 A4
Genoa = Génova I 80 B2
Genola I 80 B1
Génova = Genoa I 80 B2
Genowefa PL 54 A3
Gensingen D 60 A3
Gent = Ghent B 49 B4
Genthin D 44 C4
Gentioux F 68 C1
Genzano di Lucánia I 104 C2
Genzano di Roma I 102 B5
Georgenthal D 51 C6
Georgsmarienhütte D 50 A4
Gera D 52 C2
Geraards-bergen B 49 C4
Gerace I 106 C3
Geraci Sículo I 109 B3
Gérardmer F 60 B2
Geras A 63 B6
Gerbéviller F 60 B2
Gerbini I 109 B3
Gerbstedt D 52 B1
Gerði IS 111 C9
Gerede TR 114 B7
Gerena E 99 B4
Geretsried D 62 C2
Gérgal E 101 B3
Gergy F 69 B4
Gerindote E 94 C2
Gerjen H 74 B3
Gerlos A 72 A2
Germay F 59 B6
Germering D 62 B2
Germersheim D 61 A4
Gernika-Lumo E 89 A4
Gernrode D 52 B1
Gernsbach D 61 B4
Gernsheim D 61 A4
Geroda D 51 C5
Gerola Alta I 71 B4
Geroldsgrun D 52 C1
Gerolstein D 50 C2
Gerolzhofen D 61 A6
Gerovo HR 73 C4
Gerrards Cross GB 31 C3
Gerri de la Sal E 91 A4
Gersfeld D 51 C5
Gerstetten D 61 B6
Gersthofen D 62 B1
Gerstungen D 51 C6
Gerswalde D 45 B5
Gerzat F 68 C3
Gerze TR 16 A7
Gerzen D 62 B3
Gescher D 50 B3
Geseke D 51 B4
Geslau D 61 A6
Gespunsart F 59 A5
Gesté F 66 A3
Gestorf D 51 A5
Gesualda I 103 C8
Geta FIN 6 A5
Getafe E 94 B3
Getinge S 40 C2
Getxo E 89 A4
Geversdorf D 43 B6
Gevgelija MK 112 A4
Gevora del Caudillo E 93 C4
Gevrey-Chambertin F 69 A4
Gex F 69 B6
Gey D 50 C2
Geyikli TR 114 C1
Geysir IS 111 C5
Geyve TR 114 B5
Gföhl A 63 B6
Ghedi I 71 C5
Ghent = Gent B 49 B4
Gheorgheni RO 11 C8
Ghigo I 79 B6
Ghilarza I 110 B1
Ghisonaccia F 102 A2
Ghisoni F 102 A2
Giardinetto Vécchio I 103 B8
Giardini Naxos I 109 B4
Giarratana I 109 B3
Giarre I 109 B4
Giat F 68 C2
Giaveno I 80 A1
Giazza I 71 C6
Giba I 110 C1
Gibellina Nuova I 108 B1
Gibraleón E 99 B4
Gibraltar GBZ 99 C5
Gic H 74 A2
Gidle PL 55 C4
Giebelstadt D 61 A5
Gieboldehausen D 51 B6
Gielniów PL 55 B5
Gielow D 45 B4
Gien F 58 C3
Giengen D 61 B6
Giens F 79 C5
Giera RO 75 C5
Gieselwerder D 51 B5
Giessen D 51 C4
Gieten NL 42 B3
Giethoorn NL 42 C3
Giffaumont-Champaubert F 59 B5
Gifford GB 25 C5
Gifhorn D 44 C2
Gige H 74 B2
Giglio Porto I 102 A3
Gignac F 78 C2
Gijón E 88 A1
Gilena E 100 B1
Gilford GB 19 B5
Gillberga S 34 B4
Gilleleje DK 41 C2
Gilley F 69 A6
Gilley-sur-Loire F 68 B3
Gillingham, *Dorset* GB 29 B5
Gillingham, *Medway* GB 31 C4
Gilocourt F 59 A3
Gilserberg D 51 C5
Gilsland GB 25 D5
Gilze NL 49 B5
Gimo S 36 A5
Gimont F 77 C3
Ginasservis F 79 C4
Gingelom B 49 C6
Gingst D 45 A5
Ginosa I 104 C2
Ginzling A 72 A1
Giões P 98 B3
Gióia dei Marsi I 103 B6
Gióia del Colle I 104 C2
Gióia Sannitica I 103 B7
Gióia Tauro I 106 C2
Gioiosa Iónica I 106 C3
Gioiosa Marea I 109 A3
Giosla GB 22 C2
Giovinazzo I 104 B2
Girifalco I 106 C3
Giromagny F 60 C2
Girona E 91 B5

Györszemere H 74 A2
Gypsera CH 70 B2
Gysinge S 36 A3
Gyttorp S 36 B1
Gyula H 75 B6
Gyulafirátót H 74 A2
Gyulaj H 74 B3

H

Haacht B 49 C5
Haag, *Nieder Östereich* A 63 B5
Haag, *Ober Östereich* A 63 B4
Haag D 62 B3
Haaksbergen NL 50 A2
Haamstede NL 49 B4
Haan D 50 B3
Haapajärvi FIN 3 E26
Haapsalu EST 6 B7
Haarlem NL 42 C1
Habas F 76 C2
Habay B 60 A1
Habo S 40 B4
Habry CZ 63 A6
Habsheim F 60 C3
Hachenburg D 50 C3
Hacıbektaş TR 16 B7
Hacılar TR 16 B7
Hacinas E 89 C3
Hacketstown IRL 21 B5
Hackthorpe GB 26 A3
Hadamar D 50 C4
Haddington GB 25 C5
Hadersdorf am Kamp A 63 B6
Haderslev DK 39 D2
Hadım TR 16 C6
Hadleigh, *Essex* GB 31 C4
Hadleigh, *Suffolk* GB 30 B4
Hadlow GB 31 C4
Hadmersleben D 52 A1
Hadsten DK 39 C3
Hadsund DK 38 C3
Hadyach UA 7 F13
Hadžići BIH 84 C3
Hægebostad N 33 C4
Hægeland N 33 C4
Hafnarfjörður IS 111 C4
Hafnir IS 111 D3
Haganj HR 74 C1
Hagby S 40 C6
Hage D 43 B4
Hagen, *Niedersachsen* D 43 B5
Hagen, *Nordrhein-Westfalen* D 50 B3
Hagenbach D 61 A4
Hagenow D 44 B3
Hagetmau F 76 C2
Hagfors S 34 A5
Hagondange F 60 A2
Haguenau F 60 B3
Hahnbach D 62 A2
Hahnslätten D 50 C4
Hahót H 74 B1
Haiger D 50 C4
Haigerloch D 61 B4
Hailsham GB 31 D4
Hainburg A 64 B2
Hainfeld A 64 B1
Hainichen D 52 C3
Hajdúböszörmény H 10 C6
Hajdučica YU 75 C5
Hajdúszoboszló H 75 A6
Hajnáčka SK 65 B5
Hajnówka PL 6 E7
Hajós H 75 B4
Hakkas S 3 C24
Håksberg S 36 A2
Halaszi H 64 C3
Halberstadt D 52 B1
Halberton GB 29 C4
Hald Ege DK 39 C2
Haldem D 43 C5
Halden N 34 B3
Haldensleben D 52 A1
Halenbeck D 44 B4
Halesowen GB 26 C3
Halesworth GB 30 B5
Halfing D 62 C3
Halhjem N 32 A2
Halifax GB 27 B4
Halkirk GB 23 C5
Hall S 37 D5
Hall in Tirol A 71 A6
Hallabro S 41 C5
Hällabrottet S 37 B2
Halland GB 31 D4
Hällaryd S 41 C4
Hällberga S 36 B3
Hällbybrunn S 36 B3
Halle B 49 C5
Halle, *Nordrhein-Westfalen* D 51 A4
Halle, *Sachsen-Anhalt* D 52 B1
Hälleberga S 40 C5
Hällefors S 36 B1
Hälleforsnäs S 36 B3
Hallein A 62 C4
Hällekis S 35 C5
Hällen S 36 A4
Hallenberg D 51 B4
Hällestad S 37 C2
Hällevadsholm S 35 C3
Hällevik S 41 C4
Hälleviksstrand S 35 C3
Hallingby N 34 A2
Hällnäs S 36 A4
Hallormsstaður IS 111 B11
Hallsberg S 37 B2
Hällsta S 36 B3
Hallstahammar S 36 B3
Hallstatt A 72 A3
Hallstavik S 36 A5
Halltorp S 40 C6
Halluin F 49 C4
Hallworthy GB 28 C3
Halmstad S 40 C2
Hals DK 38 B3
Halstead GB 31 C4
Haltdalen N 2 E19
Haltern D 50 B3
Haltwhistle GB 25 D5
Halvarsgårdarna S 36 A2
Halver D 50 B3
Halvrimmen DK 38 B2
Ham F 59 A4
Hamar N 34 A3
Hamarhaug N 32 A2
Hambach F 60 A3
Hambergen D 43 B5
Hambergsund S 35 C3
Hambledon GB 31 D2
Hambuhren D 44 C1
Hamburg D 44 B2
Hamdibey TR 114 C2
Hamdorf D 43 A6
Hämeenlinna FIN 3 F26
Hameln = Hamlin D 51 A5
Hamersleben D 52 A1
Hamidiye TR 114 C5
Hamilton GB 24 C3
Hamina FIN 7 A9
Hamlin = Hameln D 51 A5
Hamm D 50 B3
Hammar S 37 C1
Hammarö S 34 B5
Hamme B 49 B5
Hammel DK 39 C2
Hammelburg D 51 C5
Hammelspring D 45 B5
Hammenhög S 41 D4
Hammerfest N 3 A25
Hammershøj DK 38 C2
Hammerum DK 39 C2
Hamminkeln D 50 B2
Hamnavoe GB 22 A7
Hamneda S 40 C3
Hamont B 49 B6
Hámor H 65 B6
Hamra S 37 E5
Hamstreet GB 31 C4
Han TR 114 C5
Han Knežica BIH 83 A5
Han Pijesak BIH 84 B3
Hanaskog S 41 C4
Hanau D 51 C4
Händelöp S 37 D3
Handlová SK 65 B4
Hanerau-Hademarschen D 43 A6
Hånger S 40 B3
Hanken S 37 C1
Hankensbüttel D 44 C2
Hanko FIN 6 B7
Hannover D 43 C6
Hannut B 49 C6
Hanstedt D 44 B2
Hanstholm DK 38 B1
Hantsavichy BY 7 E9
Hanušovice CZ 54 C1
Haparanda S 3 D26
Haradok BY 7 D10
Harads S 3 C24
Häradsbäck S 40 C4
Harbo S 36 A4
Harboør DK 38 C1
Harburg, *Bayern* D 62 B1
Harburg, *Hamburg* D 44 B1
Hårby DK 39 D3
Harc H 74 B3
Hardegarijp NL 42 B2
Hardegsen D 51 B5
Hardelot Plage F 48 C2
Hardenbeck D 45 B5
Hardenberg NL 42 C3
Harderwijk NL 42 C2
Hardheim D 61 A5
Hardt D 61 B4
Hareid N 2 E17
Haren D 43 C4
Haren NL 42 B3
Harestua N 34 A2
Harfleur F 57 A6
Harg S 36 A5
Hargicourt F 49 D4
Hargnies F 49 C5
Hargshamn S 36 A5
Harkány H 74 C3
Härkeberga S 36 B4
Harkebrügge D 43 B4
Harlech GB 26 C1
Harleston GB 30 B5
Härlev DK 41 D2
Harlingen NL 42 B2
Harlösa S 41 D3
Harlow GB 31 C4
Harmancık TR 114 C4
Härnevi S 36 B4
Härnösand S 2 E22
Haro E 89 B4
Haroldswick GB 22 A8
Háromfa H 74 B2
Haroué F 60 B2
Harpenden GB 31 C3
Harplinge S 40 C2
Harpstedt D 43 C5
Harrogate GB 27 A4
Harrow GB 31 C3
Härryda S 40 B2
Harsefeld D 43 B6
Harsewinkel D 50 B4
Hârşova RO 11 D9
Harstad N 2 B22
Harsum D 51 A5
Harta H 75 B4
Hartberg A 73 A5
Hartburn GB 25 C6
Hartennes F 59 A4
Hartest GB 30 B4
Hartha D 52 B2
Hartland GB 28 C3
Hartlepool GB 27 A4
Hartmanice CZ 63 A4
Hartmannsdorf A 73 A5
Harwell GB 31 C2
Harwich GB 31 C5
Harzgerode D 52 B1
Häselgehr A 71 A5
Haselünne D 43 C4
Hasköy TR 114 A1
Haslach D 61 B4
Haslach an der Mühl A 63 B5
Hasle DK 41 D4
Haslemere GB 31 C3
Haslev DK 39 D4
Hasloch D 61 A5
Hasparren F 76 C1
Hasselfelde D 51 B6
Hasselfors S 37 B1
Hasselt B 49 C6
Hasselt NL 42 C3
Hassfurt D 51 C6
Hassleben D 45 B5
Hässleholm S 41 C3
Hasslö S 41 C5
Hassloch D 61 A4
Hästholmen S 37 C1
Hastière-Lavaux B 49 C5
Hastigrow GB 23 C5
Hastings GB 31 D4
Hästveda S 41 C3
Hatfield, *Hertfordshire* GB 31 C3
Hatfield, *South Yorkshire* GB 27 B5
Hatherleigh GB 28 C3
Hathersage GB 27 B4
Hatlestrand N 32 A2
Hattem NL 42 C3
Hatten D 43 B5
Hatten F 60 B3
Hatting DK 39 D2
Hattingen D 50 B3
Hattstadt F 60 B3
Hattstedt D 43 A6
Hatvan H 65 C5
Hatvik N 32 A2
Hau D 50 B2
Haudainville F 59 A6
Hauganes IS 111 B7
Hauge N 32 C3
Haugesund N 32 B2
Haughom N 32 C3
Haugsdorf A 64 B2
Haukeland N 32 A2
Haukeligrend N 33 B4
Haukipudas FIN 3 D26
Haulerwijk NL 42 B3
Haunersdorf D 62 B3
Hausach D 61 B4
Hausham D 62 C2
Hausmannstätten A 73 B5
Hausvik N 32 C3
Haut-Fays B 49 C6
Hautefort F 67 C6
Hauterives F 69 C5
Hauteville-Lompnès F 69 C5
Hautmont F 49 C4
Hautrage B 49 C4
Hauzenberg D 63 B4
Havant GB 31 D3
Havdhem S 37 D5
Havdrup DK 39 D5
Havelange B 49 C6
Havelberg D 44 C4
Havelte NL 42 C3
Haverfordwest GB 28 B3
Haverhill GB 30 B4
Havering GB 31 C4
Håverud S 35 C4
Havířov CZ 65 A4
Havixbeck D 50 B3
Havlíčkův Brod CZ 63 A6
Havndal DK 38 C3
Havneby DK 39 D1
Havnsø DK 39 D4
Havøysund N 3 A26
Havran TR 114 C2
Havrebjerg DK 39 D4
Havsa TR 114 A1
Havstenssund S 35 C3
Havza TR 16 A7
Hawes GB 26 A3
Hawick GB 25 C5
Hawkhurst GB 31 C4
Hawkinge GB 31 C5
Haxey GB 27 B5
Hay-on-Wye GB 29 A4
Hayange F 60 A2
Haydon Bridge GB 25 D5
Hayle GB 28 C2
Haymana TR 114 C7
Hayrabolu TR 114 A2
Haysyn UA 11 B10
Hayvoron UA 11 B10
Haywards Heath GB 31 D3
Hazebrouck F 48 C3
Hazlov CZ 52 C2
Heacham GB 30 B4
Headcorn GB 31 C4
Headford IRL 20 A2
Heanor GB 27 B4
Héas F 76 D3
Heathfield GB 31 D4
Hebden Bridge GB 26 B3
Heberg S 40 C2
Heby S 36 B3
Hechingen D 61 B4
Hechlingen D 62 B1
Hecho E 76 D2
Hechtel B 49 B6
Hechthausen D 43 B6
Heckelberg D 45 C5
Heckington GB 27 C5
Hecklingen D 52 B1
Hed S 36 B2
Hedared S 40 B2
Heddal N 33 B6
Hédé F 57 B4
Hede S 2 E20
Hedekas S 35 C3
Hedemora S 36 A2
Hedensted DK 39 D2
Hedersleben D 52 B1
Hedesunda S 36 A4
Hedge End GB 31 D2
Hedon GB 27 B5
Heede D 43 C4
Heek D 50 A3
Heemstede NL 42 C1
Heerde NL 42 C3
's Heerenberg NL 50 B2
Heerenveen NL 42 C2
Heerhugowaard NL 42 C1
Heerlen NL 50 C1
Heeze NL 49 B6
Hegyeshalom H 64 C3
Hegyközség H 74 A1
Heide D 43 A6
Heidelberg D 61 A4
Heiden D 50 B2
Heidenau D 53 C3
Heidenheim D 61 B6
Heidenreichstein A 63 B6
Heikendorf D 44 A2
Heilam GB 22 C4
Heilbad Heiligenstadt D 51 B6
Heilbronn D 61 A5
Heiligenblut A 72 A2
Heiligendamn D 44 A3
Heiligendorf D 44 C2
Heiligengrabe D 44 B4
Heiligenhafen D 44 A2
Heiligenhaus D 50 B2
Heiligenkreuz A 73 B6
Heiligenstadt D 62 A2
Heiloo NL 42 C1
Heilsbronn D 62 A1
Heimburg D 51 B6
Heimdal N 2 E19
Heinerscheid L 50 C2
Heinersdorf D 45 C6
Heining D 63 B4
Heiningen D 61 B5
Heinola FIN 3 F27
Heinsberg D 50 B2
Heist-op-den-Berg B 49 B5
Hejde S 37 D5
Hejdeby S 37 D5
Hejls DK 39 D2
Hejnice CZ 53 C5
Hel PL 47 A4
Helchteren B 49 B6
Heldburg D 51 C6
Heldrungen D 52 B1
Helechosa E 94 C2
Helensburgh GB 24 B3
Helfenberg A 63 B5
Helgen N 33 B6
Helgeroa N 33 C6
Hella IS 111 D5
Hellas S 35 C4
Helle N 32 C3
Helleland N 32 C3
Hellendoorn NL 42 C3
Hellenthal D 50 C2
Hellesylt N 2 E17
Hellevoetsluis NL 49 B5
Hellín E 101 A4
Hellissandur IS 111 C2
Hellnar IS 111 C2
Hellvi S 37 D5
Hellvik N 32 C2
Helm-brechts D 52 C1
Helmond NL 49 B6
Helmsdale GB 23 C5
Helmsley GB 27 A4
Helmstedt D 51 A6
Hel'pa SK 65 B5
Helsa D 51 B5
Helsby GB 26 B3
Helsingborg S 41 C2
Helsinge DK 41 C2
Helsingør DK 41 C2
Helsinki FIN 6 A8
Helston GB 28 C2
Hemau D 62 A2
Hemel Hempstead GB 31 C3
Hemer D 50 B3
Héming F 60 B2
Hemmet DK 39 D1
Hemmingstedt D 43 A6
Hemmoor D 43 B6
Hemnes N 34 B3
Hemnesberget N 2 C20
Hemse S 37 D5
Hemsedal N 2 F18
Hemslingen D 43 B6
Hemsworth GB 27 B4
Hen N 34 A2
Henån S 35 C3
Hendaye F 76 C1
Hendek TR 114 B5
Hendungen D 51 C6
Henfield GB 31 D3
Hengelo, *Gelderland* NL 50 A2
Hengelo, *Overijssel* NL 50 A2
Hengersberg D 62 B4
Hengoed GB 29 B4
Hénin-Beaumont F 48 C3
Henley-on-Thames GB 31 C3
Henne Strand DK 39 D1
Henneberg D 51 C6
Hennebont F 56 C2
Hennigsdorf D 45 C5
Hennstedt D 43 A6
Henrichemont F 68 A2
Henryków PL 54 C2
Henrykowo PL 47 A6
Henstedt-Ulzburg D 44 B1
Heppenheim D 61 A4
Herad N 32 C3
Heraklion = Iráklion GR 113 G7
Herálec CZ 64 A2
Herand N 32 A3
Herbault F 58 C2
Herbern D 50 B3
Herbertstown IRL 20 B3
Herbeumont B 59 A6
Herbignac F 66 A2
Herbisse F 59 B5
Herbitzheim F 60 A3
Herbolzheim D 60 B3
Herborn D 50 C4
Herbrechtingen D 61 B6
Herby PL 54 C3
Herceg-Novi YU 105 A4
Hercegovać HR 74 C2
Hercegovacka Goleša YU 85 C4
Hercegszántó H 75 C3
Herchen D 50 C3
Heréd H 65 C5
Hereford GB 29 A5
Herefoss N 33 C5
Hereke TR 114 B4
Herencia E 95 C3
Herend H 74 A2
Herent B 49 C5
Herentals B 49 B5
Hérépian F 78 C2
Herfølge DK 41 D2
Herford D 51 A4
Herguijuela E 93 B5
Héric F 66 A3
Héricourt F 60 C2
Héricourt-en-Caux F 58 A1
Hérimoncourt F 70 A1
Heringsdorf D 44 A3
Herisau CH 71 A4
Hérisson F 68 B2
Herk-de-Stad B 49 C6
Herlufmagle DK 39 D4
Hermagor A 72 B3
Hermannsburg D 44 C2
Heřmanův Městec CZ 53 D5
Herment F 68 C2
Hermeskeil D 60 A2
Hermisende E 87 C4
Hermonville F 59 A4
Hermsdorf D 52 C1
Hernani E 76 C1
Hernansancho E 94 B2
Herne D 50 B3
Herne Bay GB 31 C5
Herning DK 39 C1
Herøya N 33 B6
Herramelluri E 89 B3
Herräng S 36 A5
Herre N 33 B6
Herrenberg D 61 B4
Herrera E 100 B1
Herrera de Alcántara E 92 B3
Herrera de los Navarros E 90 B1
Herrera de Pisuerga E 88 B2
Herrera del Duque E 94 C1
Herrerias E 98 B3
Herreros del Suso E 94 B1
Herrestad S 35 C3
Herrhamra S 37 C4
Herrlisheim F 60 B3
Herrljunga S 35 C5
Herrnhut D 53 B4
Herrsching D 62 B2
Hersbruck D 62 A2
Hersby S 36 B5
Herscheid D 50 B3
Herselt B 49 B5
Herstal B 49 C6
Herstmonceux GB 31 D4
Herten D 50 B3
Hertford GB 31 C3
's-Hertogenbosch NL 49 B6
Hervás E 93 A5
Hervik N 32 B2
Herxheim D 61 A4
Herzberg, *Brandenburg* D 45 C4
Herzberg, *Brandenburg* D 52 B3
Herzberg, *Niedersachsen* D 51 B6
Herzebrock D 50 B4
Herzfelde D 45 C5
Herzlake D 43 C4
Herzogen-aurach D 62 A1
Herzogenbuchsee CH 70 A2
Herzogenburg A 63 B6
Herzsprung D 44 B4
Hesby N 32 B2
Hesdin F 48 C3
Hesel D 43 B4
Heskestad N 32 C3
Hesselager DK 39 D3
Hessisch Lichtenau D 51 B5
Hessisch-Oldendorf D 51 A5
Hestra S 40 B3
Heswall GB 26 B2
Hettange-Grande F 60 A2
Hetton-le-Hole GB 25 D6
Hettstedt D 52 B1
Heuchin F 48 C3
Heudicourt-sous-les-Côtes F 60 B1
Heunezel F 60 B2
Heuqueville F 57 A6
Heves H 65 C6
Héviz H 74 B2
Hexham GB 25 D5
Heysham GB 26 A3
Heytesbury GB 29 B5
Hidas H 74 B3
Hieflau A 63 C5
Hiendelaencina E 95 A4
Hiersac F 67 C5
High Bentham GB 26 A3
High Hesket GB 25 D5
High Wycombe GB 31 C3
Highclere GB 31 C2
Highley GB 26 C3
Higuera de Arjona E 100 B2
Higuera de Calatrava E 100 B1
Higuera de la Serena E 93 C5
Higuera de la Sierra E 99 B4
Higuera de Vargas E 93 C4
Higuera la Real E 99 A4
Higueras de Llerena E 93 C4
Higueruela E 96 C1
Híjar E 90 B2
Hilchenbach D 50 B4
Hildburghausen D 51 C6
Hilden D 50 B2
Hilders D 51 C5
Hildesheim D 51 A5
Hilgay GB 30 B4
Hillared S 40 B3
Hille D 51 A4
Hillegom NL 49 A5
Hillerød DK 41 D2
Hillerstorp S 40 B3
Hillesheim D 50 C2
Hillestad N 34 B2
Hillmersdorf D 52 B3
Hillsborough GB 19 B5
Hillswick GB 22 A7
Hilpoltstein D 62 A2
Hiltpoltstein D 62 A2
Hilvarenbeek NL 49 B6
Hilversum NL 49 A6
Himarë AL 112 B1
Himesháza H 74 B3
Himmelberg A 73 B4
Himmelpforten D 43 B6
Himód H 74 A2
Hinckley GB 30 B2
Hindås S 40 B2
Hindelang D 71 A5
Hindelbank CH 70 A2
Hinderavåg N 32 B2
Hindhead GB 31 C3
Hinjosa del Valle E 93 C4
Hinnerup DK 39 C3
Hinneryd S 40 C3
Hinojal E 93 B4
Hinojales E 99 B4
Hinojos E 99 B4
Hinojosa del Duque E 93 C5
Hinojosas de Calatrava E 100 A1
Hinterhornbach A 71 A5
Hinterriss A 71 A6
Hintersee A 63 C4
Hintersee D 45 B6
Hinterstoder A 63 C5
Hintertux A 72 A1
Hinterweidenthal D 60 A3
Hinwil CH 70 A3
Hippolytushoef NL 42 C1
Hirschaid D 62 A1
Hirschau D 62 A2
Hirschfeld D 52 B3
Hirschhorn D 61 A4
Hirsingue F 60 C3
Hirson F 59 A5
Hirtshals DK 38 B2
Hirzenhain D 51 C5
Hisarcık TR 114 C4
Hishult S 41 C3
Hitchin GB 31 C3
Hittarp S 41 C2
Hittisau A 71 A4
Hitzacker D 44 B3
Hjallerup DK 38 B3
Hjältevad S 40 B5
Hjärnarp S 41 C2
Hjartdal N 33 B5
Hjellestad N 32 A2
Hjelmeland N 32 B3
Hjerkinn N 2 E18
Hjerm DK 38 C1
Hjerpsted DK 39 D1
Hjerting DK 39 D1
Hjo S 35 C6
Hjordkær DK 39 D2
Hjørring DK 38 B2
Hjorted S 40 B6
Hjortkvarn S 37 C2
Hjortsberga S 40 C4
Hjukse N 33 B6
Hjuksebø N 33 B6
Hliník nad Hronom. SK 65 B4
Hlinsko CZ 64 A1
Hlío IS 111 A10
Hlohovec SK 64 B3
Hluboká nad Vltavou CZ 63 A5
Hlučín CZ 64 A4
Hlukhiv UA 7 F12
Hlyboka UA 11 B8
Hlybokaye BY 7 D9
Hniezdne SK 65 A6
Hnilec SK 65 B6
Hnúšt'a SK 65 B5
Hobol H 74 B2
Hobro DK 38 C2
Hobscheid L 60 A1
Hochdonn D 43 A6
Hochdorf CH 70 A3
Hochfelden F 60 B3
Hochspeyer D 60 A3
Höchst im Odenwald D 61 A5
Höchstadt, *Bayern* D 62 A1
Höchstädt, *Bayern* D 61 B6
Hochstenbach D 50 C3
Hockenheim D 61 A4
Hoddesdon GB 31 C3
Hodejov SK 65 B5
Hodenhagen D 43 C6
Hodkovice CZ 53 C5
Hódmezővásárhely H 75 B5
Hodnet GB 26 C3
Hodonín CZ 64 B3
Hodslavice CZ 64 A4
Hoedekenskerke NL 49 B4
Hoegaarden B 49 C5
Hoek van Holland NL 49 B5
Hoenderlo NL 50 A1
Hof D 52 C1
Hof N 34 B2
Hofbieber D 51 C5
Hoff GB 26 A3
Hofgeismar D 51 B5
Hofheim, *Bayern* D 51 C6
Hofheim, *Hessen* D 51 C4
Hofkirchen im Mühlkreis A 63 B4
Höfn IS 111 C10
Hofors S 36 A3
Hofsós IS 111 B6
Höganäs S 41 C2
Hogdal S 35 B3
Högfors S 36 B2
Högklint S 37 D5
Högsäter S 35 C4
Högsby S 40 B6
Högsjö S 37 B2
Hogstad S 37 C2
Högyész H 74 B3
Hohen Neuendorf D 45 C5
Hohenau A 64 B2
Hohenberg A 63 C6
Hohenbucko D 52 B3
Hohenburg D 62 A2
Hohenems A 71 A4
Hohenhameln D 51 A6
Hohenhausen D 51 A4
Hohenkirchen D 43 B4
Hohenlinden D 62 B2
Hohenlockstedt D 43 B6
Hohenmölsen D 52 B2
Hohennauen D 44 C4
Hohenseeden D 52 A2
Hohentauern A 73 A4
Hohentengen D 70 A3
Hohenwepel D 51 B5
Hohenwestedt D 43 A6
Hohenwutzen D 45 C6
Hohenzieritz D 45 B5
Hohn D 43 A6
Hohne D 44 C2
Hohnstorf D 44 B2
Højer DK 39 E1
Højslev Stby DK 38 C2
Hok S 40 B4
Hökerum S 40 B3
Hökhuvud S 36 A5
Hokksund N 33 B6
Hökön S 40 C4
Hola Pristan UA 11 C12
Hólar IS 111 B6
Holbæk, *Aarhus Amt.* DK 38 C3
Holbæk, *Vestsjællands Amt.* DK 39 D4
Holbeach GB 30 B4
Holdenstedt D 44 C2
Holdhus N 32 A2
Holdorf D 43 C5
Holeby DK 44 A3
Hølen N 34 B2
Holešov CZ 64 A3
Holguera E 93 B4
Holíč SK 64 B3
Holice CZ 53 C5
Holice SK 64 C3
Hollabrunn A 64 B2
Hollandstoun GB 23 B6
Høllen N 33 C4
Hollfeld D 52 D1
Hollstadt D 51 C6
Hollum NL 42 B2
Höllviksnäs S 41 D2
Hólmavík IS 111 B4
Holme-on-Spalding-Moor GB 27 B5
Holmedal S 34 B3
Holmegil N 34 B3
Holmes Chapel GB 26 B3
Holmestrand N 34 B2
Holmfirth GB 27 B4
Holmsbu N 34 B2
Holmsjö S 41 C5
Holmsund S 3 E24
Holmudden S 37 D6
Hölö S 37 B4
Holsbybrunn S 40 B5
Holsljunga S 40 B2
Holstebro DK 39 C1
Holsted DK 39 D1
Holsworthy GB 28 C3
Holt, *Norfolk* GB 30 B5
Holt, *Wrexham* GB 26 B3
Holt IS 111 D6
Holt N 33 C5
Holten NL 50 A2
Holtwick D 50 A3
Holum N 33 C4
Holwerd NL 42 B2
Holycross IRL 21 B4
Holyhead GB 26 B1
Holýšov CZ 62 A4
Holywell GB 26 B2
Holywood GB 19 B6
Holzdorf D 52 B3
Holzhausen D 51 A4
Holzheim D 61 B6
Holzkirchen D 62 C2
Holzminden D 51 B5
Holzthaleben D 51 B6
Homberg, *Hessen* D 51 B5
Homberg, *Hessen* D 51 C5
Homburg D 60 A3
Hommelvik N 2 E19
Hommersåk N 32 C2
Homokmegy H 75 B4
Homokszentgyörgy H 74 B2
Homrogd H 65 B6
Homyel = Gomel BY 7 E11
Hondarribia E 76 C1
Hondón de los Frailes E 101 A5
Hondschoote F 48 C3
Hönebach D 51 C5
Hønefoss N 34 A2
Honfleur F 57 A6
Høng DK 39 D4
Honiton GB 29 C4
Hönningen D 50 C2
Honningsvåg N 3 A27
Hönö S 38 B4
Honrubia E 95 C4
Hontalbilla E 88 C2
Hontianske-Nemce SK 65 B4
Hontoria de la Cantera E 88 B3
Hontoria de Valdearados E 89 C3
Hontoria del Pinar E 89 C3
Hoofddorp NL 49 A5
Hoogerheide NL 49 B5
Hoogeveen NL 42 C3
Hoogezand-Sappemeer NL 42 B3
Hoogkarspel NL 42 C2
Hoogkerk NL 42 B3
Hoogstede D 42 C3
Hoogstraten B 49 B5
Hook GB 31 C3
Hooksiel D 43 B5
Höör S 41 D3
Hoorn NL 42 C2
Hope GB 26 B2
Hope under Dinmore GB 29 A5
Hopfgarten A 72 A2
Hopfgarten in Defereggen A 72 B2
Hopsten D 43 C4
Hoptrup DK 39 D2
Hora Svatého Sebestiána CZ 52 C3
Horaždóvice CZ 63 A4
Horb am Neckar D 61 B4
Horbelev DK 39 E5

Hørby	DK	38	B3
Hörby	S	41	D3
Horcajada de la Torre	E	95	B4
Horcajo de los Montes	E	94	C2
Horcajo de Santiago	E	95	C3
Horcajo-Medianero	E	93	A5
Horche	E	95	B3
Horda	S	40	B4
Hořesedly	CZ	52	C3
Horezu	RO	11	D8
Horgen	CH	70	A3
Horgoš	YU	75	B4
Hořice	CZ	53	C5
Horjul	SLO	73	B4
Horka	D	53	B4
Hörken	S	36	A1
Horki	BY	7	D11
Hörle	S	40	B4
Horn	A	63	B6
Horn	D	51	B4
Horn	S	40	B5
Horna	E	101	A4
Horná Mariková	SK	64	A4
Horná Streda	SK	64	B3
Horná Štrubna	SK	65	B4
Horná Súča	SK	64	B3
Hornachos	E	93	C4
Hornachuelos	E	99	B5
Hornanes	N	32	B2
Hornbæk, *Aarhus Amt.*	DK	38	C2
Hornbæk, *Frederiksværk*	DK	41	C2
Hornberg	D	61	B4
Hornburg	D	51	A6
Horncastle	GB	27	B5
Horndal	S	36	A3
Horndean	GB	31	D2
Horne, *Fyns Amt.*	DK	39	D3
Horne, *Ribe Amt.*	DK	39	D1
Hörnebo	S	35	C6
Horneburg	D	43	B6
Horní Bečva	CZ	64	A4
Horní Benešov	CZ	64	A3
Horní Cerekev	CZ	63	A6
Horní Jiřetín	CZ	52	C3
Horní Lomná	CZ	65	A4
Horní Maršov	CZ	53	C5
Horní Planá	CZ	63	B5
Horní Slavkov	CZ	52	C2
Horní Vltavice	CZ	63	B4
Horning	DK	39	C3
Hörningsholm	S	37	B4
Hornnes	N	33	C4
Horno	D	53	B4
Hornos	E	101	A3
Hornoy-le-Bourg	F	58	A2
Hornsea	GB	27	B5
Hornslet	DK	39	C3
Hornstein	A	64	C2
Hörnum	D	39	E1
Hornum	DK	38	C2
Horný Tisovník	SK	65	B5
Horodenka	UA	11	B8
Horodnya	UA	7	F11
Horodok, *Khmelnytskyy*	UA	11	B9
Horodok, *Lviv*	UA	11	B7
Horodyshche	UA	11	B11
Horokhiv	UA	11	A8
Horovice	CZ	63	A4
Horred	S	40	B2
Hörsching	A	63	B5
Horsens	DK	39	D2
Horsham	GB	31	C3
Hørsholm	DK	41	D2
Horslunde	DK	39	E4
Horšovský Týn	CZ	62	A3
Horst	NL	50	B2
Horstel	D	50	A3
Horsten	D	43	B4
Horstmar	D	50	A3
Hort	H	65	C5
Horta	P	87	C3
Horten	N	34	B2
Hortezuela	E	89	C4
Hortiguela	E	89	B3
Hortobágy	H	75	A6
Horton in Ribblesdale	GB	26	A3
Hørve	DK	39	D4
Hörvik	S	41	C4
Horwich	GB	26	B3
Hösbach	D	51	C5
Hosena	D	53	B4
Hosenfeld	D	51	C5
Hosingen	L	50	C2
Hospental	CH	70	B3
Hospital	IRL	20	B3
Hossegor	F	76	C1
Hosszuhetény	H	74	B3
Hostal de Iplés	E	90	A2
Hoštálkova	CZ	64	A3
Hostalric	E	91	B5
Hostens	F	76	B2
Hostěradice	CZ	64	B2
Hostinné	CZ	53	C5
Hostomice	CZ	63	A5
Hostouň	CZ	62	A3
Hoting	S	2	D22
Hotolisht	AL	112	A2
Hotton	B	49	C6
Houdain	F	48	C3
Houdan	F	58	B2
Houdelaincourt	F	60	B1
Houeillès	F	76	B3
Houffalize	B	50	C1
Houghton-le-Spring	GB	25	D6
Houlgate	F	57	A5
Hounslow	GB	31	C3
Hourtin	F	66	C3
Hourtin-Plage	F	66	C3
Houthalen	B	49	B6
Houyet	B	49	C5
Hov	DK	39	D3
Hova	S	35	C6
Hovåg	N	33	C5
Hovden	N	33	B4
Hove	GB	31	D3
Hovedgård	DK	39	D2
Hovelhof	D	51	B4
Hoven	DK	39	D1
Hovingham	GB	27	A5
Hovmantorp	S	40	C5
Hovsta	S	36	B2
Howden	GB	27	B5
Höxter	D	51	B5
Hoya	D	43	C6
Hoya de Santa Maria	E	99	B4
Hoya-Gonzalo	E	95	D5
Høyanger	N	2	F17
Hoyerswerda	D	53	B4
Høyjord	N	34	B2
Hoylake	GB	26	B2
Hoym	D	52	B1
Hoyo de Manzanares	E	94	B3
Hoyo de Pinares	E	94	B2
Hoyocasero	E	94	B2
Hoyos	E	93	A4
Hoyos del Espino	E	93	A5
Hrabusiče	SK	65	B6
Hradec Králové	CZ	53	C5
Hradec nad Moravicí	CZ	64	A3
Hrádek	CZ	64	B2
Hrádek nad Nisou	CZ	53	C4
Hradište	SK	65	B4
Hrafnagil	IS	111	B7
Hrafnseyri	IS	111	B2
Hranice, *Severomoravský*	CZ	64	A3
Hranice, *Západočeský*	CZ	52	C2
Hranovnica	SK	65	B6
Hrasnica	BIH	84	C3
Hrastnik	SLO	73	B5
Hrebenka	UA	11	A12
Hřensko	CZ	53	C4
Hriňová	SK	65	B5
Hrochov	CZ	64	A2
Hrochův Tynec	CZ	53	D5
Hrodna	BY	6	E7
Hrodzyanka	BY	7	E10
Hronov	CZ	53	C6
Hronský Beňadik	SK	65	B4
Hrotovice	CZ	64	A2
Hrtkovci	YU	85	B4
Hrun	IS	111	A5
Hrušov	SK	65	B5
Hrušovany nad Jevišovkou	CZ	64	B2
Hřuštin	SK	65	A5
Hrvaćani	BIH	84	B2
Hrvace	HR	83	C5
Hrymayliv	UA	11	B9
Huben	A	72	B2
Hückel-hoven	D	50	B2
Hückeswagen	D	50	B3
Hucknall	GB	27	B4
Hucqueliers	F	48	C2
Huddersfield	GB	27	B4
Huddinge	S	36	B4
Huddunge	S	36	A3
Hude	D	43	B5
Hudiksvall	S	2	F22
Huélago	E	100	B2
Huélamo	E	95	B5
Huelgoat	F	56	B2
Huelma	E	100	B2
Huelva	E	99	B4
Huéneja	E	100	B3
Huércal de Almeria	E	101	C3
Huércal-Overa	E	101	B4
Huerta de Abajo	E	89	B3
Huerta de Valdecarabanos	E	95	C3
Huerta del Rey	E	89	C3
Huertahernando	E	95	B4
Huesa	E	100	B2
Huesca	E	90	A2
Huéscar	E	101	B3
Huete	E	95	B4
Huétor Tájar	E	100	B1
Hüfingen	D	61	C4
Hufthamar	N	32	A2
Hugh Town	GB	28	D1
Huglfing	D	62	C2
Huissen	NL	50	B1
Huittinen	FIN	3	F25
Huizen	NL	49	A6
Hulín	CZ	64	A3
Hüls	D	50	B2
Hulsig	DK	38	B3
Hulst	NL	49	B5
Hult	S	40	B5
Hulterstad	S	41	C6
Hultsfred	S	40	B5
Humanes	E	95	B3
Humberston	GB	27	B5
Humble	DK	39	E3
Humenné	SK	10	B6
Humilladero	E	100	B1
Humlebæk	DK	41	D2
Humlum	DK	38	C1
Hummelsta	S	36	B3
Humpolec	CZ	63	A6
Humshaugh	GB	25	C5
Hundested	DK	39	D5
Hundvåg	N	32	B2
Hunedoara	RO	11	D7
Hünfeld	D	51	C5
Hungen	D	51	C4
Hungerford	GB	31	C2
Hunnebostrand	S	35	C3
Hunstanton	GB	30	B4
Huntingdon	GB	30	B3
Huntley	GB	29	B5
Huntly	GB	23	D6
Hünxe	D	50	B2
Hurbanovo	SK	64	C4
Hürbel	D	61	B5
Hurdal	N	34	A3
Hurezani	RO	11	D7
Hurlford	GB	24	C3
Hurstbourne Tarrant	GB	31	C2
Hurstpierpoint	GB	31	D3
Hürth	D	50	C2
Hurup	DK	38	C1
Húsafell	IS	111	C5
Húsavík	IS	111	A8
Husbands Bosworth	GB	30	B2
Husby	D	39	E2
Husby	DK	39	C1
Husey	IS	111	B11
Huşi	RO	11	C10
Husina	BIH	84	B3
Husinec	CZ	63	A4
Husinish	GB	22	D1
Huskvarna	S	40	B4
Husnes	N	32	B2
Hüsten	D	50	B3
Hustopeče	CZ	64	B2
Hustopeče nad Bečvou	CZ	64	A3
Husum	D	43	A6
Huta	PL	46	C2
Hutovo	BIH	84	D2
Hüttenberg	A	73	B4
Hüttlingen	D	61	B6
Huttoft	GB	27	B6
Hutton Cranswick	GB	27	B5
Hüttschlag	A	72	A3
Huttwil	CH	70	A2
Huy	B	49	C6
Hval	N	34	A2
Hvåle	N	33	A6
Hvaler	N	35	B3
Hvalpsund	DK	38	C2
Hvammstangi	IS	111	B5
Hvammur	IS	111	B6
Hvanneyri	IS	111	C4
Hvar	HR	83	C5
Hvarnes	N	33	B6
Hveragerði	IS	111	D4
Hvidbjerg	DK	38	C1
Hvide Sande	DK	39	D1
Hvittingfoss	N	34	B2
Hvolsvöllur	IS	111	D5
Hybe	SK	65	A5
Hycklinge	S	40	B5
Hyères	F	79	C5
Hyères Plage	F	79	C5
Hylestad	N	33	B4
Hylke	DK	39	D2
Hyllstofta	S	41	C3
Hyltebruk	S	40	B3
Hynish	GB	24	B1
Hynnekleiv	N	33	C5
Hythe, *Hampshire*	GB	31	D2
Hythe, *Kent*	GB	31	C5
Hyvinkää	FIN	3	F26

I

Iam	RO	85	A6
Iaşi	RO	11	C9
Íasmos	GR	112	A7
Ibahernando	E	93	B5
Ibarranguelua	E	89	A4
Ibbenbüren	D	50	A3
Ibeas de Juarros	E	89	B3
Ibi	E	96	C2
Ibiza = Eivissa	E	97	C1
İbriktepe	TR	114	A1
Ibros	E	100	A2
Ibstock	GB	27	C4
İçel	TR	16	C7
Ichenhausen	D	61	B6
Ichnya	UA	11	A12
Ichtegem	B	49	B4
Ichtershausen	D	51	C6
Idanha-a-Novo	P	93	B3
Idar-Oberstein	D	60	A3
Idd	N	35	B3
Ídhra	GR	113	E5
Idiazábal	E	89	B4
Idkerberget	S	36	A2
Idön	S	36	A5
Idre	S	2	F20
Idrija	SLO	73	C4
Idritsa	RUS	7	C10
Idstein	D	50	C4
Idvor	YU	75	C5
Iecca Mare	RO	75	C5
Ielsi	I	103	B7
Ieper = Ypres	B	48	C3
Ierápetra	GR	113	G7
Ierissós	GR	112	B5
Iesi	I	82	C2
Ig	SLO	73	C4
Igal	H	74	B2
Igea	E	89	B4
Igea Marina	I	82	B1
Igelfors	S	37	C2
Igersheim	D	61	A5
Iggesund	S	2	F22
Iglesias	E	88	B3
Iglésias	I	110	C1
Igls	A	71	A6
Iğneada	TR	114	A2
Igny-Comblizy	F	59	A4
Igorre	E	89	A4
Igoumenítsa	GR	112	C2
Igries	E	90	A2
Igualada	E	91	B4
Igüeña	E	86	B4
Iguerande	F	68	B4
Iharosberény	H	74	B2
Ihl'any	SK	65	A6
Ihlienworth	D	43	B5
Ihringen	D	60	B3
Ihrlerstein	D	62	B2
İhsaniye	TR	114	C5
Ii	FIN	3	D26
Iisalmi	FIN	3	E27
IJmuiden	NL	42	C1
IJsselmuiden	NL	42	C2
IJzendijke	NL	49	B4
Ikast	DK	39	C2
Ikervár	H	74	A1
il Castagno	I	81	C4
Ilandža	YU	75	C5
Ilanz	CH	71	B4
Ilava	SK	64	B4
Iława	PL	47	B5
Ilche	E	90	B3
Ilchester	GB	29	C5
Ilfracombe	GB	28	B3
Ilgaz	TR	16	A6
Ilgın	TR	16	B5
Ílhavo	P	92	A2
Ilica	TR	114	C2
Ilidža	BIH	84	C3
Ilijaš	BIH	84	C3
Ilirska Bistrica	SLO	73	C4
Ilkeston	GB	27	C4
Ilkley	GB	27	B4
Illana	E	95	B4
Illano	E	86	A4
Illar	E	101	C3
Illas	E	88	A1
Illats	F	76	B2
Ille-sur-Têt	F	91	A5
Illertissen	D	61	B6
Illescas	E	94	B3
Illfurth	F	60	C3
Illichivsk	UA	11	C11
Illiers-Combray	F	58	B2
Illkirch-Graffenstaden	F	60	B3
Illmersdorf	D	52	B3
Illmitz	A	64	C2
Íllora	E	100	B2
Illueca	E	89	C5
Ilmajoki	FIN	3	E25
Ilmenau	D	51	C6
Ilminster	GB	29	C5
Ilok	HR	75	C4
Ilomantsi	FIN	3	E29
Iłow	PL	47	C6
Iłowa	PL	53	B5
Iłowo-Osada	PL	47	B6
Ilsenburg	D	51	B6
Ilshofen	D	61	A5
Ilz	A	73	A5
Iłża	PL	55	B6
İmamoğlu	TR	16	C7
Imatra	FIN	3	F28
Imielin	PL	55	C4
Imingen	N	33	A5
Immeln	S	41	C4
Immenhausen	D	51	B5
Immenstadt	D	61	C6
Immingham	GB	27	B5
Ímola	I	81	B5
Imon	E	95	A4
Imotski	HR	84	C2
Impéria	I	80	C2
Imphy	F	68	B3
İmroz	TR	112	B7
Imsland	N	32	B2
Imst	A	71	A5
Inagh	IRL	20	B2
Inari	FIN	3	B27
Inca	E	97	B2
Inchnadamph	GB	22	C4
Incinillas	E	89	B3
Indjija	YU	85	A5
İnebolu	TR	16	A6
İnecik	TR	114	B2
İnegöl	TR	114	B4
Inerthal	CH	70	A3
Infiesto	E	88	A1
Ingatorp	S	40	B5
Ingedal	N	34	B3
Ingelheim	D	50	D4
Ingelmunster	B	49	C4
Ingelstad	S	40	C4
Ingleton	GB	26	A3
Ingolfsland	N	33	B5
Ingolstadt	D	62	B2
Ingrandes, *Maine-et-Loire*	F	66	A4
Ingrandes, *Vienne*	F	67	B5
Ingwiller	F	60	B3
Inhisar	TR	114	B5
Inhulec	UA	11	C12
Iniesta	E	95	C5
Inishannon	IRL	20	C3
Inishcrone	IRL	18	B2
Inke	H	74	B2
Innellan	GB	24	C3
Innerleithen	GB	25	C4
Innermessan	GB	24	D3
Innertkirchen	CH	70	B3
Innervillgraten	A	72	B2
Innsbruck	A	71	A6
İnönü	TR	114	C5
Inowłódz	PL	55	B5
Inowrocław	PL	47	C4
Ins	CH	70	A2
Insch	GB	23	D6
Ińsko	PL	46	B1
Instow	GB	28	B3
İntepe	TR	114	B1
Interlaken	CH	70	B2
Intragna	CH	70	B3
Introbio	I	71	C4
Inverallochy	GB	23	D7
Inveran	GB	23	D4
Inveran	IRL	20	A2
Inveraray	GB	24	B2
Inverbervie	GB	25	B5
Invergarry	GB	22	D4
Invergordon	GB	23	D4
Invergowrie	GB	25	B4
Inverkeilor	GB	25	B5
Inverkeithing	GB	25	B4
Invermoriston	GB	22	D4
Inverness	GB	23	D4
Inveruno	I	70	C3
Inverurie	GB	23	D6
Ioánnina	GR	112	C2
Iolanda di Savoia	I	81	B5
Ion Corvin	RO	11	D9
Ióppolo	I	106	C2
Íos	GR	113	F7
Ipáti	GR	112	D4
İpsala	TR	114	B1
Ipswich	GB	30	B5
Iráklia	GR	112	A5
Iráklion = Heraklion	GR	113	G7
Irdning	A	73	A4
Iregszemcse	H	74	B3
Irgoli	I	110	B2
Irig	YU	85	A4
Ironbridge	GB	26	C3
Irpin	UA	11	A11
Irrel	D	60	A2
Irsina	I	104	C2
Irthlingborough	GB	30	B3
Iruela	E	87	B4
Irún	E	76	C1
Irurita	E	76	C1
Irurzun	E	76	D1
Irvine	GB	24	C3
Irvinestown	GB	19	B4
Is-sur-Tille	F	69	A5
Isaba	E	76	D2
Isabela	E	100	A2
Ísafjörður	IS	111	A2
Isaszeg	H	75	A4
Isbister	GB	22	A7
Íscar	E	88	C2
İscehisar	TR	114	C5
Ischgl	A	71	A5
Íschia	I	103	C6
Ischia di Castro	I	102	A4
Ischitella	I	104	B1
Isdes	F	58	C3
Ise	N	34	B3
Iselle	I	70	B3
Iseltwald	CH	70	B2
Isen	D	62	B3
Isenbüttel	D	44	C2
Iseo	I	71	C5
Iserlohn	D	50	B3
Isérnia	I	103	B7
Isigny-sur-Mer	F	57	A4
Ísili	I	110	C2
Iskilip	TR	16	A7
Isla Canela	E	98	B3
Isla Cristina	E	98	B3
Islares	E	89	A3
Isle Of Whithorn	GB	24	D3
Isleham	GB	30	B4
Ismaning	D	62	B2
Isna	P	92	B3
Isny	D	61	C6
Isoba	E	88	A1
Isola	F	79	B6
Isola del Gran Sasso d'Itália	I	103	A6
Ísola del Liri	I	103	B6
Ísola della Scala	I	71	C6
Isola delle Fémmine	I	108	A2
Ísola di Capo Rizzuto	I	107	C4
Isona	E	91	A4
Ispagnac	F	78	B2
Isparta	TR	16	C5
Isperikh	BG	11	E9
Íspica	I	109	C3
Isselburg	D	50	B2
Issigeac	F	77	B3
Issogne	I	70	C2
Issoire	F	68	C3
Issoncourt	F	59	B6
Issoudun	F	68	B2
Issum	D	50	B2
Issy-l'Evêque	F	68	B3
Istán	E	100	C1
İstanbul	TR	114	A3
Istebna	PL	65	A4
Ístia d'Ombrone	I	81	D5
Istiaía	GR	112	D5
Istok	YU	85	D5
Istres, *Bouches du Rhône*	F	78	C3
Istvándi	H	74	B2
Itéa	GR	112	D4
Itháki	GR	112	D2
Itoiz	E	76	D1
Ítrabo	E	100	C2
Itri	I	103	B6
Ittireddu	I	110	B1
Íttiri	I	110	B1
Itzehoe	D	43	B6
Ivalo	FIN	3	B27
Iván	H	74	A1
Ivanava	BY	7	E8
Ivančice	CZ	64	A2
Ivančna Gorica	SLO	73	C4
Iváncsa	H	74	A3
Ivanec	HR	73	B6
Ivanić Grad	HR	73	C6
Ivanjica	YU	85	C5
Ivanjska	BIH	84	B2
Ivanka	SK	64	B4
Ivankovo	HR	74	C3
Ivano-Frankivsk	UA	11	B8
Ivanovice na Hané	CZ	64	A3
Ivanska	HR	74	C1
Ivatsevichy	BY	7	E8
Ivaylovgrad	BG	112	A8
Ivoz Ramet	B	49	C6
Ivrea	I	70	C2
Ivrindi	TR	114	C2
Ivry-en-Montagne	F	69	A4
Ivry-la-Bataille	F	58	B2
Ivybridge	GB	28	C4
Iwaniska	PL	55	C6
Iwiny	PL	53	B5
Iwuy	F	49	C4
Ixworth	GB	30	B4
Izarra	E	89	B4
Izbica Kujawska	PL	47	C4
Izbište	YU	85	A6
Izeda	P	87	C4
Izegem	B	49	C4
Izernore	F	69	B5
Izmayil	UA	11	D10
İzmir	TR	16	B3
İzmit = Kocaeli	TR	114	B4
Iznájar	E	100	B1
Iznalloz	E	100	B2
Iznatoraf	E	100	A2
İznik	TR	114	B4
Izola	SLO	72	C3
Izsák	H	75	B4
Izsófalva	H	65	B6
Izyaslav	UA	11	A9

J

Jabalquinto	E	100	A2
Jablanac	HR	83	B3
Jablanica	BIH	84	C2
Jablonec nad Jizerou	CZ	53	C5
Jablonec nad Nisou	CZ	53	C5
Jablonica	SK	64	B3
Jablonka	PL	65	A5
Jabłonna	PL	55	A5
Jablonné nad Orlicí	CZ	54	C1
Jablonne Podještědí	CZ	53	C4
Jablonov nad Turňou	SK	65	B6
Jabłonowo Pomorskie	PL	47	B5
Jablůnka	CZ	64	A3
Jablunkov	CZ	65	A4
Jabučje	YU	85	B5
Jabugo	E	99	B4
Jabuka, *Srbija*	YU	85	C4
Jabuka, *Vojvodina*	YU	85	B5
Jabukovac	HR	73	C6
Jaca	E	90	A2
Jáchymov	CZ	52	C2
Jacobidrebber	D	43	C5
Jade	D	43	B5
Jadraque	E	95	B4
Jægerspris	DK	39	D4
Jaén	E	100	B2
Jagare	BIH	84	B2
Jagel	D	43	A6
Jagenbach	A	63	B6
Jagodina	YU	85	C6
Jagodnjak	HR	74	C3
Jagodzin	PL	53	B5
Jagstheim	D	61	A6
Jagstzell	D	61	A6
Jahodna	SK	64	B3
Jajce	BIH	84	B2
Ják	H	74	A1
Jakabszálbs	H	75	B4
Jaklovce	SK	65	B6
Jakovlje	HR	73	C5
Jakšic	HR	74	C2
Jakubany	SK	65	A6
Jalance	E	96	B1
Jalasjärvi	FIN	3	E25
Jalhay	B	50	C1
Jaligny-sur-Besbre	F	68	B3
Jallais	F	66	A4
Jalón	E	96	C2
Jâlons	F	59	B5
Jamena	YU	84	B4
Jamilena	E	100	B2
Jämjö	S	41	C5
Jamnička Kiselica	HR	73	C5
Jamno	PL	46	A2
Jamoigne	B	59	A6
Jämsä	FIN	3	F26
Jämshög	S	41	C4
Janakkala	FIN	3	F26
Jandelsbrunn	D	63	B4
Jänickendorf	D	52	A3
Janikowo	PL	47	C4
Janja	BIH	85	B4
Janjina	HR	84	D2
Janki, *Łódzkie*	PL	55	B4
Janki, *Mazowieckie*	PL	55	A5
Jankov	CZ	63	A5
Jankowo Dolne	PL	46	C3
Jánoshalma	H	75	B4
Jánosháza	H	74	A2
Jánoshida	H	75	A5
Jánossomorja	H	64	C3
Janovice nad Uhlavou	CZ	63	A4
Janów	PL	55	C4
Janowiec Wielkopolski	PL	46	C3
Janowo	PL	47	B6
Janville	F	58	B2
Janzé	F	57	C4
Jarabá	SK	65	B5
Jaraczewo	PL	54	B2
Jarafuel	E	96	B1
Jaraicejo	E	93	B5
Jaraíz de la Vera	E	93	A5
Jarak	YU	85	B4
Jarandilla de la Vera	E	93	A5
Jaray	E	89	C4
Jard-sur-Mer	F	66	B3
Jaren	N	34	A2
Jargeau	F	58	C3
Jarkovac	YU	75	C5
Järlåsa	S	36	B4
Jarmen	D	45	B5
Järna	S	37	B4
Jarnac	F	67	C4
Järnforsen	S	40	B5
Jarny	F	60	A1
Jarocin	PL	54	B2
Jaroměř	CZ	53	C5
Jaroměřice nad Rokytnou	CZ	64	A1
Jaroslav	CZ	53	C6
Jaroslavice	CZ	64	B2
Jarosław	PL	11	A7
Jaroslawiec	PL	46	A2
Jarošov nad Nežarkou	CZ	63	A6
Järpås	S	35	C4
Järpen	S	2	E20
Jarrow	GB	25	D6
Järvenpää	FIN	7	A8
Jarvornik	CZ	54	C1
Jarzé	F	67	A4
Jaša Tomic	YU	75	C5
Jasenak	HR	73	C5
Jasenica	BIH	83	B5
Jasenice	HR	83	B4
Jasenovac	HR	74	C1
Jasenovo, *Srbija*	YU	85	C4
Jasenovo, *Vojvodina*	YU	85	B6
Jasień	PL	53	B5
Jasienica	PL	53	B4
Jasika	YU	85	C6
Jasło	PL	10	B6
Jásova	SK	65	C4
Jasseron	F	69	B5
Jastarnia	PL	47	A4
Jastrebarsko	HR	73	C5
Jastrowie	PL	46	B2
Jastrzębia-Góra	PL	47	A4
Jastrzębie Zdrój	PL	54	D3
Jászals-Lószentgyörgy	H	75	A5
Jászapáti	H	75	A5
Jászárokszállás	H	65	C5
Jászberény	H	75	A4
Jászdózsa	H	65	C6
Jászfényszaru	H	75	A4
Jászjákóhalma	H	75	A5
Jászkarajenő	H	75	A5
Jászkisér	H	75	A5
Jászladány	H	75	A5
Jászszentlászló	H	75	B4
Jásztelek	H	75	A5
Játar	E	100	C2
Jatznick	D	45	B5
Jaun	CH	70	B2
Jausiers	F	79	B5
Jávea	E	96	C3
Jävenitz	D	44	C3
Javerlhac	F	67	C5
Javier	E	90	A1
Javorani	BIH	84	B2
Javorina	SK	65	A6
Javron	F	57	B5
Jawor	PL	53	B6
Jaworzno	PL	55	C4
Jaworzyna Śl.	PL	54	C1
Jayena	E	100	C2
Jażow	PL	53	B4
Jebel	RO	75	C6
Jebjerg	DK	38	C2
Jedburgh	GB	25	C5
Jedlinsk	PL	55	B6
Jedlnia	PL	55	B6
Jedlnia Letnisko	PL	55	B6
Jedovnice	CZ	64	A2
Jędrychow	PL	47	B5
Jędrzejów	PL	55	C5
Jedwabno	PL	47	B6
Jegłownik	PL	47	A5
Jegun	F	77	C3
Jēkabpils	LV	7	C8
Jektevik	N	32	B2
Jelakci	YU	85	C5
Jelcz-Laskowice	PL	54	B2
Jelenec	SK	64	B4
Jelenia Góra	PL	53	C5
Jelgava	LV	6	C7
Jelka	SK	64	B3
Jelling	DK	39	D2
Jels	DK	39	D2
Jelsa	HR	83	C5
Jelsa	N	32	B3
Jelšava	SK	65	B6
Jemgum	D	43	B4
Jemnice	CZ	63	A6
Jena	D	52	C1
Jenaz	CH	71	B4
Jenbach	A	72	A1
Jenikow	PL	45	B7
Jennersdorf	A	73	B6
Jenny	S	40	B6
Jerchel	D	44	C3
Jeres del Marquesado	E	100	B2
Jerez de la Frontera	E	99	C4
Jerez de los Caballeros	E	99	A4
Jerica	E	96	B2
Jerichow	D	44	C4
Jerka	PL	54	A1
Jermenovci	YU	75	C6
Jerslev	DK	38	B3
Jerte	E	93	A5
Jerup	DK	38	B3
Jerxheim	D	51	A6
Jerzmanowice	PL	55	C4
Jerzu	I	110	C2
Jerzwałd	PL	47	B5
Jesberg	D	51	C5
Jesenice, *Středočeský*	CZ	52	C3
Jesenice, *Středočeský*	CZ	53	D4
Jesenice	SLO	73	B4
Jeseník	CZ	54	C2
Jesenké	SK	65	B6
Jésolo	I	72	C2
Jessen	D	52	B2
Jessheim	N	34	A3
Jessnitz	D	52	B2
Jesteburg	D	44	B1
Jeumont	F	49	C5
Jeven-stedt	D	43	A6
Jever	D	43	B4
Jevíčko	CZ	64	A2
Jevišovice	CZ	64	B1
Jevnaker	N	34	A2
Jezerane	HR	83	A4
Jezero	BIH	84	B2
Jezero	HR	83	A4
Jeziorany	PL	47	B6
Jezów	PL	55	B4
Jičín	CZ	53	C5
Jičíněves	CZ	53	C5
Jihlava	CZ	63	A6
Jijona	E	96	C2
Jilemnice	CZ	53	C5
Jílové	CZ	53	C4
Jílové u Prahy	CZ	63	A5
Jimbolia	RO	75	C5
Jimena	E	100	B2
Jimena de la Frontera	E	99	C5
Jimera de Libar	E	99	C5
Jimramov	CZ	64	A2
Jince	CZ	63	A4
Jindřichovice	CZ	52	C2
Jindřichův Hradec	CZ	63	A6
Jirkov	CZ	52	C3
Jistebnice	CZ	63	A5
Joachimsthal	D	45	C5
João da Loura	P	92	C2
Jobbágyi	H	65	C5
Jochberg	A	72	A2
Jódar	E	100	B2
Jodoigne	B	49	C5
Joensuu	FIN	3	E28
Jœuf	F	60	A1
Jõgeva	EST	7	B9
Johann-georgen-stadt	D	52	C2
Johannishus	S	41	C5
Johanniskirchen	D	62	B3
Johansfors	S	40	C5
John o'Groats	GB	23	C5
Johnshaven	GB	25	B5
Johnstone	GB	24	C3
Johnstown	IRL	21	B4
Jõhvi	EST	7	B9
Joigny	F	59	C4
Joinville	F	59	B6
Jokkmokk	S	3	C23
Jöllenbeck	D	51	A4
Jönåker	S	37	C3
Jonava	LT	6	D8
Jonchery-sur-Vesle	F	59	A4
Jondal	N	32	A3
Jondalen	N	33	B6
Joniškis	LT	6	C7
Jönköping	S	40	B4
Jønnbu	N	33	B6
Jonsered	S	38	B5
Jonstorp	S	41	C2
Jonzac	F	67	C4
Jorba	E	91	B4
Jordanów	PL	65	A5
Jordanów Śląski	PL	54	C1
Jordanowo	PL	46	C1
Jordbro	S	36	B5
Jördenstorf	D	45	B4
Jordøse	DK	39	D3
Jork	D	43	B6
Jörn	S	3	D24

Jørpeland N 32 B3
Jorquera E 96 B1
Jošan HR 83 B4
Jošanička Banja YU 85 C5
Jošavka BIH 84 B2
Josipdol HR 73 C5
Josipovac HR 74 C3
Jössefors S 34 B4
Josselin F 56 C3
Jósvafő H 65 B6
Jouarre F 59 B4
Joué-lès-Tours F 67 A5
Joué-sur-Erdre F 66 A3
Joure NL 42 C2
Joutseno FIN 3 F28
Joux-la-Ville F 59 C4
Jouy F 58 B2
Jouy-le-Châtel F 59 B4
Jouy-le-Potier F 58 C2
Joyeuse F 78 B3
Joze F 68 C3
Józefów PL 55 A6
Juan-les-Pins F 79 C6
Juankoski FIN 3 E28
Jübek D 43 A6
Jubera E 89 B4
Jubrique E 99 C5
Jüchsen D 51 C6
Judaberg N 32 B2
Judenburg A 73 A4
Juelsminde DK 39 D3
Jugon-les-Lacs F 56 B3
Juillac F 67 C6
Juillan F 76 C3
Juist D 43 B4
Julianadorp NL 42 C1
Julianstown IRL 19 C5
Jülich D 50 C2
Jullouville F 57 B4
Jumeaux F 68 C3
Jumièges F 58 A1
Jumilhac-le-Grand F 67 C6
Jumilla E 101 A4
Juncosa E 90 B3
Juneda E 90 B3
Jung S 35 C5
Jungingen D 61 B5
Junglingster L 60 A2
Juniville F 59 A5
Junosuando S 3 C25
Junqueira P 87 C3
Juprelle B 49 C6
Jurata PL 47 A4
Jurbarkas LT 6 D7
Jurjevo HR 83 B3
Jūrmala LV 6 C7
Juromenha P 93 C3
Jursla S 37 C3
Jussac F 77 B5
Jussey F 60 C1
Jussy F 59 A4
Juta H 74 B2
Jüterbog D 52 B3
Juuka FIN 3 E28
Juvigny-le-Terte F 57 B4
Juvigny-sous-Andaine F 57 B5
Juzennecourt F 59 B5
Jyderup DK 39 D4
Jyväskylä FIN 3 E26

K

Kaamanen FIN 3 B27
Kaarssen D 44 B3
Kaatscheuvel NL 49 B6
Kaba H 75 A6
Kåbdalis S 3 C23
Kačarevo YU 85 B5
Kačikol YU 85 D6
Kács H 65 C6
Kadan CZ 52 C3
Kadarkút H 74 B2
Kadınhanı TR 16 B6
Kaduy RUS 7 B14
Kågeröd S 41 D3
Kahl D 51 C5
Kahla D 52 C1
Kainach bei Voitsberg A 73 A5
Kaindorf A 73 A5
Kaisersesch D 50 C3
Kaiserslautern D 60 A3
Kaisheim D 62 B1
Kajaani FIN 3 D27
Kajárpéc H 74 A2
Kajdacs H 74 B3
Kakanj BIH 84 B3
Kakasd H 74 B3
Kakolewo PL 54 B1
Kál H 65 C6
Kalabáka GR 112 C3
Kalače YU 85 D5
Kalajoki FIN 3 D25
Kalámai = Kalamata GR 113 E4
Kalamariá GR 112 B4
Kalamata = Kalámai GR 113 E4
Kalándra GR 112 C5
Kalávrita GR 113 D4
Kalbe D 44 C3
Kalce SLO 73 C4
Káld H 74 A2
Kale TR 16 C4
Kalecik TR 16 A6
Kalefeld D 51 B6
Kalenić YU 85 C5
Kalesija BIH 84 B3
Kalety PL 54 C3
Kalevala RUS 3 D29
Kalhovd N 33 A5
Kali HR 83 B4
Kaliningrad RUS 47 A6
Kalinkavichy BY 7 E10
Kalinovac HR 74 B2
Kalinovik BIH 84 C3
Kalinovo SK 65 B5
Kalirrákhi GR 112 B6
Kaliska, *Pomorskie* PL 47 A4
Kaliska, *Pomorskie* PL 47 B4
Kalisko PL 55 B4
Kalisz PL 54 B3
Kalisz Pomorski PL 46 B1
Kalix S 3 D25
Kalkan TR 16 C4
Kalkar D 50 B2
Kalkım TR 114 C2
Kall D 50 C2
Källby S 35 C5
Kållered S 38 B5
Kållerstad S 40 B3
Kallinge S 41 C5
Kallmünz D 62 A2
Kalloní GR 112 C8
Källvik S 37 C4
Kalmar S 40 C6
Kalmthout B 49 B5
Kalná SK 65 B4
Kaló Neró GR 113 E3
Kalocsa H 75 B3
Káloz H 74 B3
Kals A 72 A2
Kalsdorf A 73 B5
Kaltbrunn CH 70 A4
Kaltenbach A 72 A1
Kaltenkirchen D 44 B1
Kaltennordheim D 51 C6
Kaluga RUS 7 D14
Kalundborg DK 39 D4
Kalush UA 11 B8
Kałuszyn PL 55 A6
Kalvehave DK 41 D2
Kalwang A 73 A4
Kalwaria-Zebrzydowska PL 65 A5
Kalyazin RUS 7 C14
Kam H 74 A1
Kaman TR 16 B6
Kamárai GR 113 F6
Kamen D 50 B3
Kamenice CZ 64 A1
Kamenice nad Lipou CZ 63 A6
Kameničná SK 64 C4
Kamenný Most SK 65 C4
Kamenny Ujezd CZ 63 B5
Kamenska HR 74 C2
Kamensko HR 84 C1
Kamenz D 53 B4
Kamičak BIH 84 B1
Kamień PL 55 B5
Kamień Krajeński PL 46 B3
Kamień Pomorski PL 45 B6
Kamieniec Zabk PL 54 C1
Kamienka SK 65 A6
Kamienna Góra PL 53 C6
Kamieńsk PL 55 B4
Kaminka UA 11 B12
Kamnik SLO 73 B4
Kamp-Lintfort D 50 B2
Kampen NL 42 C2
Kampinos PL 55 A5
Kampor HR 83 B3
Kamyanets-Podil's'kyy UA 11 B9
Kamyanka-Buz'ka UA 11 A8
Kamýk n Vltavou CZ 63 A5
Kanal SLO 72 B3
Kanália GR 112 C4
Kandalaksha RUS 3 C30
Kandanos GR 113 G5
Kandel D 61 A4
Kandern D 60 C3
Kandersteg CH 70 B2
Kandhila GR 113 E4
Kandıra TR 114 A5
Kandyty PL 47 A6
Kanfanar HR 82 A2
Kangasala FIN 3 F26
Kaniów PL 53 B4
Kanjiža YU 75 B5
Kankaanpää FIN 3 F25
Kannus FIN 3 E25
Kanturk IRL 20 B3
Kapaklı TR 114 A2
Kapellen A 63 C6
Kapellen B 49 B5
Kapellskär S 36 B6
Kapfenberg A 73 A5
Kapfenstein A 73 B5
Kaplice CZ 63 B5
Kapljuh BIH 83 B5
Kápolna H 65 C6
Kápolnásnyék H 74 A3
Kaposfő H 74 B2
Kaposfüred H 74 B2
Kaposszekcső H 74 B3
Kaposvár H 74 B2
Kappel D 60 B3
Kappeln D 44 A1
Kappelshamn S 37 D5
Kappl A 71 A5
Kaprun A 72 A2
Kaptol HR 74 C2
Kapuvár H 64 C3
Karabiğa TR 114 B2
Karabük TR 114 A7
Karaburun TR 16 B3
Karacabey TR 114 B3
Karacaköy TR 114 A3
Karacasu TR 16 C4
Karachev RUS 7 E13
Karácsond H 65 C6
Karád H 74 B2
Karaisali TR 16 C7
Karaman, *Balıkesir* TR 114 C3
Karaman, *Karaman* TR 16 C6
Karamürsel TR 114 B4
Karan YU 85 C4
Karancslapujto H 65 B5
Karapınar TR 16 C6
Karasjok N 3 B26
Karasu TR 114 A5
Karataş TR 16 C7
Karbenning S 36 A3
Kårberg S 37 C1
Karby D 44 A1
Karby DK 38 C1
Karby S 36 B5
Karcag H 75 A5
Karczew PL 55 A6
Karczów PL 54 C2
Karczowiska PL 53 B6
Kardašova Rečice CZ 63 A5
Kardhámila GR 112 D8
Kardhamili GR 113 F4
Kardhítsa GR 112 C3
Kärdla EST 6 B7
Kardoskút H 75 B5
Kargı TR 16 A7
Kargowa PL 53 A5
Karise DK 41 D2
Káristos GR 113 D6
Karkkila FIN 6 A8
Karl Liebknecht RUS 7 F13
Karlholmsbruk S 36 A4
Karlino PL 46 A1
Karlobag HR 83 B4
Karlovac HR 73 C5
Karlovčic YU 85 B5
Karlovice CZ 54 C2
Karlovo BG 11 E8
Karlovy Vary CZ 52 C2
Karłowice PL 54 C2
Karlsborg S 37 C1
Karlshamn S 41 C4
Karlshöfen D 43 B6
Karlshus N 34 B2
Karlskoga S 36 B1
Karlskrona S 41 C5
Karlsrud N 33 A5
Karlsruhe D 61 A4
Karlstad S 34 B5
Karlstadt D 51 D5
Karlstetten A 63 B6
Karlstift A 63 B5
Karmacs H 74 B2
Kärna S 38 B4
Karnobat BG 11 E9
Karojba HR 72 C3
Karow D 44 B4
Karpacz PL 53 C5
Karpenísion GR 112 D3
Kärrbo S 36 B3
Karrebaeksminde DK 39 D4
Karsin PL 46 B3
Kårsta S 36 B5
Karstädt D 44 B3
Kartal TR 114 B4
Kartitsch A 72 B2
Kartuzy PL 47 A4
Karup DK 39 C2
Karviná CZ 65 A4
Kås DK 38 B2
Kaş TR 16 C4
Kašava CZ 64 A3
Kasejovice CZ 63 A4
Kashin RUS 7 C14
Kašina HR 73 C6
Kasina-Wielka PL 65 A6
Kaskinen FIN 3 E24
Kašperské Hory CZ 63 A4
Kassándrinon GR 112 B5
Kassel D 51 B5
Kassiópi GR 112 C1
Kastamonu TR 16 A6
Kastav HR 73 C4
Kaštel-Stari HR 83 C5
Kaštel Zegarski HR 83 B4
Kastellaun D 50 C3
Kastéllion GR 113 G7
Kasterlee B 49 B5
Kastl D 62 A2
Kastlösa S 41 C6
Kastorf D 44 B2
Kastóri GR 113 E4
Kastoría GR 112 B3
Kastráki GR 113 F7
Kastrosikiá GR 112 C2
Kastsyukovichy BY 7 E12
Kaszaper H 75 B5
Katákolon GR 113 E3
Katápola GR 113 F7
Katastári GR 113 E2
Katerbow D 45 C4
Kateríni GR 112 B4
Katlenburg-Lindau D 51 B6
Káto Akhaïa GR 113 D3
Káto Stavros GR 112 B5
Katoúna GR 112 D3
Katovice CZ 63 A4
Katowice PL 55 C4
Katrineholm S 37 C3
Kattarp S 41 C2
Katthammarsvik S 37 D5
Kattilstorp S 35 C5
Katwijk NL 49 A5
Kąty Wrocławskie PL 54 B1
Katymár H 75 B4
Katzenelnbogen D 50 C3
Katzhütte D 52 C1
Kaub D 50 C3
Kaufbeuren D 62 C1
Kauhajoki FIN 3 E25
Kauhava FIN 3 E25
Kaulsdorf D 52 C1
Kaunas LT 6 D7
Kaupanger N 2 F17
Kautokeino N 3 B25
Kautzen A 63 B6
Kavadarci MK 112 A4
Kavajë AL 105 B5
Kavakköy TR 114 B1
Kavaklı TR 114 A2
Kavála GR 112 B6
Kavarna BG 11 E10
Kävlinge S 41 D3
Kawcze PL 46 A2
Kaxholmen S 40 B4
Kaymaz TR 114 C6
Kaynarca TR 114 A5
Kayseri TR 16 B7
Kaysersberg F 60 B3
Kazanlŭk BG 11 E8
Kazár H 65 B5
Kazimierza Wielka PL 55 C5
Kazincbarcika H 65 B6
Kaźmierz PL 46 C2
Kcynia PL 46 B3
Kdyně CZ 62 A4
Kéa GR 113 E6
Keadow IRL 18 B3
Keady GB 19 B5
Kecel H 75 B4
Kecskemét H 75 B4
Kėdainiai LT 6 D7
Kędzierzyn-Koźle PL 54 C3
Keel IRL 18 C1
Keenagh IRL 19 C4
Keerbergen B 49 B5
Kefken TR 114 A5
Keflavík IS 111 C3
Kegworth GB 27 C4
Kehl D 60 B3
Kehrigk D 53 A3
Keighley GB 27 B4
Keila EST 6 B8
Keillmore GB 24 C2
Keiss GB 23 C5
Keith GB 23 D6
Kelberg D 50 C2
Kelbra D 51 B7
Kelč CZ 64 A3
Kelchsau A 72 A2
Këlcyrë AL 112 B2
Keld GB 26 A3
Kelebia H 75 B4
Kelemér H 65 B6
Keles TR 114 C4
Kelheim D 62 B2
Kell D 60 A2
Kellas GB 23 D5
Kellinghusen D 43 B6
Kells GB 19 B5
Kells IRL 19 C5
Kelmis B 50 C2
Kelsall GB 26 B3
Kelso GB 25 C5
Kelsterbach D 51 C4
Keltneyburn GB 24 B3
Kematen A 71 A6
Kemberg D 52 B2
Kemer TR 16 C5
Kemerkaya TR 114 D6
Kemeten A 73 A6
Kemi FIN 3 D26
Kemijärvi FIN 3 C27
Kemnath D 62 A2
Kemnay GB 23 D6
Kemnitz, *Brandenburg* D 52 A2
Kemnitz, *Mecklenburg-Vorpommern* D 45 A5
Kempen D 50 B2
Kempsey GB 29 A5
Kempten D 61 C6
Kemptthal CH 70 A3
Kendal GB 26 A3
Kenderes H 75 A5
Kengyel H 75 A5
Kenilworth GB 30 B2
Kenmare IRL 20 C2
Kenmore GB 25 B4
Kennacraig GB 24 C2
Kenyeri H 74 A2
Kenzingen D 60 B3
Kepez TR 114 B1
Kępice PL 46 A2
Kępno PL 54 B3
Kepsut TR 114 C3
Keramoti GR 112 B6
Keratéa GR 113 E5
Kerava FIN 7 A8
Kerecsend H 65 C6
Kerekegyhaza H 75 B4
Kerepestarcsa H 75 A4
Keri GR 113 E2
Kérien F 56 B2
Kerkafalva H 74 B1
Kerken D 50 B2
Kérkira GR 112 C1
Kerkrade NL 50 C2
Kerlouan F 56 B1
Kernascléden F 56 B2
Kernhof A 63 C6
Kerns CH 70 B3
Kerpen D 50 C2
Kerrysdale GB 22 D3
Kerta H 74 A2
Kerteminde DK 39 D3
Kerzers CH 70 B2
Keşan TR 114 B1
Kesgrave GB 30 B5
Kesh GB 19 B4
Keskin TR 16 B6
Kesselfall A 72 A2
Kestenga RUS 3 D29
Keswick GB 26 A2
Keszthely H 74 B2
Kétegyháza H 75 B6
Kéthely H 74 B2
Kętrzyn PL 6 D6
Kettering GB 30 B3
Kettlewell GB 26 A3
Kęty PL 65 A5
Ketzin D 45 C4
Keuruu FIN 3 E26
Kevelaer D 50 B2
Kevermes H 75 B6
Kevi YU 75 C4
Keyingham GB 27 B5
Keynsham GB 29 B5
Kežmarok SK 65 A6
Khalkís GR 112 D5
Khandrá GR 113 G8
Kharmanli BG 11 F8
Khaskovo BG 11 F8
Khérson GR 112 A4
Kherson UA 11 C12
Khiliomódhion GR 113 E4
Khimki RUS 7 D14
Khíos GR 112 D8
Khisinev = Chişinău MD 11 C10
Khmelnik UA 11 B9
Khmelnytskyy UA 11 B9
Khodoriv UA 11 B8
Kholm RUS 7 C11
Khóra GR 113 E3
Khóra Sfakíon GR 113 G6
Khorol UA 11 B12
Khotyn UA 11 B9
Khoyniki BY 7 F10
Khrisoúpolis GR 112 B6
Khust UA 11 B7
Khvoynaya RUS 7 B13
Kiáton GR 113 D4
Kibæk DK 39 C1
Kicasalih TR 114 A1
Kičevo MK 112 A2
Kidderminster GB 26 C3
Kidlington GB 31 C2
Kidsgrove GB 26 B3
Kidwelly GB 28 B3
Kiefersfelden D 62 C3
Kiel D 44 A2
Kielce PL 55 C5
Kiełczygłów PL 55 B4
Kielder GB 25 C5
Kiełpino PL 47 A4
Kielpiny PL 47 B5
Kienzia PL 55 A4
Kierspe D 50 B3
Kietrz PL 54 C3
Kietz D 45 C6
Kiev = Kyyiv UA 11 A11
Kiezmark PL 47 A4
Kifino Selo BIH 84 C3
Kifisiá GR 113 D5
Kije PL 55 C5
Kijevo HR 83 C5
Kikinda YU 75 C5
Kil N 33 C6
Kil, *Örebro* S 36 B2
Kil, *Värmland* S 34 B5
Kila S 34 B4
Kilb Rabenstein A 63 B6
Kilbaha IRL 20 B2
Kilbeggan IRL 21 A4
Kilberry GB 24 C2
Kilbirnie GB 24 C3
Kilchattan GB 24 C2
Kilchoan GB 24 B1
Kilcock IRL 21 A5
Kilconnell IRL 20 A3
Kilcormac IRL 21 A4
Kilcreggan GB 24 C3
Kilcullen IRL 21 A5
Kilcurry IRL 19 B5
Kildare IRL 21 A5
Kildinstroy RUS 3 B30
Kildonan GB 23 C5
Kildorrery IRL 20 B3
Kilegrend N 33 B5
Kilen N 33 B5
Kilgarvan IRL 20 C2
Kiliya UA 11 D10
Kilkee IRL 20 B2
Kilkeel GB 19 B5
Kilkenny IRL 21 B4
Kilkieran IRL 20 A2
Kilkinlea IRL 20 B2
Kilkís GR 112 A4
Kill IRL 21 B4
Killadysert IRL 20 B2
Killala IRL 18 B2
Killaloe IRL 20 B3
Killarney IRL 20 B2
Killashandra IRL 19 B4
Killashee IRL 19 C4
Killearn GB 24 B3
Killeberg S 40 C4
Killeigh IRL 21 A4
Killenaule IRL 21 B4
Killimor IRL 20 A3
Killin GB 24 B3
Killinaboy IRL 20 B2
Killini GR 113 E3
Killinick IRL 21 B5
Killorglin IRL 20 B2
Killucan IRL 21 A4
Killybegs IRL 18 B3
Killyleagh GB 19 B6
Kilmacrenan IRL 19 A4
Kilmacthomas IRL 21 B4
Kilmaine IRL 18 C2
Kilmallock IRL 20 B3
Kilmarnock GB 24 C3
Kilmartin GB 24 B2
Kilmaurs GB 24 C3
Kilmeadan IRL 21 B4
Kilmeedy IRL 20 B3
Kilmelford GB 24 B2
Kilmore Quay IRL 21 B5
Kilmuir GB 23 D4
Kilnaleck IRL 19 C4
Kilninver GB 24 B2
Kilrea GB 19 B5
Kilrush IRL 20 B2
Kilsmo S 37 B2
Kilsyth GB 24 C3
Kiltoom IRL 20 A3
Kilwinning GB 24 C3
Kimasozero RUS 3 D29
Kími GR 112 D6
Kímolos GR 113 F6
Kimovsk RUS 7 D14
Kimratshofen D 61 C6
Kimry RUS 7 C14
Kimstad S 37 C2
Kinbrace GB 23 C5
Kincardine GB 25 B4
Kincraig GB 23 D5
Kindberg A 73 A5
Kindelbruck D 52 B1
Kingarrow IRL 18 B3
Kingisepp RUS 7 B10
King's Lynn GB 30 B4
Kingsbridge GB 28 C4
Kingsclere GB 31 C2
Kingscourt IRL 19 C5
Kingsteignton GB 29 C4
Kingston, *Greater London* GB 31 C3
Kingston, *Moray* GB 23 D5
Kingston Bagpuize GB 31 C2
Kingston upon Hull GB 27 B5
Kingswear GB 29 C4
Kingswood GB 29 B5
Kington GB 29 A4
Kingussie GB 23 D4
Kınık TR 114 C2
Kinloch, *Highland* GB 22 C4
Kinloch, *Highland* GB 22 D2
Kinloch Rannoch GB 24 B3
Kinlochbervie GB 22 C3
Kinlochewe GB 22 D3
Kinlochleven GB 24 B3
Kinlochmoidart GB 24 B2
Kinloss GB 23 D5
Kinlough IRL 18 B3
Kinna S 40 B2
Kinnared S 40 B3
Kinnarp S 35 C5
Kinne-Kleva S 35 C5
Kinnegad IRL 21 A4
Kinnitty IRL 21 A4
Kinrooi B 50 B1
Kinross GB 25 B4
Kinsale IRL 20 C3
Kintarvie GB 22 C2
Kintore GB 23 D6
Kinvarra IRL 20 A3
Kióni GR 112 D2
Kiparissía GR 113 E3
Kipfenburg D 62 B2
Kippen GB 24 B3
Kirazlı TR 114 B1
Kirberg D 50 C4
Kirchbach in Steiermark A 73 B5
Kirchberg CH 70 A2
Kirchberg, *Baden-Württemberg* D 61 A5
Kirchberg, *Rheinland-Pfalz* D 60 A3
Kirchberg am Wechsel A 64 C1
Kirchberg an der Pielach A 63 B6
Kirchberg im Tirol A 72 A2
Kirchbichl A 72 A2
Kirchdorf, *Bayern* D 63 B4
Kirchdorf, *Mecklenburg-Vorpommern* D 44 B3
Kirchdorf, *Niedersachsen* D 43 C5
Kirchdorf an der Krems A 63 C5
Kirchdorf in Tirol A 72 A2
Kirchenlamitz D 52 C1
Kirchenthumbach D 62 A2
Kirchhain D 51 C4
Kirchheim, *Baden-Württemberg* D 61 B5
Kirchheim, *Bayern* D 61 B6
Kirchheim, *Hessen* D 51 C5
Kirchheim-bolanden D 61 A4
Kirchhundem D 50 B4
Kirchlintein D 43 C6
Kirchschlag A 73 A6
Kirchweidach D 62 B3
Kirchzarten D 60 C3
Kircubbin GB 19 B6
Kireç TR 114 C3
Kırıkkale TR 16 B6
Kirillov RUS 7 B15
Kirishi RUS 7 B12
Kirk Michael GB 26 A1
Kırka TR 114 C5
Kırkağaç TR 114 C2
Kirkbean GB 25 D4
Kirkbride GB 25 D4
Kirkby GB 26 B3
Kirkby Lonsdale GB 26 A3
Kirkby Malzeard GB 27 A4
Kirkby Stephen GB 26 A3
Kirkbymoorside GB 27 A5
Kirkcaldy GB 25 B4
Kirkcolm GB 24 D2
Kirkconnel GB 24 C3
Kirkcowan GB 24 D3
Kirkcudbright GB 24 D3
Kirkehamn N 32 C3
Kirkelly IRL 18 C3
Kirkenær N 34 A4
Kirkenes N 3 B29
Kirkham GB 26 B3
Kirkintilloch GB 24 C3
Kirkjubæjarklaustur IS 111 D7
Kirkkonummi FIN 6 A8
Kırklareli TR 114 A2
Kirkmichael GB 25 B4
Kirkoswald GB 24 C3
Kirkpatrick Fleming GB 25 C4
Kirkton of Glenisla GB 25 B4
Kirkwall GB 23 C6
Kirkwhelpington GB 25 C6
Kirn D 60 A3
Kirov RUS 7 D13
Kirovohrad UA 11 B12
Kirovsk RUS 3 C30
Kirriemuir GB 25 B5
Kırşehir TR 16 B7
Kirton GB 30 B3
Kirton in Lindsey GB 27 B5
Kirtorf D 51 C5
Kiruna S 3 C24
Kisa S 37 D2
Kisač YU 75 C4
Kisbér H 74 A3
Kiseljak BIH 84 C3
Kisielice PL 47 B5
Kisköre H 75 A5
Kiskőrös H 75 B4
Kiskunfélegyháza H 75 B4
Kiskunhalas H 75 B4
Kiskunlacháza H 75 A3
Kiskunmajsa H 75 B4
Kisláng H 74 B3
Kíssamos GR 113 G5
Kisslegg D 61 C5
Kissolt H 75 B4
Kist D 61 A5
Kistanje HR 83 C4
Kistelek H 75 B4
Kisterenye H 65 B5
Kisújszállás H 75 A5
Kisvárda H 11 B7
Kisvejke H 74 B3
Kiszkowo PL 46 C3
Kiszombor H 75 B5
Kitee FIN 3 E29
Kithira GR 113 F4
Kíthnos GR 113 E6
Kittendorf D 45 B4
Kittilä FIN 3 C26
Kittsee A 64 B3
Kitzbühel A 72 A2
Kitzingen D 61 A6
Kiuruvesi FIN 3 E27
Kivertsi UA 11 A8
Kivik S 41 D4
Kivotós GR 112 B3
Kiwity PL 47 A6
Kıyıköy TR 114 A3
Kızılcahamam TR 16 A6
Kızılhisar TR 16 C4
Kızılırmak TR 16 A6
Kjellerup DK 39 C2
Kjøllefjord N 3 A27
Kjopmannskjaer N 34 B2
Kl'ačno SK 65 B4
Kladanj BIH 84 B3
Kläden D 44 C3
Klädesholmen S 38 B4
Kladnica YU 85 C5
Kladnice HR 83 C5
Kladno CZ 53 C4
Kladruby CZ 62 A3
Klagenfurt A 73 B4
Klågerup S 41 D3
Klagstorp S 41 D3
Klaipėda LT 6 D6
Klaistow D 52 A2
Klaksvík FO 2 E10
Klana HR 73 C4
Klanac HR 83 B4
Klanjec HR 73 B5
Klardorf D 62 A3
Klarup DK 38 B3
Klašnice BIH 84 B2
Klässbol S 34 B4
Klášterec nad Ohří CZ 52 C3
Klaštor pod Znievom SK 65 B4
Klatovy CZ 63 A4
Klaus an der Pyhrnbahn A 63 C5
Klazienaveen NL 42 C3
Kłecko PL 46 C3
Kleczew PL 47 C4
Klein Plasten D 45 B4
Klein Sankt Paul A 73 B4
Kleinsölk A 72 A3
Kleinzell A 64 C1
Klejtrup DK 38 C2
Klek YU 75 C5
Klemensker DK 41 D4
Klenak YU 85 B4
Klenci pod Cerchovem CZ 62 A3
Klenica PL 53 B5
Klenje YU 85 B4
Klenoec MK 112 A2
Klenovec SK 65 B5
Klenovica HR 83 A3
Klenovnik HR 73 B6
Kleppe N 32 C2
Kleptow D 45 B5
Kletnya RUS 7 E12
Kleve D 50 B2
Klevshult S 40 B4
Klewki PL 47 B6
Kličevac YU 85 B6
Kliening A 73 B4
Klietz D 44 C4
Klikuszowa PL 65 A5
Klimkovice CZ 64 A4
Klimontów PL 55 C6
Klimovichi BY 7 E11
Klin RUS 7 C14
Klinča Sela HR 73 C5
Klingenbach A 64 C2
Klingenberg D 61 A5
Klingenmunster D 61 A4
Klingenthal D 52 C2
Klintehamn S 37 D5
Klintsy RUS 7 E12
Kliny PL 55 B5
Klipley DK 39 E2
Klippan S 41 C3
Klis HR 83 C5
Klitmøller DK 38 B1
Klixbüll D 39 E1
Kljajićevo YU 75 C4
Ključ BIH 83 B5
Klobouky CZ 64 B2
Kłobuck PL 54 C3
Kłodawa, *Lubuskie* PL 45 C7
Kłodawa, *Wielkopolskie* PL 54 A3
Kłodzko PL 54 C1
Kløfta N 34 A3
Klokkarvik N 32 A2
Klokkerholm DK 38 B3
Klokočov SK 65 A4
Kłomnice PL 55 C4
Klonowa PL 54 B3
Kloosterzande NL 49 B5
Kłopot PL 53 A4
Klos AL 112 A2
Kloštar Ivanić HR 73 C6
Kloster D 45 A5
Kloster DK 39 C1
Klösterle A 71 A5
Klostermansfeld D 52 B1
Klosterneuburg A 64 B2
Klosters CH 71 B4
Kloten CH 70 A3
Klötze D 44 C3
Kluczbork PL 54 C3
Kluczewo PL 46 B2
Kluisbergen B 49 C4
Klundert NL 49 B5
Klutz D 44 B3
Klwów PL 55 B5
Klyetsk BY 7 E9
Knaben N 32 C3
Knapstad N 34 B3
Knäred S 40 C3
Knaresborough GB 27 A4
Knebworth GB 31 C3
Knesebeck D 44 C2
Knesselare B 49 B4
Knežak SLO 73 C4
Kneževi Vinogradi HR 74 C3
Kneževo HR 74 C3
Knić YU 85 C5
Knighton GB 29 A4
Knin HR 83 B5
Knislinge S 41 C4
Knittelfeld A 73 A4
Knivsta S 36 B4
Knock IRL 18 C3
Knocktopher IRL 21 B4
Knokke-Heist B 49 B4
Knowle GB 30 B2
Knurów PL 54 C3
Knutby S 36 B5
Knutsford GB 26 B3
Kobarid SLO 72 B3
København = Copenhagen DK 41 D2
Kobenz A 73 A4
Kobersdorf A 64 C2
Kobiernice PL 65 A5
Kobierzyce PL 54 C1
Kobilje SLO 73 B6
Kobiór PL 54 C3
Koblenz CH 61 C4
Koblenz D 50 C3

Kobryn BY 6 E8
Kobylanka PL 45 B6
Kobylin PL 54 B2
Kobyłka PL 55 A6
Kobylniki PL 47 C6
Kocaali TR 114 A5
Kocaeli = İzmit TR 114 B4
Kočani MK 11 F7
Koceljevo YU 85 B4
Kočerin BIH 84 C2
Kočevje SLO 73 C4
Kočevska Reka SLO 73 C4
Kochel am see D 62 C2
Kocs H 64 C4
Kocsér H 75 A4
Kocsola H 74 B3
Koczala PL 46 B3
Kodal N 34 B2
Kodersdorf D 53 B4
Kodrab PL 55 B4
Koekelare B 48 B3
Kofçaz TR 114 A2
Köflach A 73 A5
Køge DK 41 D2
Kohlberg D 62 A3
Kohtla-Järve EST 7 B9
Köinge S 40 B2
Kojetín CZ 64 A3
Kokava SK 65 B5
Kokkola FIN 3 E25
Kokori BIH 84 B2
Kokoski PL 47 A4
Koksijde B 48 B3
Kola BIH 84 B2
Kola RUS 3 B30
Köla S 34 B4
Kołacin PL 55 B4
Kolari FIN 3 C25
Kolárovo SK 64 C3
Kolašin YU 85 D4
Kolbäck S 36 B3
Kolbacz PL 45 B6
Kolbeinsstaðir IS 111 C3
Kolbermoor D 62 C3
Kołbiel PL 55 A6
Kolbnitz A 72 B3
Kolbotn N 34 B2
Kolby Kås DK 39 D3
Kolczewo PL 45 B6
Kolczyglowy PL 46 A3
Kolding DK 39 D2
Kölesd H 74 B3
Kolín CZ 53 C5
Kolind DK 39 C3
Kolinec CZ 63 A4
Koljane HR 83 C5
Kølkær DK 39 C2
Kölleda D 52 B1
Kollum NL 42 B3
Köln = Cologne D 50 C2
Koło PL 54 A3
Kołobrzeg PL 46 A1
Kolochau D 52 B3
Kolomyya UA 11 B8
Kolonowskie PL 54 C3
Koloveč CZ 62 A4
Kolpino RUS 7 B11
Kolpny RUS 7 E14
Kolrep D 44 B4
Kolsko PL 53 B5
Kolsva S 36 B2
Kolta SK 65 B4
Kolunič BIH 83 B5
Koluszki PL 55 B4
Kolut YU 75 C3
Kølvrå DK 39 C2
Komarica BIH 84 B2
Komárno SK 64 C4
Komárom H 64 C4
Kombóti GR 112 C3
Komen SLO 72 C3
Komin HR 84 C2
Komiža HR 83 C5
Komjáti H 65 B6
Komjatice SK 64 B4
Komletinci HR 75 C3
Komló, *Baranya* H 74 B3
Kömlo, *Heves* H 65 C6
Komoča SK 64 C4
Komorniki PL 54 A1
Komorzno PL 54 B3
Komotini GR 112 A7
Konak YU 75 C5
Konakovo RUS 7 C14
Konary PL 55 B6
Konarzyny PL 46 B3
Kondiá GR 112 C7
Kondorfa H 73 B6
Kondoros H 75 B5
Kondrovo RUS 7 D13
Køng DK 39 D4
Konga S 40 C5
Kongerslev DK 38 C3
Kongsberg N 33 B6
Kongshamn N 33 C5
Kongsmark DK 39 D1
Kongsvinger N 34 A4
Konice CZ 64 A2
Konie PL 55 B5
Koniecpol PL 55 C4
Königs Wusterhausen D 52 A3
Königsberg D 51 C6
Königsbronn D 61 B6
Königsbrück D 53 B3
Königsbrunn D 62 B1
Konigsdorf D 62 C2
Königsee D 52 C1
Königshorst D 45 C4
Königslutter D 51 A6
Königssee D 62 C3
Königstein, *Hessen* D 51 C4
Königstein, *Sachsen* D 53 C4
Königstetten A 64 B2
Königswartha D 53 B4
Königswiesen A 63 B5
Königswinter D 50 C3
Konin PL 54 A3
Konispol AL 112 C2
Kónitsa GR 112 B2
Köniz CH 70 B2
Konjevići BIH 85 B4
Konjevrate HR 83 C5
Konjic BIH 84 C2
Konjščina HR 73 B6
Könnern D 52 B1
Konnerud N 34 B2
Konopiska PL 54 C3
Konotop PL 53 B5
Konotop UA 7 F12
Końskie PL 55 B5
Konsmo N 33 C4
Konstancin-Jeziorna PL 55 A6
Konstantynów Łódźki PL 55 B4
Konstanz D 61 C5
Kontich B 49 B5
Kontiolahti FIN 3 E28
Konya TR 16 C6
Konz D 60 A2
Kópasker IS 111 A9
Kópavogur IS 111 C4
Kopčany SK 64 B3
Koper SLO 72 C3
Kopervik N 32 B2
Kópháza H 64 C2
Kopice PL 54 C2
Kopidlno CZ 53 C5
Köping S 36 B2
Köpingebro S 41 D3
Köpingsvik S 41 C6
Koppang N 2 F19
Kopparberg S 36 B1
Koppom S 34 B4
Koprivlen BG 112 A5
Koprivna BIH 84 B3
Koprivnica HR 74 B1
Kopřivnice CZ 64 A4
Koprzywnica PL 55 C6
Kopstal L 60 A2
Kopychyntsi UA 11 B8
Kopytkowo PL 47 B4
Korbach D 51 B4
Körbecke D 50 B4
Korçë AL 112 B2
Korčula HR 84 D2
Korczyców PL 53 A4
Korenevo RUS 7 F13
Korenita YU 85 B4
Korets UA 11 A9
Korfantów PL 54 C2
Körfez TR 114 B4
Korgen N 2 C20
Korinth DK 39 D3
Kórinthos = Corinth GR 113 E4
Korita BIH 83 B5
Korita HR 84 D2
Koríthi GR 113 E2
Korkuteli TR 16 C5
Körmend H 74 A1
Korne PL 46 A3
Korneuburg A 64 B2
Kornevo RUS 47 A6
Kórnik PL 54 A2
Kornsjø N 35 C3
Környe H 74 A3
Koromačno HR 82 B3
Koróni GR 113 F3
Koronís GR 113 E7
Koronowo PL 46 B3
Körösladány H 75 B6
Köröstarcsa H 75 B6
Korosten UA 11 A10
Korostyshev UA 11 A10
Korsberga, *Jönköping* S 40 B5
Korsberga, *Skaraborg* S 35 C6
Korshavn N 35 B3
Korsnäs S 36 A2
Korsør DK 39 D4
Korsun Shevchenkovskiy UA 11 B11
Kortrijk B 49 C4
Korucu TR 114 C2
Koryčany CZ 64 A3
Korykovka UA 7 F12
Korzeńsko PL 54 B1
Korzybie PL 46 A2
Kosanica YU 85 C4
Kosaya Gora RUS 7 D14
Kösching D 62 B2
Kościan PL 54 A1
Kościelec PL 54 A3
Kościerzyna PL 46 A3
Koserow D 45 A5
Košetice CZ 63 A6
Košice SK 10 B6
Kosjerić YU 85 C4
Koška HR 74 C3
Kosovska Mitrovica YU 85 D5
Kosta S 40 C5
Kostajnica HR 74 C1
Kostajnik YU 85 B4
Kostanjevica SLO 73 C5
Kostelec na Hané CZ 64 A3
Kostelec nad Černými Lesy CZ 53 C4
Kostice CZ 53 C3
Kostkowo PL 47 A4
Kostojevići YU 85 B4
Kostolac YU 85 B6
Kostopil UA 11 A9
Kostów PL 54 B3
Kostrzyn, *Lubuskie* PL 45 C6
Kostrzyn, *Wielkopolskie* PL 46 C3
Koszalin PL 46 A2
Koszęcin PL 54 C3
Kőszeg H 74 A1
Koszwaly PL 47 A4
Koszyce PL 55 C5
Kot SLO 73 C5
Kötelek H 75 A5
Köthen D 52 B1
Kotka FIN 7 A9
Kotomierz PL 47 B4
Kotor YU 105 A4
Kotor Varoš BIH 84 B2
Kotoriba HR 74 B1
Kotorsko BIH 84 B3
Kotovsk UA 11 C10
Kotraža YU 85 C5
Kótronas GR 113 F4
Kötschach A 72 B2
Kötzting D 62 A3
Koudum NL 42 C2
Kouřim CZ 53 C4
Kout na Šumave CZ 62 A4
Kouvola FIN 3 F27
Kovačevac YU 85 B5
Kovačica YU 85 A5
Kovdor RUS 3 C29
Kovel' UA 11 A8
Kovilj YU 75 C5
Kovin YU 85 B5
Kovren YU 85 C4
Kowal PL 47 C5
Kowalewo Pomorskie PL 47 B4
Kowalów PL 45 C6
Kowary PL 53 C5
Köyceğiz TR 16 C4
Kozan TR 16 C7
Kozáni GR 112 B3
Kozarac BIH 84 B1
Kozarac HR 73 C5
Kozárovce SK 65 B4
Kozelets UA 11 A11
Kozelsk RUS 7 D13
Kozica HR 84 C2
Koziegłowy PL 55 C4
Kozienice PL 55 B6
Kozina SLO 72 C3
Kozje SLO 73 B5
Kozlu TR 114 A6
Kozluk BIH 85 B4
Koźmin PL 54 B2
Koźminek PL 54 B3
Kozolupy CZ 63 A4
Kożuchów PL 53 B5
Kožuhe BIH 84 B3
Kozyatyn UA 11 B10
Kozyörük TR 114 A1
Krackow D 45 B6
Krąg PL 46 A2
Kragenæs DK 39 E4
Kragerø N 33 C6
Krągi PL 46 B2
Kragujevac YU 85 B5
Kraiburg D 62 B3
Krajenka PL 46 B2
Krajišnik YU 75 C5
Krajková CZ 52 C2
Krajné SK 64 B3
Krajnik Dolny PL 45 B6
Krakača BIH 83 A4
Kräklingbo S 37 D5
Kraków PL 55 C4
Krakow am See D 44 B4
Králíky CZ 54 C1
Kraljevica HR 73 C4
Kraljevo YU 85 C5
Kráľ'ov Brod SK 64 B3
Kral'ovany SK 65 A5
Kralovice CZ 52 D3
Kralupy nad Vltavou CZ 53 C4
Králův Dvůr CZ 63 A5
Kramfors S 2 E22
Kramsach A 72 A1
Kramsk PL 54 A3
Kråmvik N 33 B5
Kranenburg D 50 B2
Kraniá GR 112 C3
Kranía Elassónas GR 112 C4
Kranichfeld D 52 C1
Kranídhion GR 113 E5
Kranj SLO 73 B4
Kranjska Gora SLO 72 B3
Krapanj HR 83 C4
Krapina HR 73 B5
Krapje HR 74 C1
Krapkowice PL 54 C2
Kraselov CZ 63 A4
Krašić HR 73 C5
Krāslava LV 7 D9
Kraslice CZ 52 C2
Krasna PL 55 B5
Krasna Lipa CZ 53 C4
Kraśnik PL 11 A7
Krašnja SLO 73 B4
Krásno SK 65 A4
Krasno Polje HR 83 B4
Krásnohorské Podhradie SK 65 B6
Krasnozavodsk RUS 7 C15
Krasnystaw PL 11 A7
Krasnyy RUS 7 D11
Krasnyy Kholm RUS 7 B14
Krasocin PL 55 C5
Kraszewice PL 54 B3
Kraszkowice PL 54 B3
Krátigos GR 114 C1
Kraubath A 73 A4
Krausnick D 53 A3
Krautheim D 61 A5
Kravaře, *Severočeský* CZ 53 C4
Kravaře, *Severomoravsky* CZ 64 A4
Kravarsko HR 73 C6
Kraznějov CZ 63 A4
Krčedin YU 75 C5
Krefeld D 50 B2
Krembz D 44 B3
Kremenchuk UA 11 B12
Kremenets UA 11 A8
Kremmen D 45 C5
Kremna YU 85 C4
Kremnica SK 65 B4
Krempe D 43 B6
Krems A 63 B6
Kremsbrücke A 72 B3
Kremsmünster A 63 B5
Křemže CZ 63 B5
Křenov CZ 64 A2
Krepa PL 54 B3
Krepsko PL 46 B2
Kreševo BIH 84 C3
Kressbronn D 61 C5
Kréstena GR 113 E3
Kretinga LT 6 D6
Krettsy RUS 7 B12
Kreuth D 62 C2
Kreuzau D 50 C2
Kreuzlingen CH 61 C5
Kreuztal D 50 C3
Krewelin D 45 C5
Krezluk BIH 84 B2
Krieglach A 73 A5
Kriegsfeld D 60 A3
Kriens CH 70 A3
Krimml A 72 A2
Krimpen aan de IJssel NL 49 B5
Křinec CZ 53 C5
Kristdala S 40 B6
Kristiansand N 33 C5
Kristianstad S 41 C4
Kristiansund N 2 E17
Kristiinankaupunki FIN 3 E24
Kristinehamn S 34 B6
Kriváň SK 65 B5
Krivoy Rog = Kryvyy Rih UA 11 C12
Kriż HR 74 C1
Křižanov CZ 64 A2
Križevci HR 74 B1
Krk HR 83 A3
Krka SLO 73 C4
Krnjača YU 85 B5
Krnjak HR 73 C5
Krnjeuša BIH 83 B5
Krnjevo YU 85 B6
Krnov CZ 54 C2
Krobia PL 54 B1
Kroczyce PL 55 C4
Krøderen N 33 A6
Krokeai GR 113 F4
Krokek S 37 C3
Krokom S 2 E21
Krokowa PL 47 A4
Krokstad-elva N 33 B6
Kroksund N 34 B3
Krolevets UA 7 F12
Kroměříž CZ 64 A3
Krommenie NL 42 C1
Krompachy SK 65 B6
Kromy RUS 7 E13
Kronach D 52 C1
Kronshagen D 44 A2
Kronshtadt RUS 7 B10
Kröpelin D 44 A3
Kropp D 43 A6
Kroppenstedt D 52 B1
Kropstädt D 52 B2
Krościenko nad Dunajcem PL 65 A6
Kröslin D 45 A5
Krośnice PL 54 B2
Krośniewice PL 55 A4
Krosno PL 10 B6
Krosno Odrzańskie PL 53 A5
Krostitz D 52 B2
Krotoszyn PL 54 B2
Krottendorf A 73 A5
Krouna CZ 64 A2
Krowiarki PL 54 C3
Kršan HR 73 C4
Krško SLO 73 C5
Krstac YU 84 C3
Krstur YU 75 B5
Křtiny CZ 64 A2
Kruft D 50 C3
Kruishoutem B 49 C4
Krulyewshchyna BY 7 D9
Krumbach A 73 A6
Krumbach D 61 B6
Krumovgrad BG 112 A7
Krün D 71 A6
Krupá CZ 53 C3
Krupa na Vrbasu BIH 84 B2
Krupanj YU 85 B4
Krupina SK 65 B5
Krupka CZ 53 C3
Krupki BY 7 D10
Kruså DK 39 E2
Krušćica BIH 84 B2
Kruševac YU 85 C6
Kruševo MK 112 A3
Kruszwica PL 47 C4
Kruszyn PL 47 C5
Krychaw BY 7 E11
Krynica PL 65 A6
Krynica Morska PL 47 A5
Kryvyy Rih = Krivoy Rog UA 11 C12
Krzęcin PL 46 B1
Krzelów PL 54 B1
Krzepice PL 54 C3
Krzepielów PL 53 B6
Krzeszowice PL 55 C4
Krzeszyce PL 45 C7
Krzynowlaga Mała PL 47 B6
Krzywiń PL 54 B1
Krzyż Wielkopolski PL 46 C2
Krzyżanowice PL 54 D3
Krzyżowa PL 65 A5
Ksiaz Wielkopolski, *Małopolskie* PL 55 C5
Książ Wielkopolski, *Wielkopolskie* PL 54 A2
Kłębowiec PL 46 B2
Kübekháza H 75 B5
Küblis CH 71 B4
Kuchary PL 54 B2
Kuchl A 63 C4
Kucice PL 47 C6
Kuciste HR 84 D2
Kućište YU 85 D5
Küçükköy TR 114 C1
Küçükkuyu TR 114 C1
Kucura YU 75 C4
Kuczbork-Osada PL 47 B6
Kudowa-Zdrój PL 53 C6
Kufstein A 62 C3
Kuggeboda S 41 C5
Kühbach D 62 B2
Kuhmo FIN 3 D28
Kuhmoinen FIN 3 F26
Kuhnsdorf A 73 B4
Kuhstedt D 43 B5
Kuinre NL 42 C2
Kuivastu EST 6 B7
Kukës AL 10 E6
Kuklin PL 47 B6
Kukljica HR 83 B4
Kukujevci YU 85 A4
Kula TR 16 B4
Kula, *Srbija* YU 85 B6
Kula, *Vojvodina* YU 75 C4
Kuldīga LV 6 C6
Kulen Vakuf BIH 83 B5
Kulina BIH 84 B3
Kulmain D 62 A2
Kulmbach D 52 C1
Kulu TR 16 B6
Kumane YU 75 C5
Kumanovo MK 10 E6
Kumbağ TR 114 B2
Kumkale TR 114 C1
Kumla S 36 B2
Kumlakyrkby S 36 B3
Kumluca TR 16 C5
Kumrovec HR 73 B5
Kunadacs H 75 B4
Kunágota H 75 B6
Kunbaja H 75 B4
Kunda EST 7 B9
Kundl A 72 A1
Kunfehértó H 75 B4
Kungälv S 38 B4
Kungs-Husby S 36 B4
Kungsängen S 36 B4
Kungsäter S 40 B2
Kungsbacka S 38 B5
Kungsgården S 36 A3
Kungshamn S 35 C3
Kungsör S 36 B3
Kunhegyes H 75 A5
Kunmadaras H 75 A5
Kunovice CZ 64 A3
Kunów PL 55 C6
Kunowo PL 54 B2
Kunštát CZ 64 A2
Kunszállás H 75 B4
Kunszentmárton H 75 B5
Kunszentmiklós H 75 A4
Kunžak CZ 63 A6
Künzelsau D 61 A5
Kuolajärvi RUS 3 C28
Kuopio FIN 3 E27
Kup H 74 A2
Kup PL 54 C2
Kupa H 65 B6
Kupci YU 85 C6
Kupferzell D 61 A5
Kupinec HR 73 C5
Kupinečki Kraljevac HR 73 C5
Kupinovo YU 85 B5
Kupirovo HR 83 B5
Kupjak HR 73 C4
Kuppenheim D 61 B4
Kupres BIH 84 C2
Küps D 52 C1
Kurd H 74 B3
Kŭrdzhali BG 112 A7
Küre TR 16 A6
Kuressaare EST 6 B7
Kurikka FIN 3 E25
Kuřim CZ 64 A2
Kurki PL 47 B6
Kurort Oberwiesenthal D 52 C2
Kurort Schmalkalden D 51 C6
Kurort Stolberg D 51 B6
Kurort Wippra D 52 B1
Kurów PL 11 A7
Kurowice PL 55 B4
Kursk RUS 7 F14
Kuršumlija YU 85 C6
Kuršumlijska Banja YU 85 C6
Kurşunlu, *Bursa* TR 114 B4
Kurşunlu, *Çankırı* TR 16 A6
Kürten D 50 B3
Kurucaşile TR 16 A6
Kurzelów PL 55 C4
Kusadak YU 85 B5
Kuşadası TR 16 C3
Kusel D 60 A3
Kusey D 44 C3
Küsnacht CH 70 A3
Kütahya TR 114 C4
Kutenholz D 43 B6
Kutina HR 74 C1
Kutjevo HR 74 C2
Kutná Hora CZ 53 D5
Kutno PL 55 A4
Küttingen CH 70 A3
Kúty SK 64 B3
Kuusamo FIN 3 D28
Kuusankoski FIN 3 F27
Kuvshinovo RUS 7 C13
Kuzmin YU 85 A4
Kuźnia Raciborska PL 54 C3
Kuźnica Czarnkowska PL 46 C2
Kuźnica Żelichowska PL 46 C2
Kværndrup DK 39 D3
Kvänum S 35 C5
Kvås N 33 C4
Kvasice CZ 64 A3
Kvernaland N 32 C2
Kvibille S 40 C2
Kvicksund S 36 B3
Kvidinge S 41 C3
Kvikne N 2 E19
Kvilda CZ 63 A4
Kville S 35 C3
Kvillsfors S 40 B5
Kvinesdal N 32 C3
Kvinlog N 32 C3
Kvinnherad N 32 B3
Kvissel DK 38 B3
Kviteseid N 33 B5
Kvitsøy N 32 B2
Kwakowo PL 46 A3
Kwidzyn PL 47 B4
Kwilcz PL 46 C2
Kyjov CZ 64 B3
Kyle of Lochalsh GB 22 D3
Kyleakin GB 22 D3
Kylerhea GB 22 D3
Kylestrome GB 22 C3
Kyllburg D 50 C2
Kynšperk nad Ohří CZ 52 C2
Kyrenia CY 16 D6
Kyritz D 44 C4
Kyrkesund S 35 C3
Kyrkhult S 41 C4
Kysucké Nové Mesto SK 65 A4
Kyustendil BG 11 E7
Kyyiv = Kiev UA 11 A11
Kyyjärvi FIN 3 E26

L

La Adrada E 94 B2
La Alameda E 100 A2
La Alberca E 93 A4
La Alberca de Záncara E 95 C4
La Albergueria de Argañán E 93 A4
La Albuera E 93 C4
La Aldea del Portillo del Busto E 89 B3
La Algaba E 99 B4
La Aliseda de Tormes E 93 A5
La Almarcha E 95 C4
La Almolda E 90 B2
La Almunia de Doña Godina E 89 C5
La Antillas E 98 B3
La Arena E 86 A4
La Aulaga E 99 B4
La Balme-de-Sillingy F 69 C6
La Bañeza E 88 B1
La Barca de la Florida E 99 C5
La Barre-de-Monts F 66 B2
La Barre-en-Ouche F 58 B1
La Barrosa E 99 C4
La Barthe-de-Neste F 77 C3
La Bassée F 48 C3
La Bastide-de-Sèrou F 77 C4
La Bastide-des-Jourdans F 79 C4
La Bastide-Puylaurent F 78 B2
La Bathie F 69 C6
La Baule-Escoublac F 66 A2
La Bazoche-Gouet F 58 B1
La Bégude-de-Mazenc F 78 B3
La Bernerie-en-Retz F 66 A2
La Bisbal d'Empordà E 91 B6
La Boissière F 57 A6
La Bourboule F 68 C2
La Bóveda de Toro E 88 C1
La Brède F 76 B2
La Bresse F 60 B2
La Bridoire F 69 C5
La Brillanne F 79 C4
La Bruffière F 66 A3
La Bussière F 58 C3
La Caillère F 66 B4
La Caletta I 110 B2
La Calmette F 78 C3
La Calzada de Oropesa E 93 B5
La Campana E 99 B5
La Cañada E 94 B2
La Canourgue F 78 B2
La Capelle F 49 D4
La Cardanchosa E 99 A5
La Caridad E 86 A4
La Carlota E 100 B1
La Carolina E 100 A2
La Cava E 90 C3
La Cavalerie F 78 B2
La Celle-en-Moravan F 69 A4
La Celle-St. Avant F 67 A5
La Cerca E 89 B3
La Chaise-Dieu F 68 C3
La Chaize-le-Vicomte F 66 B3
La Chambre F 69 C6
La Chapelaude F 68 B2
La Chapelle-d'Angillon F 68 A2
La Chapelle-en-Aalgaudémar F 79 B5
La Chapelle-en-Vercors F 79 B4
La Chapelle-Glain F 57 C4
La Chapelle-la-Reine F 58 B3
La Chapelle-Laurent F 68 C3
La Chapelle-St. Luc F 59 B5
La Chapelle-sur-Erdre F 66 A3
La Chapelle-Vicomtesse F 58 C2
La Charce F 79 B4
La Charité-sur-Loire F 68 A3
La Chartre-sur-le-Loir F 58 C1
La Châtaigneraie F 67 B4
La Châtre F 68 B1
La Chaussée-sur-Marne F 59 B5
La Chaux-de-Fonds CH 70 A1
La Cheppe F 59 A5
La Chèze F 56 B3
La Ciotat F 79 C4
La Clayette F 69 B4
La Clusaz F 69 C6
La Codosera E 93 B3
La Concha E 88 A3
La Condamine-Châtelard F 79 B5
La Contienda E 99 A4
La Coquille F 67 C5
La Coronada E 93 C5
La Côte-St. André F 69 C5
La Cotinière F 66 C3
La Courtine F 68 C2
La Crau F 79 C5
La Crèche F 67 B4
La Croix F 67 A5
La Croix-Valmer F 79 C5
La Cumbre E 93 B5
La Douze F 77 A3
La Espina E 86 A4
La Estrella E 94 C1
La Farga de Moles E 91 A4
La Fatarella E 90 B3
La Felipa E 95 C5
La Fère F 59 A4
La Ferrière F 66 B3
La Ferrière-en-Parthenay F 67 B4
La-Ferté-Alais F 58 B3
La Ferté-Bernard F 58 B1
La Ferté-Frênel F 58 B1
La Ferté-Gaucher F 59 B4
La Ferté-Imbault F 68 A1
La Ferté-Macé F 57 B5
La Ferté-Milon F 59 A4
La Ferté-St. Aubin F 58 C2
La Ferté-St.Cyr F 58 C2
La Ferté-sous-Jouarre F 59 B4
La Ferté-Vidame F 58 B1
La Ferté Villeneuil F 58 C2
La Feuillie F 58 A2
La Flèche F 57 C5
La Flotte F 66 B3
La Font de la Figuera E 101 A5
La Fouillade F 77 B5
La Fregeneda E 87 D4
La Fresneda E 90 C3
La Fuencubierta E 99 B6
La Fuente de San Esteban E 87 D4
La Fulioala E 91 B4
La Gacilly F 57 C3
La Galera E 90 C3
La Garde-Freinet F 79 C5
La Garnache F 66 B3
La Garriga E 91 B5
La Garrovilla E 93 C4
La Gaubretière F 66 B3
La Gineta E 95 C4
La Granadella, *Alicante* E 96 C3
La Granadella, *Lleida* E 90 B3
La Grand-Combe F 78 B3
La Grande-Croix F 69 C4
La Grande-Motte F 78 C3
La Granja d'Escarp E 90 B3
La Granjuela E 93 C5
La Grave F 79 A5
La Gravelle F 57 B4
La Guardia E 95 C3
La Guardia de Jaén E 100 B2
La Guerche-de-Bretagne F 57 C4
La Guerche-sur-l'Aubois F 68 B2
La Guérinière F 66 B2
La Haba E 93 C5
La Haye-du-Puits F 57 A4
La Haye-Pesnel F 57 B4
La Herlière F 48 C3
La Hermida E 88 A2
La Herrera E 95 D4
La Higuera E 101 A4
La Hiniesta E 88 C1
La Horcajada E 93 A5
La Horra E 88 C3
La Hulpe B 49 C5
La Hutte F 57 B6
La Iglesuela E 94 B2
La Iglesuela del Cid E 90 C2
La Iruela E 100 B3
La Javie F 79 B5
La Jonchère-St. Maurice F 67 B6
La Jonquera E 91 A5
La Lantejuela E 99 B5
La Línea de la Concepción E 99 C5
La Llacuna E 91 B4
La Londe-les-Maures F 79 C5
La Loupe F 58 B2
La Louvière B 49 C5
La Luisiana E 99 B5
La Machine F 68 B3
la Maddalena I 110 A2
La Mailleraye-sur-Seine F 58 A1
La Malène F 78 B2
La Mamola E 100 C2
La Manresana dels Prats E 91 B4
La Masadera E 90 B2
La Mata E 94 C2
La Mata de Ledesma E 94 A1
La Mata de Monteagudo E 88 B1
La Meilleraye-de-Bretagne F 66 A3
La Ménitré F 67 A4
La Mojonera E 101 C3
La Mole F 79 C5
La Molina E 91 A4
La Monnerie-le-Montel F 68 C3
La Morera E 93 C4
La Mothe-Achard F 66 B3
La Mothe-St. Héray F 67 B4
La Motte-Chalançon F 79 B4
La Motte-du-Caire F 79 B5
La Motte-Servolex F 69 C5
La Mudarra E 88 C2
La Muela E 90 B1
La Mure F 79 B4
La Nava E 99 B4
La Nava de Ricomalillo E 94 C2
La Nava de Santiago E 93 B4
La Neuve-Lyre F 58 B1
La Neuveville CH 70 A2
La Nocle-Maulaix F 68 B3
La Nuez de Arriba E 88 B3
La Paca E 101 B4
La Pacaudière F 68 B3
La Palma d'Ebre E 90 B3
La Palma del Condado E 99 B4
La Palme F 78 D2

158

Marl D 50 B3
Marlborough, *Devon* GB 28 C4
Marlborough, *Wiltshire* GB 29 B6
Marle F 59 A4
Marlieux F 69 B5
Marlow D 45 A4
Marlow GB 31 C3
Marma S 36 A4
Marmagne F 69 B4
Marmande F 76 B3
Marmara TR 114 B2
Marmaris TR 16 C4
Marmelete P 98 B2
Marmolejo E 100 A1
Marmoutier F 60 B3
Marnay F 69 A5
Marne D 43 B6
Marnheim D 61 A4
Marnitz D 44 B3
Maroldsweisach D 51 C6
Marolles-les-Braults F 58 B1
Maromme F 58 A2
Marone I 71 C5
Marónia GR 112 B7
Maroslele H 75 B5
Maróstica I 72 C1
Marotta I 82 C2
Márpissa GR 113 E7
Marquion F 49 C4
Marquise F 48 C2
Marradi I 81 B5
Marratxi E 97 B2
Marrùbiu I 110 C1
Marrum NL 42 B2
Marrupe E 94 B2
Mars-la-Tours F 60 A1
Marsac F 77 C5
Marsac-en-Livradois F 68 C3
Marságlia I 80 B3
Marsala I 108 B1
Marsberg D 51 B4
Marsciano I 82 D1
Marseillan F 78 C2
Marseille = Marseilles F 79 C4
Marseille en Beauvaisis F 58 A2
Marseilles = Marseille F 79 C4
Mársico Nuovo I 104 C1
Marske-by-the-Sea GB 27 A4
Marson F 59 B5
Märsta S 36 B4
Marstal DK 39 E3
Marstrand S 38 B4
Marta I 102 A4
Martano I 107 A5
Martel F 77 B4
Martelange B 60 A1
Martfeld D 43 C6
Martfű H 75 A5
Martham GB 30 B5
Marthon F 67 C5
Martiago E 93 A4
Martigné-Briand F 67 A4
Martigné-Ferchaud F 57 C4
Martigny CH 70 B2
Martigny-les-Bains F 60 B1
Martigues F 79 C4
Martim-Longo P 98 B3
Martin SK 65 A4
Martin de la Jara E 100 B1
Martin Muñoz de las Posadas E 94 A2
Martina CH 71 B5
Martina Franca I 104 C3
Martinamor E 94 B1
Martinengo I 71 C4
Martinsberg A 63 B6
Martinšćica HR 82 B3
Martinshöhe D 60 A3
Martinsicuro I 82 D2
Martinszell D 61 C6
Mártis I 110 B1
Martofte DK 39 D3
Martonvásár H 74 A3
Martorell E 91 B4
Martos E 100 B2
Martres Tolosane F 77 C3
Marugán E 94 B2
Marúggio I 104 C3
Marvão P 92 B3
Marvejols F 78 B2
Marville F 60 A1
Marwałd PL 47 B5
Marykirk GB 25 B5
Marypark GB 23 D5
Maryport GB 26 A2
Marytavy GB 28 C3
Marzabotto I 81 B5
Marzahna D 52 B2
Marzahne D 45 C4
Marzamemi I 109 C4
Marzocca I 82 C2
Mas de Barberáns E 90 C3
Mas de las Matas E 90 C2
Masa E 88 B3
Máscali I 109 B4
Mascaraque E 94 C3
Mascarenhas P 87 C3
Mascioni I 103 A6
Masegosa E 101 A3
Masegoso de Tajuña E 95 B4
Masera I 70 B3
Masevaux F 60 C2
Masham GB 27 A4
Maside E 87 B2
Maslacq F 76 C2
Maslinica HR 83 C5
Maslovare BIH 84 B2
Masone I 80 B2
Massa I 81 B4
Massa Fiscáglia I 81 B6
Massa Lombarda I 81 B5
Massa Lubrense I 103 C7
Massa Maríttima I 81 C4
Massa Martana I 82 D1
Massafra I 104 C3
Massamagrell E 96 B2
Massanassa E 96 B2
Massarosa I 81 C4
Massat F 77 D4
Massay F 68 A1
Massbach D 51 C6
Masseret F 67 C6
Masseube F 77 C3
Massiac F 68 C3
Massing D 62 B3
Massmechelen B 50 C1
Masty BY 6 E8
Masúa I 110 C1
Masueco E 87 C4
Mašun SLO 73 C4
Maszewo, *Lubuskie* PL 53 A4
Maszewo, *Zachodnio-Pomorskie* PL 45 B7
Mata de Alcántara E 93 B4
Mátala GR 113 H6
Matalebreras E 89 C4
Matallana de Torio E 88 B1
Matamala E 89 C4
Mataporquera E 88 B2
Matapozuelos E 88 C2
Mataró E 91 B5
Mataruge YU 85 C4
Mataruška Banja YU 85 C5
Matélica I 82 C2
Matera I 104 C2
Mateševo YU 85 D4
Mátészalka H 11 C7
Matet E 96 B2
Matha F 67 C4
Mathay F 70 A1
Matignon F 57 B3
Matilla de los Caños del Rio E 94 B1
Matlock GB 27 B4
Matosinhos P 87 C2
Matour F 69 B4
Mátrafüred H 65 C5
Mátraterenye H 65 B5
Matre N 32 B2
Matrei am Brenner A 71 A6
Matrei in Osttirol A 72 A2
Matrice I 103 B7
Mattarello I 71 B6
Mattersburg A 64 C2
Mattighofen A 62 B4
Mattinata I 104 B2
Mattos P 92 B2
Mattsee A 62 C4
Matulji HR 73 C4
Maubert-Fontaine F 59 A5
Maubeuge F 49 C4
Maubourguet F 76 C3
Mauchline GB 24 C3
Maud GB 23 D6
Mauer-kirchen A 62 B4
Mauern D 62 B2
Mauguio F 78 C3
Maulbronn D 61 B4
Maule F 58 B2
Mauléon F 67 B4
Mauléon-Barousse F 77 D3
Mauléon-Licharre F 76 C2
Maulévrier F 67 A4
Maum IRL 18 C2
Maurach A 72 A1
Maure-de-Bretagne F 57 C4
Maureilhan F 78 C2
Mauriac F 68 C2
Mauron F 57 B3
Maurs F 77 B5
Maury F 77 D5
Maussane-les-Alpilles F 78 C3
Mautern A 63 B6
Mautern im Steiermark A 73 A4
Mauterndorf A 72 A3
Mauthausen A 63 B5
Mauthen A 72 B3
Mauvezin F 77 C3
Mauzé-sur-le-Mignon F 67 B4
Maxent F 57 C3
Maxey-sur-Vaise F 60 B1
Maxial P 92 B1
Maxieira P 92 B2
Maxwellheugh GB 25 C5
Mayalde E 88 C1
Maybole GB 24 C3
Mayen D 50 C3
Mayenne F 57 B5
Mayet F 58 C1
Maylough IRL 18 C3
Mayorga E 88 B1
Mayres F 78 B3
Mayrhofen A 72 A1
Mazagón E 99 B4
Mazaleón E 90 B3
Mazamet F 77 C5
Mazan F 79 B4
Mazara del Vallo I 108 B1
Mazarambroz E 94 C2
Mazarete E 95 B4
Mazaricos E 86 B2
Mazarrón E 101 B4
Mažeikiai LT 6 C7
Mazères F 77 C4
Mazères-sur-Salat F 77 C3
Mazières-en-Gâtine F 67 B4
Mazin HR 83 B4
Mazuelo E 88 B3
Mazyr BY 7 E10
Mazzarino I 109 B3
Mazzarrà Sant'Andrea I 109 A4
Mazzo di Valtellina I 71 B5
Mchowo PL 47 B6
Mdzewo PL 47 C6
Mealabost GB 22 C2
Mealhada P 92 A2
Meana Sardo I 110 C2
Meaulne F 68 B2
Meaux F 59 B3
Mecerreyes E 89 B3
Mechelen B 49 B5
Mechernich D 50 C2
Mechnica PL 54 C3
Mechterstädt D 51 C6
Mecidiye TR 114 B1
Mecikal PL 46 B3
Mecina-Bombarón E 100 C2
Mecitözü TR 16 A7
Meckenbeuren D 61 C5
Meckenheim, *Rheinland-Pfalz* D 50 C3
Meckenheim, *Rheinland-Pfalz* D 61 A4
Meckesheim D 61 A4
Mecseknádasd H 74 B3
Meda I 71 C4
Meda P 87 D3
Medak HR 83 B4
Mede I 80 A2
Medebach D 51 B4
Medelim P 93 A3
Medemblik NL 42 C2
Medena Selista BIH 84 B1
Medesano I 81 B4
Medevi S 37 C1
Medgidia RO 11 D10
Medgyesháza H 75 B6
Medhamn S 35 B5
Mediaş RO 11 C8
Medicina I 81 B5
Medina de las Torres E 93 C4
Medina de Pomar E 89 B3
Medina de Rioseco E 88 C1
Medina del Campo E 88 C2
Medina Sidonia E 99 C5
Medinaceli E 95 A4
Medinilla E 93 A5
Medja YU 75 C5
Medjedja BIH 85 C4
Medulin HR 82 B2
Meduno I 72 B2
Medveda YU 85 B6
Medvedja YU 85 C6
Medvedov SK 64 C3
Medvide HR 83 B4
Medvode SLO 73 B4
Medzev SK 65 B6
Medžitlija MK 112 B3
Meerane D 52 C2
Meerle B 49 B5
Meersburg D 61 C5
Meeuwen B 49 B6
Megalópolis GR 113 E4
Mégara GR 113 D5
Megève F 69 C6
Meggenhofen A 63 B4
Megra RUS 7 A14
Mehedeby S 36 A4
Mehun-sur-Yèvre F 68 A2
Meigle GB 25 B4
Meijel NL 50 B1
Meilen CH 70 A3
Meilhan F 76 C2
Meimôa P 93 A3
Meina I 70 C3
Meine D 44 C2
Meinersen D 44 C2
Meinerzhagen D 50 B3
Meiningen D 51 C6
Meira E 86 A3
Meiringen CH 70 B3
Meisenheim D 60 A3
Meissen D 52 B3
Meitingen D 62 B1
Meix-devant-Virton B 60 A1
Męka PL 54 B3
Meka Gruda BIH 84 C3
Mel I 72 B2
Melč CZ 64 A3
Méldola I 82 B1
Meldorf D 43 A6
Melegnano I 71 C4
Melenci YU 75 C5
Melendugno I 105 C4
Melfi I 104 C1
Melgaço P 87 B2
Melgar de Arriba E 88 B1
Melgar de Fernamental E 88 B2
Melgar de Yuso E 88 B2
Melhus N 2 E19
Meliana E 96 B2
Melide CH 70 C3
Melide E 86 B2
Melides P 98 A2
Meligalá GR 113 E3
Melilli I 109 B4
Melinovac HR 83 B4
Melisenda I 110 C2
Melisey F 60 C2
Mélito di Porto Salvo I 109 B4
Melk A 63 B6
Melksham GB 29 B5
Mellansel S 3 E23
Mellbystrand S 40 C2
Melle B 49 B4
Melle D 50 A4
Melle F 67 B4
Mellendorf D 43 C6
Mellerud S 35 C4
Mellieha M 107 C5
Mellösa S 37 B3
Mellrichstadt D 51 C6
Mělnické Vtelno CZ 53 C4
Mělník CZ 53 C4
Melón E 87 B2
Melrose GB 25 C5
Mels CH 71 A4
Melsungen D 51 B5
Meltham GB 27 B4
Melton Mowbray GB 30 B3
Melun F 58 B3
Melvaig GB 22 D3
Melvich GB 23 C5
Mélykút H 75 B4
Melzo I 71 C4
Memaliaj AL 112 B1
Membrilla E 95 D3
Membrio E 93 B3
Memer F 77 B4
Memmelsdorf D 51 D6
Memmingen D 61 C6
Memoria P 92 B2
Mena UA 7 F12
Menàggio I 71 B4
Menai Bridge GB 26 B1
Menasalbas E 94 C2
Menat F 68 B2
Mendavia E 89 B4
Mendaza E 89 B4
Mende F 78 B2
Menden D 50 B3
Mendig D 50 C3
Mendiga P 92 B2
Mendrisio CH 70 C3
Ménéac F 56 B3
Menemen TR 16 B3
Menen B 49 C4
Menetou-Salon F 68 A2
Menfi I 108 B1
Ménfőcsanak H 64 C3
Mengamuñoz E 94 B2
Mengen D 61 B5
Mengen TR 114 B7
Mengeš SLO 73 B4
Mengíbar E 100 B2
Mengkofen D 62 B3
Mens F 79 B4
Menslage D 43 C4
Mentana I 102 A5
Menton F 80 C1
Méntrida E 94 B2
Méounes-les-Montrieux F 79 C4
Meppel NL 42 C3
Meppen D 43 C4
Mequinenza E 90 B3
Mer F 58 C2
Mera, *Coruña* E 86 A2
Mera, *Coruña* E 86 A3
Merano I 71 B6
Merate I 71 C4
Mercadillo E 89 A3
Mercatale I 82 C1
Mercatino Conca I 82 C1
Mercato San Severino I 103 C7
Mercato Saraceno I 82 C1
Merching D 62 B1
Merchtem B 49 C5
Merdrignac F 56 B3
Merdžanići BIH 84 C2
Meré E 88 A2
Mere GB 29 B5
Meréville F 58 B3
Merfeld D 50 B3
Méribel F 69 C6
Méribel Motraret F 69 C6
Meriç TR 114 A1
Mérida E 93 C4
Mérignac F 76 B2
Měřín CZ 64 A1
Mering D 62 B1
Merkendorf D 62 A1
Merklin CZ 63 A4
Merksplas B 49 B5
Merlimont Plage F 48 C2
Mern DK 39 D5
Mernye H 74 B2
Mers-les-Bains F 48 C2
Mersch L 60 A2
Merseburg D 52 B1
Merthyr Tydfil GB 29 B4
Mertingen D 62 B1
Mértola P 98 B3
Méru F 58 A3
Merufe P 87 B2
Mervans F 69 B5
Merville F 48 C3
Méry-sur-Seine F 59 B4
Merzifon TR 16 A7
Merzig D 60 A2
Mesagne I 105 C3
Mesão Frio P 87 C3
Mesas de Ibor E 93 B5
Meschede D 50 B4
Meschers-sur-Gironde F 66 C4
Meshchovsk RUS 7 D13
Meslay-du-Maine F 57 C5
Mesocco CH 71 B4
Mésola I 82 B1
Mesolóngion GR 112 D3
Mesopótamon GR 112 C2
Mesoraca I 107 B3
Messac F 57 C4
Messancy B 60 A1
Messdorf D 44 C3
Messei F 57 B5
Messejana P 98 B2
Messina I 109 A4
Messíni GR 113 E4
Messkirch D 61 C5
Messtetten D 61 B4
Mestá GR 113 D7
Mestanza E 100 A1
Městec Králové CZ 53 C5
Mestlin D 44 B3
Město Albrechtice CZ 54 C2
Město Libavá CZ 64 A3
Město Touškov CZ 63 A4
Mestre I 72 C2
Mesvres F 69 B4
Mesztegnyő H 74 B2
Meta I 103 C7
Metajna HR 83 B3
Metelen D 50 A3
Méthana GR 113 E5
Methlick GB 23 D6
Methóni GR 113 F3
Methven GB 25 B4
Methwold GB 30 B4
Metković HR 84 C2
Metlika SLO 73 C5
Metnitz A 73 B4
Metslawier NL 42 B3
Métsovon GR 112 C3
Metten D 62 B3
Mettendorf D 50 D2
Mettet B 49 C5
Mettingen D 50 A3
Mettlach D 60 A2
Mettlen CH 70 B2
Mettmann D 50 B2
Metz F 60 A2
Metzervisse F 60 A2
Metzingen D 61 B5
Meulan F 58 A2
Meung-sur-Loire F 58 C2
Meuselwitz D 52 B2
Meuzac F 67 C6
Mevagissey GB 28 C3
Mexborough GB 27 B4
Meximieux F 69 C5
Mey GB 23 C5
Meyenburg D 44 B4
Meyerhöfen D 43 C5
Meylan F 69 C5
Meymac F 68 C2
Meyrargues F 79 C4
Meyrueis F 78 B2
Meyssac F 77 A4
Meysse F 78 B3
Meyzieu F 69 C4
Mèze F 78 C2
Mézériat F 69 B5
Mežica SLO 73 B4
Mézidon-Canon F 57 A5
Mézières-en-Brenne F 67 B6
Mézières-sur-Issoire F 67 B5
Mézilhac F 78 B3
Mézilles F 59 C4
Mézin F 76 B3
Mezőberény H 75 B6
Mezőcsát H 65 C6
Mezőfalva H 74 B3
Mezőhegyes H 75 B5
Mezőkeresztes H 65 C6
Mezőkomárom H 74 B3
Mezőkövácsháza H 75 B5
Mezőkövesd H 65 C6
Mezőörs H 74 A2
Mézos F 76 B1
Mezőszilas H 74 B3
Mezőtúr H 75 A5
Mezquita de Jarque E 90 C2
Mezzano, *Emilia Romagna* I 81 B6
Mezzano, *Trentino Alto Adige* I 72 B1
Mezzojuso I 108 B2
Mezzoldo I 71 B4
Mezzolombardo I 71 B6
Mgarr M 107 C5
Mglin RUS 7 E12
Miajadas E 93 B5
Mianowice PL 46 A3
Miasteczko Krajeńskie PL 46 B3
Miasteczko Śl. PL 54 C3
Miastko PL 46 A2
Michalovce SK 10 B6
Michałowice PL 55 C4
Michelau D 61 A6
Michelbach D 61 A6
Micheldorf A 63 C5
Michelhausen A 64 B1
Michelsneukirchen D 62 A3
Michelstadt D 61 A5
Michendorf D 52 A3
Michurin BG 11 E9
Mickleover GB 27 C4
Mid Yell GB 22 A7
Midbea GB 23 B6
Middelburg NL 49 B4
Middelfart DK 39 D2
Middelharnis NL 49 B5
Middelkerke B 48 B3
Middelstum NL 42 B3
Middlesbrough GB 27 A4
Middleton GB 24 B1
Middleton Cheney GB 30 B2
Middleton-in-Teesdale GB 26 A3
Middletown GB 19 B5
Middlewich GB 26 B3
Middlezoy GB 29 B5
Midhurst GB 31 D3
Midleton IRL 20 C3
Midlum D 43 B5
Midsomer Norton GB 29 B5
Midwolda NL 43 B4
Miechów PL 55 C5
Miedes de Aragón E 89 C5
Miedes de Atienza E 95 A3
Międzybodzie Bielskie PL 65 A5
Międzybórz PL 54 B2
Międzychód PL 46 C1
Międzylesie PL 54 C1
Międzyrzec Podlaski PL 6 F7
Międzyrzecz PL 46 C1
Międzywodzie PL 45 A6
Międzyzdroje PL 45 B6
Miejska Górka PL 54 B1
Miélan F 76 C3
Mielec PL 55 C6
Mielęcin PL 45 B6
Mielno, *Warmińsko-Mazurskie* PL 47 B6
Mielno, *Zachodnio-Pomorskie* PL 46 A2
Miengo E 88 A3
Miercurea Ciuc RO 11 C8
Mieres, *Asturias* E 88 A1
Mieres, *Girona* E 91 A5
Mieroszów PL 53 C6
Mierzyn PL 55 B4
Miesau D 60 A3
Miesbach D 62 C2
Mieścisko PL 46 C3
Mieste D 44 C3
Miesterhorst D 44 C3
Mieszków PL 54 A2
Mieszkowice PL 45 C6
Mietków PL 54 C1
Migennes F 59 C4
Miggiano I 107 B5
Migliánico I 103 A7
Migliarino I 81 B5
Miglionico I 104 C2
Mignano Monte Lungo I 103 B6
Migné F 67 B6
Miguel Esteban E 95 C3
Miguelturra E 94 D3
Mihajlovac YU 85 B5
Miháld H 74 B2
Mihalgazi TR 114 B5
Mihaliççık TR 114 C6
Mihályi H 74 A2
Mihla D 51 B6
Mihohnić HR 83 A3
Miholjsko HR 73 C5
Mihovljan HR 73 B5
Mijares E 94 B2
Mijas E 100 C1
Mijoska YU 85 D4
Mike H 74 B2
Mikhnevo RUS 7 D14
Mikínai GR 113 E4
Mikkeli FIN 3 F27
Mikleuš HR 74 C2
Mikołajki Pomorskie PL 47 B5
Mikolów PL 54 C3
Mikonos GR 113 E7
Mikorzyn PL 54 B3
Mikrón Dhérion GR 112 A8
Mikstat PL 54 B2
Mikulášovice CZ 53 C4
Mikulov CZ 64 B2
Mikulovice CZ 54 C2
Milagro E 89 B5
Miłakowo PL 47 A6
Milan = Milano I 71 C4
Miland N 33 B5
Milano = Milan I 71 C4
Milano Marittima I 82 B1
Milâs TR 16 C3
Milazzo I 109 A4
Mildenhall GB 30 B4
Milejewo PL 47 A5
Milelín CZ 53 C5
Miletić YU 75 C4
Miletićevo YU 75 C6
Mileto I 106 C3
Milevsko CZ 63 A5
Milford IRL 19 A4
Milford Haven GB 28 B2
Milford on Sea GB 31 D2
Milhão P 87 C4
Milići BIH 84 B4
Miličin CZ 63 A5
Milicz PL 54 B2
Milín CZ 63 A5
Militello in Val di Catánia I 109 B3
Miljevina BIH 84 C3
Milkowice PL 53 B6
Millançay F 68 A1
Millares E 96 B2
Millas F 91 A5
Millau F 78 B2
Millesimo I 80 B2
Millevaches F 68 C2
Millom GB 26 A2
Millport GB 24 C3
Millstatt A 72 B3
Millstreet, *Cork* IRL 20 B2
Millstreet, *Waterford* IRL 21 B4
Milltown, *Galway* IRL 18 C3
Milltown, *Kerry* IRL 20 B1
Milltown Malbay IRL 20 B2
Milly-la-Forêt F 58 B3
Milmarcos E 95 A5
Milmersdorf D 45 B5
Milna HR 83 C5
Milnthorpe GB 26 A3
Miločaj YU 85 C5
Milogórze PL 47 A6
Miłomłyn PL 47 B5
Milos GR 113 F6
Miloševo YU 85 B6
Miłosław PL 54 A2
Milówka PL 65 A5
Miltach D 62 A3
Miltenberg D 61 A5
Milton Keynes GB 31 B3
Milutovac YU 85 C6
Milverton GB 29 B4
Milzyn PL 47 C4
Mimice HR 84 C1
Mimizan F 76 B1
Mimizan-Plage F 76 B1
Mimoň CZ 53 C4
Mina de Juliana P 98 B2
Mina de São Domingos P 98 B3
Minas de Riotinto E 99 B4
Minateda E 101 A4
Minaya E 95 C4
Minde P 92 B2
Mindelheim D 61 B6
Mindelstetten D 62 B2
Minden D 51 A4
Mindszent H 75 B5
Minehead GB 29 B4
Mineo I 109 B3
Minerbe I 71 C6
Minérbio I 81 B5
Minervino Murge I 104 B2
Minglanilla E 95 C5
Mingorria E 94 B2
Minnesund N 34 A3
Miño E 86 A2
Miño de San Esteban E 89 C3
Minsen D 43 B4
Minsk BY 7 E9
Mińsk Mazowiecki PL 55 A6
Minsterley GB 26 C3
Mintlaw GB 23 D6
Minturno I 103 B6
Mionica BIH 84 B3
Mionica YU 85 B5
Mios F 76 B2
Mira E 96 B1
Mira I 72 C2
Mira P 92 A2
Mirabel E 93 B4
Mirabel-aux-Baronnies F 79 B4
Mirabella Eclano I 103 B8
Mirabella Imbáccari I 109 B3
Mirabello I 81 B5
Miradoux F 77 B3
Miraflores de la Sierra E 94 B3
Miralrio E 95 B4
Miramar P 87 C2
Miramare I 82 B1
Miramas F 78 C3
Mirambeau F 67 C4
Miramont-de-Guyenne F 77 B3
Miranda de Arga E 89 B5
Miranda de Ebro E 89 B4
Miranda do Corvo P 92 A2
Miranda do Douro P 87 C4
Mirande F 77 C3
Mirandela P 87 C3
Mirandilla E 93 C4
Mirándola I 81 B5
Miranje HR 83 B4
Mirano I 72 C2
Miras AL 112 B2
Miravet E 90 B3
Miré F 57 C5
Mirebeau F 67 B5
Mirebeau-sur-Bèze F 69 A5
Mirecourt F 60 B2
Mirepoix F 77 C4
Miribel F 69 C4
Miričina BIH 84 B3
Mirina GR 112 C7
Mirna SLO 73 C5
Miroslav CZ 64 B2
Mirosławice PL 54 C1
Mirosławiec PL 46 B2
Mirošov CZ 63 A4
Mirotice CZ 63 A5
Mirovice CZ 63 A5
Mirow D 45 B4
Mirsk PL 53 C5
Mirzec PL 55 B6
Misilmeri I 108 A2
Miske H 75 B4
Miskolc H 65 B6
Mislinja SLO 73 B5
Missanello I 104 C2
Missillac F 66 A2
Mistelbach A 64 B2
Mistelbach D 62 A2
Misterbianco I 109 B4
Misterhult S 40 B6
Mistretta I 109 B3
Misurina I 72 B2
Mitchelstown IRL 20 B3
Mithimna GR 112 C8
Mitilini GR 114 C1
Mittelberg, *Tirol* A 71 B5
Mittelberg, *Vorarlberg* A 71 A5
Mittenwald D 71 A6
Mittenwalde D 52 A3
Mitter-Kleinarl A 72 A3
Mitterback A 63 C6
Mitterdorf im Mürztal A 73 A5
Mittersheim F 60 B2
Mittersill A 72 A2
Mitterskirchen D 62 B3
Mitterteich D 62 A3
Mittweida D 52 C2
Mitwitz D 51 C6
Mizhhir'ya UA 11 B7
Mjällby S 41 C4
Mjöbäck S 40 B2
Mjölby S 37 C2
Mjøndalen N 34 B2
Mladá Boleslav CZ 53 C4
Mladá Vožice CZ 63 A5
Mladé Buky CZ 53 C5
Mladenovac YU 85 B5
Mladenovo YU 75 C4
Mladikovine BIH 84 B2
Mława PL 47 B6
Mlinište BIH 84 B1
Młodzieszyn PL 55 A5
Mlogoszyn PL 55 A4
Młynary PL 47 A5
Mnichóvice CZ 63 A5
Mnichovo Hradiště CZ 53 C4
Mniów PL 55 B5
Mnisek nad Hnilcom SK 65 B6
Mníšek pod Brdy CZ 63 A5
Mniszek PL 55 B5
Mniszków PL 55 B5
Mo, *Hedmark* N 34 A3
Mo, *Telemark* N 33 B4
Mo S 35 C3
Mo i Rana N 2 C21
Moaña E 87 B2
Moate IRL 21 A4
Mocejón E 94 C3
Močenok SK 64 B3
Mochales E 95 A4
Mochowo PL 47 C5
Mochy PL 53 A6
Mockern D 52 A1
Mockfjärd S 36 A1
Möckmühl D 61 A5
Mockrehna D 52 B2
Moclin E 100 B2
Mocsa H 64 C4
Möcsény H 74 B3
Modane F 70 C1
Modbury GB 28 C4
Módena I 81 B4
Möðrudalur IS 111 B10
Módica I 109 C3
Modigliana I 81 B5
Modlin PL 47 C6
Mödling A 64 B2
Modliszewice PL 55 B5
Modliszewko PL 46 C3
Modogno I 104 B2
Modra SK 64 B3
Modran BIH 84 B2
Modriča BIH 84 B3
Modrý Kamen SK 65 B5
Moëlan-sur-Mer F 56 C2
Moelfre GB 26 B1
Moena I 72 B1
Moerbeke B 49 B4
Moers D 50 B2
Mões P 87 D3
Moffat GB 25 C4
Mogadouro P 87 C4
Mogata S 37 C3
Móggio Udinese I 72 B3
Mogielnica PL 55 B5
Mogilany PL 65 A5

Mogilno PL 46 C3
Mogliano I 82 C2
Mogliano Véneto I 72 C2
Mogor E 87 B2
Mógoro I 110 C1
Moguer E 99 B4
Mohács H 74 C3
Moheda S 40 B4
Mohedas E 93 A4
Mohedas de la Jara E 93 B5
Mohelnice CZ 64 A2
Mohill IRL 19 C4
Möhlin CH 70 A2
Moholm S 35 C6
Mohorn D 52 B3
Mohyliv-Podil's'kyy UA 11 B9
Moi N 32 C3
Moià E 91 B5
Móie I 82 C2
Moimenta da Beira P 87 D3
Moirans F 69 C5
Moirans-en-Montagne F 69 B5
Moires GR 113 G6
Moisaküla EST 7 B8
Moisdon-la-Rivière F 57 C4
Moissac F 77 B4
Moita, *Coimbra* P 92 A2
Moita, *Guarda* P 93 A3
Moita, *Santarém* P 92 B2
Moita, *Setúbal* P 92 C1
Moita dos Ferreiros P 92 B1
Moixent E 101 A5
Mojacar E 101 B4
Mojados E 88 C2
Mojkovac YU 85 D4
Mojmírovce SK 64 B4
Mojtin SK 65 B4
Möklinta S 36 A3
Mokošica HR 84 D3
Mokra Gora YU 85 C4
Mokro Polje HR 83 B5
Mokronog SLO 73 C5
Mokrzyska PL 55 C5
Møkster N 32 A2
Mol B 49 B6
Mol YU 75 C5
Mola di Bari I 104 B3
Moláoi GR 113 F4
Molare I 80 B2
Molaretto I 70 C2
Molas F 77 C3
Molassano I 80 B2
Molbergen D 43 C4
Mold GB 26 B2
Molde N 2 E17
Møldrup DK 38 C2
Moledo do Minho P 87 C2
Molfetta I 104 B2
Molfsee D 44 A2
Molières F 77 B4
Molina de Aragón E 95 B5
Molina de Segura E 101 A4
Molinar E 89 A3
Molinaseca E 86 B4
Molinella I 81 B5
Molinet F 68 B3
Molini di Tures I 72 B1
Molinicos E 101 A3
Molinos de Duero E 89 C4
Molins de Rei E 91 B5
Moliterno I 104 C1
Molkom S 34 B5
Möllbrücke A 72 B3
Mölle S 41 C2
Molledo E 88 A2
Möllenbeck D 45 B5
Mollerussa E 90 B3
Mollet de Perelada E 91 A5
Mollina E 100 B1
Mölln D 44 B2
Molló E 91 A5
Mollösund S 35 C3
Mölltorp S 37 C1
Mölnbo S 37 B4
Mölndal S 38 B5
Mölnlycke S 38 B5
Molompize F 68 C3
Moloy F 69 A4
Molsheim F 60 B3
Moltzow D 45 B4
Molve HR 74 B2
Molveno I 71 B5
Molvizar E 100 C2
Molzbichl A 72 B3
Mombaróccio I 82 C1
Mombeltrán E 94 B1
Mombris D 51 C5
Mombuey E 87 B4
Momchilgrad BG 112 A7
Mommark DK 39 E3
Momo I 70 C3
Monaghan IRL 19 B5
Monar Lodge GB 22 D4
Monasterace Marina I 106 C3
Monasterevin IRL 21 A4
Monasterio de Rodilla E 89 B3
Monastir I 110 C2
Monbahus F 77 B3
Monbazillac F 77 B3
Moncada E 96 B2
Moncalieri I 80 A1
Moncalvo I 80 A2
Monção P 87 B2
Moncarapacho P 98 B3
Moncel-sur-Seille F 60 B2
Monchegorsk RUS 3 C30
Mönchengladbach = Munchen-Gladbach D 50 B2
Mónchio della Corti I 81 B4
Monchique P 98 B2
Monclar-de-Quercy F 77 C4
Moncofa E 96 B2
Moncontour F 56 B3
Moncoutant F 67 B4
Monda E 100 C1
Mondariz E 87 B2
Mondavio I 82 C1
Mondéjar E 95 B3
Mondello I 108 A2
Mondim de Basto P 87 C3
Mondolfo I 82 C2
Mondoñedo E 86 A3
Mondorf-les-Bains L 60 A2
Mondoubleau F 58 C1
Mondovì I 80 B1
Mondragon F 78 B3
Mondragone I 103 B6
Mondsee A 63 C4
Monéglia I 80 B3
Monegrillo E 90 B2
Monein F 76 C2
Monemvasía GR 113 F5
Mónesi I 80 B1
Monesiglio I 80 B2
Monesterio E 99 A4
Monestier-de-Clermont F 79 B4
Monestiés F 77 B5
Monéteau F 59 C4
Moneygall IRL 21 B4
Moneymore GB 19 B5
Monfalcone I 72 C3
Monfero E 86 A2
Monflanquin F 77 B3
Monflorite E 90 A2
Monforte P 92 B3
Monforte da Beira E 92 B3
Monforte da Beira P 92 B3
Monforte d'Alba I 80 B1
Monforte de Lemos E 86 B3
Monforte de Moyuela E 90 B1
Monforte del Cid E 96 C2
Monghidoro I 81 B5
Mongiana I 106 C3
Monguelfo I 72 B2
Monheim D 62 B1
Moniaive GB 25 C4
Monifieth GB 25 B5
Monikie GB 25 B5
Monistrol-d'Allier F 78 B2
Monistrol de Montserrat E 91 B4
Monistrol-sur-Loire F 68 C4
Mönkebude D 45 B5
Monkton GB 24 C3
Monmouth GB 29 B5
Monnaie F 67 A5
Monnerville F 58 B3
Monnickendam NL 42 C2
Monópoli I 104 C3
Monor H 75 A4
Monóvar E 101 A5
Monpazier F 77 B3
Monreal D 50 C3
Monreal E 76 D1
Monreal del Campo E 95 B5
Monreale I 108 A2
Monroy E 93 B4
Monroyo E 90 C2
Mons B 49 C4
Monsaraz P 92 C3
Monschau D 50 C2
Monségur F 76 B3
Monsélice I 72 C1
Monster NL 49 A5
Mönsterås S 40 B6
Monsummano Terme I 81 C4
Mont-de-Marsan F 76 C2
Mont-Louis F 91 A5
Mont-roig del Camp E 90 B3
Mont-St. Aignan F 58 A2
Mont-St. Vincent F 69 B4
Mont-sous-Vaudrey F 69 B5
Montabaur D 50 C3
Montafia I 80 B2
Montagnac F 78 C2
Montagnana I 71 C6
Montaigu F 66 B3
Montaigu-de-Quercy F 77 B4
Montaiguët-en-Forez F 68 B3
Montaigut F 68 B2
Montaigut-sur-Save F 77 C4
Montalbán E 90 C2
Montalbán de Córdoba E 100 B1
Montalbano Elicona I 109 A4
Montalbano Iónico I 104 C2
Montalbo E 95 C4
Montalcino I 81 C5
Montaldo di Cósola I 80 B3
Montalegre P 87 C3
Montalieu-Vercieu F 69 C5
Montalivet-les-Bains F 66 C3
Montallegro I 108 B2
Montalto delle Marche I 82 D2
Montalto di Castro I 102 A4
Montalto Pavese I 80 B3
Montalto Uffugo I 106 B3
Montalvão P 92 B3
Montamarta E 88 C1
Montana BG 11 E7
Montana-Vermala CH 70 B2
Montánchez E 93 B4
Montanejos E 96 A2
Montano Antilia I 106 A2
Montans F 77 C4
Montargil P 92 B2
Montargis F 58 C3
Montastruc-la-Conseillère F 77 C4
Montauban F 77 B4
Montauban-de-Bretagne F 57 B3
Montbard F 59 C5
Montbarrey F 69 A5
Montbazens F 77 B5
Montbazon F 67 A5
Montbéliard F 70 A1
Montbenoit F 69 B6
Montbeugny F 68 B3
Montblanc E 91 B4
Montbozon F 69 A6
Montbrison F 68 C4
Montbron F 67 C5
Montbrun-les-Bains F 79 B4
Montceau-les-Mines F 69 B4
Montcenis F 69 B4
Montchanin F 69 B4
Montcornet F 59 A5
Montcuq F 77 B4
Montdardier F 78 C2
Montdidier F 58 A3
Monte-Carlo MC 80 C1
Monte Clara P 92 B3
Monte Clérigo P 98 B2
Monte da Pedra P 92 B3
Monte de Goula P 92 B3
Monte do Trigo P 92 C3
Monte Gordo P 98 B3
Monte Juntos P 92 C3
Monte Porzio I 82 C2
Monte Real P 92 B2
Monte Redondo P 92 B2
Monte Romano I 102 A4
Monte San Giovanni Campano I 103 B6
Monte San Savino I 81 C5
Monte Sant'Ángelo I 104 B1
Monte Vilar P 92 B1
Monteagudo E 101 A4
Monteagudo de las Vicarias E 89 C4
Montealegre E 88 C2
Montealegre del Castillo E 101 A4
Montebello Iónico I 109 B4
Montebello Vicentino I 71 C6
Montebelluna I 72 C2
Montebourg F 57 A4
Montebruno I 80 B3
Montecarotto I 82 C2
Montecassiano I 82 C2
Montecastrilli I 102 A5
Montecatini Terme I 81 C4
Montécchio I 82 C1
Montécchio Emilia I 81 B4
Montécchio Maggiore I 71 C6
Montech F 77 C4
Montechiaro d'Asti I 80 A2
Montecórice I 103 C7
Montecorvino Rovella I 103 C7
Montederramo E 87 B3
Montedoro I 108 B2
Montefalco I 82 D1
Montefalcone di Val Fortore I 103 B8
Montefalcone nel Sánnio I 103 B7
Montefano I 82 C2
Montefiascone I 102 A5
Montefiorino I 81 B4
Montefortino I 82 D2
Montefranco I 102 A5
Montefrío E 100 B2
Montegiordano Marina I 106 A3
Montegiórgio I 82 C2
Montegranaro I 82 C2
Montehermoso E 93 A4
Montejicar E 100 B2
Montejo de la Sierra E 95 A3
Montejo de Tiermes E 89 C3
Monteleone di Púglia I 103 B8
Monteleone di Spoleto I 102 A5
Monteleone d'Orvieto I 81 D6
Montelepre I 108 A2
Montelibretti I 102 A5
Montelier F 79 B4
Montélimar F 78 B3
Montella E 91 A4
Montella I 103 C8
Montellano E 99 B5
Montelupo Fiorentino I 81 C5
Montemaggiore Belsito I 108 B2
Montemagno I 80 B2
Montemayor E 100 B1
Montemayor de Pinilla E 88 C2
Montemésola I 104 C3
Montemilleto I 103 B7
Montemilone I 104 B1
Montemolín E 99 A4
Montemónaco I 82 D2
Montemor-o-Novo P 92 C2
Montemor-o-Velho P 92 A2
Montemurro I 104 C1
Montendre F 67 C4
Montenegro de Cameros E 89 B4
Montenero di Bisáccia I 103 B7
Monteneuf F 57 C3
Monteparano I 104 C3
Montepescali I 81 D5
Montepiano I 81 B5
Montepulciano I 81 C5
Montereale I 103 A6
Montereale Valcellina I 72 B2
Montereau-Faut-Yonne F 59 B3
Monterénzio I 81 B5
Monteroni d'Arbia I 81 C5
Monteroni di Lecce I 105 C4
Monterosso al Mare I 80 B3
Monterosso Almo I 109 B3
Monterosso Grana I 79 B6
Monterotondo I 102 A5
Monterotondo Maríttimo I 81 C4
Monterrey E 87 C3
Monterroso E 86 B3
Monterrubio de la Serena E 93 C5
Monterubbiano I 82 C2
Montes Velhos P 98 B2
Montesa E 96 C2
Montesalgueiro E 86 A2
Montesano sulla Marcellana I 104 C1
Montesárchio I 103 B7
Montescaglioso I 104 C2
Montesclaros E 94 B2
Montesilvano I 103 A7
Montespértoli I 81 C5
Montesquieu-Volvestre F 77 C4
Montesquiou F 77 C3
Montestruc-sur-Gers F 77 C3
Montevarchi I 81 C5
Montéveglio I 81 B5
Montfaucon F 66 A3
Montfaucon-d'Argonne F 59 A6
Montfaucon-en-Velay F 69 C4
Montferrat, *Isère* F 69 C5
Montferrat, *Var* F 79 C5
Montfort-en-Chalosse F 76 C2
Montfort-l'Amaury F 58 B2
Montfort-le-Gesnois F 58 B1
Montfort-sur-Meu F 57 B4
Montfort-sur-Risle F 58 A1
Montgai E 90 B3
Montgaillard F 76 C3
Montgenèvre F 79 B5
Montgiscard F 77 C4
Montgomery GB 26 C2
Montguyon F 67 C4
Monthermé F 59 A5
Monthey CH 70 B1
Monthois F 59 A5
Monthureux-sur-Saône F 60 B1
Monti I 110 B2
Monticelli d'Ongina I 81 A3
Montichiari I 71 C5
Monticiano I 81 C5
Montiel E 100 A3
Montier-en-Der F 59 B5
Montieri I 81 C5
Montiglio I 80 A2
Montignac F 77 A4
Montigny-le-Roi F 60 C1
Montigny-lès-Metz F 60 A2
Montigny-sur-Aube F 59 C5
Montijo E 93 C4
Montijo P 92 C2
Montilla E 100 B1
Montillana E 100 B2
Montilly F 68 B3
Montivilliers F 57 A6
Montjaux F 78 B1
Montjean-sur-Loire F 66 A4
Montlhéry F 58 B3
Montlieu-la-Garde F 67 C4
Montlouis-sur-Loire F 67 A5
Montluçon F 68 B2
Montluel F 69 C5
Montmarault F 68 B2
Montmartin-sur-Mer F 57 B4
Montmédy F 59 A6
Montmélian F 69 C6
Montmeyran F 78 B3
Montmirail, *Marne* F 59 B4
Montmirail, *Sarthe* F 58 B1
Montmirat F 78 C3
Montmirey-le-Château F 69 A5
Montmoreau-St. Cybard F 67 C5
Montmorency F 58 B3
Montmorillon F 67 B5
Montmort-Lucy F 59 B4
Montoir-de-Bretagne F 66 A2
Montoire-sur-le-Loir F 58 C1
Montoito P 92 C3
Montolieu F 77 C5
Montório al Vomano I 103 A6
Montoro E 100 A1
Montpellier F 78 C2
Montpezat-de-Quercy F 77 B4
Montpezat-sous-Bouzon F 78 B3
Montpon-Ménestérol F 76 A3
Montpont-en-Bresse F 69 B5
Montréal, *Aude* F 77 C5
Montréal, *Gers* F 76 C3
Montredon-Labessonnié F 77 C5
Montréjeau F 77 C3
Montrésor F 67 A6
Montresta I 110 B1
Montret F 69 B5
Montreuil, *Pas de Calais* F 48 C2
Montreuil, *Seine St. Denis* F 58 B3
Montreuil-aux-Lions F 59 A4
Montreuil-Bellay F 67 A4
Montreux CH 70 B1
Montrevault F 66 A3
Montrevel-en-Bresse F 69 B5
Montrichard F 67 A6
Montricoux F 77 B4
Montrond-les-Bains F 69 C4
Montrose GB 25 B5
Montroy E 96 B2
Monts-sur-Guesnes F 67 B5
Montsalvy F 77 B5
Montsauche-les-Settons F 68 A4
Montseny E 91 B5
Montsoreau F 67 A5
Montsûrs F 57 B5
Montuenga E 94 A2
Montuïri E 97 B3
Monturque E 100 B1
Monza I 71 C4
Monzón E 90 B3
Monzón de Campos E 88 B2
Moorbad Lobenstein D 52 C1
Moordorf D 43 B4
Moorslede B 49 C4
Moosburg D 62 B2
Moosburg im Kärnten A 73 B4
Mór H 74 A3
Mora E 94 C3
Móra P 92 C2
Mora S 2 F21
Mora de Rubielos E 96 A2
Mòra d'Ebre E 90 B3
Mòra la Nova E 90 B3
Moraby S 36 A2
Moradillo de Roa E 88 C3
Morąg PL 47 B5
Mórahalom H 75 B4
Moraime E 86 A1
Morais P 87 C4
Moral de Calatrava E 100 A2
Moraleda de Zafayona E 100 B2
Moraleja E 93 A4
Moraleja del Vino E 88 C1
Morales de Toro E 88 C1
Morales de Valverde E 88 C1
Morales del Vino E 88 C1
Moralina E 87 C4
Morano Cálabro I 106 B3
Mörarp S 41 C2
Morasverdes E 93 A4
Morata de Jalón E 89 C5
Morata de Jiloca E 89 C5
Morata de Tajuña E 95 B3
Moratalla E 101 A4
Moravče SLO 73 B4
Moravec CZ 64 A2
Moraviţa RO 75 C6
Morávka CZ 65 A4
Moravská Třebová CZ 64 A2
Moravské Budějovice CZ 64 A1
Moravské Lieskové SK 64 B3
Moravske Toplice SLO 73 B6
Moravský-Beroun CZ 64 A3
Moravský Krumlov CZ 64 A2
Moravský Svätý Ján SK 64 B3
Morawica PL 55 C5
Morawin PL 54 B3
Morbach D 60 A3
Morbegno I 71 B4
Morbier F 69 B6
Mörbisch am See A 64 C2
Mörbylånga S 41 C6
Morcenx F 76 B2
Morciano di Romagna I 82 C1
Morcone I 103 B7
Morcuera E 89 C3
Mordelles F 57 B4
Moréac F 56 C3
Morebattle GB 25 C5
Morecambe GB 26 A3
Moreda, *Granada* E 100 B2
Moreda, *Oviedo* E 88 A1
Morée F 58 C2
Moreles de Rey E 88 B1
Morella E 90 C2
Moreruela de los Infanzones E 88 C1
Morés E 89 C5
Móres I 110 B1
Morestel F 69 C5
Moret-sur-Loing F 58 B3
Moreton-in-Marsh GB 29 B6
Moretonhampstead GB 28 C4
Moretta I 80 B1
Moreuil F 58 A3
Morez F 69 B6
Mörfelden D 51 D4
Morgano I 72 C2
Morgat F 56 B1
Morges CH 69 B6
Morgex I 70 C2
Morgongåva S 36 B3
Morhange F 60 B2
Morhet B 49 D6
Mori I 71 C5
Morialmé B 49 C5
Morianes P 98 B3
Moriani Plage F 102 A2
Móricháida H 74 A2
Moriles E 100 B1
Morille E 94 B1
Moringen D 51 B5
Morjärv S 3 C25
Morkarla S 36 A4
Morke DK 39 C3
Mørkøv DK 39 D4
Morkovice-Slížany CZ 64 A3
Morlaàs F 76 C2
Morlaix F 56 B2
Mörlunda S 40 B5
Mormanno I 106 B2
Mormant F 59 B3
Mornant F 69 C4
Morokovo YU 85 D4
Morón de Almazán E 89 C4
Morón de la Frontera E 99 B5
Morović YU 85 A4
Morozzo I 80 B1
Morpeth GB 25 C6
Morphou CY 16 D6
Mörrum S 41 C4
Morsbach D 50 C3
Mörsch D 61 B4
Mörsil S 2 E20
Morsum D 39 E1
Mortagne-au-Perche F 58 B1
Mortagne-sur-Gironde F 66 C4
Mortagne-sur-Sèvre F 66 B4
Mortágua P 92 A2
Mortain F 57 B5
Mortara I 70 C3
Morteau F 69 A6
Mortegliano I 72 C3
Mortelle I 109 A4
Mortemart F 67 B5
Mortimer's Cross GB 29 A5
Mortrée F 57 B6
Mörtschach A 72 B2
Mortsel B 49 B5
Morwenstow GB 28 C3
Moryń PL 45 C6
Morzeszczyn PL 47 B4
Morzewo PL 47 B5
Morzine F 70 B1
Mosalsk RUS 7 D13
Mosbach D 61 A5
Mosby N 33 C4
Mosca P 87 C4
Moscavide P 92 C1
Moščenica HR 73 C6
Moščenice HR 73 C4
Moščenicka Draga HR 73 C4
Mosciano Sant'Ángelo I 82 D2
Mościsko PL 54 C1
Moscow = Moskva RUS 7 D14
Mosina PL 54 A1
Mosjøen N 2 D20
Moskorzew PL 55 C4
Moskva = Moscow RUS 7 D14
Moslavina Podravska HR 74 C2
Moşniţa Nouă RO 75 C6
Moso in Passíria I 71 B6
Mosonmagyaróvár H 64 C3
Mošorin YU 75 C5
Mošovce SK 65 B4
Mosqueruela E 90 C2
Moss N 34 B2
Mossfellsbær IS 111 C4
Mössingen D 61 B5
Mosstrand N 33 B5
Most CZ 52 C3
Most na Soči SLO 72 B3
Mosta M 107 C5
Mostar BIH 84 C2
Mosterhamn N 32 B2
Mostki PL 53 A5
Móstoles E 94 B3
Mostová SK 64 B3
Mostowo PL 46 A2
Mostuéjouls F 78 B2
Mosty PL 45 B6
Mostys'ka UA 11 B7
Mota del Cuervo E 95 C4
Mota del Marqués E 88 C1
Motala S 37 C2
Motherwell GB 25 C4
Möthlow D 45 C4
Motilla del Palancar E 95 C5
Motnik SLO 73 B4
Motovun HR 72 C3
Motril E 100 C2
Motta I 71 C6
Motta di Livenza I 72 C2
Motta Montecorvino I 103 B8
Motta Visconti I 70 C3
Mottisfont GB 31 C2
Móttola I 104 C3
Mou DK 38 C3
Mouchard F 69 B5
Moúdhros GR 112 C7
Moudon CH 70 B1
Mougins F 79 C5
Mouilleron en-Pareds F 66 B4
Mouliherne F 67 A5
Moulinet F 80 C1
Moulins F 68 B3
Moulins-Engilbert F 68 B3
Moulins-la-Marche F 58 B1
Moulismes F 67 B5
Moult F 57 A5
Mount Bellew Bridge IRL 20 A3
Mountain Ash GB 29 B4
Mountfield GB 19 B4
Mountmellick IRL 21 A4
Mountrath IRL 21 A4
Mountsorrel GB 30 B2
Moura P 98 A3
Mourão P 92 C3
Mourenx F 76 C2
Mouriés F 78 C3
Mourmelon-le-Grand F 59 A5
Mouronho P 92 A2
Mouscron B 49 C4
Mousehole GB 28 C2
Moussac F 78 C3
Moussey F 60 B2
Mousteru F 56 B2
Moustey F 76 B2
Moustiers-Ste. Marie F 79 C5
Mouthe F 69 B6
Mouthier-Haute-Pierre F 69 A6
Mouthoumet F 77 D5
Moutier CH 70 A2
Moûtiers F 69 C6
Moutiers-les-Mauxfaits F 66 B3
Mouy F 58 A3
Mouzáki GR 112 C3
Mouzon F 59 A6
Møvik N 32 A2
Moville IRL 19 A4
Moy, *Highland* GB 23 D4
Moy, *Tyrone* GB 19 B5
Moycullen IRL 20 A2
Moyenmoutier F 60 B2
Moyenvic F 60 B2
Mózar E 88 C1
Mozhaysk RUS 7 D14
Mozirje SLO 73 B4
Mözs H 74 B3
Mozzanica I 71 C4
Mramorak YU 85 B5
Mrčajevci YU 85 C5
Mrkonjić Grad BIH 84 B2
Mrkopalj HR 73 C4
Mrmoš YU 85 C6
Mrocza PL 46 B3
Mroczeń PL 54 B2
Mroczno PL 47 B5
Mrozy PL 55 A6
Mrzezyno PL 45 A7
Mšec CZ 53 C3
Mšeno CZ 53 C4
Mstów PL 55 C4
Mstsislaw BY 7 D11
Mszana Dolna PL 65 A6
Mszczonów PL 55 B5
Mtsensk RUS 7 E14
Muć HR 83 C5
Múccia I 82 C2
Much D 50 C3
Much Marcle GB 29 B5
Much Wenlock GB 26 C3
Mücheln D 52 B1
Muchów PL 53 B6
Mucientes E 88 C2
Muckross IRL 20 B2
Mucur TR 16 B7
Muda P 98 B2
Mudanya TR 114 B3
Mudau D 61 A5
Müden D 44 C2
Mudersbach D 50 C3
Mudurnu TR 114 B6
Muel E 90 B1
Muelas del Pan E 88 C1
Muess D 44 B3
Muff IRL 19 A4
Mugardos E 86 A2
Muge P 92 B2
Mügeln, *Sachsen-Anhalt* D 52 B3
Mügeln, *Sachsen* D 52 B3
Múggia I 72 C3
Muğla TR 16 C4
Mugnano I 82 C1
Mugron F 76 C2
Mugueimes E 87 C3
Muhi H 65 C6
Mühlacker D 61 B4
Mühlbach am Hochkönig A 72 A3
Mühlberg, *Brandenburg* D 52 B3
Mühlberg, *Thüringen* D 51 C6
Mühldorf A 72 B3
Mühldorf D 62 B3
Muhleberg CH 70 B2
Mühleim D 61 B4
Muhlen-Eichsen D 44 B3
Mühlhausen, *Bayern* D 62 A1
Mühlhausen, *Thüringen* D 51 B6
Mühltroff D 52 C1
Muhos FIN 3 D27
Muhr A 72 A3
Muine Bheag IRL 21 B5
Muir of Ord GB 23 D4
Muirkirk GB 24 C3
Muirteira P 92 B1
Mukacheve UA 11 B7
Muker GB 26 A3
Mula E 101 A4
Mulben GB 23 D5
Mulegns CH 71 B4
Mules I 71 B6
Mülheim D 50 B2
Mulhouse F 60 C3
Muljava SLO 73 C4
Mullany's Cross IRL 18 B3
Müllheim D 60 C3
Mullhyttan S 36 B1
Mullinavat IRL 21 B4
Mullingar IRL 21 A4
Mullion GB 28 C2
Müllrose D 53 A4
Mullsjö S 40 B3
Mulseryd S 40 B3
Munaðarnes IS 111 A4
Munana E 94 B1
Muñás E 86 A4
Münchberg D 52 C1
Müncheberg D 45 C6
München = Munich D 62 B2
Munchen-Gladbach = Mönchengladbach D 50 B2

Osterburg D 44 C3
Osterburken D 61 A5
Österbybruk S 36 A4
Østerbyhavn DK 38 B4
Österbymo S 40 B5
Ostercappeln D 43 C5
Österfärnebo S 36 A3
Osterfeld D 52 B1
Osterhofen D 62 B4
Osterholz-Scharmbeck D 43 B5
Østerild DK 38 B1
Österlövsta S 36 A4
Ostermiething A 62 B3
Osterode am Harz D 51 B6
Östersund S 2 E21
Östervåla S 36 A4
Östervallskog S 34 B3
Osterwieck D 51 B6
Osterzell D 62 C1
Ostffyasszonyfa H 74 A2
Östhammar S 36 A5
Ostheim F 60 B3
Ostheim vor der Rhön D 51 C6
Osthofen D 61 A4
Ostiano I 71 C5
Ostiglia I 81 A5
Ostiz E 76 D1
Östmark S 34 A4
Ostojićevo YU 75 C5
Ostra I 82 C2
Östra Amtervik S 34 B5
Östra Husby S 37 C3
Östra Ljungby S 41 C3
Östra Ryd S 37 C3
Östraby S 41 D3
Ostrach D 61 C5
Ostrau D 52 B3
Ostrava CZ 64 A4
Østre Halsen N 35 B2
Ostrhauderfehn D 43 B4
Ostritz D 53 B4
Ostróda PL 47 B5
Ostroh UA 11 A9
Ostrołęka PL 6 E6
Ostropole PL 46 B2
Ostroróg PL 46 C2
Ostrošovac BIH 83 B4
Ostrov CZ 52 C2
Ostrov RUS 7 C10
Ostrov nad Oslavou CZ 64 A1
Ostrów Mazowiecka PL 6 E6
Ostrów Wielkopolski PL 54 B2
Ostrówek PL 54 B3
Ostrowice PL 46 A2
Ostrowiec-Świętokrzyski PL 55 C6
Ostrowite PL 47 B5
Ostrowo PL 47 C4
Ostrožac BIH 84 C2
Ostrzeszów PL 54 B2
Ostseebad Kühlungsborn D 44 A3
Ostuni I 104 C3
Osuna E 99 B5
Osvětimany CZ 64 A3
Oswestry GB 26 C2
Oświęcim PL 55 C4
Osztopán H 74 B2
Oteiza E 89 B5
Otelec RO 75 C5
Oteo E 89 A3
Oterbekk N 34 B2
Otero de Herreros E 94 B2
Otero de O Bodas E 87 C4
Othem S 37 D5
Otley GB 27 B4
Otmuchów PL 54 C2
Otočac HR 83 B4
Otok, *Splitsko-Dalmatinska* HR 83 C5
Otok, *Vukovarsko-Srijemska* HR 74 C3
Otoka BIH 83 B5
Otranto I 107 A5
Otrić HR 83 B5
Otrícoli I 102 A5
Otrokovice CZ 64 A3
Ottana I 110 B2
Ottaviano I 103 C7
Ottenby S 41 C6
Ottendorf-Okrilla D 53 B3
Ottenhöfen D 61 B4
Ottenschlag A 63 B6
Ottensheim A 63 B5
Otter Ferry GB 24 B2
Otterbach D 60 A3
Otterbäcken S 35 C6
Otterberg D 60 A3
Otterburn GB 25 C5
Otterndorf D 43 B5
Ottersburg D 43 B6
Ottersweier D 61 B4
Otterup DK 39 D3
Ottery St. Mary GB 29 C4
Ottignies B 49 C5
Ottmarsheim F 60 C3
Ottobeuren D 61 C6
Öttömös H 75 B4
Ottone I 80 B3
Ottweiler D 60 A3
Ötvöskónyi H 74 B2
Otwock PL 55 A6
Ouanne F 59 C4
Ouarville F 58 B2
Oucques F 58 C2
Oud-Beijerland NL 49 B5
Oud Gastel NL 49 B5
Ouddorp NL 49 B4
Oude-Pekela NL 43 B4
Oude-Tonge NL 49 B5
Oudemirdum NL 42 C2
Oudenaarde B 49 C4
Oudenbosch NL 49 B5
Oudenburg B 48 B3
Oudewater NL 49 A5
Oudon F 66 A3
Oughterard IRL 20 A2
Ouguela P 93 B3
Ouistreham F 57 A5
Oulainen FIN 3 D26
Oulchy-le-Château F 59 A4
Oullins F 69 C4
Oulmes F 67 B4
Oulton GB 30 B5
Oulton Broad GB 30 B5
Oulu FIN 3 D26
Oulx I 79 A5
Oundle GB 30 B3
Ouranópolis GR 112 B6
Ourense E 87 B3
Ourique P 98 B2
Ourol E 86 A3
Ouroux-en-Morvan F 68 A3
Ousdale GB 23 C5
Oust F 77 D4
Outeiro P 92 A2
Outeiro de Rei E 86 A3
Outes E 86 B2
Outokumpu FIN 3 E28
Outreau F 48 C2
Outwell GB 30 B4
Ouzouer-le-Marché F 58 C2
Ouzouer-sur-Loire F 58 C3
Ovada I 80 B2
Ovar P 87 D2
Ove DK 38 C2
Ovelgönne D 43 B5
Over-jerstal DK 39 D2
Overath D 50 C3
Overbister GB 23 B6
Overdinkel NL 50 A3
Överenhörna S 36 B4
Overijse B 49 C5
Överkalix S 3 C25
Overlade DK 38 C2
Överlida S 40 B2
Overpelt B 49 B6
Overton GB 26 C3
Övertorneå S 3 C25
Överum S 37 D3
Ovidiopol UA 11 C11
Oviedo E 88 A1
Oviglio I 80 B2
Ovindoli I 103 A6
Ovodda I 110 B2
Øvre Årdal N 2 F17
Øvre Sirdal N 32 C3
Övre Ullerud S 34 B5
Øvrebygd N 32 C3
Ovruch UA 7 F10
Ovtrup DK 39 D1
Owińska PL 46 C2
Oxelösund S 37 C4
Oxenholme GB 26 A3
Oxford GB 31 C2
Oxie S 41 D3
Oxilithos GR 112 D4
Oxted GB 31 C4
Oyaca TR 114 C7
Øyenkilen N 34 B2
Oyfiell N 33 B5
Øygärdslia N 33 C5
Oykel Bridge GB 22 D4
Øymark N 34 B3
Oyonnax F 69 B5
Øyslebø N 33 C4
Oyten D 43 B6
Øyuvsbu N 33 B4
Ozaeta E 89 B4
Ozalj HR 73 C5
Ożarów PL 55 C6
Ożarów Maz PL 55 A5
Ožbalt SLO 73 B5
Ózd H 65 B6
Ožďany SK 65 B5
Ozieri I 110 B2
Ozimek PL 54 C3
Ozimica BIH 84 B3
Ozora H 74 B3
Ozorków PL 55 B4
Ozzano Monferrato I 80 A2

P

Paal B 49 B6
Pabianice PL 55 B4
Pacanów PL 55 C6
Paceco I 108 B1
Pachino I 109 C4
Pačir YU 75 C4
Pack A 73 A5
Paços de Ferreira P 87 C2
Pacov CZ 63 A6
Pacsa H 74 B2
Pacy-sur-Eure F 58 A2
Paczków PL 54 C2
Padany RUS 3 E30
Padborg DK 39 E2
Padej YU 75 C5
Padene HR 83 B5
Paderborn D 51 B4
Paderne P 98 B2
Padiham GB 26 B3
Padina YU 75 C5
Padinska Skela YU 85 B5
Padornelo P 87 C2
Pádova I 72 C1
Padragkút H 74 A2
Padria I 110 B1
Padrón E 86 B2
Padru I 110 B2
Padstow GB 28 C3
Padul E 100 B2
Padula I 104 C1
Paduli I 103 B7
Paesana I 79 B6
Paese I 72 C2
Pag HR 83 B4
Pagani I 103 C7
Pagánica I 103 A6
Pagánico I 81 D5
Paglieta I 103 A7
Pagny-sur-Moselle F 60 B1
Páhi H 75 B4
Pahl D 62 C2
Paide EST 7 B8
Paignton GB 29 C4
Pailhès F 77 C4
Paimboeuf F 66 A2
Paimpol F 56 B2
Paimpont F 57 B3
Painswick GB 29 B5
Painten D 62 B2
Paisley GB 24 C3
Pajala S 3 C25
Pajares E 88 A1
Pajares de los Oteros E 88 B1
Pajęczno PL 54 B3
Páka H 74 B1
Pakość PL 47 C4
Pakosławice PL 54 C2
Pakoštane HR 83 C4
Pakrac HR 74 C2
Paks H 74 B3
Palacios de la Sierra E 89 C3
Palaciòs de la Valduerna E 88 B1
Palacios de Sanabria E 87 B4
Palacios del Sil E 86 B4
Palaciosrubios E 94 A1
Palafrugell E 91 B6
Palagiano I 104 C3
Palagonia I 109 B3
Paláia I 81 C4
Palaiókastron GR 113 G8
Palaiokhóra GR 113 G5
Pálairos GR 112 D2
Palaiseau F 58 B3
Palamás GR 112 C4
Palamós E 91 B6
Palanga LT 6 D6
Palanzano I 81 B4
Palárikovo SK 64 B4
Palas de Rei E 86 B3
Palata I 103 B7
Palatna YU 85 C6
Palau I 110 A2
Palavas-les-Flots F 78 C2
Palazuelos de la Sierra E 89 B3
Palazzo Adriano I 108 B2
Palazzo del Pero I 81 C5
Palazzo San Gervásio I 104 C1
Palazzolo Acréide I 109 B3
Palazzolo sull Oglio I 71 C4
Palazzuolo sul Senio I 81 B5
Paldiski EST 6 B8
Pale BIH 84 C3
Palena I 103 B7
Palencia E 88 B2
Palenciana E 100 B1
Palermo I 108 A2
Palestrina I 102 B5
Pálfa H 74 B3
Palfau A 63 C5
Palhaça P 92 A2
Palheiros da Tocha P 92 A2
Palheiros de Quiaios P 92 A2
Paliaópolis GR 113 E6
Palić YU 75 B4
Palidoro I 102 B5
Palinuro I 106 A2
Paliouri GR 112 C5
Paliseul B 59 A6
Pallanza I 70 C3
Pallares E 99 A4
Pallaruelo de Monegros E 90 B2
Pallas Green IRL 20 B3
Pallerols E 91 A4
Palling D 62 B3
Palluau F 66 B3
Palma P 92 C2
Palma Campánia I 103 C7
Palma de Mallorca E 97 B2
Palma del Rio E 99 B5
Palma di Montechiaro I 108 B2
Palma Nova E 97 B2
Palmanova I 72 C3
Palmela P 92 C2
Palmerola E 91 A5
Palmi I 106 C2
Pálmonostora H 75 B4
Palo del Colle I 104 B2
Palomares E 101 B4
Palomares del Campo E 95 C4
Palomas E 93 C4
Palombara Sabina I 102 A5
Palos de la Frontera E 99 B4
Palotaboszok H 74 B3
Palotás H 65 C5
Pals E 91 B6
Pålsboda S 37 B2
Paluzza I 72 B3
Pamhagen A 64 C2
Pamiers F 77 C4
Pamiętowo PL 46 B3
Pampaneira E 100 C2
Pamparato I 80 B1
Pampilhosa, *Aveiro* P 92 A2
Pampilhosa, *Coimbra* P 92 A3
Pampliega E 88 B3
Pamplona E 76 D1
Pamukçu TR 114 C2
Pamukova TR 114 B5
Panagyurishte BG 11 E8
Pancalieri I 80 B1
Pančevo YU 85 B5
Pancey F 59 B6
Pancorvo E 89 B3
Pancrudo E 90 C1
Pandino I 71 C4
Pandrup DK 38 B2
Panenský-Týnec CZ 53 C3
Panes E 88 A2
Panevėžys LT 6 D8
Pangbourne GB 31 C2
Panissières F 69 C4
Panki PL 54 C3
Pannes F 58 B3
Panningen NL 50 B1
Pannonhalma H 74 A2
Pánormos GR 113 E7
Panschwitz-Kuckau D 53 B4
Pansdorf D 44 B2
Pantano de Cíjara E 94 C2
Panticosa E 76 D2
Pantín E 86 A2
Pantoja E 94 B3
Pantón E 86 B3
Panxon E 87 B2
Páola I 106 B3
Paola M 107 C5
Pápa H 74 A2
Papasidero I 106 B2
Pápateszér H 74 A2
Papenburg D 43 B4
Paphos CY 16 D6
Pappenheim D 62 B1
Paprotnia PL 55 A5
Parábita I 107 A5
Paraćin YU 85 C6
Parád H 65 C6
Parada, *Bragança* P 87 C4
Parada, *Viseu* P 92 A2
Paradas E 99 B5
Paradela E 86 B3
Parades de Rubiales E 94 A1
Paradinas de San Juan E 94 B1
Paradiso di Cevadale I 71 B5
Paradyż PL 55 B5
Parainen FIN 6 A7
Parakhino Paddubye RUS 7 B12
Paramé F 57 B4
Paramithiá GR 112 C2
Páramo E 86 A4
Páramo del Sil E 86 B4
Parandaça P 87 C3
Paravadella E 86 A3
Paray-le-Monial F 68 B4
Parceiros P 92 B2
Parcey F 69 A5
Parchim D 44 B3
Parcice PL 54 B3
Pardilla E 88 C3
Pardubice CZ 53 C5
Paredes E 95 B4
Paredes P 87 C2
Paredes de Coura P 87 C2
Paredes de Nava E 88 B2
Paredes de Siguenza E 95 A4
Pareja E 95 B4
Parennes F 57 B5
Parenti I 106 B3
Parentis-en-Born F 76 B1
Parey D 44 C3
Parfino RUS 7 C11
Parga GR 112 C2
Pargny-sur-Saulx F 59 B5
Parigné-l'Évêque F 58 C1
Parikkala FIN 3 F28
Paris F 58 B3
Parisot F 77 B4
Parkano FIN 3 E25
Parknasilla IRL 20 C2
Parla E 94 B3
Parlavá E 91 A6
Parma I 81 B4
Parndorf A 64 C2
Párnica SK 65 A5
Parnu EST 6 B8
Parolis E 101 A3
Páros GR 113 E7
Parrillas E 94 B1
Parsberg D 62 A2
Parstein D 45 C6
Partakko FIN 3 B27
Partanna I 108 B1
Parthenay F 67 B4
Partinico I 108 A2
Partizani YU 85 B5
Partizánske SK 65 B4
Partney GB 27 B6
Påryd S 40 C5
Parysów PL 55 B6
Parzymiechy PL 54 B3
Paşcani RO 11 C9
Pasewalk D 45 B5
Pasina Voda YU 85 C4
Påskallavik S 40 B6
Pasłęk PL 47 A5
Pašman HR 83 C4
Passage East IRL 21 B5
Passage West IRL 20 C3
Passail A 73 A5
Passais F 57 B5
Passau D 63 B4
Passegueiro P 92 A2
Passignano sul Trasimeno I 82 C1
Passo di Tréia I 82 C2
Passopisciaro I 109 B4
Passow D 45 B6
Passy F 70 C1
Pastavy BY 7 D9
Pástena I 103 B7
Pastrana E 95 B4
Pastrengo I 71 C5
Pasym PL 47 B6
Pásztó H 65 C5
Pata SK 64 B3
Patay F 58 B2
Pateley Bridge GB 27 A4
Paterek PL 46 B3
Paterna E 96 B2
Paterna de Rivera E 99 C5
Paterna del Campo E 99 B4
Paterna del Madera E 101 A3
Paternion A 72 B3
Paternò I 109 B3
Paternópoli I 103 C8
Patersdorf D 62 A3
Paterswolde NL 42 B3
Patitirion GR 112 C5
Patna GB 24 C3
Pątnow PL 54 A3
Patos AL 105 C5
Pátrai = Patras GR 113 D3
Patras = Pátrai GR 113 D3
Patreksfjörður IS 111 B2
Patrickswell IRL 20 B3
Patrimonio F 102 A2
Patrington GB 27 B5
Pattada I 110 B2
Pattensen, *Niedersachsen* D 44 B2
Pattensen, *Niedersachsen* D 51 A5
Patterdale GB 26 A3
Patti I 109 A3
Páty H 74 A3
Pau F 76 C2
Pauillac F 66 C4
Paularo I 72 B3
Paulhaguet F 68 C3
Paulhan F 78 C2
Paulilátino I 110 B1
Paulström S 40 B5
Paullo I 71 C4
Paulstown IRL 21 B4
Pausa D 52 C1
Pavia I 71 C4
Pavia P 92 C2
Pavias E 96 B2
Pavilly F 58 A1
Pāvilosta LV 6 C6
Pavino Polje YU 85 C4
Pavullo nel Frignano I 81 B4
Pawłowice, *Opolskie* PL 54 B2
Pawlowice, *Śląskie* PL 54 D3
Paxoí GR 112 C2
Payerne CH 70 B1
Paymogo E 98 B3
Payrac F 77 B4
Pazardzhik BG 11 E8
Pazaryeri TR 114 B4
Pazin HR 72 C3
Paziols F 78 D1
Pčelić HR 74 C2
Peal de Becerro E 100 B2
Peasmarsh GB 31 D4
Peć YU 85 D5
Péccioli I 81 C4
Pécel H 75 A4
Pechao P 98 B3
Pechenga RUS 3 B29
Pechenizhyn UA 11 B8
Pecica RO 75 B6
Pećinci YU 85 B4
Pecka YU 85 B4
Peckelsheim D 51 B5
Pečory RUS 7 C9
Pécs H 74 B3
Pécsvárad H 74 B3
Peczniew PL 54 B3
Pedaso I 82 C2
Pedavena I 72 B1
Pedérobba I 72 C1
Pedersker DK 41 D4
Pedescala I 71 C6
Pedrafita E 86 B3
Pedrajas de San Esteban E 88 C2
Pedralba E 96 B2
Pedralba de la Praderia E 87 B4
Pedraza E 94 A3
Pedreguer E 96 C3
Pedrera E 100 B1
Pedro Abad E 100 B1
Pedro Bernardo E 94 B2
Pedro-Martinez E 100 B2
Pedro Muñoz E 95 C4
Pedroche E 100 A1
Pedrógão, *Beja* P 98 A3
Pedrógão, *Castelo Branco* P 92 A3
Pedrógão, *Leiria* P 92 B2
Pedrógão Grande P 92 B2
Pedrola E 90 B1
Pedrosa de Tobalina E 89 B3
Pedrosa del Rey E 88 C1
Pedrosa del Rio Urbel E 88 B3
Pedrosillo de los Aires E 94 B1
Pedrosillo el Ralo E 94 A1
Pędzewo PL 47 B4
Peebles GB 25 C4
Peel GB 26 A1
Peenemünde D 45 A5
Peer B 49 B6
Pega P 93 A3
Pegalajar E 100 B2
Pegau D 52 B2
Peggau A 73 A5
Pegli I 80 B2
Pegnitz D 62 A2
Pego E 96 C2
Pegões-Estação P 92 C2
Pegões Velhos P 92 C2
Pęgów PL 54 B1
Pegswood GB 25 C6
Peguera E 97 B2
Pehlivanköy TR 114 A1
Peine D 51 A6
Peisey-Nancroix F 70 C1
Peissenberg D 62 C2
Peiting D 62 C1
Peitz D 53 B4
Péjo I 71 B5
Pelagićevo BIH 84 B3
Pelahustán E 94 B2
Pełczyce PL 46 B1
Pelhřimov CZ 63 A6
Pélissanne F 79 C4
Pelkosenniemi FIN 3 C27
Pellegrino Parmense I 81 B3
Pellegrue F 76 B3
Pellérd H 74 B3
Pellestrina I 72 C2
Pellevoisin F 67 B6
Pellizzano I 71 B5
Pello FIN 3 C26
Peloche E 93 B5
Pelplin PL 47 B4
Pelussin F 69 C4
Pély H 75 A5
Pembroke GB 28 B3
Pembroke Dock GB 28 B3
Peña de Cabra E 94 B1
Peñacerrada E 89 B4
Penacova P 92 A2
Peñafiel E 88 C2
Penafiel P 87 C2
Peñaflor E 99 B5
Peñalba de Santiago E 86 B4
Peñalsordo E 93 C5
Penalva do Castelo P 92 A3
Penamacôr P 93 A3
Peñaparda E 93 A4
Peñaranda de Bracamonte E 94 B1
Peñaranda de Duero E 89 C3
Peñarroya de Tastavins E 90 C3
Peñarroya-Pueblonuevo E 93 C5
Peñarrubla E 86 B3
Penarth GB 29 B4
Peñas de San Pedro E 101 A4
Peñascosa E 101 A3
Peñausende E 88 C1
Penc H 65 C5
Pencoed GB 29 B4
Pendálofon GR 112 B3
Pendeen GB 28 C2
Pendine GB 28 B3
Pendueles E 88 A2
Penedono P 87 D3
Penela P 92 A2
Penhas Juntas P 87 C3
Peniche P 92 B1
Penicuik GB 25 C4
Penig D 52 C2
Penilhos P 98 B3
Peñíscola E 90 C3
Penistone GB 27 B4
Penkridge GB 26 C3
Penkun D 45 B6
Penmarch F 56 C1
Pennabilli I 82 C1
Penne I 103 A6
Penne-d'Agenais F 77 B3
Pennes I 71 B6
Pennyghael GB 24 B1
Peno RUS 7 C12
Penpont GB 25 C4
Penrhyndeudraeth GB 26 C1
Penrith GB 26 A3
Penryn GB 28 C2
Pentraeth GB 26 B1
Penybontfawr GB 26 C2
Penygroes, *Carmarthenshire* GB 28 B3
Penygroes, *Gwynedd* GB 26 B1
Penzance GB 28 C2
Penzberg D 62 C2
Penzlin D 45 B5
Pepeljevac YU 85 C6
Pepinster B 50 C1
Pér H 64 C3
Pera Boa P 92 A3
Perafita P 87 C2
Perakhóra GR 113 D4
Peraleda de la Mata E 93 B5
Peraleda de San Román E 93 B5
Peraleda del Zaucejo E 93 C5
Perales de Alfambra E 90 C1
Perales de Tajuña E 95 B3
Perales del Puerto E 93 A4
Peralta E 89 B5
Peralta de la Sal E 90 B3
Peralva P 98 B3
Peralveche E 95 B4
Pérama GR 113 G6
Perbál H 65 C4
Perchtoldsdorf A 64 B2
Percy F 57 B4
Perdasdefogu I 110 C2
Perdiguera E 90 B2
Peredo P 87 C4
Peregu Mare RO 75 B5
Pereiro, *Faro* P 98 B3
Pereiro, *Guarda* P 87 D3
Pereiro, *Santarém* P 92 B2
Pereiro de Aguiar E 87 B3
Perelada E 91 A6
Perelejos de las Truchas E 95 B5
Pereña E 87 C4
Pereruela E 88 C1
Pereyaslav-Khmelnytskyy UA 11 A11
Pérfugas I 110 B1
Perg A 63 B5
Pérgine Valsugana I 71 B6
Pérgola I 82 C1
Pergusa I 109 B3
Periam RO 75 B5
Periana E 100 C1
Périers F 57 A4
Périgueux F 67 C5
Perino I 80 B3
Perjasica HR 73 C5
Perkáta H 74 A3
Perković HR 83 C5
Perleberg D 44 B3
Perlez YU 75 C5
Përmet AL 112 B2
Pernarec CZ 62 A4
Pernek SK 64 B3
Pernes P 92 B2
Pernes-les-Fontaines F 79 B4
Pernik BG 11 E7
Pernink CZ 52 C2
Pernitz A 64 C1
Pero Pinheiro P 92 C1
Peroguarda P 98 A2
Pérols F 78 C2
Péronne F 59 A3
Péronnes B 49 C5
Perorrubio E 94 A3
Perosa Argentina I 79 B6
Perozinho P 87 C2
Perpignan F 91 A5
Perranporth GB 28 C2
Perranzabuloe GB 28 C2
Perrecy-les-Forges F 69 B4
Perrero I 79 B6
Perrignier F 69 B6
Perros-Guirec F 56 B2
Persan F 58 A3
Persberg S 34 B6
Persenbeug A 63 B6
Pershore GB 29 A5
Perstorp S 41 C3
Perth GB 25 B4
Pertisau A 72 A1
Pertoča SLO 73 B6
Pertuis F 79 C4
Perućac YU 85 C4
Perúgia I 82 C1
Perušić HR 83 B4
Péruwelz B 49 C4
Pervomaysk UA 11 B11
Perwez B 49 C5
Pesadas de Burgos E 89 B3
Pesaguero E 88 A2
Pésaro I 82 C1
Pescantina I 71 C5
Pescara I 103 A7
Pescasséroli I 103 B6
Peschici I 104 B2
Peschiera del Garda I 71 C5
Péscia I 81 C4
Pescina I 103 A6
Pesco Sannita I 103 B7
Pescocostanzo I 103 B7
Pescopagano I 103 C8
Peshkopi AL 112 A2
Pesmes F 69 A5
Pesnica SLO 73 B5
Peso da Régua P 87 C3
Pesquera de Duero E 88 C2
Pessac F 76 B2
Pestovo RUS 7 B13
Péta GR 112 C3
Petalídhion GR 113 F3
Pétange L 60 A1
Peteranec HR 74 B1
Peterborough GB 30 B3
Peterculter GB 23 D6
Peterhead GB 23 D7
Peterlee GB 25 D6
Petersfield GB 31 C3
Petershagen, *Brandenburg* D 45 C5
Petershagen, *Brandenburg* D 45 C6
Petershagen, *Nordrhein-Westfalen* D 43 C5
Petershausen D 62 B2
Peterswell IRL 20 A3
Pétervására H 65 B6
Petília Policastro I 107 B3
Petín E 87 B3
Petkus D 52 B3
Petlovac HR 74 C3
Petlovača YU 85 B4
Petöfiszállás H 75 B4
Petra E 97 B3
Petralia Sottana I 109 B3
Petrčane HR 83 B4
Petrella Tifernina I 103 B7
Petrer E 101 A5
Petreto-Bicchisano F 102 B1
Petrich BG 112 A5
Petrijevci HR 74 C3
Petrinja HR 73 C6
Petrodvorets RUS 7 B10
Pétrola E 101 A4
Petronà I 107 B3
Petronell A 64 B2
Petroşani RO 11 D7
Petrovac YU 85 B6
Petrovaradin YU 75 C4
Petrovice BIH 84 B3
Petrovice CZ 53 C3
Pettenbach A 63 C5
Pettigo IRL 19 B4
Petworth GB 31 D3
Peuerbach A 63 B4
Peuntenansa E 88 A2
Pevensey Bay GB 31 D4
Peveragno I 80 B1
Pewsey GB 29 B6
Pewsum D 43 B4
Peyrat-le-Château F 68 C1
Peyrehorade F 76 C1
Peyriac-Minervois F 77 C5
Peyrins F 79 A4
Peyrissac F 67 C6
Peyrolles-en-Provence F 79 C4
Peyruis F 79 B4
Pézarches F 59 B3
Pézenas F 78 C2
Pezinok SK 64 B3
Pezuls F 77 B3
Pfaffenhausen D 61 B6
Pfaffenhofen, *Bayern* D 61 B6
Pfaffenhofen, *Bayern* D 62 B2
Pfaffenhoffen F 60 B3
Pfäffikon CH 70 A3
Pfarrkirchen D 62 B3
Pfeffenhausen D 62 B2
Pfetterhouse F 70 A2
Pforzheim D 61 B4
Pfreimd D 62 A3
Pfronten D 61 C6
Pfullendorf D 61 C5
Pfullingen D 61 B5
Pfunds A 71 B5
Pfungstadt D 61 A4
Pfyn CH 61 C4
Phalsbourg F 60 B3
Philippeville B 49 C5
Philippsreut D 63 B4
Philippsthal D 51 C5
Piacenza I 81 A3
Piacenza d'Adige I 72 C1
Piádena I 71 C5
Piana F 102 A1
Piana Crixia I 80 B2
Piana degli Albanesi I 108 B2

Resuttano I 109 B3
Retamal E 93 C4
Retford GB 27 B5
Rethel F 59 A5
Rethem D 43 C6
Réthimnon GR 113 G6
Retie B 49 B6
Retiers F 57 C4
Retortillo E 87 D4
Retortillo de Soria E 89 C3
Retournac F 68 C4
Rétság H 65 C5
Rettenegg A 73 A5
Retuerta del Bullaque E 94 C2
Retz A 64 B1
Retzbach D 61 A5
Reuden D 52 A2
Reuilly F 68 A2
Reus E 91 B4
Reusel NL 49 B6
Reuterstadt Stavenhagen D 45 B4
Reuth D 62 A3
Reutlingen D 61 B5
Reutte A 71 A5
Reuver NL 50 B2
Revel F 77 C4
Revello I 80 B1
Revenga E 94 B2
Revest-du-Bion F 79 B4
Révfülöp H 74 B2
Revigny-sur-Ornain F 59 B5
Revin F 59 A5
Řevnice CZ 63 A5
Řevničov CZ 53 C3
Revo I 71 B6
Revúca SK 65 B6
Rewa PL 47 A4
Rewal PL 45 A7
Reyðarfjörður IS 111 B11
Reyero E 88 B1
Reykhólar IS 111 B3
Reykholt, *Árnessýsla* IS 111 C5
Reykholt, *Borgarfjarðarsýsla* IS 111 C4
Reykjahlið IS 111 B9
Reykjavík IS 111 C4
Rezé F 66 A3
Rēzekne LV 7 C9
Rezovo BG 11 F10
Rezzato I 71 C5
Rezzoáglio I 80 B3
Rhaunen D 60 A3
Rhayader GB 29 A4
Rheda-Wiedenbrück D 50 B4
Rhede, *Niedersachsen* D 43 B4
Rhede, *Nordrhein-Westfalen* D 50 B2
Rheinau D 60 B3
Rheinbach D 50 C2
Rheinberg D 50 B2
Rheine D 50 A3
Rheinfelden D 70 A2
Rheinsberg D 45 B4
Rhêmes-Notre-Dame I 70 C2
Rhenen NL 49 B6
Rhens D 50 C3
Rheydt D 50 B2
Rhiconich GB 22 C4
Rhinow D 44 C4
Rhiw GB 26 C1
Rho I 70 C4
Rhoden D 51 B5
Rhondda GB 29 B4
Rhosllanerchrugog GB 26 B2
Rhosneigr GB 26 B1
Rhossili GB 28 B3
Rhubodach GB 24 C2
Rhuddlan GB 26 B2
Rhyl GB 26 B2
Rhynie GB 23 D6
Riala S 36 B5
Riallé F 66 A3
Riaño E 88 B1
Riano I 102 A5
Rians F 79 C4
Rianxo E 86 B2
Riaza E 89 C3
Riba E 89 A3
Riba de Saelices E 95 B4
Riba-Roja de Turia E 96 B2
Riba-roja d'Ebre E 90 B3
Ribadavia E 87 B2
Ribadeo E 86 A3
Ribadesella E 88 A1
Ribaflecha E 89 B4
Ribaforada E 89 C5
Ribare YU 85 B6
Ribariće YU 85 D5
Ribe DK 39 D1
Ribeauvillé F 60 B3
Ribécourt-Dreslincourt F 59 A3
Ribeira da Pena P 87 C3
Ribeira de Piquín E 86 A3
Ribemont F 59 A4
Ribera I 108 B2
Ribera de Cardós E 91 A4
Ribera del Fresno E 93 C4
Ribérac F 67 C5
Ribes de Freser E 91 A5
Ribesalbes E 96 A2
Ribiers F 79 B4
Ribnica BIH 84 B3
Ribnica SLO 73 C4
Ribnica YU 85 C5
Ribnica na Potorju SLO 73 B5
Ribnik HR 73 C5
Rîbnița MD 11 C10
Ribnitz-Damgarten D 44 A4
Ribolla I 81 D5
Říčany, *Jihomoravský* CZ 64 A2
Říčany, *Středočeský* CZ 53 D4
Ríccia I 103 B7
Riccione I 82 B1
Ricco Del Golfo I 81 B3
Richebourg F 59 B6
Richelieu F 67 A5
Richisau CH 70 A3
Richmond, *Greater London* GB 31 C3
Richmond, *North Yorkshire* GB 27 A4
Richtenberg D 45 A4
Richterswil CH 70 A3
Rickling D 44 A2
Rickmansworth GB 31 C3
Ricla E 89 C5
Riddarhyttan S 36 B2
Ridderkerk NL 49 B5
Riddes CH 70 B2
Ridjica YU 75 C4
Riec-sur-Bélon F 56 C2
Ried A 63 B4
Ried im Oberinntal A 71 A5
Riedenburg D 62 B2
Riedlingen D 61 B5
Riedstadt D 61 A4
Riegersburg A 73 B5
Riego de la Vega E 88 B1
Riego del Camino E 88 C1
Riello E 88 B1
Riemst B 49 C6
Rienne B 49 D5
Riénsena E 88 A2
Riesa D 52 B3
Riese Pio X I 72 C1
Riesi I 109 B3
Riestedt D 52 B1
Rietberg D 51 B4
Rieti I 102 A5
Rietschen D 53 B4
Rieumes F 77 C4
Rieupeyroux F 77 B5
Rieux F 77 C4
Riez F 79 C5
Rīga LV 6 C8
Riggisberg CH 70 B2
Rignac F 77 B5
Rignano Gargánico I 104 B1
Rigolato I 72 B2
Rigside GB 25 C4
Rigutino I 81 C5
Riihimäki FIN 3 F26
Rijeka HR 73 C4
Rijen NL 49 B5
Rijkevorsel B 49 B5
Rijssen NL 50 A2
Rilić BIH 84 C2
Rilievo I 108 B1
Rillo de Gallo E 95 B5
Rimavská Baňa SK 65 B5
Rimavská Seč SK 65 B6
Rimavská Sobota SK 65 B6
Rimbo S 36 B5
Rimforsa S 37 C2
Rímini I 82 B1
Rîmnicu Sărat RO 11 D9
Rimogne F 59 A5
Rimpar D 61 A5
Rimske Toplice SLO 73 B5
Rincón de la Victoria E 100 C1
Rincón de Soto E 89 B5
Ringarum S 37 C3
Ringaskiddy IRL 20 C3
Ringe DK 39 D3
Ringkøbing DK 39 C1
Ringsted DK 39 D4
Ringwood GB 29 C6
Rinkaby S 41 D4
Rinkabyholm S 40 C6
Rinlo E 86 A3
Rinn A 71 A6
Rinteln D 51 A5
Rio E 86 B3
Rio do Coures P 92 B2
Rio Douro P 87 C3
Rio Frio P 92 C2
Rio frio de Riaza E 95 A3
Rio Maior P 92 B2
Rio Marina I 81 D4
Rio Tinto P 87 C2
Riobo E 86 B2
Riodeva E 96 A1
Riofrio E 94 B2
Riofrio de Aliste E 87 C4
Riogordo E 100 C1
Rioja E 101 C3
Riola I 81 B5
Riola Sardo I 110 C1
Riolobos E 93 B4
Riom F 68 C3
Riom-ès-Montagnes F 68 C2
Riomaggiore I 81 B3
Rion-des-Landes F 76 C2
Rionegro del Puente E 87 B4
Rionero in Vúlture I 104 C1
Riopar E 101 A3
Riós E 87 C3
Rioseco E 88 A1
Rioseco de Tapia E 88 B1
Riotord F 69 C4
Riotorto E 86 A3
Rioz F 69 A6
Ripač BIH 83 B4
Ripacándida I 104 C1
Ripanj YU 85 B5
Ripatransone I 82 D2
Ripley GB 27 B4
Ripoll E 91 A5
Ripon GB 27 A4
Riposto I 109 B4
Risan YU 105 A4
Risca GB 29 B4
Rischenau D 51 B5
Riscle F 76 C2
Rišňovce SK 64 B3
Risør N 33 C6
Risøyhamn N 2 B21
Ritterhude D 43 B5
Riva del Garda I 71 C5
Riva Lígure I 80 C1
Rivanazzano I 80 B3
Rivarolo Canavese I 70 C2
Rivarolo Mantovano I 81 A4
Rive-de-Gier F 69 C4
Rivedoux-Plage F 66 B3
Rivello I 106 A2
Rivergaro I 80 B3
Rives F 69 C5
Rivesaltes F 78 D1
Rivignano I 72 C3
Rivne UA 11 A9
Rivoli I 80 A1
Rivolta d'Adda I 71 C4
Rixheim F 60 C3
Rixo S 35 C3
Rjukan N 33 B5
Rø DK 41 D4
Rö S 36 B5
Roa E 88 C3
Roa N 34 A2
Roade GB 30 B3
Roager DK 39 D1
Roaldkvam N 32 B3
Roanne F 68 B4
Robakowo PL 47 B4
Róbbio I 70 C3
Röbel D 45 B4
Roberton GB 25 C5
Robertville B 50 C2
Robin Hood's Bay GB 27 A5
Robleda E 93 A4
Robledillo de Trujillo E 93 B5
Robledo, *Albacete* E 101 A3
Robledo, *Orense* E 86 B4
Robledo de Chavela E 94 B2
Robledo del Buey E 94 C2
Robledo del Mazo E 94 C2
Robledollano E 93 B5
Robles de la Valcueva E 88 B1
Robliza de Cojos E 87 D5
Robres E 90 B2
Robres del Castillo E 89 B4
Rocafort de Queralt E 91 B4
Rocamadour F 77 B4
Rocca di Mezzo I 103 A6
Rocca di Papa I 102 B5
Rocca Imperiale I 106 A3
Rocca Priora I 82 C2
Rocca San Casciano I 81 B5
Rocca Sinibalda I 102 A5
Roccabernarda I 107 B3
Roccabianca I 81 A4
Roccadáspide I 103 C8
Roccagorga I 102 B6
Roccalbegna I 81 D5
Roccalumera I 109 B4
Roccamena I 108 B2
Roccamonfina I 103 B6
Roccanova I 106 A3
Roccapalumba I 108 B2
Roccapassa I 103 A6
Roccaraso I 103 B7
Roccasecca I 103 B6
Roccastrada I 81 C5
Roccatederighi I 81 C5
Roccella Iónica I 106 C3
Rocchetta Sant'Antònio I 103 B8
Rocester GB 27 C4
Rochdale GB 26 B3
Roche-lez-Beaupré F 69 A6
Rochechouart F 67 C5
Rochefort B 49 C6
Rochefort F 66 C4
Rochefort-en-Terre F 56 C3
Rochefort-Montagne F 68 C2
Rochefort-sur-Nenon F 69 A5
Rochemaure F 78 B3
Rocheservière F 66 B3
Rochester, *Medway* GB 31 C4
Rochester, *Northumberland* GB 25 C5
Rochlitz D 52 B2
Rociana del Condado E 99 B4
Rockenhausen D 60 A3
Rockhammar S 36 B2
Rockneby S 40 C6
Ročko Polje HR 73 C4
Rocroi F 59 A5
Roda de Bara E 91 B4
Roda de Ter E 91 B5
Rodach D 51 C6
Rodalben D 60 A3
Rødberg N 33 A5
Rødby DK 44 A3
Rødbyhavn DK 44 A3
Rødding, *Sonderjyllands Amt.* DK 39 D2
Rødding, *Viborg Amt.* DK 38 C1
Rödeby S 41 C5
Rodeiro E 86 B3
Rødekro DK 39 D2
Roden NL 42 B3
Ródenas E 95 B5
Rodenkirchen D 43 B5
Rödental D 52 C1
Rödermark D 51 D4
Rodewisch D 52 C2
Rodez F 77 B5
Rodholívas GR 112 B5
Ródhos GR 16 C4
Rodi Gargánico I 104 B1
Roding D 62 A3
Rødkærsbro DK 39 C2
Rodoñá E 91 B4
Rødvig DK 41 D2
Roermond NL 50 B1
Roesbrugge B 48 C3
Roeschwoog F 61 B4
Roeselare B 49 C4
Roetgen D 50 C2
Roffiac F 78 A2
Röfors S 37 C1
Rofrano I 106 A2
Rogač HR 83 C5
Rogačica YU 85 B4
Rogalinek PL 54 A1
Rogaška Slatina SLO 73 B5
Rogatec SLO 73 B5
Rogatica BIH 84 C4
Rogatyn UA 11 B8
Rogätz D 52 A1
Roggendorf D 44 B3
Roggiano Gravina I 106 B3
Roghadal GB 22 D2
Rogliano F 102 A2
Rogliano I 106 B3
Rognes F 79 C4
Rogny-les-7-Ecluses F 59 C3
Rogowo PL 46 C3
Rogóz PL 47 A6
Rogoznica HR 83 C4
Rogoźnica PL 53 B6
Rogoźno PL 46 C2
Rohan F 56 B3
Röhlingen D 61 B6
Rohožník SK 64 B3
Rohr D 51 C6
Rohr im Gebirge A 63 C6
Rohrbach A 63 B4
Rohrbach-lès-Bitche F 60 A3
Rohrberg D 44 C3
Röhrnbach D 63 B4
Roisel F 59 A4
Roja LV 6 C7
Rojales E 96 C2
Rokiciny PL 55 B4
Rokietnica PL 46 C2
Rokiškis LT 7 D8
Rokitki PL 53 B5
Rokitno RUS 7 F13
Rokycany CZ 63 A4
Rolampont F 59 C6
Rold DK 38 C2
Røldal N 32 B3
Rolde NL 42 C3
Rollag N 33 A6
Rollán E 94 B1
Rolle CH 69 B6
Roma = Rome I 102 B5
Roma S 37 D5
Romagnano Sésia I 70 C3
Romagné F 57 B4
Romakloster S 37 D5
Roman RO 11 C9
Romana I 110 B1
Romanèche-Thorins F 69 B4
Romano di Lombardia I 71 C4
Romans-sur-Isère F 79 A4
Romanshorn CH 71 A4
Rombas F 60 A2
Rome = Roma I 102 B5
Romeán E 86 B3
Romenay F 69 B5
Romeral E 95 C3
Römerstein D 61 B5
Rometta I 109 A4
Romford GB 31 C4
Romhány H 65 C5
Römhild D 51 C6
Romilly-sur-Seine F 59 B4
Romny UA 11 A12
Romodan UA 11 B12
Romont CH 70 B1
Romorantin-Lanthenay F 68 A1
Romrod D 51 C5
Romsey GB 31 D2
Rømskog N 34 B3
Rønbjerg DK 38 C1
Roncal E 76 D2
Ronce-les-Bains F 66 C3
Ronchamp F 60 C2
Ronchi dei Legionari I 72 C3
Ronciglione I 102 A5
Ronco Canavese I 70 C2
Ronco Scrivia I 80 B2
Ronda E 99 C5
Rønde DK 39 C3
Rone S 37 D5
Ronehamn S 37 D5
Rönnäng S 38 B4
Rønne DK 41 D4
Ronneburg D 52 C2
Ronneby S 41 C5
Rönneshytta S 37 C2
Rönninge S 36 B4
Rönö S 37 C3
Ronov nad Doubravou CZ 63 A6
Ronse B 49 C4
Roosendaal NL 49 B5
Roosky IRL 19 C4
Ropczyce PL 55 C6
Ropeid N 32 B3
Ropuerelos del Páramo E 88 B1
Roquebilière F 79 B6
Roquebrun F 78 C2
Roquecourbe F 77 C5
Roquefort F 76 B2
Roquemaure F 78 B3
Roquesteron F 79 C5
Roquetas de Mar E 101 C3
Roquetes E 90 C3
Roquevaire F 79 C4
Rørbæk DK 38 C2
Rore BIH 83 B5
Röro S 38 B4
Røros N 2 E19
Rorschach CH 71 A4
Rørvig DK 39 D4
Rørvik N 2 D19
Rörvik S 40 B4
Rosà I 72 C1
Rosa Marina I 104 C3
Rosal de la Frontera E 98 B3
Rosalina Mare I 72 C2
Rosans F 79 B4
Rosário P 98 B2
Rosarno I 106 C2
Rosbach D 50 C3
Rosche D 44 C2
Rościszewo PL 47 C5
Roscoff F 56 B2
Roscommon IRL 18 C3
Roscrea IRL 21 B4
Rosdorf D 51 B5
Rose I 106 B3
Rosegg A 73 B4
Rosehall GB 22 D4
Rosehearty GB 23 D6
Rosel GB 57 A3
Rosell E 90 C3
Roselló E 90 B3
Rosendal N 32 B3
Rosenfeld D 61 B4
Rosenfors S 40 B5
Rosenheim D 62 C3
Rosenow D 45 B5
Rosenthal D 51 B4
Rosersberg S 36 B4
Roses E 91 A6
Roseto degli Abruzzi I 103 A7
Roseto Valfortore I 103 B8
Rosheim F 60 B3
Rosia I 81 C5
Rosice CZ 64 A2
Rosières-en-Santerre F 58 A3
Rosignano Maríttimo I 81 C4
Rosignano Solvay I 81 C4
Roşiori-de-Vede RO 11 D8
Roskhill GB 22 D2
Roskilde DK 39 D5
Röslau D 52 C1
Roslavl RUS 7 E12
Roslev DK 38 C1
Rosmaninhal P 93 B3
Rosmult IRL 21 B4
Rosnowo PL 46 A2
Rosolini I 109 C3
Rosova YU 85 C4
Rosoy F 59 B4
Rosporden F 56 C2
Rosquete P 92 B2
Rosrath D 50 C3
Ross-on-Wye GB 29 B5
Rossa CH 71 B4
Rossano I 106 B3
Rossas, *Aveiro* P 87 D2
Rossas, *Braga* P 87 C2
Rossdorf D 51 C6
Rossett GB 26 B3
Rosshaupten D 62 C1
Rossiglione I 80 B2
Rossignol B 60 A1
Rossla D 52 B1
Rosslare IRL 21 B5
Rosslare Harbour IRL 21 B5
Rosslau D 52 B2
Rosslea GB 19 B4
Rossleben D 52 B1
Rossoszyca PL 54 B3
Rosswein D 52 B3
Röstånga S 41 C3
Roštár SK 65 B6
Rostock D 44 A4
Rostrenen F 56 B2
Rosyth GB 25 B4
Röszke H 75 B5
Rot am See D 61 A5
Rota E 99 C4
Rota Greca I 106 B3
Rotella I 82 D2
Rotenburg, *Hessen* D 51 C5
Rotenburg, *Niedersachsen* D 43 B6
Roth, *Bayern* D 62 A2
Roth, *Rheinland-Pfalz* D 50 C3
Rothbury GB 25 C6
Rothemühl D 45 B5
Rothenkempenow D 45 B6
Röthenbach D 62 A2
Rothenburg D 53 B4
Rothenburg ob der Tauber D 61 A6
Rothéneuf F 57 B4
Rothenstein D 62 B2
Rotherham GB 27 B4
Rothes GB 23 D5
Rothesay GB 24 C2
Rothwell GB 30 B3
Rotnes N 34 A2
Rotonda I 106 B3
Rotondella I 106 A3
Rotova E 96 C2
Rott, *Bayern* D 62 C1
Rott, *Bayern* D 62 C3
Rottach-Egern D 62 C2
Röttenbach D 62 A2
Rottenbuch D 62 C1
Rottenburg, *Baden-Württemberg* D 61 B4
Rottenburg, *Bayern* D 62 B3
Rottenmann A 73 A4
Rotterdam NL 49 B5
Rotthalmünster D 63 B4
Rottingdean GB 31 D3
Röttingen D 61 A5
Rottleberode D 51 B6
Rottne S 40 B4
Rottneros S 34 B5
Rottofreno I 80 A3
Rottweil D 61 B4
Rötz D 62 A3
Roubaix F 49 C4
Roudnice nad Labem CZ 53 C4
Roudouallec F 56 B2
Rouen F 58 A2
Rouffach F 60 C3
Rougé F 57 C4
Rougemont F 69 A6
Rougemont le-Château F 60 C2
Rouillac F 67 C4
Rouillé F 67 B5
Roujan F 78 C2
Roulans F 69 A6
Roundwood IRL 21 A5
Rousínov CZ 64 A2
Roussac F 67 B6
Roussennac F 77 B5
Rousses F 78 B2
Roussillon F 69 C4
Rouvroy-sur-Audry F 59 A5
Rouy F 68 A3
Rovaniemi FIN 3 C26
Rovato I 71 C4
Rovensko pod Troskami CZ 53 C5
Roverbella I 71 C5
Rovereto I 71 C6
Rövershagen D 44 A4
Roverud N 34 A4
Rovigo I 81 A5
Rovinj HR 82 A2
Rovišce HR 74 C1
Rów PL 45 C6
Rowy PL 46 A3
Royal Leamington Spa GB 30 B2
Royal Tunbridge Wells GB 31 C4
Royan F 66 C3
Royat F 68 C3
Roybon F 69 C5
Roybridge GB 24 B3
Roye F 58 A3
Røykenvik N 34 A2
Royos E 101 B3
Royston GB 30 B3
Rozadas E 86 A4
Rožaj YU 85 D5
Rozalén del Monte E 95 C4
Różańsko PL 45 C6
Rožanstvo YU 85 C4
Rozay-en-Brie F 59 B3
Roždalovice CZ 53 C5
Rozdilna UA 11 C11
Rozental PL 47 B5
Rozhyshche UA 11 A8
Rožmitál pod Třemšínem CZ 63 A4
Rožňava SK 65 B6
Rožnov pod Radhoštěm CZ 64 A4
Rozoy-sur-Serre F 59 A5
Rozprza PL 55 B4
Roztoky CZ 53 C4
Rozvadov CZ 62 A3
Rozzano I 71 C4
Ruanes E 93 B5
Rubbestadnesset N 32 B2
Rubi E 91 B5
Rubiá E 86 B4
Rubiacedo de Abajo E 89 B3
Rubielos Bajos E 95 C4
Rubielos de Mora E 96 A2
Rubiera I 81 B4
Rucandio E 89 B3
Rud, *Akershus* N 34 A3
Rud, *Buskerud* N 34 A2
Ruda PL 54 B3
Ruda S 40 B6
Ruda Maleniecka PL 55 B5
Ruda Pilczycka PL 55 B5
Ruda Śl. PL 54 C3
Rudabánya H 65 B6
Ruden A 73 B4
Rudersberg D 61 B5
Rudersdorf A 73 A6
Rüdersdorf D 45 C5
Ruderting D 63 B4
Rüdesheim D 50 D3
Rudkøbing DK 39 E3
Rudmanns A 63 B6
Rudna CZ 53 C4
Rudna PL 53 B6
Rudnik, *Kosovo* YU 85 D5
Rudnik, *Srbija* YU 85 B5
Rudniki, *Opolskie* PL 54 B3
Rudniki, *Śląskie* PL 55 C4
Rudno, *Dolnośląskie* PL 54 B1
Rudno, *Pomorskie* PL 47 B4
Rudnya RUS 7 D11
Rudo BIH 85 C4
Rudolstadt D 52 C1
Rudowica PL 53 B5
Rudozem BG 112 A6
Ruds Vedby DK 39 D4
Rudskoga S 35 B6
Rudston GB 27 A5
Rudy PL 54 C3
Rue F 48 C2
Rueda E 88 C2
Rueda de Jalón E 90 B1
Ruelle-sur-Touvre F 67 C5
Ruerrero E 88 B3
Ruffano I 107 B5
Ruffec F 67 B5
Rufina I 81 C5
Rugby GB 30 B2
Rugeley GB 27 C4
Rugles F 58 B1
Rugozero RUS 3 D30
Rühen D 44 C2
Ruhla D 51 C6
Ruhland D 53 B3
Ruhle D 43 C4
Ruhpolding D 62 C3
Ruhstorf D 63 B4
Ruidera E 95 D4
Ruillé-sur-le-Loir F 58 C1
Ruinen NL 42 C3
Ruiselede B 49 B4
Rulles B 60 A1
Rülzheim D 61 A4
Rum H 74 A1
Ruma YU 85 A4
Rumboci BIH 84 C2
Rumburk CZ 53 C4
Rumenka YU 75 C4
Rumia PL 47 A4
Rumigny F 59 A5
Rumilly F 69 C5
Rumney GB 29 B4
Rumont F 59 B6
Rumy PL 47 B6
Runa P 92 B1
Runcorn GB 26 B3
Rungsted DK 41 D2
Runhällen S 36 A3
Runowo PL 47 A6
Ruokolahti FIN 3 F28
Ruoms F 78 B3
Ruoti I 104 C1
Rupa HR 73 C4
Ruppichteroth D 50 C3
Rupt-sur-Moselle F 60 C2
Rus E 100 A2
Ruse BG 11 E9
Ruše SLO 73 B5
Ruševo HR 74 C3
Rush IRL 21 A5
Rushden GB 30 B3
Rusiec PL 54 B3
Rusinowo, *Zachodnio-Pomorskie* PL 46 B1
Rusinowo, *Zachodnio-Pomorskie* PL 46 B2
Ruski Krstur YU 75 C4
Ruskington GB 27 B5
Rusovce SK 64 B3
Rüsselsheim D 51 D4
Russi I 81 B6
Rust A 64 C2
Rustrel F 79 C4
Ruszki PL 55 A5
Ruszów PL 53 B5
Rute E 100 B1
Rüthen D 51 B4
Rutherglen GB 24 C3
Ruthin GB 26 B2
Ruthven GB 23 D4
Ruthwell GB 25 D4
Rüti CH 70 A3
Rutigliano I 104 B3
Rutoši YU 85 C4
Rutuna S 37 C4
Ruurlo NL 50 A2
Ruvo del Monte I 104 C1
Ruvo di Púglia I 104 B2
Ružić HR 83 C5
Ružomberok SK 65 A5
Ruzsa H 75 B4
Ry DK 39 C2
Rybany SK 64 B4
Rybina PL 47 A5
Rybinsk RUS 7 B15
Rybnik PL 54 C3
Rychliki PL 47 B5
Rychlocice PL 54 B3
Rychnov nad Kněžnou CZ 53 C6
Rychnowo PL 47 B6
Rychtal PL 54 B2
Rychwał PL 54 A3
Ryczywół, *Mazowieckie* PL 55 B6
Ryczywół, *Wielkopolskie* PL 46 C2
Ryd S 40 C4
Rydaholm S 40 C4
Rydal S 40 B2
Rydbo S 36 B5
Rydboholm S 40 B2
Ryde GB 31 D2
Rydöbruk S 40 C3
Rydsgård S 41 D3
Rydsnäs S 40 B5
Rydultowy PL 54 C3
Rydzyna PL 54 B1
Rye GB 31 D4
Rygge N 34 B2
Ryjewo PL 47 B4
Rykene N 33 C5
Rylsk RUS 7 F13
Rymań PL 46 B1
Rýmařov CZ 64 A3
Rynarzewo PL 46 B3
Ryomgård DK 39 C3
Rypin PL 47 B5
Ryssby S 40 C4
Rytel PL 46 B3
Rytro PL 65 A6
Rywociny PL 47 B6
Rzeczenica PL 46 B3
Rzeczniów PL 55 B6
Rzeczyca PL 55 B5
Rzęgnowo PL 47 B6
Rzejowice PL 55 B4
Rzemień PL 55 C6
Rzepin PL 45 C6
Rzesznikowo PL 46 B1
Rzeszów PL 10 A6
Rzgów PL 55 B4
Rzhev RUS 7 C13

S

Sa Pobla E 97 B3
Sa Savina E 97 C1
Saal, *Bayern* D 51 C6
Saal, *Bayern* D 62 B2
Saalbach A 72 A2
Saalburg D 52 C1
Saales F 60 B3
Saalfeld D 52 C1
Saalfelden am Steinernen Meer A 72 A2
Saanen CH 70 B2
Saarbrücken D 60 A2
Saarburg D 60 A2
Saarijärvi FIN 3 E26
Saarlouis D 60 A2
Saas-Fee CH 70 B2
Šabac YU 85 B4
Sabadell E 91 B5
Sabáudia I 102 B6
Sabbioneta I 81 B4
Sabero E 88 B1
Sabiñánigo E 90 A2
Sabiote E 100 A2
Sablé-sur-Sarthe F 57 C5
Sables-d'Or-les-Pins F 56 B3
Sabóia P 98 B2
Saborsko HR 83 A4
Sabres F 76 B2
Sabrosa P 87 C3
Sabugal P 93 A3
Sabuncu TR 114 C5
Săcălaz RO 75 C6
Sacecorbo E 95 B4
Saceda del Rio E 95 B4

Sacedón E 95 B4
Săcele RO 11 D8
Saceruela E 94 D2
Sachsenburg A 72 B3
Sachsenhagen D 43 C6
Sacile I 72 C2
Sacramenia E 88 C3
Sada E 86 A2
Sádaba E 90 A1
Saddell GB 24 C2
Sadernes E 91 A5
Sadki PL 46 B3
Sadkowice PL 55 B5
Sadów PL 53 A4
Sadská CZ 53 C4
Sæbøvik N 32 B2
Sæby DK 38 B3
Saelices E 95 C4
Saelices de Mayorga E 88 B1
Saerbeck D 50 A3
Særslev DK 39 D3
Sætre N 34 B2
Saeul L 60 A1
Sævareid N 32 A2
Safaalan TR 114 A3
Safara P 98 A3
Säffle S 34 B4
Saffron Walden GB 31 B4
Safonovo RUS 7 D12
Safranbolu TR 16 A6
Säfsnäs S 36 A1
Şag RO 75 C6
Sagard D 45 A5
S'Agaro E 91 B6
Sagone F 102 A1
Sagres P 98 C2
Ságújfalu H 65 B5
Sagunt E 96 B2
Sagvåg N 32 B2
Ságvár H 74 B3
Sagy F 69 B5
Sahagún E 88 B1
Šahy SK 65 B4
Saignelégier CH 70 A1
Saignes F 68 C2
Saillagouse F 91 A5
Saillans F 79 B4
Sains F 59 A4
St. Abb's GB 25 C5
St. Affrique F 78 C1
St. Agnan F 68 B3
St. Agnant F 66 C4
St. Agnes GB 28 C2
St. Agrève F 78 A3
St. Aignan F 67 A6
St. Aignan-sur-Roë F 57 C4
St. Alban-sur-Limagnole F 78 B2
St. Albans GB 31 C3
St. Amand-en-Puisaye F 68 A3
St. Amand-les-Eaux F 49 C4
St. Amand-Longpré F 58 C2
St. Amand-Montrond F 68 B2
St. Amans F 78 B2
St. Amans-Soult F 77 C5
St. Amant-Roche-Savine F 68 C3
St. Amarin F 60 C2
St. Ambroix F 78 B3
St. Amé F 60 B2
St. Amour F 69 B5
St. André-de-Corcy F 69 C4
St. André-de-Cubzac F 76 B2
St. André-de-l'Eure F 58 B5
St. André-de-Sangonis F 78 C2
St. André-de-Valborgne F 78 B2
St. André-les-Alpes F 79 C5
St. Andrews GB 25 B5
St. Angel F 68 C2
St. Anthème F 68 C3
St. Antoine-de-Ficalba F 77 B3
St. Antönien CH 71 B4
St. Antonin-Noble-Val F 77 B4
St. Août F 68 B1
St. Armant-Tallende F 68 C3
St. Arnoult F 58 B2
St. Asaph GB 26 B2
St. Astier F 67 C5
St. Athan GB 29 B4
St. Auban F 79 C5
St. Aubin CH 70 B1
St. Aubin F 69 A5
St. Aubin GB 57 A3
St. Aubin-d'Aubigné F 57 B4
St. Aubin-du-Cormier F 57 B4
St. Aubin-sur-Aire F 60 B1
St. Aubin-sur-Mer F 57 A5
St. Aulaye F 67 C5
St. Austell GB 28 C3
St. Avit F 68 C2
St. Avold F 60 A2
St. Aygulf F 79 C5
St. Bauzille-de-Putois F 78 C2
St. Béat F 77 D3
St. Bees GB 26 A2
St. Benim-d'Azy F 68 B3
St. Benoît-du-Sault F 67 B6
St. Benoit-en-Woëvre F 60 B1
St. Berthevin F 57 B5
St. Blaise-la-Roche F 60 B3
St. Blazey GB 28 C3
St. Blin F 59 B6
St. Bonnet F 79 B5
St. Bonnet-de-Joux F 69 B4
St. Bonnet-le-Château F 68 C4
St. Bonnet-le-Froid F 69 C4
St. Brévin-les-Pins F 66 A2
St. Briac-sur-Mer F 57 B3
St. Brice-en-Coglès F 57 B4
St. Brieuc F 56 B3
St. Bris-le-Vineux F 59 C4
St. Broladre F 57 B4
St. Calais F 58 C1
St. Cannat F 79 C4
St. Cast-le-Guildo F 57 B3
St. Céré F 77 B4
St. Cergue CH 69 B6
St. Cergues F 69 B6
St. Cernin F 77 A5
St. Chamant F 68 C1
St. Chamas F 79 C4
St. Chamond F 69 C4
St. Chély-d'Apcher F 78 B2
St. Chély-d'Aubrac F 78 B1
St. Chinian F 78 C1
St. Christol-lès-Alès F 78 B3
St. Christoly-Médoc F 66 C4
St. Christophe-du-Ligneron F 66 B3
St. Christophe-en-Brionnais F 69 B4
St. Ciers-sur-Gironde F 67 C4
St. Clair-sur-Epte F 58 A2
St. Clar F 77 C3
St. Claud F 67 C5
St. Claude F 69 B5
St. Clears GB 28 B3
St. Columb Major GB 28 C3
St. Come-d'Olt F 78 B1
St. Cosme-en-Vairais F 58 B1
St. Cyprien, *Dordogne* F 77 B4
St. Cyprien, *Pyrenées-Orientales* F 91 A6
St. Cyr-sur-Loire F 67 A5
St. Cyr-sur-Mer F 79 C4
St. Cyr-sur-Methon F 69 B4
St. David's GB 28 B2
St. Denis F 58 B3
St. Denis-d'Oléron F 66 B3
St. Denis d'Orques F 57 B5
St. Didier F 69 B4
St. Didier-en-Velay F 69 C4
St. Dié F 60 B2
St. Dizier F 59 B5
St. Dizier-Leyrenne F 68 B1
St. Dogmaels GB 28 A3
St. Efflam F 56 B2
St. Égrève F 69 C5
St. Eloy-les-Mines F 68 B2
St. Émilion F 76 B2
St. Enoder GB 28 C3
St. Esteben F 76 C1
St. Estèphe F 66 C4
St. Étienne F 69 C4
St. Etienne-de-Baigorry F 76 C1
St. Étienne-de-Cuines F 69 C6
St. Etienne-de-Fursac F 67 B6
St. Etienne-de-Montluc F 66 A3
St. Etienne-de-St. Geoirs F 69 C5
St. Étienne-de-Tinée F 79 B5
St. Étienne-du-Bois F 69 B5
St. Étienne-du-Rouvray F 58 A2
St. Etienne-les-Orgues F 79 B4
St. Fargeau F 59 C4
St. Félicien F 78 A3
St. Felix-de-Sorgues F 78 C1
St. Félix-Lauragais F 77 C4
St. Fillans GB 24 B3
St. Firmin F 79 B5
St. Florent F 102 A2
St. Florent-le-Vieil F 66 A3
St. Florent-sur-Cher F 68 B2
St. Florentin F 59 C4
St. Flour F 78 A2
St. Flovier F 67 B6
St. Fort-sur-le-Né F 67 C4
St. Fulgent F 66 B3
St. Galmier F 69 C4
St. Gaudens F 77 C3
St. Gaultier F 67 B6
St. Gély-du-Fesc F 78 C2
St. Genest-Malifaux F 69 C4
St. Gengoux-le-National F 69 B4
St. Geniez F 79 B5
St. Geniez-d'Olt F 78 B1
St. Genis-de-Saintonge F 67 C4
St. Genis-Pouilly F 69 B6
St. Genix-sur-Guiers F 69 C5
St. Georges Buttavent F 57 B5
St. Georges-d'Aurac F 68 C3
St. Georges-de-Commiers F 79 A4
St. Georges-de-Didonne F 66 C4
St. Georges-de-Luzençon F 78 B1
St. Georges-de Mons F 68 C2
St. Georges-de-Reneins F 69 B4
St. Georges d'Oléron F 66 C3
St. Georges-en-Couzan F 68 C3
St. Georges-lès-Baillargeaux F 67 B5
St. Georges-sur-Loire F 66 A4
St. Georges-sur-Meuse B 49 C6
St. Geours-de-Maremne F 76 C1
St. Gérand-de-Vaux F 68 B3
St. Gérand-le-Puy F 68 B3
St. Germain F 60 C2
St. Germain-Chassenay F 68 B3
St. Germain-de-Calberte F 78 B2
St. Germain-de-Confolens F 67 B5
St. Germain-de-Joux F 69 B5
St. Germain-des-Fossés F 68 B3
St. Germain-du-Bois F 69 B5
St. Germain-du-Plain F 69 B4
St. Germain-du Puy F 68 A2
St. Germain-en-Laye F 58 B3
St. Germain-Laval F 68 C4
St. Germain-Lembron F 68 C3
St. Germain-les-Belles F 67 C6
St. Germain-Lespinasse F 68 B3
St. Germain-l'Herm F 68 C3
St. Gervais-d'Auvergne F 68 B2
St. Gervais-les-Bains F 70 C1
St. Gervais-sur-Mare F 78 C2
St. Gildas-de-Rhuys F 66 A2
St. Gildas-des-Bois F 66 A2
St. Gilles, *Gard* F 78 C3
St. Gilles, *Ille-et-Vilaine* F 57 B4
St. Gilles-Croix-de-Vie F 66 B3
St. Gingolph F 70 B1
St. Girons, *Ariège* F 77 D4
St. Girons, *Landes* F 76 C1
St. Girons-Plage F 76 C1
St. Gobain F 59 A4
St. Guénolé F 56 C1
St. Harmon GB 29 A4
St. Helens GB 26 B3
St. Helier GB 57 A3
St. Herblain F 66 A3
St. Hilaire, *Allier* F 68 B3
St. Hilaire, *Aude* F 77 C5
St. Hilaire-de-Riez F 66 B3
St. Hilaire-de-Villefranche F 67 C4
St. Hilaire-des-Loges F 67 B4
St. Hilaire-du-Harcouët F 57 B4
St. Hilaire-du-Rosier F 79 A4
St. Hippolyte, *Aveyron* F 77 B5
St. Hippolyte, *Doubs* F 70 A1
St. Hippolyte-du-Fort F 78 C2
St. Honoré-les-Bains F 68 B3
St. Hubert B 49 C6
St. Imier CH 70 A2
St. Issey GB 28 C3
St. Ives, *Cambridgeshire* GB 30 B3
St. Ives, *Cornwall* GB 28 C2
St. Izaire F 78 C1
St. Jacques-de-la-Lande F 57 B4
St. Jacut-de-la-Mer F 57 B3
St. James F 57 B4
St. Jaume d'Enveja E 90 C3
St. Jean-Brévelay F 56 C3
St. Jean-d'Angély F 67 C4
St. Jean-de-Belleville F 69 C6
St. Jean-de-Bournay F 69 C5
St. Jean-de-Braye F 58 C2
St. Jean-de-Côle F 67 C5
St. Jean-de-Daye F 57 A4
St. Jean de Losne F 69 A5
St. Jean-de-Luz F 76 C1
St. Jean-de-Maurienne F 69 C6
St. Jean-de-Monts F 66 B2
St. Jean-d'Illac F 76 B2
St. Jean-du-Bruel F 78 B2
St. Jean-du-Gard F 78 B2
St. Jean-en-Royans F 79 A4
St. Jean-la-Riviere F 79 C6
St. Jean-Pied-de-Port F 76 C1
St. Jean-Poutge F 77 C3
St. Jeoire F 69 B6
St. Joachim F 66 A2
St. Johnstown IRL 19 B4
St. Jorioz F 69 C6
St. Joris Winge B 49 C5
St. Jouin-de-Marnes F 67 B4
St. Juéry F 77 C5
St. Julien-Chapteuil F 78 A3
St. Julien-de-Vouvantes F 57 C4
St. Julien-du-Sault F 59 B4
St. Julien-du-Verdon F 79 C5
St. Julien-en-Born F 76 B1
St. Julien-en-Genevois F 69 B6
St. Julien la-Vêtre F 68 C3
St. Julien-l'Ars F 67 B5
St. Julien-Mont-Denis F 69 C6
St. Julien-sur-Reyssouze F 69 B5
St. Junien F 67 C5
St. Just F 78 B3
St. Just GB 28 C2
St. Just-en-Chaussée F 58 A3
St. Just-en-Chevalet F 68 C3
St. Just-St. Rambert F 69 C4
St. Justin F 76 C2
St. Keverne GB 28 C2
St. Lary-Soulan F 77 D3
St. Laurent-d'Aigouze F 78 C3
St. Laurent-de-Chamousset F 69 C4
St. Laurent-de-Condel F 57 A5
St. Laurent-de-la-Cabrerisse F 78 C1
St. Laurent-de-la-Salanque F 78 D1
St. Laurent-des-Autels F 66 A3
St. Laurent-du-Pont F 69 C5
St. Laurent-en-Caux F 58 A1
St. Laurent-en-Grandvaux F 69 B5
St. Laurent-Médoc F 76 A2
St. Laurent-sur-Gorre F 67 C5
St. Laurent-sur-Mer F 57 A5
St. Laurent-sur-Sèvre F 66 B4
St. Leger B 60 A1
St. Léger-de-Vignes F 68 B3
St. Léger-sous-Beuvray F 68 B4
St. Léger-sur-Dheune F 69 B4
St. Léonard-de-Noblat F 67 C6
St. Leonards GB 31 D4
St. Lô F 57 A4
St. Lon-les-Mines F 76 C1
St. Louis F 60 C3
St. Loup F 68 B3
St. Loup-de-la-Salle F 69 B4
St. Loup-sur-Semouse F 60 C2
St. Lunaire F 57 B3
St. Lupicin F 69 B5
St. Lyphard F 66 A2
St. Lys F 77 C4
St. Macaire F 76 B2
St. Maclou F 58 A1
St. Maixent-l'École F 67 B4
St. Malo F 57 B3
St. Mamet-la-Salvetat F 77 B5
St. Mandrier-sur-Mer F 79 C4
St. Marcel, *Drôme* F 78 B3
St. Marcel, *Saône-et-Loire* F 69 B4
St. Marcellin F 69 C5
St. Marcellin sur Loire F 68 C4
St. Marcet F 77 C3
St. Mards-en-Othe F 59 B4
St. Margaret's-at-Cliffe GB 31 C5
St. Margaret's Hope GB 23 C6
St. Mars-la-Jaille F 66 A3
St. Martin-d'Ablois F 59 B4
St. Martin-d'Auxigny F 68 A2
St. Martin-de-Belleville F 69 C6
St. Martin-de-Bossenay F 59 B4
St. Martin-de-Crau F 78 C3
St. Martin-de-Londres F 78 C2
St. Martin-de-Queyrières F 79 B5
St. Martin-de-Ré F 66 B3
St. Martin-de-Valamas F 78 B3
St. Martin-d'Entraunes F 79 B5
St. Martin des Besaces F 57 A5
St. Martin-d'Estreaux F 68 B3
St. Martin-d'Hères F 69 C5
St. Martin-du-Frêne F 69 B5
St. Martin-en-Bresse F 69 B5
St. Martin-en-Haut F 69 C4
St. Martin-la-Méanne F 68 C1
St. Martin-sur-Ouanne F 59 C4
St. Martin-Valmeroux F 77 A5
St. Martin-Vésubie F 79 B6
St. Martory F 77 C3
St. Mary's GB 23 C6
St. Mathieu F 67 C5
St. Mathieu-de-Tréviers F 78 C2
St. Maurice CH 70 B1
St. Maurice-Navacelles F 78 C2
St. Maurice-sur-Moselle F 60 C2
St. Mawes GB 28 C2
St. Maximin-la-Ste. Baume F 79 C4
St. Méard-de-Gurçon F 76 B3
St. Médard-de-Guizières F 76 A2
St. Médard-en-Jalles F 76 B2
St. Méen-le-Grand F 57 B3
St. Menges F 59 A5
St. Město CZ 54 C1
St. M'Hervé F 57 B4
St. Michel, *Aisne* F 59 A5
St. Michel, *Gers* F 77 C3
St. Michel-Chef-Chef F 66 A2
St. Michel-de-Maurienne F 69 C6
St. Michel-en-Grève F 56 B2
St. Michel-en-l'Herm F 66 B3
St. Michel-Mont-Mercure F 66 B4
St. Mihiel F 60 B1
St. Monance GB 25 B5
St. Montant F 78 B3
St. Moritz CH 71 B4
St. Nazaire F 66 A2
St. Nazaire-en-Royans F 79 A4
St. Nazaire-le-Désert F 79 B4
St. Nectaire F 68 C2
St. Neots GB 30 B3
St. Nicolas-de-Port F 60 B2
St. Nicolas-de-Redon F 57 C3
St. Nicolas-du-Pélem F 56 B2
St. Niklaas B 49 B5
St. Omer F 48 C3
St. Pair-sur-Mer F 57 B4
St. Palais F 76 C1
St. Palais-sur-Mer F 66 C3
St. Pardoux-la-Rivière F 67 C5
St. Paul-Cap-de-Joux F 77 C4
St. Paul-de-Fenouillet F 77 D5
St. Paul-de-Varax F 69 B5
St. Paul-le-Jeune F 78 B3
St. Paul-lès-Dax F 76 C1
St. Paul-Trois-Châteaux F 78 B3
St. Paulien F 68 C3
St. Pé-de-Bigorre F 76 C2
St. Pée-sur-Nivelle F 76 C1
St. Péravy-la-Colombe F 58 C2
St. Péray F 78 B3
St. Père-en-Retz F 66 A2
St. Peter Port GB 56 A3
St. Petersburg = Sankt-Peterburg RUS 7 B11
St. Philbert-de-Grand-Lieu F 66 A3
St. Pierre F 78 C1
St. Pierre-d'Albigny F 69 C6
St. Pierre-d'Allevard F 69 C6
St. Pierre-de-Chartreuse F 69 C5
St. Pierre-de-Chignac F 77 A3
St. Pierre-de-la-Fage F 78 C2
St. Pierre-d'Entremont F 69 C5
St. Pierre-d'Oléron F 66 C3
St. Pierre-Eglise F 57 A4
St. Pierre-en-Port F 58 A1
St. Pierre-le-Moûtier F 68 B3
St. Pierre Montlimart F 66 A3
St. Pierre-Quiberon F 66 A1
St. Pierre-sur-Dives F 57 A5
St. Pierreville F 78 B3
St. Pieters-Leeuw B 49 C5
St. Plancard F 77 C3
St. Poix F 57 C4
St. Pol-de-Léon F 56 B2
St. Pol-sur-Ternoise F 48 C3
St. Polgues F 68 C3
St. Pons-de-Thomières F 78 C1
St. Porchaire F 66 C4
St. Pourçain-sur-Sioule F 68 B3
St. Priest F 69 C4
St. Privat F 68 C2
St. Quay-Portrieux F 56 B3
St. Quentin F 59 A4
St. Quentin-la-Poterie F 78 B3
St. Quentin-les-Anges F 57 C5
St. Rambert-d'Albon F 69 C4
St. Rambert-en-Bugey F 69 C5
St. Raphaël F 79 C5
St. Rémy-de-Provence F 78 C3
St. Rémy-du-Val F 57 B6
St. Remy-en-Bouzemont F 59 B5
St. Renan F 56 B1
St. Révérien F 68 A3
St. Riquier F 48 C2
St. Romain-de-Colbosc F 58 A1
St. Rome-de-Cernon F 78 B1
St. Rome-de-Tarn F 78 B1
St Sadurní d'Anoia E 91 B4
St. Saëns F 58 A2
St. Sampson GB 56 A3
St. Samson-la-Poterie F 58 A2
St. Saturnin-de-Lenne F 78 B2
St. Saturnin-lès-Apt F 79 C4
St. Sauflieu F 58 A3
St. Saulge F 68 A3
St. Sauveur, *Finistère* F 56 B2
St. Sauveur, *Haute-Saône* F 60 C2
St. Sauveur-de-Montagut F 78 B3
St. Sauveur-en-Puisaye F 59 C4
St. Sauveur-en-Rue F 69 C4
St. Sauveur-le-Vicomte F 57 A4
St. Sauveur-Lendelin F 57 A4
St. Sauveur-sur-Tinée F 79 B6
St. Savin, *Gironde* F 76 A2
St. Savin, *Vienne* F 67 B5
St. Savinien F 67 C4
St. Savournin F 79 C4
St. Seine-l'Abbaye F 69 A4
St. Sernin-sur-Rance F 77 C5
St. Sevan-sur-Mer F 57 B3
St. Sever F 76 C2
St. Sever-Calvados F 57 B4
St. Sorlin-d'Arves F 69 C6
St. Soupplets F 58 A3
St. Sulpice F 77 C4
St. Sulpice-Laurière F 67 B6
St. Sulpice-les-Feuilles F 67 B6
St. Symphorien F 76 B2
St. Symphorien-de-Lay F 69 C4
St. Symphorien d'Ozon F 69 C4
St. Symphorien-sur-Coise F 69 C4
St. Teath GB 28 C3
St. Thégonnec F 56 B2
St. Thiébault F 60 B1
St. Trivier-de-Courtes F 69 B5
St. Trivier sur-Moignans F 69 B4
St. Trojan-les-Bains F 66 C3
St. Tropez F 79 C5
St. Truiden B 49 C6
St. Vaast-la-Hougue F 57 A4
St. Valérien F 59 B4
St. Valery-en-Caux F 58 A1
St. Valéry-sur-Somme F 48 C2
St. Vallier, *Drôme* F 69 C4
St. Vallier, *Saône-et-Loire* F 69 B4
St. Vallier-de-Thiey F 79 C5
St. Varent F 67 B4
St. Vaury F 68 B1
St. Venant F 48 C3
St. Vincent I 70 C2
St. Vincent-de-Tyrosse F 76 C1
St. Vit F 69 A5
St. Vith B 50 C2
St. Vivien-de-Médoc F 66 C3
St. Yan F 68 B4
St. Yorre F 68 B3
St. Yrieix-la-Perche F 67 C6
Ste. Adresse F 57 A6
Ste. Anne F 58 B1
Ste. Anne-d'Auray F 56 C3
Ste. Croix CH 69 B6
Ste. Croix-Volvestre F 77 C4
Ste. Engrâce F 76 C2
Ste. Enimie F 78 B2
Ste. Foy-de-Peyrolières F 77 C4
Ste. Foy-la-Grande F 76 B3
Ste. Foy l'Argentiere F 69 C4
Ste. Gauburge-Ste. Colombe F 58 B1
Ste. Gemme la Plaine F 66 B3
Ste. Geneviève F 58 A3
Ste. Hélène F 76 B2
Ste. Hélène-sur-Isère F 69 C6
Ste. Hermine F 66 B3
Ste. Jalle F 79 B4
Ste. Livrade-sur-Lot F 77 B3
Ste. Marie-aux-Mines F 60 B3
Ste. Marie-du-Mont F 57 A4
Ste. Maure-de-Touraine F 67 A5
Ste. Maxime F 79 C5
Ste. Ménéhould F 59 A5
Ste. Mère-Église F 57 A4
Ste. Ode B 49 C6
Ste. Savine F 59 B5
Ste. Sévère-sur-Indre F 68 B2
Ste. Sigolène F 69 C4
Ste. Suzanne F 57 B5
Ste. Tulle F 79 C4
Sainteny F 57 A4
Saintes F 67 C4
Stes. Maries-de-la-Mer F 78 C3
Saintfield GB 19 B6
Saissac F 77 C5
Saja E 88 A2
Sajan YU 75 C5
Šajkaš YU 75 C5
Sajókaza H 65 B6
Sajószentpéter H 65 B6
Sajóvámos H 65 B6
Sakarya TR 114 B5
Šakiai LT 6 D7
Sakskøbing DK 39 E4
Sakule YU 75 C5
Sala S 36 B3
Šal'a SK 64 B3
Sala Baganza I 81 B4
Sala Consilina I 104 C1
Salakovac YU 85 B6
Salamanca E 94 B1
Salamís GR 113 E5
Salandra I 104 C2
Salaparuta I 108 B1
Salar E 100 B1
Salardú E 90 A3
Salas E 86 A4
Salas de los Infantes E 89 B3
Salau F 77 D4
Salavaux CH 70 B2
Salbertrand I 79 A5
Salbohed S 36 B3
Salbris F 68 A2
Salce E 86 B4
Salching D 62 B3
Salcombe GB 28 C4
Saldaña E 88 B2
Saldus LV 6 C7
Sale I 80 B2
Saleby S 35 C5
Salem D 61 C5
Salemi I 108 B1
Salen, *Highland* GB 24 B2
Salen, *Highland* GB 24 B2
Sälen S 2 F20
Salernes F 79 C5
Salerno I 103 C7
Salers F 68 C2
Salford GB 26 B3
Salgótarján H 65 B5
Salgueiro P 92 B3
Sali HR 83 C4
Sálice Salentino I 105 C3
Salientes E 86 B4
Salies-de-Béarn F 76 C2
Salies-du-Salat F 77 C3
Salignac-Eyvigues F 77 B4
Saligney-sur-Roudon F 68 B3
Salihli TR 16 B4
Salihorsk BY 7 E9
Salinas, *Alicante* E 101 A5
Salinas, *Huesca* E 90 A3
Salinas de Medinaceli E 95 A4
Salinas de Pisuerga E 88 B2
Saline di Volterra I 81 C4
Salins-les-Bains F 69 B5
Salir P 98 B2
Salisbury GB 29 B6
Salla A 73 A4
Salla FIN 3 C28
Sallachy GB 23 C4
Sallanches F 70 C1
Sallent E 91 B4
Sallent de Gállego E 76 D2
Salles F 76 B2
Salles-Curan F 78 B1
Salles-sur-l'Hers F 77 C4
Sallins IRL 21 A5
Salmerón E 95 B4
Salmiech F 77 B5
Salmoral E 94 B1
Salo FIN 6 A7
Salò I 71 C5
Salobreña E 100 C2
Salon-de-Provence F 79 C4
Salonica = Thessaloníki GR 112 B4
Salonta RO 10 C6
Salorino E 93 B3
Salornay-sur-Guye F 69 B4
Salorno I 71 B6
Salou E 91 B4
Šalovci SLO 73 B6
Salses-le-Chateau F 78 D1
Salsomaggiore Terme I 81 B3
Salt E 91 B5
Saltara I 82 C1
Saltash GB 28 C3
Saltburn-by-the-Sea GB 27 A5

Seynes F 78 B3
Seyssel F 69 C5
Sežana SLO 72 C3
Sézanne F 59 B4
Sezulfe P 87 C3
Sezze I 102 B6
Sfântu Gheorghe RO 11 D8
Sforzacosta I 82 C2
Sgarasta Mhor GB 22 D1
Shaftesbury GB 29 B5
Shaldon GB 29 C4
Shanagolden IRL 20 B2
Shanklin GB 31 D2
Shap GB 26 A3
Sharpness GB 29 B5
Shawbury GB 26 C3
Shchekino RUS 7 D14
Shchigry RUS 7 F14
Shchors UA 7 F11
Sheerness GB 31 C4
Sheffield GB 27 B4
Shefford GB 31 B3
Shenfield GB 31 C4
Shëngjergj AL 112 A2
Shepetivka UA 11 A9
Shepshed GB 27 C4
Shepton Mallet GB 29 B5
Sherborne GB 29 C5
Shercock IRL 19 C5
Sheringham GB 30 B5
Shiel Bridge GB 22 D3
Shieldaig GB 22 D3
Shillelagh IRL 21 B5
Shimsk RUS 7 B11
Shipston-on-Stour GB 29 A6
Shklow BY 7 D11
Shkodër AL 105 A5
Shoeburyness GB 31 C4
Shoreham-by-Sea GB 31 D3
Shostka UA 7 F12
Shotley Gate GB 31 C5
Shpola UA 11 B11
Shrewsbury GB 26 C3
Shugozero RUS 7 B13
Shumen BG 11 E9
Siabost GB 22 C2
Sianów PL 46 A2
Siátista GR 112 B3
Siauges-St. Romain F 78 A2
Šiauliai LT 6 D7
Sibari I 106 B3
Sibbhult S 41 C4
Šibenik HR 83 C4
Sibinj HR 74 C2
Sibiu RO 11 D8
Sibnica YU 85 B5
Sibsey GB 27 B6
Siculiana I 108 B2
Šid YU 85 A4
Sidari GR 112 C1
Siddeburen NL 42 B3
Siderno I 106 C3
Sidhirókastron GR 112 A5
Sidmouth GB 29 C4
Sidzina PL 65 A5
Siebenlehn D 52 B3
Siedlce PL 6 E7
Siedlce PL 46 B1
Siedlinghausen D 51 B4
Siedlisko PL 46 C2
Siegburg D 50 C3
Siegen D 50 C4
Siegenburg D 62 B2
Sieghartskirchen A 64 B2
Siegsdorf D 62 C3
Siekierki PL 45 C6
Sielpia PL 55 B5
Siemiany PL 47 B5
Siena I 81 C5
Sieniawka PL 53 C4
Siennica PL 55 A6
Sienno PL 55 B6
Sieradz PL 54 B3
Sieraków, *Śląskie* PL 54 C3
Sieraków, *Wielkopolskie* PL 46 C2
Sierakowice PL 46 A3
Sierck-les-Bains F 60 A2
Sierentz F 60 C3
Sierning A 63 B5
Sierpc PL 47 C5
Sierra de Fuentes E 93 B4
Sierra de Luna E 90 A2
Sierra de Yeguas E 100 B1
Sierre CH 70 B2
Siestrzeń PL 55 A5
Sietamo E 90 A2
Siewierz PL 55 C4
Sigdal N 33 A6
Sigean F 78 C1
Sighetu-Marmatiei RO 11 C7
Sighişoara RO 11 C8
Sigillo I 82 C1
Siglufjörður IS 111 A7
Sigmaringen D 61 B5
Signa I 81 C5
Signes F 79 C4
Signy-l'Abbaye F 59 A5
Signy-le-Petit F 59 A5
Sigogne F 67 C4
Sigri GR 112 C7
Sigtuna S 36 B4
Sigueiro E 86 B2
Sigüenza E 95 A4
Sigües E 90 A1
Sigulda LV 6 C8
Siilinjärvi FIN 3 E27
Sikenica SK 65 B4
Sikiá GR 112 B5
Sikinos GR 113 F7
Siklós H 74 C3
Sikórz PL 47 C5
Silandro I 71 B5
Silánus I 110 B1
Silbaš YU 75 C4
Silbersted D 43 A6
Şile TR 114 A4
Siles E 101 A3
Silgueiros P 92 A3
Silifke TR 16 C6
Siliqua I 110 C1
Silistra BG 11 D9
Silivri TR 114 A3
Siljan N 33 B6
Silkeborg DK 39 C2
Silla E 96 B2
Sillamäe EST 7 B9
Sillé-le-Guillaume F 57 B5
Silleda E 86 B2
Sillenstede D 43 B4
Sillerud S 34 B4
Sillian A 72 B2
Silloth GB 25 D4
Silno PL 46 B3
Silnowo PL 46 B2
Silo HR 73 C4
Sils E 91 B5
Silte S 37 D5
Šilute LT 6 D6
Silvaplana CH 71 B4
Silvares P 92 A3
Silverdalen S 40 B5
Silvermines IRL 20 B3
Silverstone GB 30 B2
Silverton GB 29 C4
Silves P 98 B2
Silvi Marina I 103 A7
Simandre F 69 B4
Šimanovci YU 85 B5
Simard F 69 B5
Simat de Valldigna E 96 B2
Simav TR 114 C3
Simbach, *Bayern* D 62 B3
Simbach, *Bayern* D 62 B4
Simbário I 106 C3
Simeria RO 11 D7
Simićevo YU 85 B6
Simlångsdalen S 40 C3
Simmerath D 50 C2
Simmerberg D 61 C5
Simmern D 50 D3
Simo FIN 3 D26
Šimonovce SK 65 B6
Simonsbath GB 28 B4
Simonstorp S 37 C3
Simontornya H 74 B3
Simplon CH 70 B3
Simrishamn S 41 D4
Sinaia RO 11 D8
Sinalunga I 81 C5
Sinarcas E 96 B1
Sincan TR 114 C7
Sindal DK 38 B3
Sindelfingen D 61 B5
Sindia I 110 B1
Sındırgı TR 114 C3
Sinekli TR 114 A3
Sines P 98 B2
Sineu E 97 B3
Singen D 61 C4
Singleton GB 31 D3
Siniscóla I 110 B2
Sinj HR 83 C5
Sinlabajos E 94 A2
Sinn D 50 C4
Sinnai I 110 C2
Sinnes N 32 C3
Sinop TR 16 A7
Sins CH 70 A3
Sinsheim D 61 A4
Sint Annaland NL 49 B5
Sint Annaparochie NL 42 B2
Sint Athonis NL 50 B1
Sint Nicolaasga NL 42 C2
Sint Oedenrode NL 49 B6
Sintra P 92 C1
Sinzheim D 61 B4
Sinzig D 50 C3
Siófok H 74 B3
Sion CH 70 B2
Sion Mills GB 19 B4
Siorac-en-Périgord F 77 B3
Šipanska Luka HR 84 D2
Šipovo BIH 84 B2
Sira N 32 C3
Siracusa I 109 B4
Siret RO 11 C9
Sirevåg N 32 C2
Sirig YU 75 C4
Sirmione I 71 C5
Sirok H 65 C6
Široké SK 65 B6
Široki Brijeg BIH 84 C2
Sirolo I 82 C2
Siruela E 94 D1
Sisak HR 73 C6
Sisante E 95 C4
Šišljavić HR 73 C5
Sissach CH 70 A2
Sissonne F 59 A4
Sistelo P 87 C2
Sisteron F 79 B4
Sistiana I 72 C3
Sitges E 91 B4
Sitia GR 113 G8
Sittard NL 50 B1
Sittensen D 43 B6
Sittingbourne GB 31 C4
Sitzenroda D 52 B2
Sivac YU 75 C4
Siverić HR 83 C5
Sivrihisar TR 114 C6
Sixt-Fer-á-Cheval F 70 B1
Siziano I 71 C4
Sizun F 56 B1
Sjenica YU 85 C5
Sjöbo S 41 D3
Sjømarken S 40 B2
Sjørring DK 38 C1
Sjötofta S 40 B3
Sjötorp S 35 C5
Sjuntorp S 35 C4
Skadovsk UA 11 C12
Skælskør DK 39 D4
Skærbæk DK 39 D1
Skafså N 33 B5
Skaftafell IS 111 D9
Skagaströnd IS 111 B5
Skagen DK 38 B3
Skagersvik S 35 C6
Skála GR 113 D2
Skała PL 55 C4
Skála Oropoú GR 113 D5
Skala-Podilska UA 11 B9
Skalat UA 11 B8
Skalbmierz PL 55 C5
Skålevik N 33 C5
Skalica SK 64 B3
Skalité SK 65 A4
Skalná CZ 52 C2
Skals DK 38 C2
Skanderborg DK 39 C2
Skåne-Tranås S 41 D3
Skånes-Fagerhult S 41 C3
Skånevik N 32 B2
Skänninge S 37 C2
Skanör med Falsterbo S 41 D2
Skåpafors S 35 B4
Skąpe PL 53 A5
Skara S 35 C5
Skarberget N 2 B22
Skärblacka S 37 C2
Skarð IS 111 B3
Skare N 32 B3
Skåre S 34 B5
Skärhamn S 38 B4
Skarnes N 34 A3
Skarp Salling DK 38 C2
Skärplinge S 36 A4
Skarrild DK 39 D1
Skärstad S 40 B4
Skarszewy PL 47 A4
Skårup DK 39 D3
Skaryszew PL 55 B6
Skarżysko-Kamienna PL 55 B5
Skarzysko Ksiazece PL 55 B5
Skatøy N 33 C6
Skattkärr S 34 B5
Skave DK 39 C1
Skawina PL 55 D4
Skebobruk S 36 B5
Skebokvarn S 37 B3
Skedala S 40 C2
Skedevi S 37 C2
Skedsmokorset N 34 A3
Skee S 35 C3
Skegness GB 27 B6
Skela YU 85 B5
Skelani BIH 85 C4
Skellefteå S 3 D24
Skelleftehamn S 3 D24
Skelmersdale GB 26 B3
Skelmorlie GB 24 C3
Skelund DK 38 C3
Skender Vakuf BIH 84 B2
Skene S 40 B2
Skępe PL 47 C5
Skepplanda S 40 B2
Skeppshult S 40 B3
Skerries IRL 19 C5
Ski N 34 B2
Skiathos GR 112 C5
Skibbereen IRL 20 C2
Skídhra GR 112 B4
Skien N 33 B6
Skierniewice PL 55 B5
Skillingaryd S 40 B4
Skillinge S 41 D4
Skillingmark S 34 B4
Skinnardai S 37 B5
Skinnskatteberg S 36 B2
Skipness GB 24 C2
Skipsea GB 27 B5
Skipton GB 26 B3
Skiptvet N 34 B3
Skiros GR 112 D6
Skivarp S 41 D3
Skive DK 38 C2
Skjærhalden N 35 B3
Skjeberg N 34 B3
Skjeggedal N 32 A3
Skjeljavik N 32 B2
Skjern DK 39 D1
Skjold N 32 B2
Skjoldastraumen N 32 B2
Skjolden N 2 F17
Skjønhaug N 34 B3
Škocjan SLO 73 C5
Skoczów PL 65 A4
Skodborg DK 39 D2
Škofja Loka SLO 73 B4
Škofljica SLO 73 C4
Skoghall S 34 B5
Skogstorp, *Halland* S 40 C2
Skogstorp, *Södermanland* S 36 B3
Skoki PL 46 C3
Skokloster S 36 B4
Sköldinge S 37 B3
Skole UA 11 B7
Skollenborg N 33 B6
Sköllersta S 36 B2
Skomlin PL 54 B3
Skópelos GR 112 C5
Skopje MK 10 E6
Skoppum N 34 B2
Skórcz PL 47 B4
Skorogoszcz PL 54 C2
Skoroszów PL 54 B2
Skørping DK 38 C2
Skotfoss N 33 B6
Skotniki PL 55 B4
Skotselv N 33 B6
Skotterud N 34 B4
Skottorp S 40 C2
Skovby DK 39 E2
Skövde S 35 C5
Skovsgård DK 38 B2
Skrad HR 73 C4
Skradin HR 83 C4
Skradnik HR 73 C5
Škrdlovice CZ 64 A1
Skrea S 40 C2
Skruv S 40 C5
Skrwilno PL 47 B5
Skrydstrup DK 39 D2
Skucani BIH 84 C1
Skudeneshavn N 32 B2
Skui N 34 B2
Skulsk PL 47 C4
Skultorp S 35 C5
Skultuna S 36 B3
Skuodas LT 6 C6
Skurup S 41 D3
Skuteč CZ 64 A1
Skutskär S 36 A4
Skvyra UA 11 B10
Skwierzyna PL 46 C1
Skýcov SK 65 B4
Skyllberg S 37 C1
Skyttorp S 36 A4
Sládkovičovo SK 64 B3
Slagelse DK 39 D4
Slagharen NL 42 C3
Slaidburn GB 26 B3
Slane IRL 19 C5
Slangerup DK 41 D2
Slano HR 84 D2
Slantsy RUS 7 B10
Slaný CZ 53 C4
Slap SLO 72 B3
Šlapanice CZ 64 A2
Slatina BIH 84 C2
Slatina HR 74 C2
Slatina RO 11 D8
Slatina YU 85 C5
Slatiňany CZ 64 A1
Slatinice CZ 64 A3
Slattum N 34 B2
Slavičin CZ 64 A3
Slavkov CZ 64 B3
Slavkov u Brna CZ 64 A2
Slavkovica YU 85 B5
Slavonice CZ 63 B6
Slavonski Brod HR 74 C3
Slavonski Kobas HR 84 A2
Slavõsovce SK 65 B6
Slavskoye RUS 47 A6
Slavuta UA 11 A9
Sława, *Lubuskie* PL 53 B6
Sława, *Zachodnio-Pomorskie* PL 46 B1
Slawharad BY 7 E11
Sławków PL 55 C4
Sławno, *Wielkopolskie* PL 46 C3
Sławno, *Zachodnio-Pomorskie* PL 46 A2
Sławoborze PL 46 B1
Sl'ažany SK 64 B4
Sleaford GB 27 C5
Sleðbrjótur IS 111 B11
Sledmere GB 27 A5
Sleights GB 27 A5
Slemmestad N 34 B2
Ślesin PL 47 C4
Sliač SK 65 B5
Sliema M 107 C5
Sligo IRL 18 B3
Slite S 37 D5
Slitu N 34 B3
Sliven BG 11 E9
Śliwice PL 47 B4
Slobozia RO 11 D9
Slochteren NL 42 B3
Slöinge S 40 C2
Słomniki PL 55 C5
Slonim BY 7 E8
Słońsk PL 45 C6
Slottsbron S 34 B5
Slough GB 31 C3
Slovenj Gradec SLO 73 B5
Slovenska Bistrica SLO 73 B5
Slovenská L'upča SK 65 B5
Slovenská-Ves SK 65 A6
Slovenské Darmoty SK 65 B5
Slovenske Konjice SLO 73 B5
Słubice PL 45 C6
Sluderno I 71 B5
Sluis NL 49 B4
Šluknov CZ 53 B4
Slunj HR 83 A4
Słupca PL 54 A2
Słupiec PL 54 C1
Słupsk PL 46 A3
Slutsk BY 7 E9
Smålandsstenar S 40 B3
Smardzewo PL 53 A5
Smarhon BY 7 D9
Šmarje SLO 73 B5
Šmarjeta SLO 73 C5
Šmartno SLO 73 B4
Smečno CZ 53 C4
Smedby S 40 C6
Smědec CZ 63 B5
Smederevo YU 85 B5
Smederevska Palanka YU 85 B5
Smedjebacken S 36 A2
Smęgorzów PL 55 C6
Smeland N 33 C5
Smidary CZ 53 C5
Śmigiel PL 54 A1
Smila UA 11 B11
Smilde NL 42 C3
Smiřice CZ 53 C5
Smithfield GB 25 D5
Śmiłowo PL 46 B2
Smögen S 35 C3
Smogulec PL 46 B3
Smolenice SK 64 B3
Smolensk RUS 7 D12
Smolnik SK 65 B6
Smolyan BG 112 A6
Smuka SLO 73 C4
Smygehamn S 41 D3
Smykow PL 55 B5
Snainton GB 27 A5
Snaith GB 27 B4
Snaptun DK 39 D3
Snarum N 33 A6
Snedsted DK 38 C1
Sneek NL 42 B2
Sneem IRL 20 C2
Snejbjerg DK 39 C1
Snihurivka UA 11 C12
Snjegotina BIH 84 B2
Snøde DK 39 D3
Snogebaek DK 41 D5
Snyatyn UA 11 B8
Soave I 71 C6
Sober E 86 B3
Sobernheim D 60 A3
Soběslav CZ 63 A5
Sobienie Jeziory PL 55 B6
Sobota, *Dolnośląskie* PL 53 B5
Sobota, *Łódzkie* PL 55 A4
Sobotište SK 64 B3
Sobotka CZ 53 C5
Sobótka, *Dolnośląskie* PL 54 C1
Sobótka, *Wielkopolskie* PL 54 B2
Sobra HR 84 D2
Sobrado, *Coruña* E 86 A2
Sobrado, *Lugo* E 86 B3
Sobral da Adica P 98 A3
Sobral de Monte Argraço P 92 C1
Sobreira Formosa P 92 B3
Søby DK 39 E3
Soca SLO 72 B3
Sočanica YU 85 C5
Sochaczew PL 55 A5
Socol RO 85 B6
Socovos E 101 A4
Socuéllamos E 95 C4
Sodankylä FIN 3 C27
Soderåkra S 40 C6
Söderbärke S 36 A2
Söderby-Karl S 36 B5
Söderfors S 36 A4
Söderhamn S 2 F22
Söderköping S 37 C3
Södertälje S 36 B4
Södingberg A 73 A5
Södra Finnö S 37 C3
Södra Ny S 34 B5
Södra Råda S 35 B6
Södra Sandby S 41 D3
Södra Vi S 40 B5
Sodražica SLO 73 C4
Sodupe E 89 A3
Soengas P 87 C2
Soest D 50 B4
Soest NL 49 A6
Sofádhes GR 112 C4
Sofia = Sofiya BG 11 E7
Sofikón GR 113 E5
Sofiya = Sofia BG 11 E7
Şofronea RO 75 B6
Sögel D 43 C4
Sogliano al Rubicone I 82 B1
Sogndalsfjøra N 2 F17
Søgne N 33 C4
Söğüt TR 114 B5
Söğütlu TR 114 B5
Soham GB 30 B4
Sohland D 53 B4
Sohren D 60 A3
Soignies B 49 C5
Soissons F 59 A4
Söjtör H 74 B1
Sokal' UA 11 A8
Söke TR 16 C3
Sokhós GR 112 B5
Sokna N 33 A6
Sokndal N 32 C3
Soko BIH 84 B3
Sokolac BIH 84 C3
Sokółka PL 6 E7
Sokolov CZ 52 C2
Sokołów Podlaski PL 6 E7
Sokołowo PL 54 A3
Sola N 32 C2
Solana de los Barros E 93 C4
Solana del Pino E 100 A1
Solares E 88 A3
Solarino I 109 B4
Solarussa I 110 C1
Solas GB 22 D1
Solber-gelva N 34 B2
Solberga S 40 B4
Solčany SK 64 B4
Solčava SLO 73 B4
Solda I 71 B5
Sölden A 71 B6
Solec Kujawski PL 47 B4
Solec nad Wisła PL 55 B6
Soleils F 79 C5
Solenzara F 102 B2
Solera E 100 B2
Solesmes F 49 C4
Soleto I 107 A5
Solgne F 60 B2
Solheimsvik N 32 B3
Solignac F 67 C6
Solihull GB 27 C4
Solin HR 83 C5
Solingen D 50 B3
Solivella E 91 B4
Solkan SLO 72 C3
Söll A 72 A2
Sollana E 96 B2
Sollebrunn S 35 C4
Sollefteå S 2 E22
Sollen-tuna S 36 B4
Sollenau A 64 C2
Sóller E 97 B2
Søllested DK 39 E4
Solliès-Pont F 79 C5
Sollihøgda N 34 B2
Solnechnogorsk RUS 7 C14
Solnice CZ 53 C6
Solofra I 103 C7
Solomiac F 77 C3
Solopaca I 103 B7
Solórzano E 89 A3
Solothurn CH 70 A2
Solre-le-Château F 49 C5
Solsona E 91 B4
Solt H 75 B4
Soltau D 44 C1
Soltsy RUS 7 B11
Soltszentimre H 75 B4
Soltvadkert H 75 B4
Solumsmoen N 33 B6
Solva GB 28 B2
Sölvesborg S 41 C4
Solymár H 65 C4
Soma TR 114 C2
Somain F 49 C4
Somberek H 74 B3
Sombernon F 69 A4
Sombor YU 75 C4
Sombreffe B 49 C5
Someren NL 50 B1
Somero FIN 6 A7
Somersham GB 30 B3
Somerton GB 29 B5
Sominy PL 46 A3
Somma Lombardo I 70 C3
Sommariva del Bosco I 80 B1
Sommatino I 109 B3
Somme-Tourbe F 59 A5
Sommeilles F 59 B5
Sommen S 37 C1
Sommepy-Tahure F 59 A5
Sömmerda D 52 B1
Sommerfeld D 45 C5
Sommersted DK 39 D2
Sommesous F 59 B5
Sommières F 78 C3
Sommières-du-Clain F 67 B5
Somo E 88 A3
Somogyfajsz H 74 B2
Somogyjád H 74 B2
Somogysámson H 74 B2
Somogysárd H 74 B2
Somogyszil H 74 B3
Somogyszob H 74 B2
Somogyvár H 74 B2
Somontin E 101 B3
Somosiero E 95 A3
Somosköújifalu H 65 B5
Sompolno PL 47 C4
Sompuis F 59 B5
Son N 34 B2
Son Bou E 97 B4
Son en Breugel NL 49 B6
Son Servera E 97 B3
Sonceboz CH 70 A2
Soncillo E 88 B3
Soncino I 71 C4
Sóndalo I 71 B5
Søndeled N 33 C6
Sønder Bjert DK 39 D2
Sønder Felding DK 39 D1
Sønder Hygum DK 39 D1
Sønder Omme DK 39 D1
Sønderborg DK 39 E2
Sønderho DK 39 D1
Sondershausen D 51 B6
Søndersø DK 39 D3
Søndervig DK 39 C1
Søndre Enningdal Kappel N 35 C3
Sóndrio I 71 B4
Soneja E 96 B2
Songe N 33 C6
Songeons F 58 A2
Sonkovo RUS 7 C14
Sönnarslöv S 41 D4
Sonneberg D 52 C1
Sonnefeld D 52 C1
Sonnewalde D 52 B3
Sonnino I 102 B6
Sonogno CH 70 B3
Sonsbeck D 50 B2
Sonseca E 94 C3
Sonstorp S 37 C3
Sonta YU 75 C4
Sontheim D 61 B6
Sonthofen D 71 A5
Sontra D 51 B5
Sopelana E 89 A4
Sopje HR 74 C2
Šoporňa SK 64 B3
Sopot PL 47 A4
Sopot YU 85 B5
Sopotnica MK 112 A3
Sopron H 64 C2
Šor YU 85 B4
Sora I 103 B6
Soragna I 81 B4
Sorano I 81 D5
Sorbara I 81 B5
Sorbas E 101 B3
Sórbolo I 81 B4
Sordal N 33 C4
Sordale GB 23 C5
Sore F 76 B2
Sörenberg CH 70 B3
Soresina I 71 C4
Sorèze F 77 C5
Sorges F 67 C5
Sórgono I 110 B2
Sorgues F 78 B3
Sorgun TR 16 B7
Soria E 89 C4
Soriano Cálabro I 106 C3
Soriano nel Cimino I 102 A5
Sorihuela del Guadalimar E 100 A2
Sorisdale GB 24 B1
Sormás H 74 B1
Sorø DK 39 D4
Soroca MD 11 B10
Sorrento I 103 C7
Sorsele S 2 D22
Sorso I 110 B1
Sort E 91 A4
Sortavala RUS 3 F29
Sortino I 109 B4
Sortland N 2 B21
Sørum N 34 A2
Sørumsand N 34 B3
Sorunda S 37 B4
Sörup D 44 A1
Sørvågen N 2 C20
Sorvik S 36 A2
Sos F 76 B3
Sos del Rey Católico E 90 A1
Sösdala S 41 C3
Sošice HR 73 C5
Sośnica PL 46 B2
Sośnicowice PL 54 C3
Sośno PL 46 B3
Sosnovyy Bor RUS 7 B10
Sosnowiec PL 55 C4
Sospel F 80 C1
Šoštanj SLO 73 B5
Sotillo de Adrada E 94 B2
Sotillo de la Ribera E 88 C3
Sotin HR 75 C4
Sotkamo FIN 3 D28
Soto de la Marina E 88 A3
Soto de los Infantes E 86 A4
Soto de Real E 94 B3
Soto de Ribera E 88 A1
Soto del Barco E 86 A4
Soto y Amio E 88 B1
Sotobañado y Priorato E 88 B2
Sotoserrano E 93 A4
Sotresgudo E 88 B2
Sotrondio E 88 A1
Sotta F 102 B2
Sottomarina I 72 C2
Sottrum D 43 B6
Sotuelamos E 95 C4
Souain F 59 A5
Soual F 77 C5
Soucy F 59 B4
Soúdha GR 113 G6
Soudron F 59 B5
Souesmes F 68 A2
Soufflenheim F 60 B3
Souflion GR 112 A8
Souillac F 77 B4
Souilly F 59 A6
Soulac-sur-Mer F 66 C3
Soulaines-Dhuys F 59 B5
Soultz-Haut-Rhin F 60 C3
Soultz-sous-Forêts F 60 B3
Soumagne B 50 C1
Soumoulou F 76 C2
Souppes-sur-Loing F 58 B3
Souprosse F 76 C2
Sourdeval F 57 B5
Soure P 92 A2
Sournia F 77 D5
Souro Pires P 87 D3
Soúrpi GR 112 C4
Sours F 58 B2
Sousceyrac F 77 B5
Sousel P 92 C3
Soustons F 76 C1
Soutelo de Montes E 86 B2
South Brent GB 28 C4
South Cave GB 27 B5
South Hayling GB 31 D3
South Molton GB 28 B4
South Ockendon GB 31 C4
South Petherton GB 29 C5
South Shields GB 25 D6
South Tawton GB 28 C4
South Woodham Ferrers GB 31 C4
Southam GB 30 B2
Southampton GB 31 D2
Southborough GB 31 C4
Southend GB 24 C2
Southend-on-Sea GB 31 C4
Southport GB 26 B2
Southwell GB 27 B5
Southwold GB 30 B5
Souto P 92 A3
Souto da Carpalhosa P 92 B2
Soutochao E 87 C3
Souvigny F 68 B3
Souzay-Champigny F 67 A4
Soverato I 106 C3
Soveria Mannelli I 106 B3
Sövestad S 41 D3
Sovetsk RUS 6 D6
Sovići BIH 84 C2
Sovicille I 81 C5
Sowerby GB 27 A4
Soyaux F 67 C5
Søyland N 32 C2
Spa B 50 C1
Spadafora I 109 A4
Spaichingen D 61 B4
Spakenburg NL 49 A6
Spalding GB 30 B3
Spálené Poříčí CZ 63 A4
Spalt D 62 A1
Spangenberg D 51 B5
Spangereid N 33 C4
Spantekow D 45 B5
Sparanise I 103 B7
Sparkær DK 38 C2
Sparkford GB 29 B5
Sparreholm S 37 B3
Sparta = Spárti GR 113 E4
Spartà I 109 A4
Spárti = Sparta GR 113 E4
Spas-Demensk RUS 7 D13
Spean Bridge GB 24 B3
Speicher D 60 A2
Speichersdorf D 62 A2
Speke GB 26 B3
Spello I 82 D1
Spenge D 51 A4
Spennymoor GB 25 D6
Spentrup DK 38 C3
Sperenberg D 52 A3
Sperlinga I 109 B3
Sperlonga I 103 B6
Spetalen N 34 B2
Spétsai GR 113 E5
Speyer D 61 A4
Spezzano Albanese I 106 B3
Spezzano della Sila I 106 B3
Spiddle IRL 20 A2
Spiegelau D 63 B4
Spiekeroog D 43 B4
Spiez CH 70 B2
Spigno Monferrato I 80 B2
Spijk NL 42 B3
Spijkenisse NL 49 B5
Spilamberto I 81 B5
Spili GR 113 G6
Spilimbergo I 72 B2
Spilsby GB 27 B6
Spinazzola I 104 C2
Spincourt F 60 A1
Spind N 32 C3
Spindleruv-Mlyn CZ 53 C5
Spinoso I 104 C1
Špišjć Bukovica HR 74 C2
Spišská Belá SK 65 A6
Spišská Nová Ves SK 65 B6
Spisská Stará Ves SK 65 A6
Spišské-Hanušovce SK 65 A6
Spišské Podhradie SK 65 B6
Spišské Vlachy SK 65 B6
Spišský-Štvrtok SK 65 B6
Spital A 63 C5
Spital am Semmering A 63 C6
Spittal an der Drau A 72 B3

Talavera de la Reina E 94 C2
Talavera la Real E 93 C4
Talayuela E 93 B5
Talayuelas E 96 B1
Talgarth GB 29 B4
Talgje N 32 B2
Talhadas P 92 A2
Táliga E 93 C3
Talizat F 78 A2
Tálknafjörður IS 111 B2
Talla I 81 C5
Talladale GB 22 D3
Tallaght IRL 21 A5
Tallard F 79 B5
Tallinn EST 6 B8
Talloires F 69 C6
Tallow IRL 21 B4
Talmay F 69 A5
Talmont-St. Hilaire F 66 B3
Talmont-sur-Gironde F 66 C4
Talne UA 11 B11
Talsano I 104 C3
Talsi LV 6 C7
Talvik N 3 A25
Talybont GB 26 C2
Tamajón E 95 B3
Tamame E 88 C1
Tamames E 93 A4
Tamarit de Mar E 91 B4
Tamarite de Litera E 90 B3
Tamariu E 91 B6
Tamási H 74 B3
Tambach-Dietharz D 51 C6
Tameza E 86 A4
Tammisaari FIN 6 A7
Tampere FIN 3 F25
Tamsweg A 72 A3
Tamurejo E 94 D2
Tamworth GB 27 C4
Tana N 3 A28
Tañabueyes E 89 B3
Tanakajd H 74 A1
Tananger N 32 C2
Tanaunella I 110 B2
Tancarville F 58 A1
Tånga S 41 C2
Tangelic H 74 B3
Tangerhütte D 44 C3
Tangermünde D 44 C3
Taninges F 69 B6
Tann D 51 C6
Tanna D 52 C1
Tannadice GB 25 B5
Tannåker S 40 C3
Tännäs S 2 E20
Tannay, *Ardennes* F 59 A5
Tannay, *Nièvre* F 68 A3
Tannenbergsthal D 52 C2
Tännesberg D 62 A3
Tannheim A 71 A5
Tanowo PL 45 B6
Tanum S 35 C3
Tanumshede S 35 C3
Tanus F 77 B5
Tanvald CZ 53 C5
Taormina I 109 B4
Tapa EST 7 B8
Tapfheim D 62 B1
Tapia de Casariego E 86 A4
Tápióbicske H 75 A4
Tápiógyörgye H 75 A4
Tápióság H 75 A4
Tápiószecsö H 75 A4
Tápiószele H 75 A4
Tápiószentmárton H 75 A4
Tapolca H 74 B2
Tapolcafö H 74 A2
Tar HR 72 C3
Taradell E 91 B5
Taraklı TR 114 B5
Taramundi E 86 A3
Tarancón E 95 B3
Táranto I 104 C3
Tarare F 69 C4
Tarascon F 78 C3
Tarascon-sur-Ariège F 77 D4
Tarashcha UA 11 B11
Tarazona E 89 C5
Tarazona de la Mancha E 95 C5
Tarbena E 96 C2
Tarbert GB 24 C2
Tarbert IRL 20 B2
Tarbes F 76 C3
Tarbet GB 24 B3
Tarbolton GB 24 C3
Tarcento I 72 B3
Tarčin BIH 84 C3
Tarczyn PL 55 B5
Tardajos E 88 B3
Tardelcuende E 89 C4
Tardets-Sorholus F 76 C2
Tardienta E 90 B2
Targon F 76 B2
Târgovişte RO 11 D8
Târgu-Jiu RO 11 D7
Târgu Mureş RO 11 C8
Târgu Ocna RO 11 C9
Târgu Secuiesc RO 11 D9
Tarifa E 99 C5
Tariquejas E 98 B3
Tarján H 65 C4
Tárkany H 64 C4
Tarland GB 23 D6
Tarłów PL 55 B6
Tarm DK 39 D1
Tarmstedt D 43 B6
Tärnaby S 2 D21
Tarnalelesz H 65 B6
Tarnaörs H 65 C6
Târnăveni RO 11 C8
Tarnobrzeg PL 55 C6
Tarnos F 76 C1
Tarnów, *Lubuskie* PL 45 C6
Tarnów, *Małopolskie* PL 55 C5
Tarnowo Podgórne PL 46 C2
Tarnowskie Góry PL 54 C3
Tärnsjö S 36 A3
Tarouca P 87 C3
Tarp D 43 A6
Tarquínia I 102 A4
Tarquínia Lido I 102 A4
Tarragona E 91 B4
Tàrrega E 91 B4
Tarrenz A 71 A5
Tårs, *Nordjyllands* DK 38 B3
Tårs, *Storstrøms* DK 39 E4
Tarsia I 106 B3
Tarsus TR 16 C7
Tartas F 76 C2
Tartu EST 7 B9
Tarussa RUS 7 D14
Tarves GB 23 D6
Tarvisio I 72 B3
Täsch CH 70 B2
Taşköprü TR 16 A7
Tasov CZ 64 A2
Tasovčići BIH 84 C2
Tåstrup DK 41 D2
Taşucu TR 16 C6
Tát H 65 C4
Tata H 65 C4
Tatabánya H 74 A3
Tataháza H 75 B4
Tatarbunary UA 11 D10
Tatárszentgyörgy H 75 A4
Tatranská-Lomnica SK 65 A6
Tau N 32 B2
Tauber-bischofsheim D 61 A5
Taucha D 52 B2
Taufkirchen D 62 B3
Taufkirchen an der Pram A 63 B4
Taulé F 56 B2
Taulignan F 78 B3
Taulov DK 39 D2
Taunton GB 29 B4
Taunusstein D 50 C4
Tauragė LT 6 D7
Taurianova I 106 C3
Taurisano I 107 B5
Tauste E 90 B1
Tauves F 68 C2
Tavankut YU 75 B4
Tavannes CH 70 A2
Tavarnelle val di Pesa I 81 C5
Tavas TR 16 C4
Tavaux F 69 A5
Taverna I 106 B3
Taverne CH 70 B3
Tavernelle I 82 C1
Tavernes de la Valldigna E 96 B2
Tavérnola Bergamasca I 71 C5
Taverny F 58 A3
Tavescan E 91 A4
Taviano I 107 B5
Tavira P 98 B3
Tavistock GB 28 C3
Tavnik YU 85 C5
Tavşanlı TR 114 C4
Tayinloan GB 24 C2
Taynuilt GB 24 B2
Tayport GB 25 B5
Tázlár H 75 B4
Tazones E 88 A1
Tczew PL 47 A4
Tczów PL 55 B6
Teangue GB 22 D3
Teano I 103 B7
Teba E 100 C1
Tebay GB 26 A3
Techendorf A 72 B3
Tecklenburg D 50 A3
Tecko-matorp S 41 D3
Tecuci RO 11 D9
Tefenni TR 16 C4
Tegelsmora S 36 A4
Tegernsee D 62 C2
Teggiano I 104 C1
Tegoleto I 81 C5
Teichel D 52 C1
Teignmouth GB 29 C4
Teillay F 57 C4
Teisendorf D 62 C3
Teistungen D 51 B6
Teixeiro E 86 A2
Tejada de Tiétar E 93 A5
Tejado E 89 C4
Tejares E 94 B1
Tejn DK 41 D4
Teke TR 114 A4
Tekirdağ TR 114 B2
Tekovské-Lužany SK 65 B4
Telavåg N 32 A1
Telč CZ 63 A6
Telese Terme I 103 B7
Telford GB 26 C3
Telfs A 71 A6
Telgárt SK 65 B6
Telgte D 50 B3
Tellingstedt D 43 A6
Telšiai LT 6 D7
Telti I 110 B2
Teltow D 45 C5
Tembleque E 95 C3
Temelin CZ 63 A5
Temerin YU 75 C4
Temiño E 89 B3
Témpio Pausánia I 110 B2
Temple Sowerby GB 26 A3
Templederry IRL 20 B3
Templemore IRL 21 B4
Templin D 45 B5
Temse B 49 B5
Ten Boer NL 42 B3
Tenay F 69 C5
Tenbury Wells GB 29 A5
Tenby GB 28 B3
Tence F 78 A3
Tende F 80 B1
Tenhult S 40 B4
Tenja HR 74 C3
Tenneville B 49 C6
Tensta S 36 A4
Tenterden GB 31 C4
Teo E 86 B2
Teora I 103 C8
Tepelenë AL 112 B2
Teplá CZ 52 D2
Teplice CZ 53 C3
Teplička nad Váhom SK 65 A4
Ter Apel NL 43 C4
Tera E 89 C4
Téramo I 103 A6
Terborg NL 50 B2
Terchová SK 65 A5
Terebovlya UA 11 B8
Teremia Mare RO 75 C5
Terena P 92 C3
Teresa de Cofrentes E 96 B1
Terešov CZ 63 A4
Terezino Polje HR 74 C2
Tergnier F 59 A4
Teriberka RUS 3 B31
Terlizzi I 104 B2
Termas de Monfortinho P 93 A4
Terme di Súio I 103 B6
Terme di Valdieri I 79 B6
Termens E 90 B3
Termes F 78 B2
Términi Imerese I 108 B2
Terminillo I 102 A5
Térmoli I 103 B8
Termonfeckin IRL 19 C5
Ternberg A 63 C5
Terndrup DK 38 C3
Terneuzen NL 49 B4
Terni I 102 A5
Ternitz A 64 C2
Ternopil UA 11 B8
Terpní GR 112 B5
Terracina I 102 B6
Terralba I 110 C1
Terranova di Pollino I 106 B3
Terranova di Sibari I 106 B3
Terras do Bouro P 87 C2
Terrasini I 108 A2
Terrassa E 91 B5
Terrasson-la-Villedieu F 77 A4
Terrazos E 89 B3
Terriente E 95 B5
Terrugem P 92 C3
Tertenía I 110 C2
Teruel E 90 C1
Tervola FIN 3 C26
Tervuren B 49 C5
Terzaga E 95 B5
Tešanj BIH 84 B2
Tesáske-Mlyňany SK 65 B4
Teslić BIH 84 B2
Tessin D 44 A4
Tessy-sur-Vire F 57 B4
Tét H 74 A2
Tetbury GB 29 B5
Teterchen F 60 A2
Teterow D 45 B4
Teteven BG 11 E8
Tetiyev UA 11 B10
Tetovo MK 10 E6
Tettau D 52 C1
Tettnang D 61 C5
Teublitz D 62 A3
Teuchern D 52 B2
Teulada E 96 C3
Teulada I 110 D1
Teupitz D 52 A3
Teutschenthal D 52 B1
Tevel H 74 B3
Teviothead GB 25 C5
Tewkesbury GB 29 B5
Thale D 52 B1
Thalfang D 60 A2
Thalgau A 63 C4
Thalkirch CH 71 B4
Thalmässing D 62 A2
Thalwil CH 70 A3
Thame GB 31 C3
Thann F 60 C3
Thannhausen D 61 B6
Thaon-les-Vosges F 60 B2
Tharandt D 52 C3
Tharsis E 99 B3
Thásos GR 112 B6
Thatcham GB 31 C2
Thaxted GB 31 C4
Thayngen CH 61 C4
The Barony GB 23 B5
The Hague = 's-Gravenhage NL 49 A5
The Mumbles GB 28 B4
Theale GB 31 C2
Thebes = Thívai GR 113 D5
Theding-hausen D 43 C6
Theessen D 52 A2
Themar D 51 C6
Thénezay F 67 B4
Thenon F 67 C6
Thermí GR 114 C1
Therouanne F 48 C3
Thessaloniki = Salonica GR 112 B4
Thetford GB 30 B4
Theux B 50 C1
Thézar-les-Corbières F 78 C1
Thèze F 76 C2
Thiberville F 58 A1
Thibie F 59 B5
Thiéblemont-Farémont F 59 B5
Thiendorf D 53 B3
Thiene I 71 C6
Thierrens CH 70 B1
Thiers F 68 C3
Thiesi I 110 B1
Thiessow D 45 A5
Thiezac F 77 A5
Þingeyri IS 111 B2
Þingvellir IS 111 C4
Thionville F 60 A2
Thira GR 113 F7
Thiron-Gardais F 58 B1
Thirsk GB 27 A4
Thisted DK 38 C1
Thívai = Thebes GR 113 D5
Thivars F 58 B2
Thiviers F 67 C5
Thizy F 69 B4
Tholen NL 49 B5
Tholey D 60 A3
Thomas Street IRL 20 A3
Thomastown IRL 21 B4
Thônes F 69 C6
Thonnance-les-Joinville F 59 B6
Thonon-les-Bains F 69 B6
Thorame-Haute F 79 B5
Thorens-Glières F 69 C6
Thorigny-sur-Oreuse F 59 B4
Thörl A 73 A5
Þorlákshöfn IS 111 D4
Thornaby on Tees GB 27 A4
Thornbury GB 29 B5
Thorne GB 27 B5
Thornhill, *Dumfries & Galloway* GB 25 C4
Thornhill, *Stirling* GB 24 B3
Thornthwaite GB 26 A2
Thornton Dale GB 27 A5
Þórshöfn IS 111 A10
Thouarcé F 67 A4
Thouars F 67 B4
Thrapston GB 30 B3
Threlkeld GB 26 A2
Thrumster GB 23 C5
Thueyts F 78 B3
Thuin B 49 C5
Thuir F 91 A5
Thumau D 52 C1
Thun CH 70 B2
Thuret F 68 C3
Thurey F 69 B5
Thüringen A 71 A4
Thurins F 69 C4
Thürkow D 45 B4
Thurles IRL 21 B4
Thurmaston GB 30 B2
Thurø By DK 39 D3
Thursby GB 25 D4
Thurso GB 23 C5
Thury-Harcourt F 57 B5
Thusis CH 71 B4
Thyborøn DK 38 C1
Þykkvibær IS 111 D5
Thyregod DK 39 D2
Tibi E 96 C2
Tibro S 35 C6
Tidaholm S 35 C5
Tidan S 35 C6
Tidersrum S 40 B5
Tiedra E 88 C1
Tiefenbach D 62 A3
Tiefencastel CH 71 B4
Tiefenort D 51 C6
Tiefensee D 45 C5
Tiel NL 49 B6
Tielmes E 95 B3
Tielt B 49 B4
Tienen B 49 C5
Tiengen D 61 C4
Tiercé F 57 C5
Tierga E 89 C5
Tiermas E 90 A1
Tierp S 36 A4
Tierrantona E 90 A3
Tighina MD 11 C10
Tighnabruaich GB 24 C2
Tignes F 70 C1
Tigy F 58 C3
Tihany H 74 B2
Tijnje NL 42 B2
Tijola E 101 B3
Tikhvin RUS 7 B12
Til Châtel F 69 A5
Tilburg NL 49 B6
Tilh F 76 C2
Tillac F 76 C3
Tillberga S 36 B3
Tille F 58 A3
Tillicoultry GB 25 B4
Tilloy Bellay F 59 A5
Tilly-sur-Seulles F 57 A5
Tim DK 39 C1
Timau I 72 B3
Timbákion GR 113 G6
Timişoara RO 75 C6
Timmele S 40 B3
Timmendorfer Strand D 44 B2
Timmernabben S 40 C6
Timmersdala S 35 C5
Timoleague IRL 20 C3
Timolin IRL 21 B5
Timsfors S 40 C3
Timsgearraidh GB 22 C1
Tinajas E 95 B4
Tinalhas P 92 B3
Tinchebray F 57 B5
Tineo E 86 A4
Tinglev DK 39 E2
Tingsryd S 40 C4
Tingstäde S 37 D5
Tingvoll N 2 E18
Tinnoset N 33 B6
Tinos GR 113 E7
Tintagel GB 28 C3
Tinténiac F 57 B4
Tintern GB 29 B5
Tintigny B 60 A1
Tione di Trento I 71 B5
Tipperary IRL 20 B3
Tiptree GB 31 C4
Tirana = Tiranë AL 105 B5
Tiranë = Tirana AL 105 B5
Tirano I 71 B5
Tiraspol MD 11 C10
Tire TR 16 B3
Tires I 71 B6
Tiriez E 95 D4
Tirig E 90 C3
Tiriolo I 106 C3
Tírnavos GR 112 C4
Tirrénia I 81 C4
Tirschenreuth D 62 A3
Tirstrup DK 39 C3
Tirteafuera E 100 A1
Tishono RUS 47 A6
Tisno HR 83 C4
Tišnov CZ 64 A2
Tisovec SK 65 B5
Tisselskog S 35 C4
Tistedal N 34 B3
Tistrup DK 39 D1
Tisvildeleje DK 39 C5
Tiszaalpár H 75 B4
Tiszabö H 75 A5
Tiszadorogma H 65 C6
Tiszaföldvár H 75 B5
Tiszafüred H 65 C6
Tiszajenö H 75 A5
Tiszakécske H 75 B5
Tiszakürt H 75 B5
Tiszanána H 75 A5
Tiszaörs H 75 A5
Tiszaroff H 75 A5
Tiszasüly H 75 A5
Tiszasziget H 75 B5
Tiszaszölös H 75 A5
Titaguas E 96 B1
Titel YU 75 C5
Titisee-Neustadt D 61 C4
Tito I 104 C1
Titova Korenica HR 83 B4
Tittling D 63 B4
Tittmoning D 62 B3
Titz D 50 B2
Tived S 37 C1
Tiverton GB 29 C4
Tivisa E 90 B3
Tívoli I 102 B5
Tjæreborg DK 39 D1
Tjällmo S 37 C2
Tjøme N 34 B2
Tjonnefoss N 33 C5
Tjörn IS 111 B5
Tjörnarp S 41 D3
Tkon HR 83 C4
Tlmače SK 65 B4
Tłuchowo PL 47 C5
Tlumačov CZ 64 A3
Tóalmas H 75 A4
Toano I 81 B4
Toba D 51 B6
Tobarra E 101 A4
Tobercurry IRL 18 B3
Tobermore GB 19 B5
Tobermory GB 24 B1
Toberonochy GB 24 B2
Tobha Mor GB 22 D1
Tobo S 36 A4
Tocane-St. Apre F 67 C5
Tocha P 92 A2
Tocina E 99 B5
Töcksfors S 34 B3
Tocón E 100 B2
Todi I 82 D1
Todmorden GB 26 B3
Todorici BIH 84 B2
Todtmoos D 61 C4
Todtnau D 60 C3
Toén E 87 B3
Tofta, *Gotland* S 37 D5
Tofta, *Skaraborg* S 35 C5
Tofte N 34 B2
Töftedal S 35 C3
Tofterup DK 39 D1
Toftlund DK 39 D2
Tófü H 74 B3
Tokarnia PL 55 C5
Tokary PL 54 B3
Tokod H 65 C4
Tököl H 75 A3
Tolastadh bho Thuath GB 22 C2
Toledo E 94 C2
Tolentino I 82 C2
Tolfa I 102 A4
Tolg S 40 B4
Tolkmicko PL 47 A5
Tolko PL 47 A6
Tollarp S 41 D3
Tollered S 40 B2
Tølløse DK 39 D4
Tolmachevo RUS 7 B10
Tolmezzo I 72 B3
Tolmin SLO 72 B3
Tolna H 74 B3
Tolnanémedi H 74 B3
Tolob GB 22 B7
Tolosa E 89 A4
Tolosa P 92 B3
Tolox E 100 C1
Tolpuddle GB 29 C5
Tolva E 90 A3
Tolve I 104 C2
Tomar P 92 B2
Tomarza TR 16 B7
Tomaševac YU 75 C5
Tomašica BIH 83 B5
Tomášikovo SK 64 B3
Tomašouka BY 6 F7
Tomášovce SK 65 B5
Tomaszów Mazowiecki PL 55 B5
Tomatin GB 23 D5
Tombeboeuf F 77 B3
Tomdoun GB 22 D3
Tomelilla S 41 D3
Tomellosa E 95 B4
Tomelloso E 95 C3
Tomiño E 87 C2
Tomintoul GB 23 D5
Tomislavgrad BIH 84 C2
Tomisław PL 53 B5
Tomisławice PL 47 C4
Tomnavoulin GB 23 D5
Tompa H 75 B4
Tompaládony H 74 A1
Tomter N 34 B2
Tona E 91 B5
Tonara I 110 B2
Tonbridge GB 31 C4
Tondela P 92 A2
Tønder DK 39 E1
Tongeren B 49 C6
Tongue GB 23 C4
Tönisvorst D 50 B2
Tonnay-Boutonne F 67 C4
Tonnay-Charente F 66 C4
Tonneins F 77 B3
Tonnerre F 59 C4
Tönning D 43 A5
Tønsberg N 34 B2
Tonstad N 32 C3
Toomyvara IRL 20 B3
Toormore IRL 20 C2
Topares E 101 B3
Topas E 94 A1
Toplița RO 11 C8
Topola YU 85 B5
Topolčani MK 112 A3
Topoľčany SK 64 B4
Topoľčianky SK 65 B4
Topolje HR 73 C6
Topólka PL 47 C4
Topoľníky SK 64 C3
Toponár H 74 B2
Toporów PL 53 A5
Topsham GB 29 C4
Topusko HR 73 C5
Toques E 86 B3
Tor Vaiánica I 102 B5
Torà E 91 B4
Toral de los Guzmanes E 88 B1
Toral de los Vados E 86 B4
Torbalı TR 16 B3
Torbjörntorp S 35 C5
Torbole I 71 C5
Torchiarolo I 105 C4
Torcross GB 29 C4
Torcy-le-Petit F 58 A2
Torda YU 75 C5
Tørdal N 33 B5
Tordehumos E 88 C1
Tordera E 91 B5
Tordesillas E 88 C1
Tordesilos E 95 B5
Töre S 3 D25
Töreboda S 35 C6
Toreby DK 39 E4
Torekov S 41 C2
Torella dei Lombardi I 103 C8
Torellò E 91 A5
Toreno E 86 B4
Torfou F 66 A3
Torgau D 52 B3
Torgelow D 45 B6
Torgueda P 87 C3
Torhamn S 41 C5
Torhout B 49 B4
Torigni-sur-Vire F 57 A5
Torija E 95 B3
Toril E 95 B5
Torino = Turin I 80 A1
Toritto I 104 C2
Torkovichi RUS 7 B11
Torla E 90 A2
Tormestorp S 41 C3
Tórmini I 71 C5
Tornada P 92 B1
Tornal'a SK 65 B6
Tornavacas E 93 A5
Tornby DK 38 B2
Tornesch D 43 B6
Torness GB 23 D4
Torniella I 81 C5
Tornimparte I 103 A6
Torning DK 39 C2
Tornio FIN 3 D26
Tornjoš YU 75 C4
Tornos E 95 B5
Toro E 88 C1
Törökszentmiklós H 75 A5
Toropets RUS 7 C11
Torpè I 110 B2
Torphins GB 23 D6
Torpoint GB 28 C3
Torpsbruk S 40 B4
Torquay GB 29 C4
Torquemada E 88 B2
Torralba de Burgo E 89 C4
Torralba de Calatrava E 94 C3
Torrão P 98 A2
Torre Annunziata I 103 C7
Torre Canne I 104 C3
Torre Cardela E 100 B2
Torre das Vargens P 92 B3
Torre de Coelheiros P 92 C3
Torre de Dom Chama P 87 C3
Torre de Juan Abad E 100 A2
Torre de la Higuera E 99 B4
Torre de Miguel Sesmero E 93 C4
Torre de Moncorvo P 87 C3
Torre de Santa Maria E 93 B4
Torre del Bierzo E 86 B4
Torre del Burgo E 95 B3
Torre del Campo E 100 B2
Torre del Greco I 103 C7
Torre del Lago Puccini I 81 C4
Torre del Mar E 100 C1
Torre dell'Orso I 105 C4
Torre do Terranho P 87 D3
Torre Faro I 109 A4
Torre la Ribera E 90 A3
Torre los Negros E 90 C1
Torre Orsáia I 106 A2
Torre-Pacheco E 101 B5
Torre Pellice I 79 B6
Torre Santa Susanna I 105 C3
Torreblacos E 89 C4
Torreblanca E 96 A3
Torreblascopedro E 100 A2
Torrecaballeros E 94 A2
Torrecampo E 100 A1
Torrecilla E 95 B4
Torrecilla de la Jara E 94 C2
Torrecilla de la Orden E 94 A1
Torrecilla del Pinar E 88 C2
Torrecilla en Cameros E 89 B4
Torrecillas de la Tiesa E 93 B5
Torredembarra E 91 B4
Torredonjimeno E 100 B2
Torregrosa E 90 B3
Torreira P 87 D2
Torrejón de Ardoz E 95 B3
Torrejón de la Calzada E 94 B3
Torrejón del Rey E 95 B3
Torrejon el Rubio E 93 B4
Torrejoncillo E 93 B4
Torrelaguna E 95 B3
Torrelapaja E 89 C5
Torrelavega E 88 A2
Torrelobatón E 88 C1
Torrelodones E 94 B3
Torremaggiore I 103 B8
Torremanzanas E 96 C2
Torremayor E 93 C4
Torremezzo di Falconara I 106 B3
Torremocha E 93 B4
Torremolinos E 100 C1
Torrenieri I 81 C5
Torrenostra E 96 A3
Torrenova I 102 B5
Torrent E 96 B2
Torrente de Cinca E 90 B3
Torrenueva, *Ciudad Real* E 100 A2
Torrenueva, *Granada* E 100 C2
Torreorgaz E 93 B4
Torreperogil E 100 A2
Torres E 100 B2
Torres-Cabrera E 100 B1
Torres de la Alameda E 95 B3
Torres Novas P 92 B2
Torres Vedras P 92 B1
Torresandino E 88 C3
Torrevieja E 96 D2
Torri del Benaco I 71 C5
Torricella I 104 C3
Torridon GB 22 D3
Torriglia I 80 B3
Torrijos E 94 C2
Tørring DK 39 D2
Torrita di Siena I 81 C5
Torroal P 92 C2
Torroella de Montgrì E 91 A6
Torrox E 100 C2
Torrskog S 34 B4
Torsåker S 36 A3
Torsang S 36 A2
Torsås S 41 C6
Torsby S 34 A4
Torshälla S 36 B3
Tórshavn FO 2 E10
Torslanda S 38 B4
Torsminde DK 39 C1
Törtel H 75 A4
Tórtoles E 93 A5
Tórtoles de Esgueva E 88 C2
Tortoli I 110 C2
Tortona I 80 B2
Tórtora I 106 B2
Tortoreto Lido I 82 D2
Tortorici I 109 A3
Tortosa E 90 C3
Tortosendo P 92 A3
Tortuera E 95 B5
Tortuero E 95 B3
Toruń PL 47 B4
Torup S 40 C3
Torver GB 26 A2
Tørvikbygde N 32 A3
Torviscón E 100 C2
Torzhok RUS 7 C13
Torzym PL 53 A5
Toscelanor-Maderno I 71 C5
Tosno RUS 7 B11
Tossa de Mar E 91 B5
Tosse F 76 C1
Tösse S 35 C4
Tossicia I 103 A6
Tostedt D 43 B6
Tosya TR 16 A7
Tószeg H 75 A5
Toszek PL 54 C3
Totana E 101 B4
Totebo S 40 B6
Tôtes F 58 A2
Tótkomlós H 75 B5
Tøtlandsvik N 32 B3
Totnes GB 28 C4
Tótszerdahely H 74 B1
Totton GB 31 D2
Touça P 87 C3
Toucy F 59 C4
Toul F 60 B1
Toulon F 79 C4
Toulon-sur-Allier F 68 B3
Toulon-sur-Arroux F 68 B4
Toulouse F 77 C4
Tourcoing F 49 C4
Tourlaville F 57 A4
Tournai B 49 C4
Tournan-en-Brie F 58 B3
Tournay F 76 C3
Tournon-d'Agenais F 77 B3
Tournon-St. Martin F 67 B5
Tournon-sur-Rhône F 78 A3
Tournus F 69 B4
Touro E 86 B2
Touro P 87 D3
Tourouvre F 58 B1
Tourriers F 67 C5
Tours F 67 A5
Tourteron F 59 A5
Tourves F 79 C4
Toury F 58 B2
Touvedo P 87 C2
Touvois F 66 B3
Toužim CZ 52 C2
Tovačov CZ 64 A3
Tovariševo YU 75 C4
Tovarnik HR 75 C4
Tovdal N 33 C5
Tovrljane YU 85 C6
Towcester GB 30 B3
Town Yetholm GB 25 C5
Trabada E 86 A3
Trabadelo E 86 B4
Trabanca E 87 C4
Trabazos E 87 C4
Traben-Trarbach D 50 D3
Trabia I 108 B2
Tradate I 70 C3
Trädet S 40 B3

Trafaria P 92 C1
Tragacete E 95 B5
Tragwein A 63 B5
Traiguera E 90 C3
Trainel F 59 B4
Traisen A 63 B6
Traismauer A 64 B1
Traitsching D 62 A3
Tralee IRL 20 B2
Tramacastilla de Tena E 76 D2
Tramagal P 92 B2
Tramariglio I 110 B1
Tramatza I 110 B1
Tramelan CH 70 A2
Tramonti di Sopra I 72 B2
Tramore IRL 21 B4
Trana I 80 A1
Tranås S 37 C1
Tranbjerg DK 39 C3
Tranby N 34 B2
Trancoso P 87 D3
Tranebjerg DK 39 D3
Tranekær DK 39 E3
Tranemo S 40 B3
Tranent GB 25 C5
Tranevåg N 32 C3
Trani I 104 B2
Trans-en-Provence F 79 C5
Tranvik S 36 B5
Trápani I 108 A1
Trappes F 58 B3
Traryd S 40 C3
Trasacco I 103 B6
Trasierra E 99 A4
Träslövsläge S 40 B2
Trasmiras E 87 B3
Traspinedo E 88 C2
Trate SLO 73 B5
Trauchgau D 62 C1
Traun A 63 B5
Traunreut D 62 C3
Traunstein D 62 C3
Traunwalchen D 62 C3
Tråvad S 35 C5
Travemünde D 44 B2
Traversétolo I 81 B4
Travnik BIH 84 B2
Travnik SLO 73 C4
Travo I 80 B3
Trawsfynydd GB 26 C2
Trbovlje SLO 73 B5
Trbušani YU 85 C5
Treban F 68 B3
Třebařov CZ 64 A2
Trebatsch D 53 A4
Trebbin D 52 A3
Třebechovice pod Orebem CZ 53 C5
Trebel D 44 C3
Třebenice CZ 53 C3
Trébeurden F 56 B2
Třebíč CZ 64 A1
Trebinje BIH 84 D3
Trebisacce I 106 B3
Trebitz D 52 B2
Trebnje SLO 73 C5
Třeboň CZ 63 A5
Třebovice CZ 64 A2
Trebsen D 52 B2
Trebujena E 99 C4
Trecastagni I 109 B4
Trecate I 70 C3
Trecenta I 81 A5
Tredegar GB 29 B4
Tredózio I 81 B5
Treffen A 72 B3
Treffort F 69 B5
Treffurt D 51 B6
Trefnant GB 26 B2
Tregaron GB 28 A4
Trégastel-Plage F 56 B2
Tregnago I 71 C6
Tregony GB 28 C3
Tréguier F 56 B2
Trégunc F 56 C2
Treharris GB 29 B4
Tréia I 82 C2
Treignac F 68 C1
Treignat F 68 B2
Treignes B 49 C5
Treis-Karden D 50 C3
Trekanten S 40 C6
Trélazé F 67 A4
Trelech GB 28 B3
Trélissac F 67 C5
Trelleborg S 41 D3
Trélon F 49 C5
Trélou-sur-Marne F 59 A4
Tremblay-le-Vicomte F 58 B2
Tremês P 92 B2
Tremezzo I 71 C4
Třemošná CZ 63 A4
Tremp E 90 A3
Trenčianska Stankovce SK 64 B3
Trenčianska Turná SK 64 B4
Trenčianske Teplá SK 64 B4
Trenčianske Teplice SK 64 B4
Trenčín SK 64 B4
Trendelburg D 51 B5
Trensacq F 76 B2
Trent D 45 A5
Trento I 71 B6
Treorchy GB 29 B4
Trepča YU 85 D5
Trept F 69 C5
Trepuzzi I 105 C4
Trescore Balneário I 71 C4
Tresenda I 71 B5
Tresigallo I 81 B5
Trešnjevica YU 85 C6
Tresnurághes I 110 B1
Trespaderne E 89 B3
Třešť CZ 63 A6
Trestina I 82 C1
Tretower GB 29 B4
Trets F 79 C4
Tretten N 2 F19
Treuchtlingen D 62 B1
Treuen D 52 C2
Treuenbrietzen D 52 A2
Treungen N 33 B5
Trevelez E 100 C2
Trevi I 82 D1
Trevi nel Lázio I 102 B6
Treviana E 89 B3
Treviglio I 71 C4
Trevignano Romano I 102 A5
Treviso I 72 C2
Trévoux F 69 C4
Treysa D 51 C5
Trézelles F 68 B3
Trezzo sull'Adda I 71 C4
Trhová Kamenice CZ 64 A1
Trhové Sviny CZ 63 B5
Triacastela E 86 B3
Triaize F 66 B3
Triaucourt-en-Argonne F 59 B6
Tribanj Kruščica HR 83 B4
Triberg D 61 B4
Tribsees D 45 A4
Tribuče SLO 73 C5
Tricárico I 104 C2
Tricase I 107 B5
Tricésimo I 72 B3
Trie-sur-Baïse F 77 C3
Trieben A 73 A4
Triebes D 52 C2
Triepkendorf D 45 B5
Trier D 60 A2
Trieste I 72 C3
Triggiano I 104 B2
Triglitz D 44 B4
Trignac F 66 A2
Trigueros E 99 B4
Trigueros del Valle E 88 C2
Trijebine YU 85 C4
Trikeri GR 112 C5
Trikkala GR 112 C3
Trilj HR 83 C5
Trillo E 95 B4
Trilport F 59 B3
Trim IRL 21 A5
Trimdon GB 25 D6
Trindade, *Beja* P 98 B3
Trindade, *Bragança* P 87 C3
Třinec CZ 65 A4
Tring GB 31 C3
Trinità d'Agultu I 110 B1
Trinitápoli I 104 B2
Trino I 70 C3
Trinta P 92 A3
Triora I 80 C1
Trípolis GR 113 E4
Triponzo I 82 D1
Triptis D 52 C1
Triste E 90 A2
Trittau D 44 B2
Trivento I 103 B7
Trivero I 70 C3
Trivigno I 104 C1
Trn BIH 84 B2
Trnava HR 74 C3
Trnava SK 64 B3
Trnovec SK 64 B3
Trnovo BIH 84 C3
Trnovska vas SLO 73 B5
Troarn F 57 A5
Trochtelfingen D 61 B5
Troense DK 39 D3
Trofa P 87 C2
Trofaiach A 73 A5
Trofors N 2 D20
Trogir HR 83 C5
Trøgstad N 34 B3
Tróia I 103 B8
Troia P 92 C2
Troina I 109 B3
Trois-Ponts B 50 C1
Troisdorf D 50 C3
Troisvierges L 50 C2
Trojane SLO 73 B4
Trojanów PL 55 B6
Troldhede DK 39 D1
Trollhättan S 35 C4
Trolog BIH 84 C1
Tromello I 70 C3
Tromøy N 33 C5
Tromsø N 3 B23
Trondheim N 2 E19
Tronget F 68 B3
Trönninge S 40 C2
Trönningeby S 40 B2
Tronzano-Vercellese I 70 C3
Trôo F 58 C1
Troon GB 24 C3
Tropea I 106 C2
Tropy Sztumskie PL 47 B5
Trosa S 37 C4
Trosly-Breuil F 59 A3
Trossingen D 61 B4
Trostberg D 62 B3
Trostyanets UA 7 F13
Trouville-sur-Mer F 57 A6
Trowbridge GB 29 B5
Troyes F 59 B5
Trpanj HR 84 C2
Trpezi YU 85 D5
Trpinja HR 74 C3
Tršće HR 73 C4
Tršice CZ 64 A3
Trstená SK 65 A5
Trstenci BIH 84 A2
Trstenik, *Kosovo* YU 85 D5
Trstenik, *Srbija* YU 85 C5
Trsteno HR 84 D2
Trstice SK 64 B3
Trstín SK 64 B3
Trubchevsk RUS 7 E12
Trubia E 88 A1
Trubjela YU 84 D3
Truchas E 87 B4
Trujillanos E 93 C4
Trujillo E 93 B5
Trumieje PL 47 B5
Trun CH 70 B3
Trun F 57 B6
Truro GB 28 C2
Trusetal D 51 C6
Truskavets' UA 11 B7
Trustrup DK 39 C3
Trutnov CZ 53 C5
Tryserum S 37 C3
Trysil N 2 F20
Tryszczyn PL 46 B3
Trzcianka PL 46 B2
Trzciel PL 46 C1
Trzcińsko Zdrój PL 45 C6
Trzebiatów PL 45 A7
Trzebiel PL 53 B4
Trzebielino PL 46 A3
Trzebień PL 53 B5
Trzebiez PL 45 B6
Trzebinia PL 55 C4
Trzebnica PL 54 B2
Trzebnice PL 53 B6
Trzeciewiec PL 47 B4
Trzemeszno PL 46 C3
Trzemeszno-Lubuskie PL 46 C1
Trzetrzewina PL 65 A6
Tržič SLO 73 B4
Tsamandás GR 112 C2
Tschagguns A 71 A4
Tschernitz D 53 B4
Tsebrykove UA 11 C11
Tsvetkovo UA 11 B11
Tsyelyakhany BY 7 E8
Tua P 87 C3
Tuam IRL 20 A3
Tubbergen NL 42 C3
Tubilla del Lago E 89 C3
Tübingen D 61 B5
Tubize B 49 C5
Tučapy CZ 63 A5
Tučepi HR 84 C2
Tuchan F 78 D1
Tüchen D 44 B4
Tuchola PL 46 B3
Tuchomie PL 46 A3
Tuczno PL 46 B2
Tuddal N 33 B5
Tudela E 89 B5
Tudela de Duero E 88 C2
Tudweiliog GB 26 C1
Tuejar E 96 B1
Tuffé F 58 B1
Tufsingdalen N 2 E19
Tuhaň CZ 53 C4
Tui E 87 B2
Tukums LV 6 C7
Tula I 110 B1
Tula RUS 7 D14
Tulcea RO 11 D10
Tul'chyn UA 11 B10
Tulette F 78 B3
Tuliszków PL 54 A3
Tulla IRL 20 B3
Tullamore IRL 21 A4
Tulle F 68 C1
Tullins F 69 C5
Tulln A 64 B2
Tullow IRL 21 B5
Tułowice PL 54 C2
Tulsk IRL 18 C3
Tumba S 36 B4
Tummel Bridge GB 24 B3
Tun S 35 C4
Tuna, *Kalmar* S 40 B6
Tuna, *Uppsala* S 36 A5
Tuna Hästberg S 36 A2
Tunçbilek TR 114 C4
Tunes P 98 B2
Tungelsta S 37 B5
Tunnerstad S 35 C6
Tunstall GB 30 B5
Tuohikotti FIN 3 F27
Tuoro sul Trasimeno I 82 C1
Tupadły PL 47 C4
Tupanari BIH 84 B3
Tupik RUS 7 D12
Tuplice PL 53 B4
Tura H 65 C5
Turanj HR 83 C4
Turany SK 65 A5
Turbe BIH 84 B2
Turbenthal CH 70 A3
Turcia E 88 B1
Turčianske Teplice SK 65 B4
Turcifal P 92 B1
Turckheim F 60 B3
Turda RO 11 C7
Turégano E 94 A3
Turek PL 54 A3
Tŭrgovishte BG 11 E9
Turgutlu TR 16 B3
Turi I 104 C3
Turin = Torino I 80 A1
Turis E 96 B1
Türje H 74 B2
Turka UA 11 B7
Túrkeve H 75 A5
Türkheim D 62 B1
Türkmenli TR 114 C1
Turku FIN 6 A7
Turleque E 94 C3
Turňa nad Bodvou SK 65 B6
Turnberry GB 24 C3
Turnhout B 49 B5
Türnitz A 63 C6
Turnov CZ 53 C5
Turnu RO 75 B6
Turnu Măgurele RO 11 E8
Turón E 100 C2
Turoszów PL 53 C4
Turowo PL 47 B6
Turquel P 92 B1
Turri I 110 C1
Turries F 79 B5
Turriff GB 23 D6
Tursi I 104 C2
Turtmann CH 70 B2
Turze PL 54 B2
Turzovka SK 65 A4
Tusa I 109 B3
Tuscánia I 102 A4
Tušilovic HR 73 C5
Tuszyn PL 55 B4
Tutin YU 85 D5
Tutow D 45 B5
Tutrakan BG 11 D9
Tuttlingen D 61 C4
Tutzing D 62 C2
Tuzla BIH 84 B3
Tuzla TR 16 C7
Tvååker S 40 B2
Tvärskog S 40 C6
Tvedestrand N 33 C5
Tver RUS 7 C13
Tversted DK 38 B3
Tving S 41 C5
Tvrdošin SK 65 A5
Tvrdošovce SK 64 B4
Twardogóra PL 54 B2
Twatt GB 23 B5
Twello NL 50 A2
Twimberg A 73 B4
Twist D 43 C4
Twistringen D 43 C5
Tworóg PL 54 C3
Twyford, *Hampshire* GB 31 C2
Twyford, *Wokingham* GB 31 C3
Tyachiv UA 11 B7
Tychówka PL 46 B2
Tychowo PL 46 B2
Tychy PL 54 C3
Týec nad Labem CZ 53 C5
Tygelsjö S 41 D2
Tylstrup DK 38 B2
Tymbark PL 65 A6
Tymowa PL 65 A6
Týn nad Vltavou CZ 63 A5
Tyndrum GB 24 B3
Týnec nad Sázavou CZ 63 A5
Tynemouth GB 25 C6
Tyngsjö S 34 A5
Týniště nad Orlicí CZ 53 C6
Tynset N 2 E19
Tyresö S 36 B5
Tyringe S 41 C3
Tyrislöt S 37 C3
Tyristrand N 34 A2
Tyrrellspass IRL 21 A4
Tysnes N 32 A2
Tyssedal N 32 A3
Tystberga S 37 C4
Tysvær N 32 B2
Tywyn GB 26 C1
Tzermiadhes GR 113 G7
Tzummarum NL 42 B2

U

Ub YU 85 B5
Ubby DK 39 D4
Úbeda E 100 A2
Überlingen D 61 C5
Ubidea E 89 A4
Ubli HR 84 D1
Ubrique E 99 C5
Ucero E 89 C3
Uchaud F 78 C3
Uchte D 43 C5
Uckerath D 50 C3
Uckfield GB 31 D4
Uclés E 95 C4
Ucria I 109 A3
Udbina HR 83 B4
Uddebo S 40 B3
Uddeholm S 34 A5
Uddevalla S 35 C3
Uddheden S 34 B4
Uden NL 49 B6
Uder D 51 B6
Udiča SK 65 A4
Údine I 72 B3
Udvar H 74 C3
Ueckermünde D 45 B6
Uelsen D 42 C3
Uelzen D 44 C2
Uetendorf CH 70 B2
Uetersen D 43 B6
Uetze D 44 C2
Uffculme GB 29 C4
Uffenheim D 61 A6
Ugarana E 89 A4
Ugento I 107 B5
Ugerløse DK 39 D4
Uggerslev DK 39 D3
Uggiano la Chiesa I 107 A5
Ugijar E 100 C2
Ugine F 69 C6
Uglejevik BIH 84 B4
Uglenes N 32 A2
Uglich RUS 7 C15
Ugljane HR 84 C1
Ugod H 74 A2
Uherské Hradiště CZ 64 A3
Uherský Brod CZ 64 A3
Uherský Ostroh CZ 64 B3
Uhingen D 61 B5
Uhliřské-Janovice CZ 63 A6
Uhřiněves CZ 53 C4
Uhyst D 53 B4
Uig GB 22 D2
Uitgeest NL 42 C1
Uithoorn NL 49 A5
Uithuizen NL 42 B3
Uithuizermeeden NL 42 B3
Uivar RO 75 C5
Ujazd, *Łódzkie* PL 55 B4
Ujazd, *Opolskie* PL 54 C3
Újezd u Brna CZ 64 A2
Ujhartyán H 75 A4
Újkigyós H 75 B6
Ujpetre H 74 C3
Ujście PL 46 B2
Ujsolt H 75 B4
Újszász H 75 A5
Ujué E 89 B5
Ukanc SLO 72 B3
Ukmergė LT 6 D8
Ukna S 37 C3
Ul'anka SK 65 B5
Ulaş TR 114 A2
Ulássai I 110 C2
Ulbster GB 23 C5
Ulceby GB 27 B5
Ulcinj YU 105 B5
Uldum DK 39 D2
Ulefoss N 33 B6
Uleila del Campo E 101 B3
Ulfborg DK 39 C1
Uljma YU 85 A6
Ullapool GB 22 D3
Ullared S 40 B2
Ullatun N 32 B3
Ulldecona E 90 C3
Ulldemolins E 90 B3
Ullerslev DK 39 D3
Ullervad S 35 C5
Üllés H 75 B4
Üllö H 75 A4
Ullvi S 36 B3
Ulm D 61 B5
Ulme P 92 B2
Ulmen D 50 C2
Ulog BIH 84 C3
Ulricehamn S 40 B3
Ulrichstein D 51 C5
Ulrika S 37 C2
Ulrum NL 42 B3
Ulsberg N 2 E19
Ulsta GB 22 A7
Ulsted DK 38 B3
Ulstrup, *Vestsjællands Amt.* DK 39 D3
Ulstrup, *Viborg Amt.* DK 39 C2
Ulubey TR 16 B4
Uluborlu TR 16 B5
Ulukışla TR 16 C7
Ulverston GB 26 A2
Umag HR 72 C3
Uman UA 11 B11
Umba RUS 3 C31
Umbértide I 82 C1
Umbriático I 107 B3
Umčari YU 85 B5
Umeå S 3 E24
Umhausen A 71 A5
Umka YU 85 B5
Umljanovic HR 83 C5
Umurbey TR 114 B1
Unaðsdalur IS 111 A3
Unapool GB 22 C3
Uncastillo E 90 A1
Undenäs S 35 C6
Unecha RUS 7 E12
Unešić HR 83 C5
Úněšov CZ 62 A4
Ungheni MD 11 C9
Unhais da Serra P 92 A3
Unhošt CZ 53 C4
Unichowo PL 46 A3
Uničov CZ 64 A3
Uniejów PL 54 B3
Unisław PL 47 B4
Unkel D 50 C3
Unken A 62 C3
Unna D 50 B3
Unnaryd S 40 C3
Unquera E 88 A2
Unter Langkampfen A 72 A2
Unter-steinbach D 61 A6
Unterach A 63 C4
Unterägeri CH 70 A3
Unterammergau D 62 C2
Unterhaching D 62 B2
Unteriberg CH 70 A3
Unterkochen D 61 B6
Unterlaussa A 63 C5
Unterlüss D 44 C2
Untermünkheim D 61 A5
Unterschächen CH 70 B3
Unterschleissheim D 62 B2
Unterschwaningen D 62 A1
Untersiemau D 51 C6
Unterweissenbach A 63 B5
Unterzell D 62 A3
Upavon GB 29 B6
Úpice CZ 53 C6
Upphärad S 35 C4
Uppingham GB 30 B3
Upplands-Väsby S 36 B4
Uppsala S 36 B4
Upton-upon-Severn GB 29 A5
Ur F 91 A4
Uras I 110 C1
Uraz PL 54 B1
Urbánia I 82 C1
Urbino I 82 C1
Urçay F 68 B2
Urda E 94 C3
Urdax E 76 C1
Urdilde E 86 B2
Urdos F 76 D2
Urk NL 42 C2
Úrkút H 74 A2
Urla TR 16 B3
Urlingford IRL 21 B4
Urnäsch CH 71 A4
Uroševac YU 10 E6
Urracal E 101 B3
Urries E 90 A1
Urroz E 76 D1
Ursensollen D 62 A2
Urshult S 40 C4
Uršna Sela SLO 73 C5
Urszulewo PL 47 C5
Ury F 58 B3
Urziceni RO 11 D9
Urzulei I 110 B2
Usagre E 93 C4
Uşak TR 16 B4
Ušće YU 85 C5
Usedom D 45 B5
Useldange L 60 A1
Usellus I 110 C1
Ushakovo RUS 47 A6
Usingen D 51 C4
Usini I 110 B1
Usk GB 29 B5
Uskedal N 32 B2
Üsküdar TR 114 A4
Uslar D 51 B5
Úsov CZ 64 A3
Usquert NL 42 B3
Ussássai I 110 C2
Ussé F 67 A5
Usséglio I 70 C2
Ussel, *Cantal* F 78 A1
Ussel, *Corrèze* F 68 C2
Usson-du-Poitou F 67 B5
Usson-en-Forez F 68 C3
Usson-les-Bains F 77 D5
Ust Luga RUS 7 B10
Ustaritz F 76 C1
Úštěk CZ 53 C4
Uster CH 70 A3
Ústi CZ 64 A3
Ústí nad Labem CZ 53 C4
Ústí nad Orlicí CZ 54 D1
Ustibar BIH 85 C4
Ustikolina BIH 84 C3
Ustiprača BIH 84 C4
Ustka PL 46 A2
Ustroń PL 65 A4
Ustronie Morskie PL 46 A1
Ustyuzhna RUS 7 B14
Uszód H 74 B3
Utåker N 32 B2
Utebo E 90 B2
Utena LT 7 D8
Utery CZ 62 A4
Utiel E 96 B1
Utö S 37 C5
Utrecht NL 49 A6
Utrera E 99 B5
Utrillas E 90 C2
Utsjoki FIN 3 B27
Utstein kloster N 32 B2
Uttendorf A 72 A2
Uttenweiler D 61 B5
Utterslev DK 39 E4
Uttoxeter GB 27 C4
Utvälinge S 41 C2
Uusikaarlepyy FIN 3 E25
Uusikaupunki FIN 3 F24
Uvac BIH 85 C4
Uvaly CZ 53 C4
Uvdal N 33 A5
Uzdin YU 75 C5
Uzdowo PL 47 B6
Uzel F 56 B3
Uzerche F 67 C6
Uzès F 78 B3
Uzhhorod UA 11 B7
Uzhok UA 11 B7
Užice YU 85 C4
Uznach CH 70 A3
Uzunköprü TR 114 A1

V

Vaas F 58 C1
Vaasa FIN 3 E24
Vaasen NL 50 A1
Vabre F 77 C5
Vác H 65 C5
Vacha D 51 C6
Váchartyán H 65 C5
Väckelsång S 40 C4
Vacqueyras F 78 B3
Vad S 36 A2
Vada I 81 C4
Väddö S 36 B5
Väderstad S 37 C1
Vadheim N 2 F16
Vadillo de la Sierra E 93 A5
Vadillos E 95 B4
Vadla N 32 B3
Vado I 81 B5
Vado Lígure I 80 B2
Vadsø N 3 A28
Vadstena S 37 C1
Vadum DK 38 B2
Vaduz FL 71 A4
Væggerløse DK 44 A3
Vafos N 33 C6
Vág H 74 A2
Vaggeryd S 40 B4
Vaglia I 81 C5
Váglio Basilicata I 104 C1
Vagney F 60 B2
Vagnhärad S 37 C4
Vagnsunda S 36 B5
Vagos P 92 A2
Vái GR 113 G8
Vaiano I 81 C5
Vaiges F 57 B5
Vaihingen D 61 B4
Vaillant F 59 C6
Vailly-sur-Aisne F 59 A4
Vailly-sur Sauldre F 68 A2
Vairano Scalo I 103 B7
Vaison-la-Romaine F 79 B4
Vaite F 60 C1
Väjern S 35 C3
Vajszló H 74 C2
Vál H 74 A3
Val de San Lorenzo E 86 B4
Val de Santo Domingo E 94 B2
Val d'Esquières F 79 C5
Val-d'Isère F 70 C1
Val-Suzon F 69 A4
Val Thorens F 69 C6
Valaam RUS 3 F29
Valada P 92 B2
Valadares P 87 C2
Valado P 92 B1
Valandovo MK 112 A4
Valaská SK 65 B5
Valaská Belá SK 65 B4
Valaská Dubová SK 65 A5
Valašská Polanka CZ 64 A3
Valašské Klobouky CZ 64 A4
Valašské Meziříčí CZ 64 A3
Valberg F 79 B5
Vålberg S 34 B5
Valbo S 36 A4
Valbom P 87 C2
Valbondione I 71 B5
Valbonnais F 79 B4
Valbuena de Duero E 88 C2
Vălcani RO 75 C5
Valdagno I 71 C6
Valdahon F 69 A6
Valdaracete E 95 B3
Valday RUS 7 C12
Valdealgorfa E 90 C2
Valdecaballeros E 93 B5
Valdecabras E 95 B4
Valdecarros E 94 B1
Valdeconcha E 95 B4
Valdeflores E 99 B4
Valdefresno E 88 B1
Valdeganga E 95 C5
Valdelacasa E 93 A5
Valdelacasa de Tajo E 93 B5
Valdelarco E 99 B4
Valdelosa E 94 A1
Valdeltormo E 90 C3
Valdelugeros E 88 B1
Valdemanco de Esteras E 94 D2
Valdemarsvik S 37 C3
Valdemorillo E 94 B2
Valdemoro E 94 B3
Valdemoro Sierra E 95 B5
Valdenoceda E 89 B3
Valdeobispo E 93 A4
Valdeolivas E 95 B4
Valdepeñas E 100 A2
Valdepeñas de Jaén E 100 B2
Valdepiélago E 88 B1
Valdepolo E 88 B1
Valderas E 88 B1
Valdérice I 108 A1
Valderrobres E 90 C3
Valderrueda E 88 B2
Valdestillas E 88 C2
Valdetorres E 93 C4
Valdetorres de Jarama E 95 B3
Valdeverdeja E 93 B5
Valdevimbre E 88 B1
Valdieri I 80 B1
Valdilecha E 95 B3
Valdobbiádene I 72 C1
Valdocondes E 89 C3
Valdoviño E 86 A2
Vale de Açor, *Beja* P 98 B3
Vale de Açor, *Portalegre* P 92 B3
Vale de Agua P 98 B2
Vale de Cambra P 87 D2
Vale de Lobo P 98 B2
Vale de Prazeres P 92 A3
Vale de Reis P 92 C2
Vale de Rosa P 98 B3
Vale de Santarém P 92 B2
Vale de Vargo P 98 B3
Vale do Peso P 92 B3
Valea lui Mihai RO 11 C7
Valega P 87 D2
Valéggio sul Mincio I 71 C5
Valeiro P 92 C2
Valença P 87 B2
Valençay F 67 A6
Valence, *Charente* F 67 C5
Valence, *Drôme* F 78 B3
Valence d'Agen F 77 B3
Valence-d'Albigeois F 77 B5
Valence-sur-Baïse F 77 C3
Valencia E 96 B2
Valencia de Alcántara E 93 B3
Valencia de Don Juan E 88 B1
Valencia de las Torres E 93 C4
Valencia de Mombuey E 99 A3
Valencia del Ventoso E 99 A4
Valenciennes F 49 C4
Valensole F 79 C4
Valentano I 102 A4
Valentigney F 70 A1
Valentine F 77 C3
Valenza I 80 A2
Valenzuela E 100 B1
Valenzuela de Calatrava E 100 A2
Våler N 34 B2
Valera de Abajo E 95 C4
Valeria E 95 C4
Valestrand N 32 B2
Valevåg N 32 B2
Valfabbrica I 82 C1
Valflaunes F 78 C2
Valga EST 7 C9
Valgorge F 78 B3
Valgrisenche I 70 C2
Valguarnera Caropepe I 109 B3
Valhelhas P 92 A3
Valjevo YU 85 B4
Valka LV 7 C8
Valkeakoski FIN 3 F26
Valkenburg NL 50 C1
Valkenswaard NL 49 B6
Valkó H 75 A4
Vall d'Alba E 96 A2
Valla S 37 B3
Vallada E 96 C2
Vallado E 86 A4
Valladolid E 88 C2
Vallåkra S 41 D2
Vallata I 103 B8
Vallberga S 40 C3
Valldemossa E 97 B2
Valle N 33 B4
Valle Castellana I 82 D2
Valle de Abdalajís E 100 C1
Valle de Cabuérniga E 88 A2
Valle de la Serena E 93 C5
Valle de Matamoros E 93 C4
Valle de Santa Ana E 93 C4
Valle Mosso I 70 C3
Valledolmo I 108 B2
Valledoria I 110 B1
Vallelado E 88 C2
Vallelunga Pratameno I 108 B2
Vallendar D 50 C3
Vallentuna S 36 B5
Valleraugue F 78 B2
Vallermosa I 110 C1
Vallet F 66 A3
Valletta M 107 C5
Valley GB 26 B1
Vallfogona de Riucorb E 91 B4
Valli del Pasúbio I 71 C6
Vallo della Lucánia I 103 C8

Villanueva del Duque E 100 A1
Villanueva del Fresno E 93 C3
Villanueva del Huerva E 90 B1
Villanueva del Rey E 99 A5
Villanueva del Rio E 99 B5
Villanueva del Rio y Minas E 99 B5
Villanueva del Rosario E 100 C1
Villanueva del Trabuco E 100 B1
Villány H 74 C3
Villaputzu I 110 C2
Villaquejida E 88 B1
Villaquilambre E 88 B1
Villaquiran de los Infantes E 88 B2
Villar de Barrio E 87 B3
Villar de Cañas E 95 C4
Villar de Chinchilla E 96 C1
Villar de Ciervo E 87 D4
Villar de Domingo Garcia E 95 B4
Villar de los Navarros E 90 B1
Villar de Rena E 93 B5
Villar del Arzobispo E 96 B2
Villar del Buey E 87 C4
Villar del Cobo E 95 B5
Villar del Humo E 95 C5
Villar del Pedroso E 93 B5
Villar del Rey E 93 B4
Villar del Rio E 89 B4
Villar del Saz de Navalón E 95 B4
Villar Perosa I 79 B6
Villaralto E 100 A1
Villarcayo E 89 B3
Villard-de-Lans F 79 A4
Villardeciervos E 87 C4
Villardefrades E 88 C1
Villarejo E 95 A3
Villarejo de Fuentes E 95 C4
Villarejo de Orbigo E 88 B1
Villarejo de Salvanes E 95 B3
Villarejo-Periesteban E 95 C4
Villares del Saz E 95 C4
Villaretto I 79 A6
Villargordo del Cabriel E 96 B1
Villarino E 87 C4
Villarino de Conso E 87 B3
Villarluengo E 90 C2
Villarobe E 89 B3
Villarosa I 109 B3
Villarramiel E 88 B2
Villarrasa E 99 B4
Villarreal de San Carlos E 93 B4
Villarrin de Campos E 88 C1
Villarrobledo E 95 C4
Villarroya de la Sierra E 89 C5
Villarroya de los Pinares E 90 C2
Villarrubia de los Ojos E 95 C3
Villarrubia de Santiago E 95 C3
Villarrubio E 95 C4
Villars-les-Dombes F 69 B5
Villarta E 95 C5
Villarta de los Montes E 94 C2
Villarta de San Juan E 95 C3
Villasana de Mena E 89 A3
Villasandino E 88 B2
Villasante E 89 A3
Villasarracino E 88 B2
Villasayas E 89 C4
Villasdardo E 87 C4
Villaseca de Henares E 95 B4
Villaseca de la Sagra E 94 C3
Villaseca de Laciana E 86 B4
Villaseco de los Gamitos E 87 C4
Villaseco de los Reyes E 87 C4
Villasequilla de Yepes E 94 C3
Villasimius I 110 C2
Villasmundo I 109 B4
Villasor I 110 C1
Villastar E 90 C1
Villastellone I 80 B1
Villatobas E 95 C3
Villatorp E 93 A5
Villatoya E 96 B1
Villavaliente E 96 B1
Villavelayo E 89 B4
Villavella E 87 B3
Villaver de de Guadalimar E 101 A3
Villaverde del Rio E 99 B5
Villaviciosa E 88 A1
Villaviciosa de Córdoba E 99 A6
Villaviciosa de Odón E 94 B3
Villavieja de Yeltes E 87 D4
Villayón E 86 A4
Villé F 60 B3
Ville-di-Pietrabugno F 102 A2
Ville-sous-la-Ferté F 59 B5
Ville-sur-Illon F 60 B2
Ville-sur-Tourbe F 59 A5
Villebois-Lavalette F 67 C5
Villecerf F 59 B3
Villecomtal F 77 B5
Villedieu-les-Poêles F 57 B4
Villedieu-sur-Indre F 67 B6
Villefagnan F 67 B5
Villefontaine F 69 C5
Villefort F 78 B2
Villefranche-d'Albigeois F 77 C5
Villefranche-d'Allier F 68 B2
Villefranche-de-Lauragais F 77 C4
Villefranche-de-Lonchat F 76 B3
Villefranche-de-Panat F 78 B1
Villefranche-de-Rouergue F 77 B5
Villefranche-du-Périgord F 77 B4
Villefranche-sur-Cher F 68 A1
Villefranche-sur-Mer F 80 C1
Villefranche-sur-Saône F 69 B4
Villegenon F 68 A2
Villel E 96 A1
Villemaur-sur-Vanne F 59 B4
Villemur-sur-Tarn F 77 C4
Villena E 101 A5
Villenauxe-la-Grande F 59 B4
Villenave-d'Ornon F 76 B2
Villeneuve CH 70 B1
Villeneuve F 77 B5
Villeneuve-d'Ascq F 49 C4
Villeneuve-de-Berg F 78 B3
Villeneuve-de-Marsan F 76 C2
Villeneuve-de-Rivière F 77 C3
Villeneuve-la-Guyard F 59 B4
Villeneuve-l'Archevêque F 59 B4
Villeneuve-le-Comte F 58 B3
Villeneuve-lès-Avignon F 78 C3
Villeneuve-les-Corbières F 78 D1
Villeneuve-St. Georges F 58 B3
Villeneuve-sur-Allier F 68 B3
Villeneuve-sur-Lot F 77 B3
Villeneuve-sur-Yonne F 59 B4
Villeréal F 77 B3
Villerias E 88 C2
Villeromain F 58 C2
Villers-Bocage, *Calvados* F 57 A5
Villers-Bocage, *Somme* F 48 D3
Villers-Bretonneux F 58 A3
Villers-Carbonnel F 59 A3
Villers-Cotterêts F 59 A4
Villers-Farlay F 69 B5
Villers-le-Gambon B 49 C5
Villers-le-Lac F 70 A1
Villers-sur-Mer F 57 A6
Villersexel F 60 C2
Villerupt F 60 A1
Villerville F 57 A6
Villeseneux F 59 B5
Villetrun F 58 C2
Villetta Barrea I 103 B6
Villeurbanne F 69 C4
Villeveyrac F 78 C2
Villevocance F 69 C4
Villia GR 113 D5
Villiers-St. Benoit F 59 C4
Villiers-St. Georges F 59 B4
Villingen D 61 B4
Villmar D 50 C4
Villoldo E 88 B2
Villoria E 94 B1
Vilnius LT 7 D8
Vils A 62 C1
Vils DK 38 C1
Vilsbiburg D 62 B3
Vilseck D 62 A2
Vilshofen D 63 B4
Vilshult S 41 C4
Vilusi YU 84 D3
Vilvestre E 87 C4
Vilvoorde B 49 C5
Vimeiro P 92 B1
Vimercate I 71 C4
Vimianzo E 86 A1
Vimieiro P 92 C3
Vimioso P 87 C4
Vimmerby S 40 B5
Vimoutiers F 57 B6
Vimperk CZ 63 A4
Vimy F 48 C3
Vinadi CH 71 B5
Vinadio I 79 B6
Vinaixa E 90 B3
Vinarós E 90 C3
Vinay F 69 C5
Vinberg S 40 C2
Vinca F 91 A5
Vinča YU 85 B5
Vinchiaturo I 103 B7
Vinci I 81 C4
Vindeby DK 39 D3
Vindeln S 3 D23
Vinderup DK 38 C1
Vindsvik N 32 B3
Vinets F 59 B5
Vineuil F 58 C2
Vinga RO 75 B6
Vingåker S 37 B2
Vingrau F 78 D1
Vinhais P 87 C4
Vinica HR 73 B6
Vinica SK 65 B5
Vinica SLO 73 C5
Vinicka YU 85 D4
Viniegra de Arriba E 89 B4
Vinje, *Sør-Trøndelag* N 2 E18
Vinje, *Telemark* N 33 B4
Vinkovci HR 74 C3
Vinninga S 35 C5
Vinnytsya UA 11 B10
Vinon-sur-Verdon F 79 C4
Vinslöv S 41 C3
Vintrosa S 36 B1
Viñuela de Sayago E 87 C5
Viñuelas E 95 B3
Vinuesa E 89 C4
Vinzelberg D 44 C3
Viöl D 43 A6
Viola I 80 B1
Violay F 69 C4
Vipava SLO 72 C3
Vipiteno I 71 B6
Vipperow D 45 B4
Vir BIH 84 C2
Vir HR 83 B4
Vira CH 70 B3
Vire F 57 B5
Vireux F 49 C5
Virgen A 72 A2
Virgen de la Cabeza E 100 A1
Virginia IRL 19 C4
Virieu F 69 C5
Virieu-le-Grand F 69 C5
Virje HR 74 B1
Virklund DK 39 C2
Virovitica HR 74 C2
Virsbo S 36 B3
Virserum S 40 B5
Virton B 60 A1
Virtsu EST 6 B7
Viry F 69 B6
Vis HR 83 C5
Visbek D 43 C5
Visby DK 39 D1
Visby S 37 D5
Visé B 50 C1
Višegrad BIH 85 C4
Viserba I 82 B1
Viseu P 92 A3
Visiedo E 90 C1
Viskafors S 40 B2
Visland N 32 C3
Vislanda S 40 C4
Visnes N 32 B2
Višnja Gora SLO 73 C4
Višnjan HR 72 C3
Višnové CZ 64 B2
Visnums-Kil S 34 B6
Viso del Marqués E 100 A2
Visoko BIH 84 C3
Visoko SLO 73 B4
Visone I 80 B2
Visp CH 70 B2
Vissefjärda S 40 C5
Visselhövede D 43 C6
Vissenbjerg DK 39 D3
Visso I 82 D2
Vistabella del Maestrat E 96 A2
Vita I 108 B1
Vitanje SLO 73 B5
Vitanovac YU 85 C5
Vitebsk = Vitsyebsk BY 7 D11
Viterbo I 102 A5
Vitez BIH 84 B2
Vithkuq AL 112 B2
Vitigudino E 87 C4
Vitina BIH 84 C2
Vitina GR 113 E4
Vitis A 63 B6
Vitkov CZ 64 A3
Vitkovac YU 85 C5
Vitomirica YU 85 D5
Vitoria-Gasteiz E 89 B4
Vitré F 57 B4
Vitrey-sur-Mance F 60 C1
Vitry-en-Artois F 48 C3
Vitry-le-François F 59 B5
Vitry-sur-Seine F 58 B3
Vitsand S 34 A4
Vitsyebsk = Vitebsk BY 7 D11
Vittangi S 3 C24
Vittaryd S 40 C3
Vitteaux F 69 A4
Vittel F 60 B1
Vittinge S 36 B4
Vittória I 109 C3
Vittório Véneto I 72 C2
Vittsjö S 41 C3
Viù I 70 C2
Viul N 34 A2
Vivario F 102 A2
Viveiro E 86 A3
Vivel del Rio Martin E 90 C2
Viver E 96 B2
Viverols F 68 C3
Viveros E 101 A3
Viviers F 78 B3
Vivonne F 67 B5
Vivy F 67 A4
Vize TR 114 A2
Vizille F 79 A4
Viziñada HR 72 C3
Viziru RO 11 D9
Vizovice CZ 64 A3
Vizvár H 74 B2
Vizzavona F 102 A2
Vizzini I 109 B3
Vlachovice CZ 64 A3
Vlachovo SK 65 B6
Vláchovo Březi CZ 63 A4
Vladimirci YU 85 B4
Vladimirovac YU 85 A5
Vladislav CZ 64 A1
Vlagtwedde NL 43 B4
Vlajkovac YU 85 A6
Vlakhiótis GR 113 F4
Vlasenica BIH 84 B3
Vlašim CZ 63 A5
Vlatkovići BIH 84 B2
Vledder NL 42 C3
Vlissingen NL 49 B4
Vlorë AL 105 C5
Vlotho D 51 A4
Vnanje Gorice SLO 73 C4
Vobarno I 71 C5
Voćin HR 74 C2
Vöcklabruck A 63 B4
Vöcklamarkt A 63 C4
Vodanj YU 85 B5
Voderady SK 64 B3
Vodice, *Istarska* HR 73 C4
Vodice, *Šibenska* HR 83 C4
Vodice SLO 73 B4
Vodňany CZ 63 A5
Vodnjan HR 82 B2
Vodskov DK 38 B3
Voe GB 22 A7
Voerså DK 38 B3
Voghera I 80 B3
Vogogna I 70 B3
Vogošća BIH 84 C3
Vogüé F 78 B3
Vohburg D 62 B2
Vohenstrauss D 62 A3
Vöhl D 51 B4
Vöhrenbach D 61 B4
Vöhringen D 61 B6
Void-Vacon F 60 B1
Voiron F 69 C5
Voise F 58 B2
Voisey F 60 C1
Voiteg RO 75 C6
Voiteur F 69 B5
Voitsberg A 73 A5
Vojens DK 39 D2
Vojka YU 85 B5
Vojlovica YU 85 B5
Vojnić HR 73 C5
Vojnice SK 65 C4
Vojnik SLO 73 B5
Vojvoda Stepa YU 75 C5
Volargne I 71 C5
Volary CZ 63 B4
Volče SLO 72 B3
Volda N 2 E17
Volendam NL 42 C2
Volga RUS 7 B15
Volimai GR 113 E2
Volissós GR 112 D7
Volkach D 61 A6
Völkermarkt A 73 B4
Volkhov RUS 7 B12
Völklingen D 60 A2
Volkmarsen D 51 B5
Vollenhove NL 42 C2
Vollore-Montagne F 68 C3
Vollsjö S 41 D3
Volodymyr-Volyns'kyy UA 11 A8
Volokolamsk RUS 7 C13
Vólos GR 112 C4
Volosovo RUS 7 B10
Volovets UA 11 B7
Volta Mantovana I 71 C5
Voltággio I 80 B2
Volterra I 81 C4
Voltri I 80 B2
Volturara Áppula I 103 B8
Volturara Irpina I 103 C7
Volvic F 68 C3
Volyně CZ 63 A4
Vónitsa GR 112 D2
Vönöck H 74 A2
Vonsild DK 39 D2
Voorschoten NL 49 A5
Vopnafjörður IS 111 B11
Vorau A 73 A5
Vorbasse DK 39 D2
Vorchdorf A 63 C4
Vorden NL 50 A2
Vordernberg A 73 A4
Vordingborg DK 39 D4
Voreppe F 69 C5
Vorey F 68 C3
Vorgod DK 39 C1
Vormsund N 34 A3
Voronezh UA 7 F12
Võru EST 7 C9
Voskopojë AL 112 B2
Voss N 2 F17
Votice CZ 63 A5
Voué F 59 B5
Vouillé F 67 B5
Voulx F 59 B3
Voussac F 68 B3
Vouvray F 67 A5
Vouvry CH 70 B1
Vouzela P 87 D2
Vouziers F 59 A5
Voves F 58 B2
Voy GB 23 B5
Voynitsa RUS 3 D29
Voznesensk UA 11 C11
Voznesenye RUS 7 A13
Vrå DK 38 B2
Vrå S 40 C3
Vráble SK 64 B4
Vračenovići YU 84 D3
Vračev Gaj YU 85 B6
Vraćevsnica YU 85 B5
Vrådal N 33 B5
Vrakhnéika GR 113 D3
Vrana HR 83 B3
Vranduk BIH 84 B2
Vrångö S 38 B4
Vrani RO 85 A6
Vranić YU 85 B5
Vranići BIH 84 C3
Vranja HR 73 C4
Vranjak BIH 84 B3
Vranje YU 10 E6
Vranov nad Dyje CZ 64 B1
Vranovice CZ 64 B2
Vransko SLO 73 B4
Vrapčići BIH 84 C2
Vratimov CZ 64 A4
Vratsa BG 11 E7
Vrbanja HR 84 B3
Vrbanjci BIH 84 B2
Vrbas YU 75 C4
Vrbaška BIH 84 A2
Vrbnik, *Primorsko-Goranska* HR 83 A3
Vrbnik, *Zadarsko-Kninska* HR 83 B5
Vrbno p. Pradědem CZ 54 C2
Vrboska HR 83 C5
Vrbov SK 65 A6
Vrbovce SK 64 B3
Vrbové SK 64 B3
Vrbovec HR 73 C6
Vrbovski YU 85 B5
Vrbovsko HR 73 C5
Vrchlabí CZ 53 C5
Vrčin YU 85 B5
Vrdy CZ 63 A6
Vrebac HR 83 B4
Vreden D 50 A2
Vrela YU 85 D5
Vreoci YU 85 B5
Vretstorp S 37 B1
Vrginmost HR 73 C5
Vrgorac HR 84 C2
Vrhnika SLO 73 C4
Vrhovine HR 83 B4
Vrhpolie YU 85 B4
Vriezenveen NL 42 C3
Vrigne-aux-Bois F 59 A5
Vrigstad S 40 B4
Vrlika HR 83 C5
Vrmbaje YU 85 C5
Vrnjačka Banja YU 85 C5
Vrnograč BIH 73 C5
Vron F 48 C2
Vroomshoop NL 42 C3
Vroutek CZ 52 C3
Vrpolje HR 74 C3
Vršac YU 85 A6
Vrsar HR 82 A2
Vrsi HR 83 B4
Vrtoče BIH 83 B5
Vrútky SK 65 A4
Všeruby CZ 62 A3
Všestary CZ 53 C5
Vsetín CZ 64 A3
Vuča YU 85 D5
Vučitrn YU 85 D5
Vučkovica YU 85 C5
Vught NL 49 B6
Vuillafans F 69 A6
Vukovar HR 75 C4
Vulcan RO 11 D7
Vulcanești MD 11 D10
Vuolijoki FIN 3 D27
Vuzenica SLO 73 B5
Vy-lès Lure F 60 C2
Vyartsilya RUS 3 E29
Vyazma RUS 7 D13
Vyborg RUS 3 F28
Výčapy CZ 64 A1
Výčapy-Opatovce SK 64 B4
Východna SK 65 A5
Vydrany SK 64 B3
Vyerkhnyadzvinsk BY 7 D9
Vyhne SK 65 B4
Vylkove UA 11 D10
Vynohradiv UA 11 B7
Vyshniy Volochek RUS 7 C13
Vyškov CZ 64 A3
Vysoká nad Kysucou SK 65 A4
Vysoké Mýto CZ 53 D6
Vysokovsk RUS 7 C14
Vyšší Brod CZ 63 B5
Vytegra RUS 7 A14

W

Waabs D 44 A1
Waalwijk NL 49 B6
Waarschoot B 49 B4
Wabern D 51 B5
Wąbrzeźno PL 47 B4
Wąchock PL 55 B6
Wachow D 45 C4
Wąchów PL 54 C3
Wächtersbach D 51 C5
Wackersdorf D 62 A3
Waddington GB 27 B5
Wadebridge GB 28 C3
Wadelsdorf D 53 B4
Wädenswil CH 70 A3
Wadern D 60 A2
Wadersloh D 50 B4
Wadlew PL 55 B4
Wadowice PL 65 A5
Wagenfeld D 43 C5
Wageningen NL 49 B6
Waghäusel D 61 A4
Waging D 62 C3
Wagrain A 72 A3
Wągrowiec PL 46 C3
Wahlsdorf D 52 B3
Wahlstedt D 44 B2
Wahrenholz D 44 C2
Waiblingen D 61 B5
Waidhaus D 62 A3
Waidhofen an der Thaya A 63 B6
Waidhofen an der Ybbs A 63 C5
Waimes B 50 C2
Wainfleet All Saints GB 27 B6
Waizenkirchen A 63 B4
Wakefield GB 27 B4
Wałbrzych PL 53 C6
Walchensee D 62 C2
Walchsee A 62 C3
Wałcz PL 46 B2
Wald CH 70 A3
Wald-Michelbach D 61 A4
Waldaschaff D 51 D5
Waldbach A 73 A5
Waldböckelheim D 60 A3
Waldbröl D 50 C3
Waldeck D 51 B5
Waldenburg D 52 C2
Waldfischbach-Burgalben D 60 A3
Waldheim D 52 B3
Waldkappel D 51 B5
Waldkirch D 60 B3
Waldkirchen D 63 B4
Waldkirchen am Wesen A 63 B4
Waldkraiburg D 62 B3
Waldmohr D 60 A3
Waldmünchen D 62 A3
Waldring A 62 C3
Waldsassen D 52 C2
Waldshut D 61 C4
Waldstatt CH 71 A4
Waldwisse F 60 A2
Walenstadt CH 71 A4
Walentynów PL 55 B6
Walichnowy PL 54 B3
Walincourt F 49 C4
Walkenried D 51 B6
Walkeringham GB 27 B5
Wallasey GB 26 B2
Walldürn D 61 A5
Wallenfells D 52 C1
Wallenhorst D 43 C5
Wallers F 49 C4
Wallersdorf D 62 B3
Wallerstein D 61 B6
Wallingford GB 31 C2
Wallitz D 45 B4
Walls GB 22 A7
Wallsbüll D 39 E2
Walmer GB 31 C5
Walsall GB 27 C4
Walshoutem B 49 C6
Walsrode D 43 C6
Waltenhofen D 61 C6
Waltershausen D 51 C6
Waltham Abbey GB 31 C4
Waltham on the Wolds GB 30 B3
Walton-on-Thames GB 31 C3
Walton-on-the-Naze GB 31 C5
Wamba E 88 C2
Wanderup D 43 A6
Wandlitz D 45 C5
Wanfried D 51 B6
Wangen im Allgäu D 61 C5
Wangerooge D 43 B4
Wangersen D 43 B6
Wängi CH 70 A3
Wanna D 43 B5
Wansford GB 30 B3
Wantage GB 31 C2
Wanzleben D 52 A1
Waplewo PL 47 B6
Wapnica PL 46 B1
Wapno PL 46 C3
Warburg D 51 B5
Wardenburg D 43 B5
Ware GB 31 C3
Waregem B 49 C4
Wareham GB 29 C5
Waremme B 49 C6
Waren D 45 B4
Warendorf D 50 B3
Warga NL 42 B2
Warin D 44 B3
Wark GB 25 C5
Warka PL 55 B6
Warkworth GB 25 C6
Warlubie PL 47 B4
Warminster GB 29 B5
Warnemünde D 44 A4
Warnow D 44 B3
Warnsveld NL 50 A2
Warrenpoint GB 19 B5
Warrington GB 26 B3
Warsaw = Warszawa PL 55 A6
Warsingsfehn D 43 B4
Warsow D 44 B3
Warstein D 51 B4
Warszawa = Warsaw PL 55 A6
Warta PL 54 B4
Wartberg A 63 C5
Warth A 71 A5
Warwick GB 30 B2
Warza D 51 C6
Wasbister GB 23 B5
Washington GB 25 D6
Wąsosz PL 54 B1
Wasselonne F 60 B3
Wassen CH 70 B3
Wassenaar NL 49 A5
Wasserauen CH 71 A4
Wasserburg D 62 B3
Wassertrüdingen D 62 A1
Wassy F 59 B5
Wasungen D 51 C6
Watchet GB 29 B4
Waterford IRL 21 B4
Watergrasshill IRL 20 B3
Waterloo B 49 C5
Waterville IRL 20 C1
Watford GB 31 C3
Wathlingen D 44 C2
Watten F 48 C3
Watten GB 23 C5
Wattens A 72 A1
Watton GB 30 B4
Wattwil CH 71 A4
Waunfawr GB 26 B1
Wavignies F 58 A3
Wavre B 49 C5
Wearhead GB 25 D5
Węchadlow PL 55 C5
Wedel D 43 B6
Wedemark D 43 C6
Weedon Bec GB 30 B2
Weener D 43 B4
Weert NL 50 B1
Weesp NL 49 A6
Weeze D 50 B2
Weferlingen D 52 A1
Wegeleben D 52 B1
Weggis CH 70 A3
Węgierska-Górka PL 65 A5
Węgliniec PL 53 B5
Węgorzyno PL 46 B1
Węgrzynice PL 53 A5
Wegscheid D 63 B4
Wehdel D 43 B5
Wehr D 60 C3
Weibersbrunn D 61 A5
Weichering D 62 B2
Weida D 52 C2
Weiden D 62 A3
Weidenberg D 52 D1
Weidenhain D 52 B2
Weidenstetten D 61 B5
Weierbach D 60 A3
Weikersheim D 61 A5
Weil D 62 B1
Weil am Rhein D 60 C3
Weil der Stadt D 61 B4
Weilburg D 50 C4
Weilerswist D 50 C2
Weilheim, *Baden-Württemberg* D 61 B5
Weilheim, *Bayern* D 62 C2
Weilmünster D 51 C4
Weitensfeld A 73 B4
Weimar D 52 C1
Weinberg D 61 A6
Weinfelden CH 71 A4
Weingarten, *Baden-Württemberg* D 61 A4
Weingarten, *Baden-Württemberg* D 61 C5
Weinheim D 61 A4
Weinstadt D 61 B5
Weismain D 52 C1
Weissbriach A 72 B3
Weissenbach A 71 A5
Weissenberg D 53 B4
Weissenbrunn D 52 C1
Weissenburg D 62 A1
Weissenfels D 52 B1
Weissenhorn D 61 B6
Weissenkirchen A 63 B6
Weissensee D 52 B1
Weissenstadt D 52 C1
Weisskirchen im Steiermark A 73 A4
Weisstannen CH 71 B4
Weisswasser D 53 B4
Weitendorf D 44 B4
Weitersfeld A 64 B1
Weitersfelden A 63 B5
Weitnau D 61 C6
Wéitra A 63 B5
Weiz A 73 A5
Wejherowo PL 47 A4
Welkenraedt B 50 C1
Wellaune D 52 B2
Wellin B 49 C6
Wellingborough GB 30 B3
Wellington, *Somerset* GB 29 C4
Wellington, *Telford & Wrekin* GB 26 C3
Wellingtonbridge IRL 21 B5
Wells GB 29 B5
Wells-next-the-Sea GB 30 B4
Wels A 63 B5
Welschenrohr CH 70 A2
Welshpool GB 26 C2
Welver D 50 B3
Welwyn Garden City GB 31 C3
Welzheim D 61 B5
Welzow D 53 B4
Wem GB 26 C3
Wembury GB 28 C3
Wemding D 62 B1
Wenden D 50 C3
Wendisch Rietz D 53 A4
Wendlingen D 61 B5
Weng A 63 B4
Weng bei Admont A 63 C5
Wengen CH 70 B2
Wenigzell A 73 A5
Wennigsen D 51 A5
Wenns A 71 A5
Wenzenbach D 62 A3
Weppersdorf A 64 C2
Werben D 44 C3
Werbig D 52 B3
Werdau D 52 C2
Werder D 45 C4
Werdohl D 50 B3
Werfen A 72 A3
Werkendam NL 49 B5
Werl D 50 B3
Werlte D 43 C4
Wermelskirchen D 50 B3
Wermsdorf D 52 B2
Wernberg Köblitz D 62 A3
Werne D 50 B3
Werneck D 51 D6
Werneuchen D 45 C5
Wernigerode D 51 B6
Wertach D 61 C6
Wertheim D 61 A5
Wertingen D 62 B1
Weseke D 50 B2
Wesel D 50 B2
Wesenberg D 45 B4
Wesendorf D 44 C2
Wesołowo PL 47 B6
Wesselburen D 43 A5
Wesseling D 50 C2
West Bridgford GB 27 C4
West Bromwich GB 27 C4
West Haddon GB 30 B2
West Kilbride GB 24 C3
West Linton GB 25 C4
West Lulworth GB 29 C5
West Mersea GB 31 C4
West-Terschelling NL 42 B2
West Woodburn GB 25 C5
Westbury, *Shropshire* GB 26 C3
Westbury, *Wiltshire* GB 29 B5
Westbury-on-Severn GB 29 B5
Westendorf A 72 A2
Westensee D 44 A1
Westerbork NL 42 C3
Westerburg D 50 C3
Westerhaar NL 42 C3
Westerholt D 43 B4
Westerkappeln D 50 A3
Westerland D 39 E1
Westerlo B 49 B5
Westerstede D 43 B4
Westheim D 62 A1
Westhill GB 23 D6
Westkapelle B 49 B4
Westkapelle NL 49 B4
Westminster GB 31 C3
Weston GB 26 C3
Weston-super-Mare GB 29 B5
Westport IRL 18 C2
Westruther GB 25 C5
Westward Ho! GB 28 B3